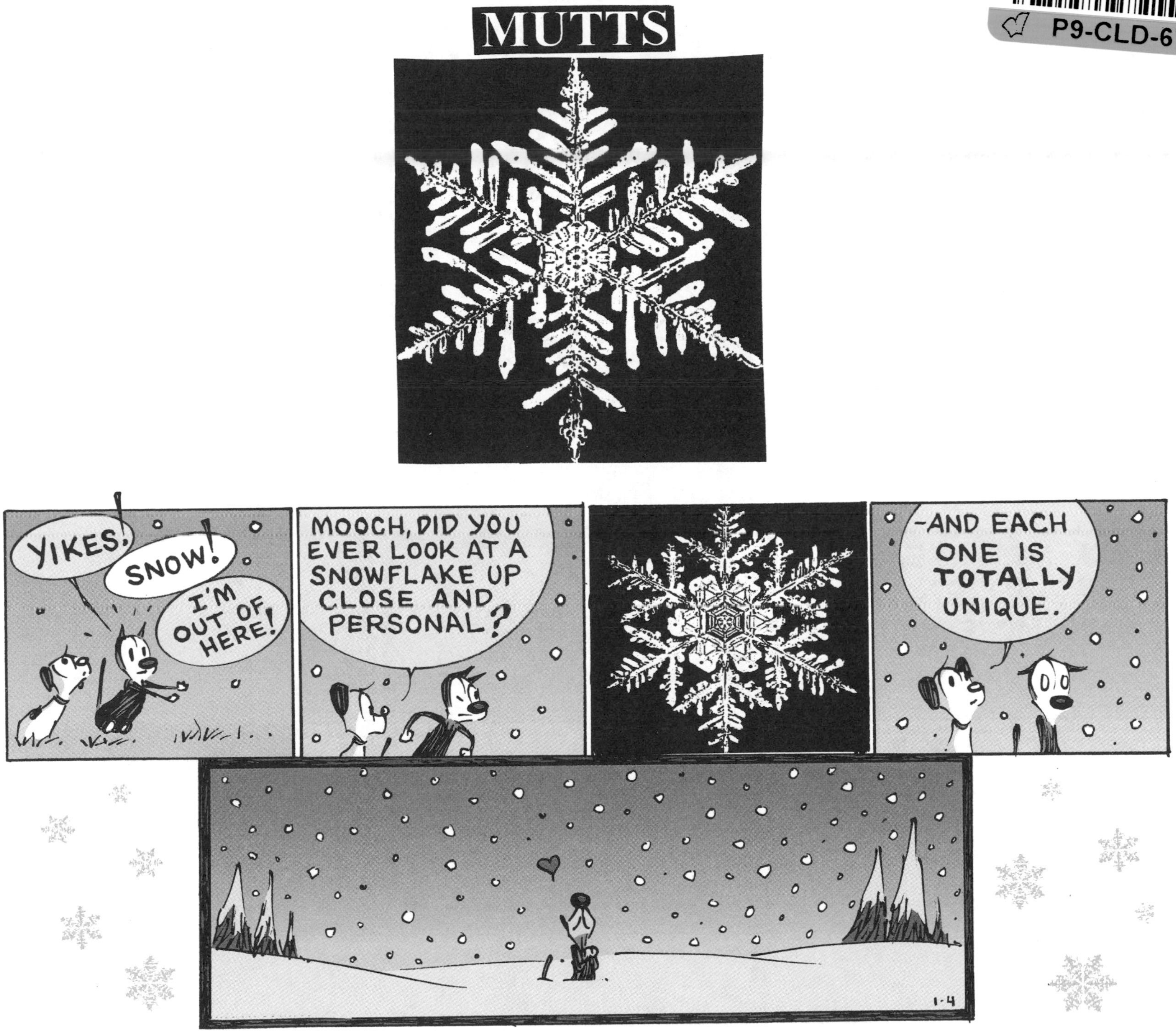
MUTTS
YIKES!
SNOW!
I'M OUT OF HERE!
MOOCH, DID YOU EVER LOOK AT A SNOWFLAKE UP CLOSE AND PERSONAL?
-AND EACH ONE IS TOTALLY UNIQUE.
1-4

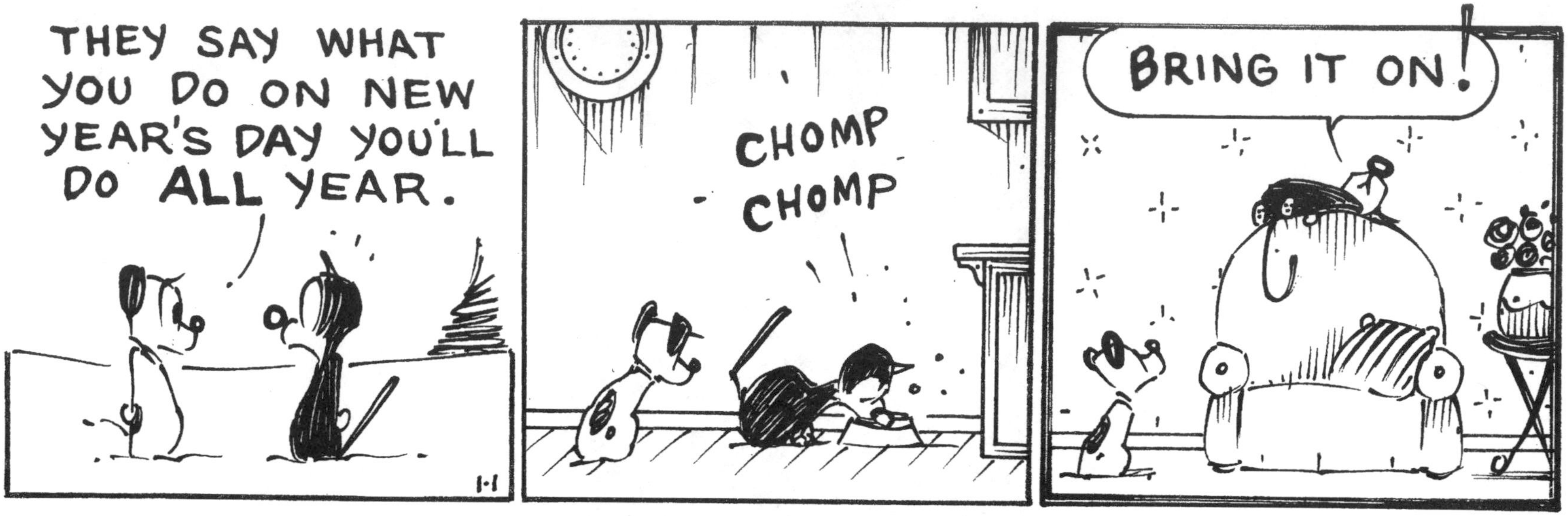
THEY SAY WHAT YOU DO ON NEW YEAR'S DAY YOU'LL DO ALL YEAR.
1·1
CHOMP
CHOMP
BRING IT ON!

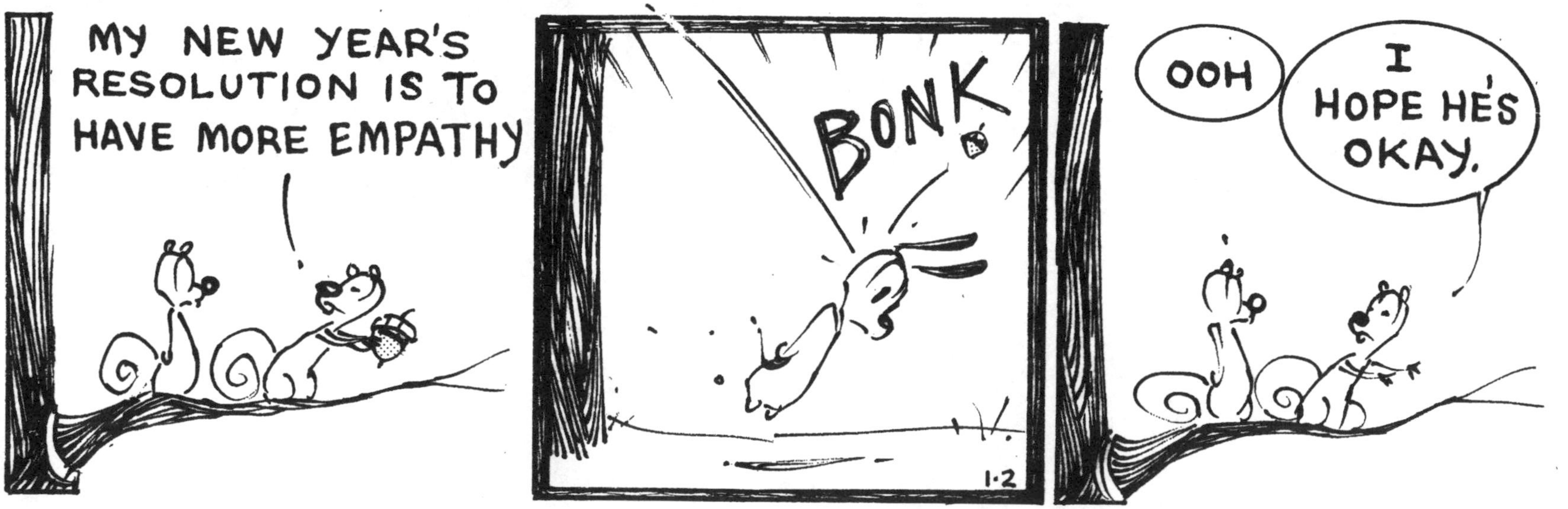
MY NEW YEAR'S RESOLUTION IS TO HAVE MORE EMPATHY
BONK
1·2
OOH
I HOPE HE'S OKAY.

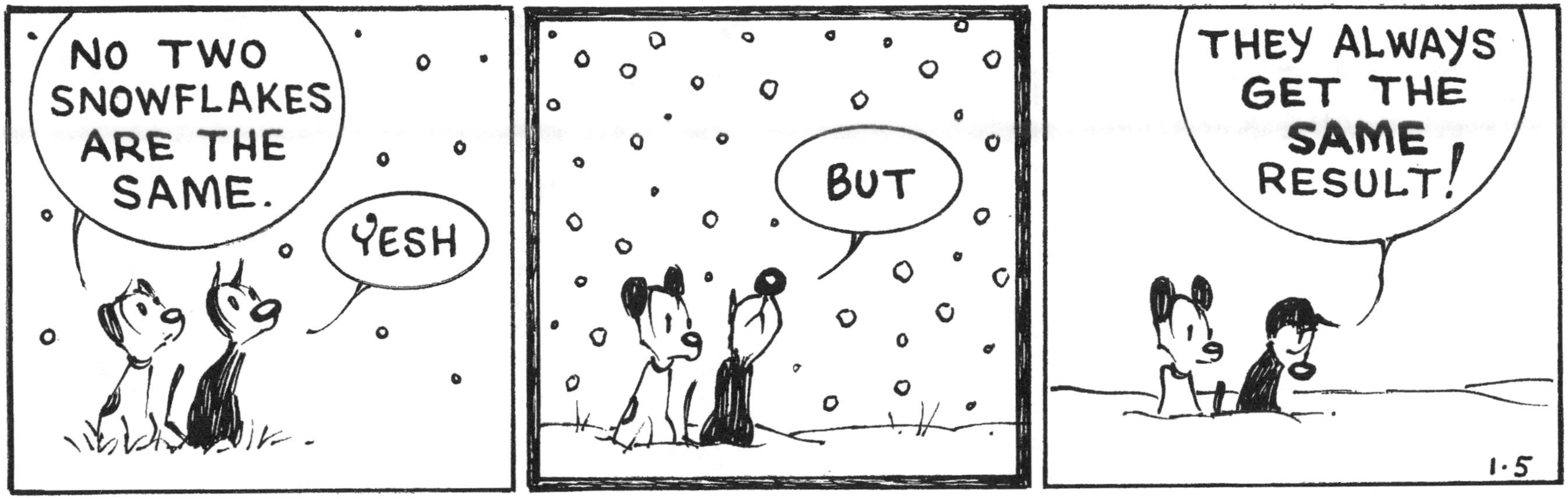
NO TWO SNOWFLAKES ARE THE SAME.
YESH
BUT
THEY ALWAYS GET THE SAME RESULT!
1·5

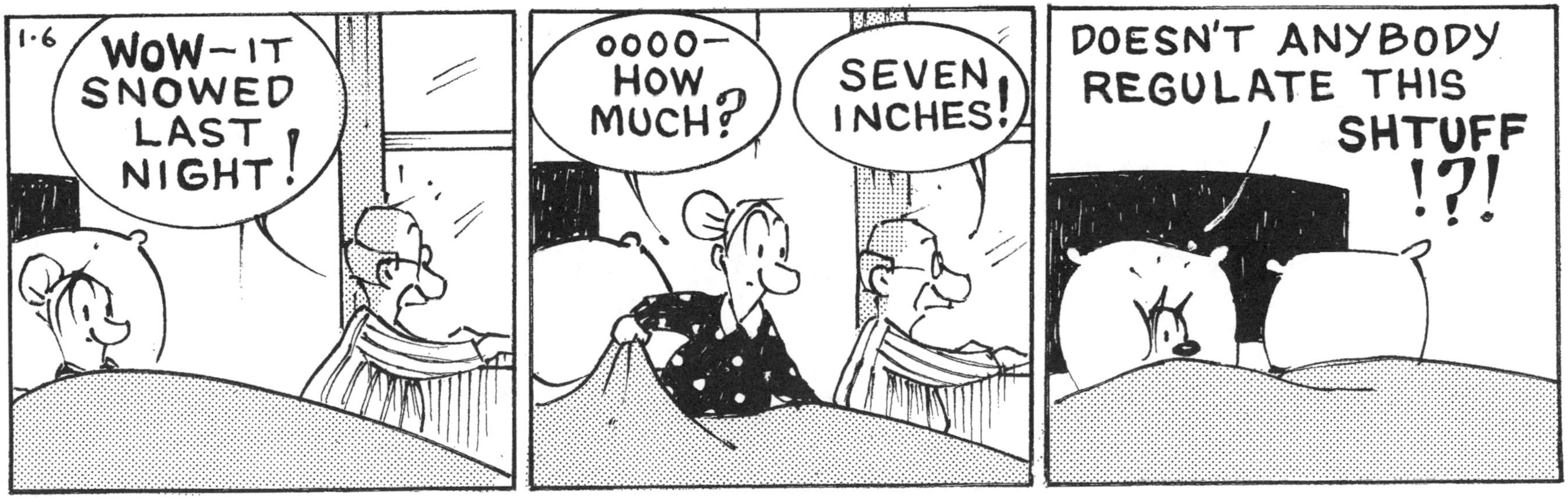
1·6
WOW—IT SNOWED LAST NIGHT!
OOOO—HOW MUCH?
SEVEN INCHES!
DOESN'T ANYBODY REGULATE THIS SHTUFF !?!

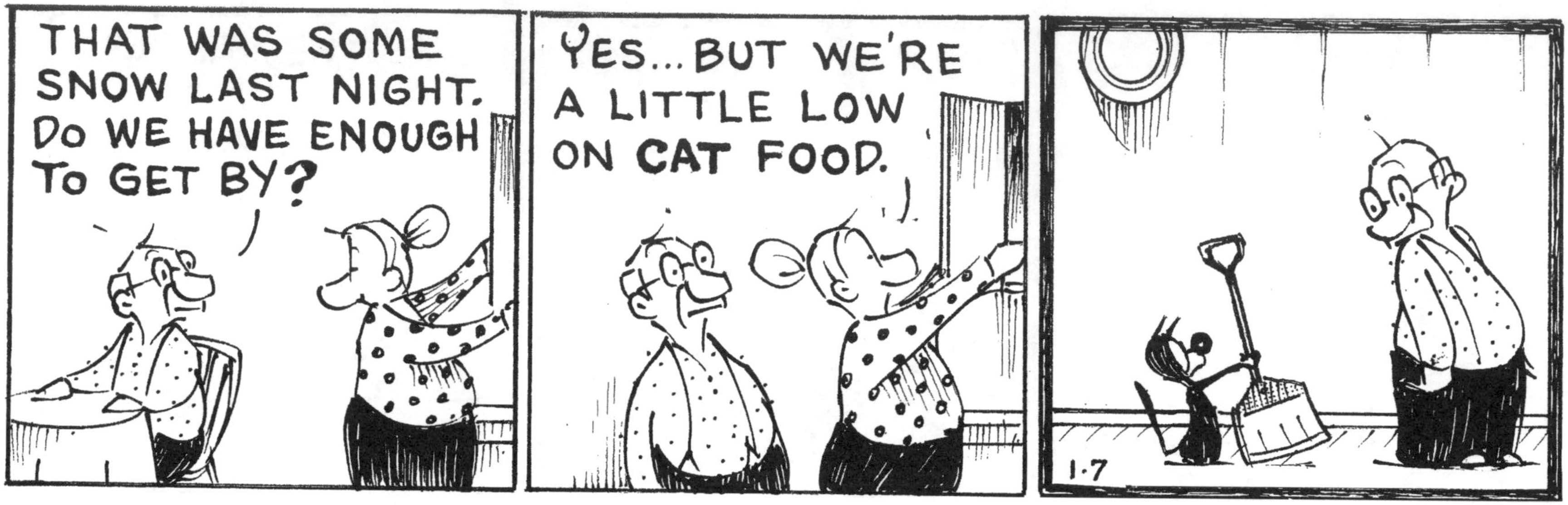
THAT WAS SOME SNOW LAST NIGHT. DO WE HAVE ENOUGH TO GET BY?
YES... BUT WE'RE A LITTLE LOW ON CAT FOOD.
1·7

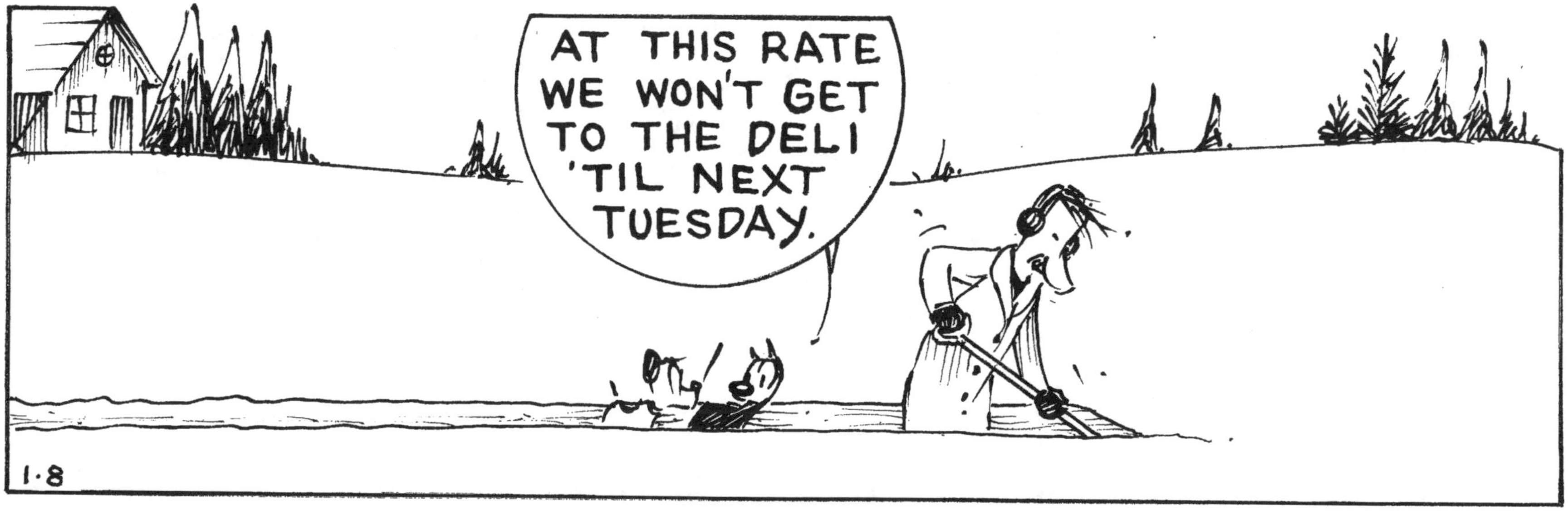
AT THIS RATE WE WON'T GET TO THE DELI 'TIL NEXT TUESDAY.
1·8

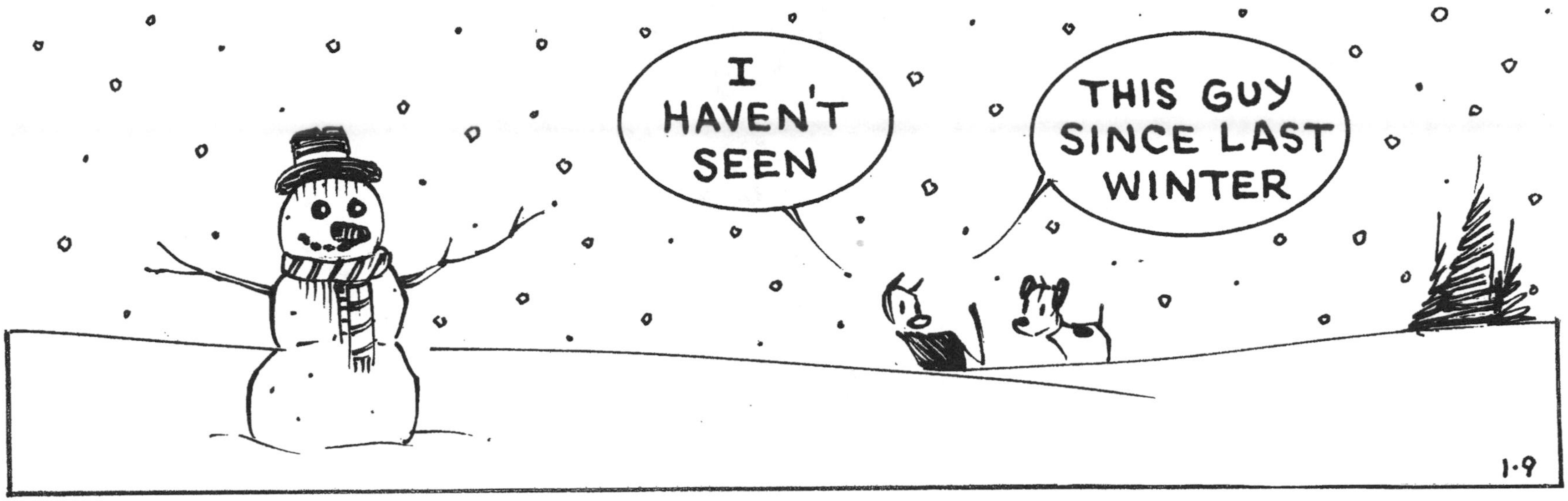
I HAVEN'T SEEN
THIS GUY SINCE LAST WINTER
1·9

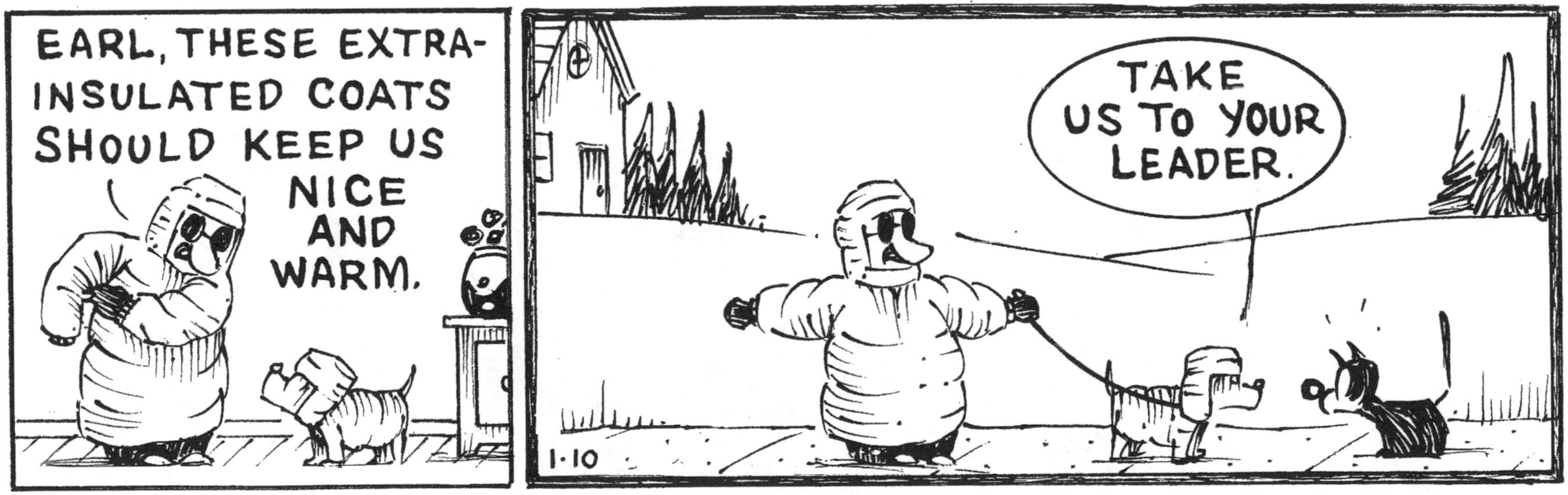
EARL, THESE EXTRA-INSULATED COATS SHOULD KEEP US NICE AND WARM.
TAKE US TO YOUR LEADER.
1·10

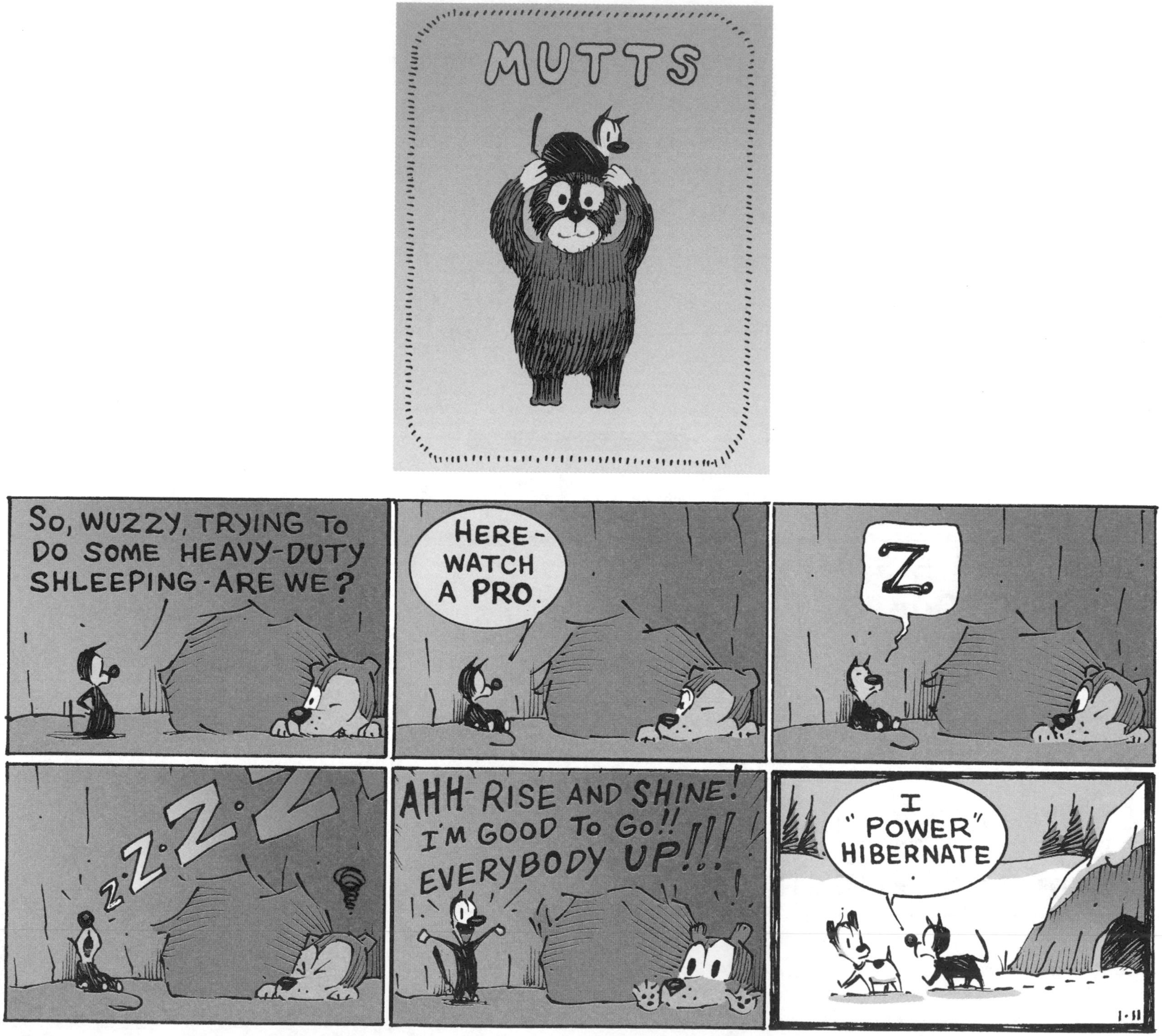
MUTTS
SO, WUZZY, TRYING TO DO SOME HEAVY-DUTY SHLEEPING-ARE WE?
HERE-WATCH A PRO.
Z
z Z Z Z
AHH-RISE AND SHINE! I'M GOOD TO GO!! EVERYBODY UP!!!
I "POWER" HIBERNATE
1-11

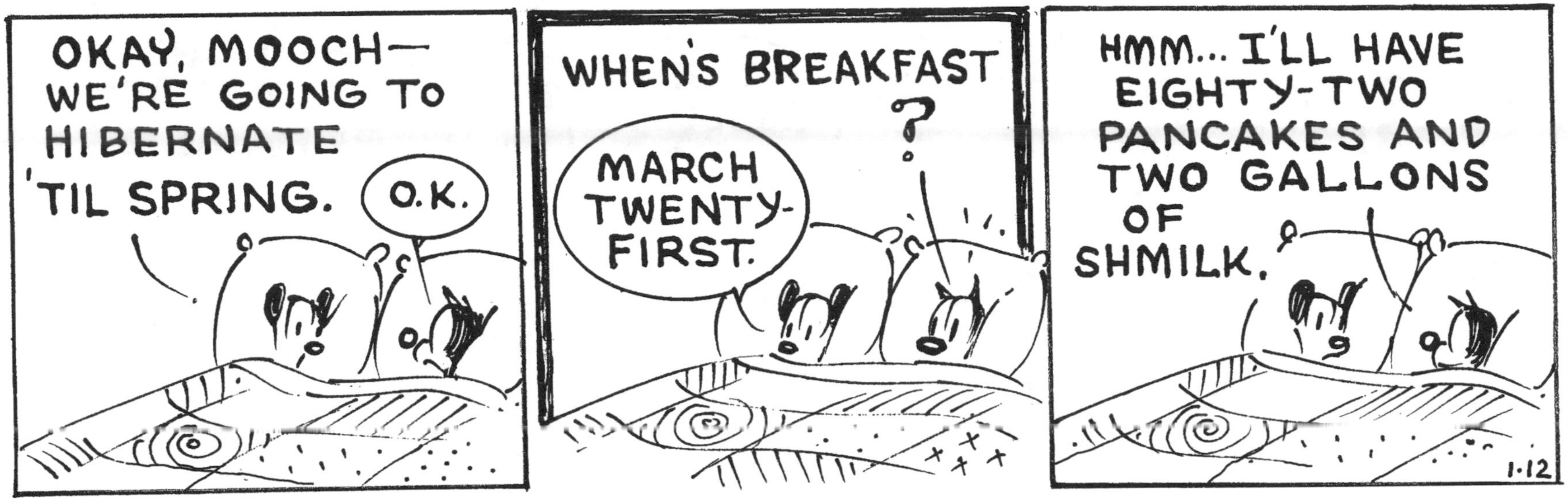
OKAY, MOOCH— WE'RE GOING TO HIBERNATE 'TIL SPRING.
O.K.
WHEN'S BREAKFAST ?
MARCH TWENTY-FIRST.
HMM... I'LL HAVE EIGHTY-TWO PANCAKES AND TWO GALLONS OF SHMILK.
1.12

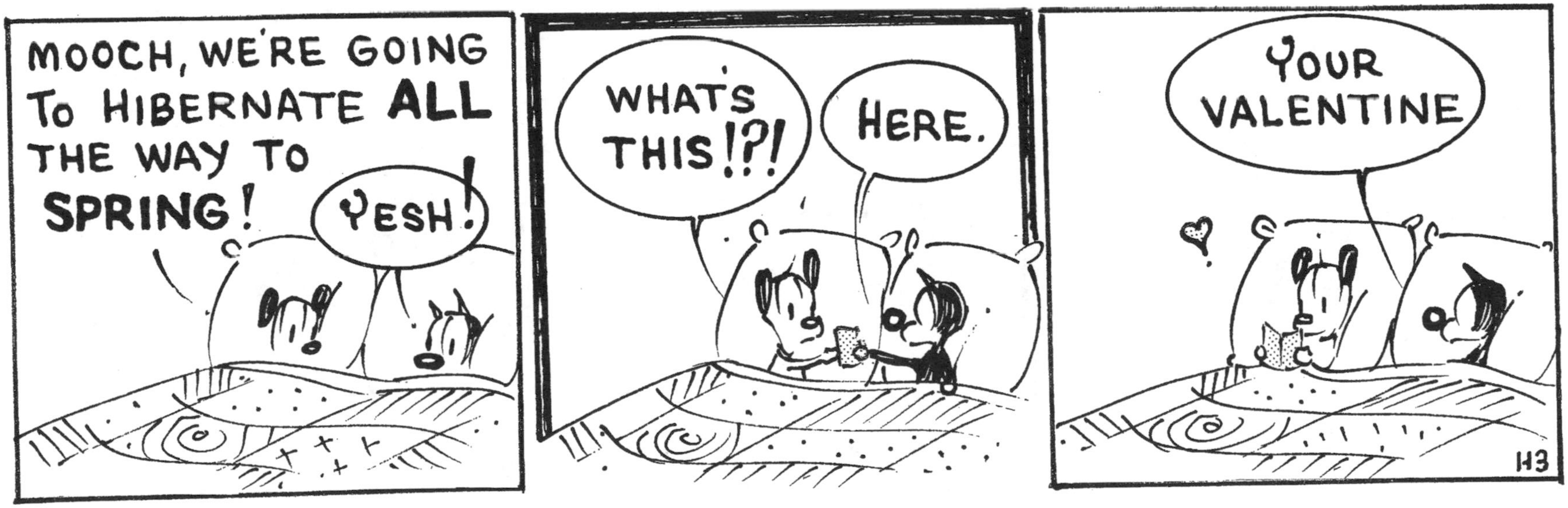
MOOCH, WE'RE GOING TO HIBERNATE ALL THE WAY TO SPRING!
YESH!
WHAT'S THIS!?!
HERE.
YOUR VALENTINE
1-13

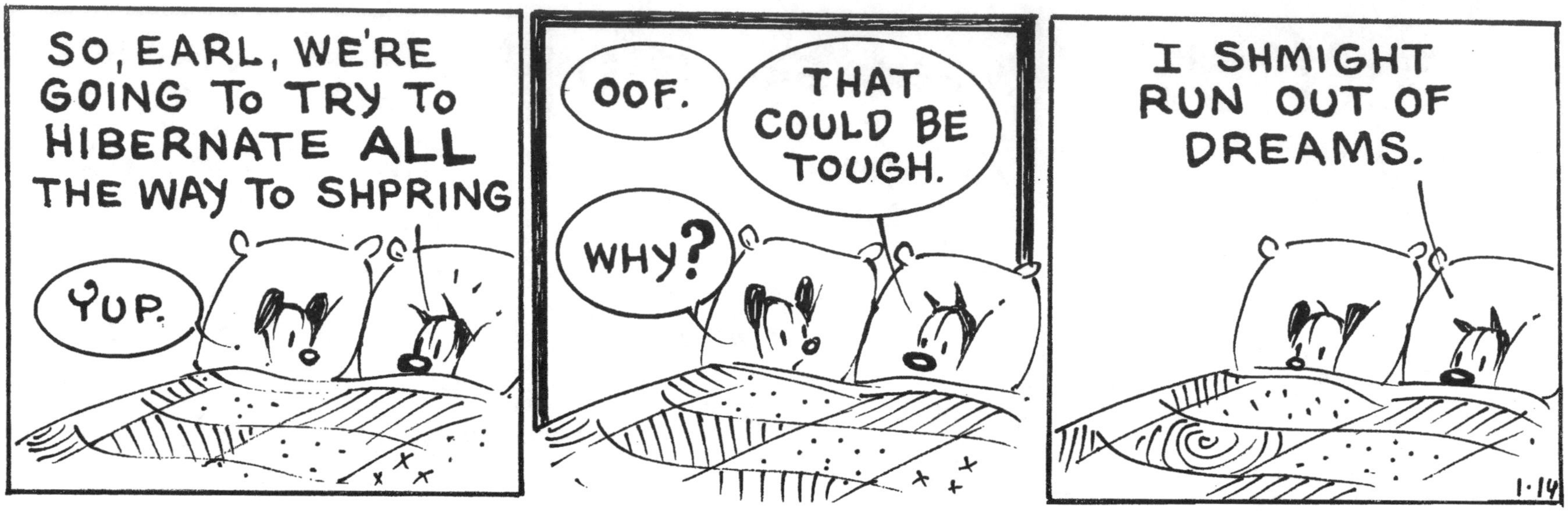
SO, EARL, WE'RE GOING TO TRY TO HIBERNATE ALL THE WAY TO SHPRING
YUP.
OOF.
THAT COULD BE TOUGH.
WHY?
I SHMIGHT RUN OUT OF DREAMS.
1·14

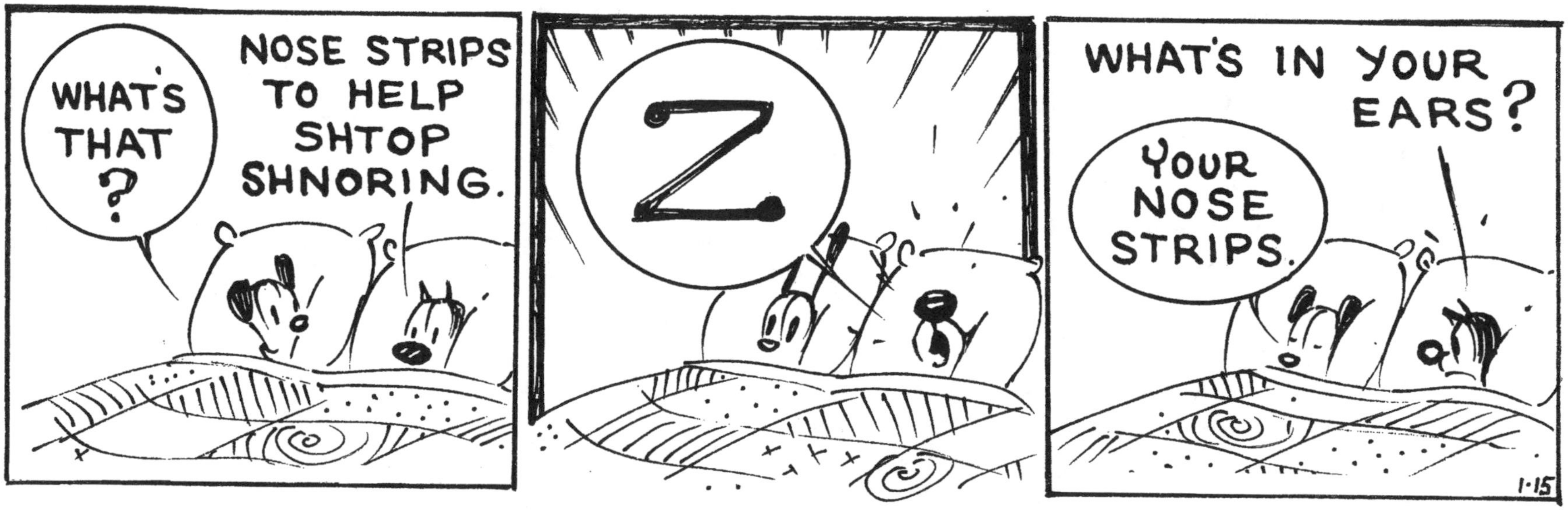
WHAT'S THAT ?
NOSE STRIPS TO HELP SHTOP SHNORING.
Z
WHAT'S IN YOUR EARS?
YOUR NOSE STRIPS.
1·15

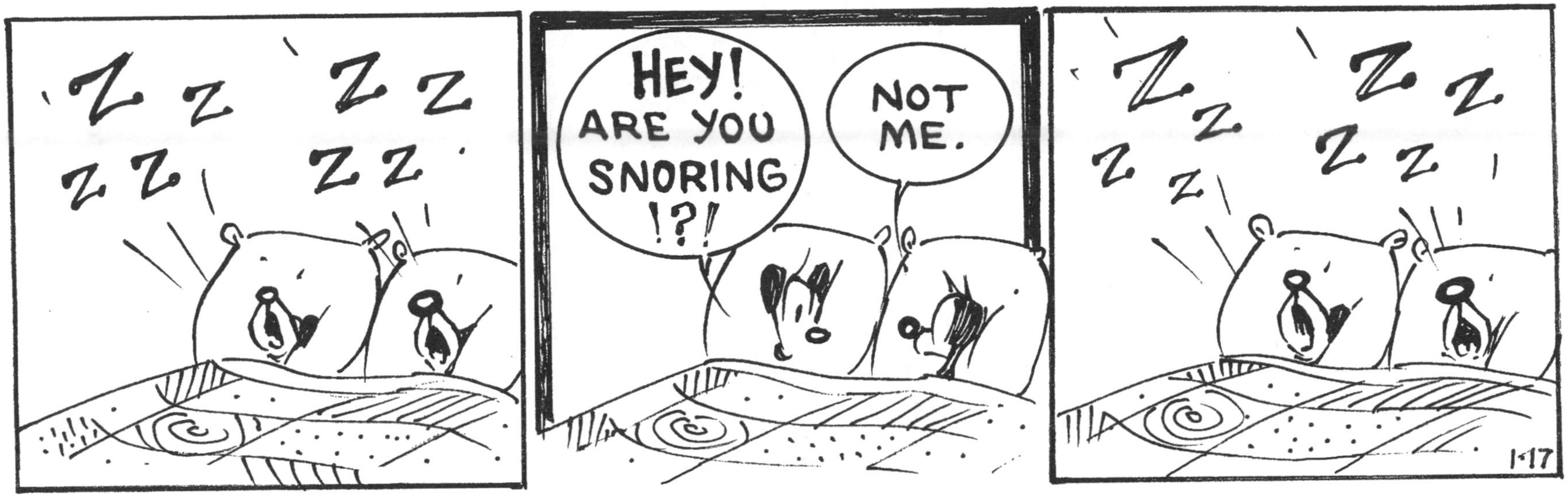
Z Z Z Z Z Z
HEY! ARE YOU SNORING !?!
NOT ME.
Z Z Z Z Z Z Z Z
1·17

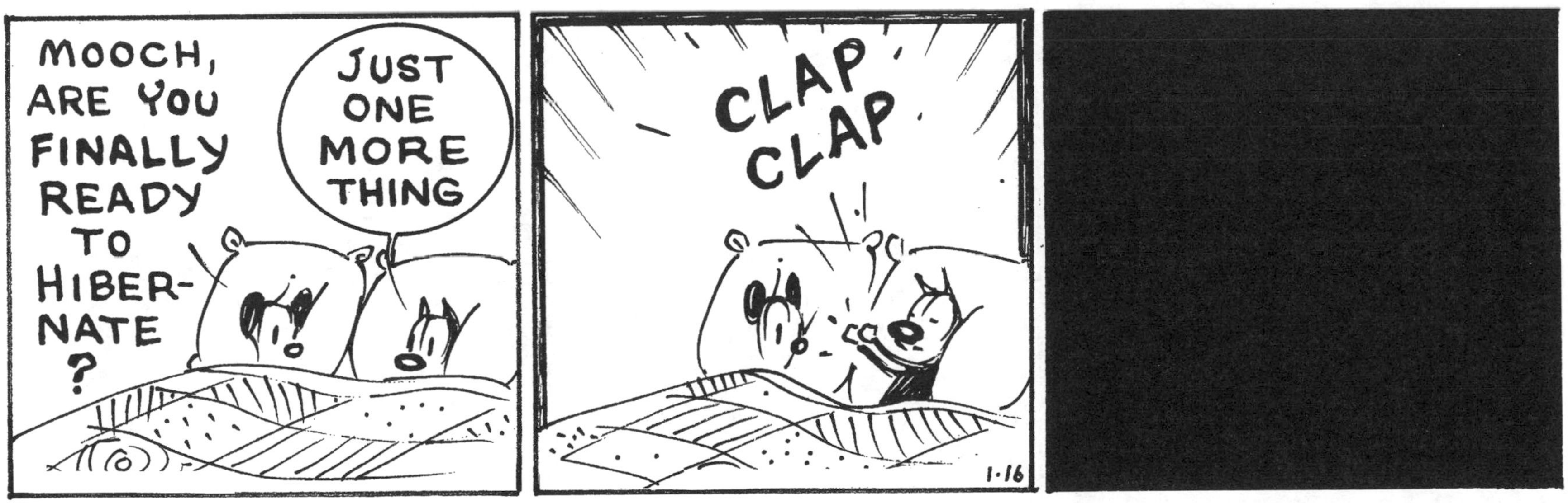
MOOCH, ARE YOU FINALLY READY TO HIBER-NATE ?
JUST ONE MORE THING
CLAP CLAP
1·16

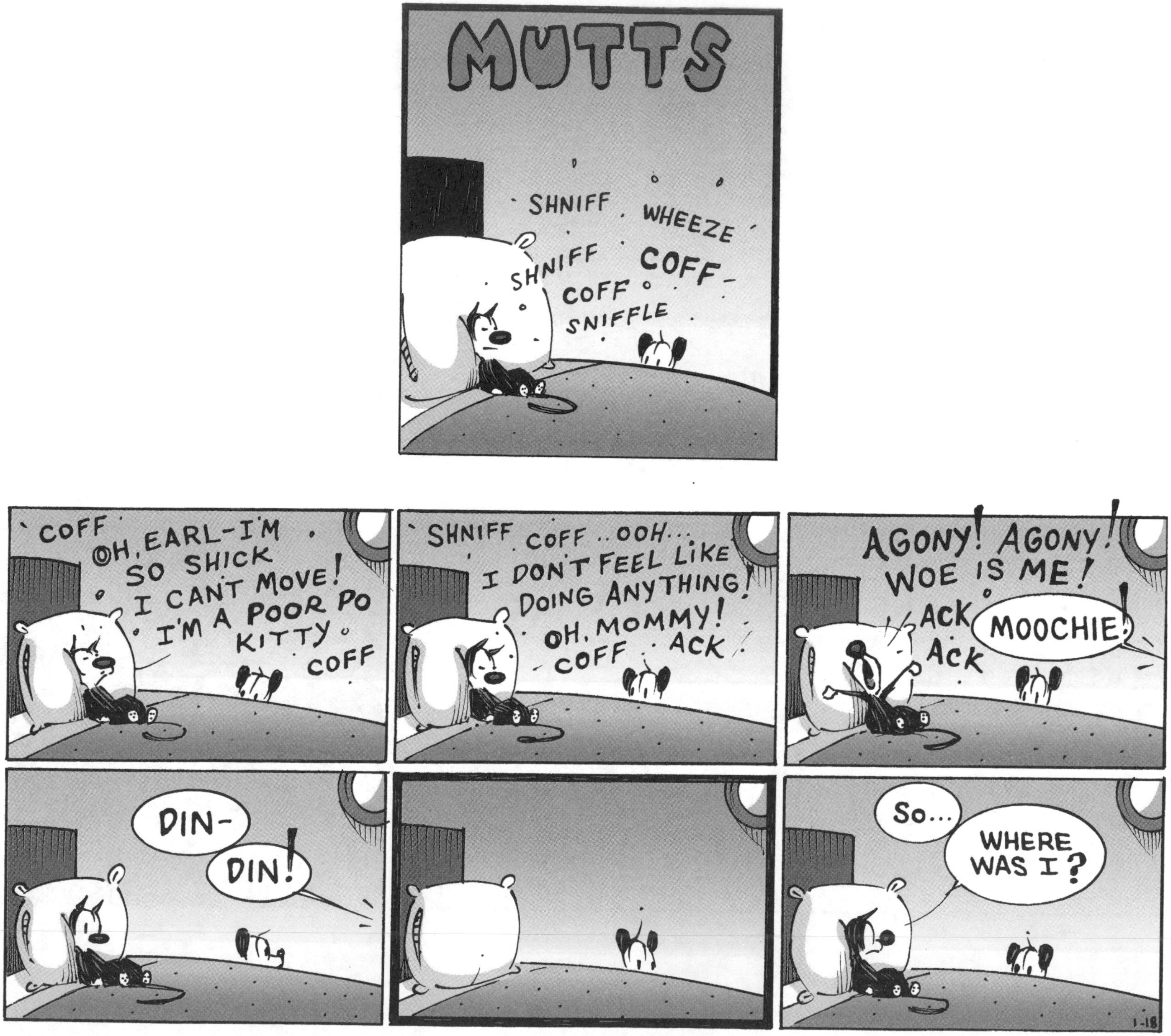
MUTTS
SHNIFF
WHEEZE
SHNIFF
COFF
COFF
SNIFFLE
COFF
OH, EARL- I'M SO SHICK
I CAN'T MOVE!
I'M A POOR PO KITTY
COFF
SHNIFF
COFF .. OOH...
I DON'T FEEL LIKE DOING ANYTHING!
OH, MOMMY!
COFF
ACK
AGONY! AGONY! WOE IS ME!
ACK
ACK
MOOCHIE!
DIN-
DIN!
SO...
WHERE WAS I?
1-18

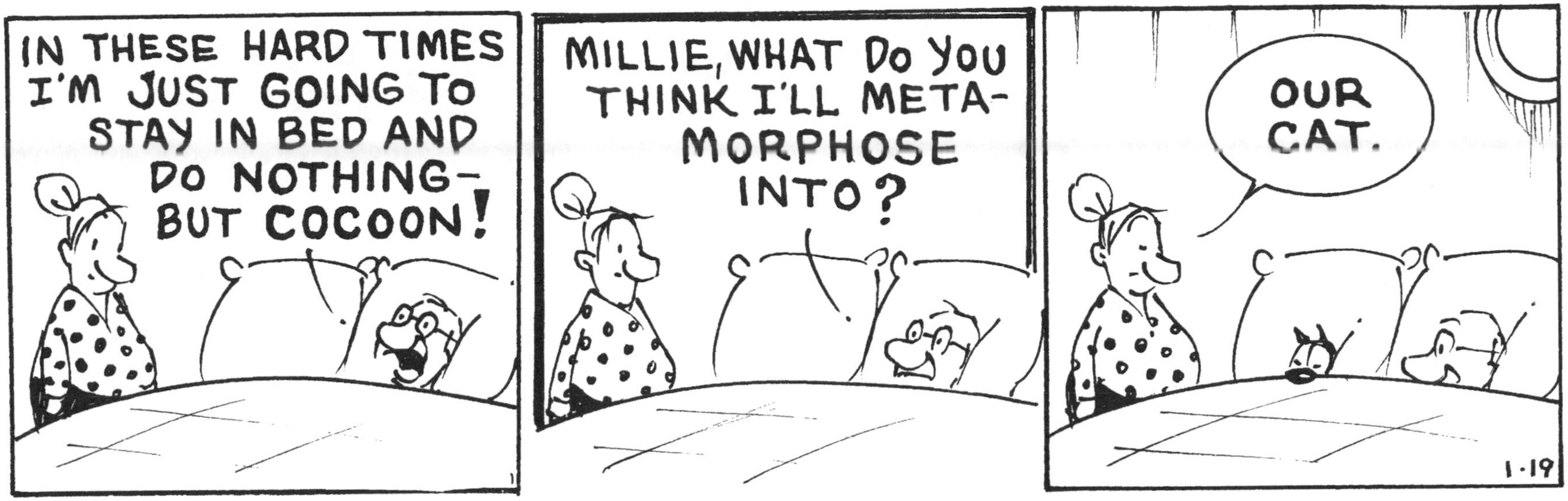
IN THESE HARD TIMES I'M JUST GOING TO STAY IN BED AND DO NOTHING- BUT COCOON!
MILLIE, WHAT DO YOU THINK I'LL META-MORPHOSE INTO?
OUR CAT.
1-19

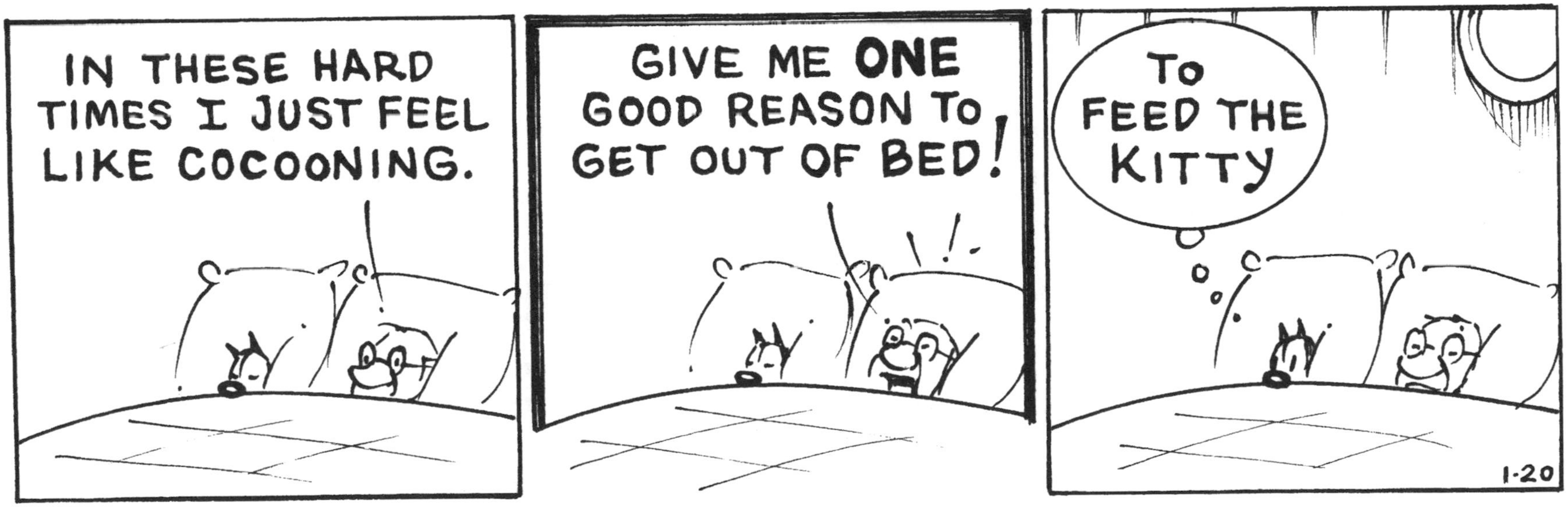
IN THESE HARD TIMES I JUST FEEL LIKE COCOONING.
GIVE ME ONE GOOD REASON TO GET OUT OF BED!
TO FEED THE KITTY
1-20

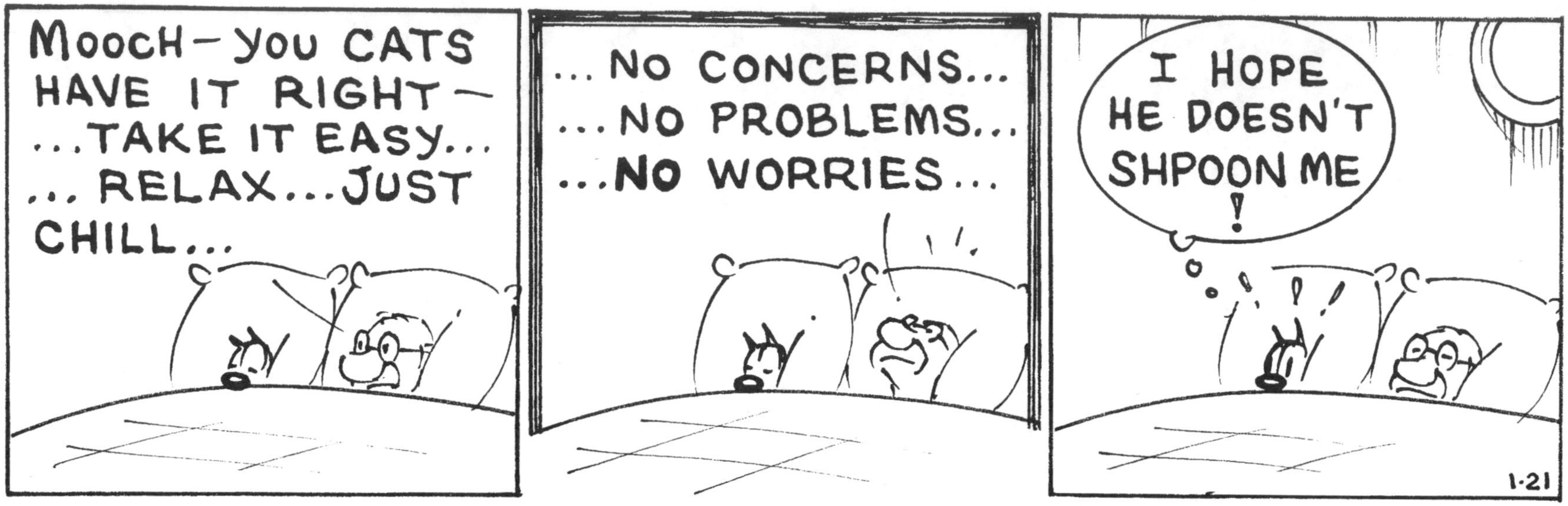
MOOCH—YOU CATS HAVE IT RIGHT—
...TAKE IT EASY...
...RELAX...JUST CHILL...
...NO CONCERNS...
...NO PROBLEMS...
...NO WORRIES...
I HOPE HE DOESN'T SHPOON ME!
1·21

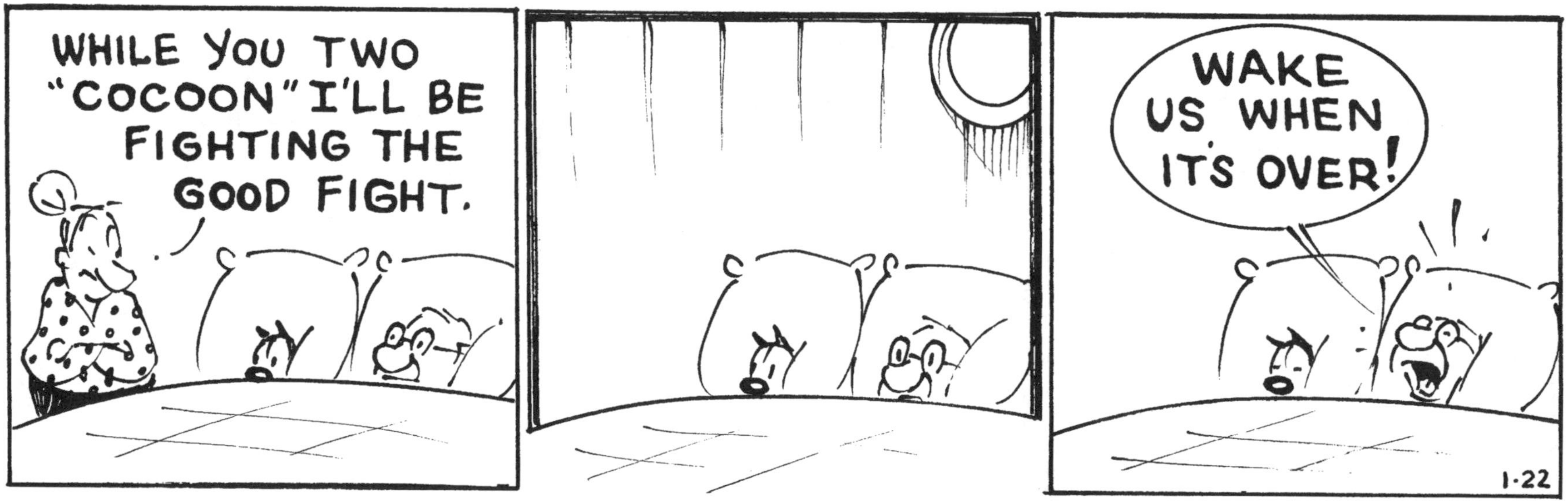
WHILE YOU TWO "COCOON" I'LL BE FIGHTING THE GOOD FIGHT.
WAKE US WHEN IT'S OVER!
1·22

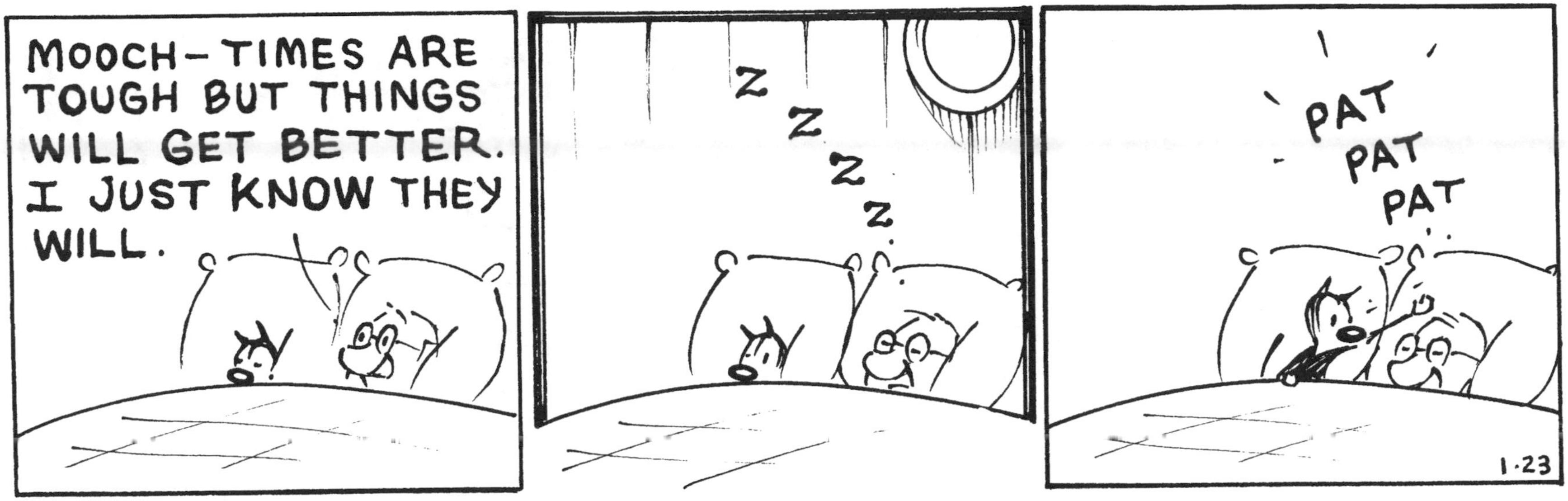
MOOCH– TIMES ARE TOUGH BUT THINGS WILL GET BETTER. I JUST KNOW THEY WILL.
Z Z Z Z
PAT PAT PAT
1·23

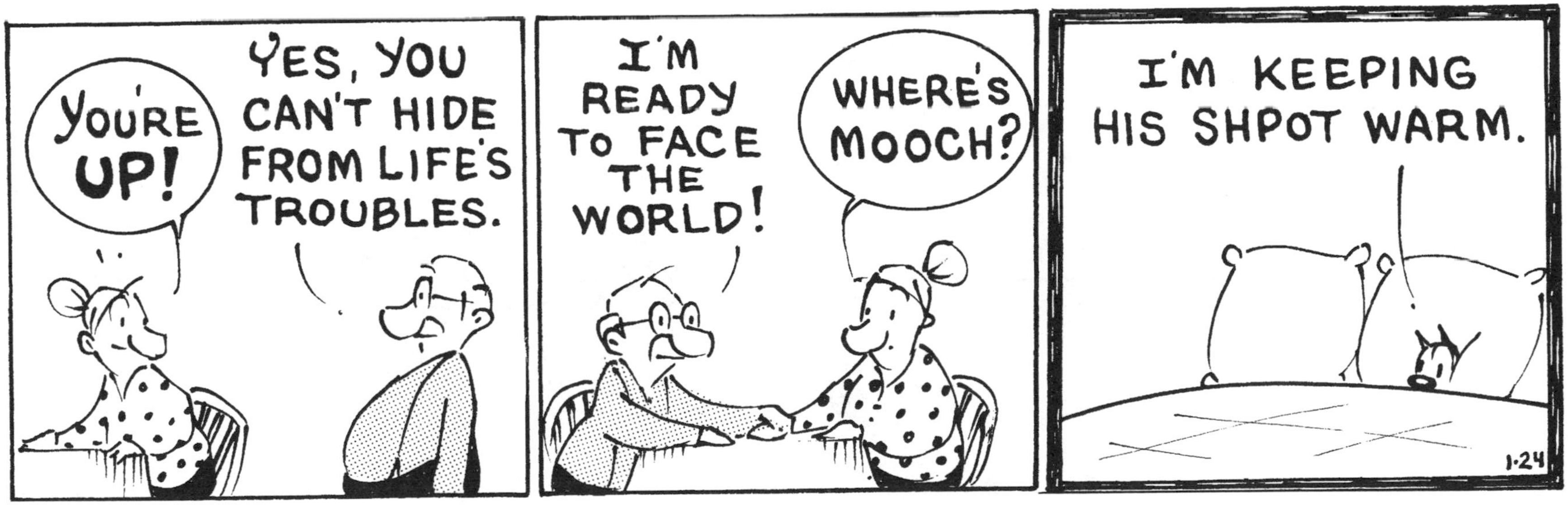
YOU'RE UP!
YES, YOU CAN'T HIDE FROM LIFE'S TROUBLES.
I'M READY TO FACE THE WORLD!
WHERE'S MOOCH?
I'M KEEPING HIS SHPOT WARM.
1·24

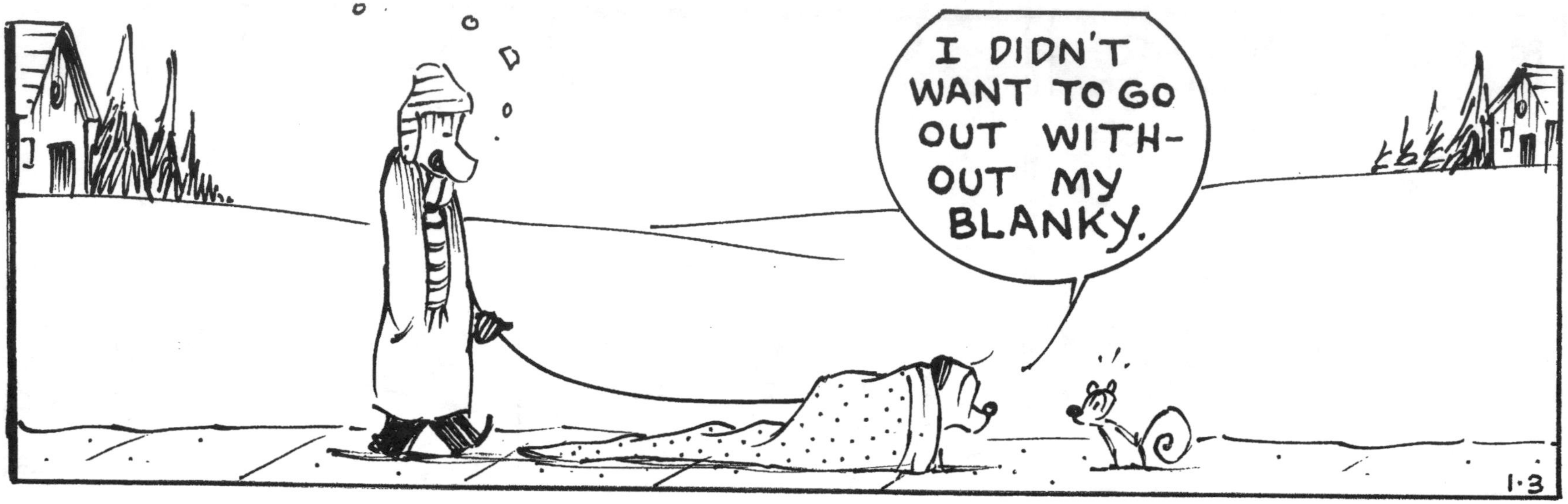
I DIDN'T WANT TO GO OUT WITH-OUT MY BLANKY.
1·3

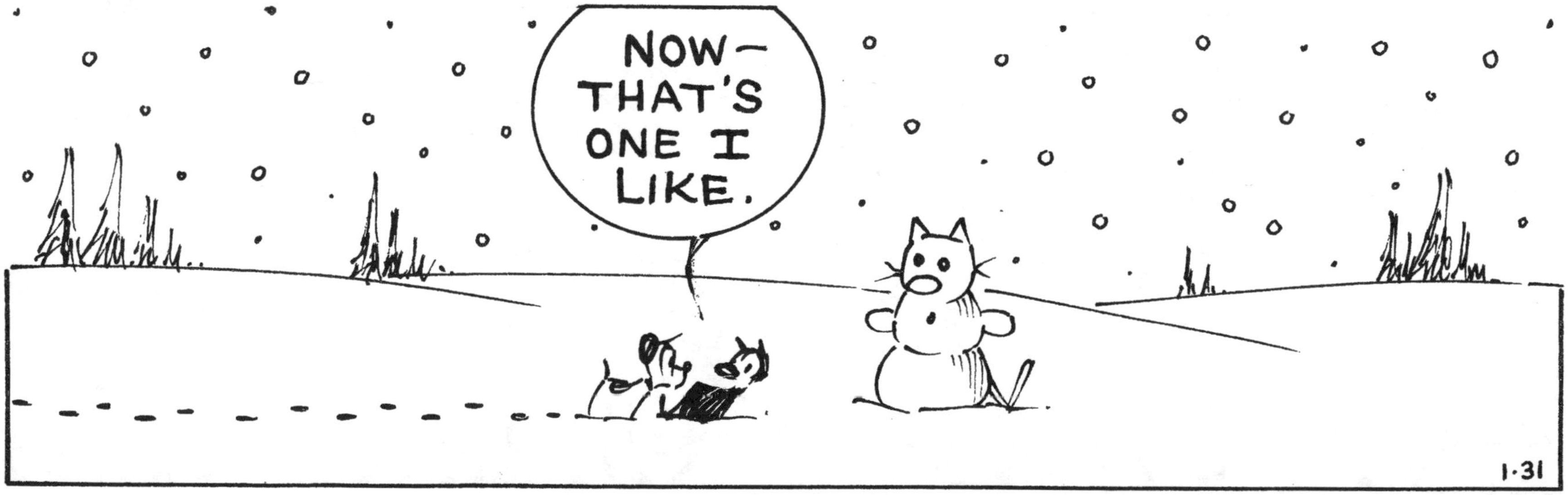
NOW—THAT'S ONE I LIKE.
1·31

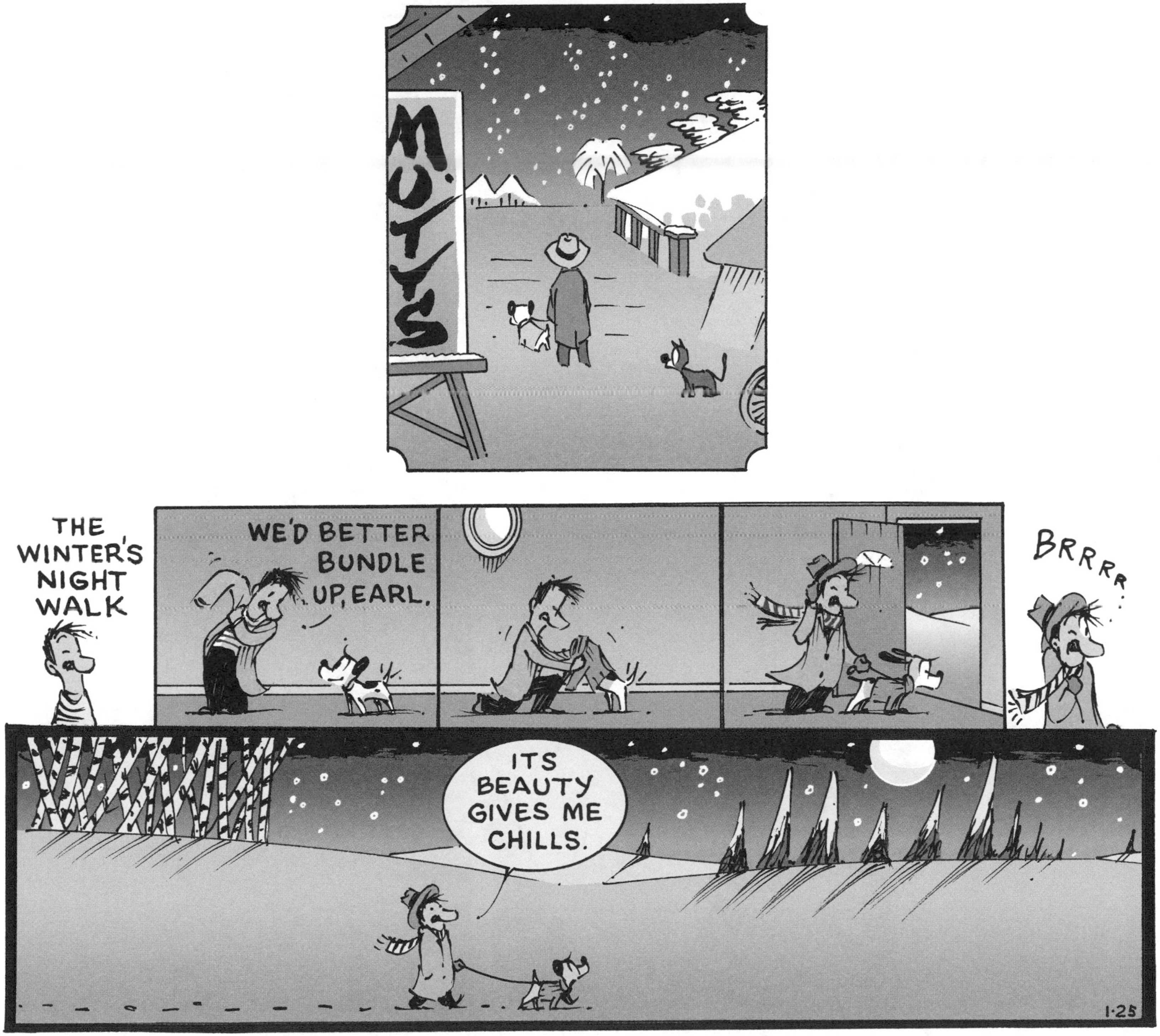
MUTTS
THE WINTER'S NIGHT WALK
WE'D BETTER BUNDLE UP, EARL.
BRRRRR
ITS BEAUTY GIVES ME CHILLS.
1·25

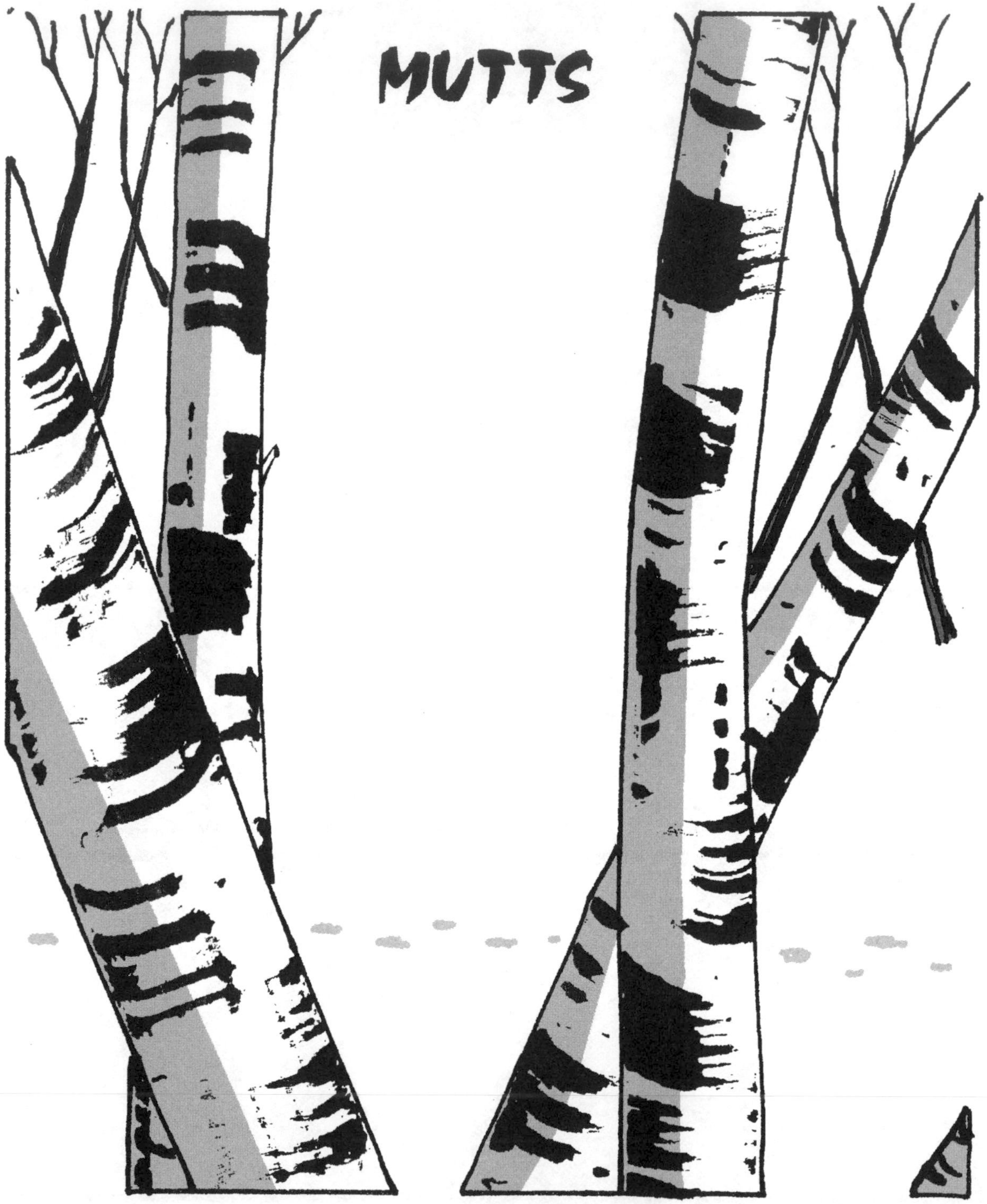
MUTTS

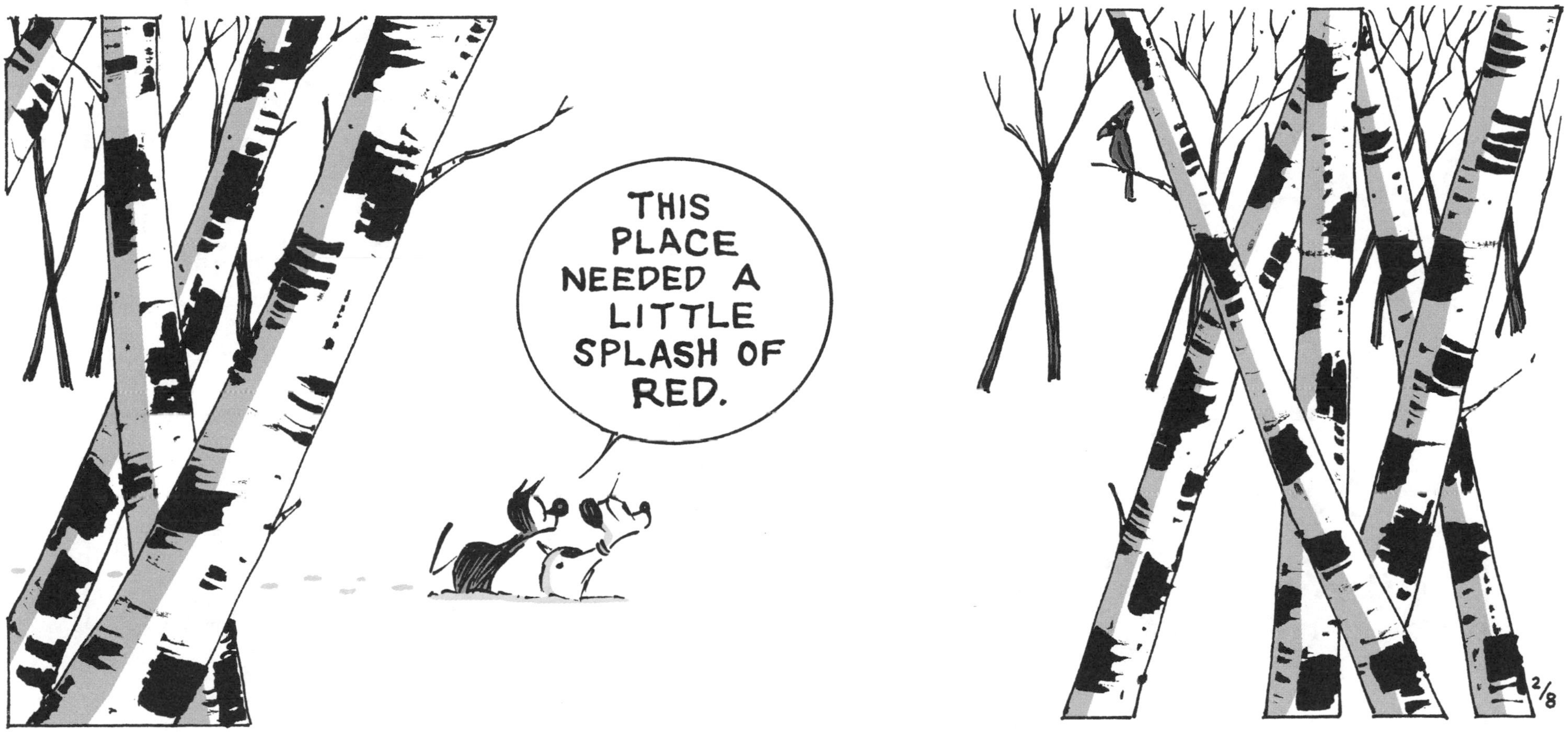
THIS PLACE NEEDED A LITTLE SPLASH OF RED.

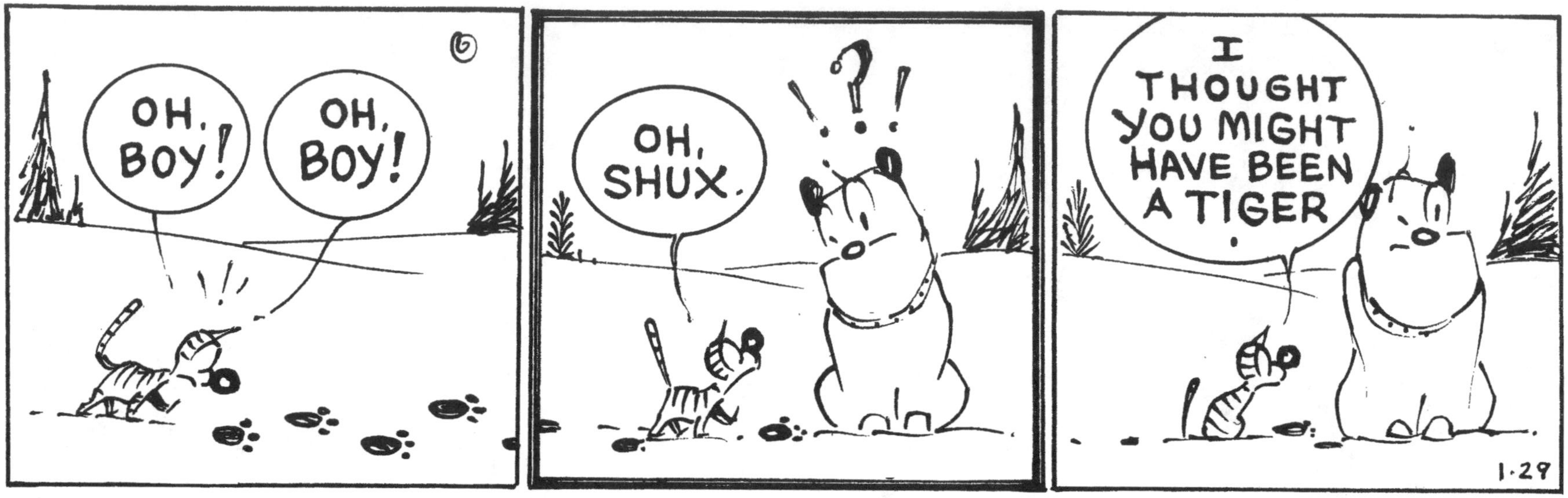
OH, BOY!
OH, BOY!
OH, SHUX.
!?!
I THOUGHT YOU MIGHT HAVE BEEN A TIGER.
1·29

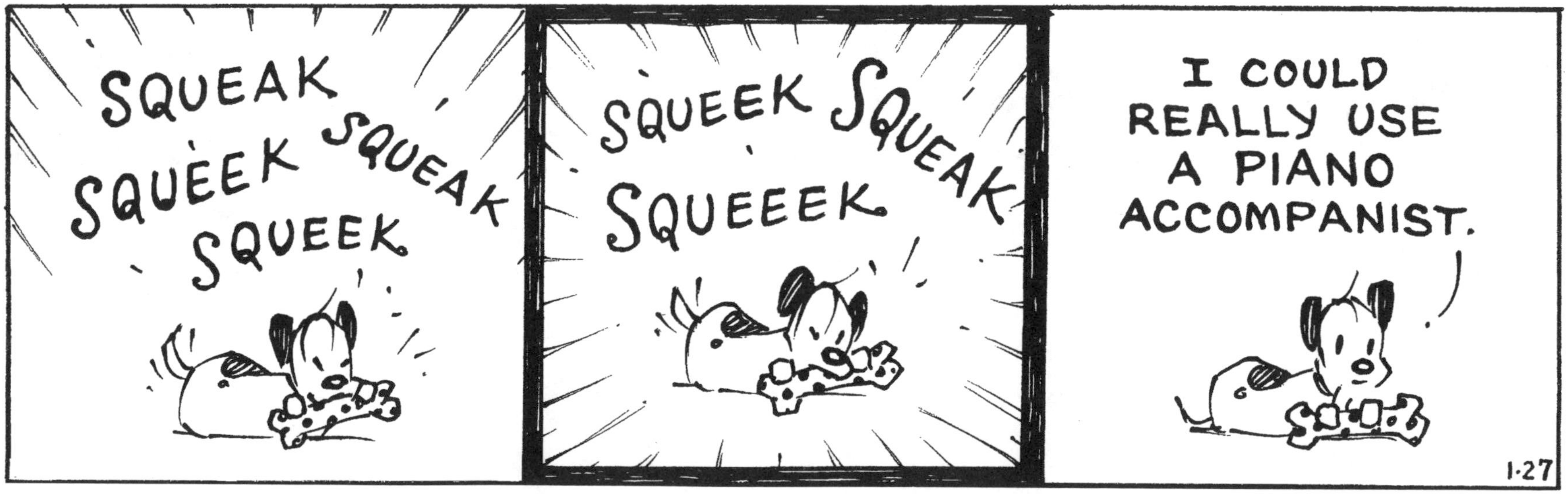
SQUEAK SQUEEK SQUEAK SQUEEK
SQUEEK SQUEAK SQUEEEK
I COULD REALLY USE A PIANO ACCOMPANIST.
1·27

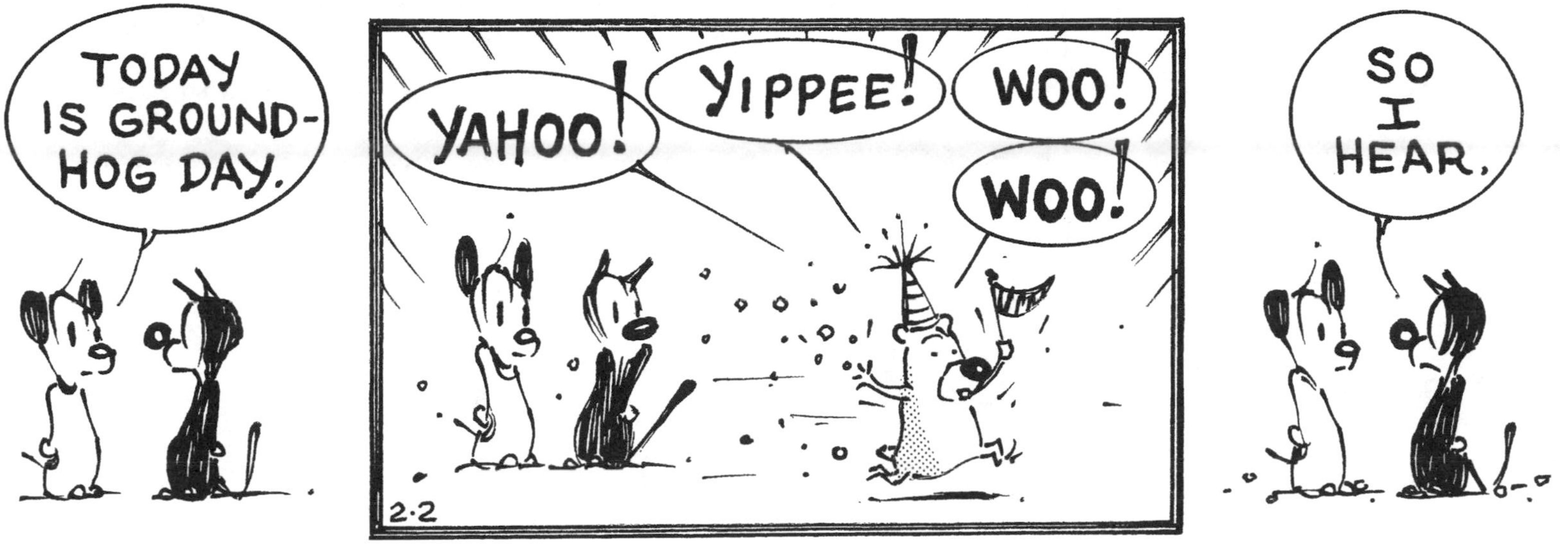
TODAY IS GROUND-HOG DAY.
YAHOO!
YIPPEE!
WOO!
WOO!
2.2
SO I HEAR.

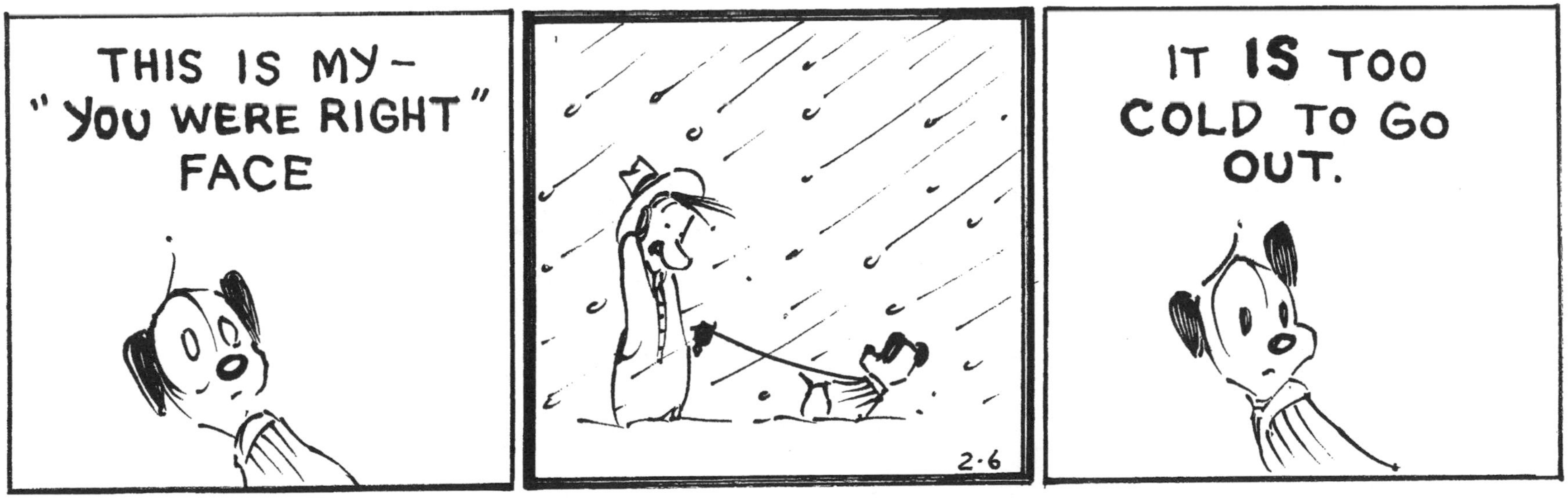
THIS IS MY- "YOU WERE RIGHT" FACE
2.6
IT IS TOO COLD TO GO OUT.

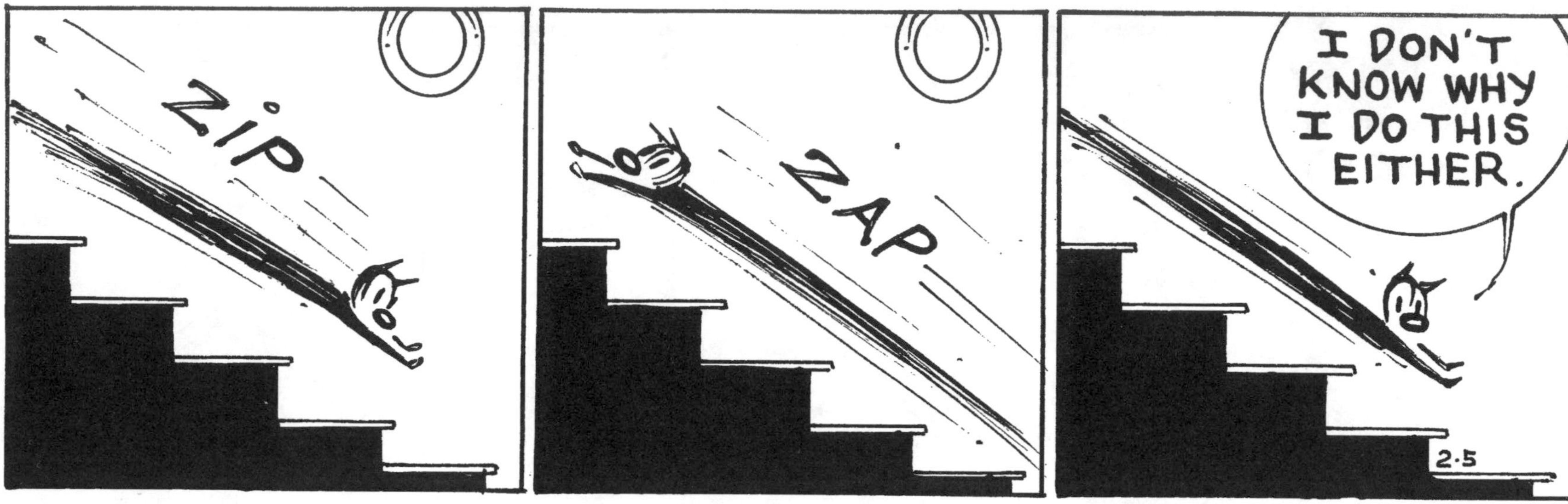
ZIP
ZAP
I DON'T KNOW WHY I DO THIS EITHER.
2·5

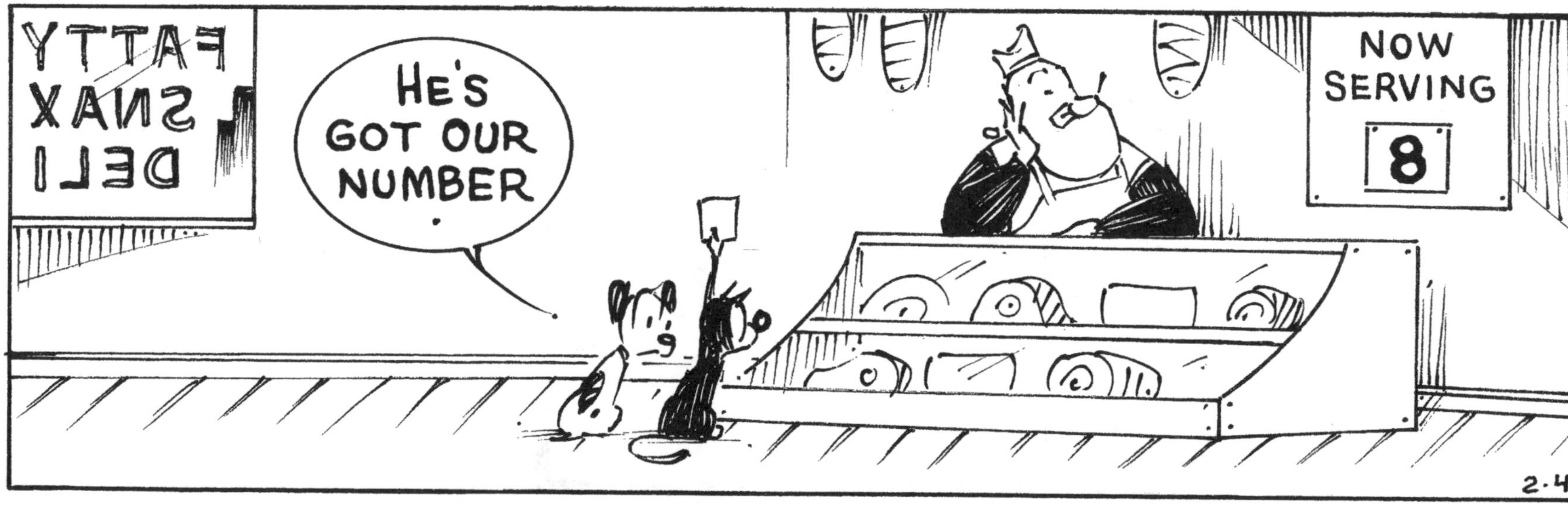
FATTY SNAX DELI
HE'S GOT OUR NUMBER
NOW SERVING
8
2·4

Love is, above all,

the gift of oneself.

~ Jean Anouilh

2·9

Love is the only force capable of

transforming an enemy into friend.

~ Martin Luther King, Jr.

PAT
PAT

2·10

The heart that loves
is forever young.

– Greek proverb

2·11

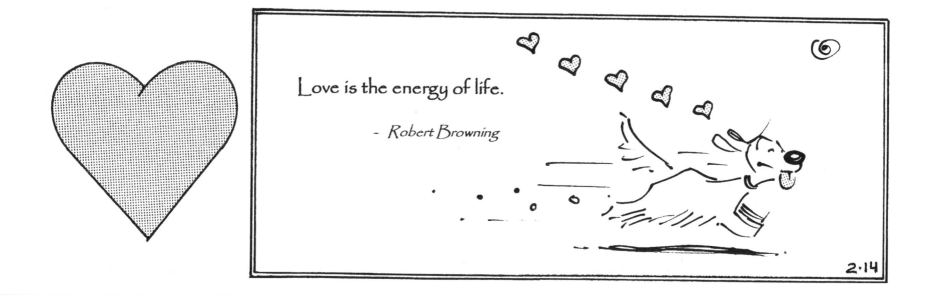

Love is the energy of life.

– Robert Browning

2·14

To the world you may be one person,

but to one person you may be the world.

– Heather Cortez

2·13

The more I think about it,

the more I realize there is nothing more artistic

than to love others.

– Vincent van Gogh

2·12

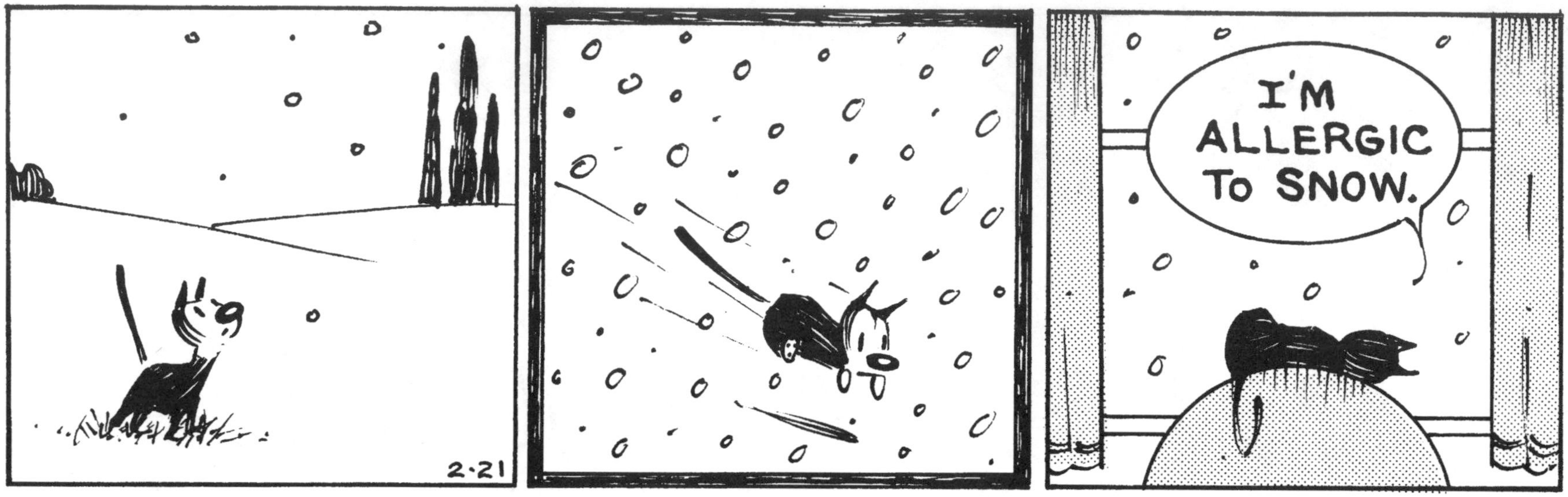
2·21
I'M ALLERGIC TO SNOW.

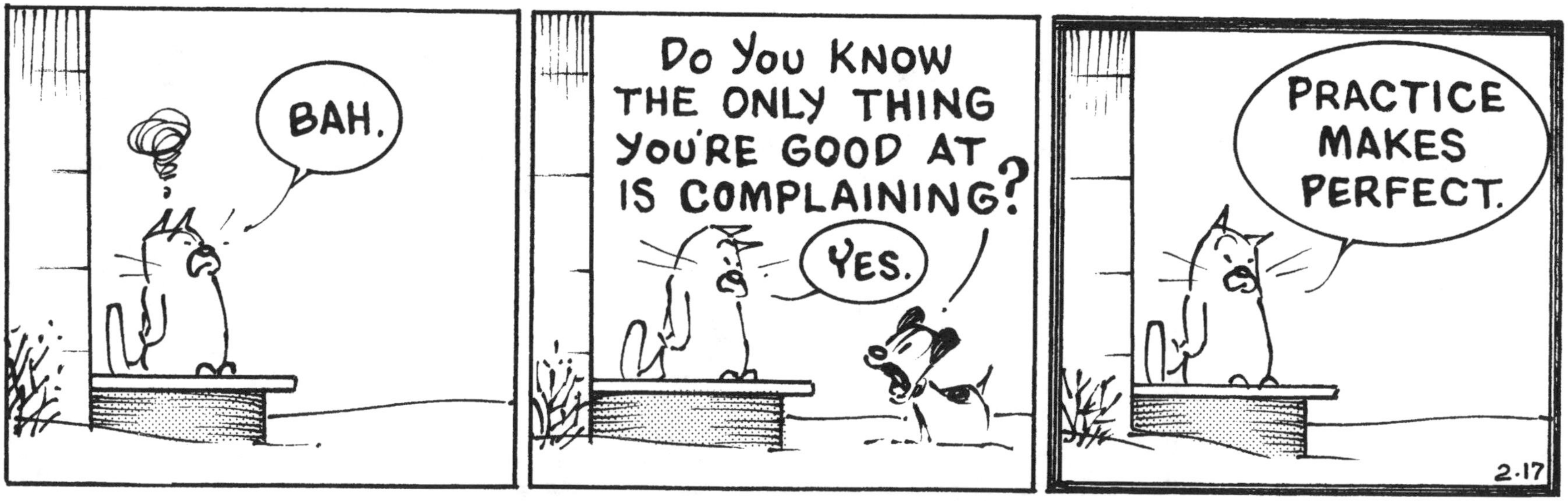
BAH.
DO YOU KNOW THE ONLY THING YOU'RE GOOD AT IS COMPLAINING?
YES.
PRACTICE MAKES PERFECT.
2·17

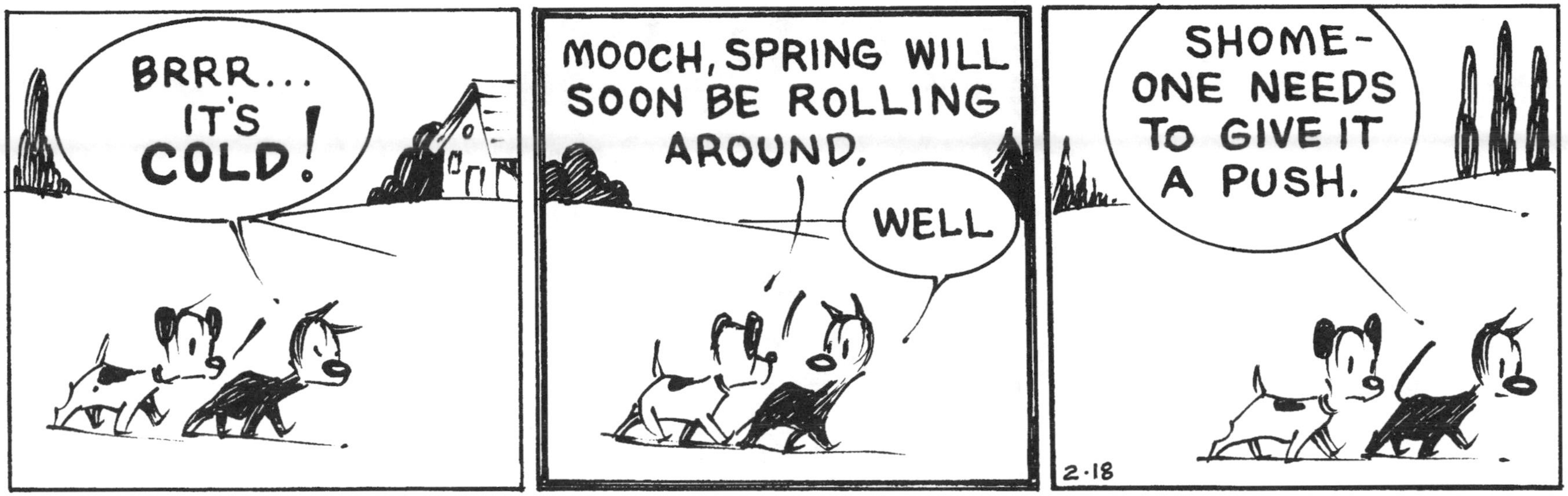
BRRR... IT'S COLD!
MOOCH, SPRING WILL SOON BE ROLLING AROUND.
WELL
SHOME-ONE NEEDS TO GIVE IT A PUSH.
2·18

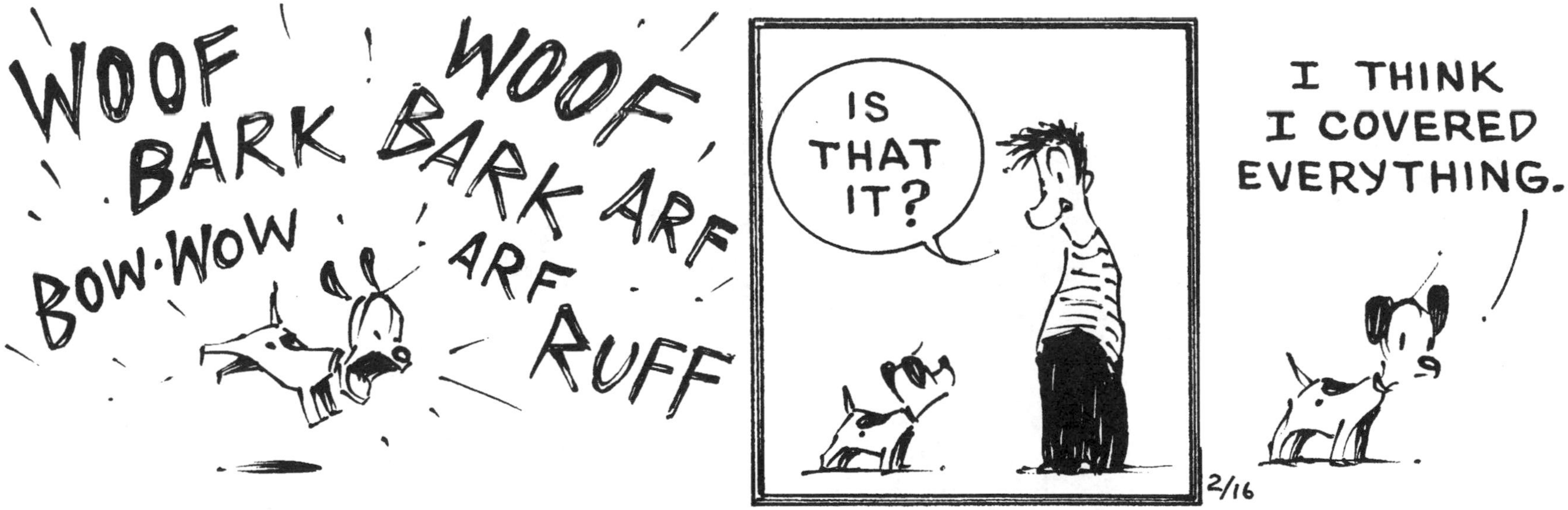
WOOF BARK WOOF BARK ARF BOW·WOW ARF RUFF
IS THAT IT?
I THINK I COVERED EVERYTHING.
2/16

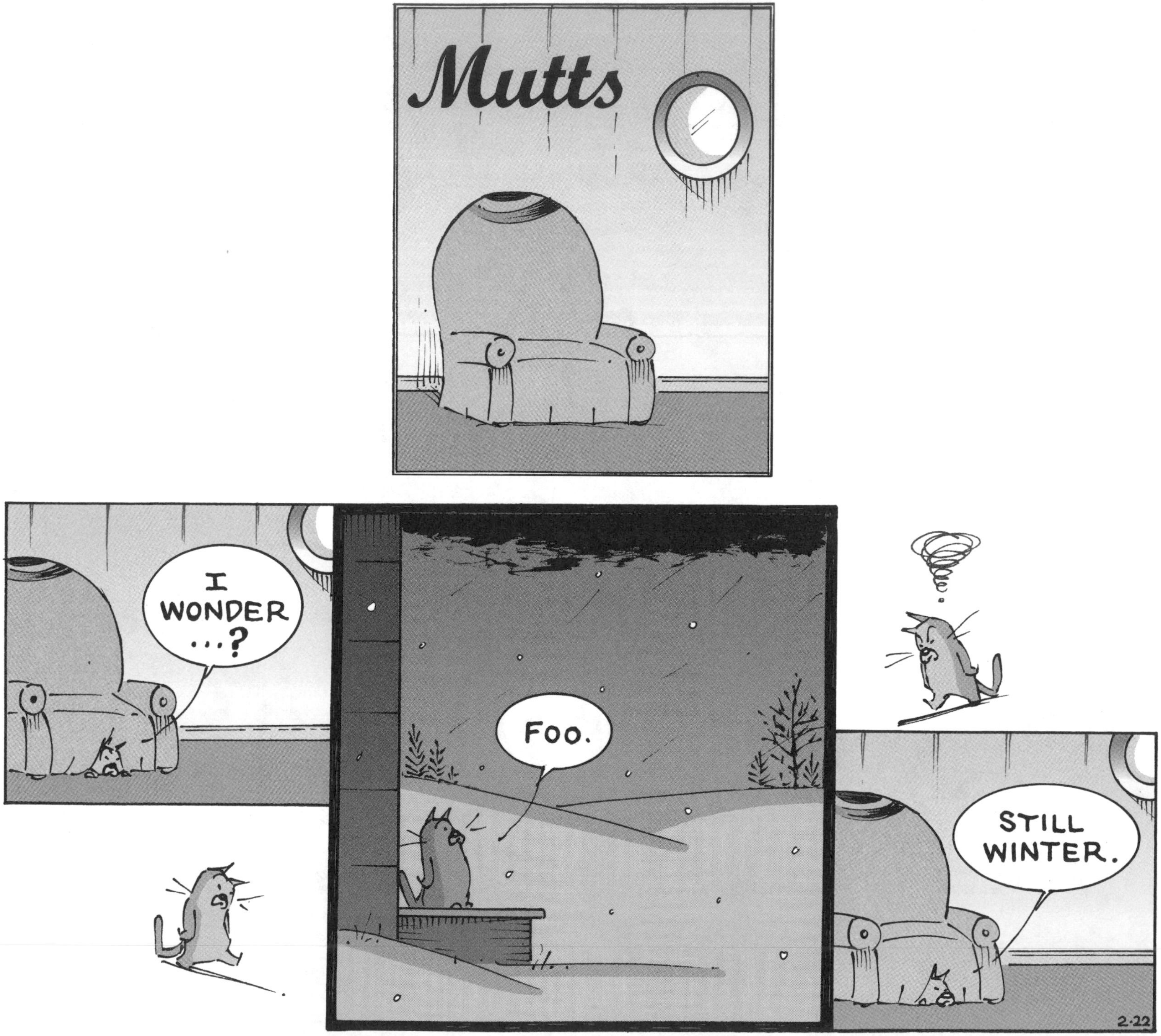
Mutts
I WONDER ...?
FOO.
STILL WINTER.
2·22

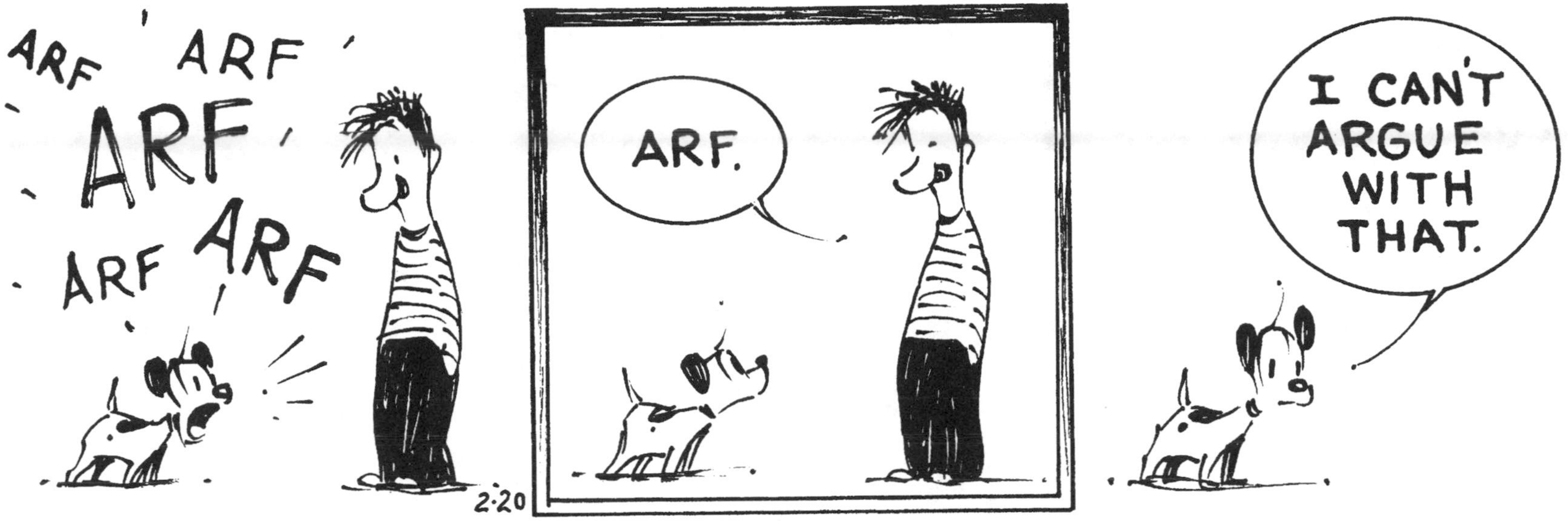
ARF ARF ARF ARF ARF
ARF.
I CAN'T ARGUE WITH THAT.
2·20

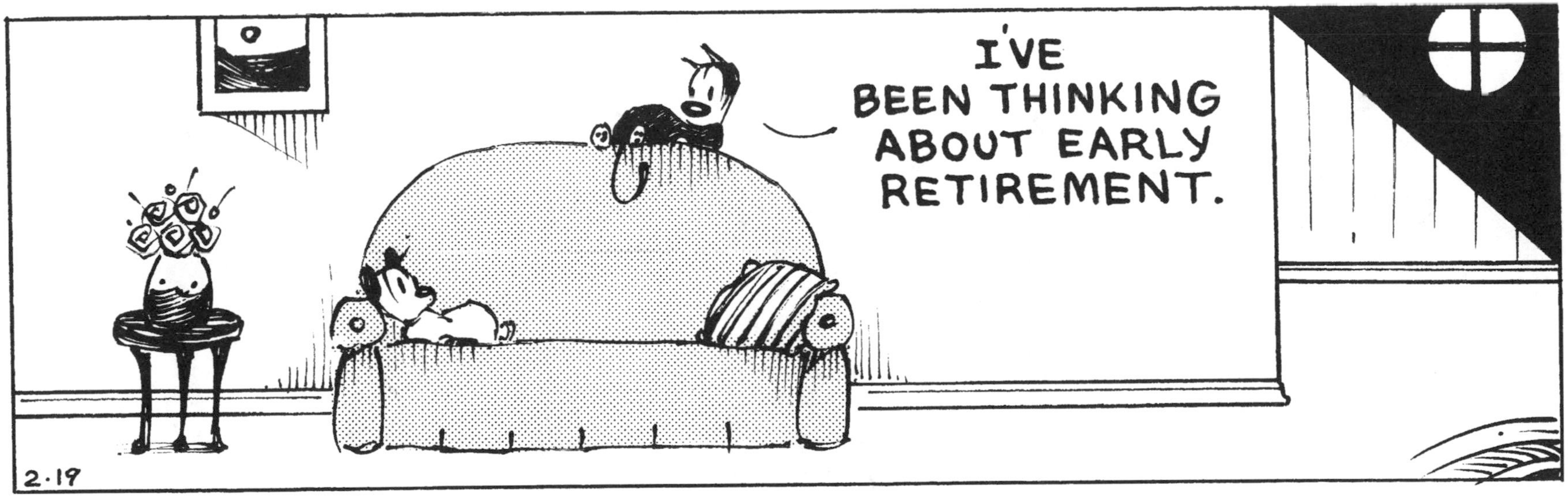
I'VE BEEN THINKING ABOUT EARLY RETIREMENT.
2·19

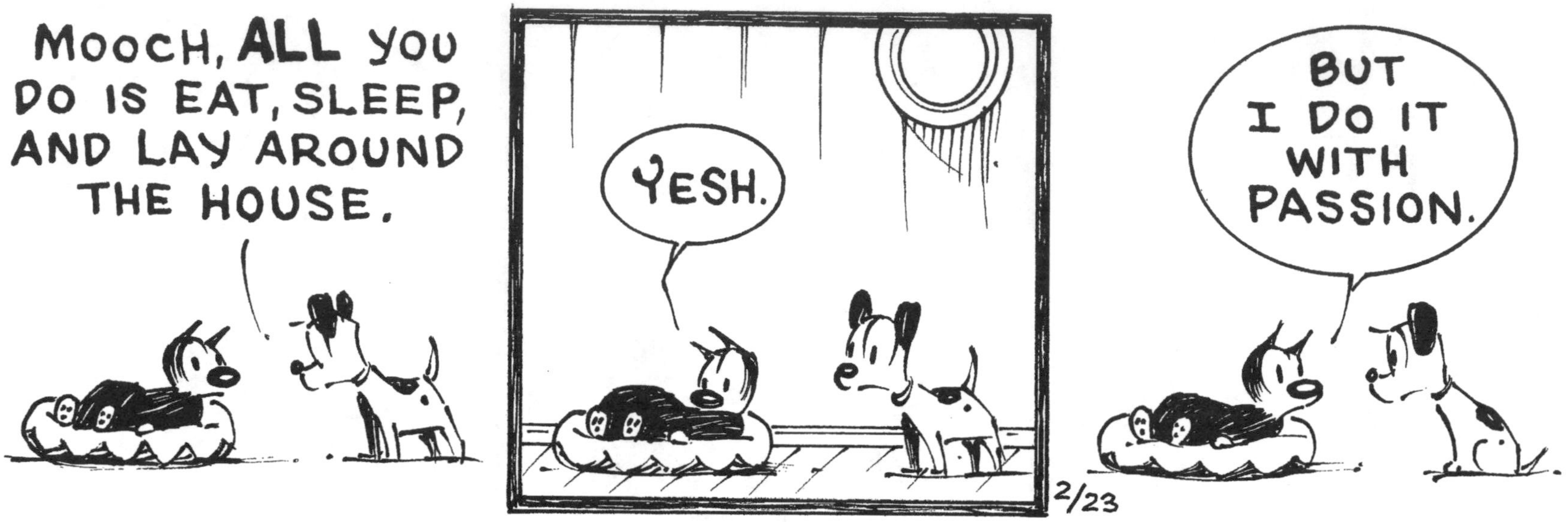
MOOCH, ALL YOU DO IS EAT, SLEEP, AND LAY AROUND THE HOUSE.
YESH.
BUT I DO IT WITH PASSION.
2/23

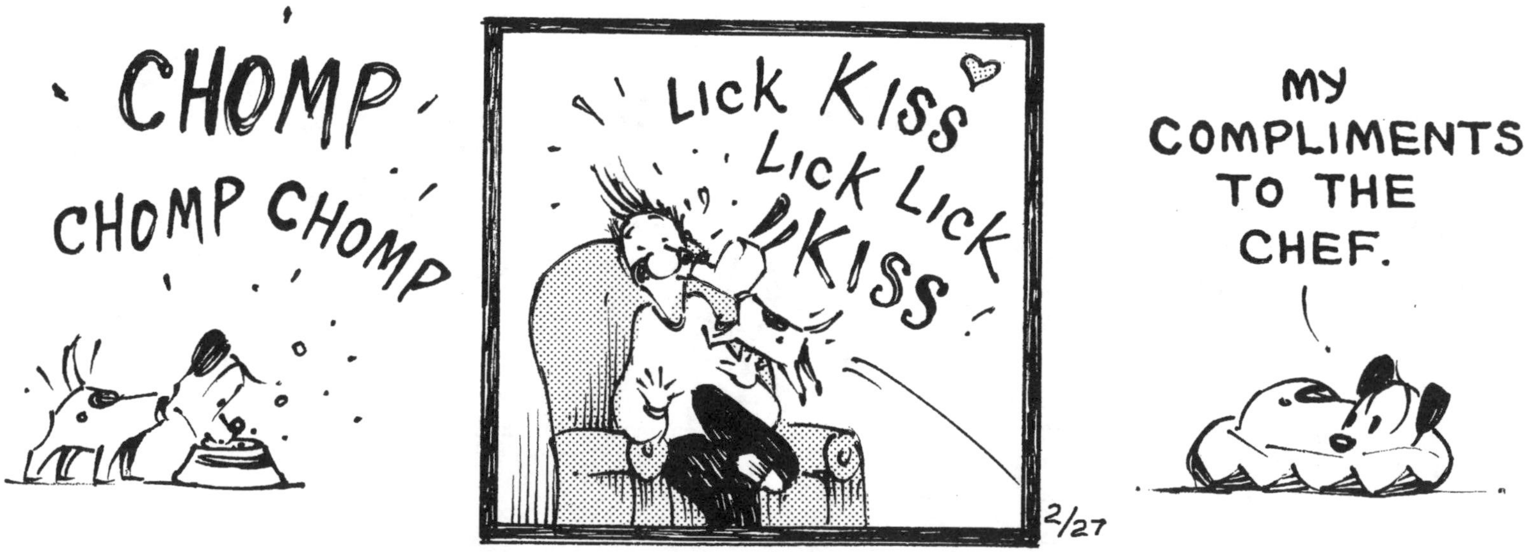
CHOMP
CHOMP CHOMP
LICK KISS
LICK LICK
KISS
MY COMPLIMENTS TO THE CHEF.
2/27

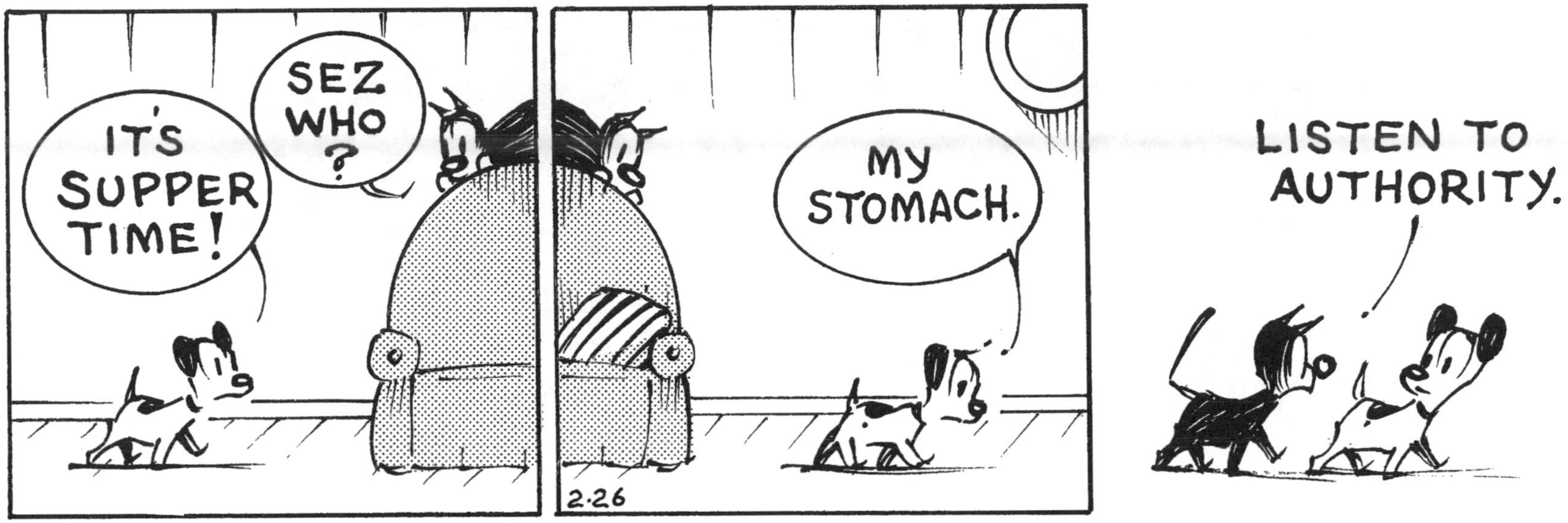
IT'S SUPPER TIME!
SEZ WHO?
MY STOMACH.
LISTEN TO AUTHORITY.
2.26

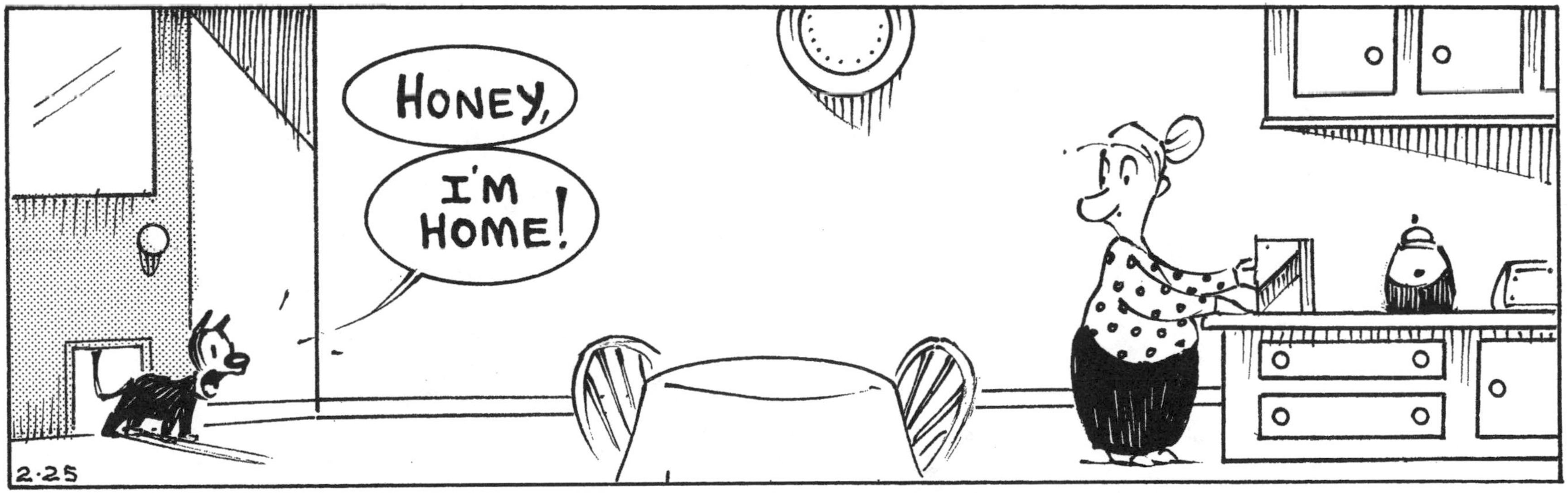
HONEY,
I'M HOME!
2.25

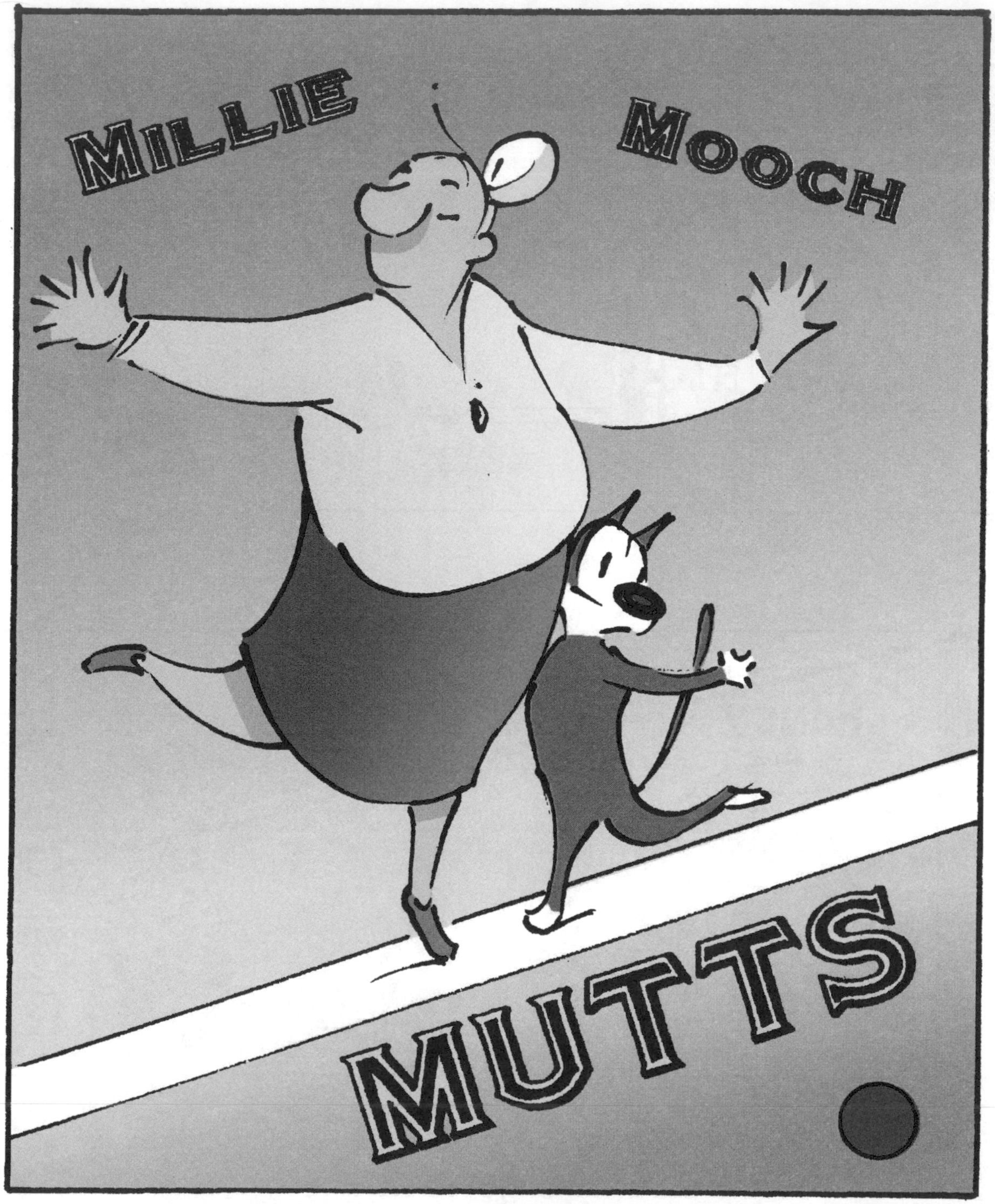
MILLIE
MOOCH
MUTTS

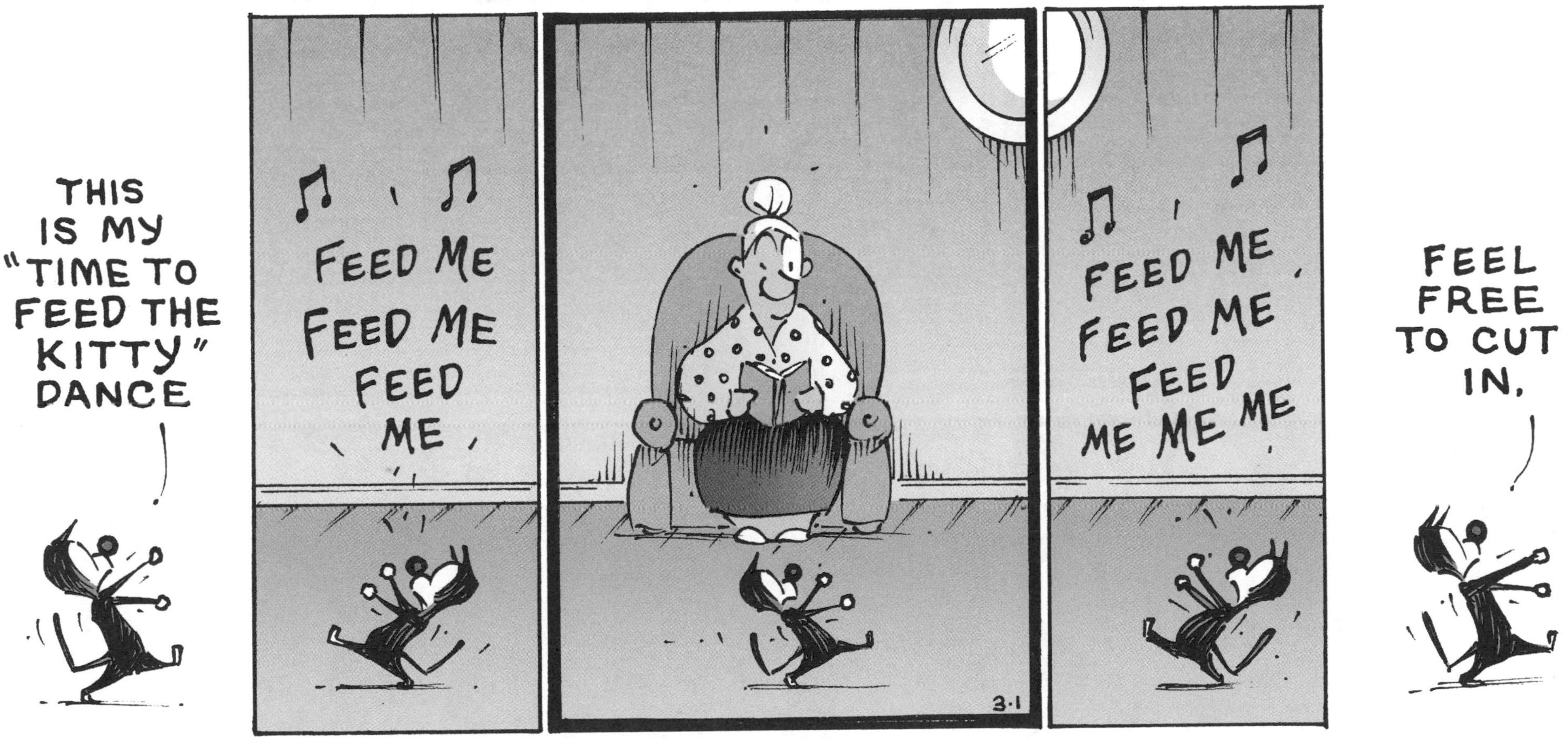
THIS IS MY "TIME TO FEED THE KITTY" DANCE
FEED ME FEED ME FEED ME
FEED ME FEED ME FEED ME ME ME
FEEL FREE TO CUT IN.

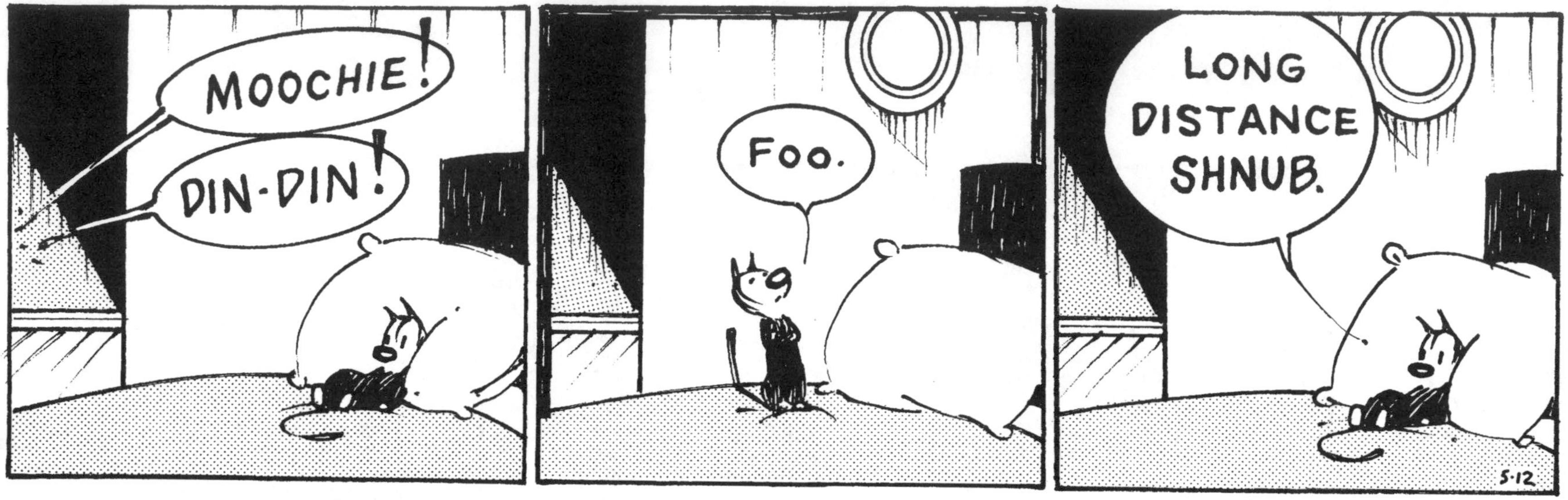
MOOCHIE!
DIN-DIN!
Foo.
LONG DISTANCE SHNUB.
5·12

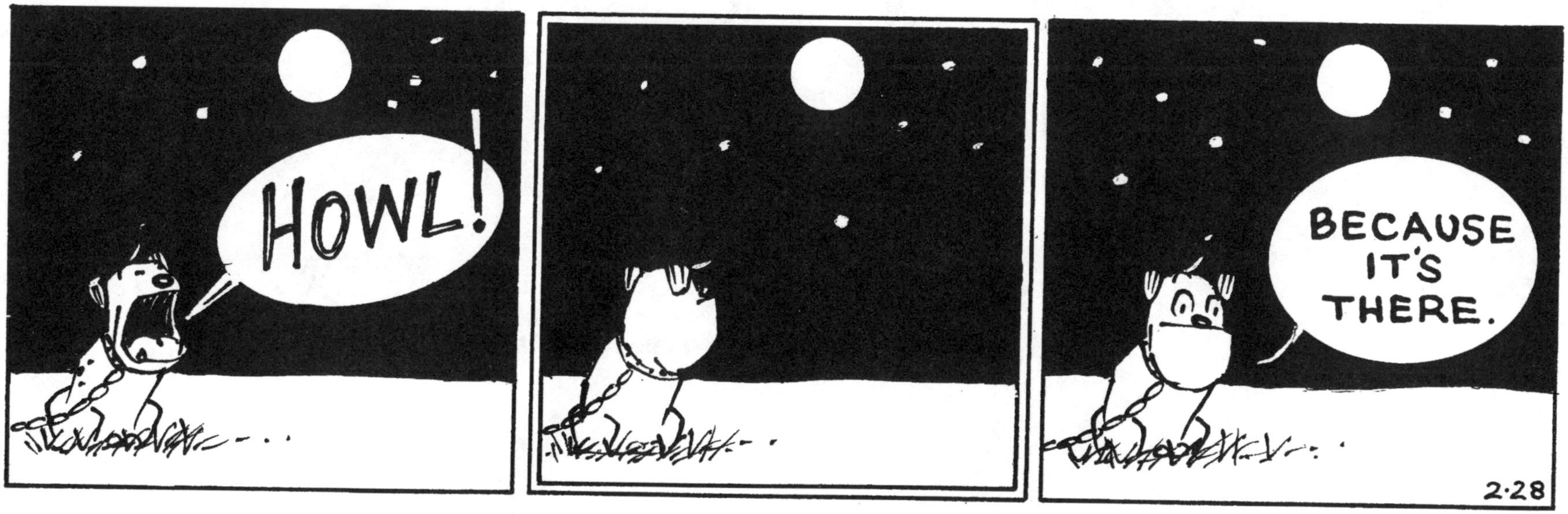
HOWL!
BECAUSE IT'S THERE.
2·28

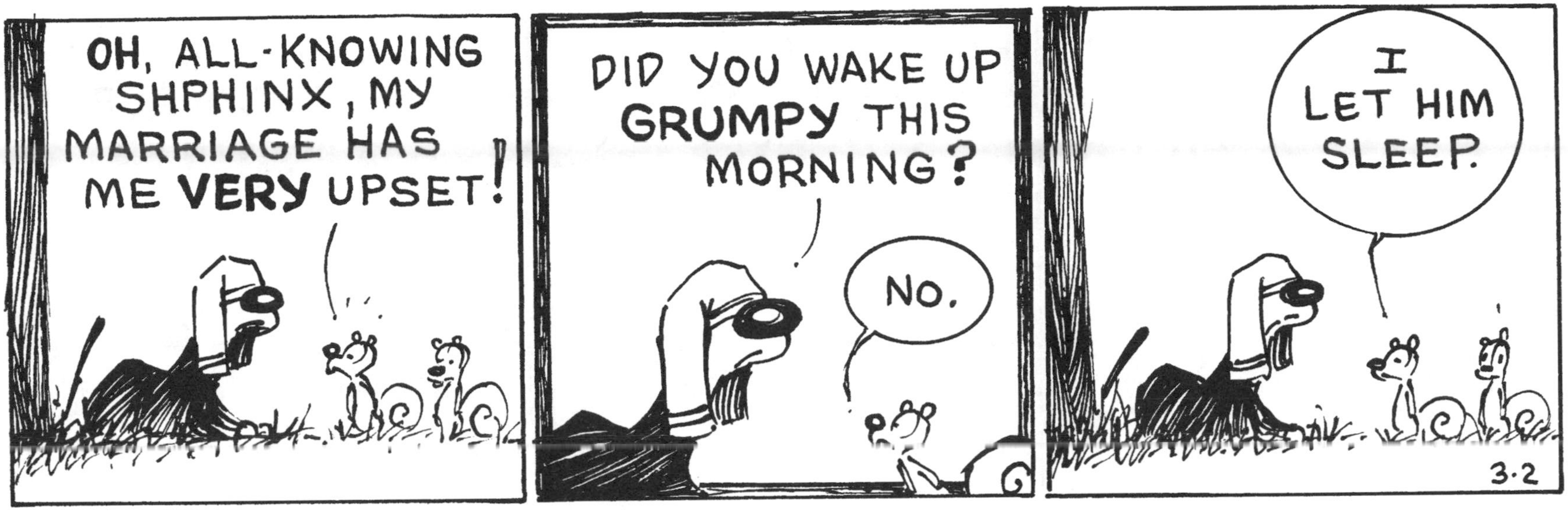
OH, ALL-KNOWING SHPHINX, MY MARRIAGE HAS ME VERY UPSET!
DID YOU WAKE UP GRUMPY THIS MORNING?
NO.
I LET HIM SLEEP.
3-2

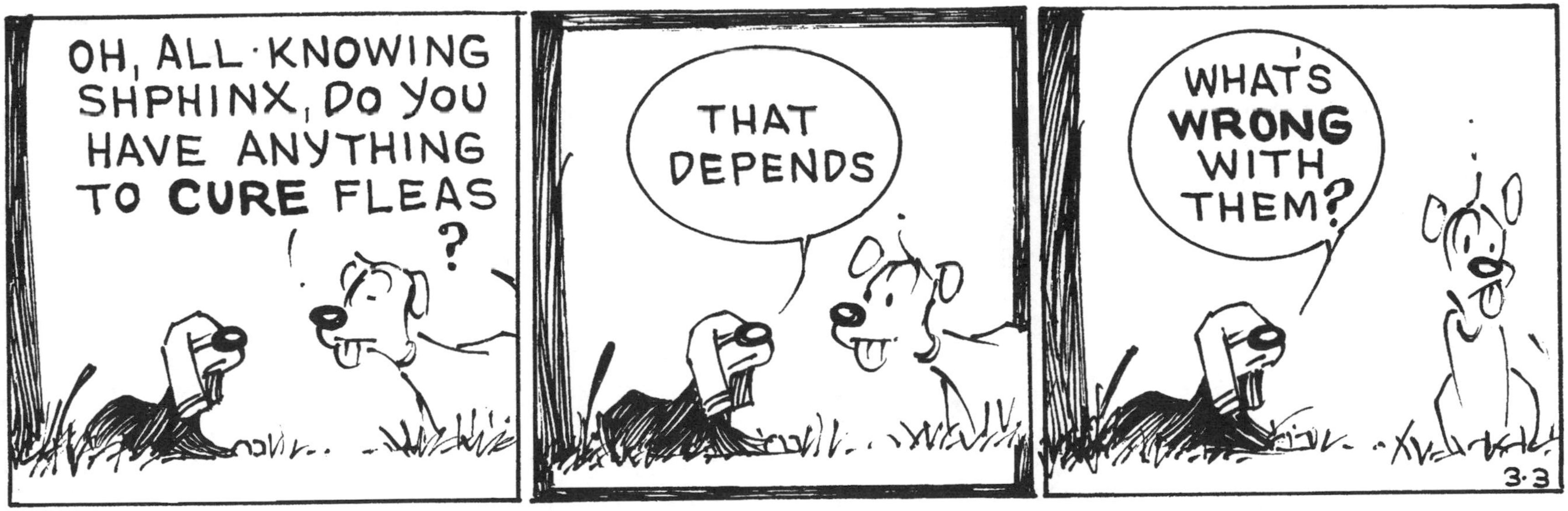
OH, ALL-KNOWING SHPHINX, DO YOU HAVE ANYTHING TO CURE FLEAS?
THAT DEPENDS
WHAT'S WRONG WITH THEM?
3-3

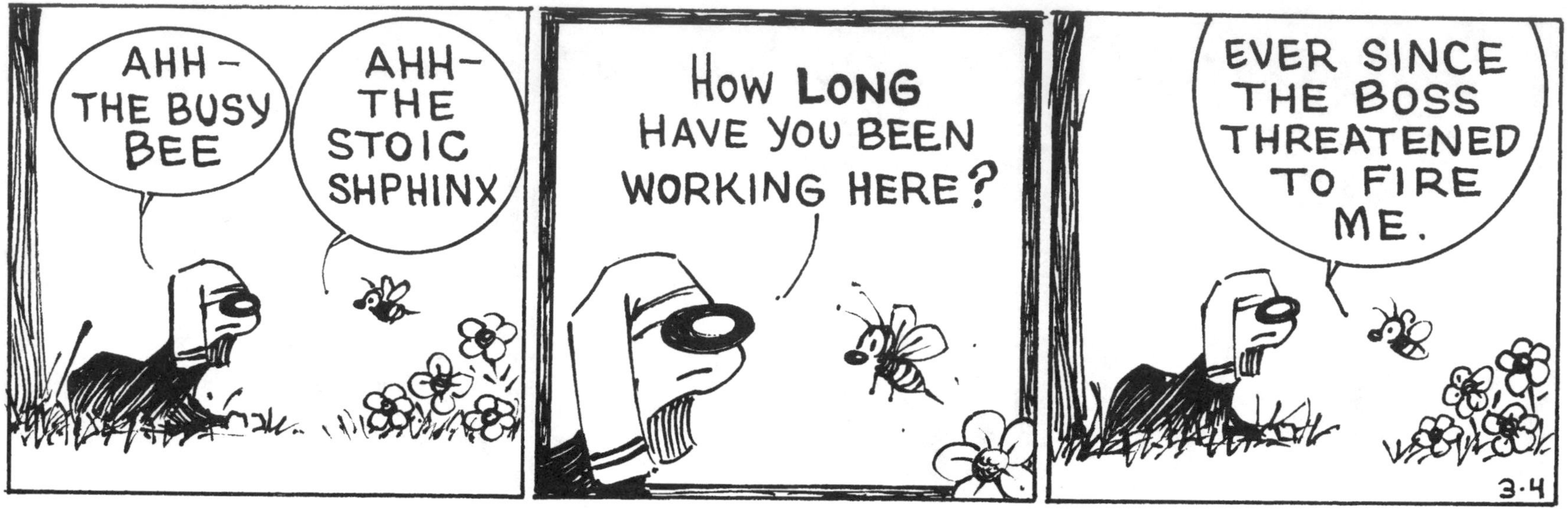
AHH- THE BUSY BEE
AHH- THE STOIC SHPHINX
HOW LONG HAVE YOU BEEN WORKING HERE?
EVER SINCE THE BOSS THREATENED TO FIRE ME.
3·4

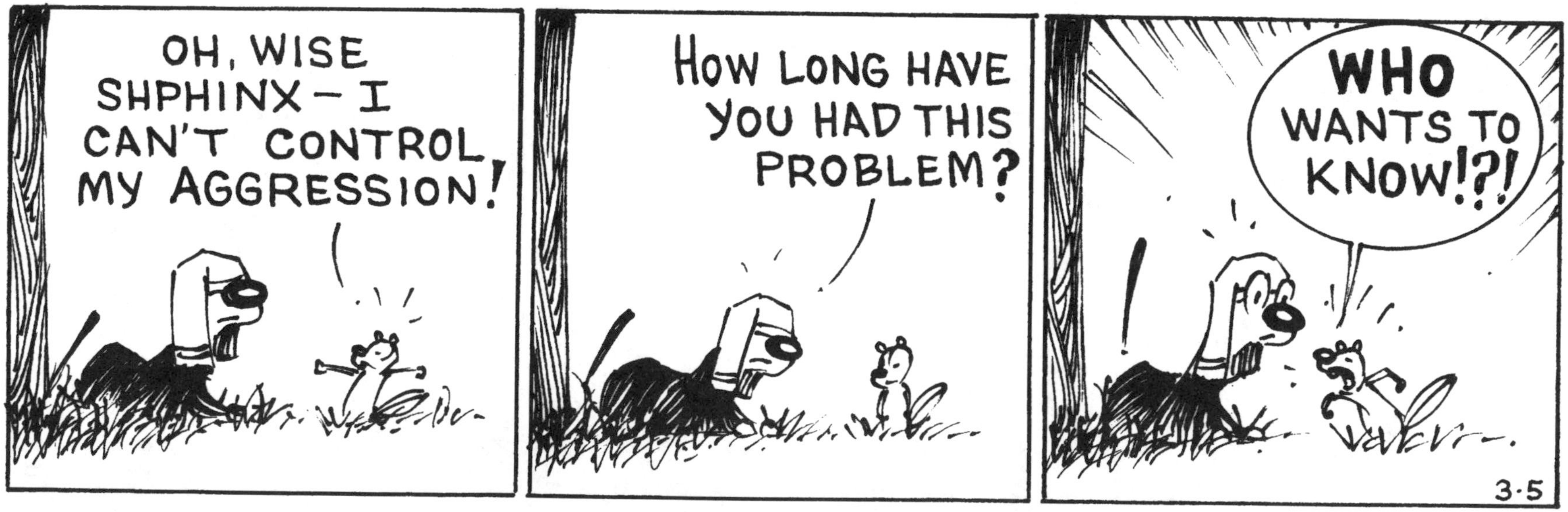
OH, WISE SHPHINX - I CAN'T CONTROL MY AGGRESSION!
HOW LONG HAVE YOU HAD THIS PROBLEM?
WHO WANTS TO KNOW!?!
3·5

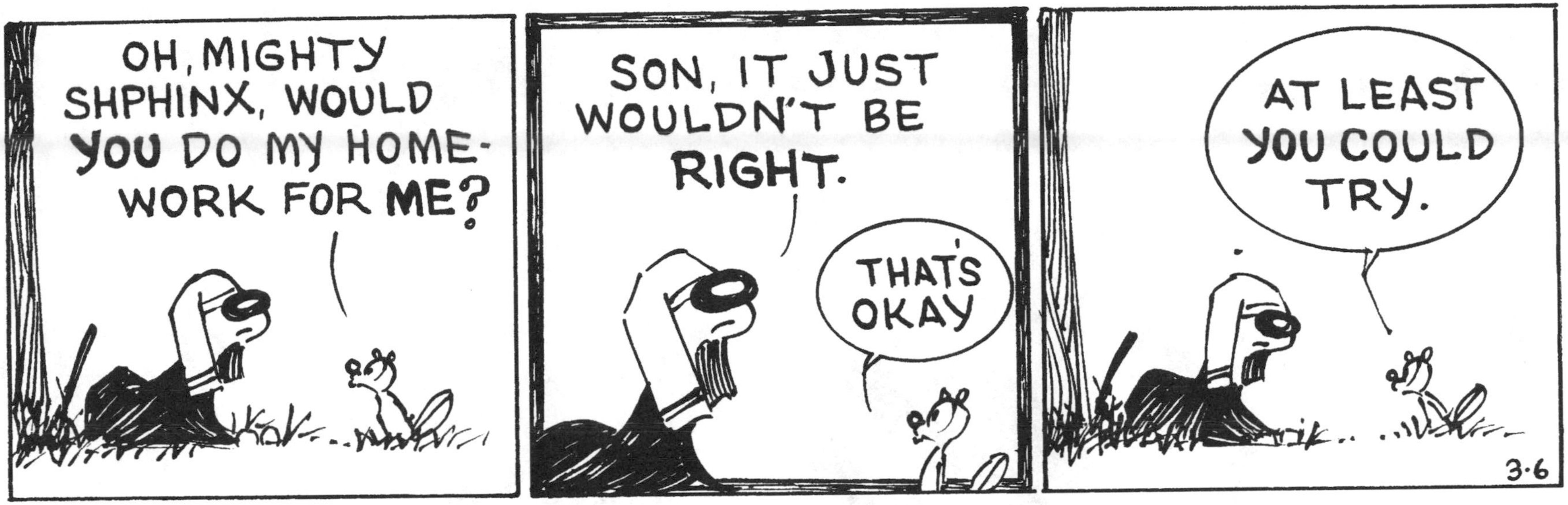
OH, MIGHTY SHPHINX, WOULD YOU DO MY HOME-WORK FOR ME?
SON, IT JUST WOULDN'T BE RIGHT.
THAT'S OKAY
AT LEAST YOU COULD TRY.
3·6

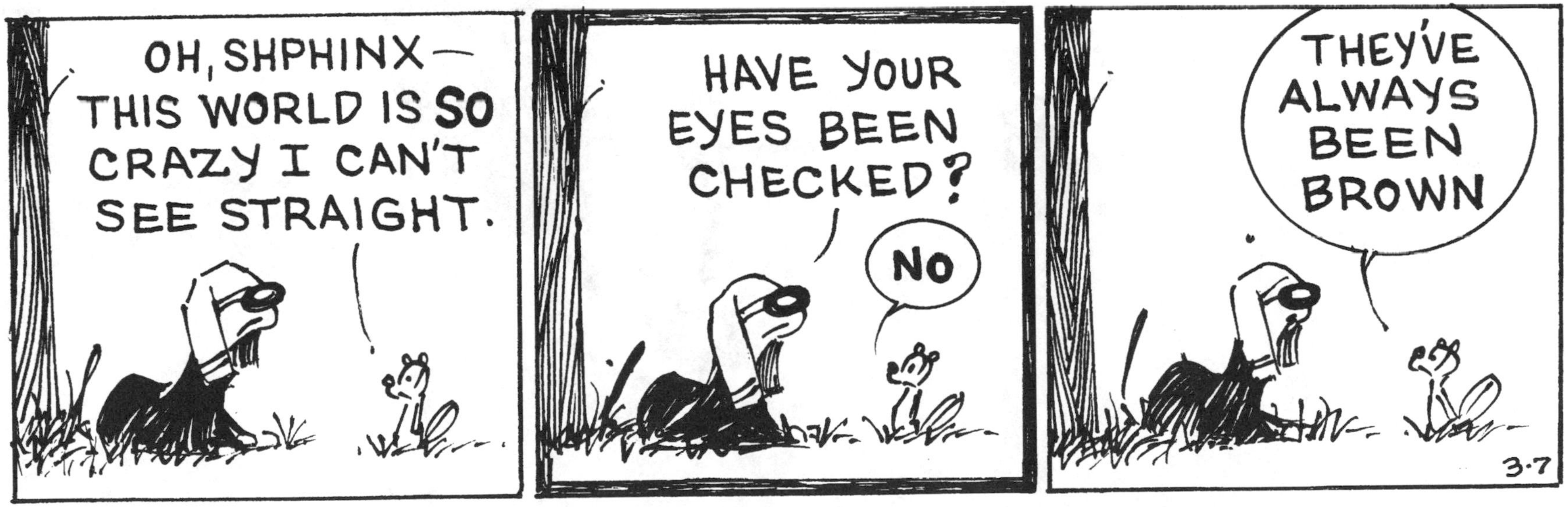
OH, SHPHINX— THIS WORLD IS SO CRAZY I CAN'T SEE STRAIGHT.
HAVE YOUR EYES BEEN CHECKED?
NO
THEY'VE ALWAYS BEEN BROWN
3·7

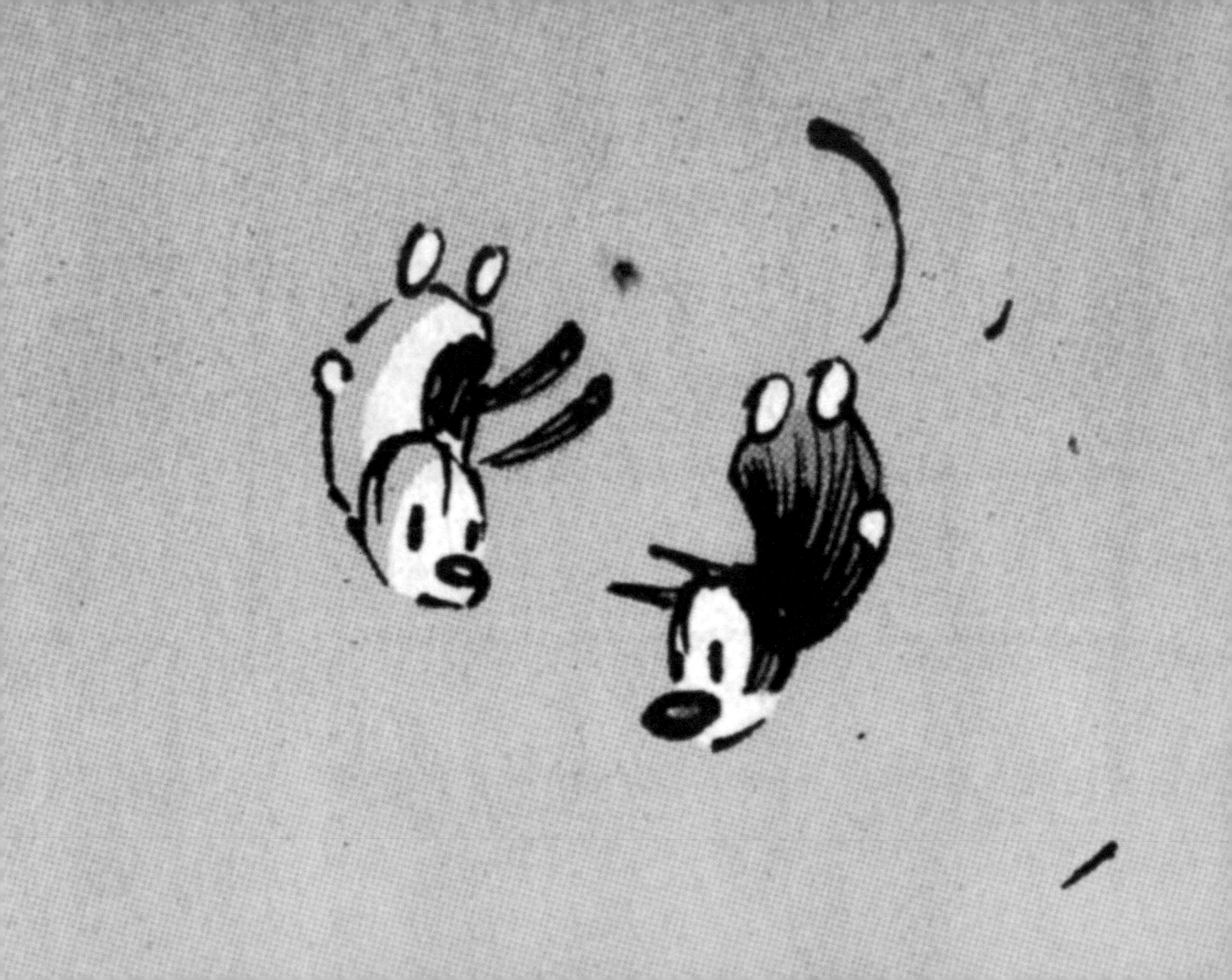

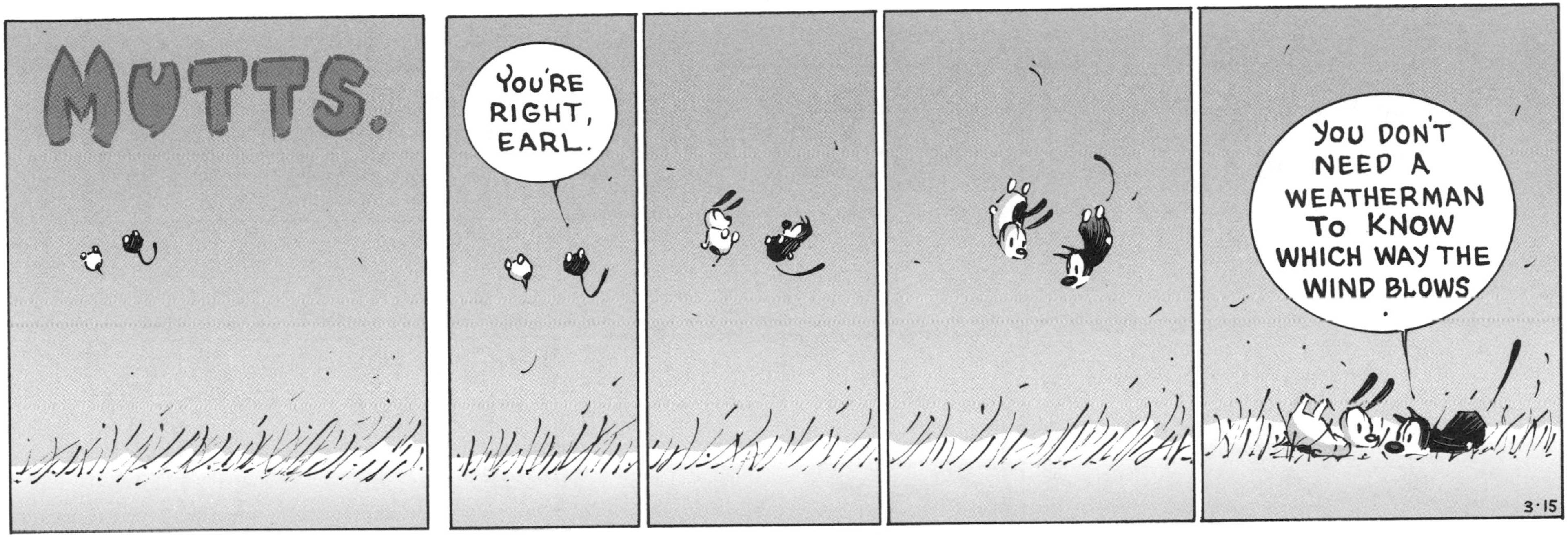
MUTTS.
YOU'RE RIGHT, EARL.
YOU DON'T NEED A WEATHERMAN TO KNOW WHICH WAY THE WIND BLOWS.
3·15

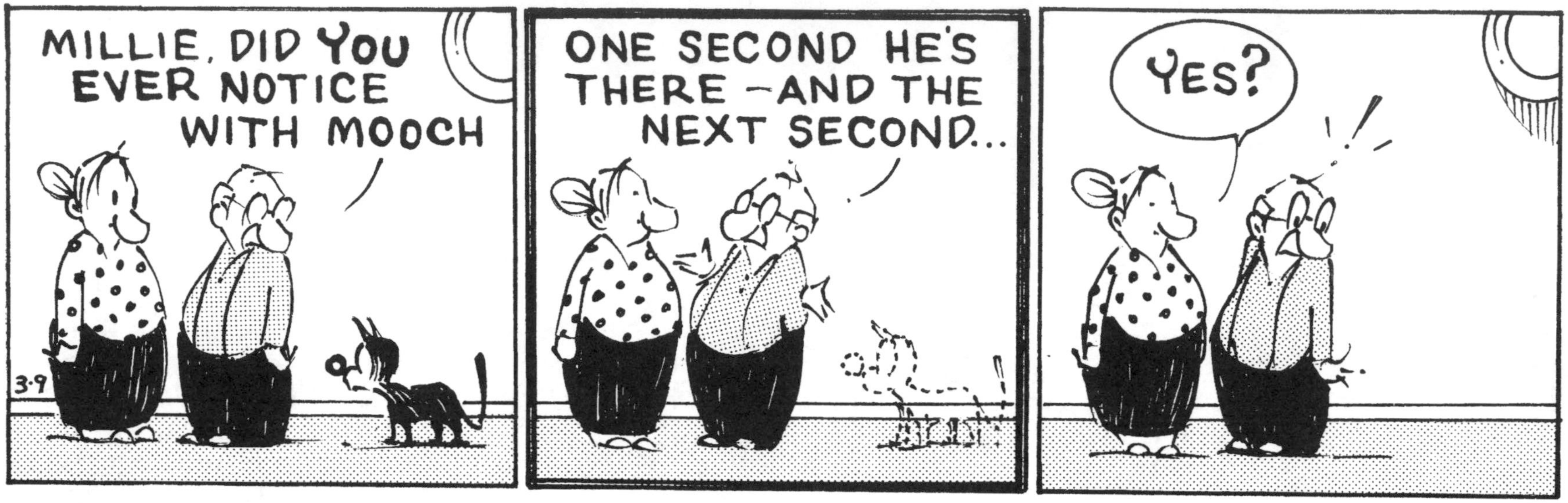
MILLIE, DID YOU EVER NOTICE WITH MOOCH
3·9
ONE SECOND HE'S THERE —AND THE NEXT SECOND...
YES?

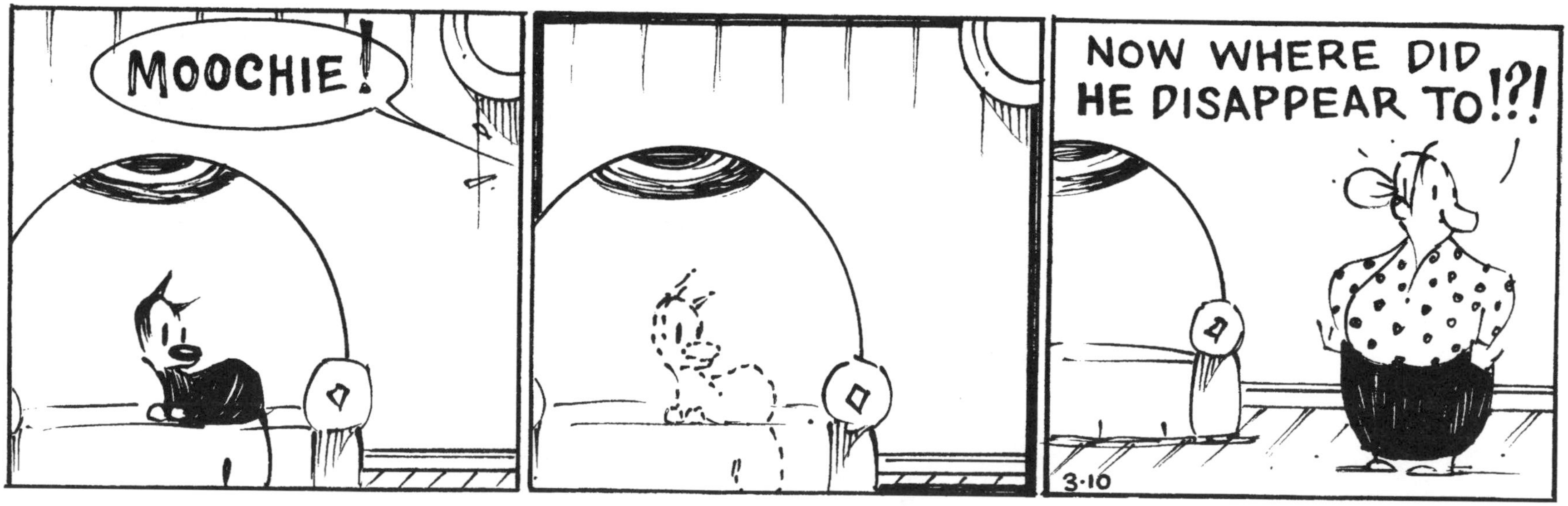
MOOCHIE!
NOW WHERE DID HE DISAPPEAR TO!?!
3·10

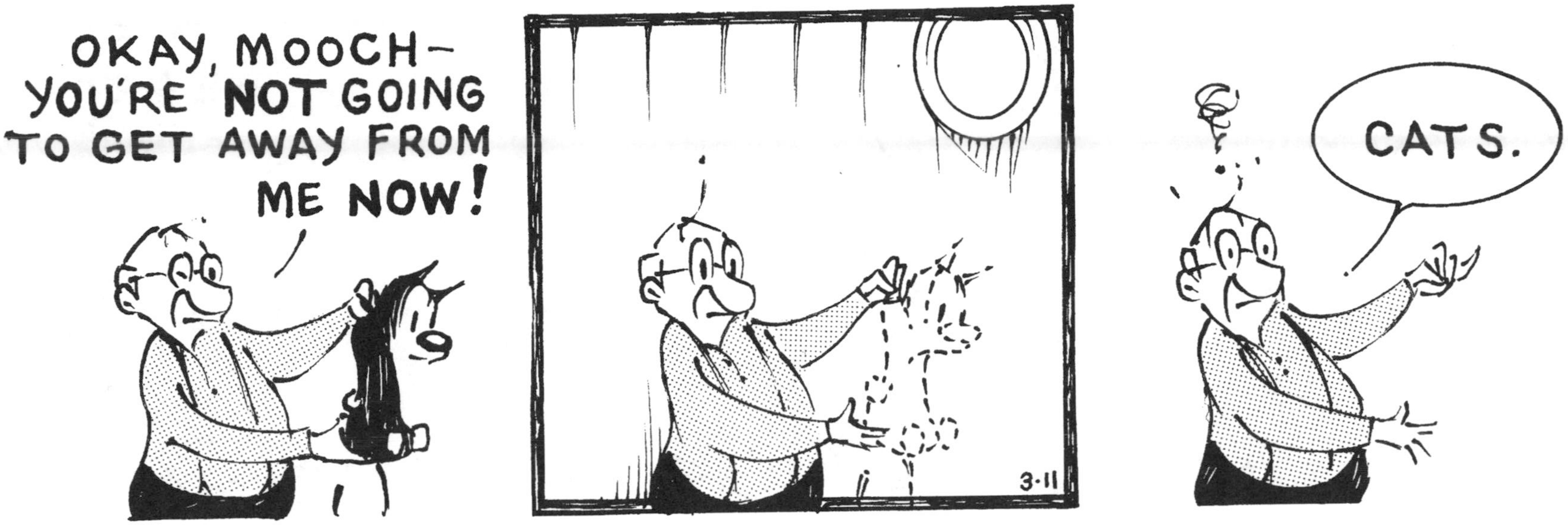
OKAY, MOOCH-
YOU'RE NOT GOING
TO GET AWAY FROM
ME NOW!
3-11
CATS.

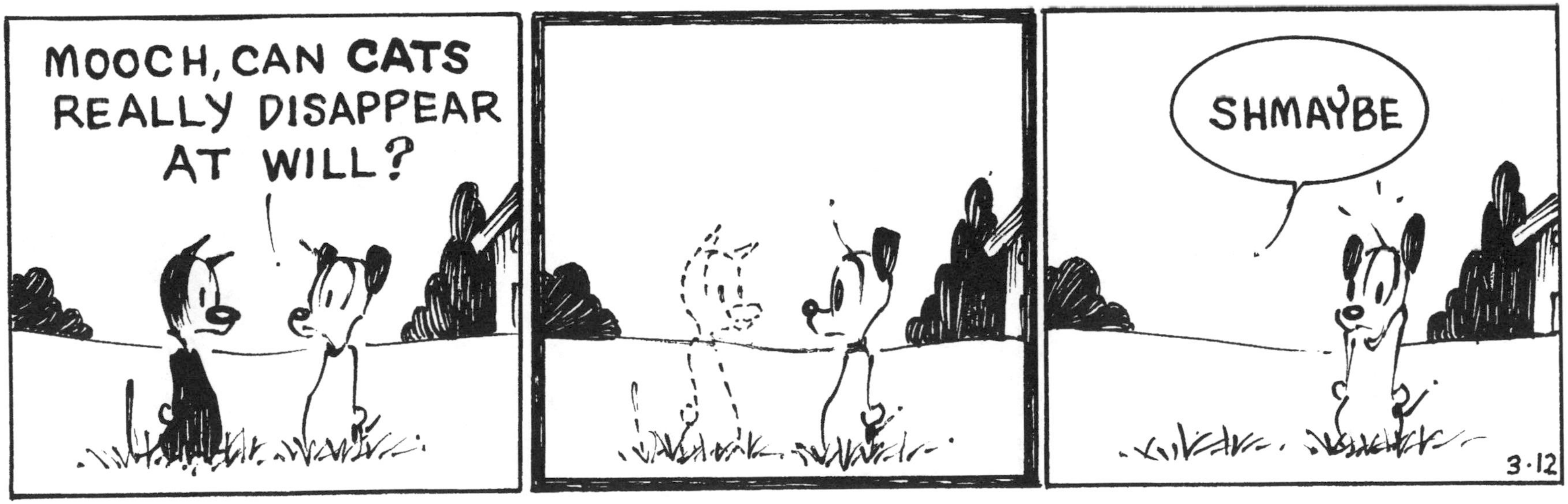
MOOCH, CAN CATS
REALLY DISAPPEAR
AT WILL?
SHMAYBE
3-12

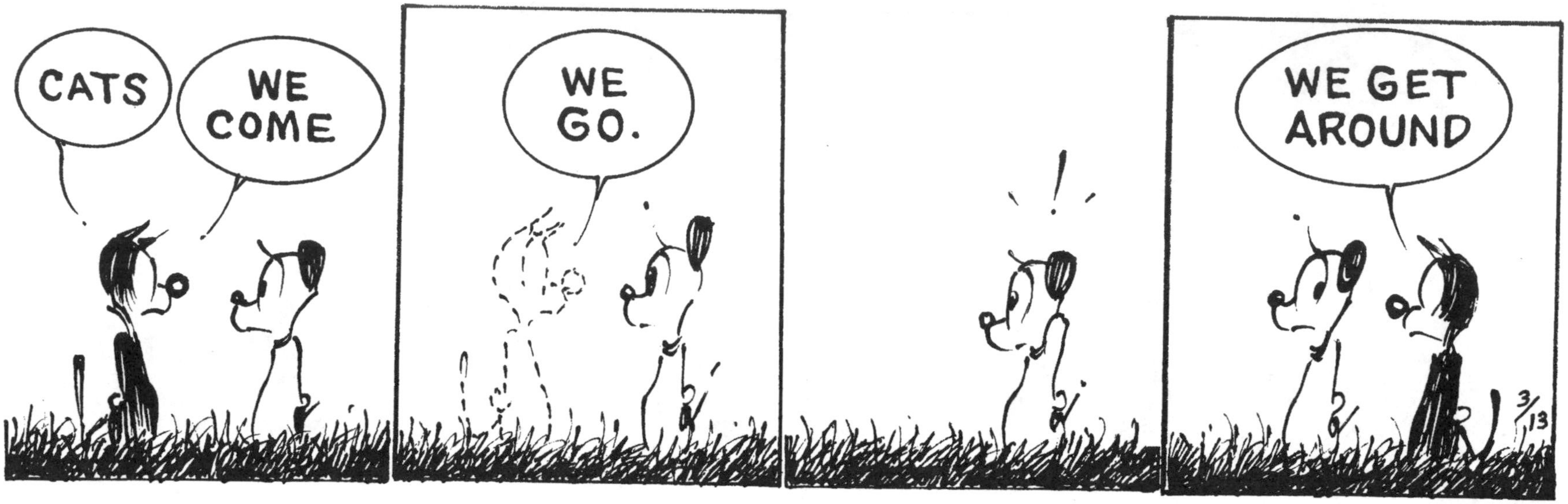
CATS
WE COME
WE GO.
!
WE GET AROUND
3/13

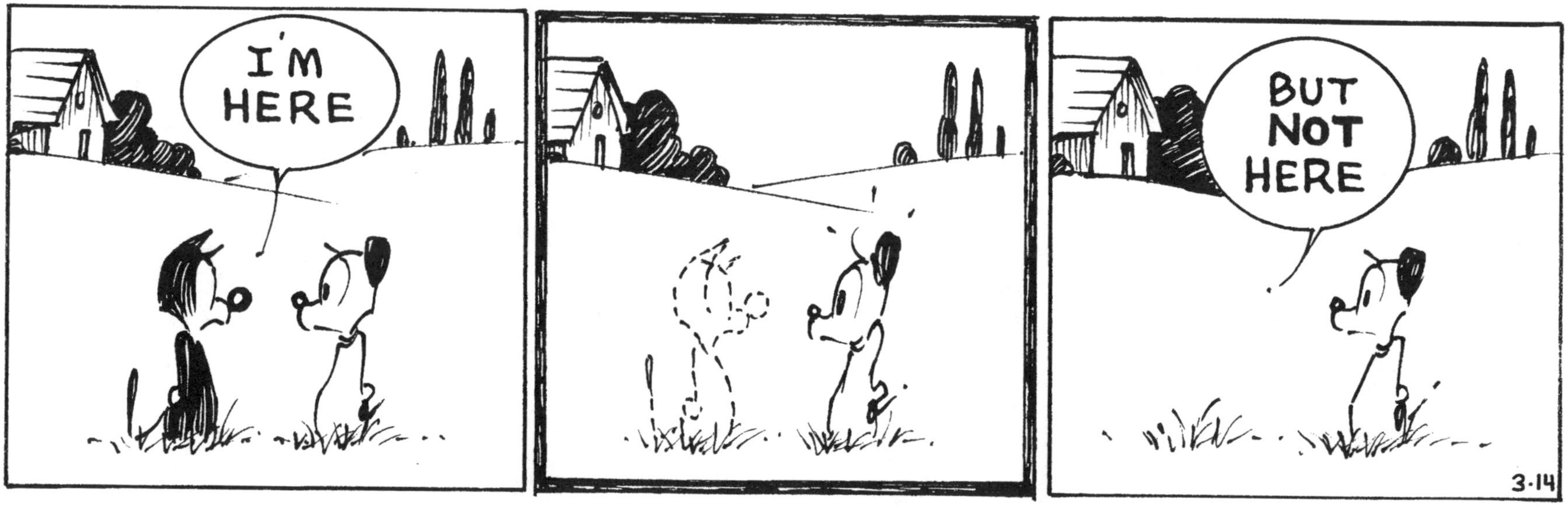
I'M HERE
BUT NOT HERE
3·14

MUTTS

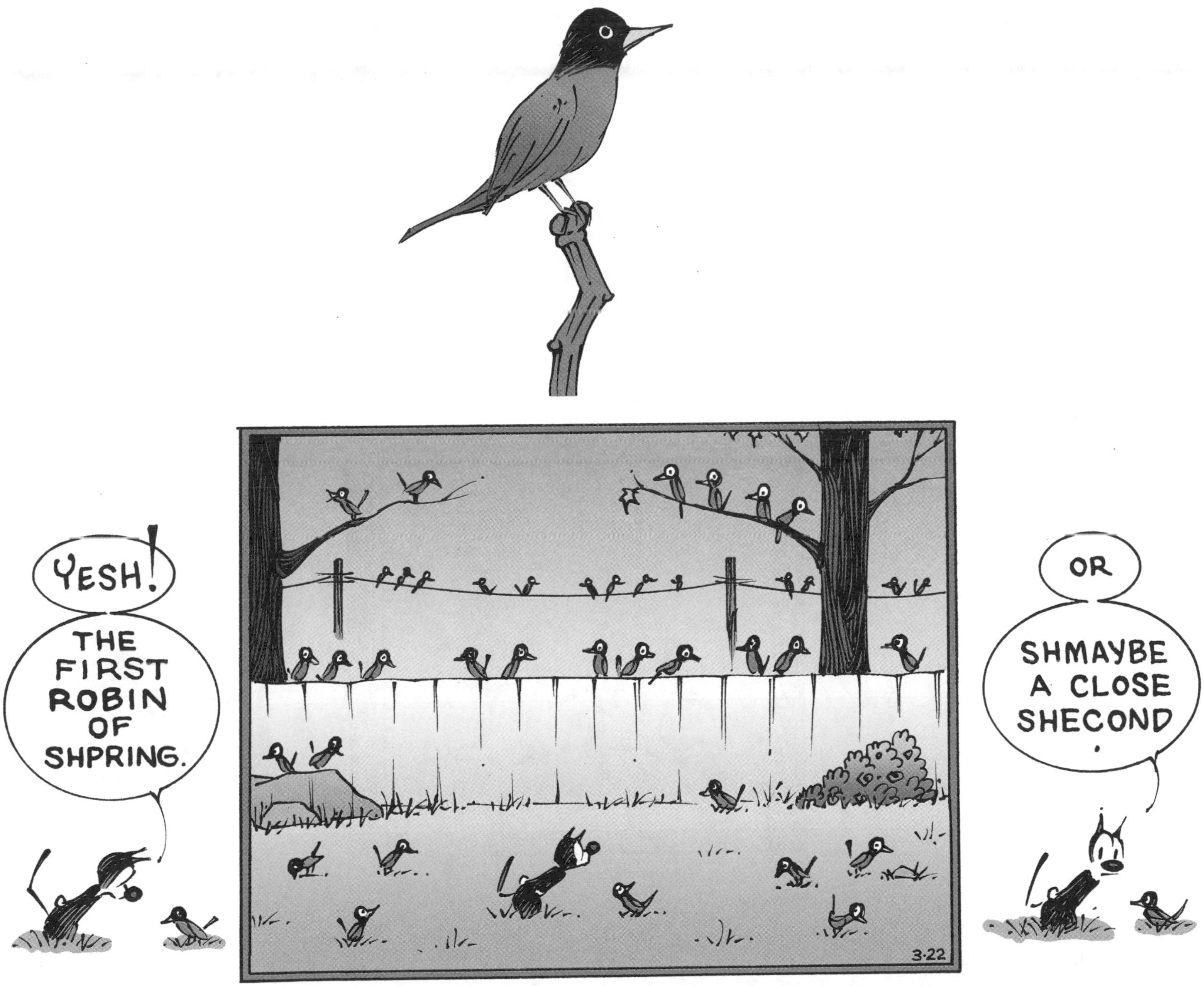
YESH!
THE FIRST ROBIN OF SHPRING.
OR
SHMAYBE A CLOSE SHECOND.
3·22

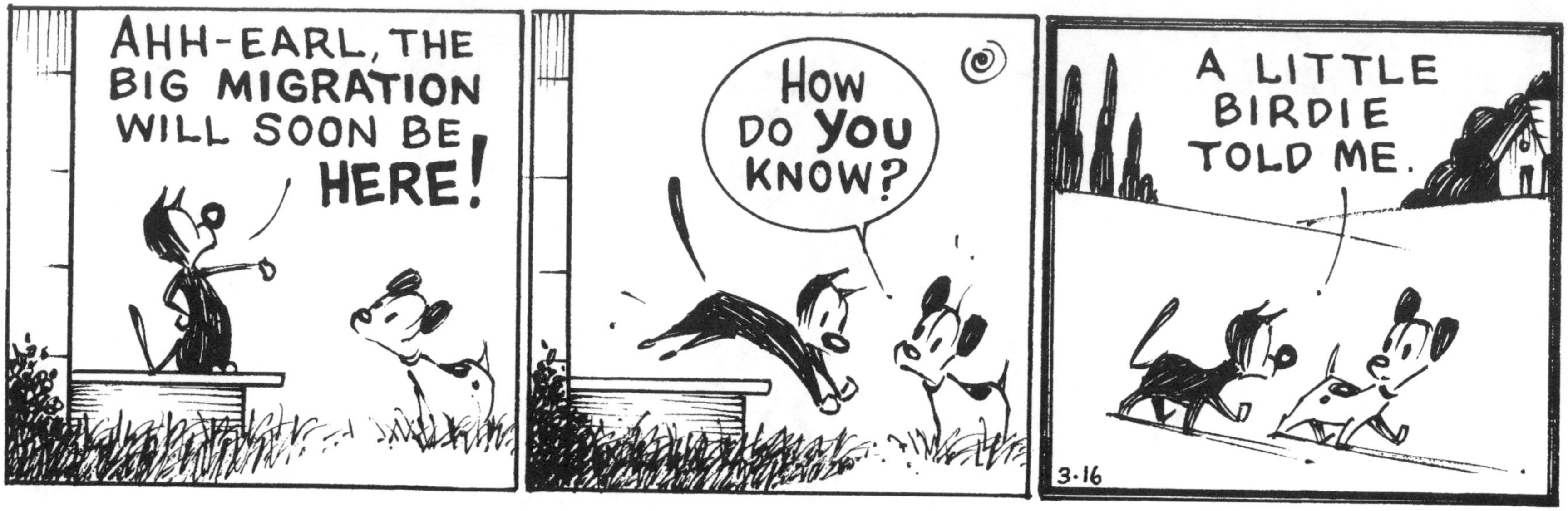
AHH-EARL, THE BIG MIGRATION WILL SOON BE HERE!
HOW DO YOU KNOW?
A LITTLE BIRDIE TOLD ME.
3·16

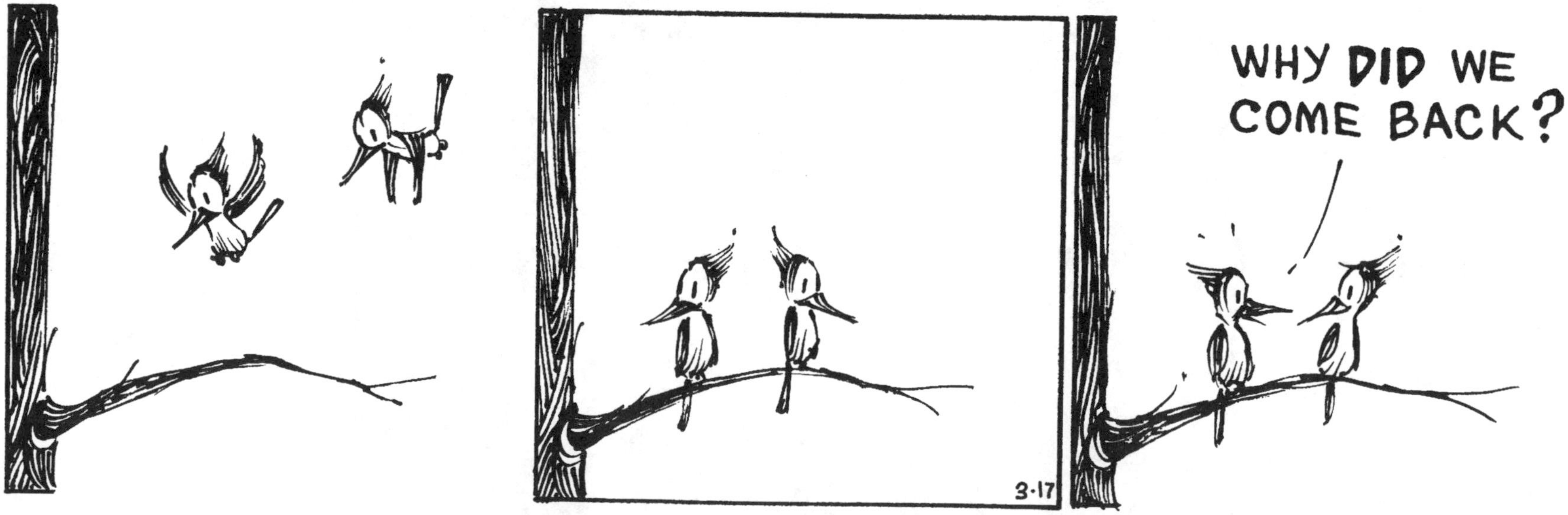
3·17
WHY DID WE COME BACK?

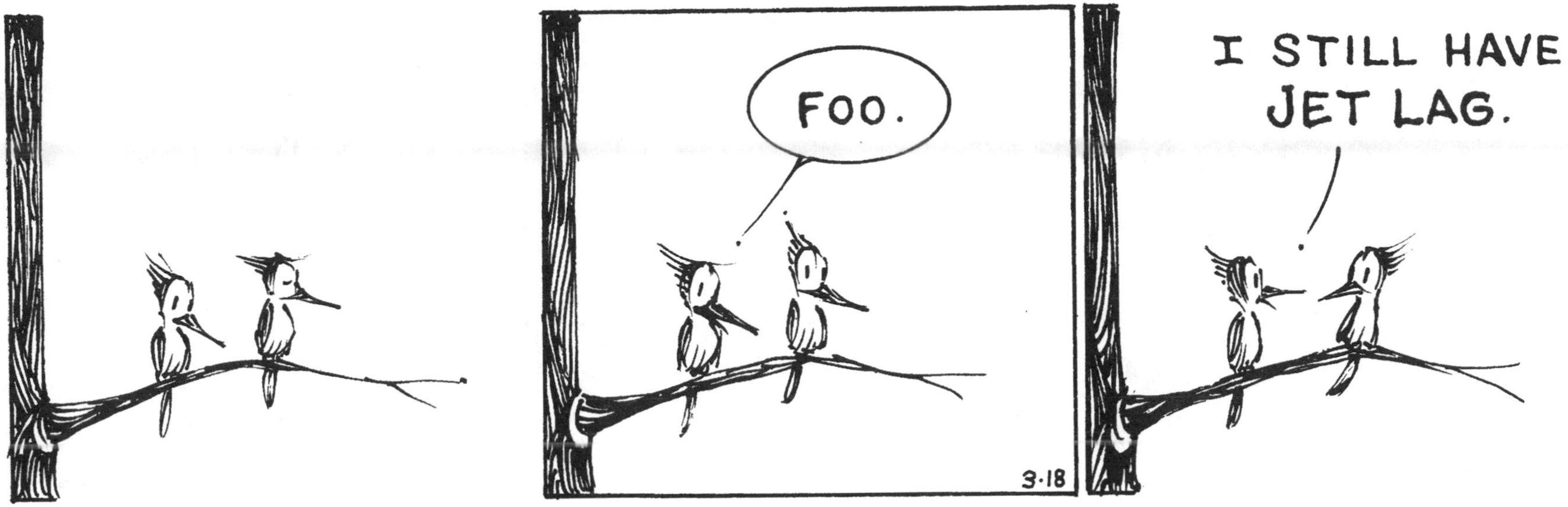
FOO.
I STILL HAVE JET LAG.
3·18

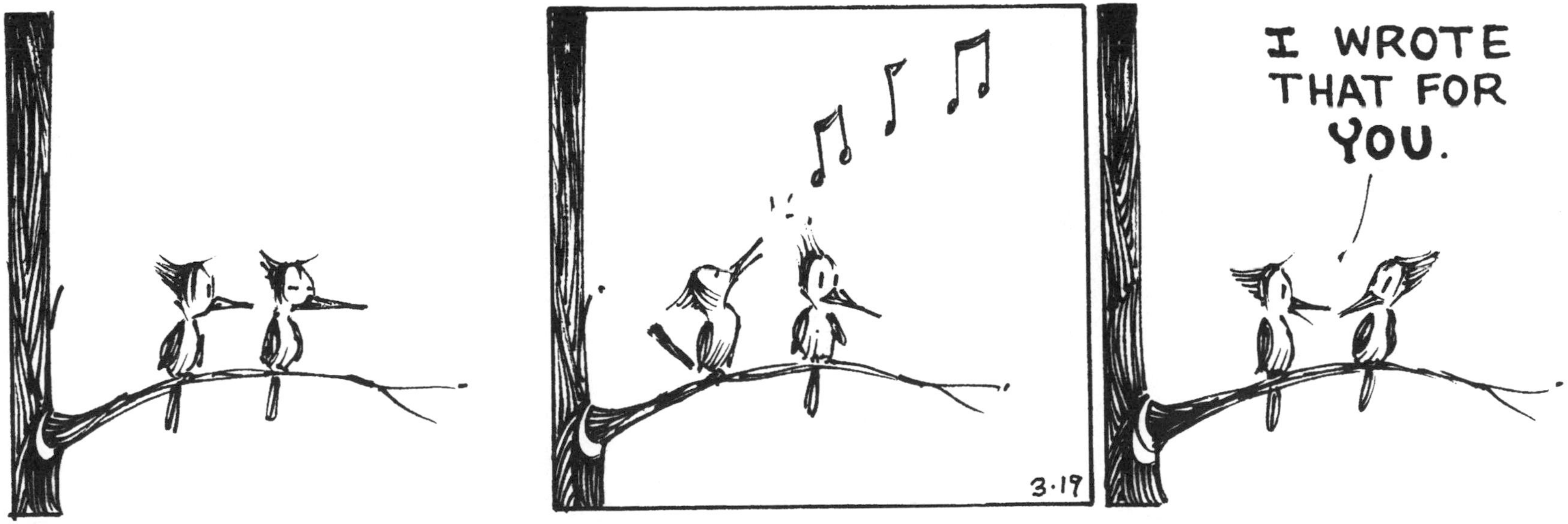
I WROTE THAT FOR YOU.
3·19

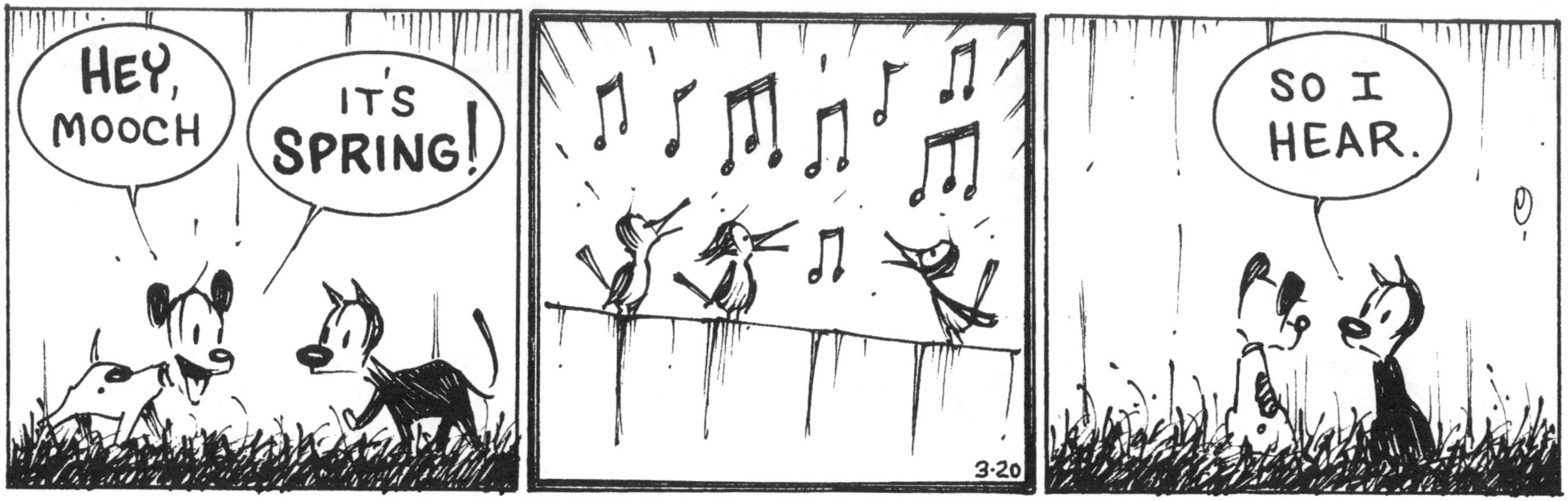
HEY, MOOCH
IT'S SPRING!
3·20
SO I HEAR.

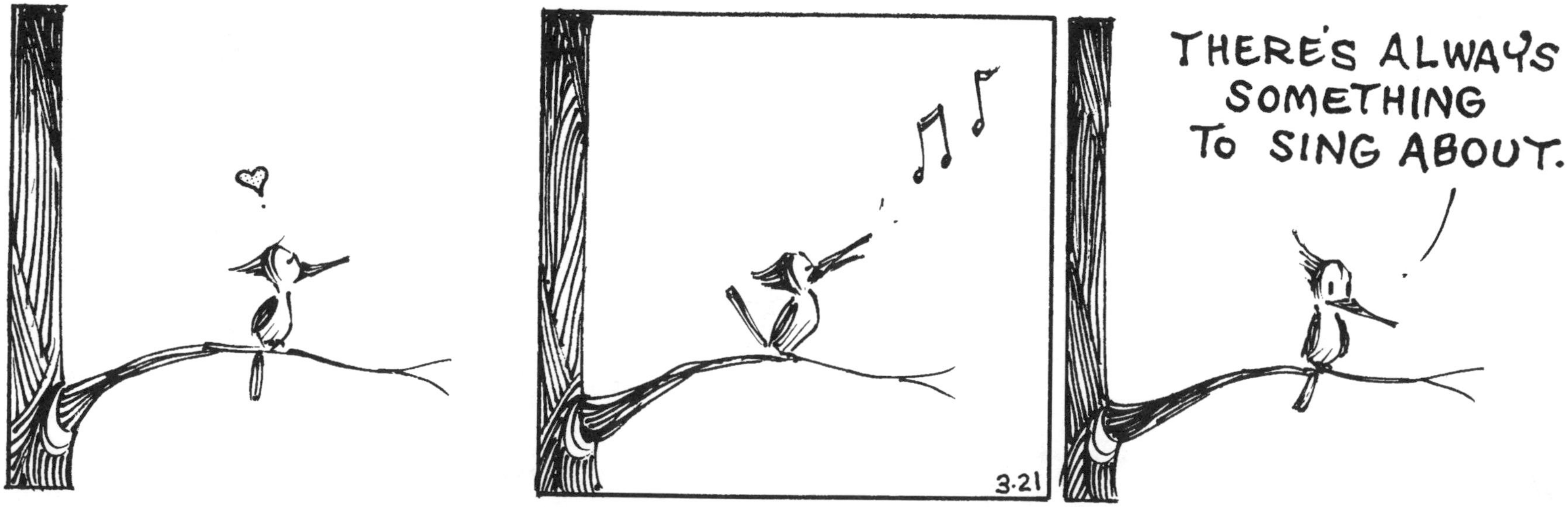
3·21
THERE'S ALWAYS SOMETHING TO SING ABOUT.

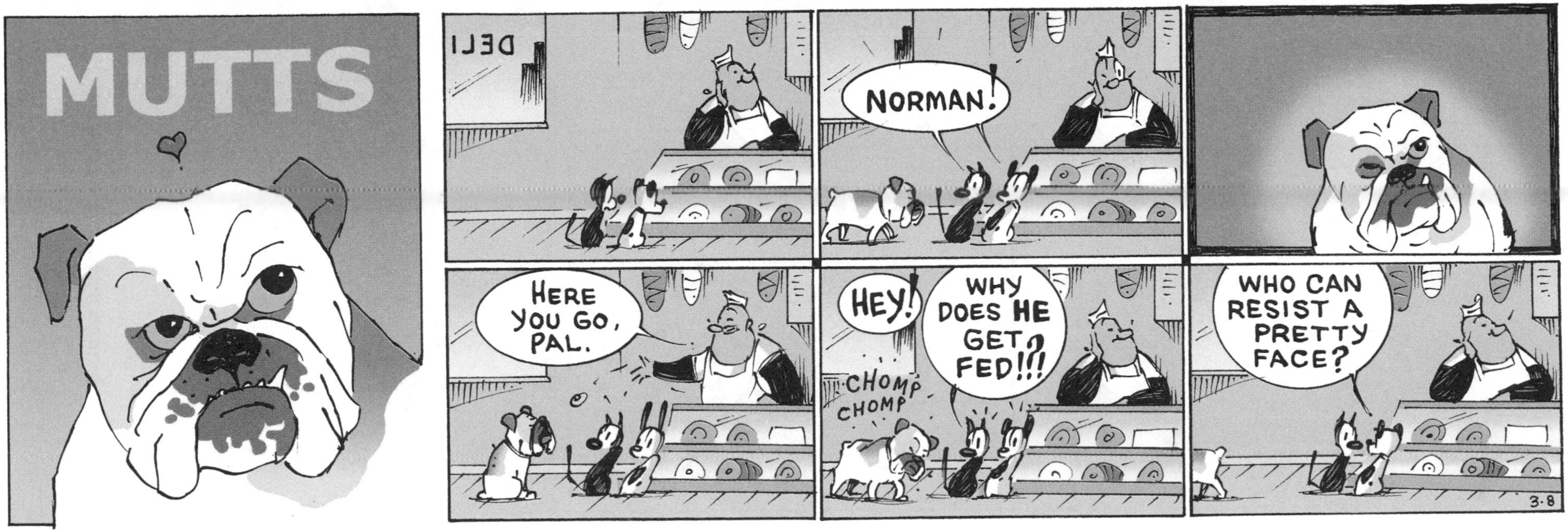
MUTTS
DELI
NORMAN!
HERE YOU GO, PAL.
HEY!
WHY DOES HE GET FED!?!
CHOMP CHOMP
WHO CAN RESIST A PRETTY FACE?
3·8

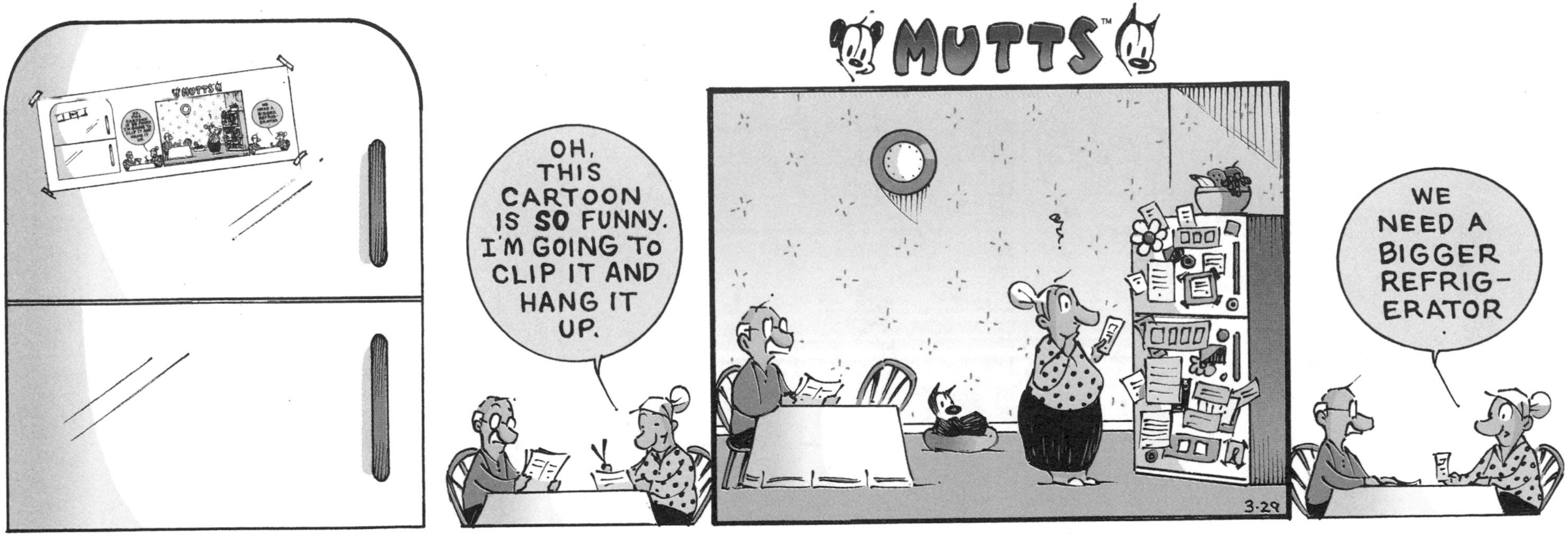
MUTTS
OH, THIS CARTOON IS SO FUNNY. I'M GOING TO CLIP IT AND HANG IT UP.
WE NEED A BIGGER REFRIG- ERATOR
3·29

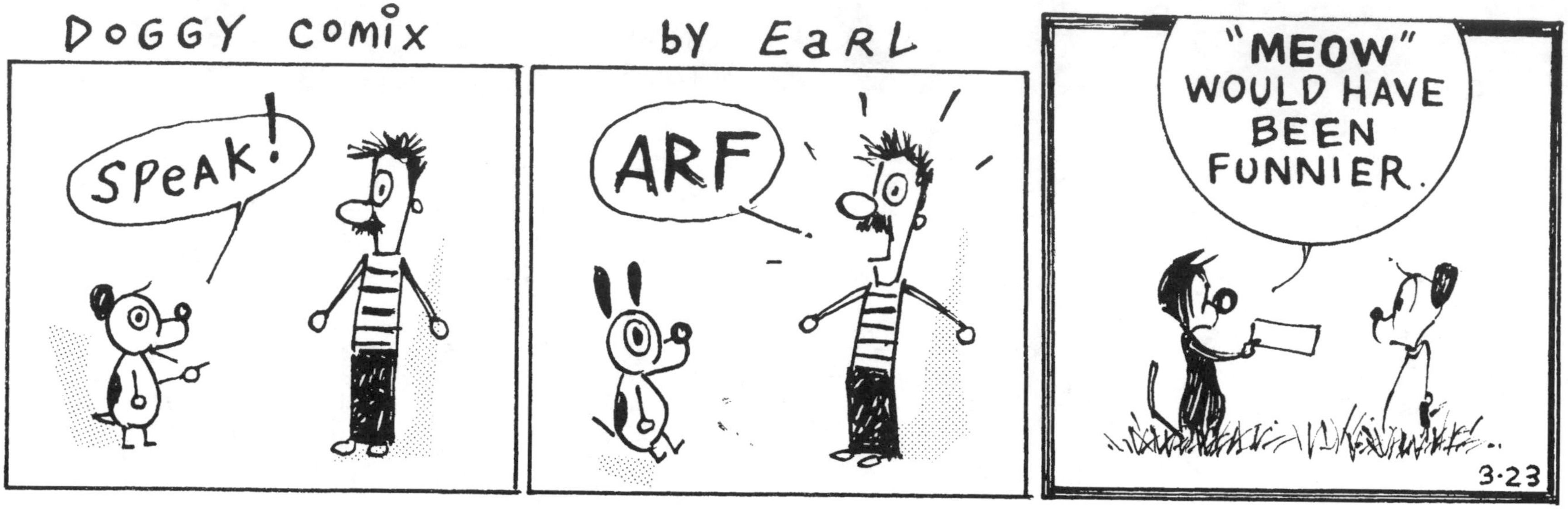
DOGGY COMIX
by EARL
SPEAK!
ARF
"MEOW" WOULD HAVE BEEN FUNNIER.
3-23

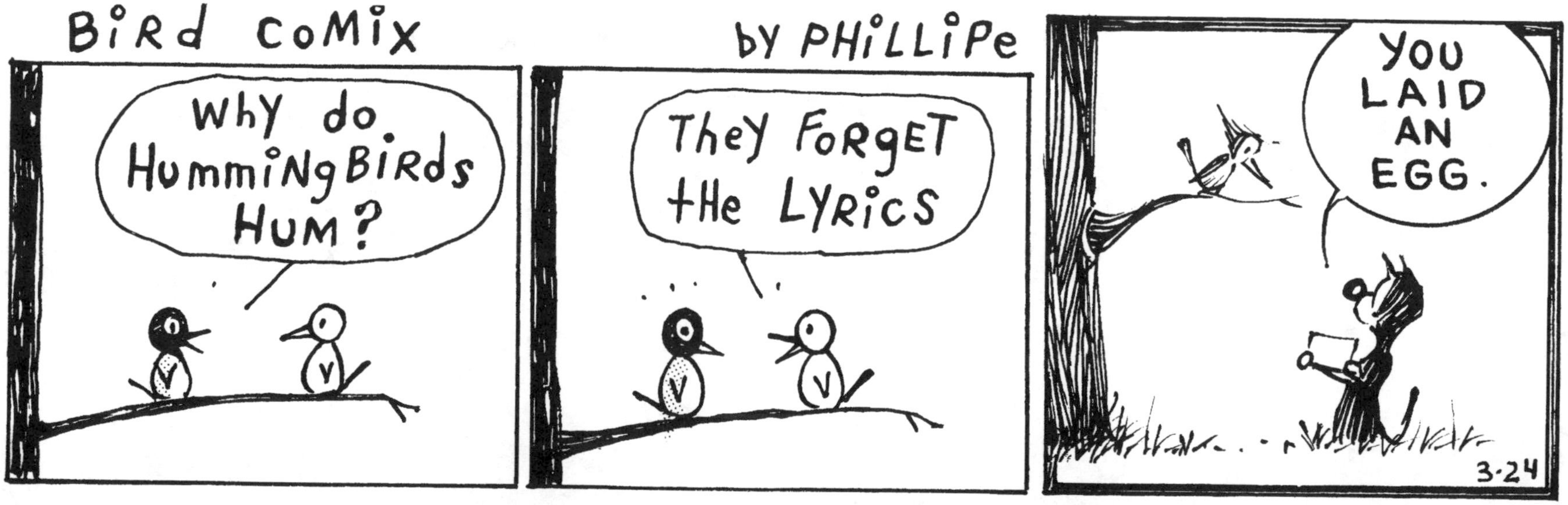
BIRD COMIX
by PHILLIPE
Why do HummingBirds Hum?
They Forget the Lyrics
YOU LAID AN EGG.
3-24

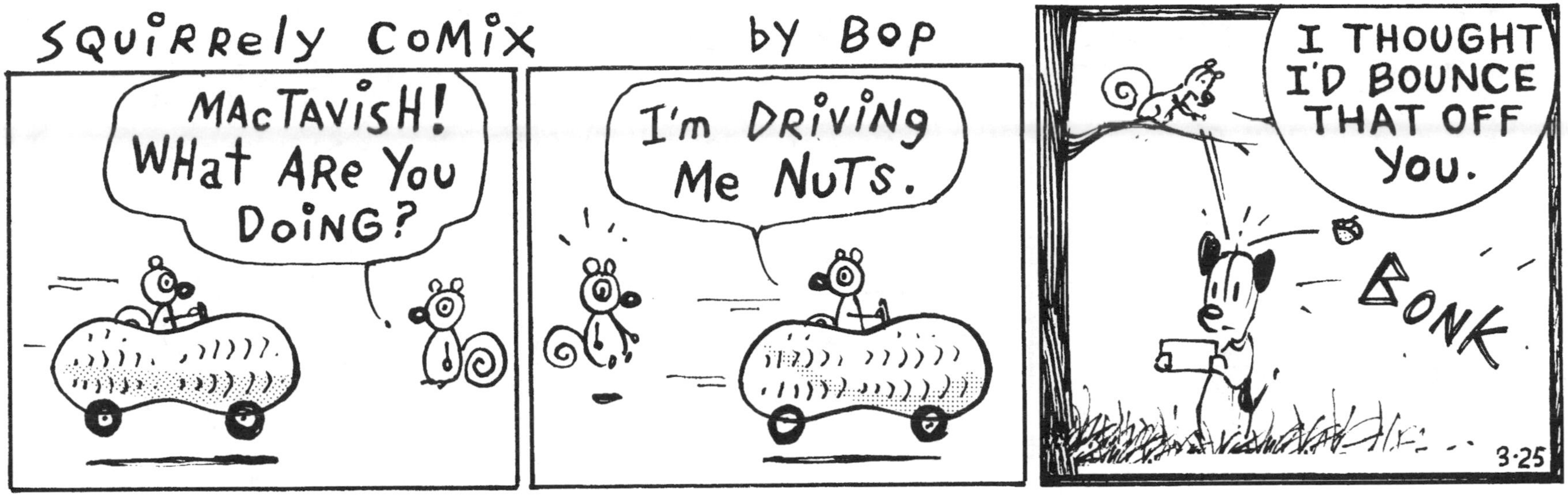
SQUIRRELY COMIX by BOP
MACTAVISH! WHAT ARE YOU DOING?
I'M DRIVING ME NUTS.
I THOUGHT I'D BOUNCE THAT OFF YOU.
BONK
3·25

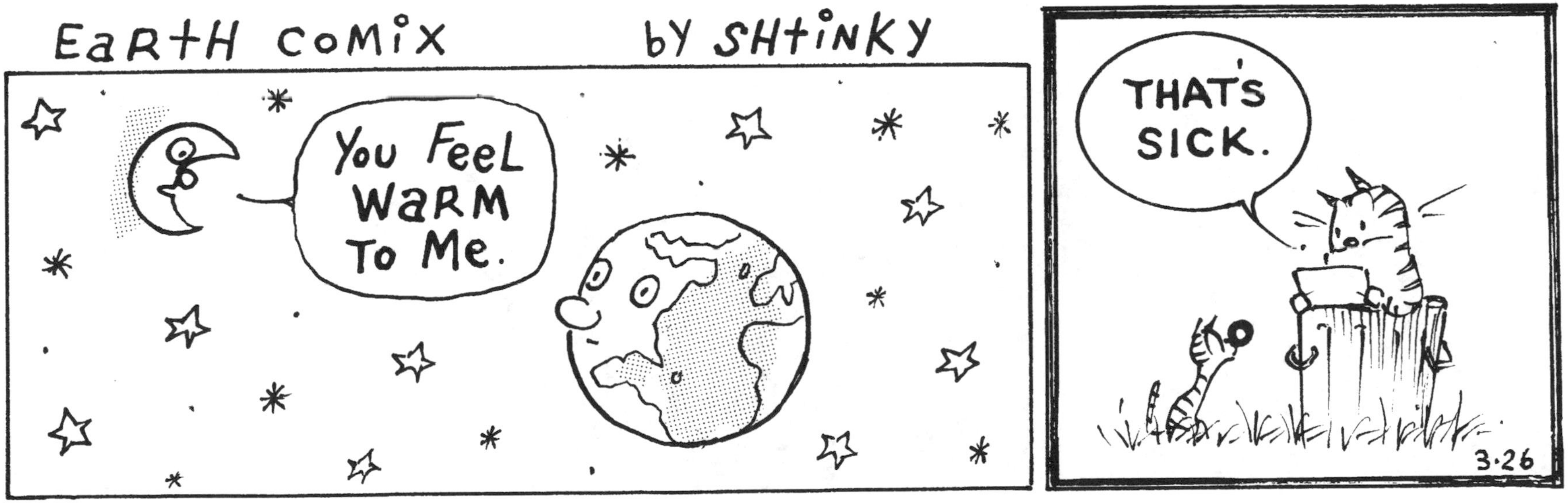
EARTH COMIX by SHTINKY
YOU FEEL WARM TO ME.
THAT'S SICK.
3·26

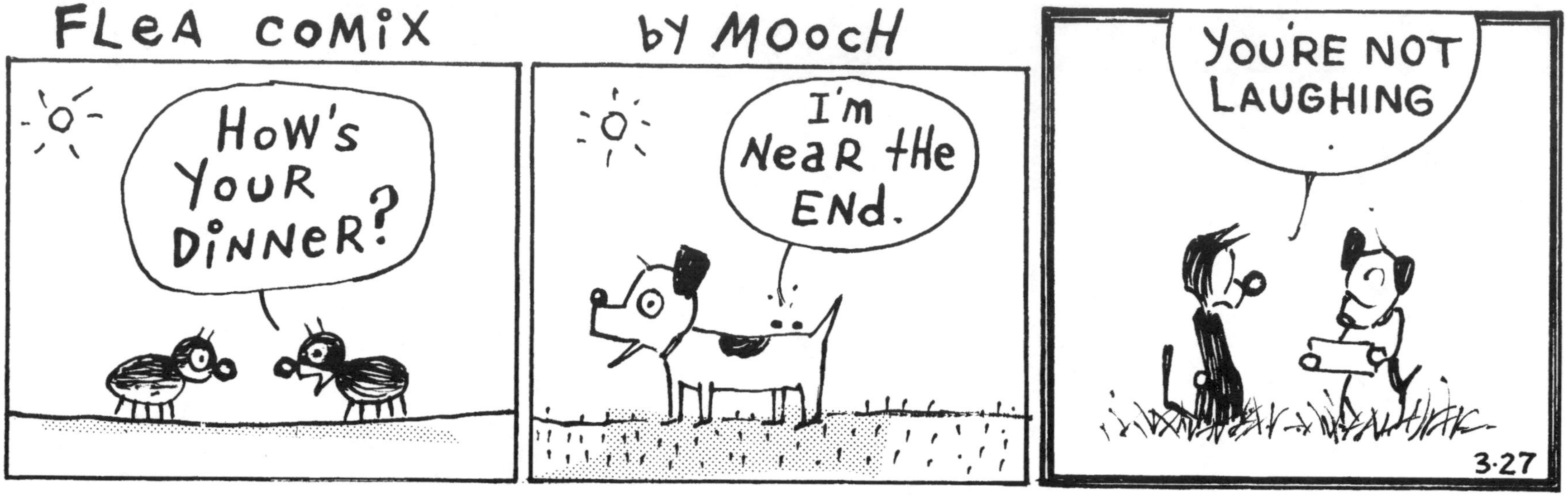
FLEA COMIX
by MOOCH
HOW'S YOUR DINNER?
I'M NEAR THE END.
YOU'RE NOT LAUGHING.
3·27

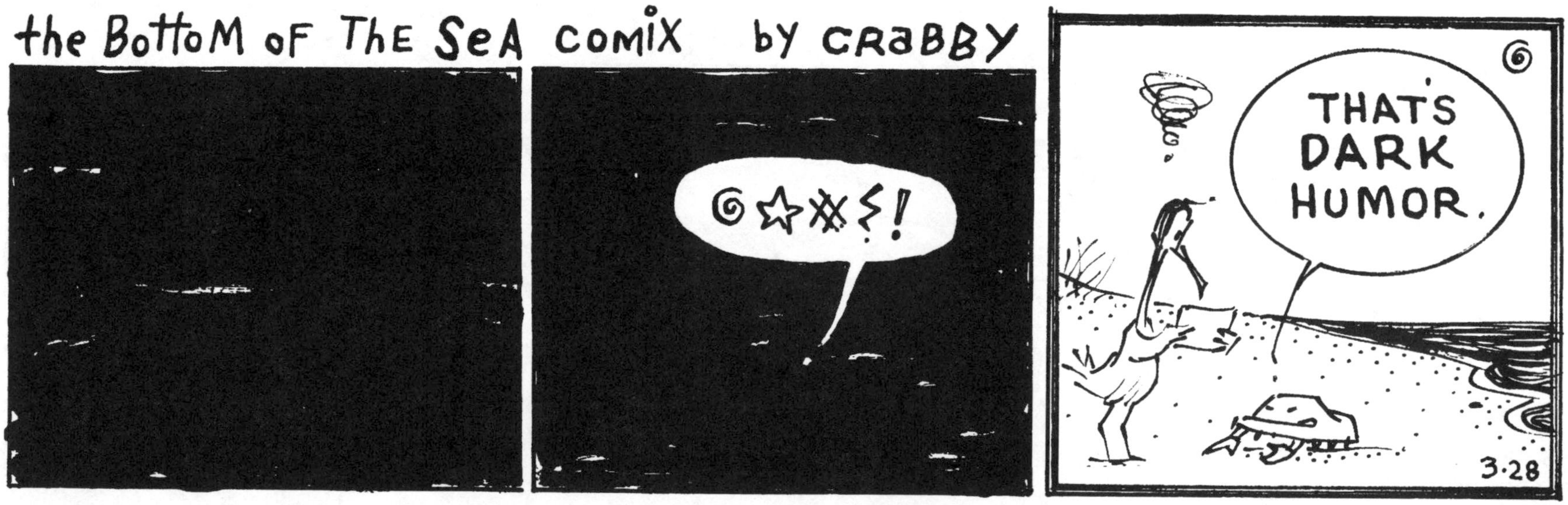
the BOTTOM OF THE SEA COMIX
by CRABBY
THAT'S DARK HUMOR.
3·28

LOOKS LIKE RAIN.
4.5

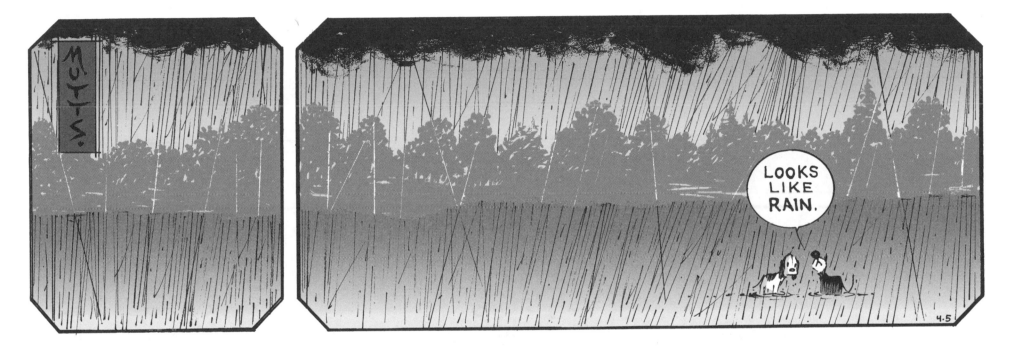

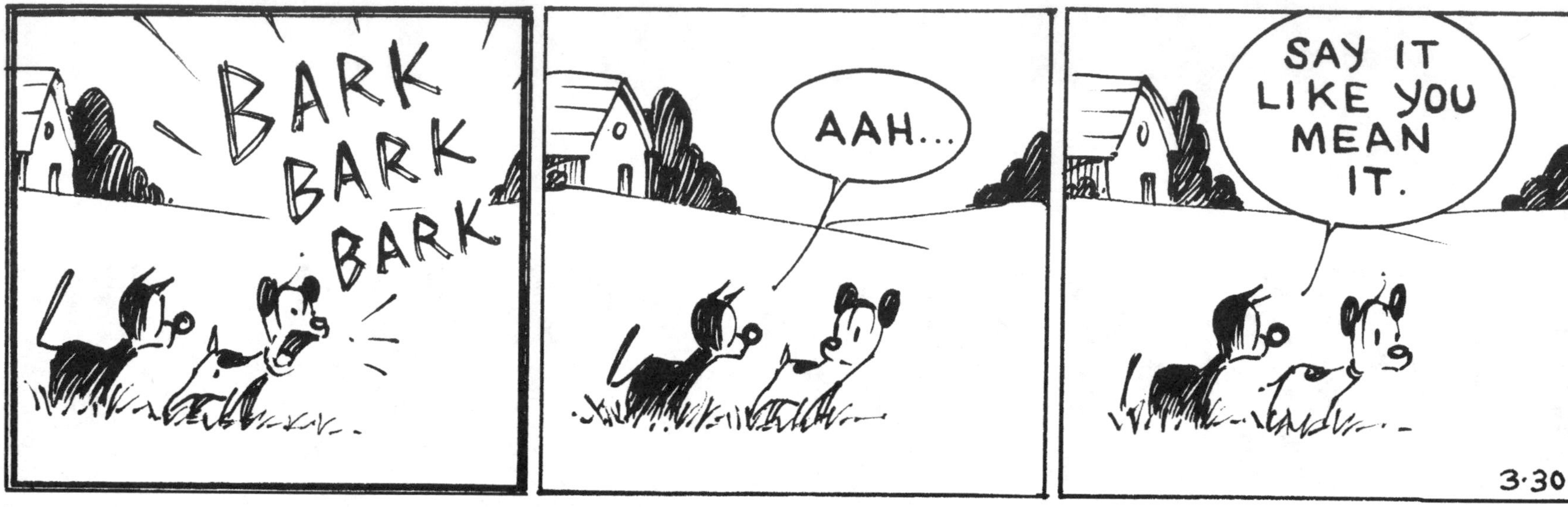
BARK
BARK
BARK
AAH...
SAY IT LIKE YOU MEAN IT.
3·30

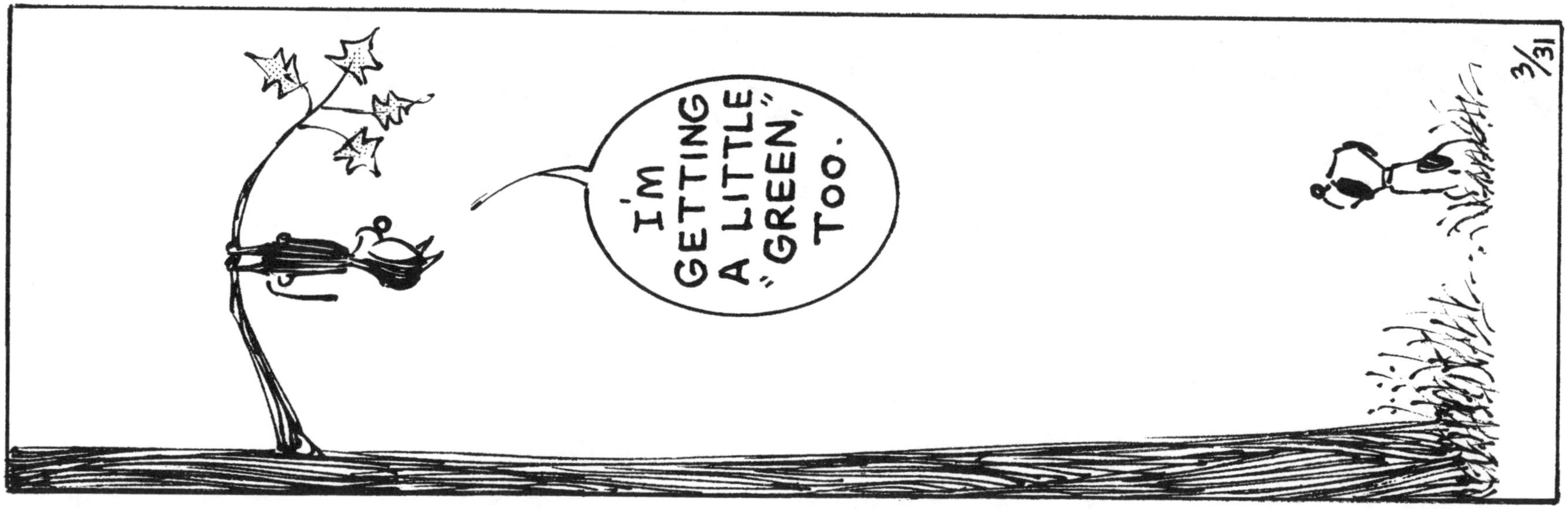
I'M GETTING A LITTLE "GREEN," TOO.
3/31

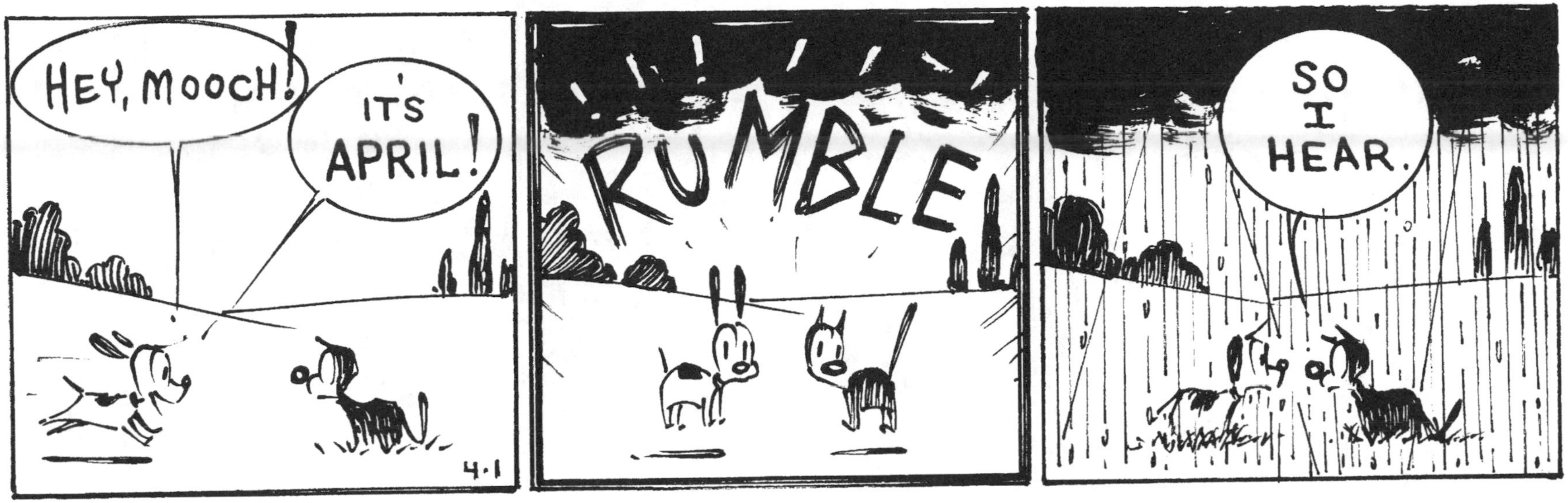
HEY, MOOCH!
IT'S APRIL!
RUMBLE
SO I HEAR.
4·1

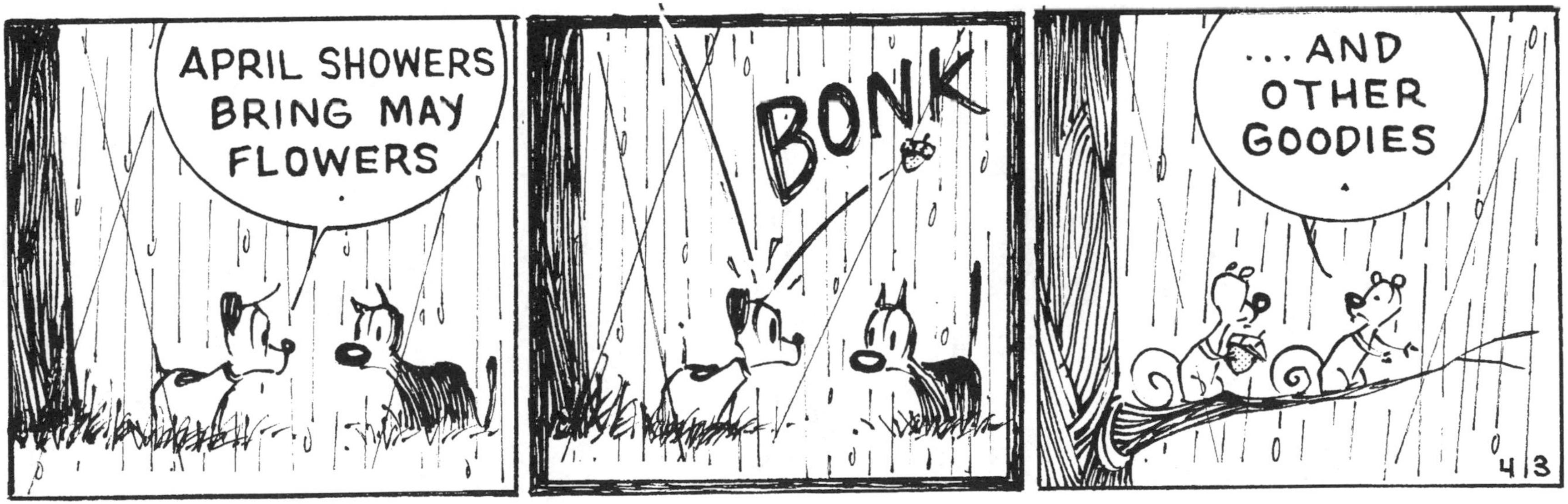
APRIL SHOWERS BRING MAY FLOWERS.
BONK
...AND OTHER GOODIES.
4 3

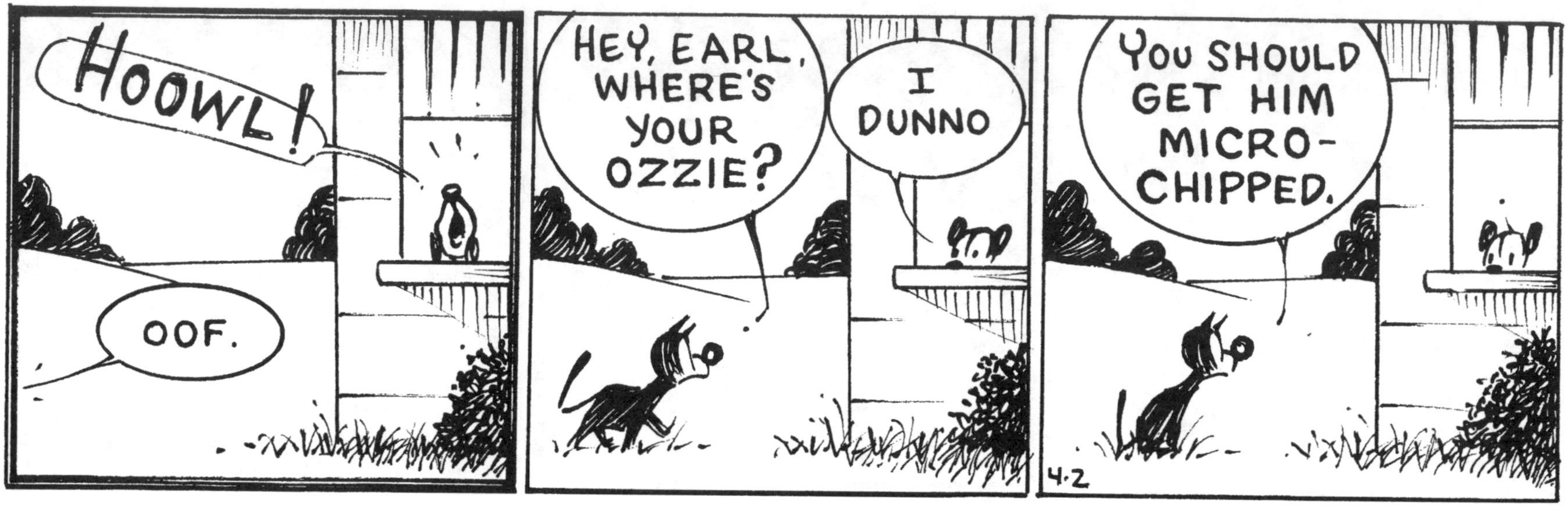
HOOWL!
OOF.
HEY, EARL, WHERE'S YOUR OZZIE?
I DUNNO
YOU SHOULD GET HIM MICRO-CHIPPED.
4·2

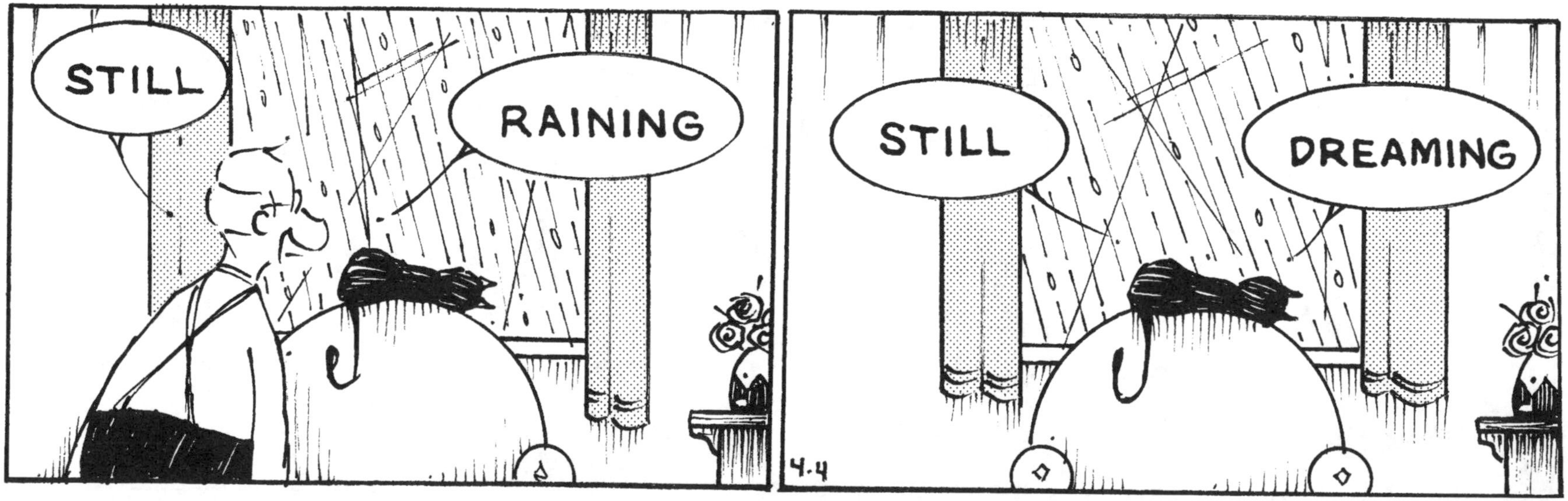
STILL
RAINING
STILL
DREAMING
4·4

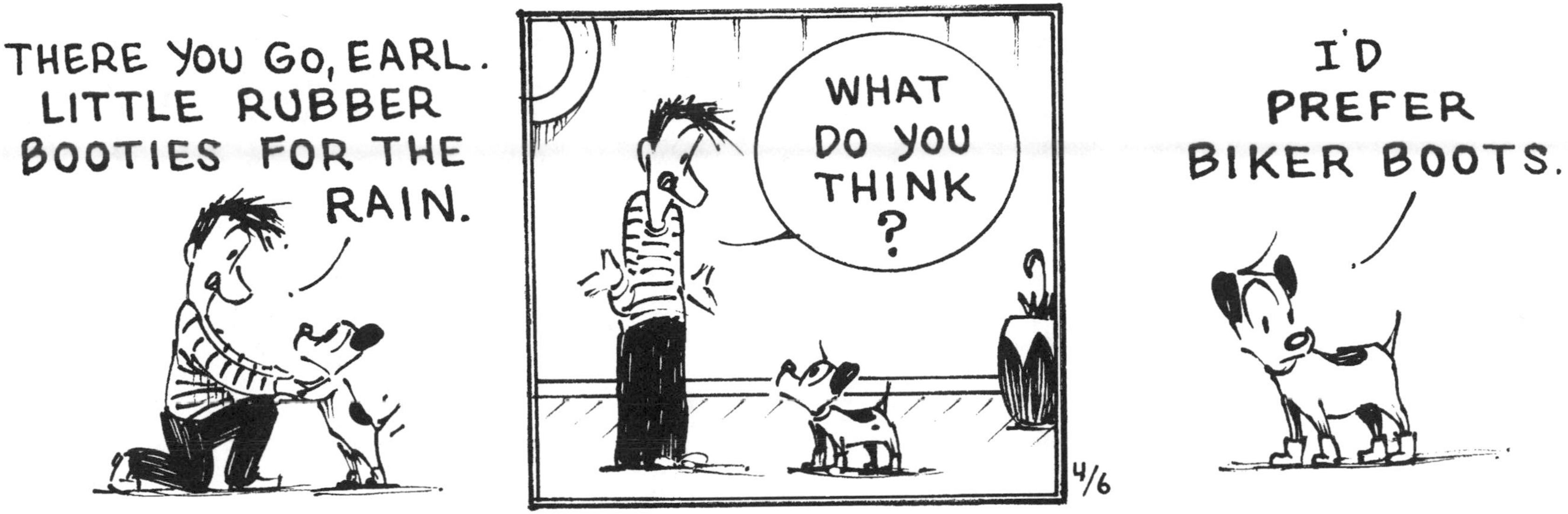
THERE YOU GO, EARL. LITTLE RUBBER BOOTIES FOR THE RAIN.
WHAT DO YOU THINK?
4/6
I'D PREFER BIKER BOOTS.

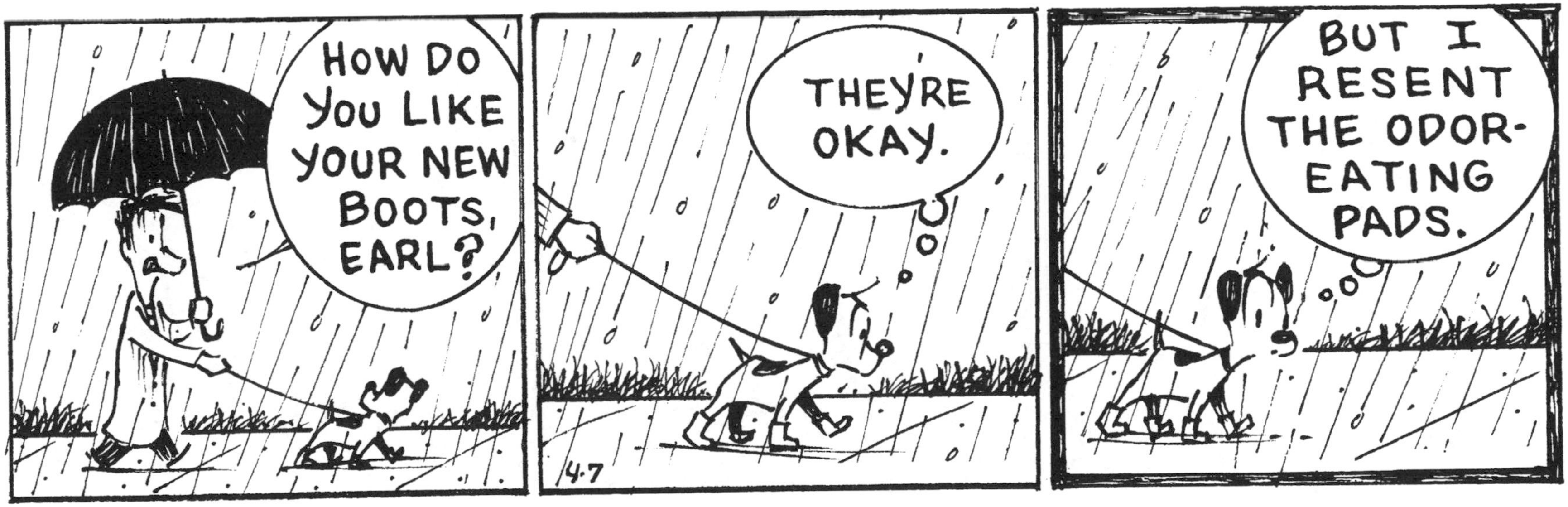
HOW DO YOU LIKE YOUR NEW BOOTS, EARL?
THEY'RE OKAY.
4·7
BUT I RESENT THE ODOR-EATING PADS.

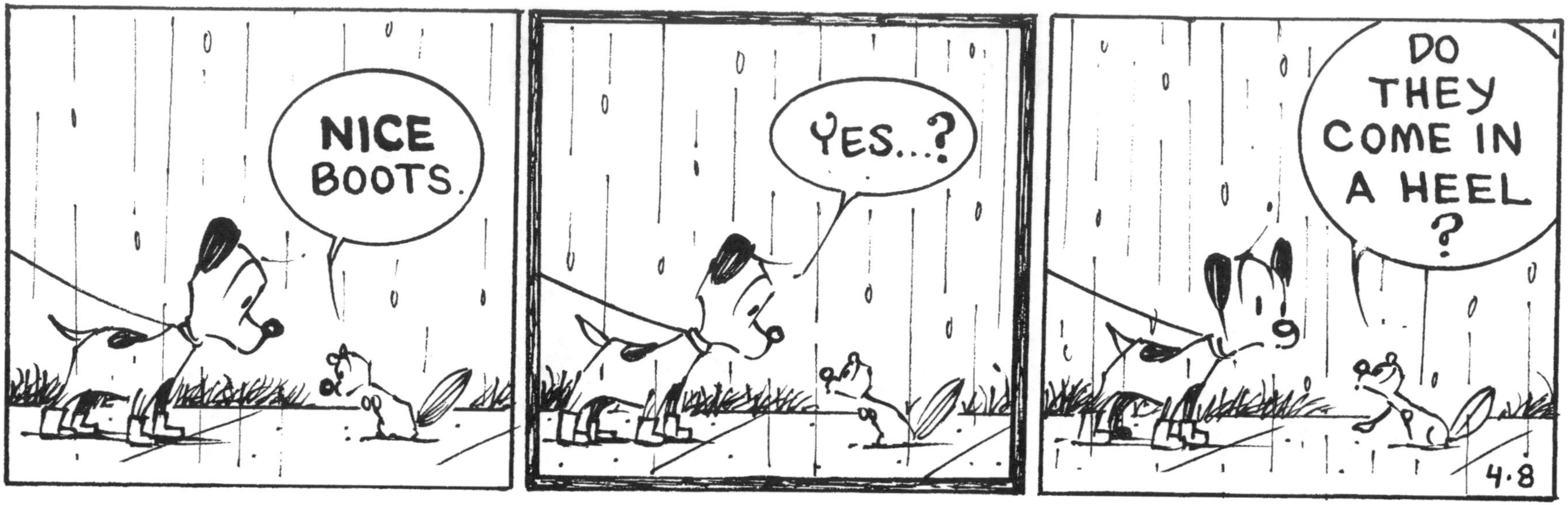
NICE BOOTS.
YES...?
DO THEY COME IN A HEEL ?
4·8

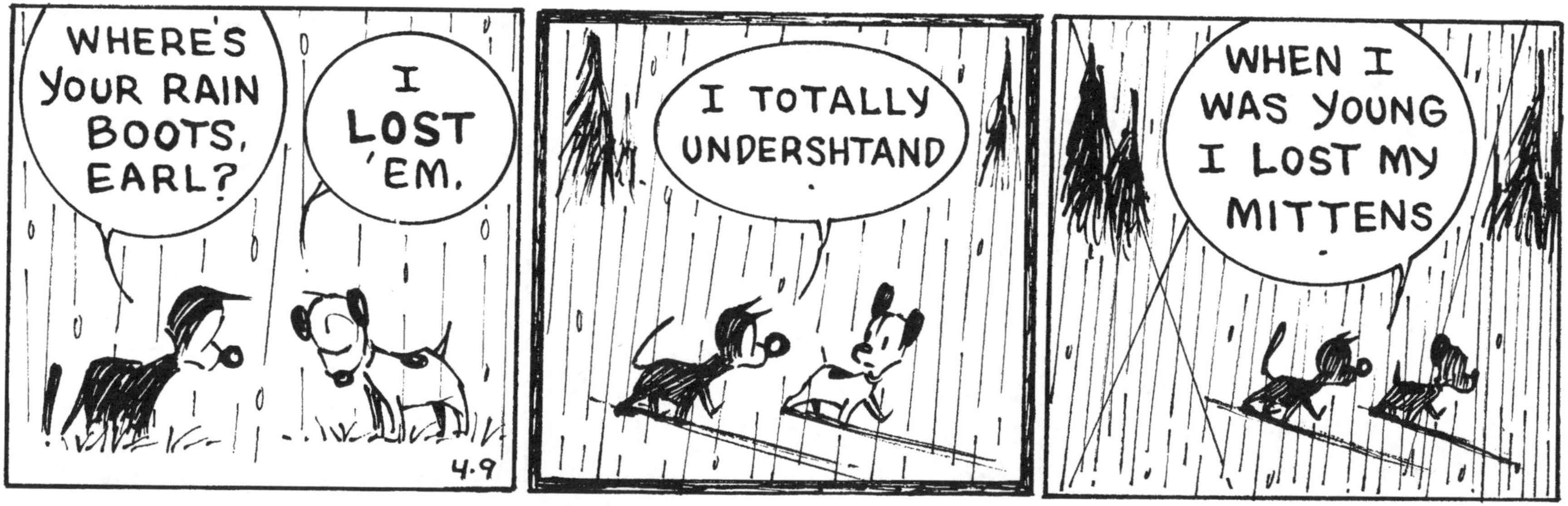
WHERE'S YOUR RAIN BOOTS, EARL?
I LOST 'EM.
4·9
I TOTALLY UNDERSHTAND.
WHEN I WAS YOUNG I LOST MY MITTENS.

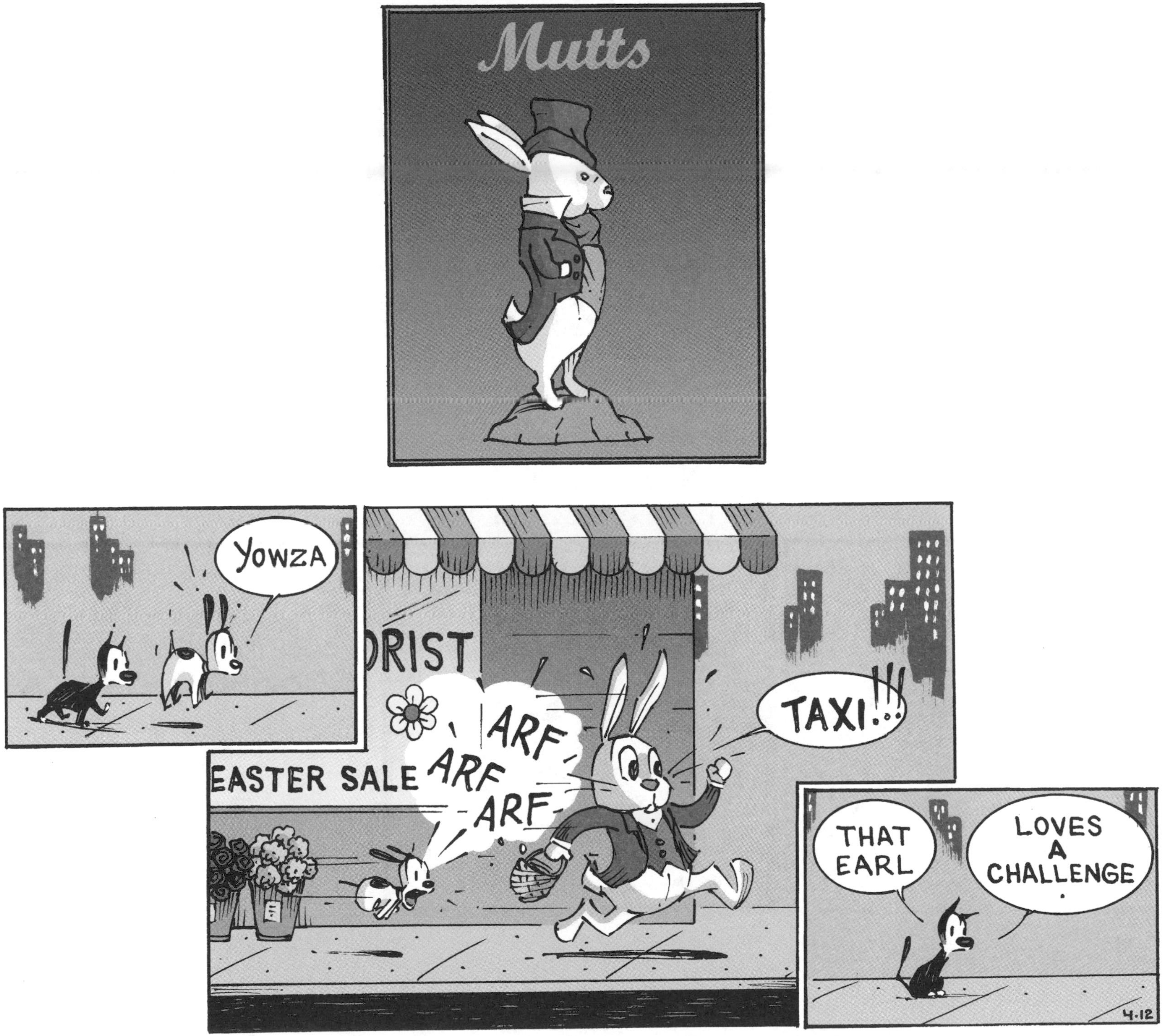

Mutts
YOWZA
ORIST
EASTER SALE
ARF ARF ARF
TAXI!!!
THAT EARL
LOVES A CHALLENGE.
4·12

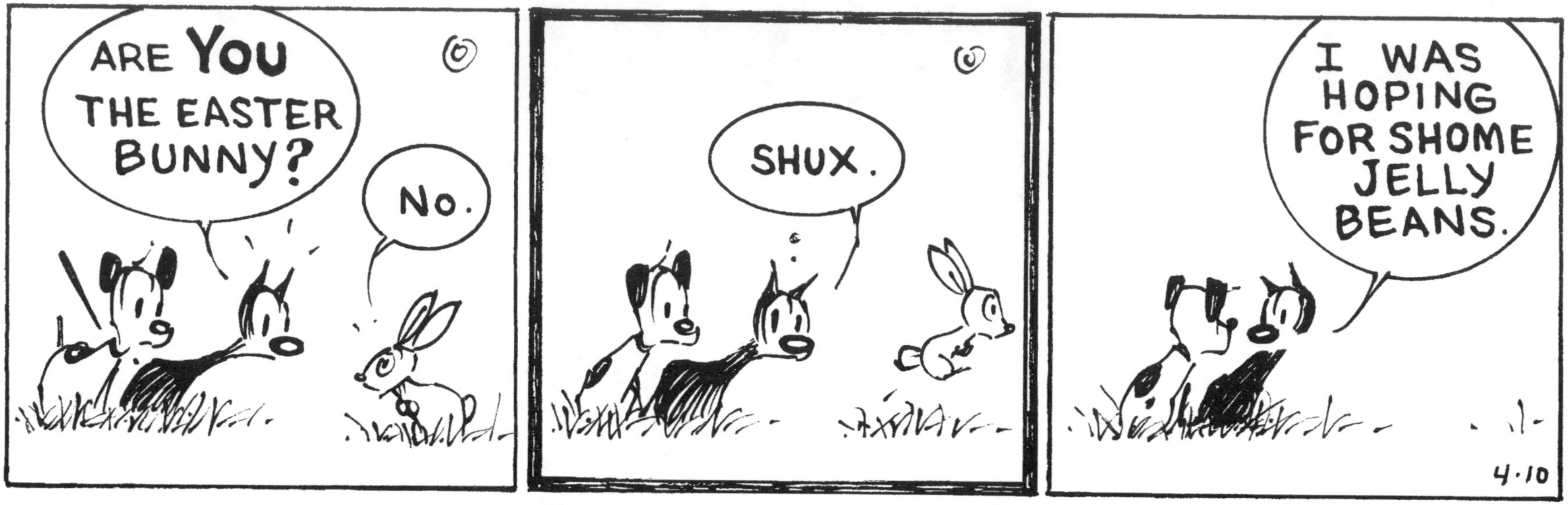
ARE YOU THE EASTER BUNNY?
No.
SHUX.
I WAS HOPING FOR SHOME JELLY BEANS.
4·10

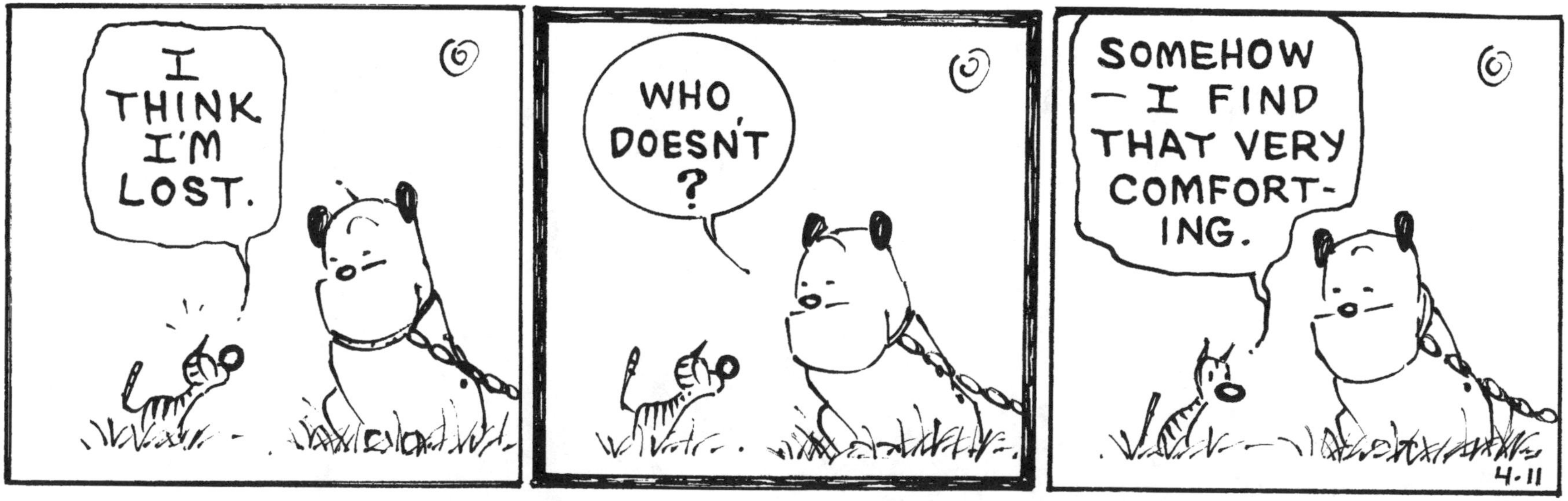
I THINK I'M LOST.
WHO DOESN'T?
SOMEHOW — I FIND THAT VERY COMFORT-ING.
4·11

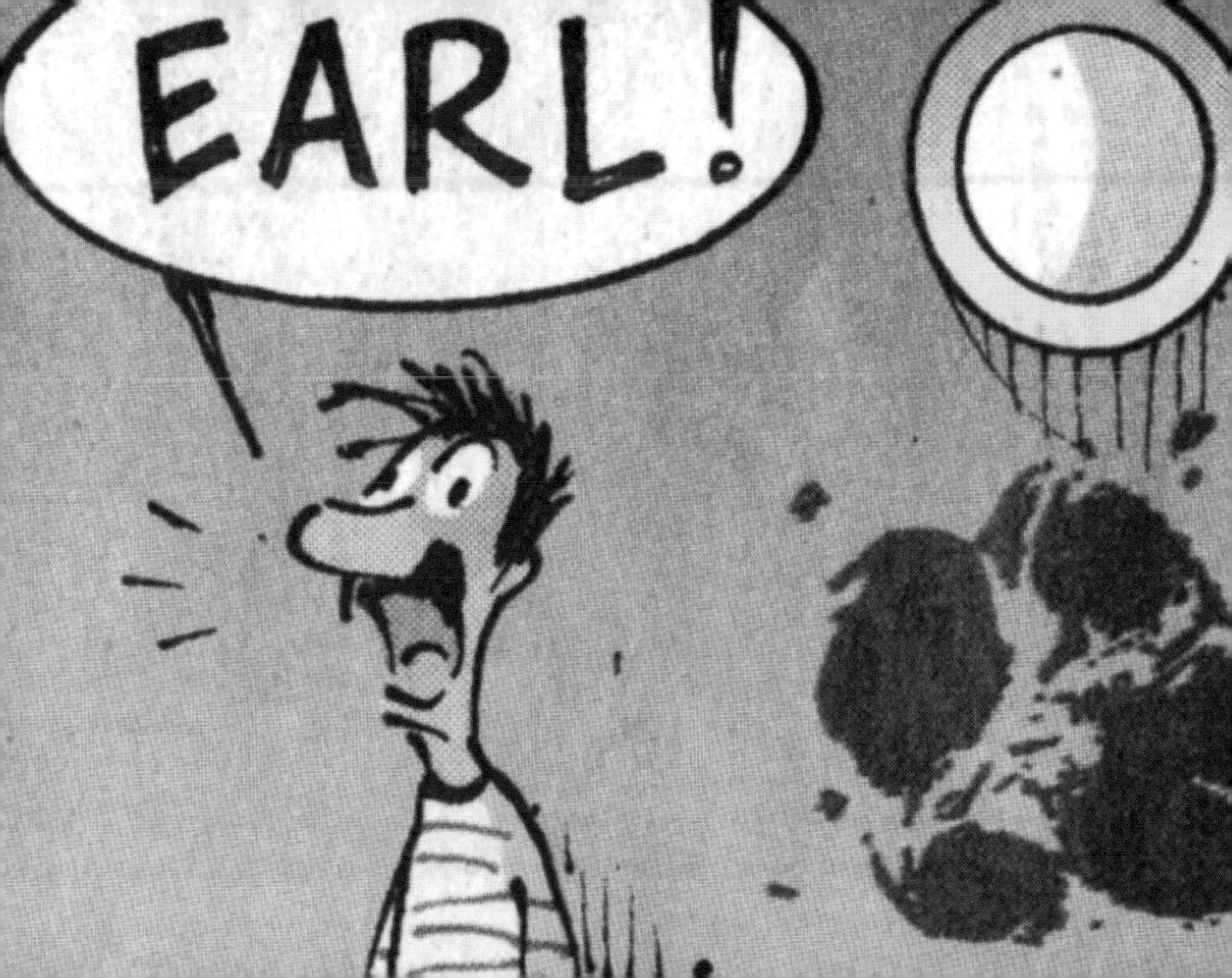
EARL!

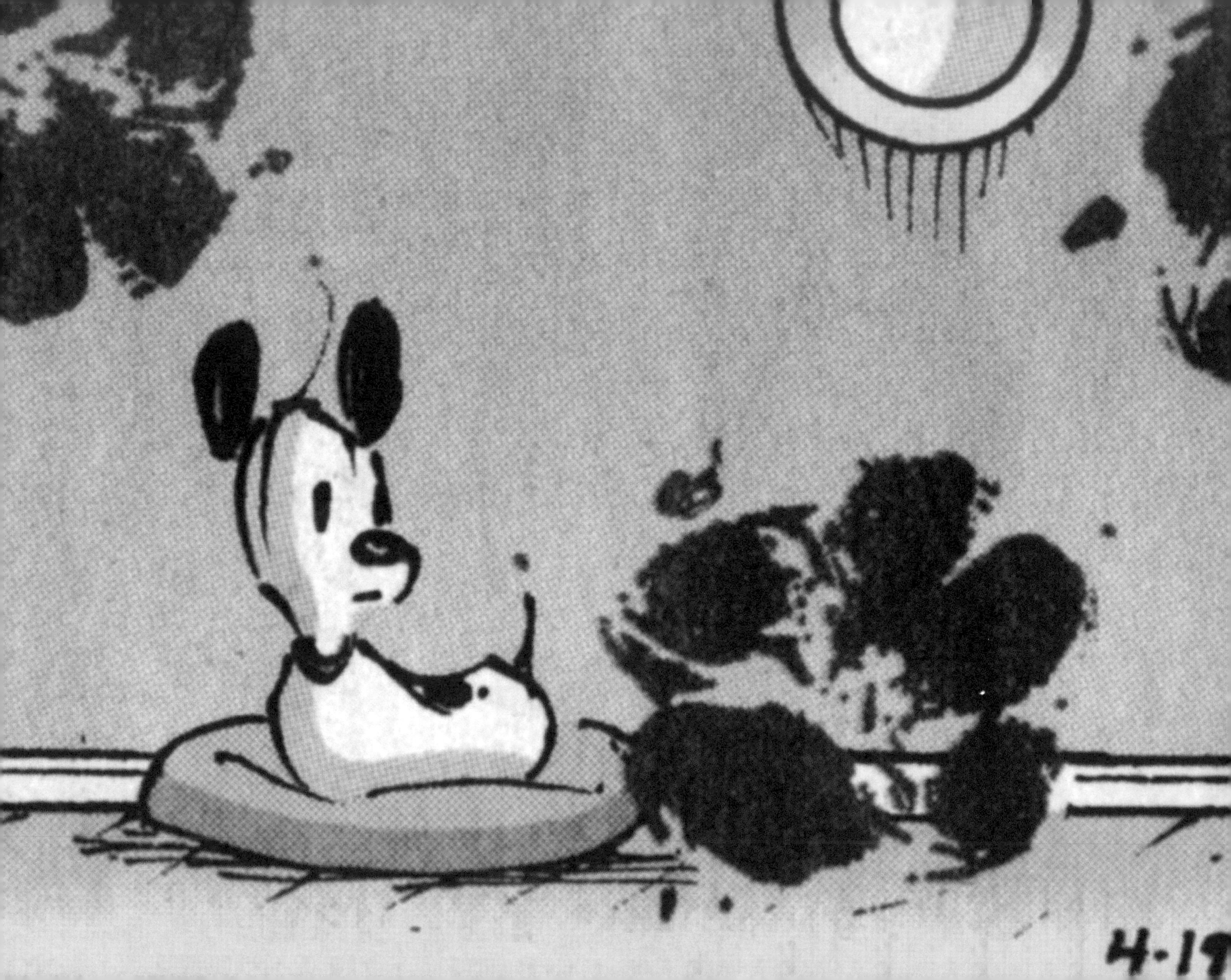
4-19

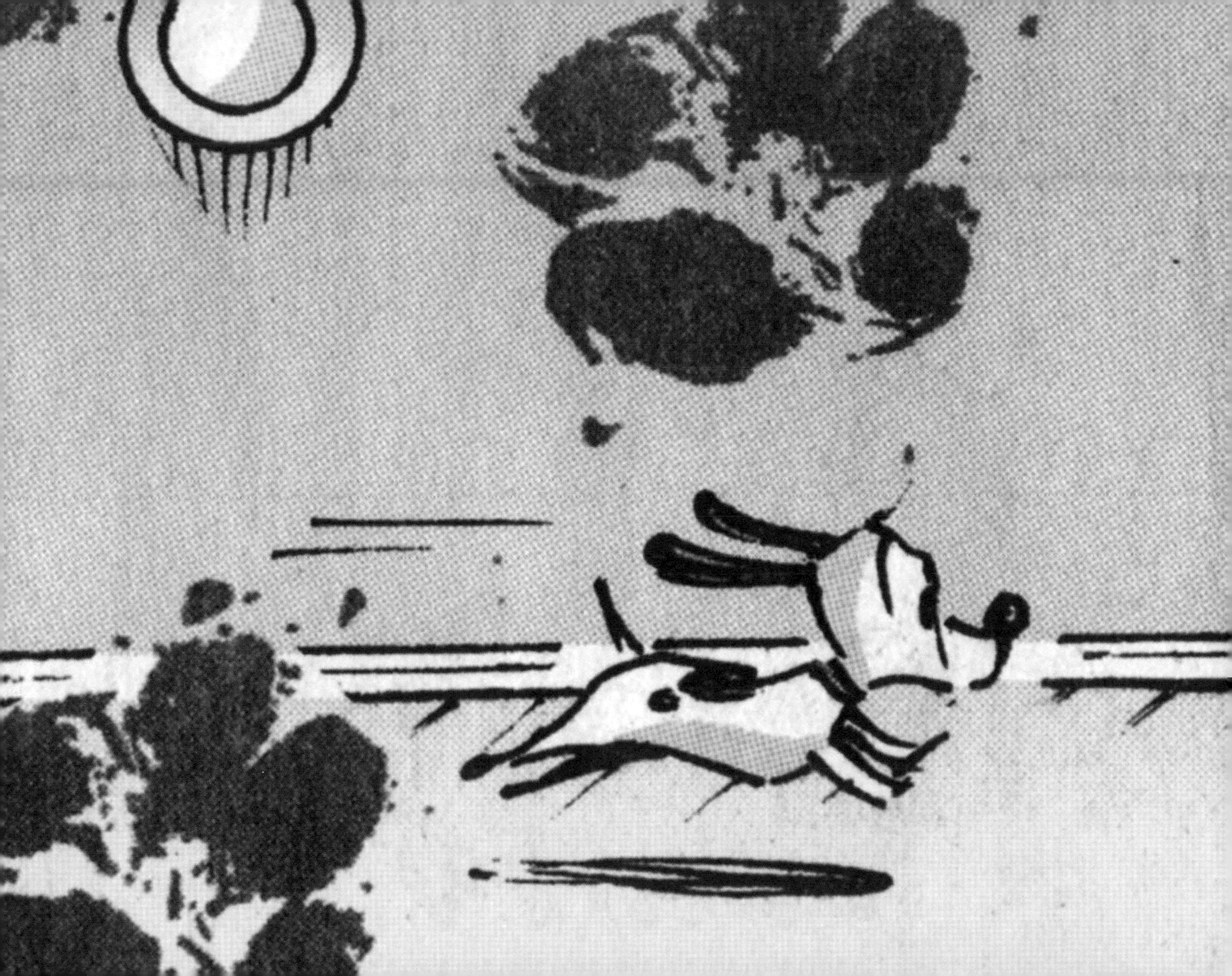

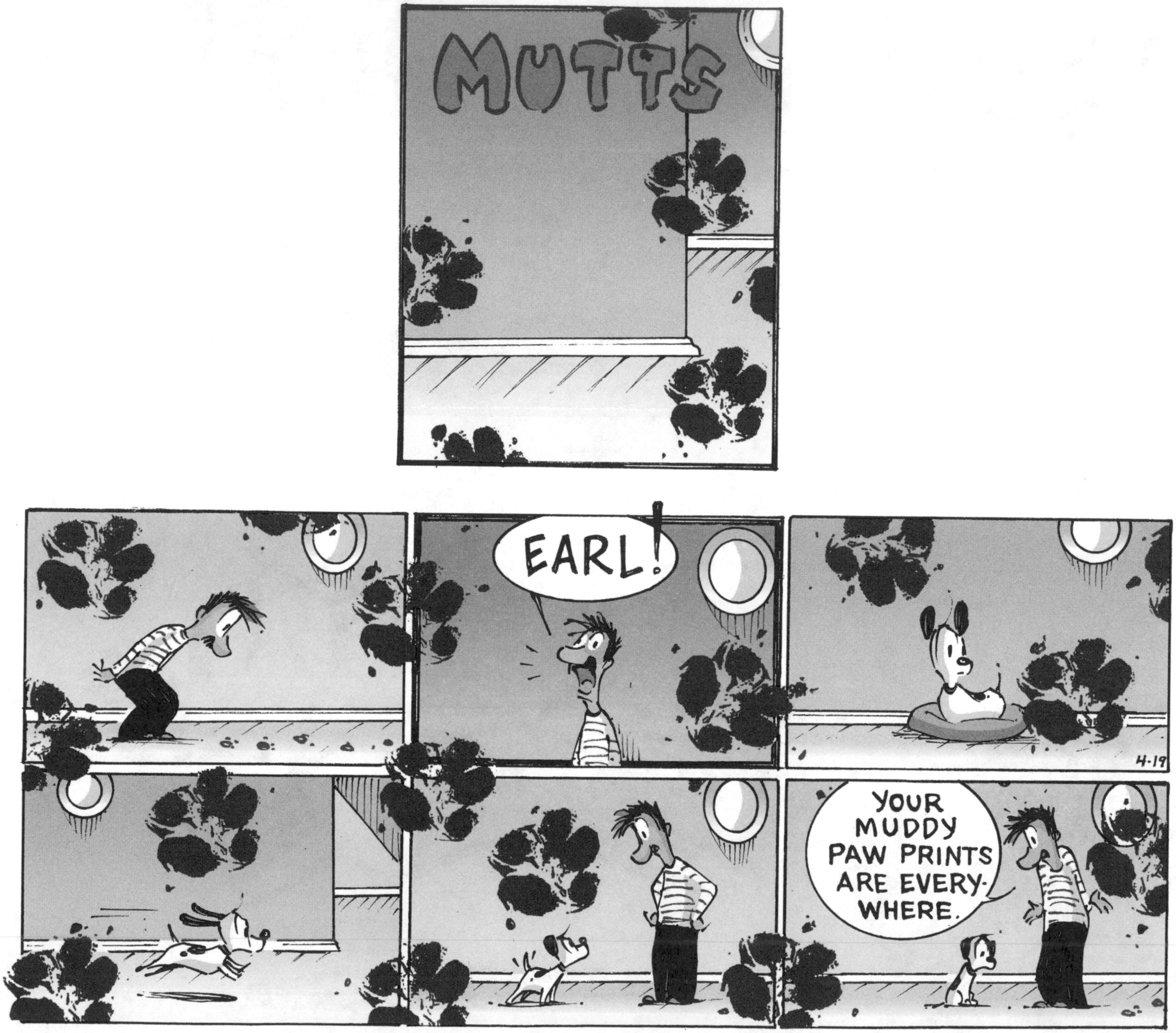
MUTTS
EARL!
4-19
YOUR MUDDY PAW PRINTS ARE EVERY-WHERE.

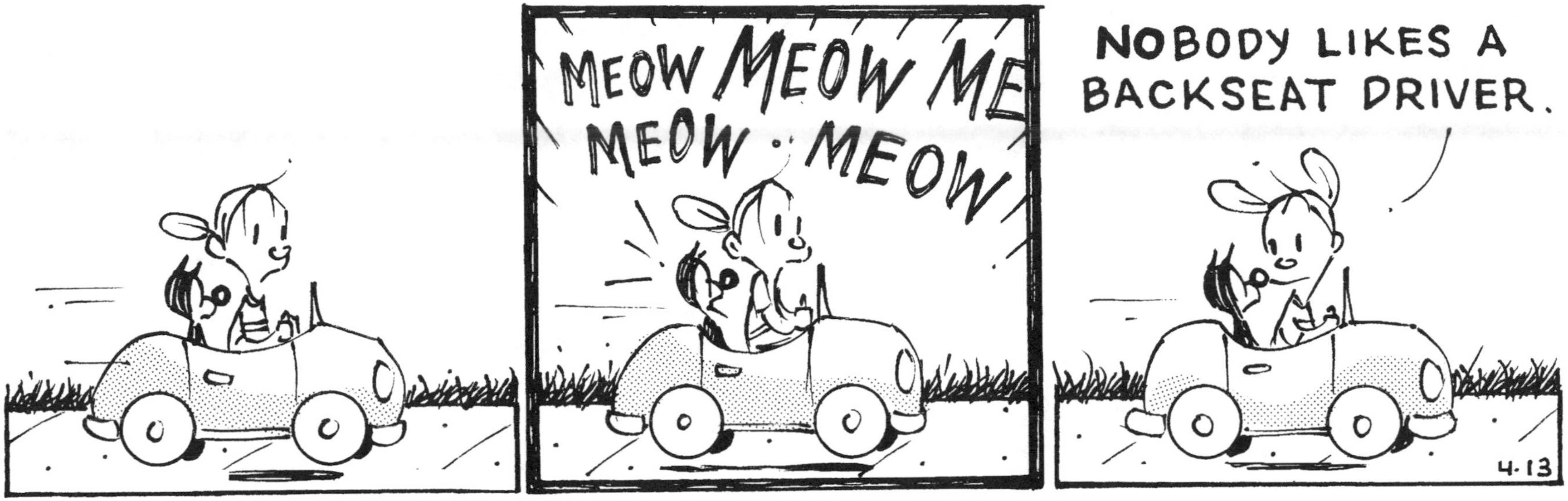
MEOW MEOW ME
MEOW · MEOW
NOBODY LIKES A BACKSEAT DRIVER.
4.13

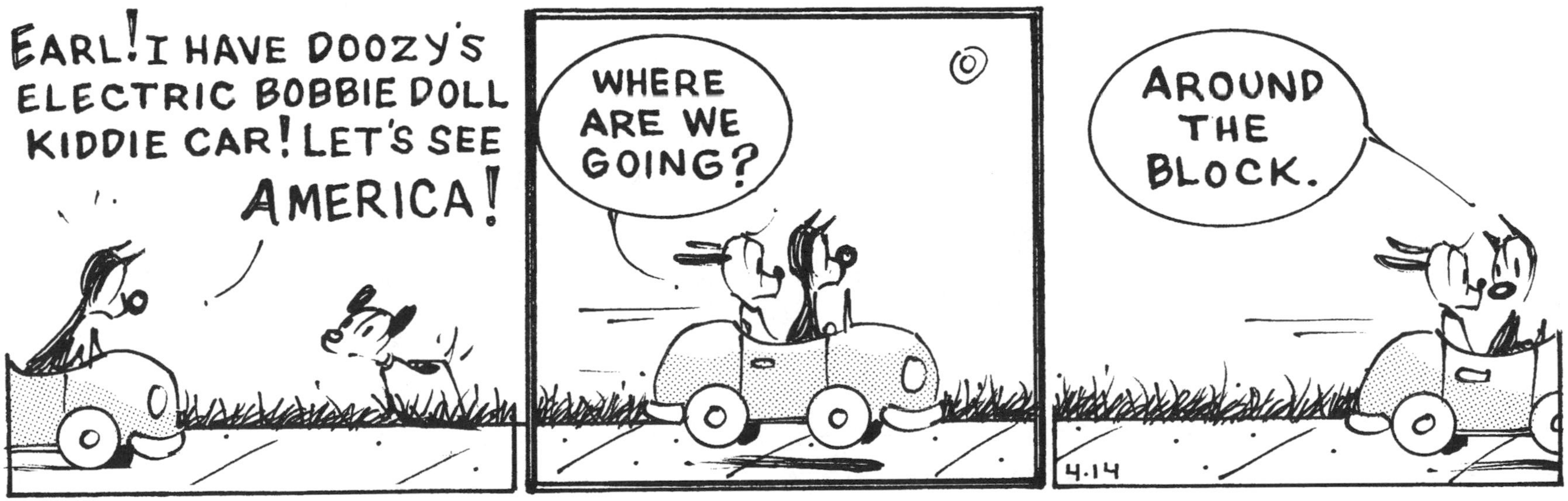
EARL! I HAVE DOOZY'S ELECTRIC BOBBIE DOLL KIDDIE CAR! LET'S SEE AMERICA!
WHERE ARE WE GOING?
AROUND THE BLOCK.
4.14

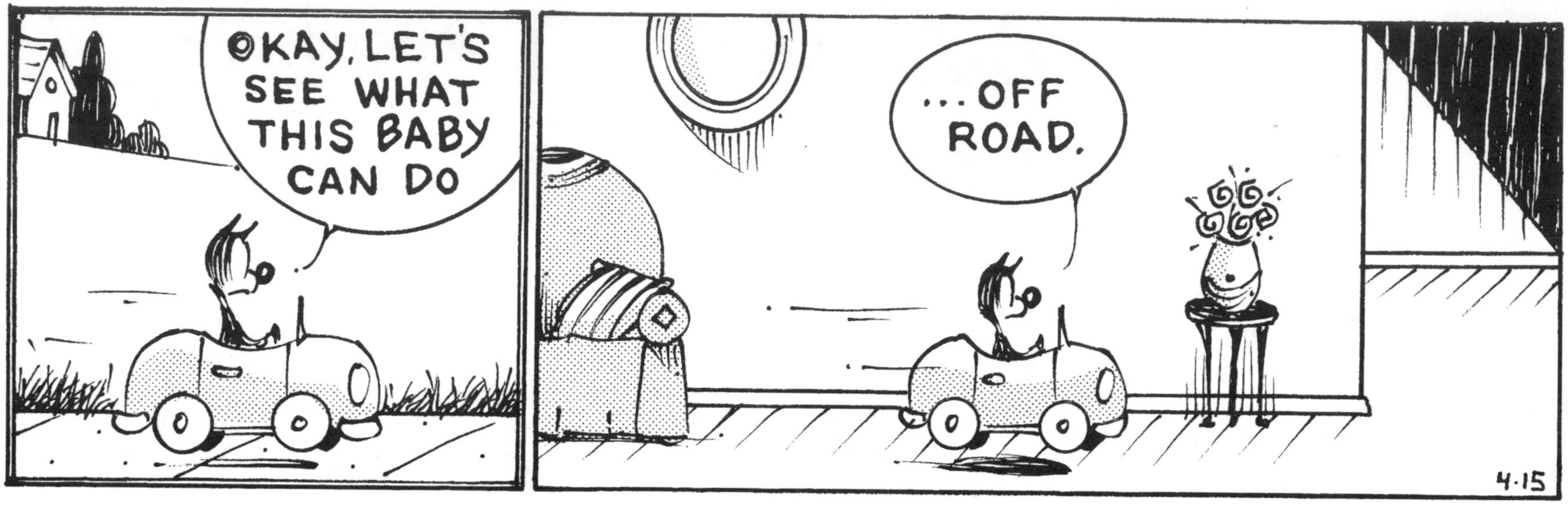
OKAY, LET'S SEE WHAT THIS BABY CAN DO
...OFF ROAD.
4·15

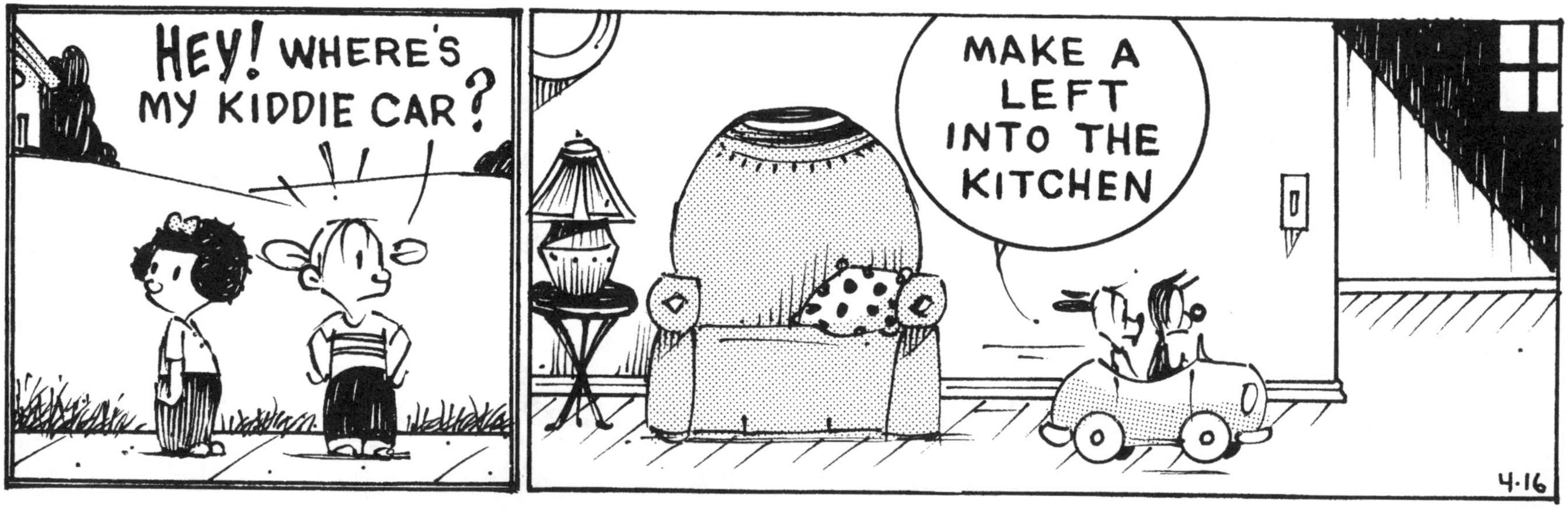
HEY! WHERE'S MY KIDDIE CAR?
MAKE A LEFT INTO THE KITCHEN
4·16

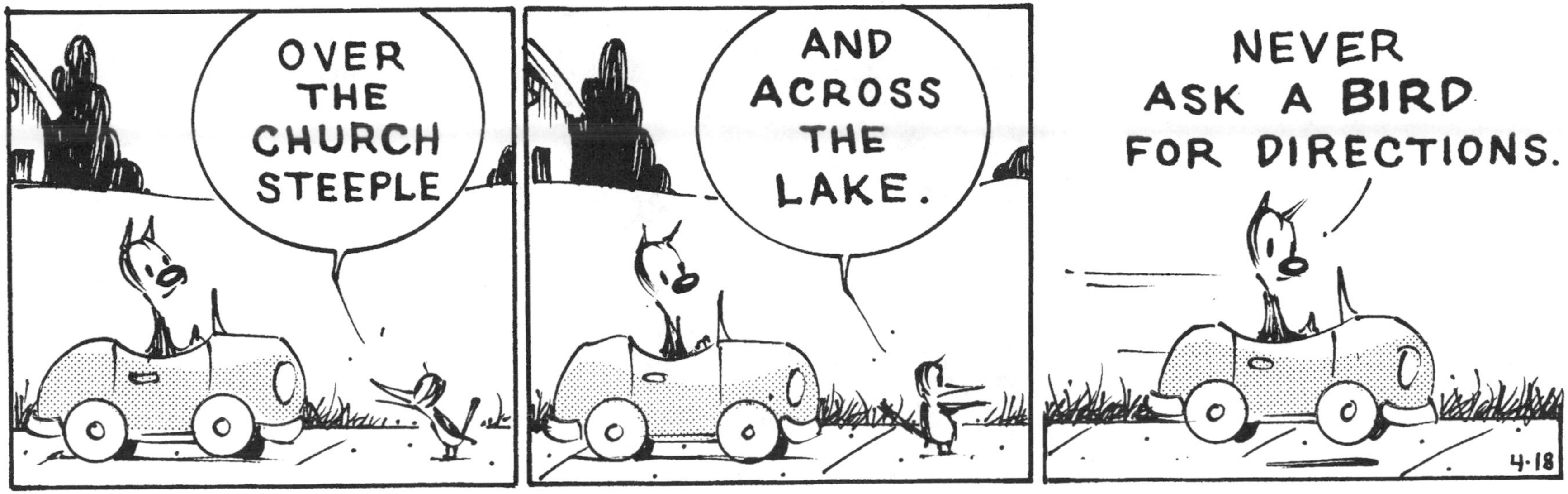
OVER THE CHURCH STEEPLE
AND ACROSS THE LAKE.
NEVER ASK A BIRD FOR DIRECTIONS.
4·18

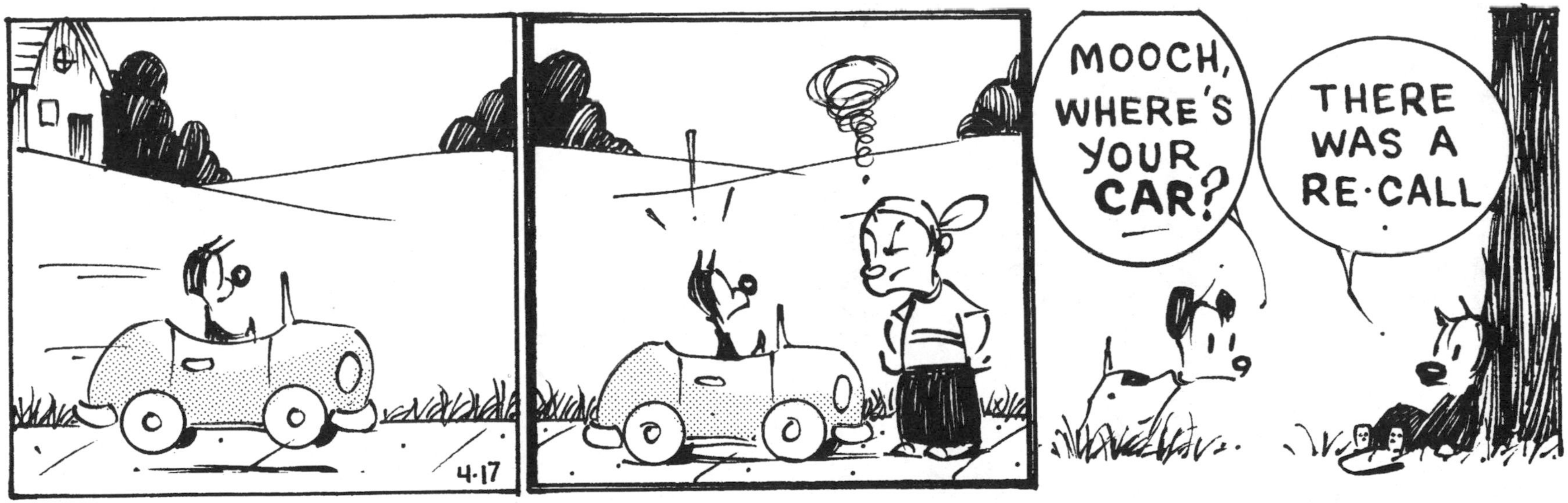
4·17
MOOCH, WHERE'S YOUR CAR?
THERE WAS A RE·CALL

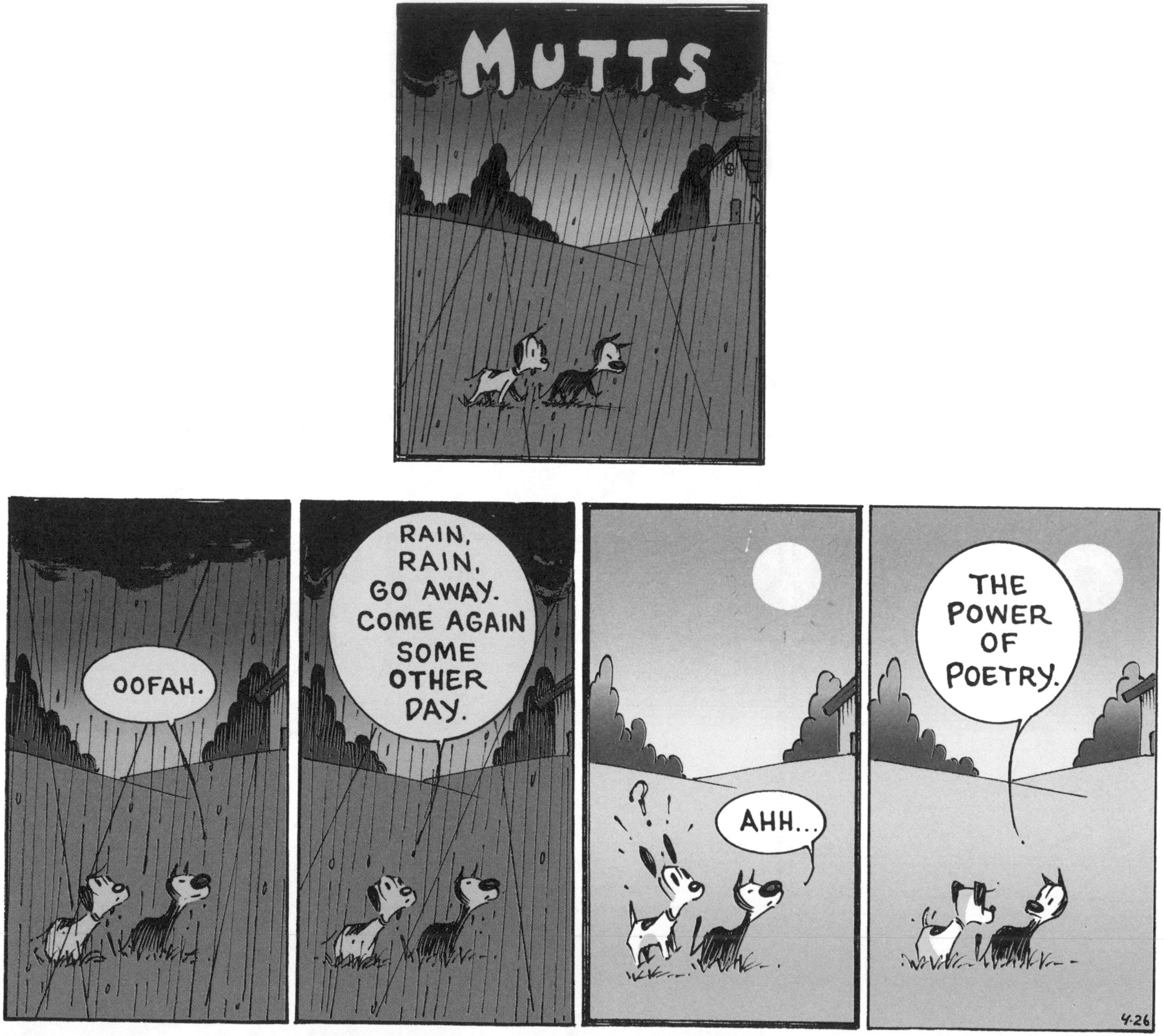
MUTTS
OOFAH.
RAIN, RAIN, GO AWAY. COME AGAIN SOME OTHER DAY.
?
!
AHH...
THE POWER OF POETRY.
4·26

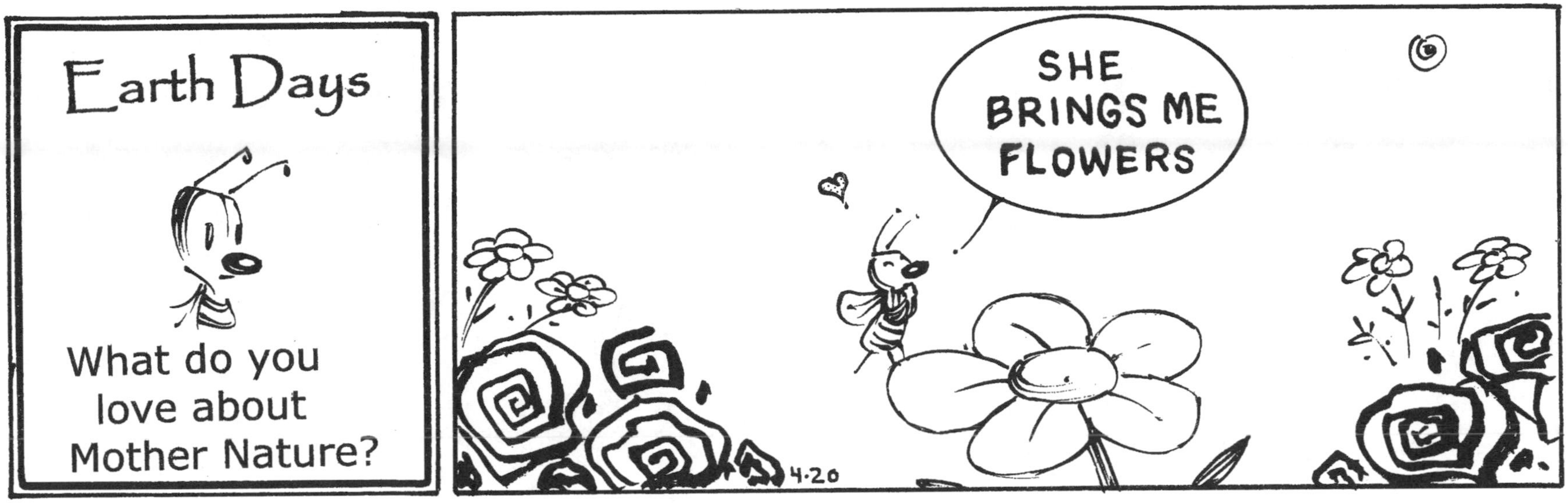
Earth Days
What do you love about Mother Nature?
SHE BRINGS ME FLOWERS
4·20

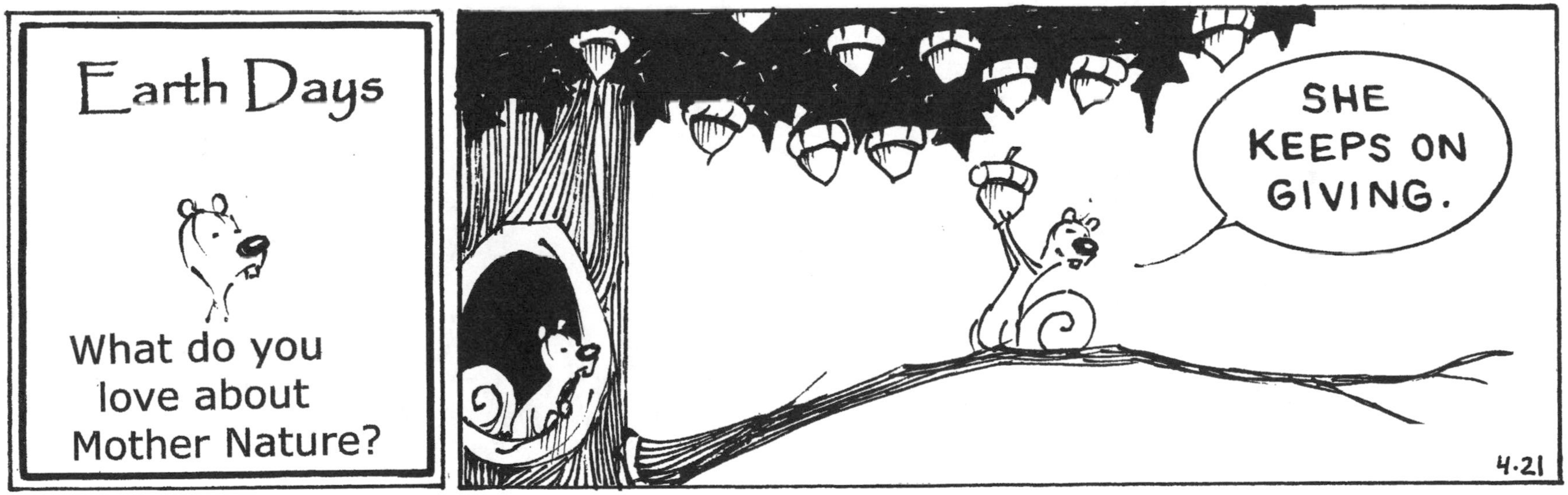
Earth Days
What do you love about Mother Nature?
SHE KEEPS ON GIVING.
4·21

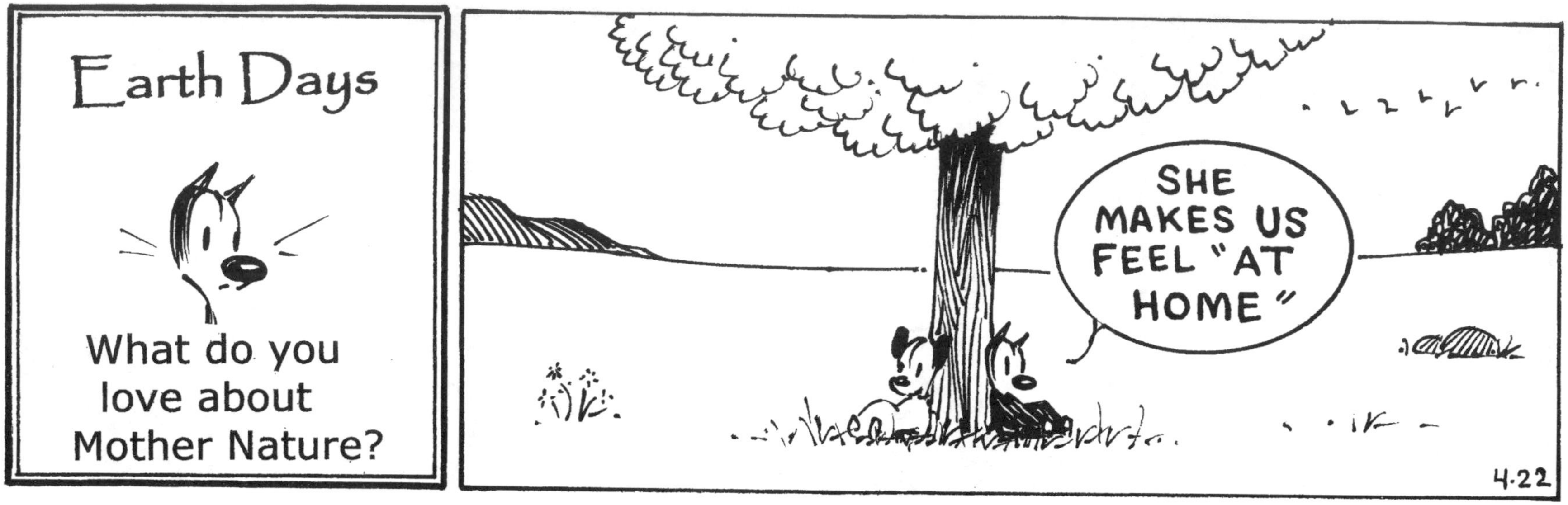
Earth Days
What do you love about Mother Nature?
SHE MAKES US FEEL "AT HOME"
4·22

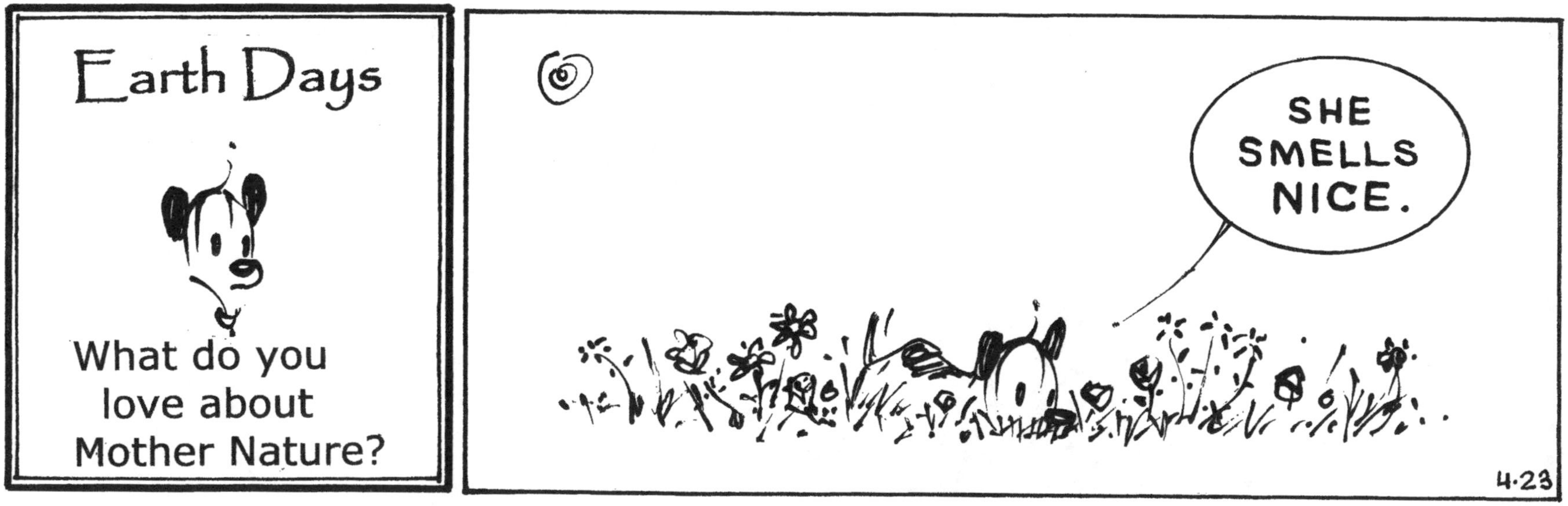
Earth Days
What do you love about Mother Nature?
SHE SMELLS NICE.
4·23

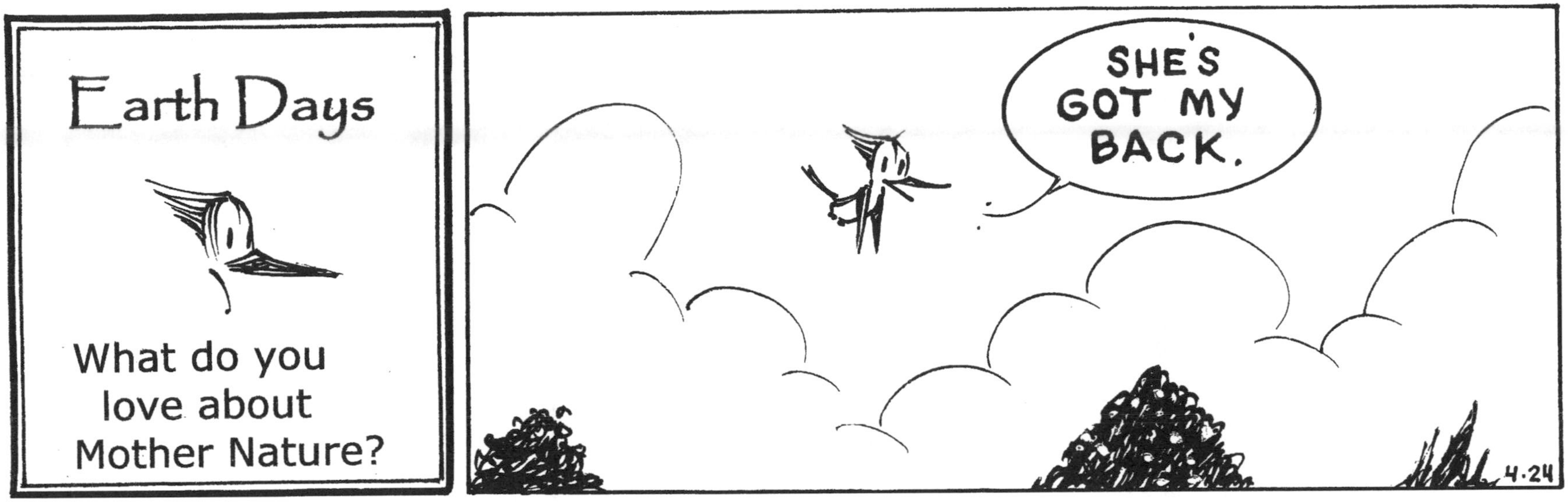
Earth Days
What do you love about Mother Nature?
SHE'S GOT MY BACK.
4·24

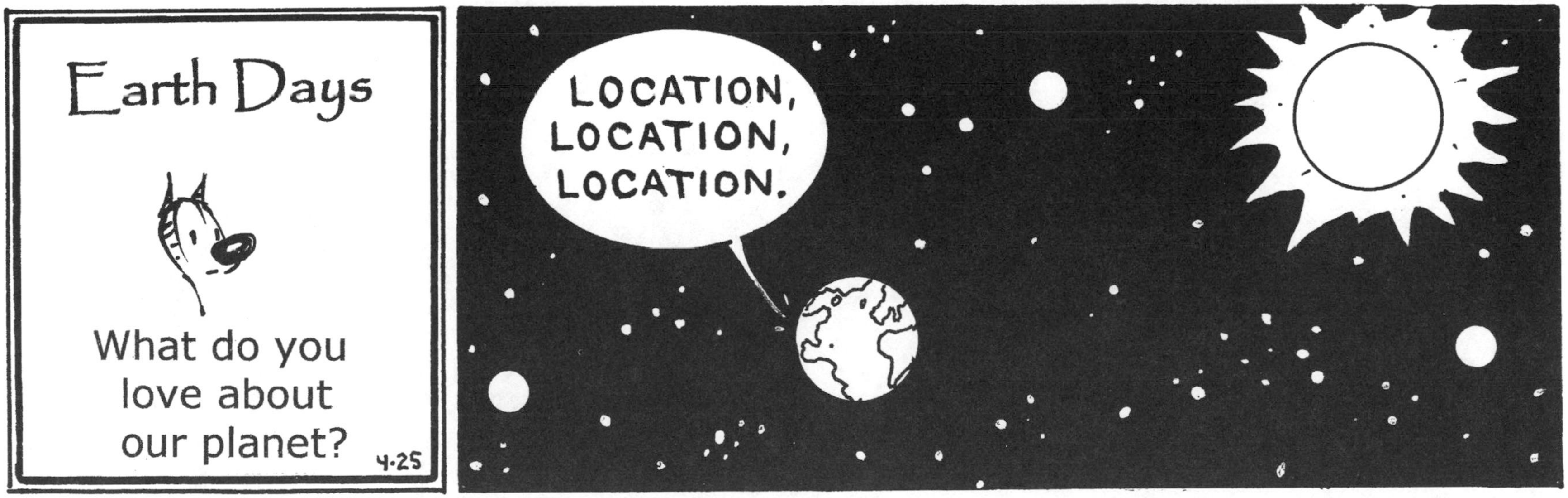
Earth Days
What do you love about our planet?
4·25
LOCATION, LOCATION, LOCATION.

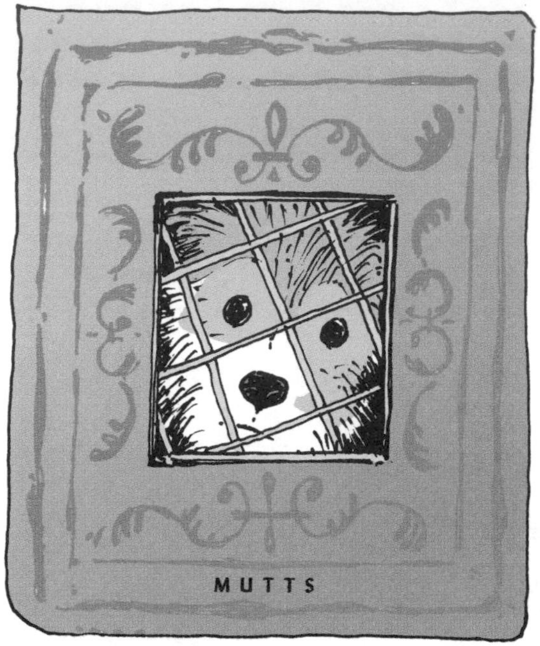
MUTTS

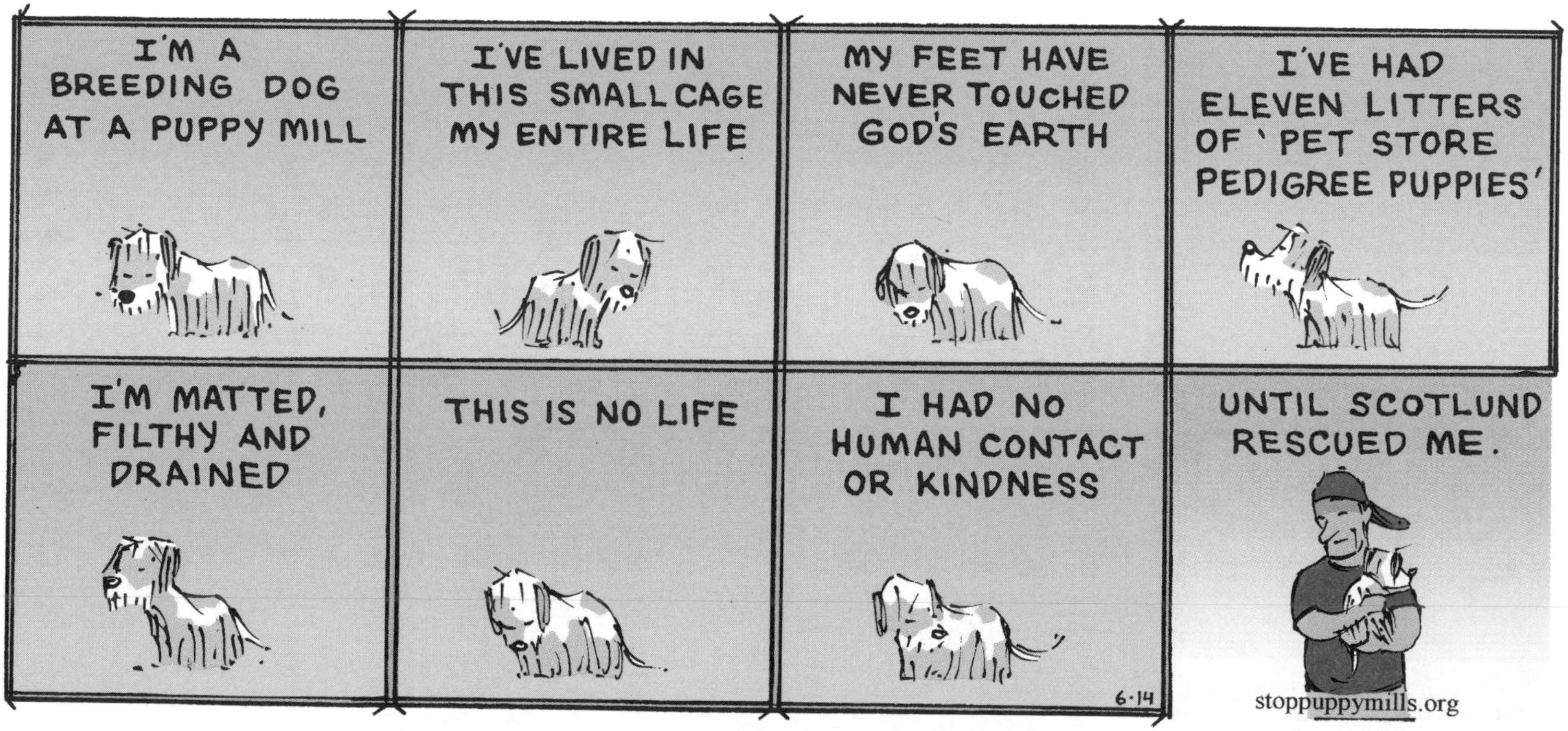
I'M A BREEDING DOG AT A PUPPY MILL
I'VE LIVED IN THIS SMALL CAGE MY ENTIRE LIFE
MY FEET HAVE NEVER TOUCHED GOD'S EARTH
I'VE HAD ELEVEN LITTERS OF 'PET STORE PEDIGREE PUPPIES'
I'M MATTED, FILTHY AND DRAINED
THIS IS NO LIFE
I HAD NO HUMAN CONTACT OR KINDNESS
6·14
UNTIL SCOTLUND RESCUED ME.
stoppuppymills.org

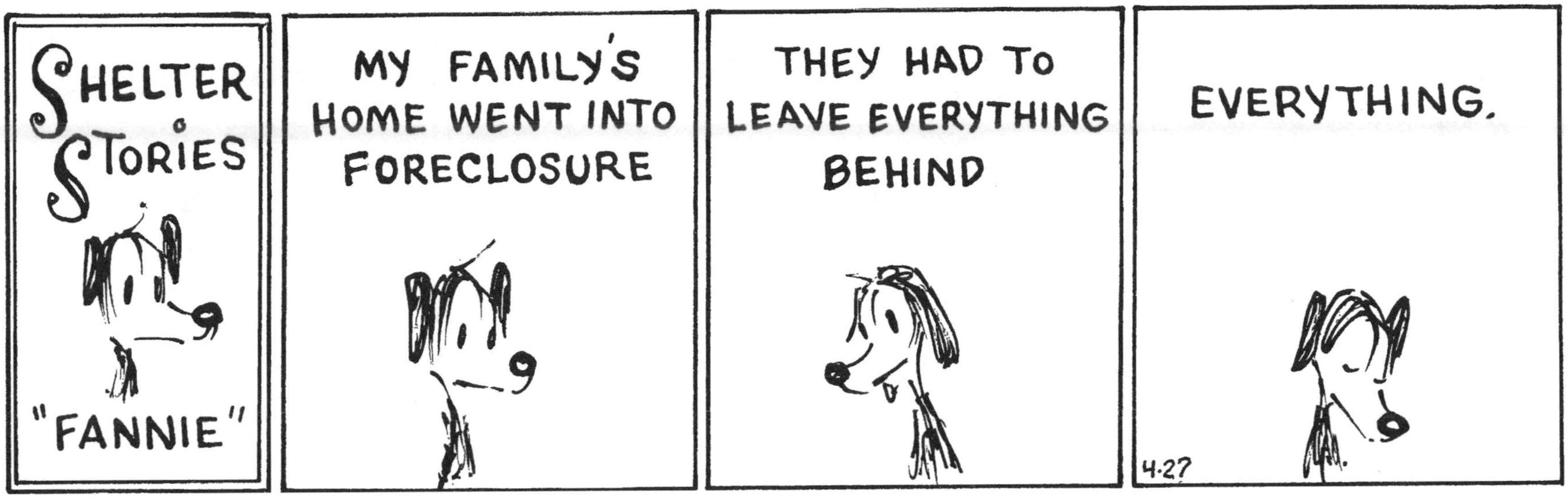
SHELTER STORIES
"FANNIE"
MY FAMILY'S HOME WENT INTO FORECLOSURE
THEY HAD TO LEAVE EVERYTHING BEHIND
EVERYTHING.
4·27

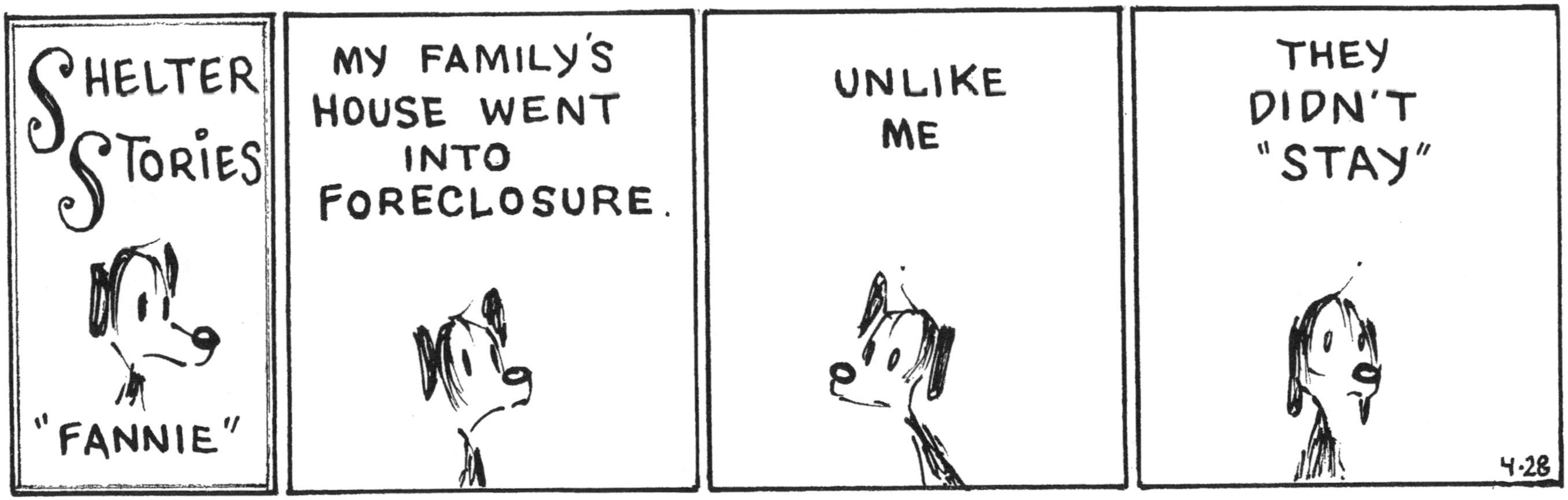
SHELTER STORIES
"FANNIE"
MY FAMILY'S HOUSE WENT INTO FORECLOSURE.
UNLIKE ME
THEY DIDN'T "STAY"
4·28

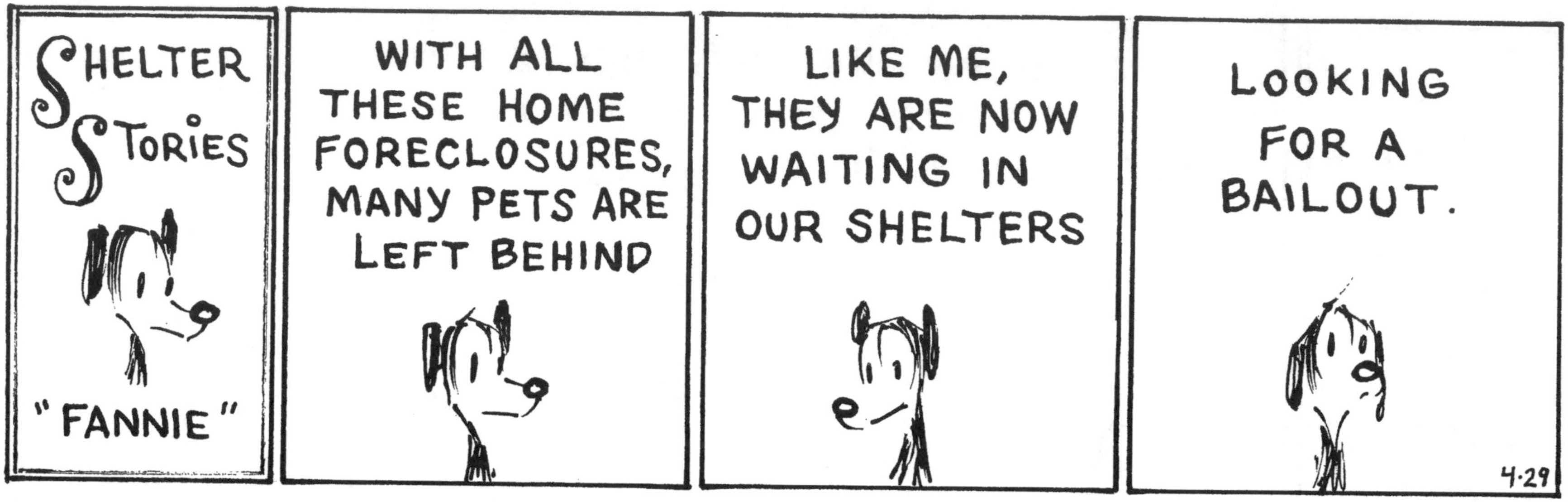
SHELTER STORIES
"FANNIE"
WITH ALL THESE HOME FORECLOSURES, MANY PETS ARE LEFT BEHIND
LIKE ME, THEY ARE NOW WAITING IN OUR SHELTERS
LOOKING FOR A BAILOUT.
4·29

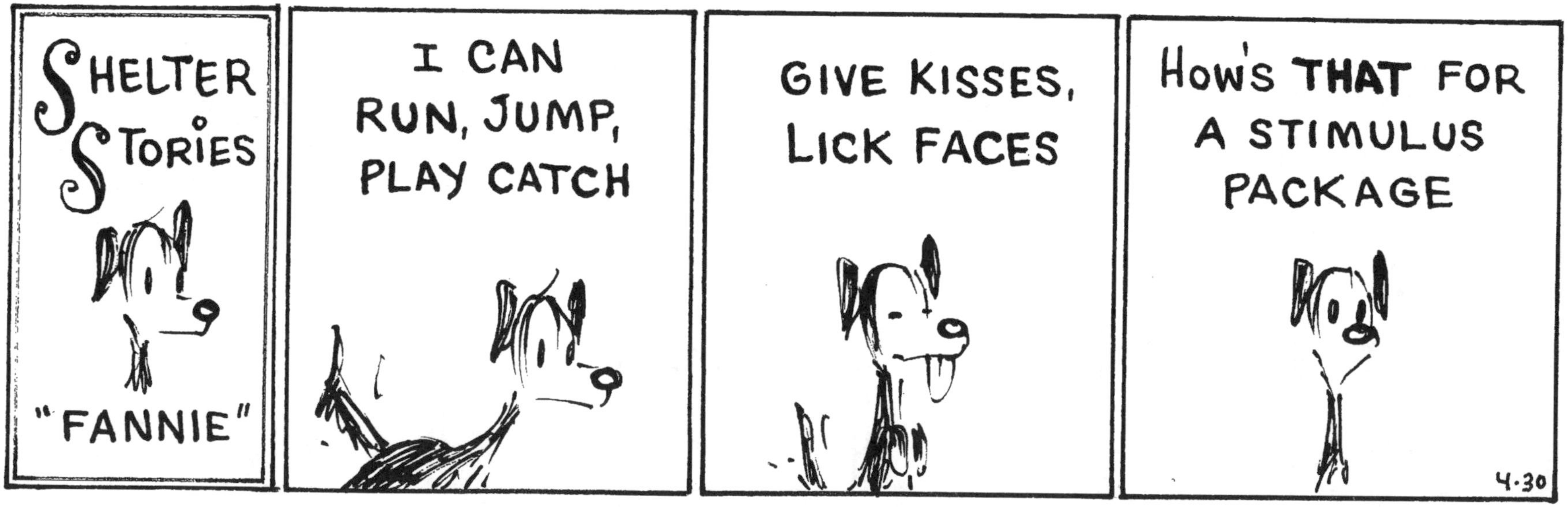
SHELTER STORIES
"FANNIE"
I CAN RUN, JUMP, PLAY CATCH
GIVE KISSES, LICK FACES
HOW'S THAT FOR A STIMULUS PACKAGE
4·30

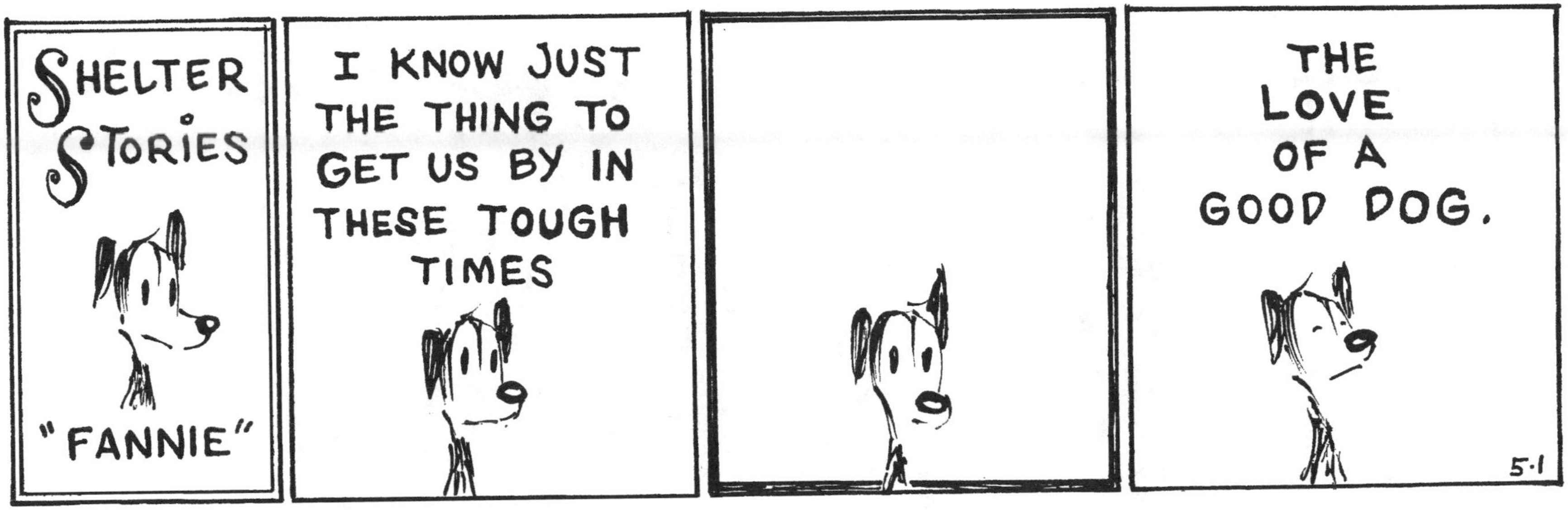
SHELTER STORIES
"FANNIE"
I KNOW JUST THE THING TO GET US BY IN THESE TOUGH TIMES
THE LOVE OF A GOOD DOG.
5·1

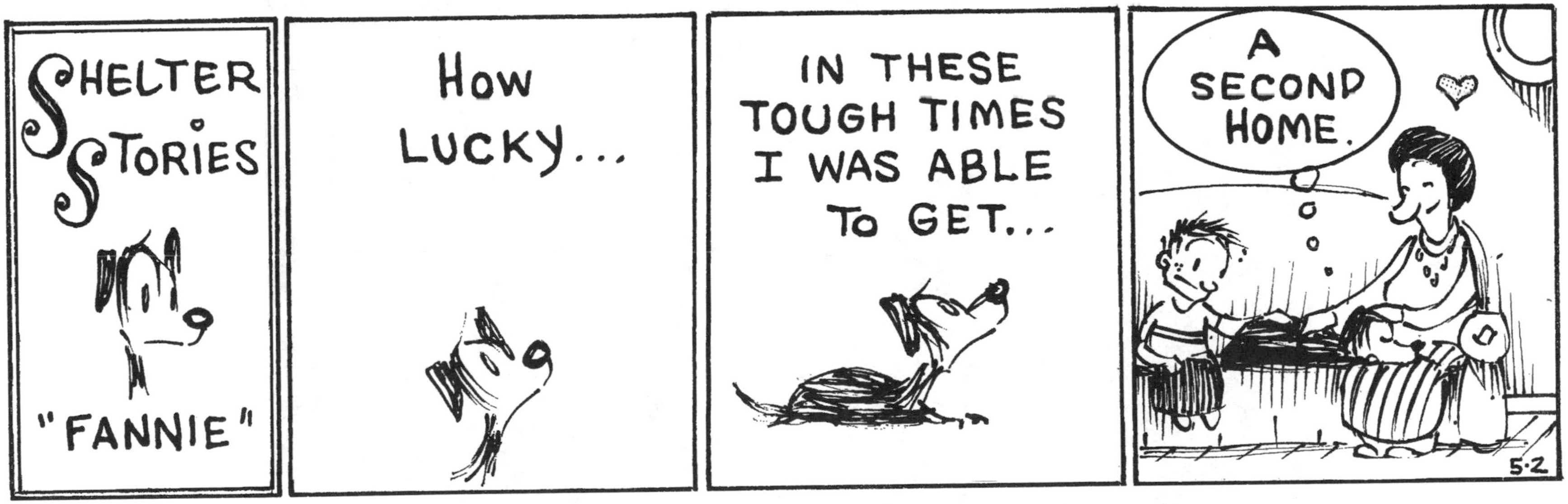
SHELTER STORIES
"FANNIE"
HOW LUCKY...
IN THESE TOUGH TIMES I WAS ABLE TO GET...
A SECOND HOME.
5·2

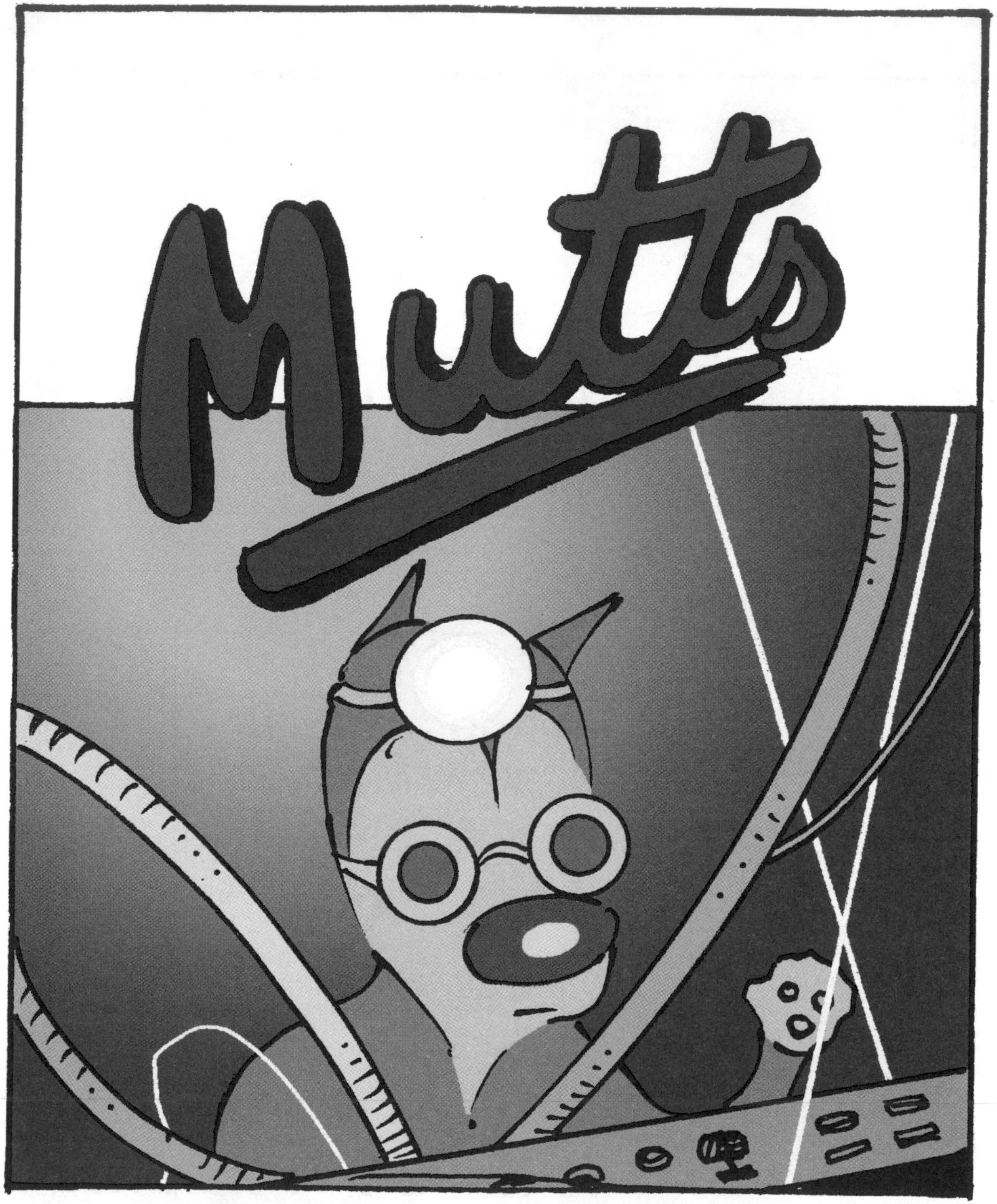
Mutts

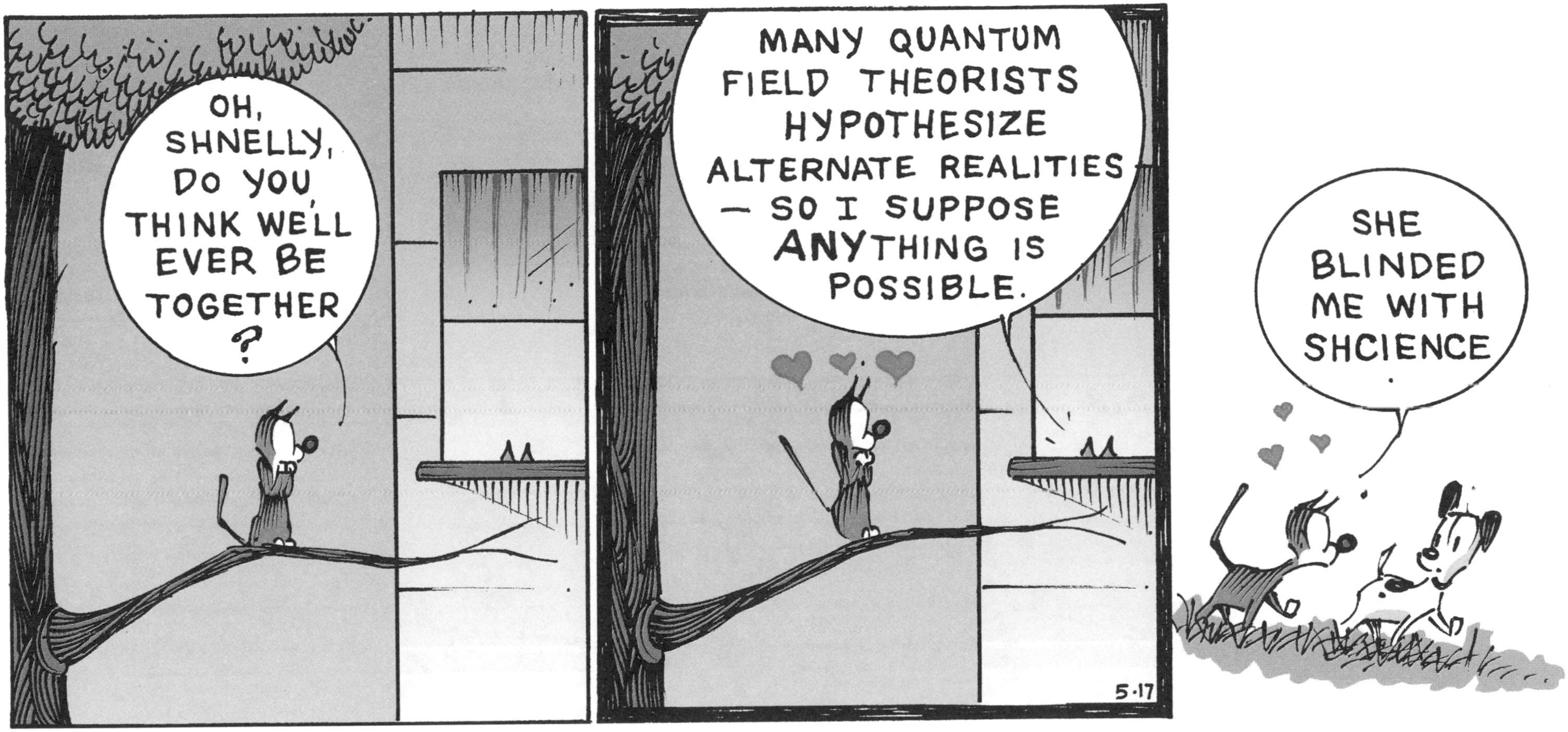
OH, SHNELLY, DO YOU THINK WE'LL EVER BE TOGETHER?
MANY QUANTUM FIELD THEORISTS HYPOTHESIZE ALTERNATE REALITIES — SO I SUPPOSE ANYTHING IS POSSIBLE.
5·17
SHE BLINDED ME WITH SHCIENCE.

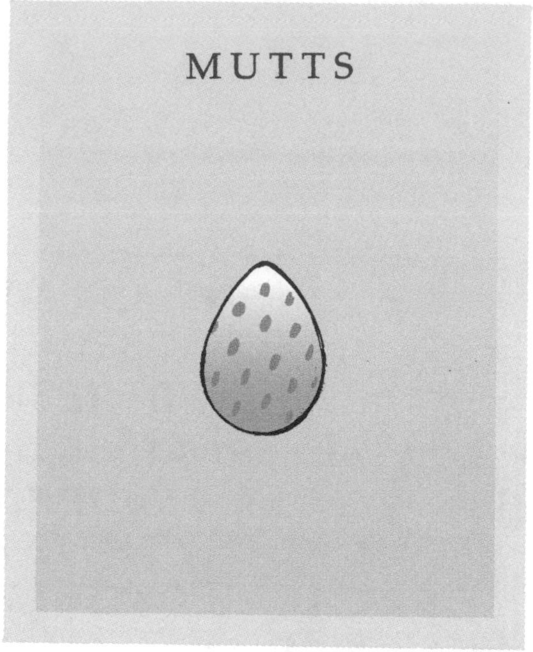
MUTTS

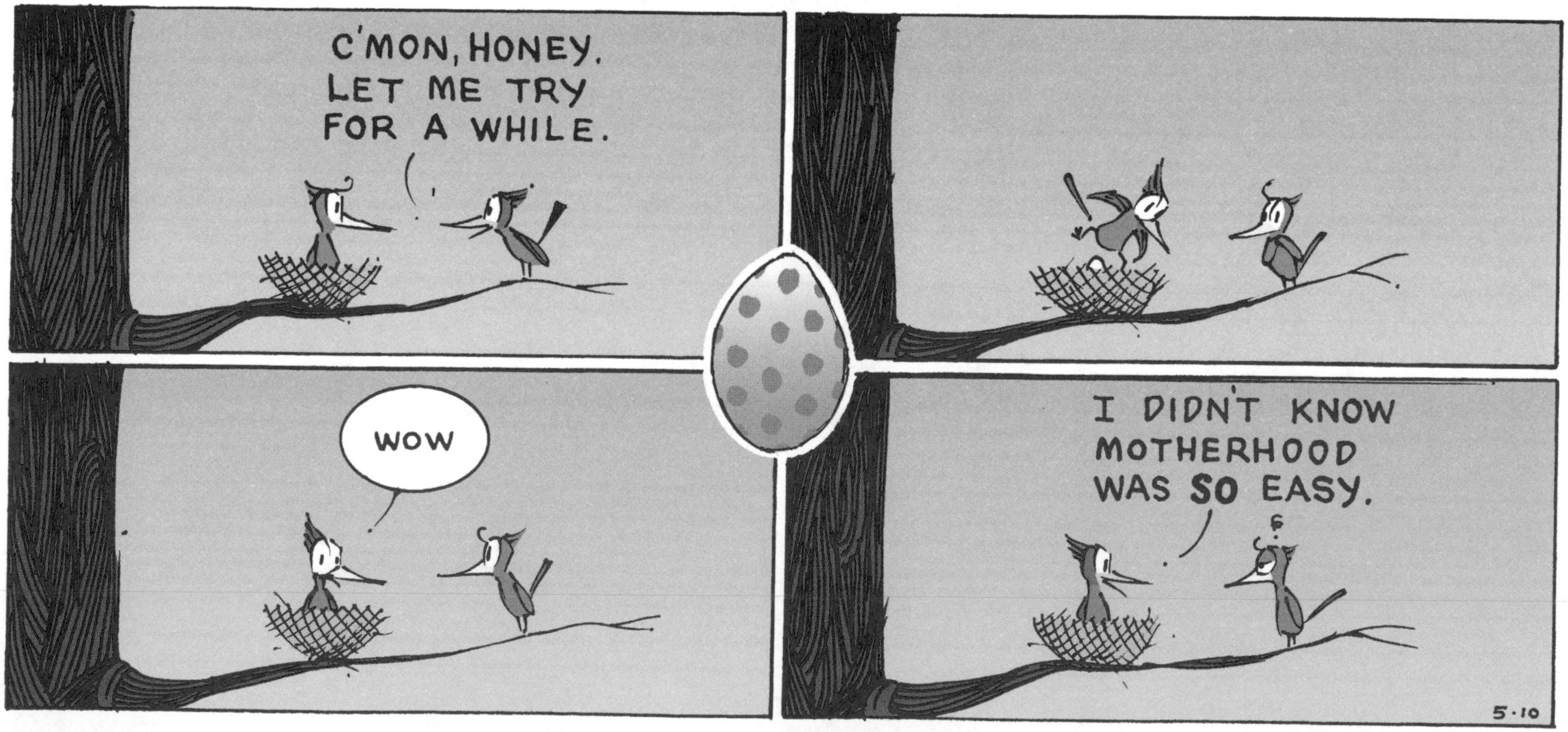
C'MON, HONEY. LET ME TRY FOR A WHILE.
WOW
I DIDN'T KNOW MOTHERHOOD WAS **SO** EASY.
5·10

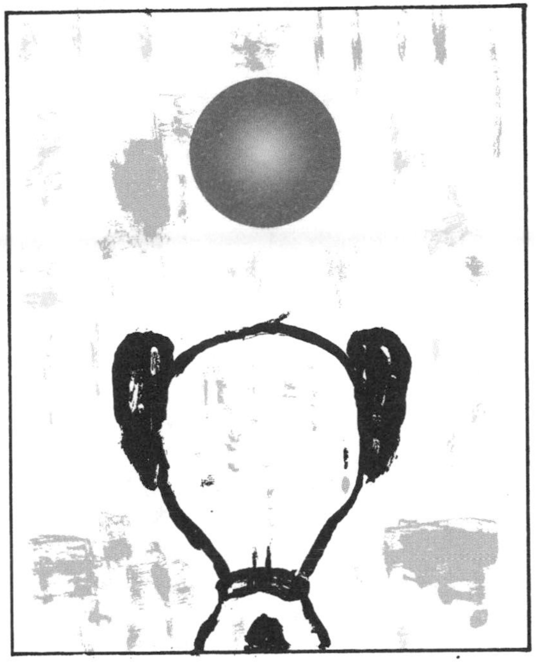

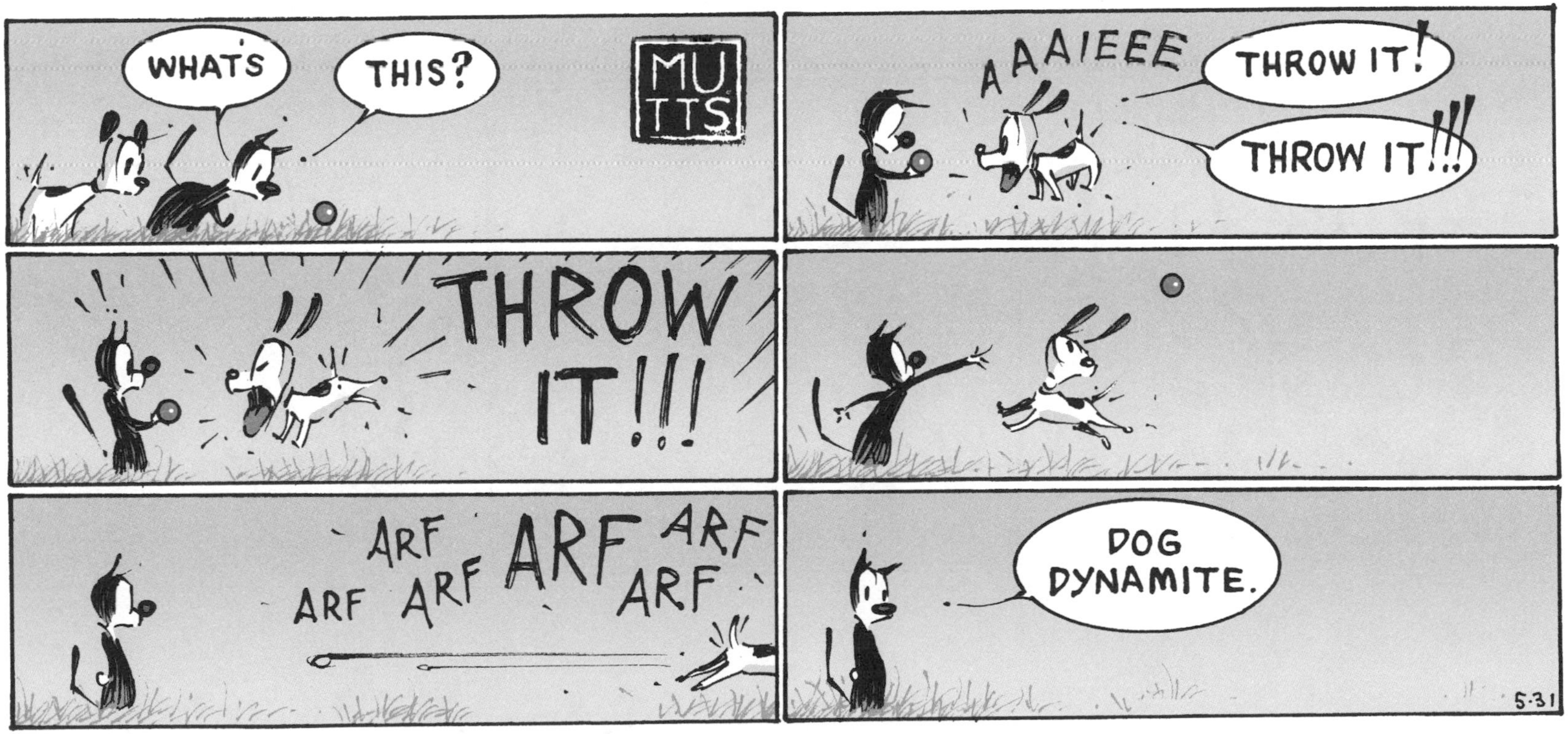
WHAT'S
THIS?
MUTTS
AAAIEEE
THROW IT!
THROW IT!!!
THROW IT!!!
ARF ARF ARF ARF ARF ARF ARF
DOG DYNAMITE.
5-31

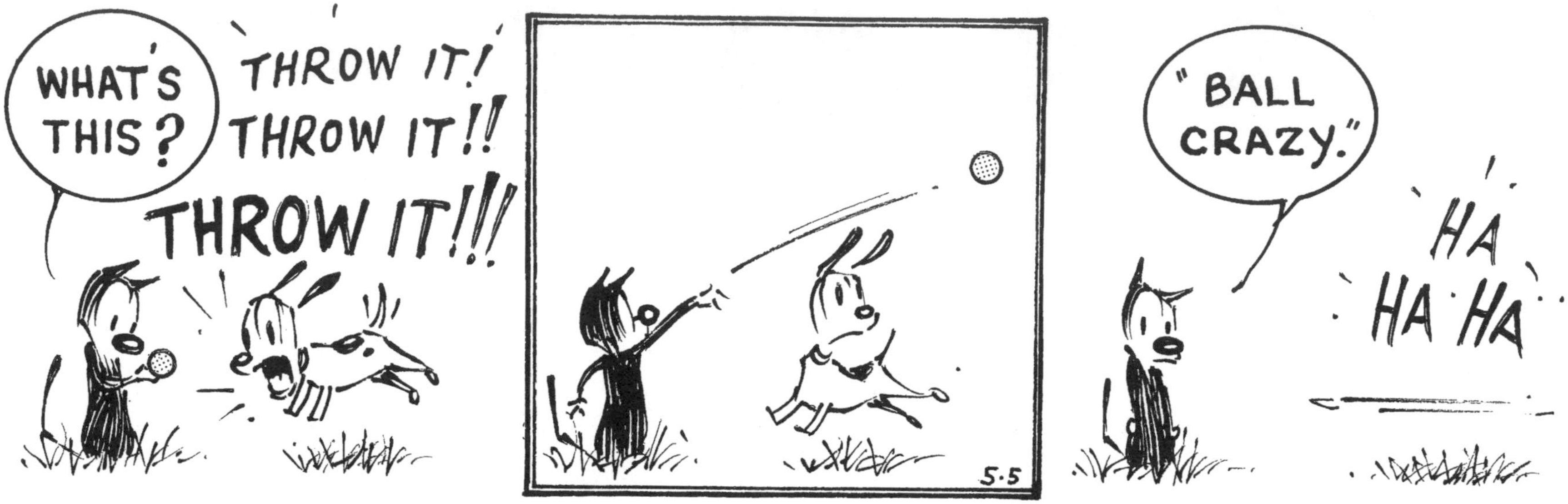
WHAT'S THIS?
THROW IT! THROW IT!! THROW IT!!!
"BALL CRAZY."
HA HA HA
5·5

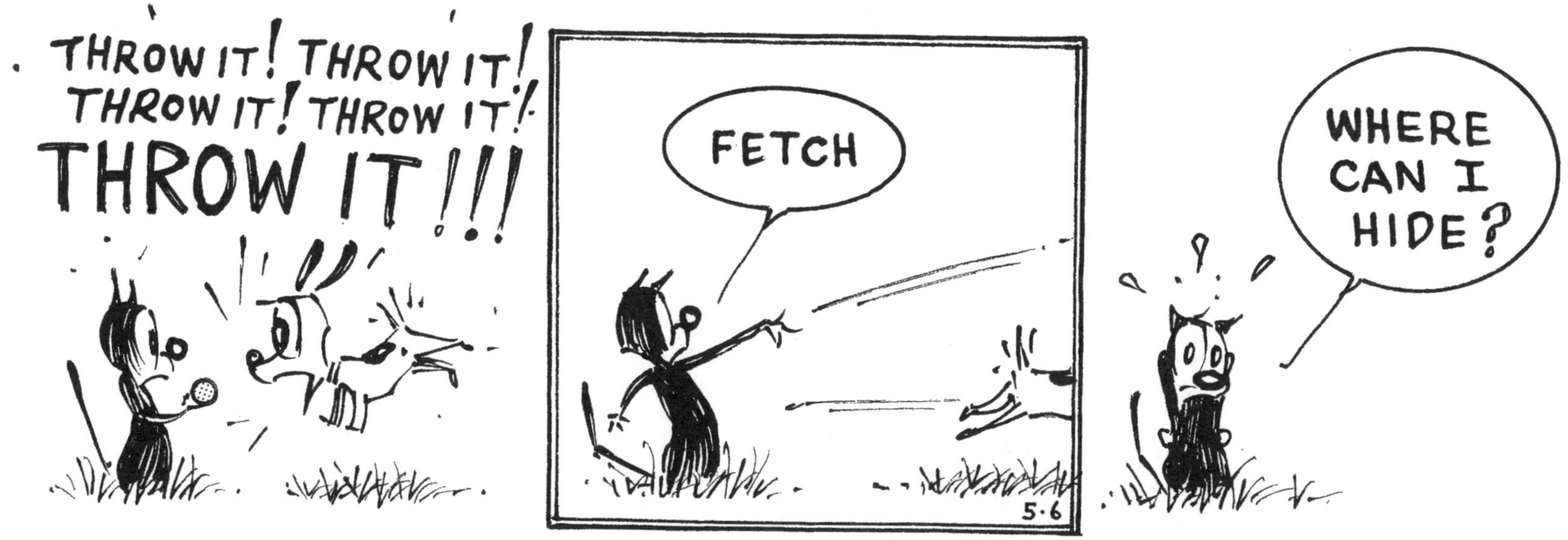
THROW IT! THROW IT! THROW IT! THROW IT! THROW IT!!!
FETCH
WHERE CAN I HIDE?
5·6

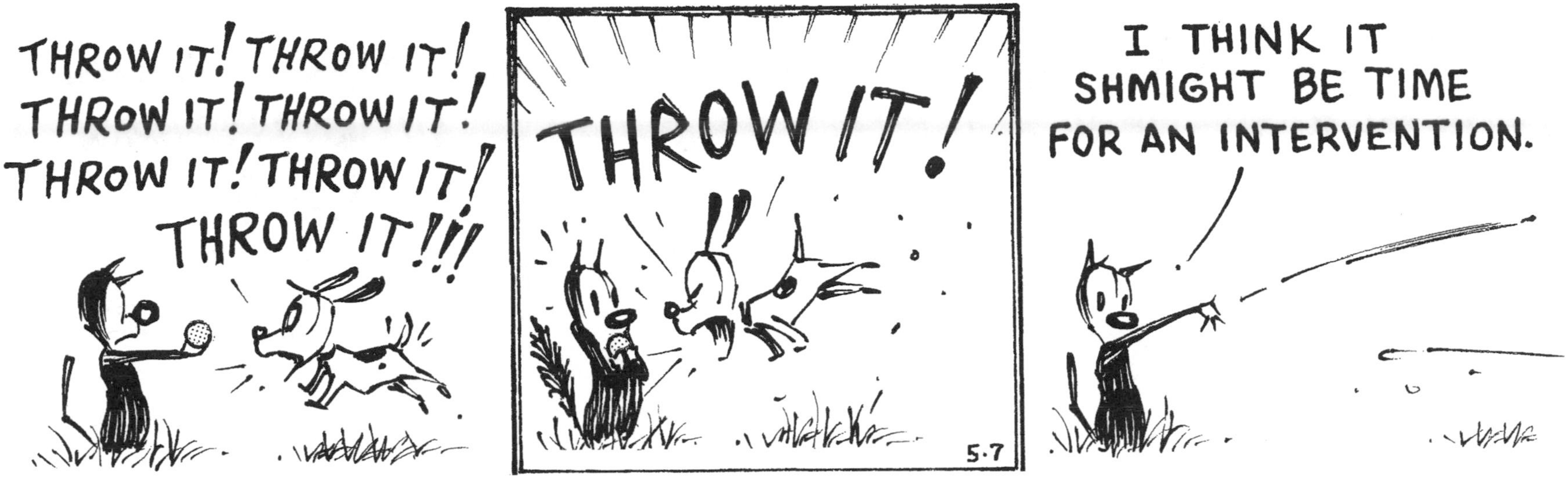
THROW IT! THROW IT! THROW IT! THROW IT! THROW IT! THROW IT! THROW IT!!!
THROW IT!
5·7
I THINK IT SHMIGHT BE TIME FOR AN INTERVENTION.

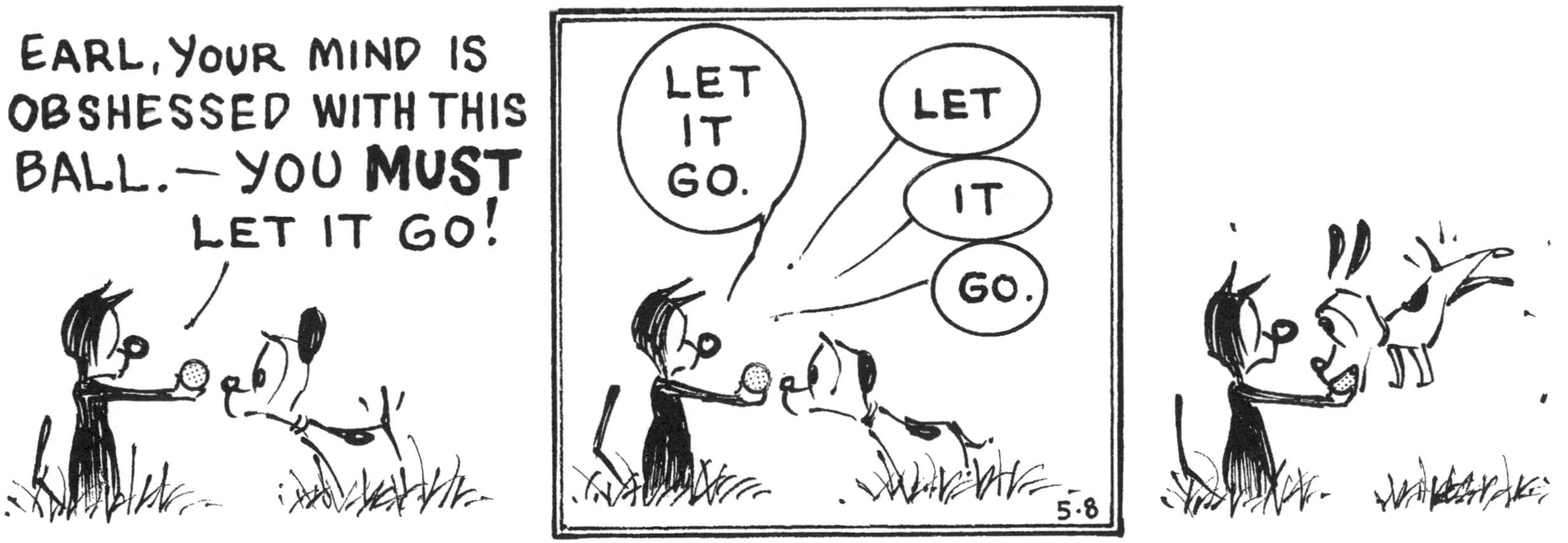
EARL, YOUR MIND IS OBSHESSED WITH THIS BALL.— YOU **MUST** LET IT GO!
LET IT GO.
LET
IT
GO.
5·8

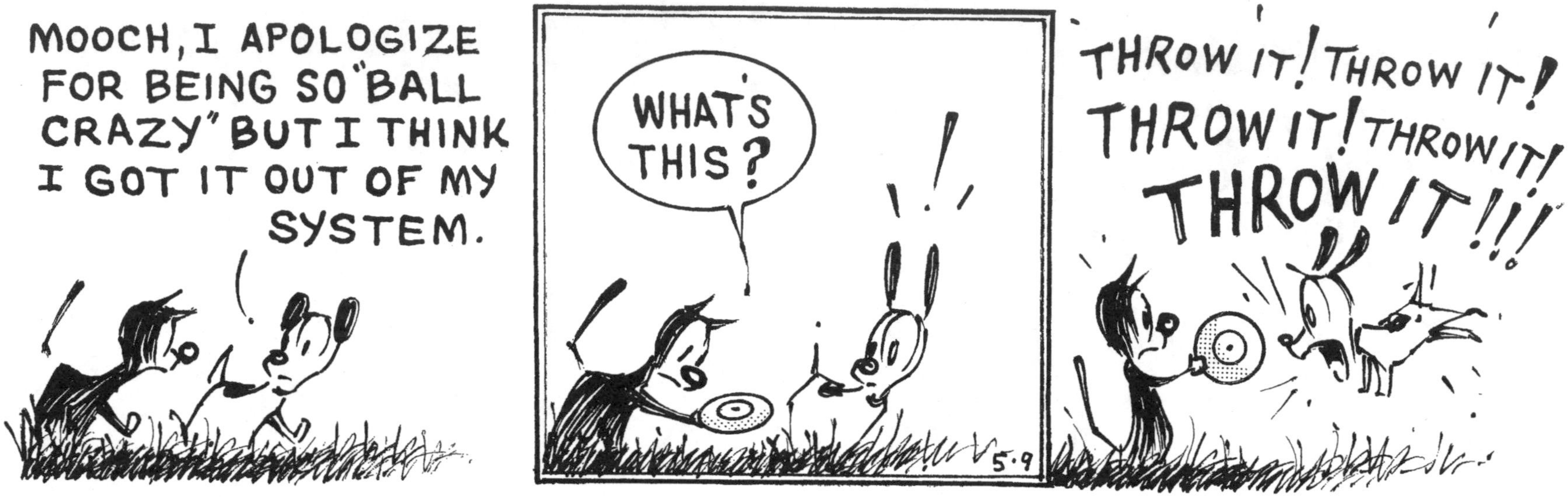
MOOCH, I APOLOGIZE FOR BEING SO "BALL CRAZY" BUT I THINK I GOT IT OUT OF MY SYSTEM.
WHAT'S THIS?
THROW IT! THROW IT! THROW IT! THROW IT! THROW IT!!!
5·9

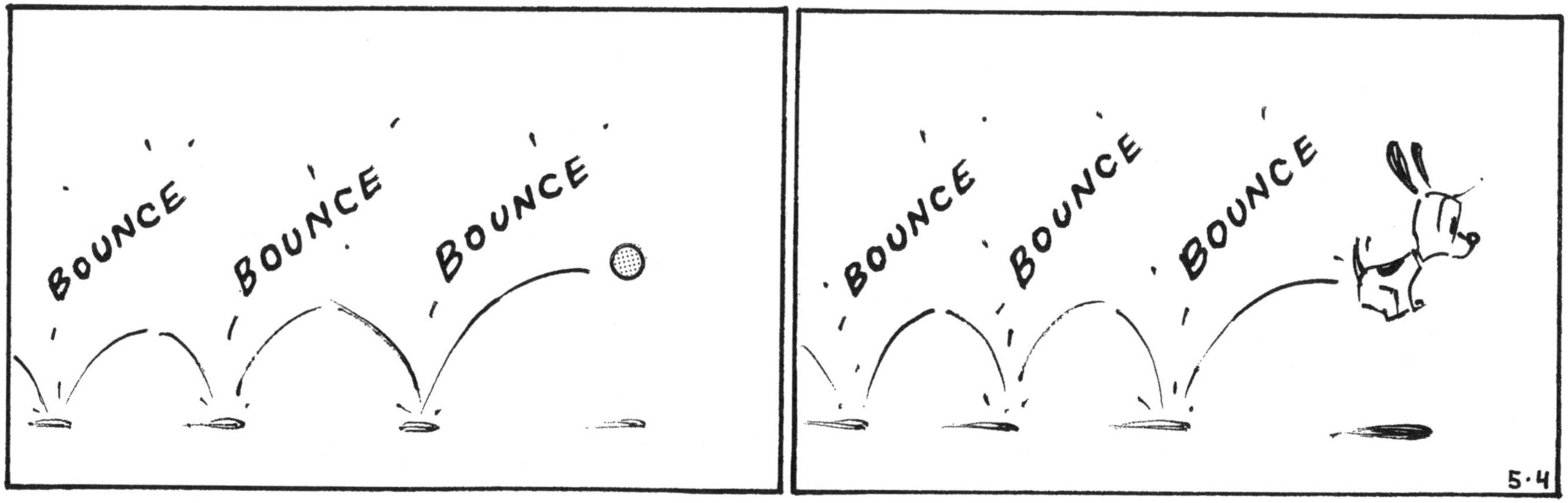
BOUNCE BOUNCE BOUNCE
BOUNCE BOUNCE BOUNCE
5·4

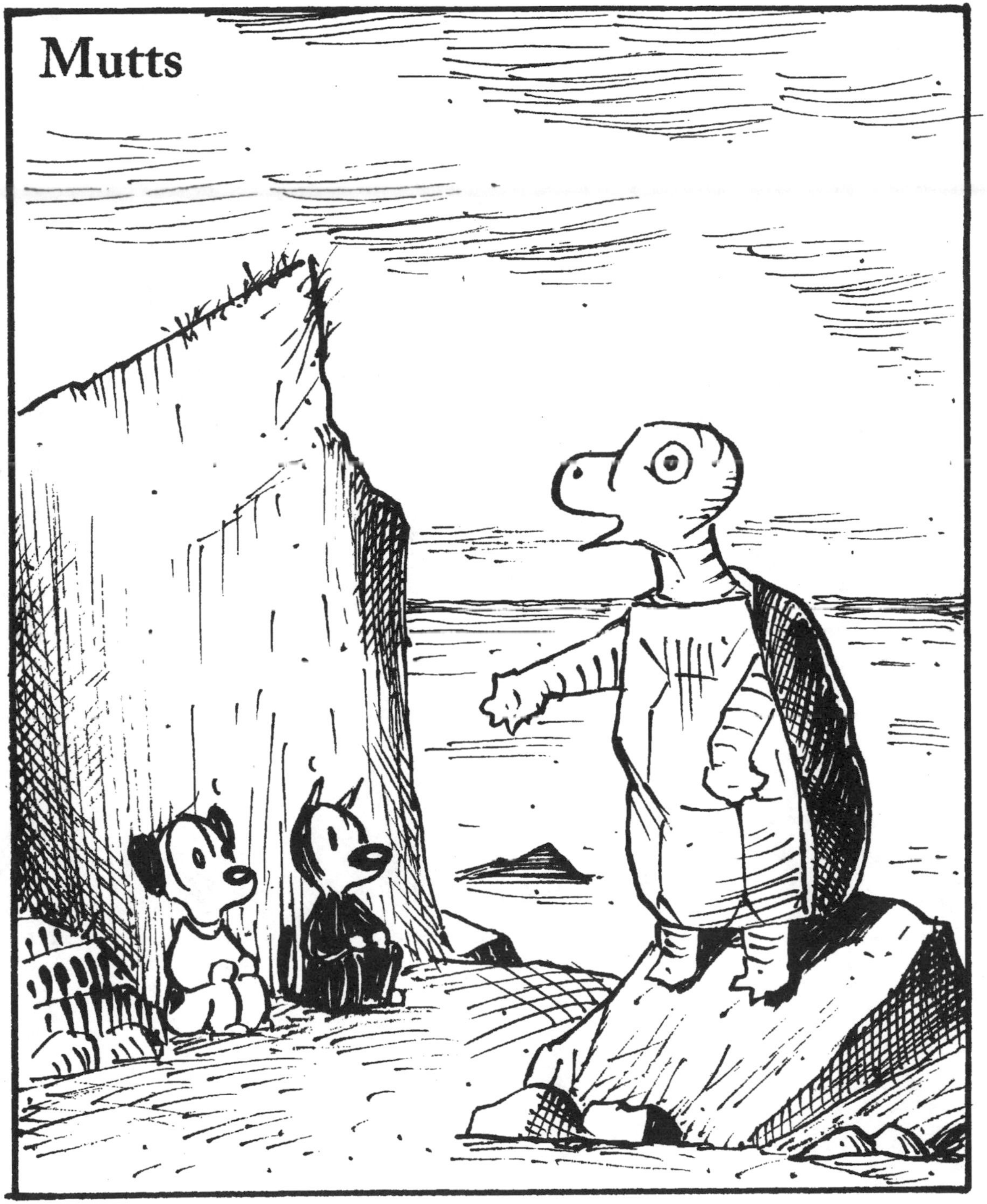
Mutts

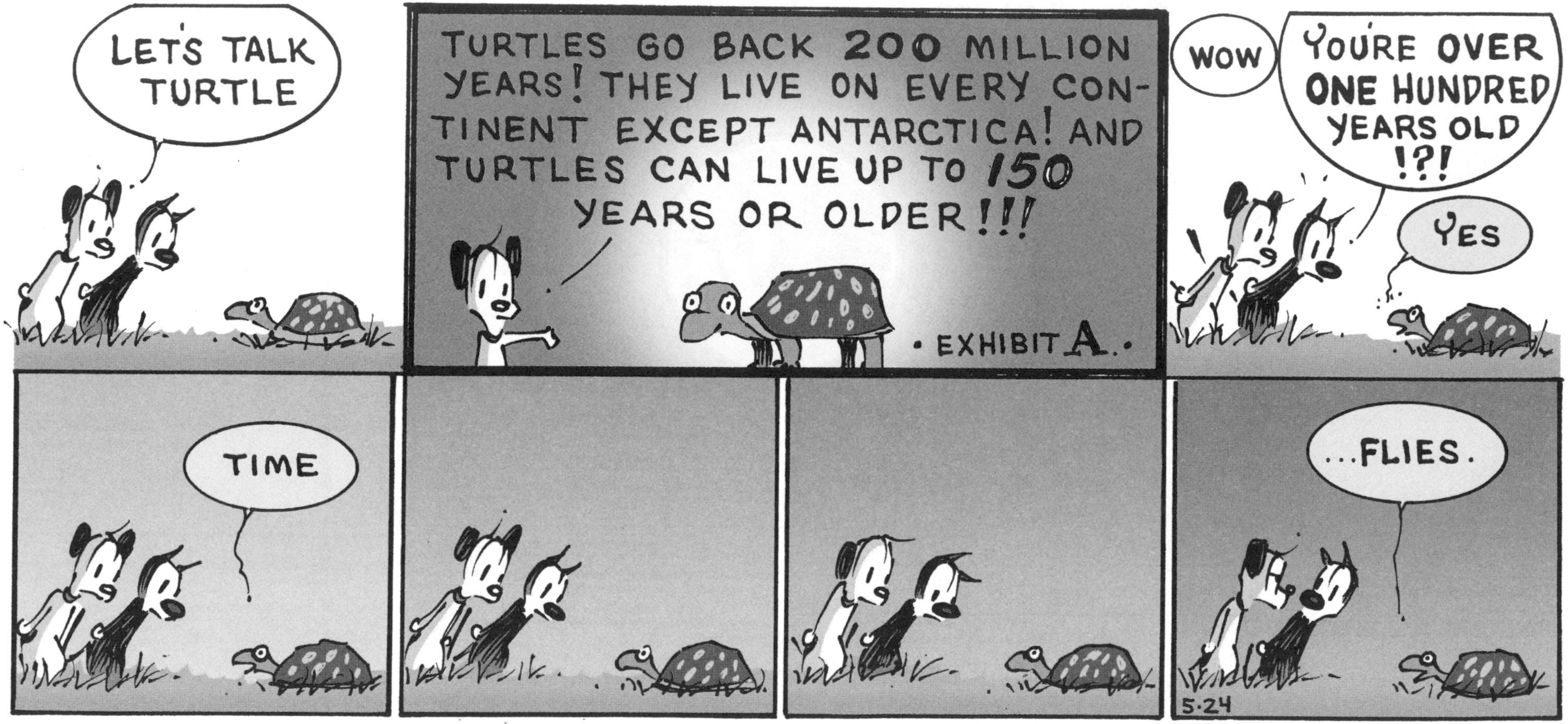
LET'S TALK TURTLE
TURTLES GO BACK 200 MILLION YEARS! THEY LIVE ON EVERY CONTINENT EXCEPT ANTARCTICA! AND TURTLES CAN LIVE UP TO 150 YEARS OR OLDER!!!
• EXHIBIT A. •
WOW
YOU'RE OVER ONE HUNDRED YEARS OLD !?!
YES
TIME
...FLIES.
5·24

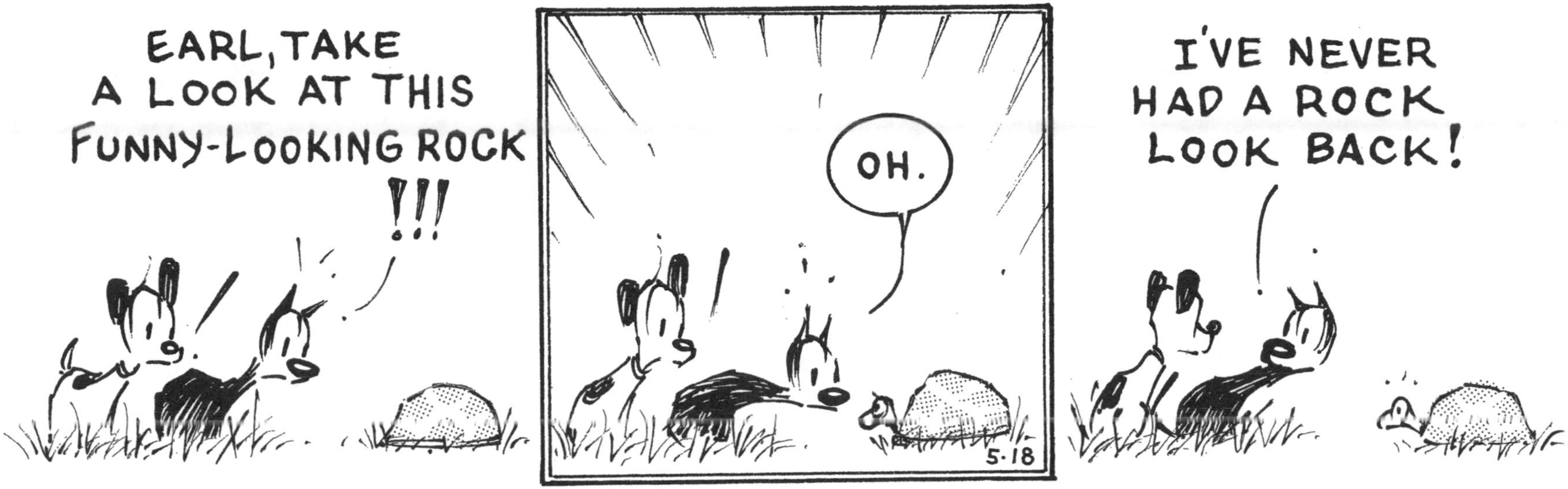
EARL, TAKE A LOOK AT THIS FUNNY-LOOKING ROCK !!!
OH.
I'VE NEVER HAD A ROCK LOOK BACK!
5·18

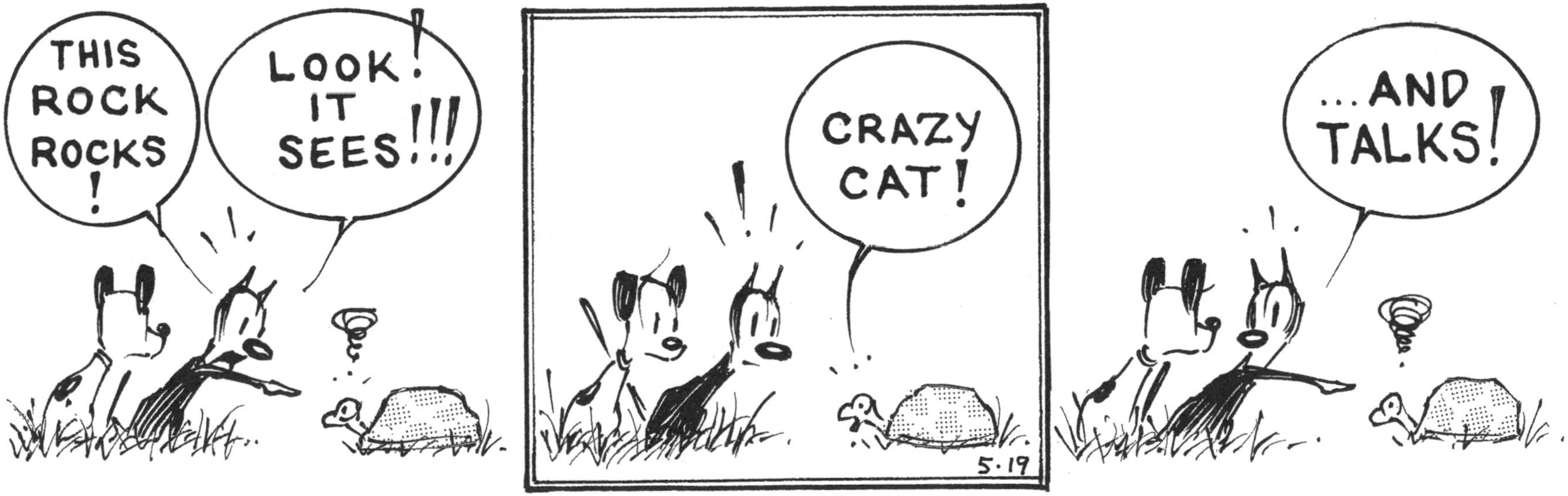
THIS ROCK ROCKS !
LOOK! IT SEES!!!
CRAZY CAT!
...AND TALKS!
5·19

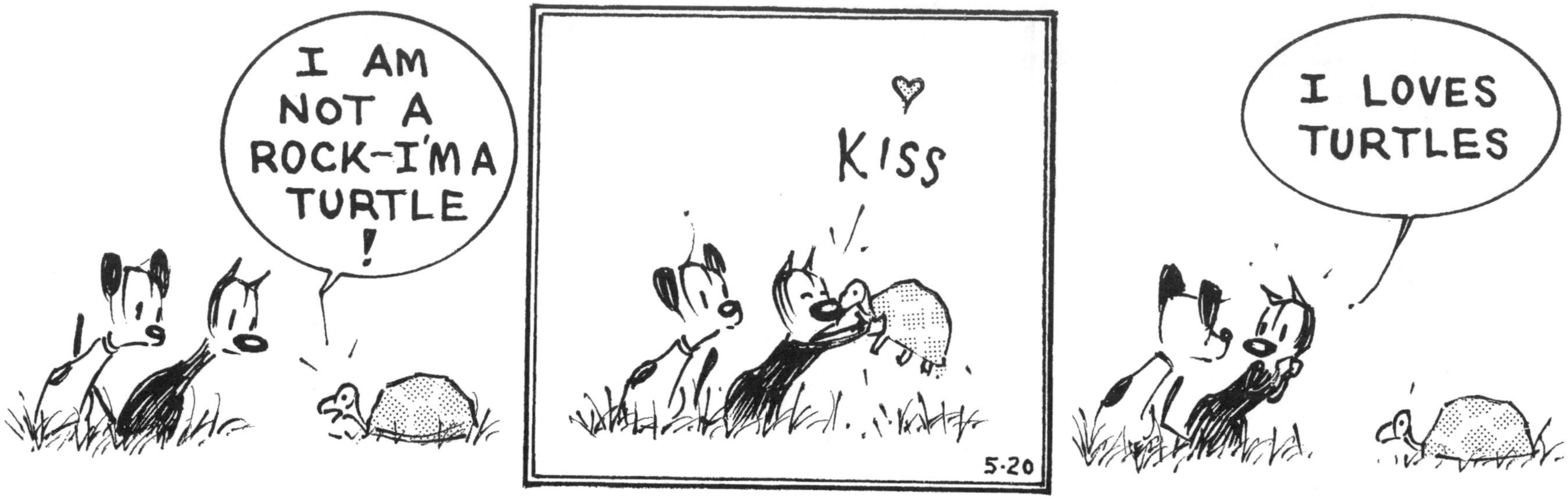
I AM NOT A ROCK–I'M A TURTLE!
KISS
5·20
I LOVES TURTLES

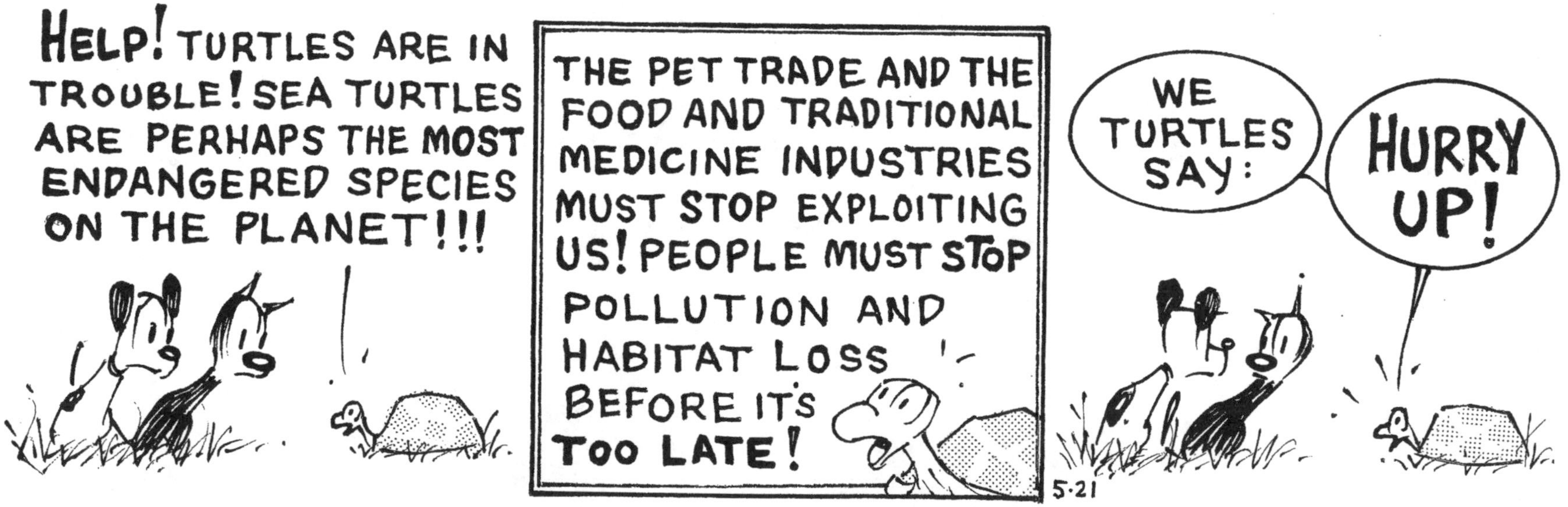
HELP! TURTLES ARE IN TROUBLE! SEA TURTLES ARE PERHAPS THE MOST ENDANGERED SPECIES ON THE PLANET!!!
THE PET TRADE AND THE FOOD AND TRADITIONAL MEDICINE INDUSTRIES MUST STOP EXPLOITING US! PEOPLE MUST STOP POLLUTION AND HABITAT LOSS BEFORE IT'S TOO LATE!
5·21
WE TURTLES SAY:
HURRY UP!

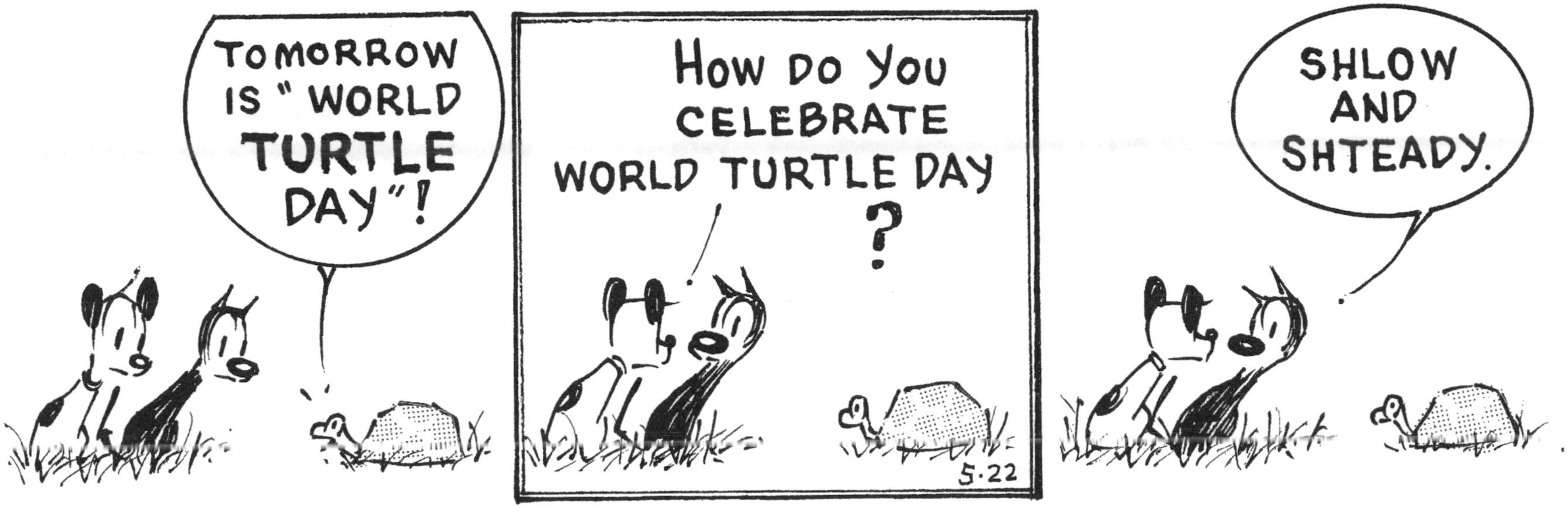
TOMORROW IS "WORLD TURTLE DAY"!
HOW DO YOU CELEBRATE WORLD TURTLE DAY ?
SHLOW AND SHTEADY.

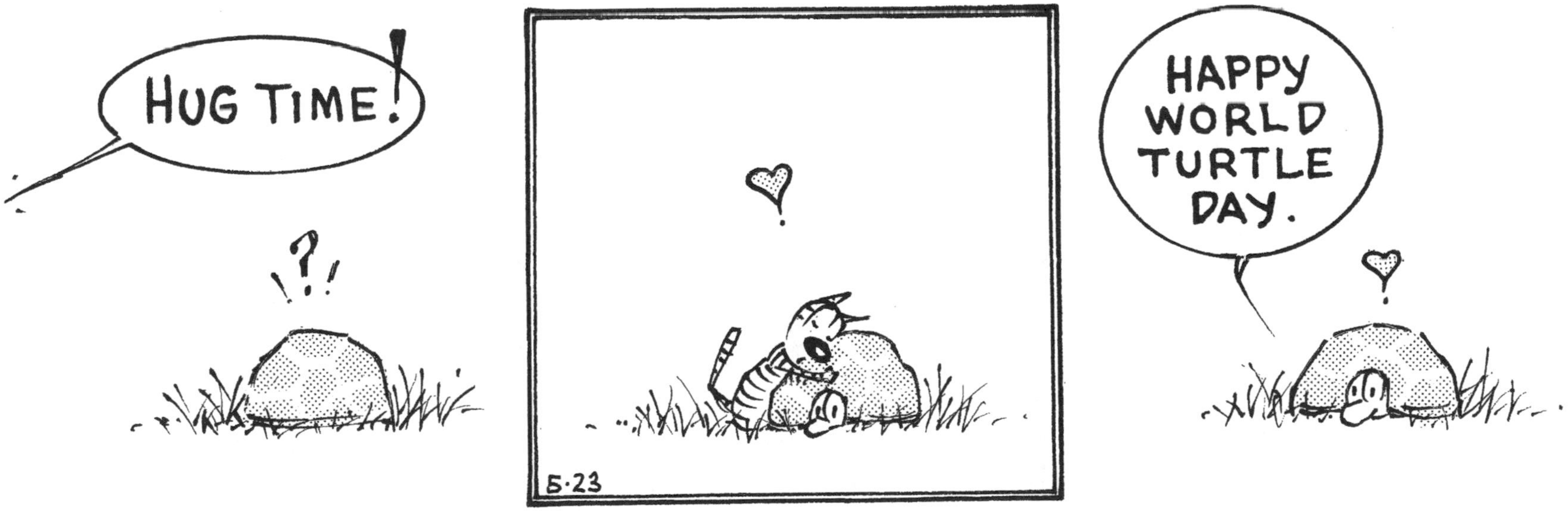
HUG TIME!
HAPPY WORLD TURTLE DAY.

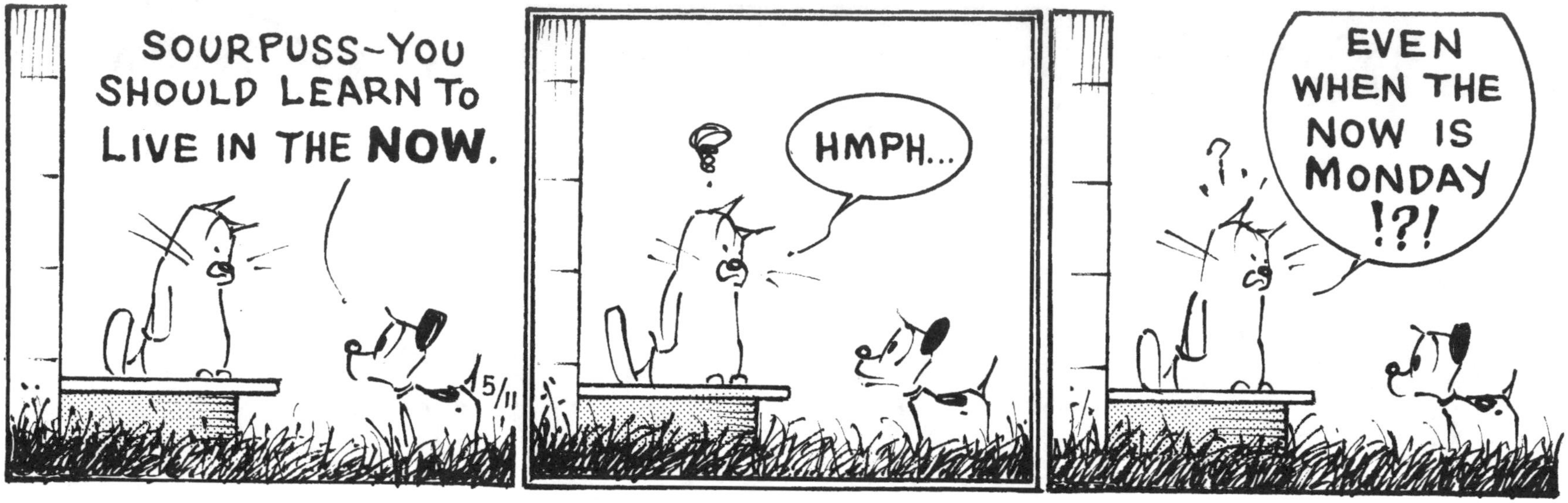
SOURPUSS~YOU SHOULD LEARN TO LIVE IN THE **NOW**.
5/11
HMPH...
EVEN WHEN THE NOW IS MONDAY !?!

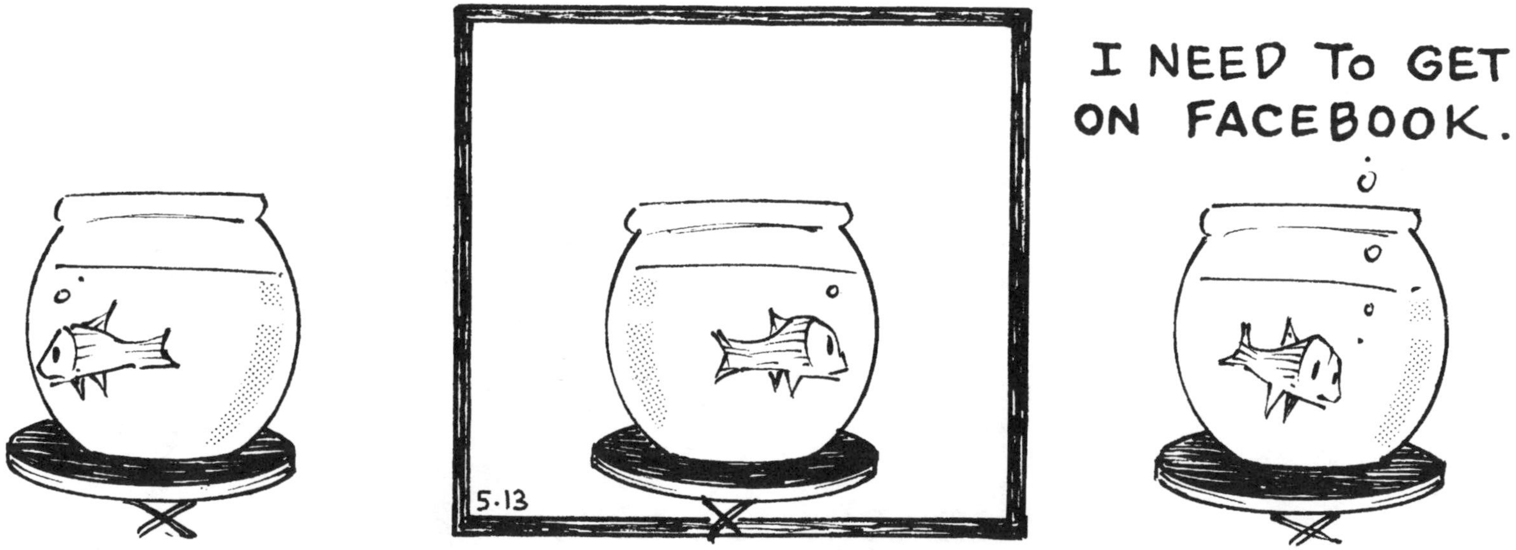
5.13
I NEED TO GET ON FACEBOOK.

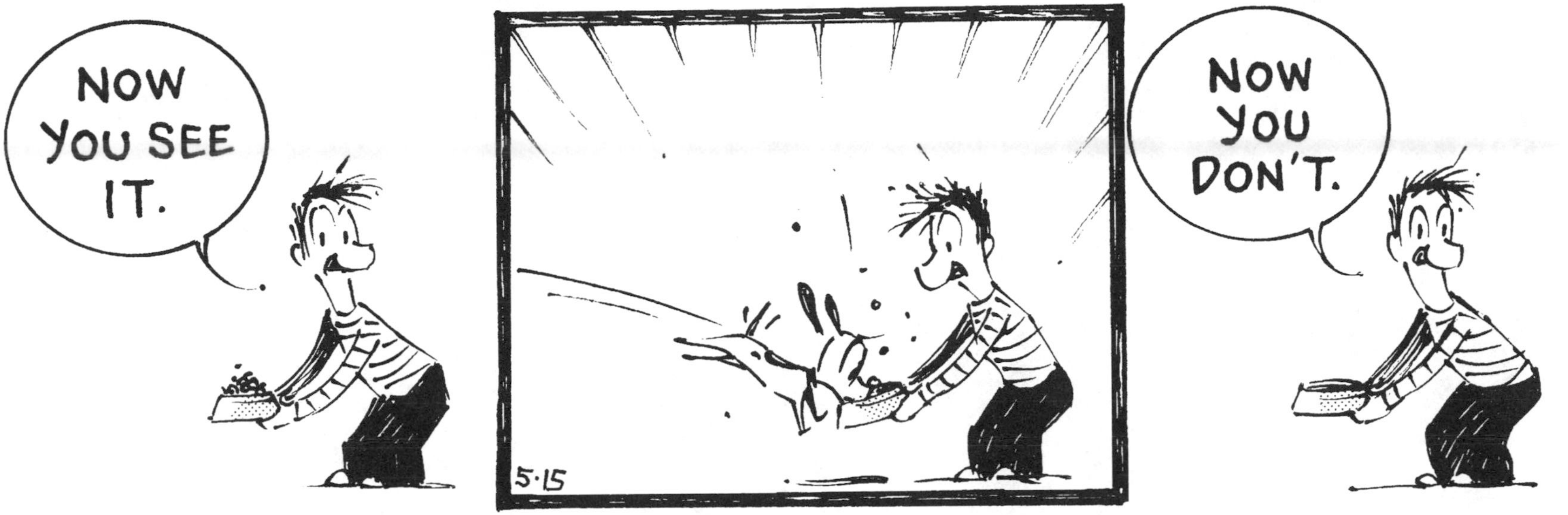
NOW YOU SEE IT.
5·15
NOW YOU DON'T.

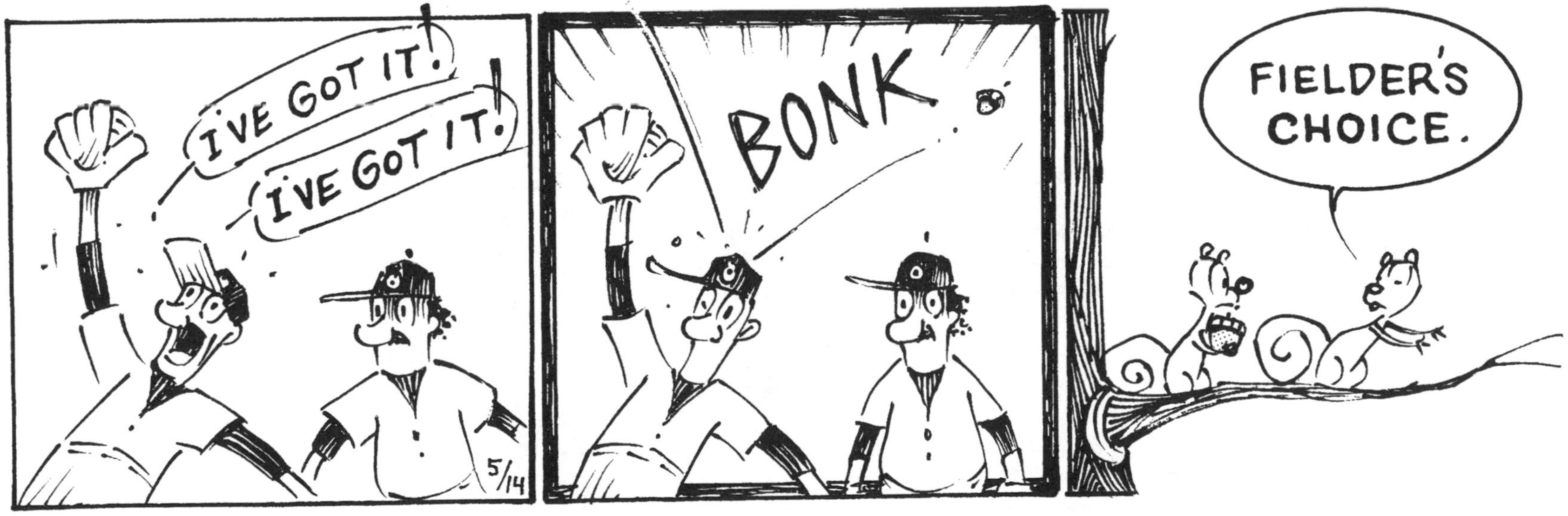
I'VE GOT IT!
I'VE GOT IT!
5/14
BONK
FIELDER'S CHOICE.

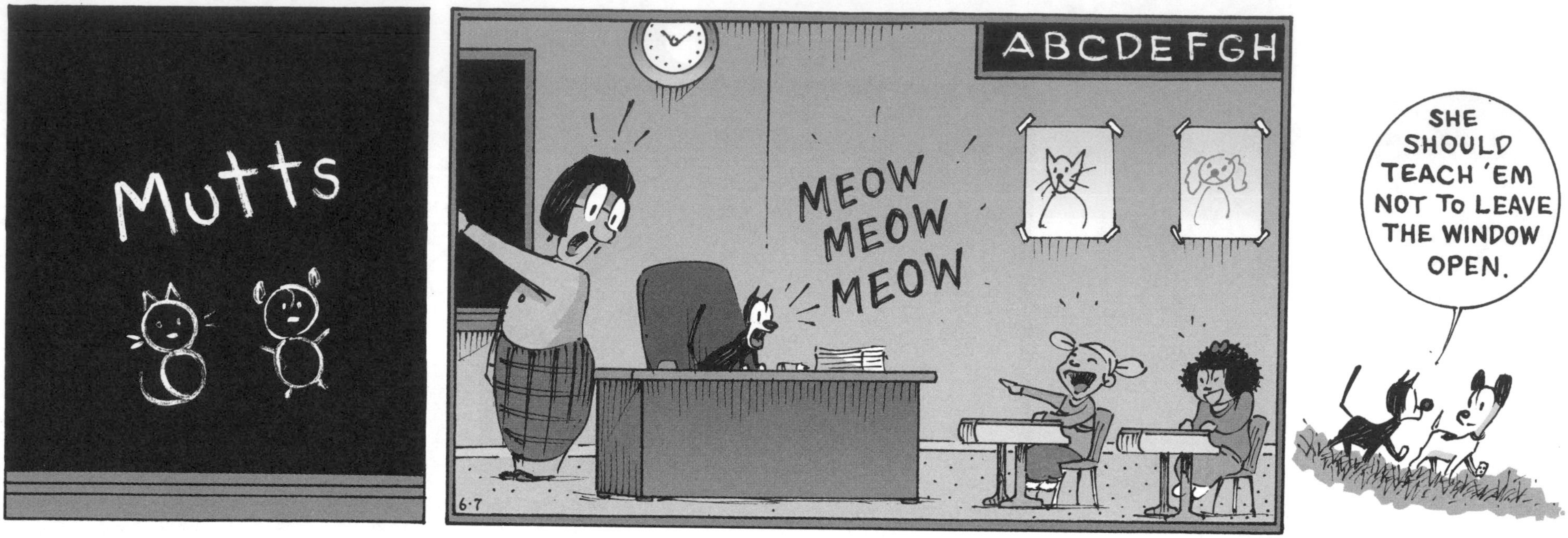
Mutts
ABCDEFGH
MEOW
MEOW
MEOW
SHE SHOULD TEACH 'EM NOT TO LEAVE THE WINDOW OPEN.
6·7

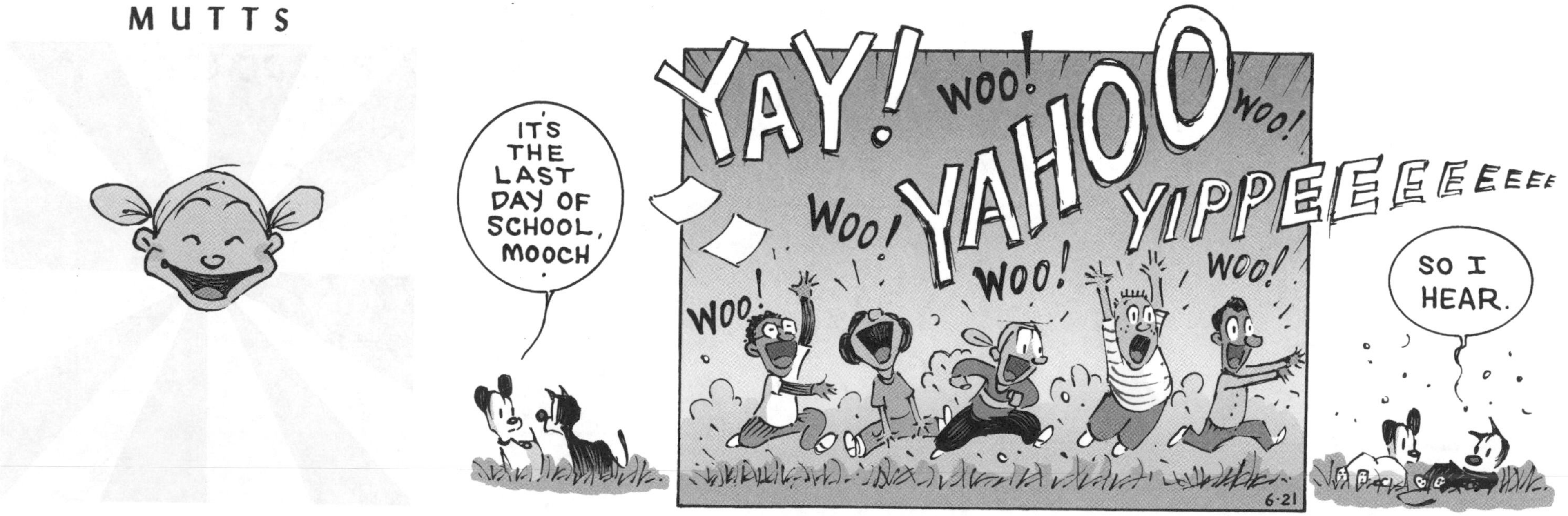
MUTTS
IT'S THE LAST DAY OF SCHOOL, MOOCH.
YAY!
WOO!
YAHOO
WOO!
WOO!
YIPPEEEEEEEE
WOO!
WOO!
WOO!
SO I HEAR.
6·21

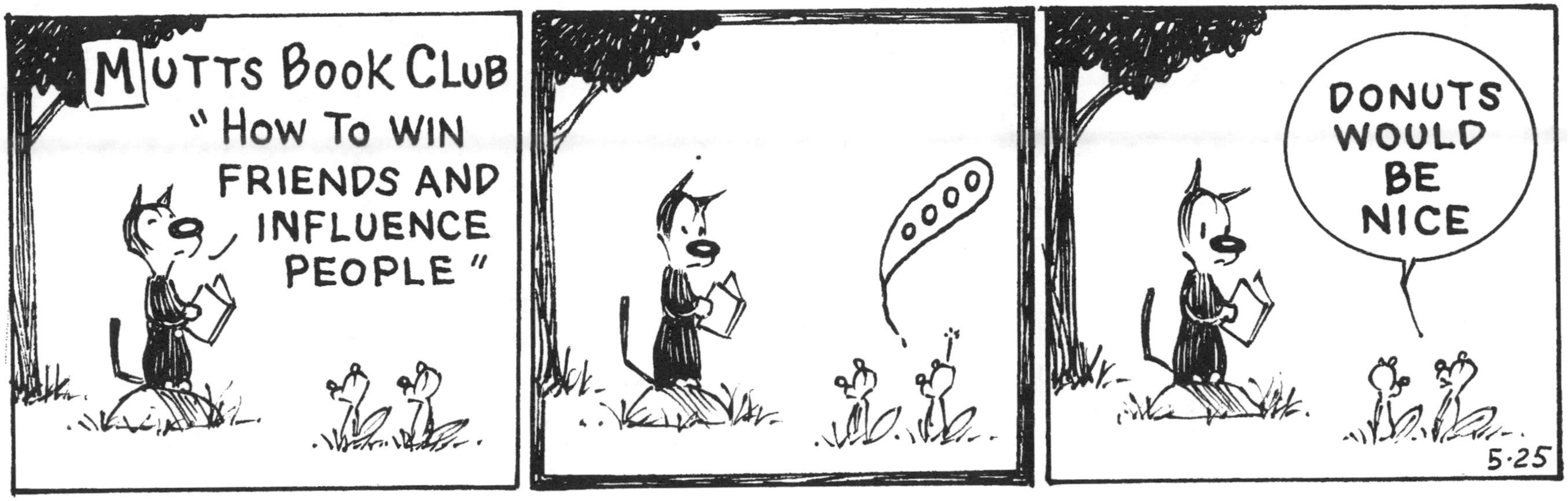
MUTTS BOOK CLUB
"HOW TO WIN FRIENDS AND INFLUENCE PEOPLE"
OOOO
DONUTS WOULD BE NICE
5·25

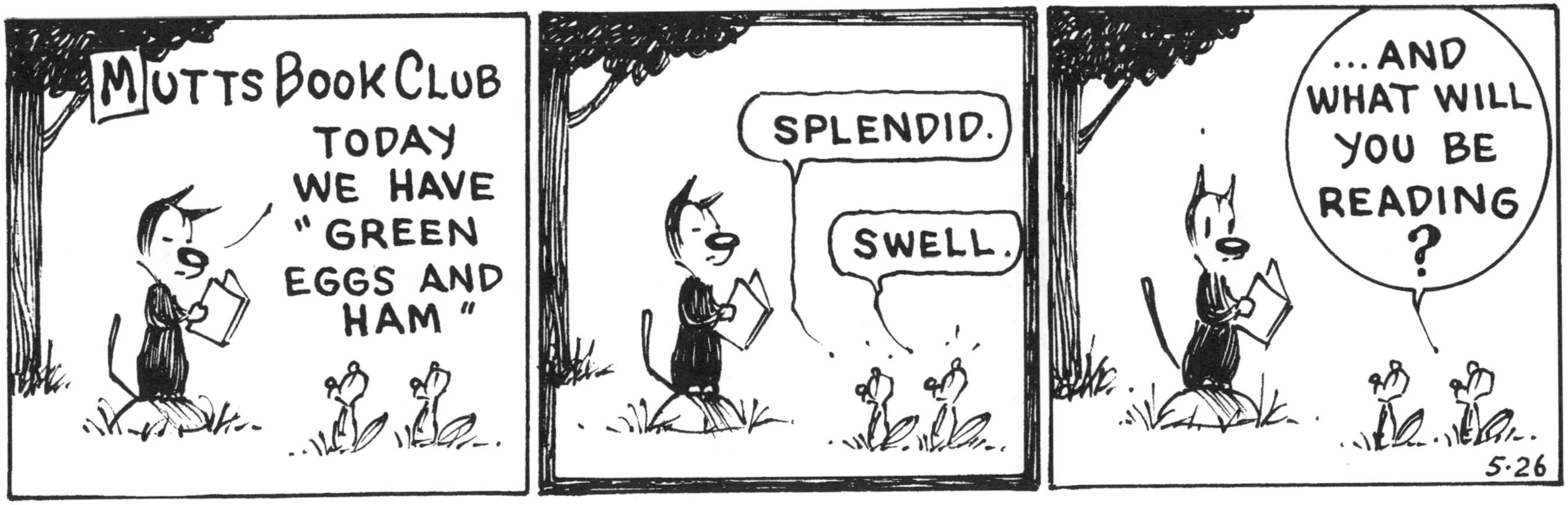
MUTTS BOOK CLUB
TODAY WE HAVE "GREEN EGGS AND HAM"
SPLENDID.
SWELL.
...AND WHAT WILL YOU BE READING?
5·26

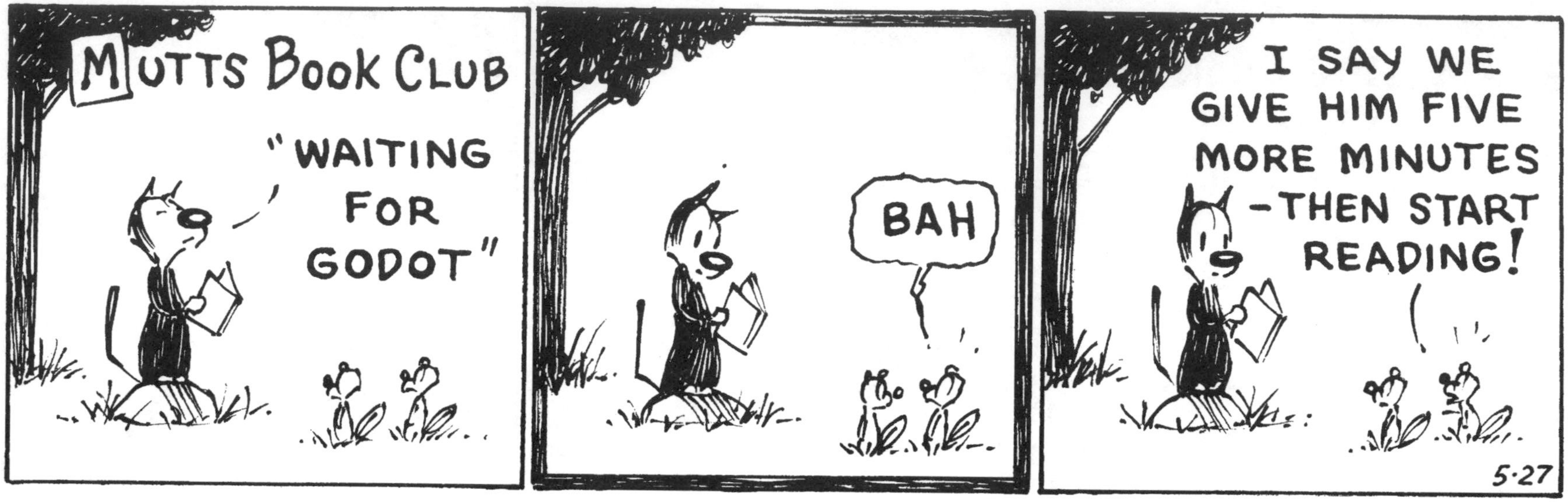
MUTTS BOOK CLUB
"WAITING FOR GODOT"
BAH
I SAY WE GIVE HIM FIVE MORE MINUTES -THEN START READING!
5·27

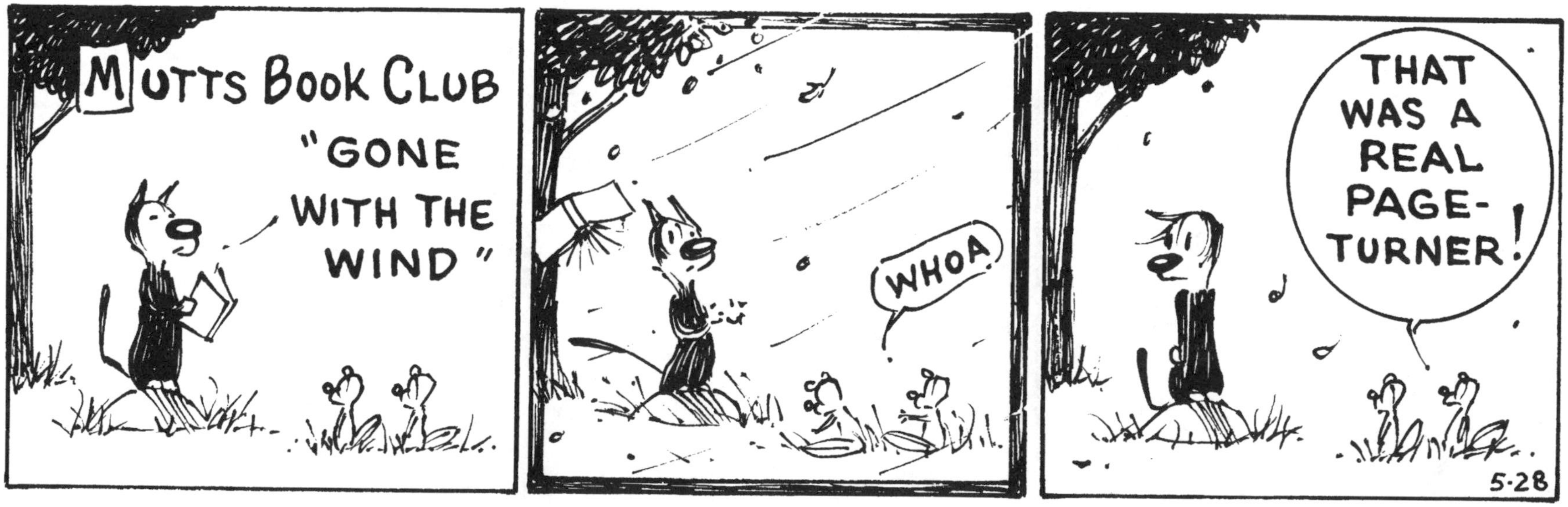
MUTTS BOOK CLUB
"GONE WITH THE WIND"
WHOA
THAT WAS A REAL PAGE-TURNER!
5·28

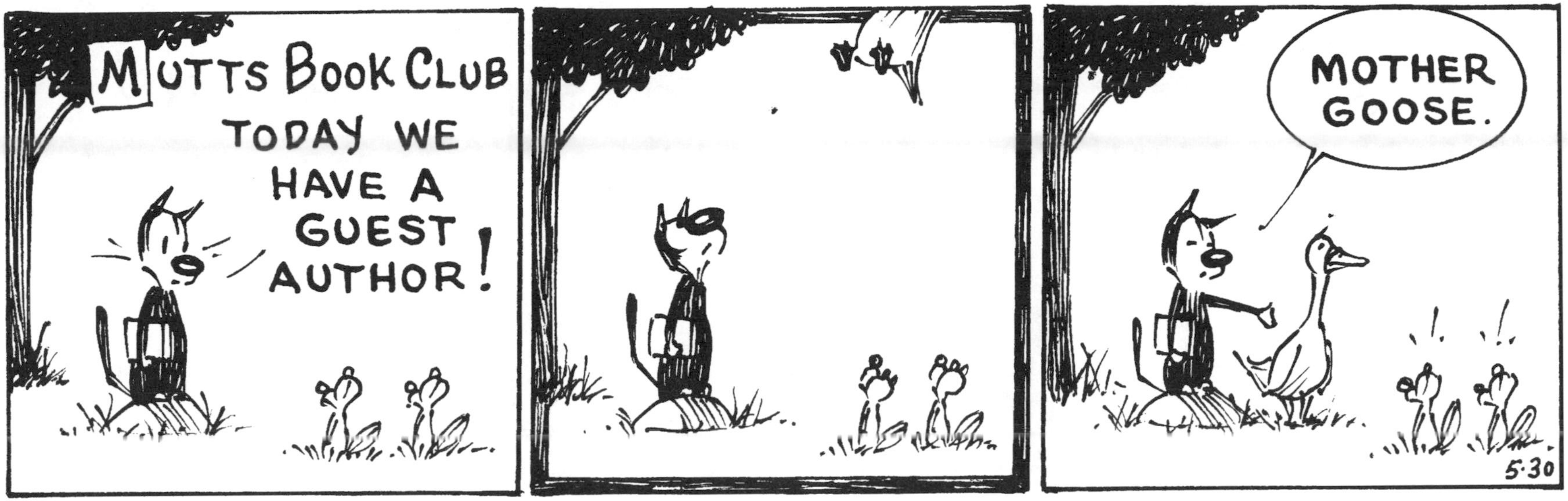
MUTTS BOOK CLUB
TODAY WE HAVE A GUEST AUTHOR!
MOTHER GOOSE.
5·30

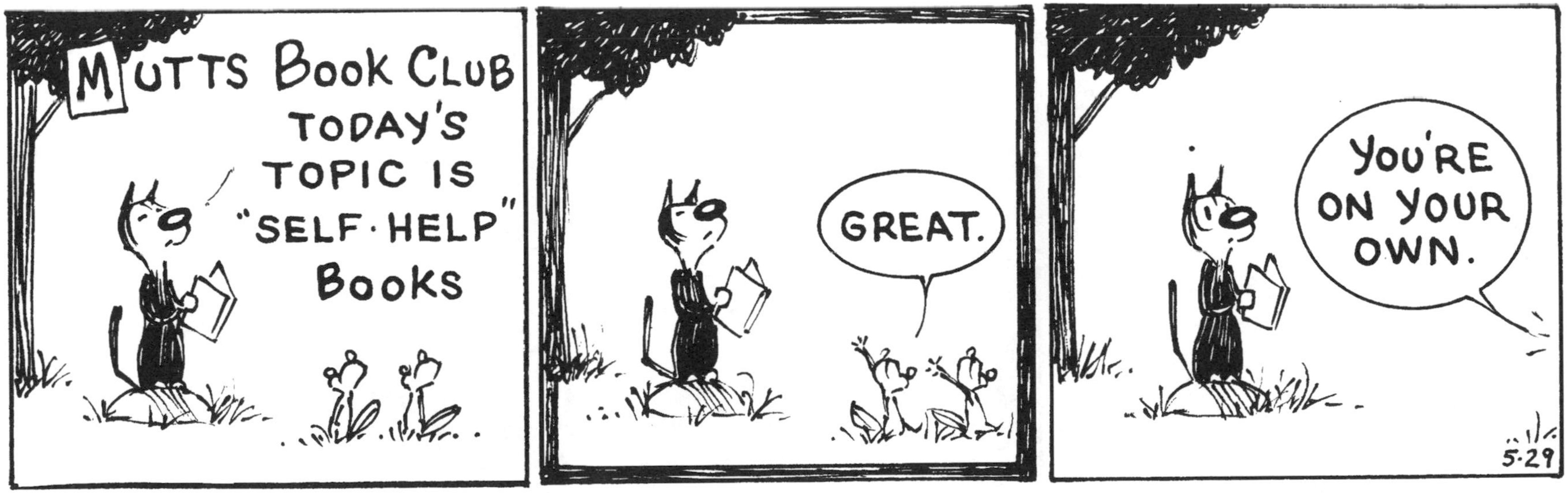
MUTTS BOOK CLUB
TODAY'S TOPIC IS "SELF·HELP" BOOKS
GREAT.
YOU'RE ON YOUR OWN.
5·29

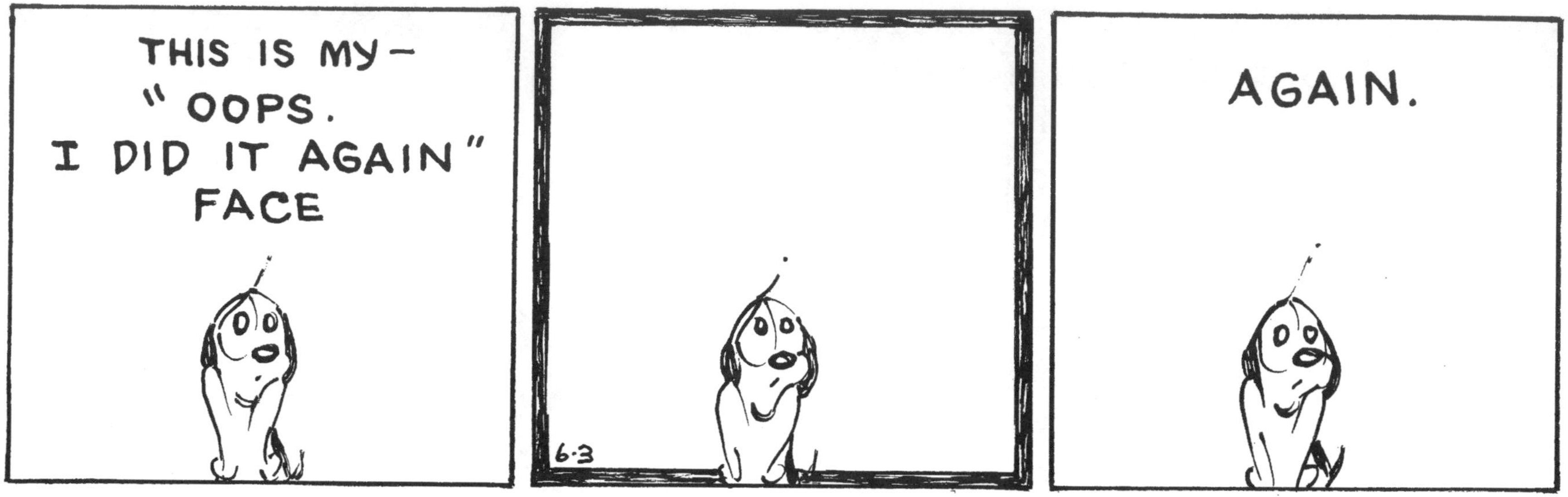
THIS IS MY—
"OOPS.
I DID IT AGAIN"
FACE
6·3
AGAIN.

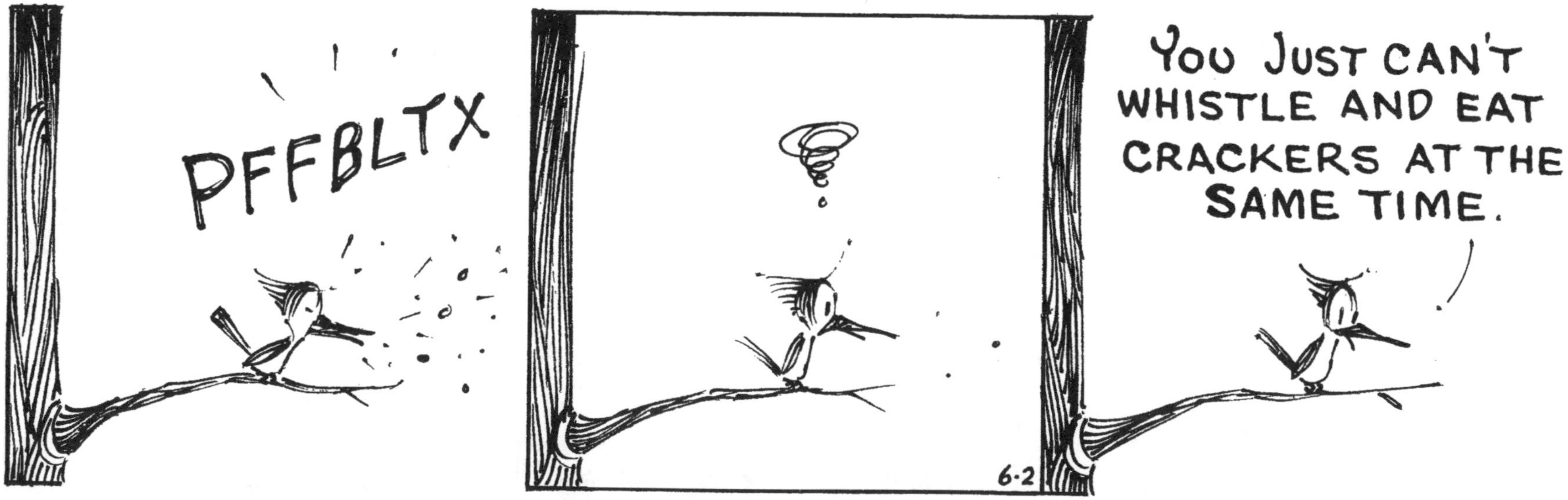
PFFBLTX
6·2
YOU JUST CAN'T WHISTLE AND EAT CRACKERS AT THE SAME TIME.

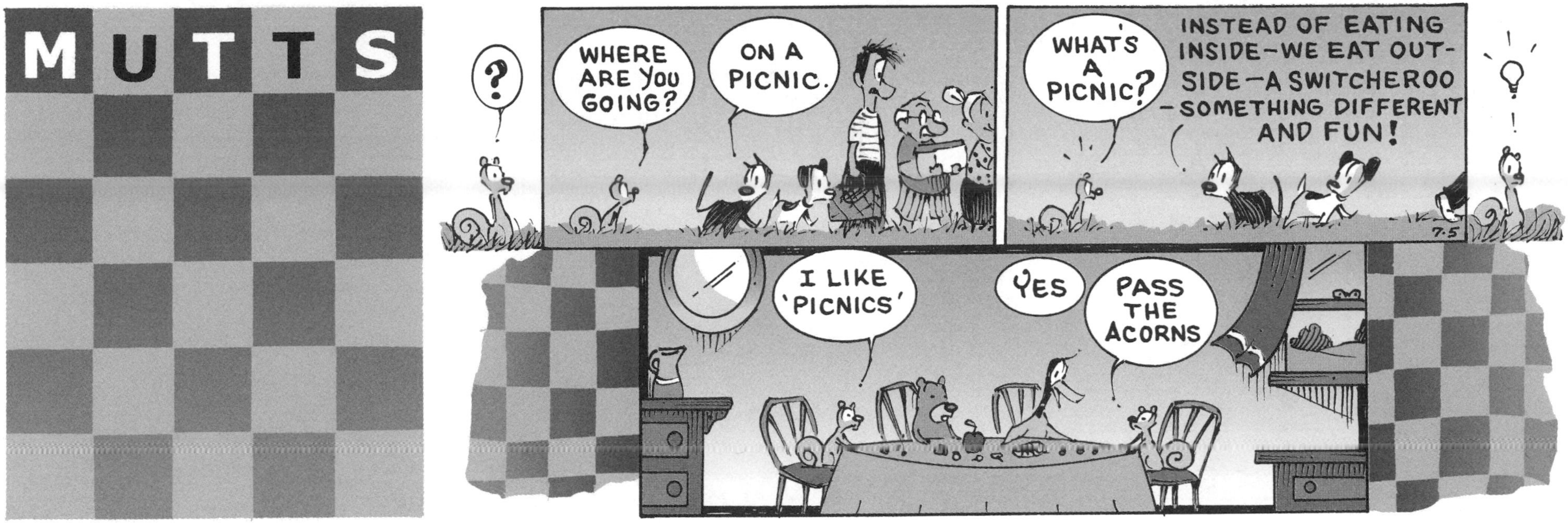
MUTTS
?
WHERE ARE YOU GOING?
ON A PICNIC.
WHAT'S A PICNIC?
INSTEAD OF EATING INSIDE—WE EAT OUT-SIDE—A SWITCHEROO—SOMETHING DIFFERENT AND FUN!
!
7·5
I LIKE 'PICNICS'
YES
PASS THE ACORNS

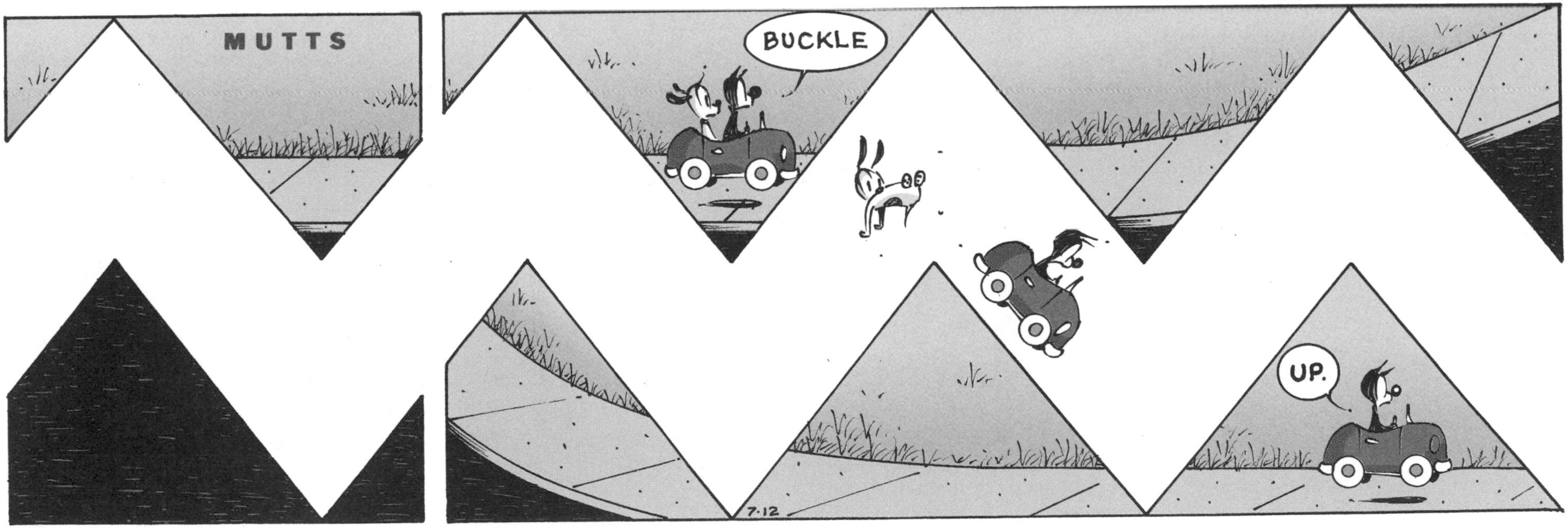
MUTTS
BUCKLE
UP.
7·12

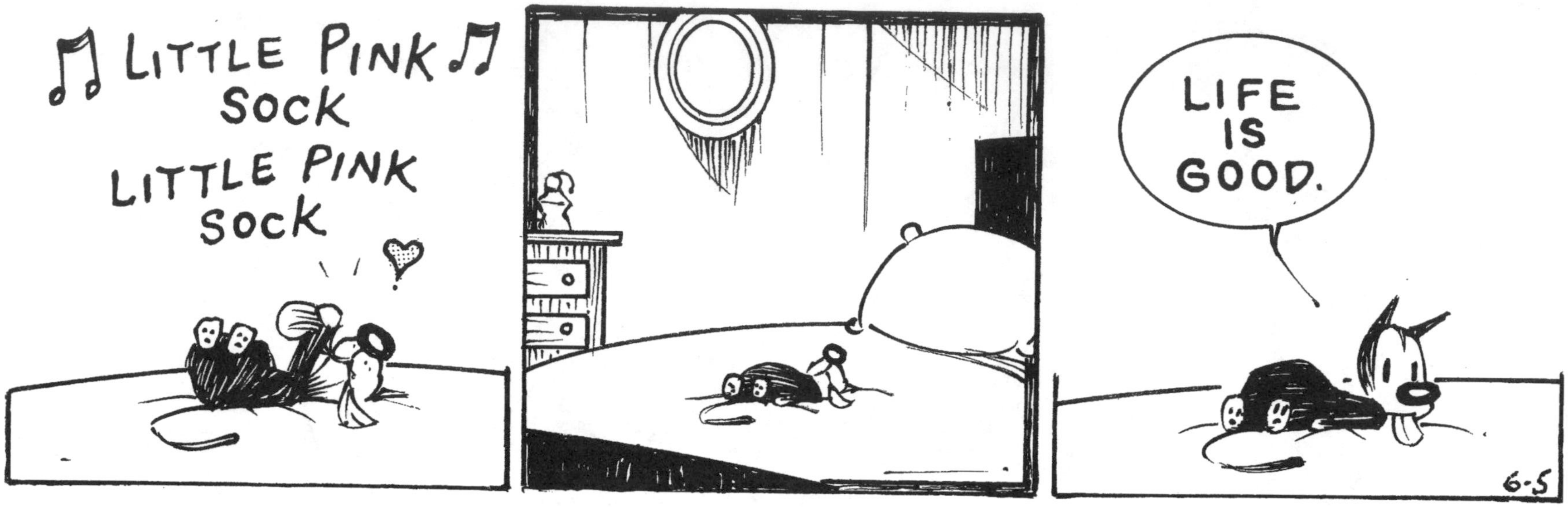
♫ LITTLE PINK ♫
SOCK
LITTLE PINK
SOCK
LIFE IS GOOD.
6-5

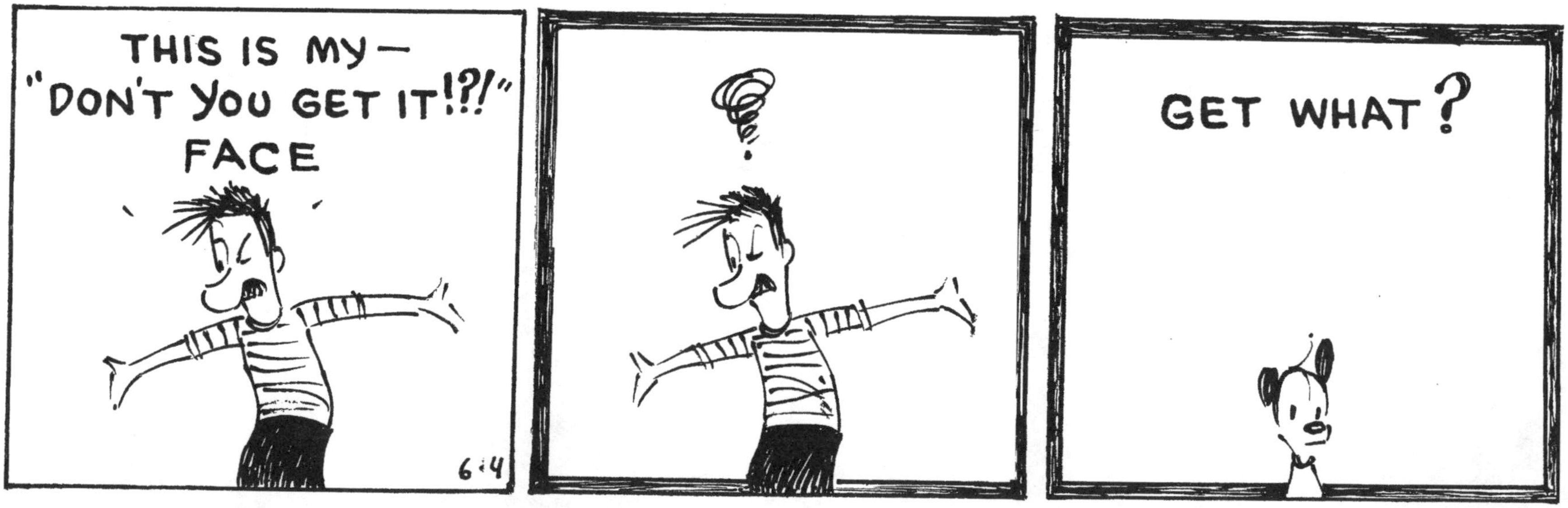
THIS IS MY—
"DON'T YOU GET IT!?!"
FACE
6-4
GET WHAT?

Mutts

[redacted]

[redacted]

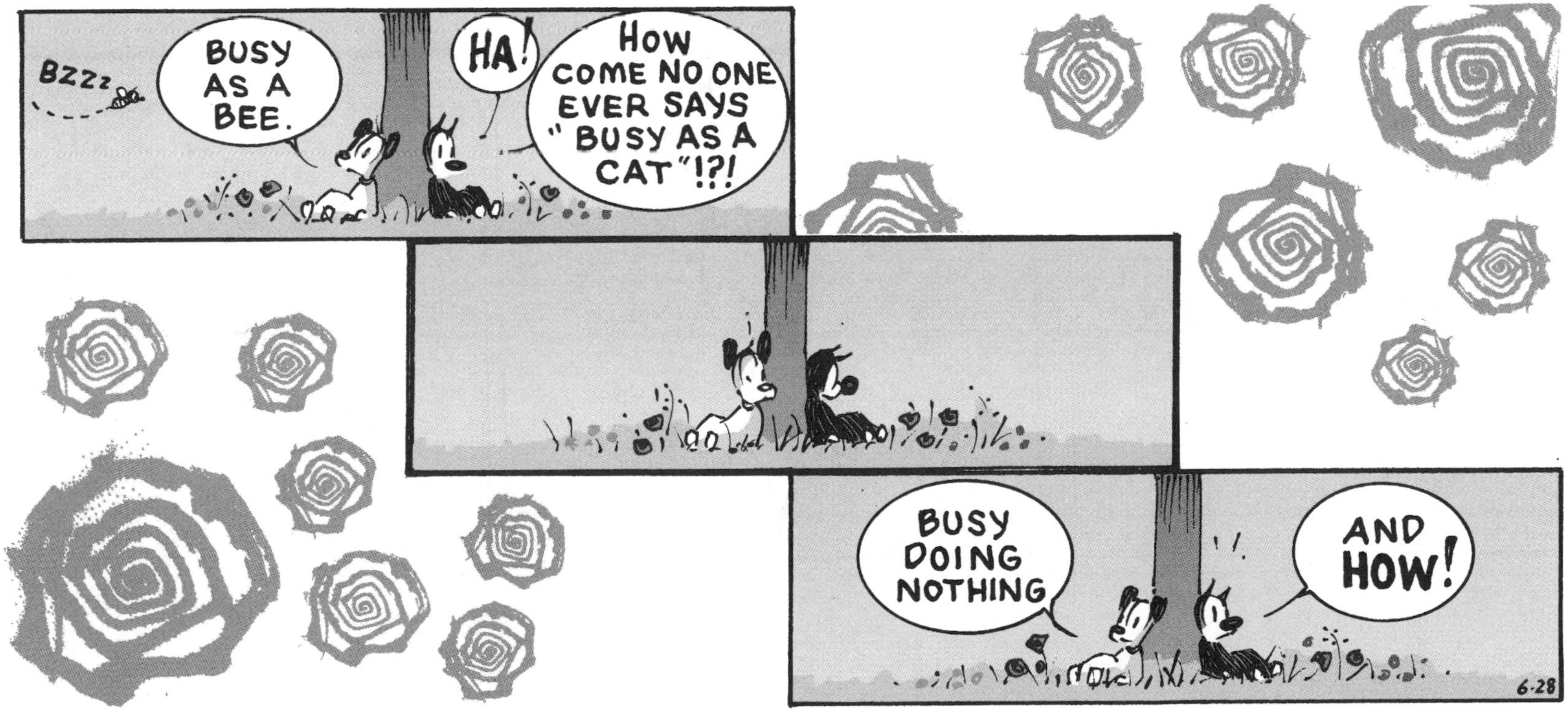
BZZZ
BUSY AS A BEE.
HA!
HOW COME NO ONE EVER SAYS "BUSY AS A CAT"!?!
BUSY DOING NOTHING
AND HOW!
6-28

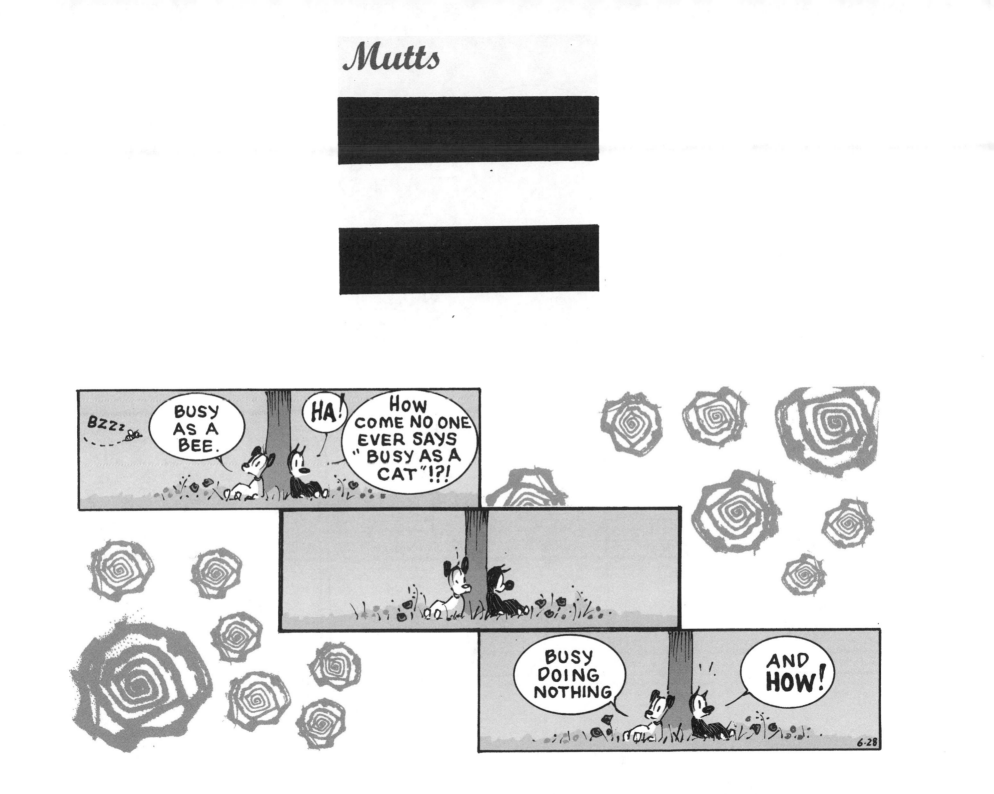

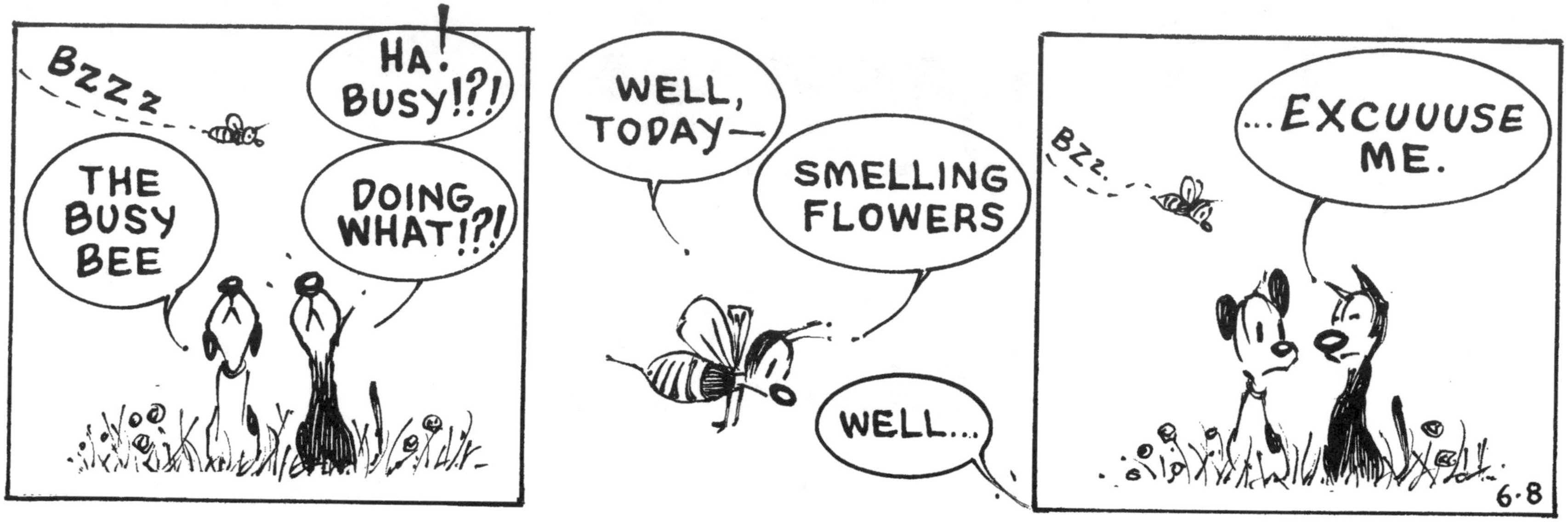
Bzzzz
THE BUSY BEE
HA! BUSY!?!
DOING WHAT!?!
WELL, TODAY—
SMELLING FLOWERS
WELL...
BZZ
...EXCUUUSE ME.
6·8

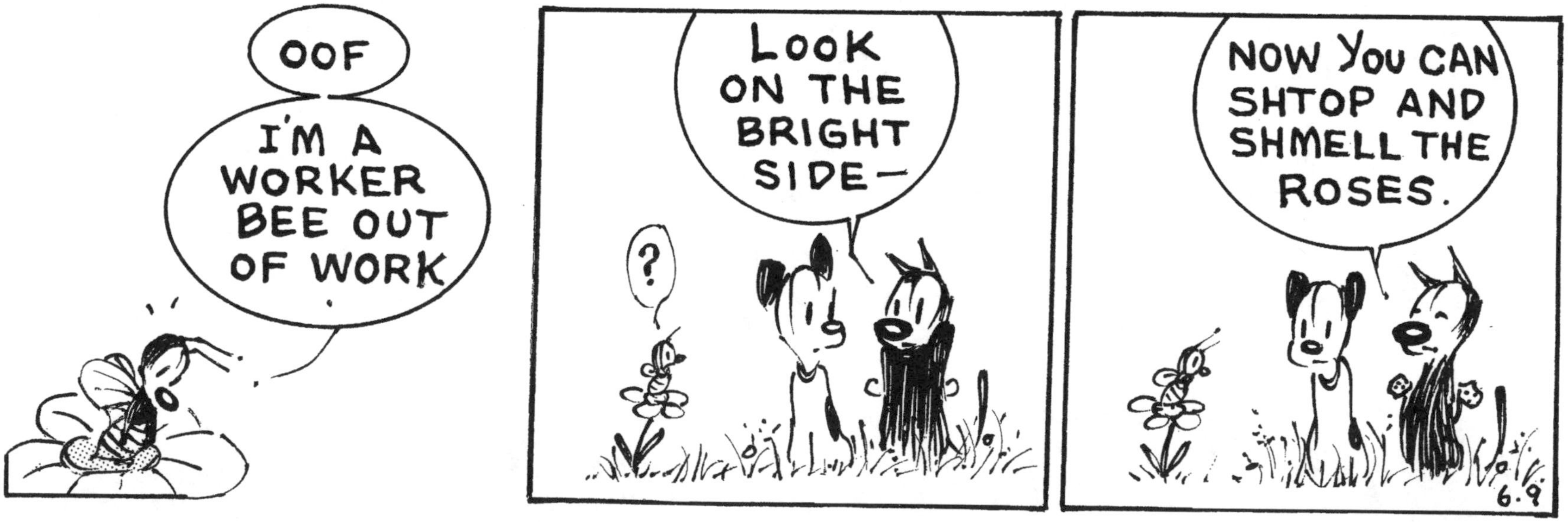
OOF
I'M A WORKER BEE OUT OF WORK
LOOK ON THE BRIGHT SIDE—
?
NOW YOU CAN SHTOP AND SHMELL THE ROSES.
6·9

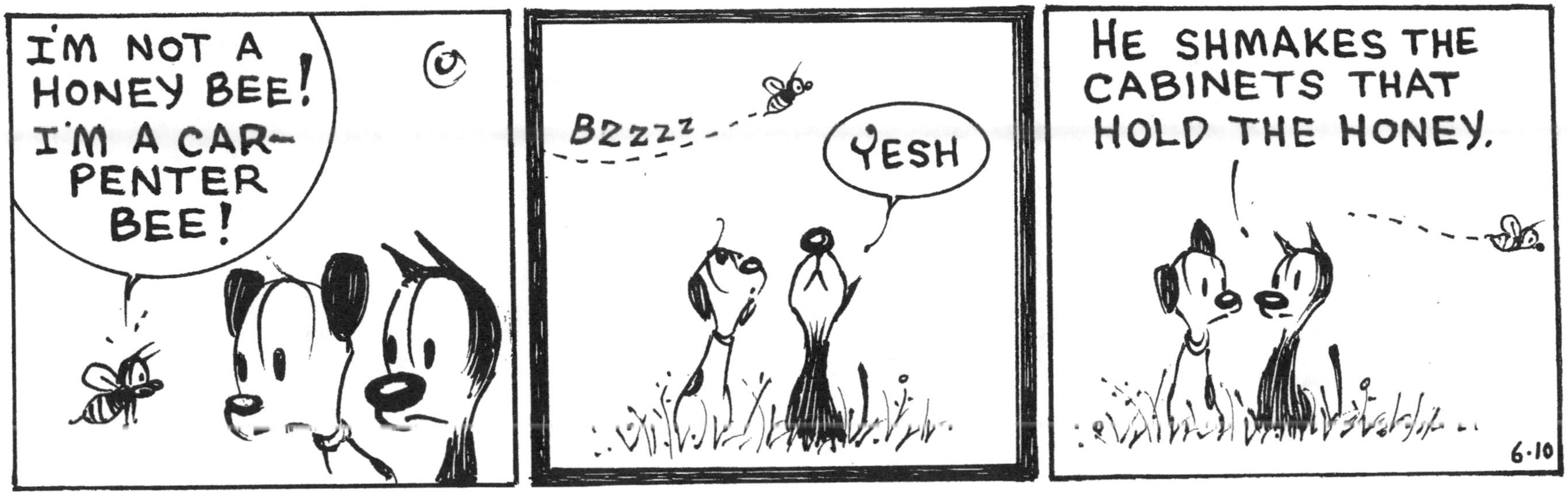
I'M NOT A HONEY BEE! I'M A CAR-PENTER BEE!
BZZZZ
YESH
HE SHMAKES THE CABINETS THAT HOLD THE HONEY.
6·10

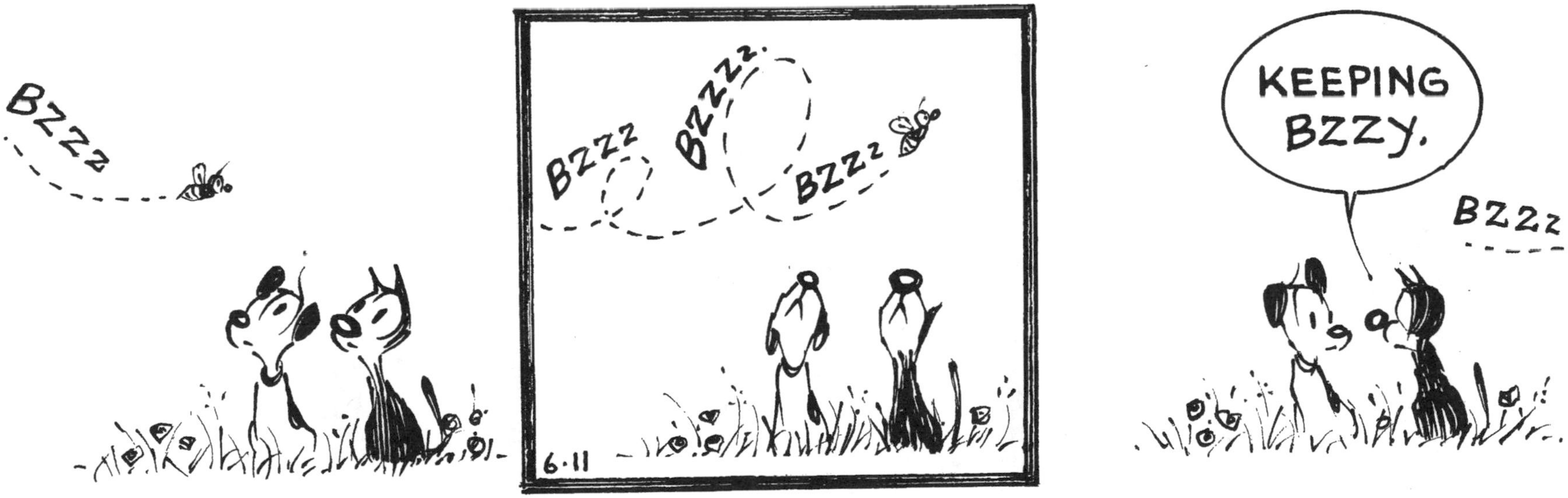
BZZZ
BZZZ
BZZZZZ
BZZZ
6·11
KEEPING BZZY.
BZZZ

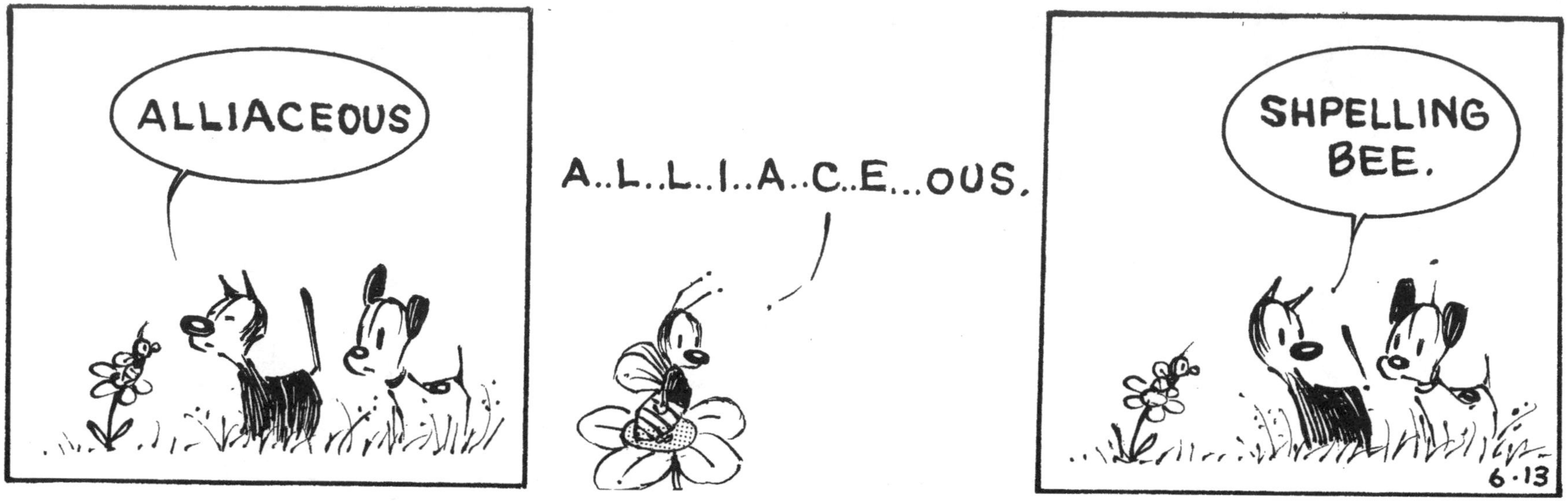
ALLIACEOUS
A..L..L..I..A..C..E...OUS.
SHPELLING BEE.
6·13

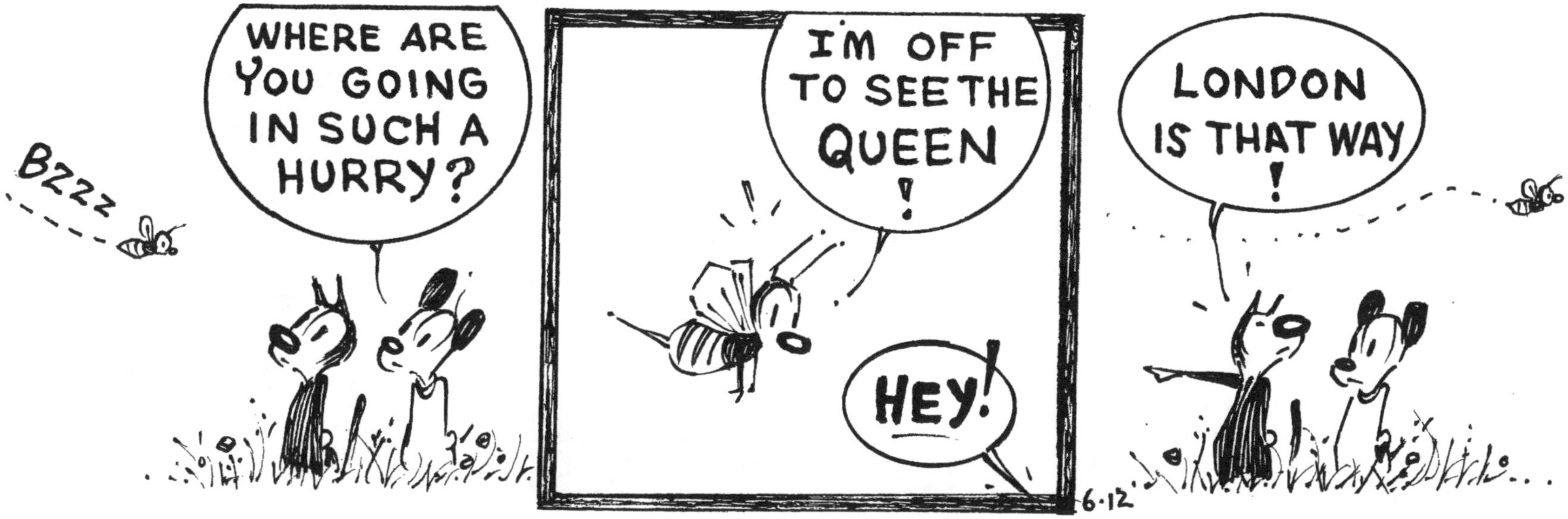
Bzzz
WHERE ARE YOU GOING IN SUCH A HURRY?
I'M OFF TO SEE THE QUEEN !
HEY!
6·12
LONDON IS THAT WAY !

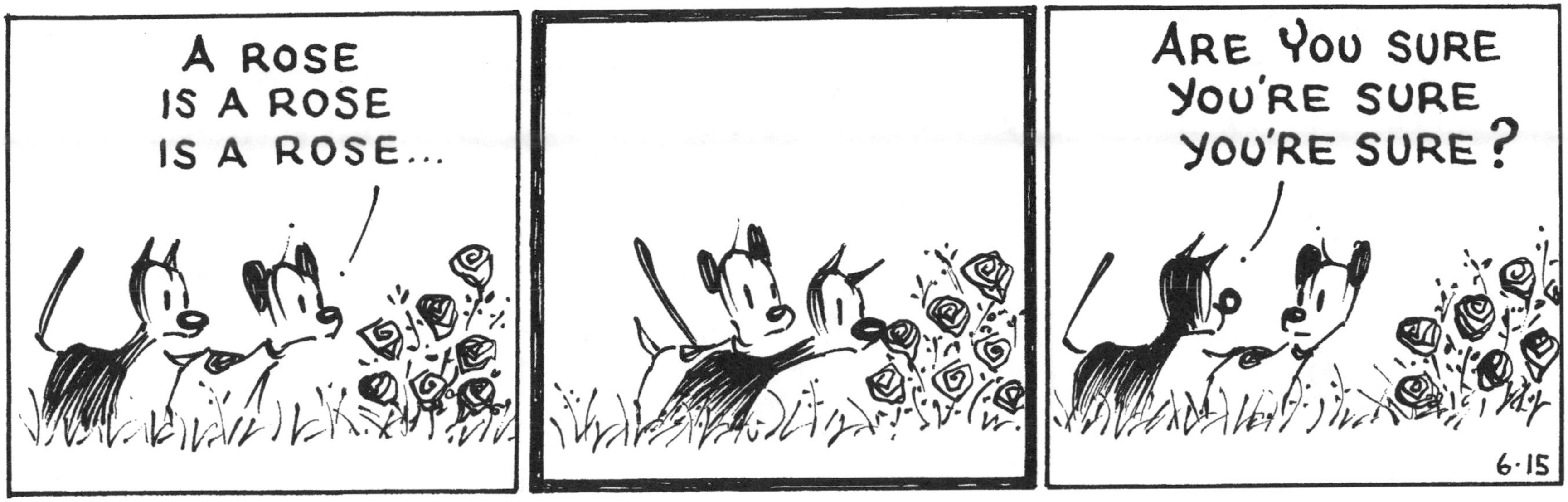
A ROSE
IS A ROSE
IS A ROSE...
ARE YOU SURE
YOU'RE SURE
YOU'RE SURE?
6·15

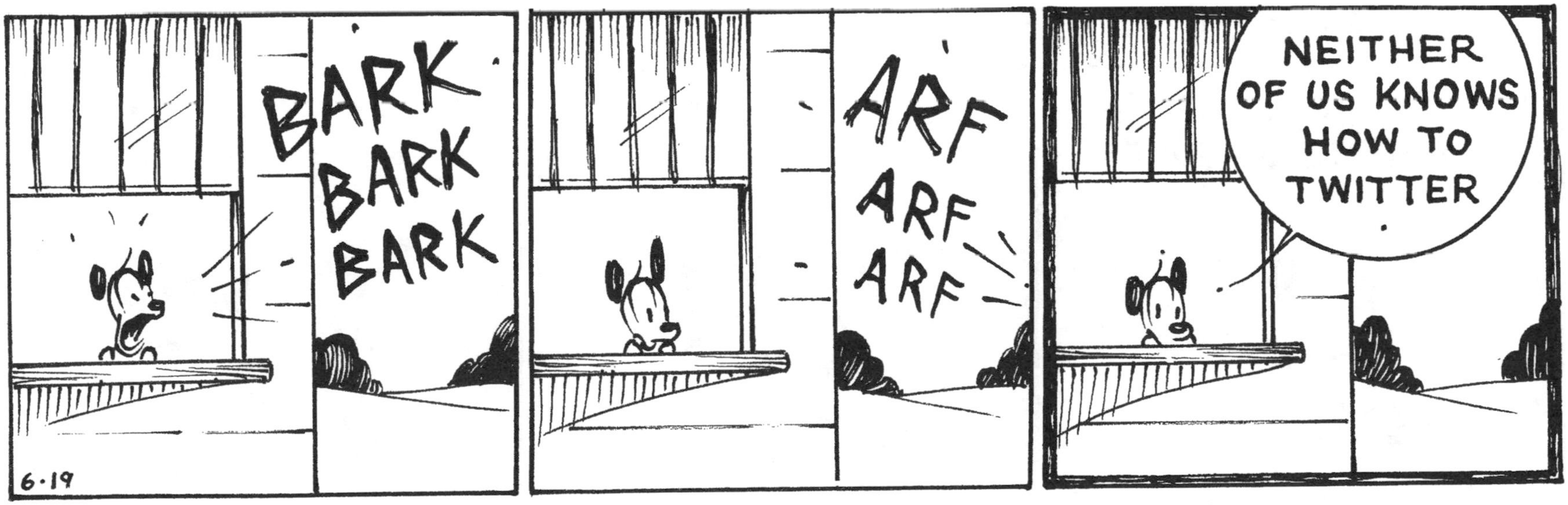
BARK
BARK
BARK
6·19
ARF
ARF
ARF
NEITHER
OF US KNOWS
HOW TO
TWITTER

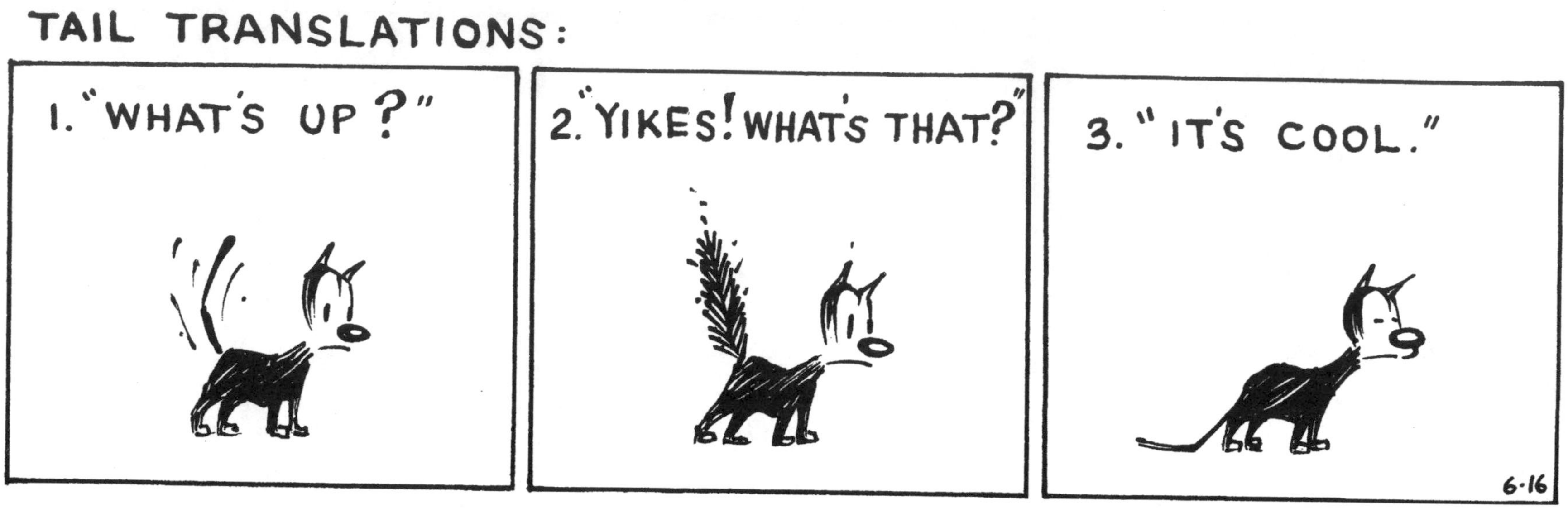
TAIL TRANSLATIONS:
1. "WHAT'S UP?"
2. "YIKES! WHAT'S THAT?"
3. "IT'S COOL."
6·16

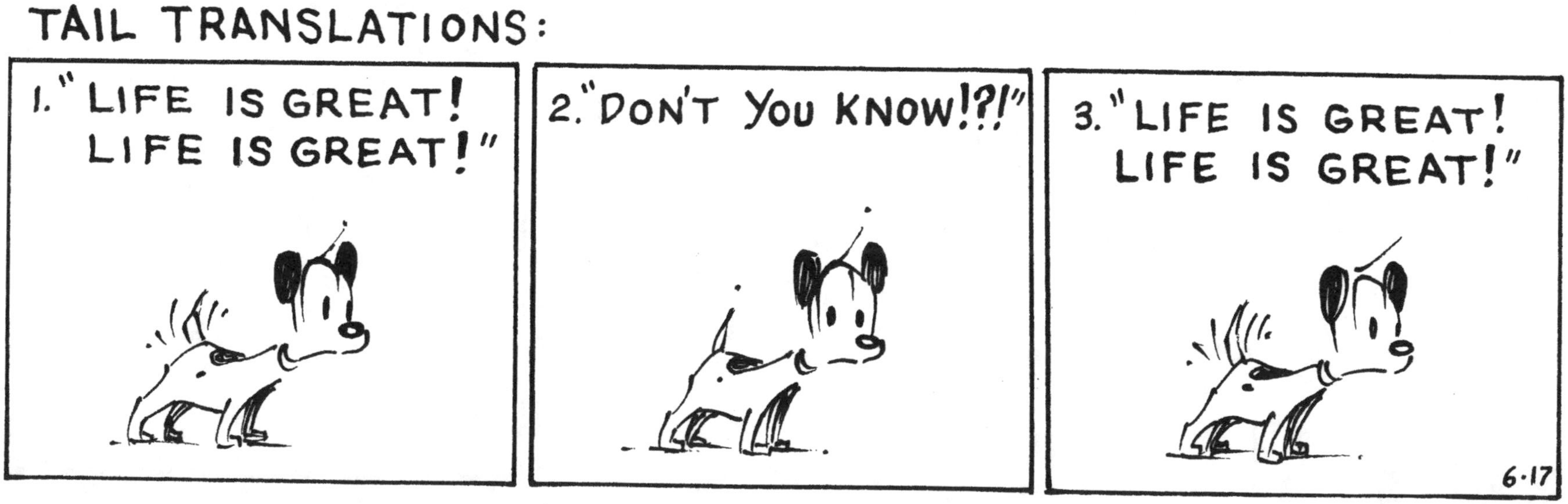
TAIL TRANSLATIONS:
1. "LIFE IS GREAT! LIFE IS GREAT!"
2. "DON'T YOU KNOW!?!"
3. "LIFE IS GREAT! LIFE IS GREAT!"
6·17

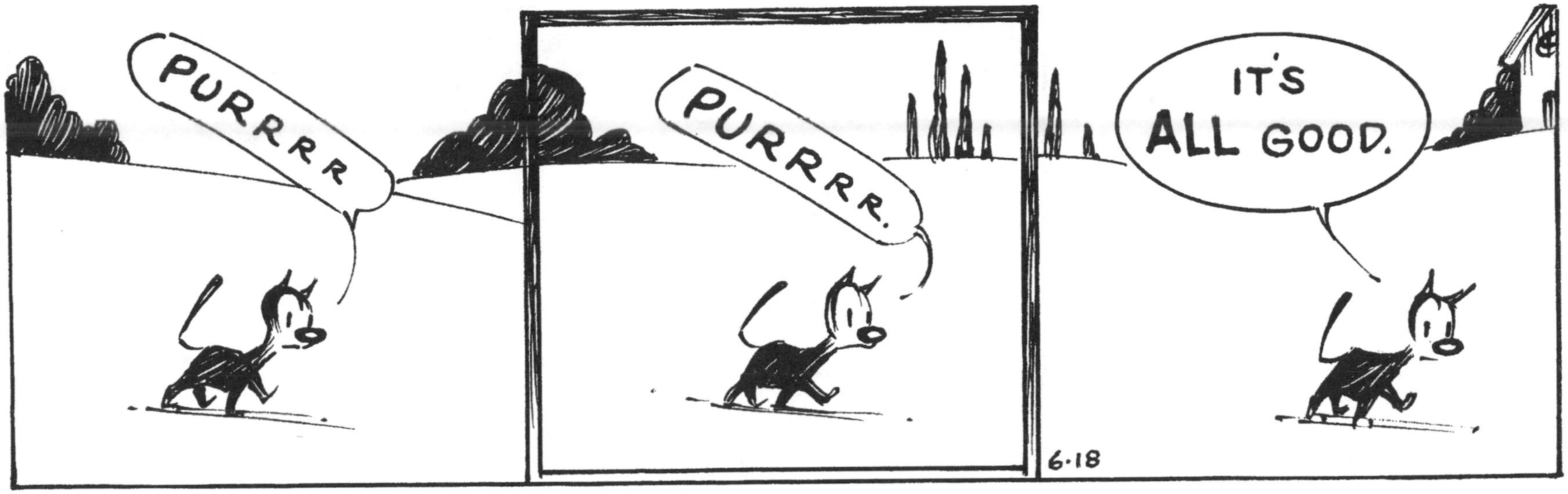
PURRRRR
PURRRRR.
IT'S ALL GOOD.
6·18

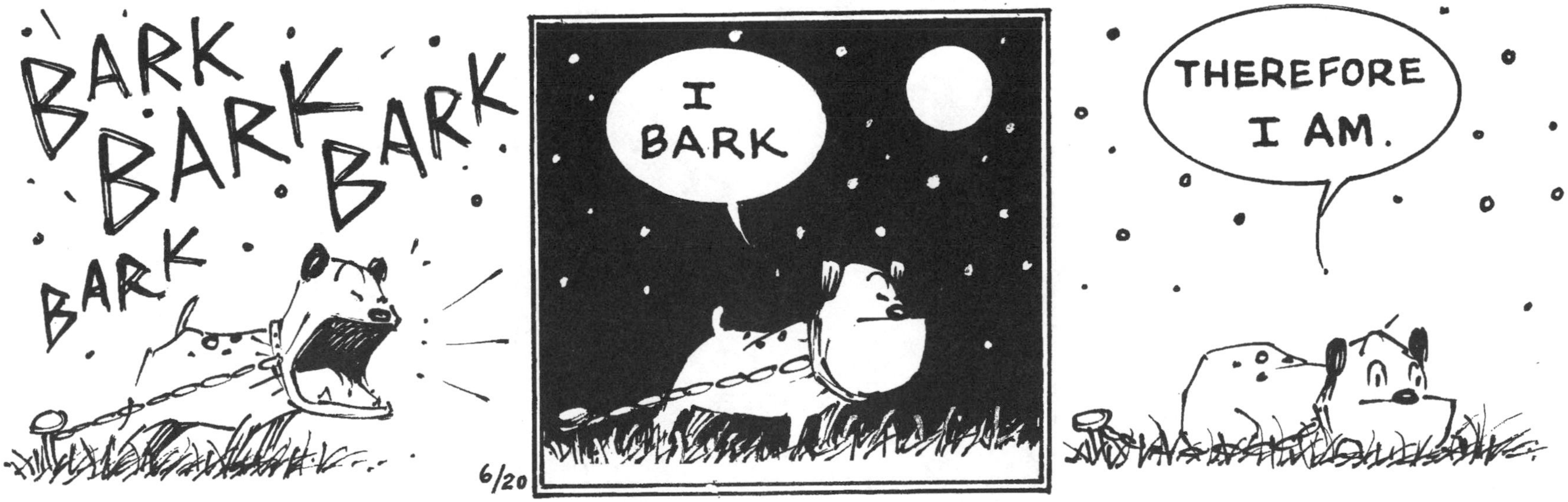
BARK BARK BARK BARK
6/20
I BARK
THEREFORE I AM.

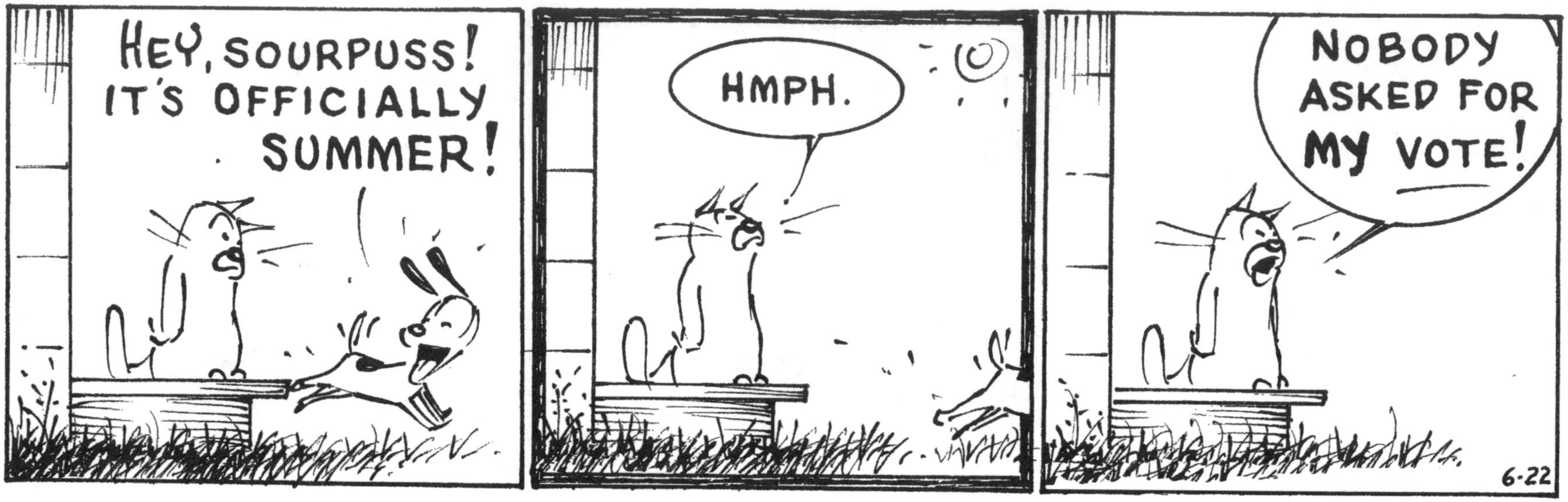
HEY, SOURPUSS! IT'S OFFICIALLY SUMMER!
HMPH.
NOBODY ASKED FOR MY VOTE!
6-22

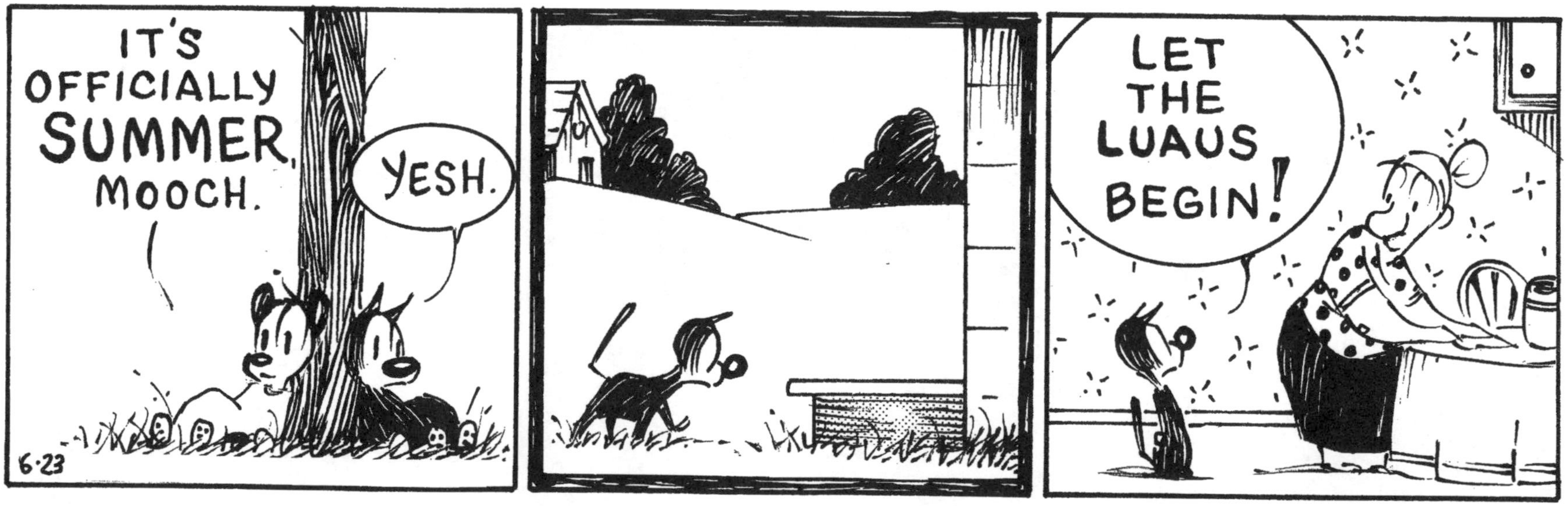
IT'S OFFICIALLY SUMMER, MOOCH.
YESH.
LET THE LUAUS BEGIN!
6-23

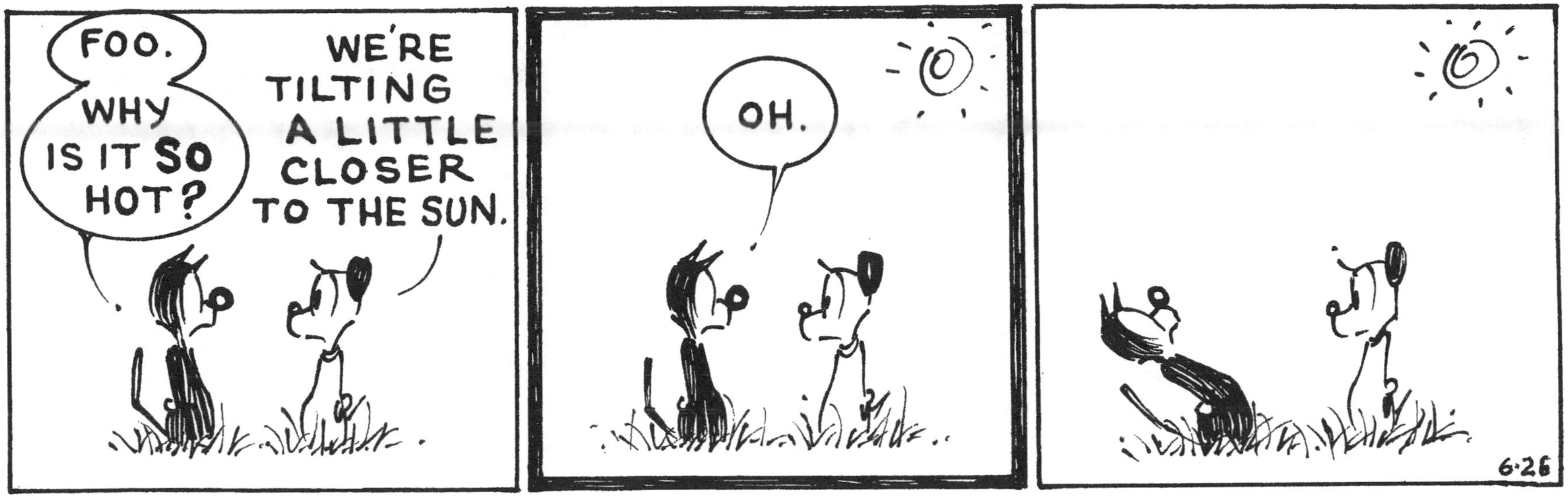
FOO.
WHY IS IT SO HOT?
WE'RE TILTING A LITTLE CLOSER TO THE SUN.
OH.
6·26

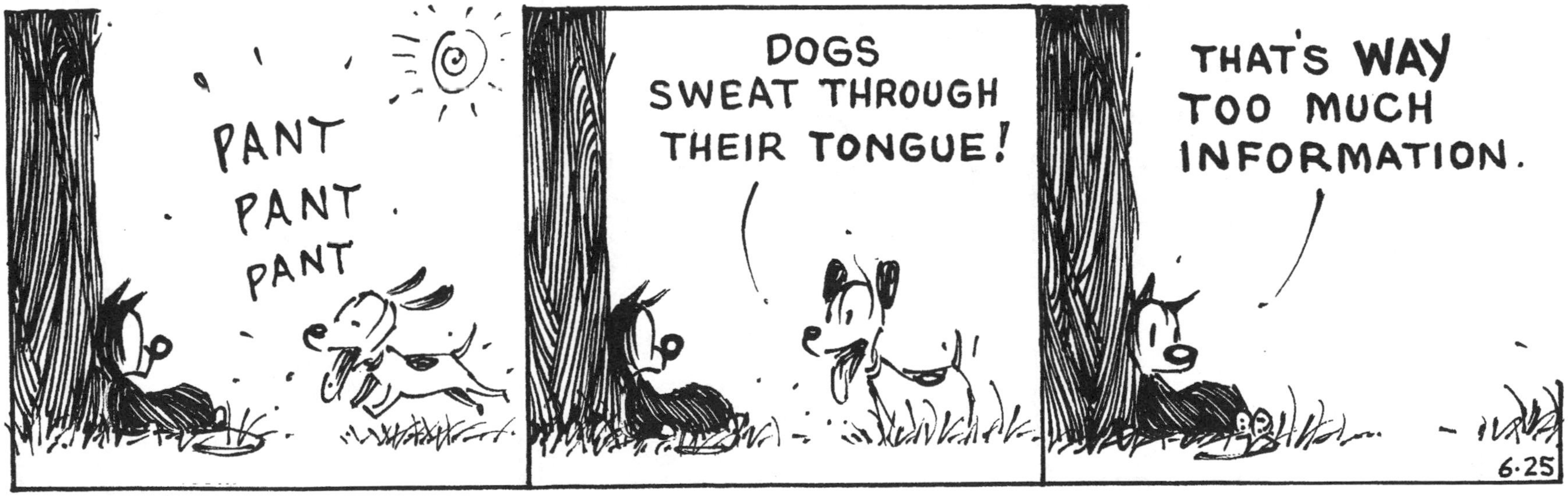
PANT
PANT
PANT
DOGS SWEAT THROUGH THEIR TONGUE!
THAT'S WAY TOO MUCH INFORMATION.
6·25

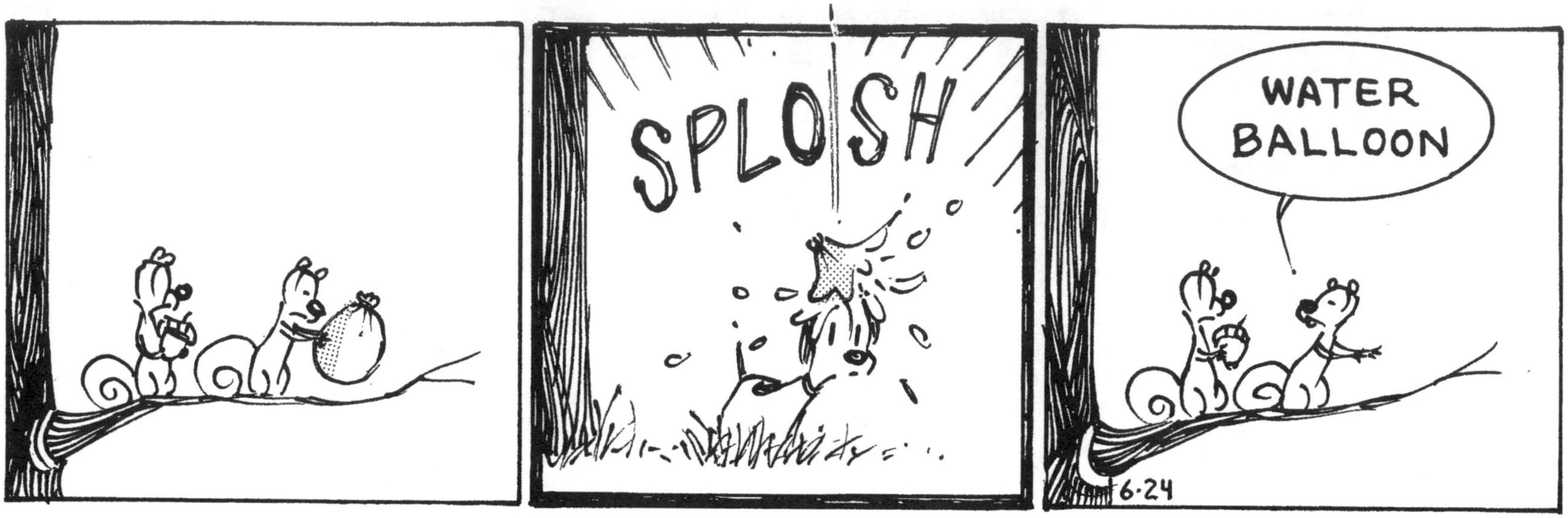
SPLOSH
WATER BALLOON
6-24

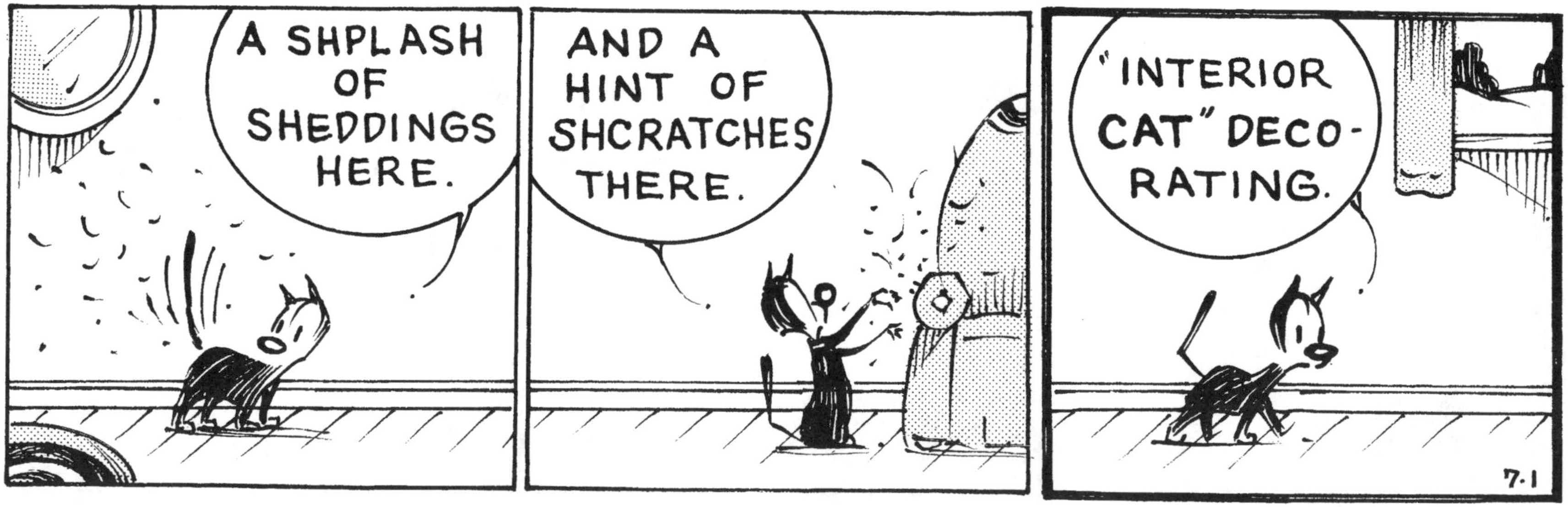
A SHPLASH OF SHEDDINGS HERE.
AND A HINT OF SHCRATCHES THERE.
"INTERIOR CAT" DECO-RATING.
7-1

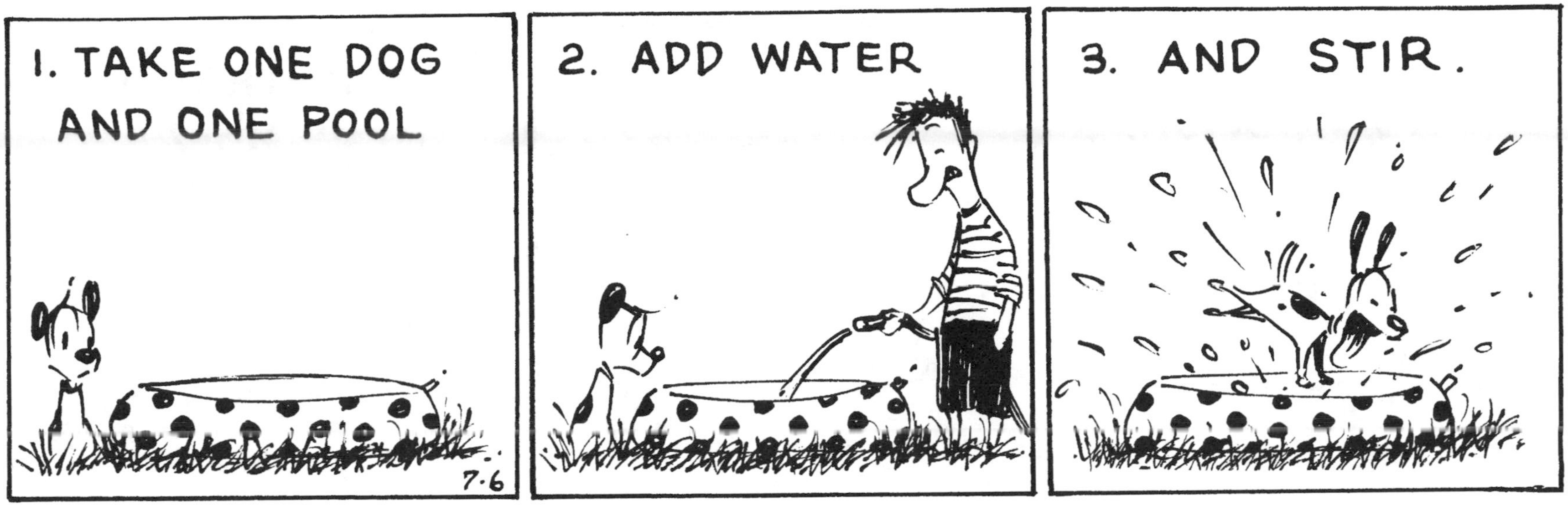
1. TAKE ONE DOG AND ONE POOL
7·6
2. ADD WATER
3. AND STIR.

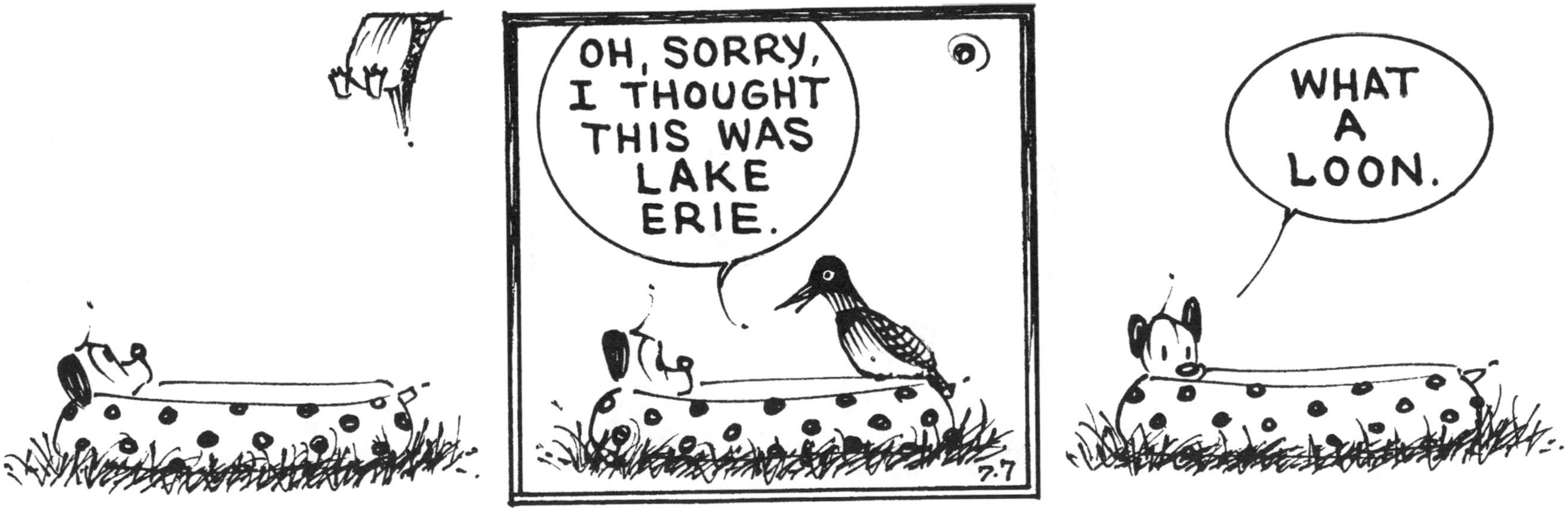
OH, SORRY, I THOUGHT THIS WAS LAKE ERIE.
7·7
WHAT A LOON.

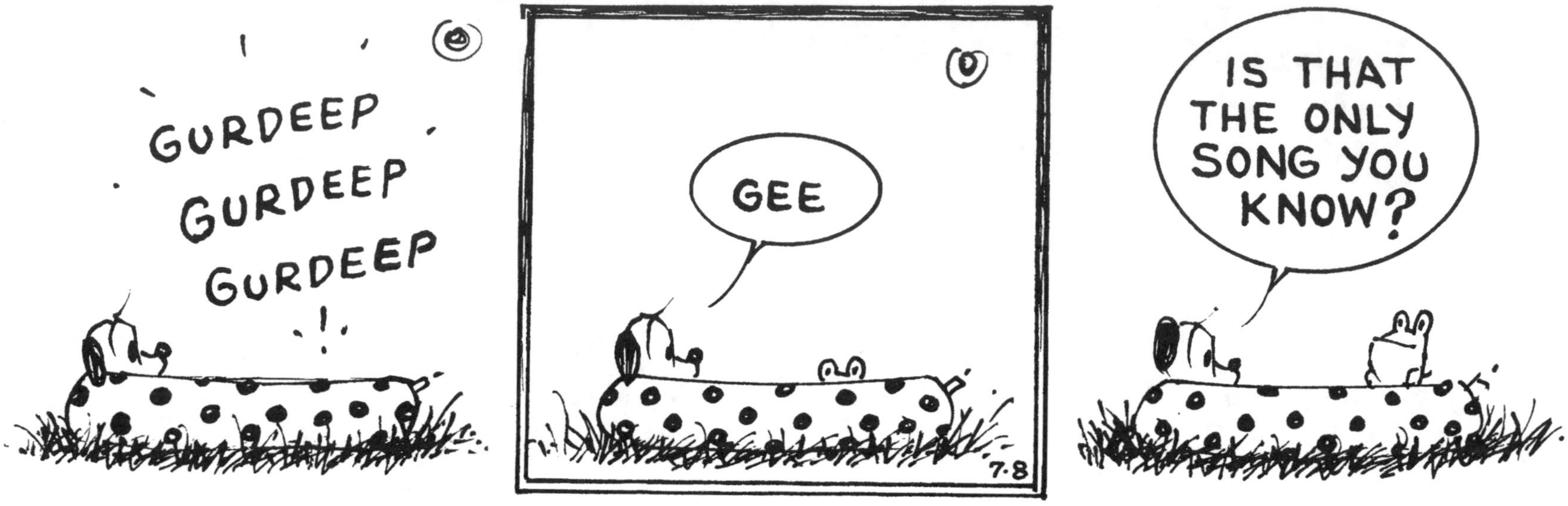
GURDEEP
GURDEEP
GURDEEP
GEE
7·8
IS THAT THE ONLY SONG YOU KNOW?

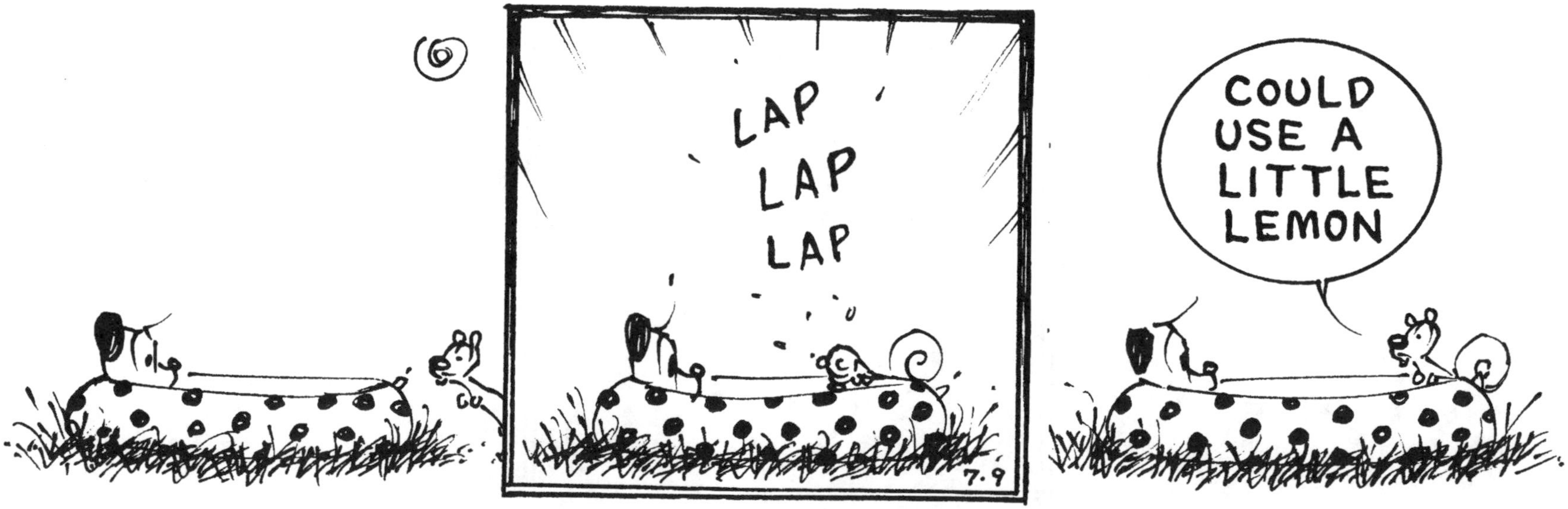
LAP
LAP
LAP
7·9
COULD USE A LITTLE LEMON

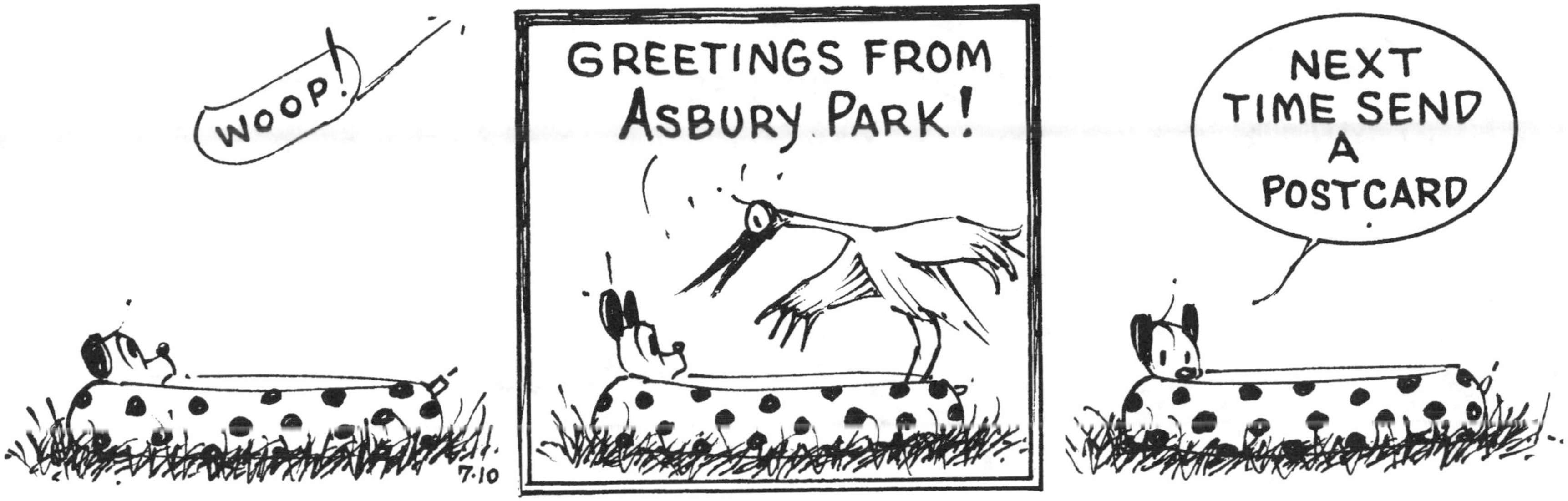
WOOP!
GREETINGS FROM ASBURY PARK!
NEXT TIME SEND A POSTCARD
7·10

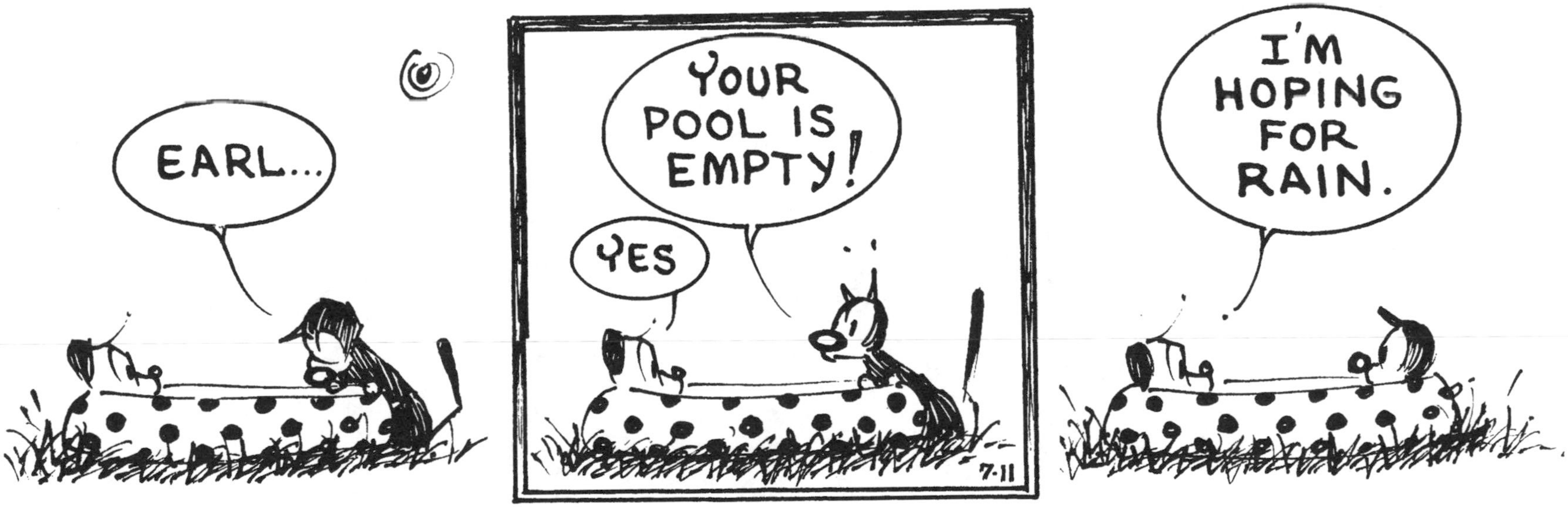
EARL...
YES
YOUR POOL IS EMPTY!
I'M HOPING FOR RAIN.
7·11

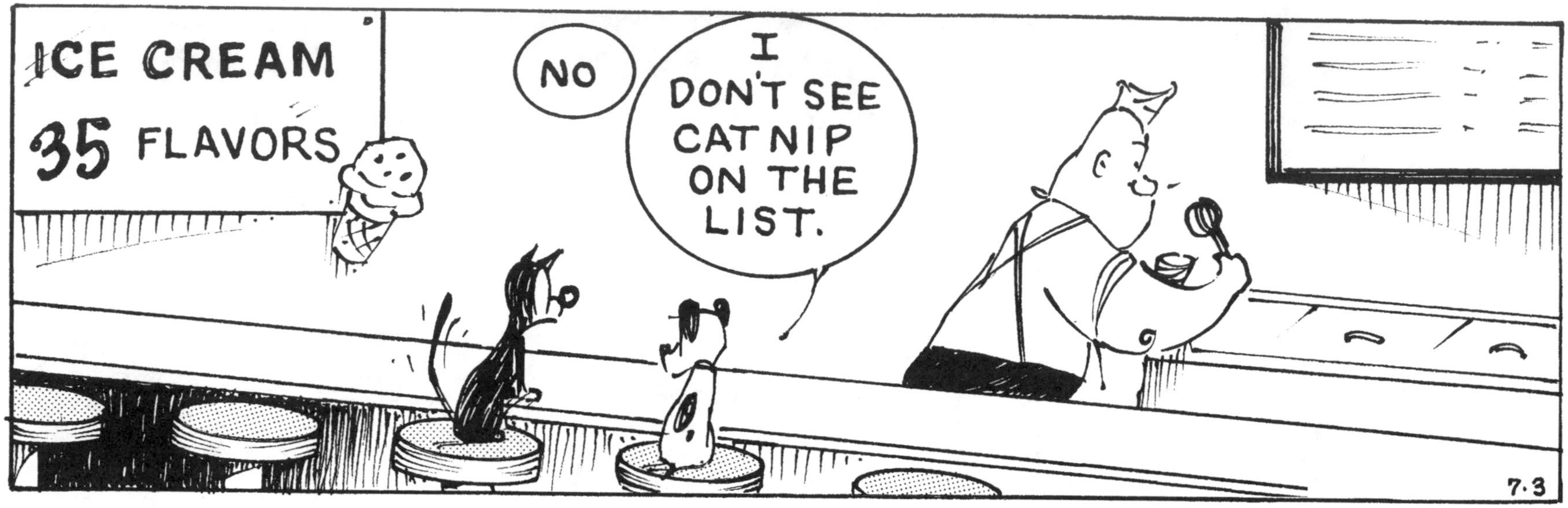
ICE CREAM
35 FLAVORS
NO
I DON'T SEE CATNIP ON THE LIST.

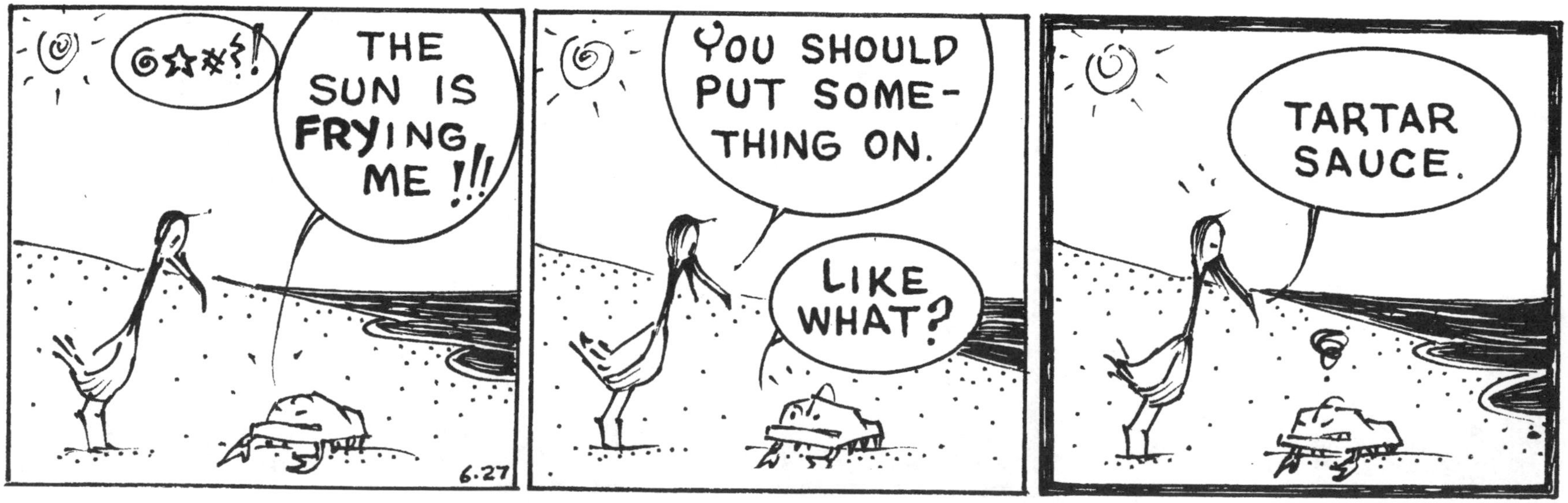
THE SUN IS FRYING ME!!!
YOU SHOULD PUT SOME-THING ON.
LIKE WHAT?
TARTAR SAUCE.

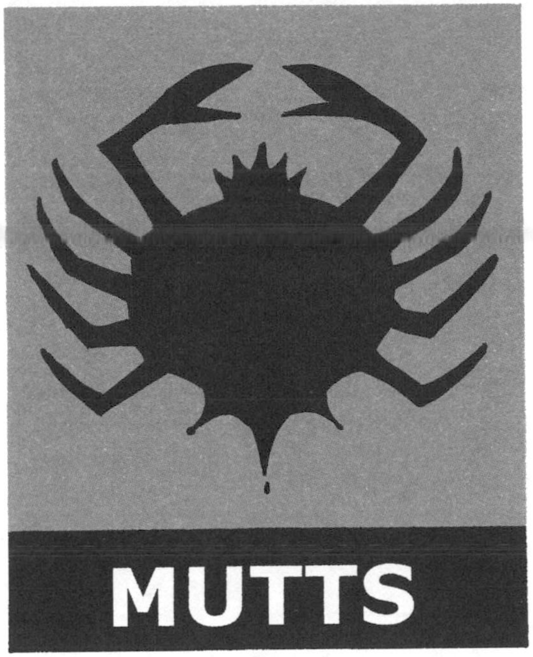
MUTTS

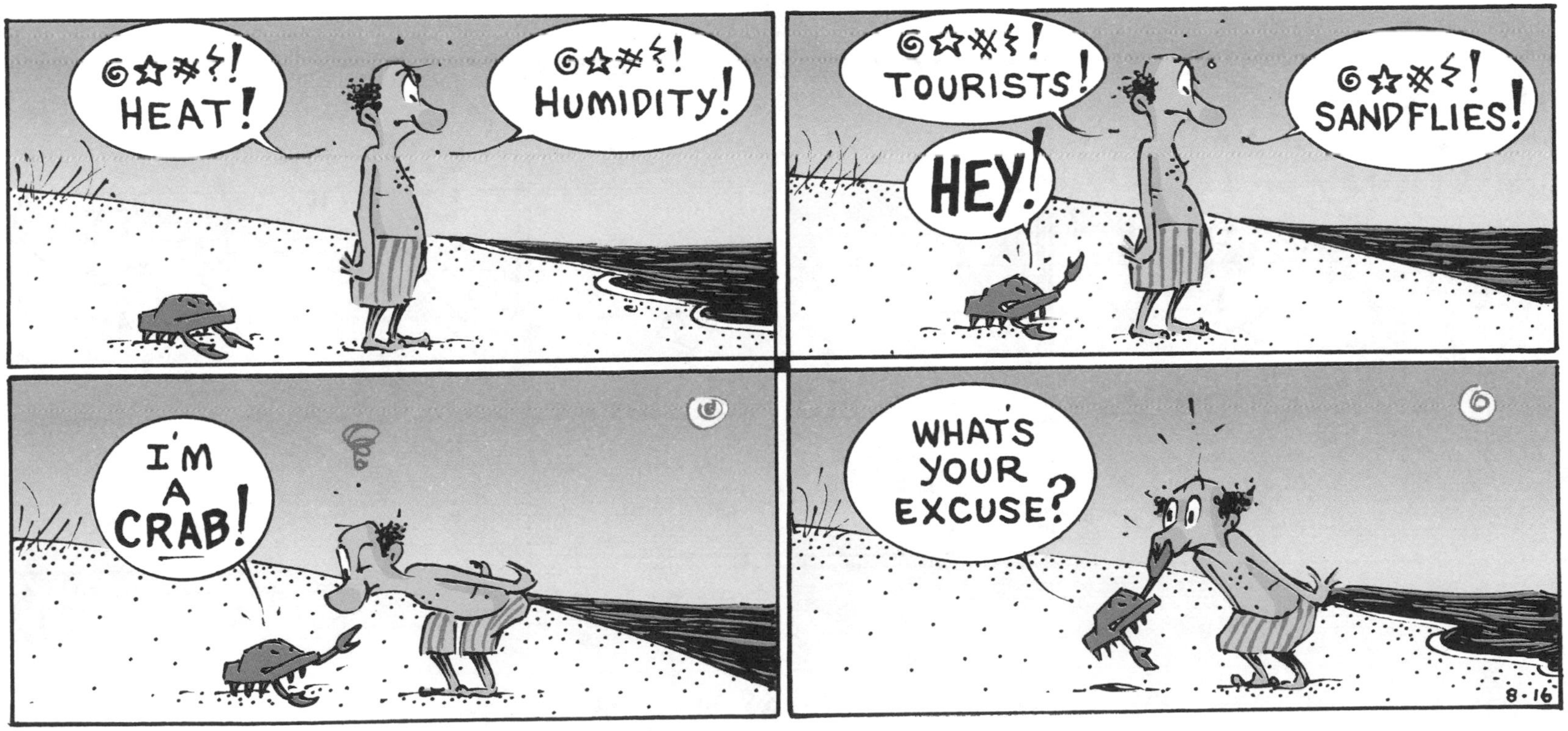
HEAT!
HUMIDITY!
TOURISTS!
SANDFLIES!
HEY!
I'M A CRAB!
WHAT'S YOUR EXCUSE?
8-16

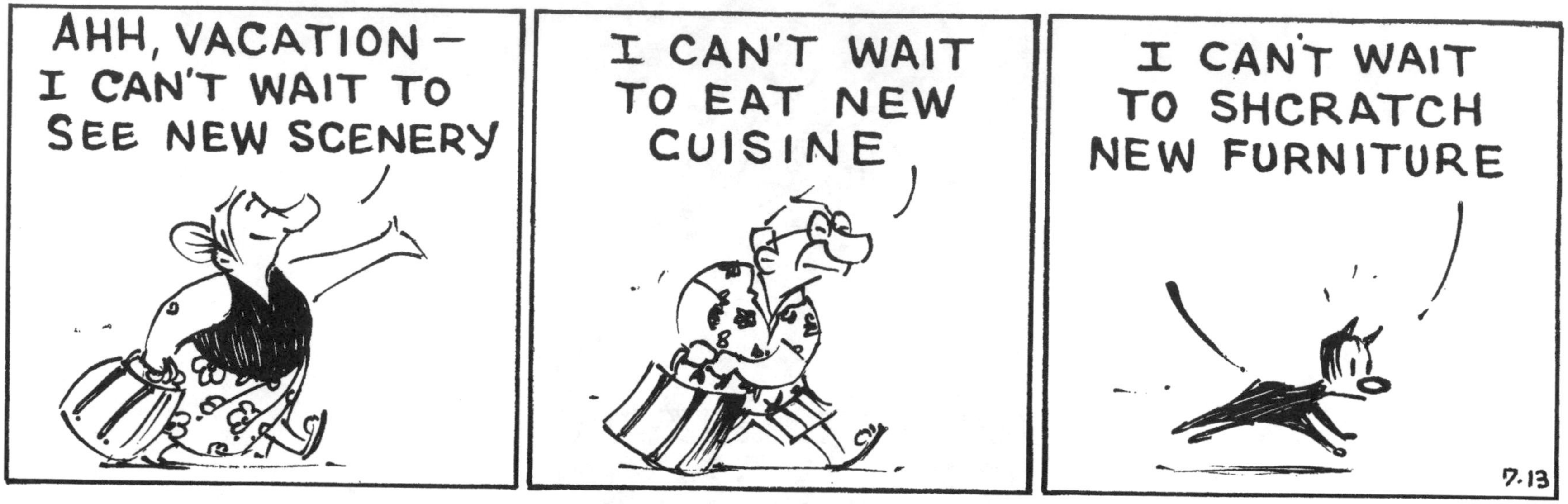
AHH, VACATION - I CAN'T WAIT TO SEE NEW SCENERY
I CAN'T WAIT TO EAT NEW CUISINE
I CAN'T WAIT TO SHCRATCH NEW FURNITURE
7.13

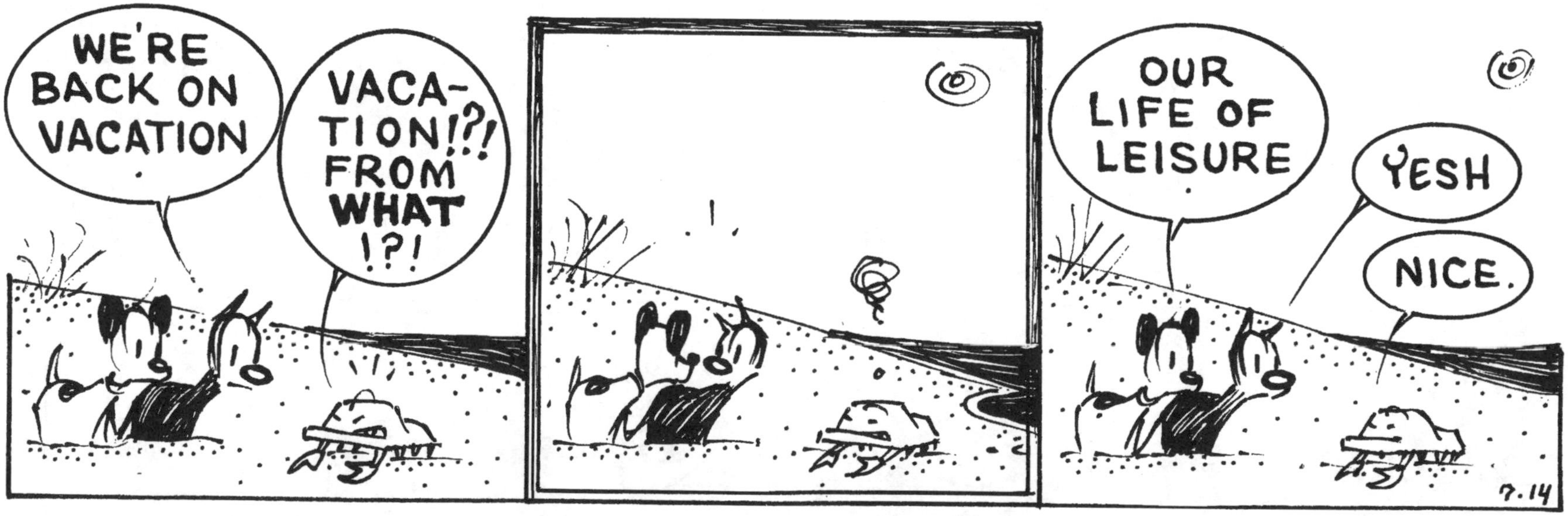
WE'RE BACK ON VACATION
VACA-TION!?! FROM WHAT !?!
OUR LIFE OF LEISURE
YESH
NICE.
7.14

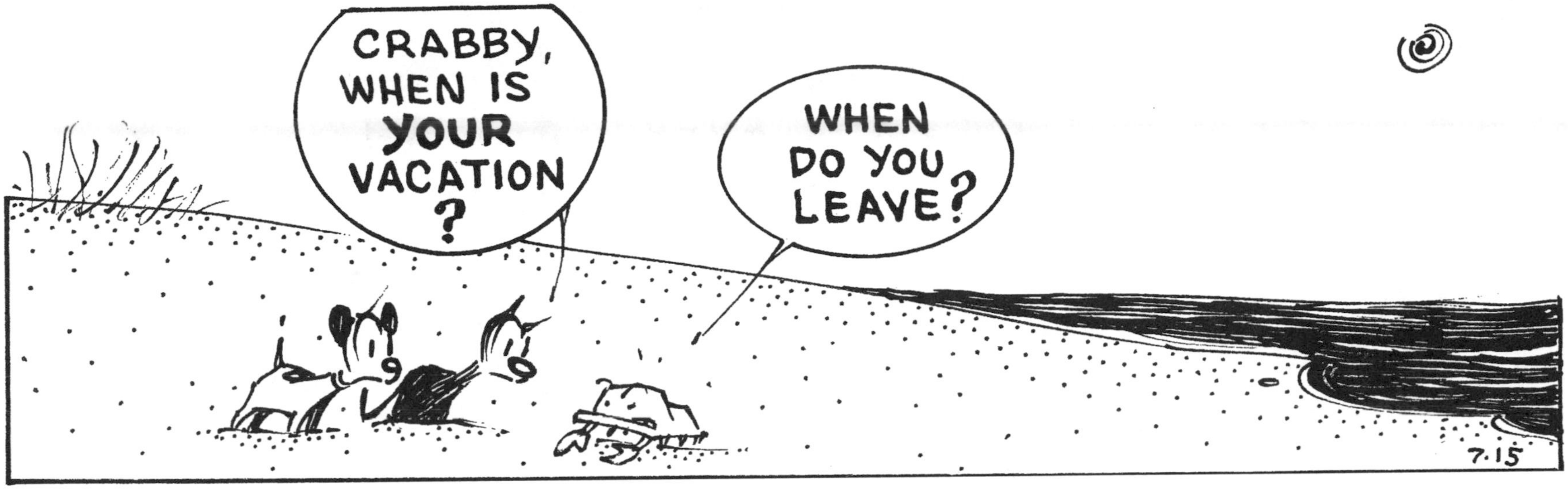
CRABBY, WHEN IS YOUR VACATION?
WHEN DO YOU LEAVE?
7.15

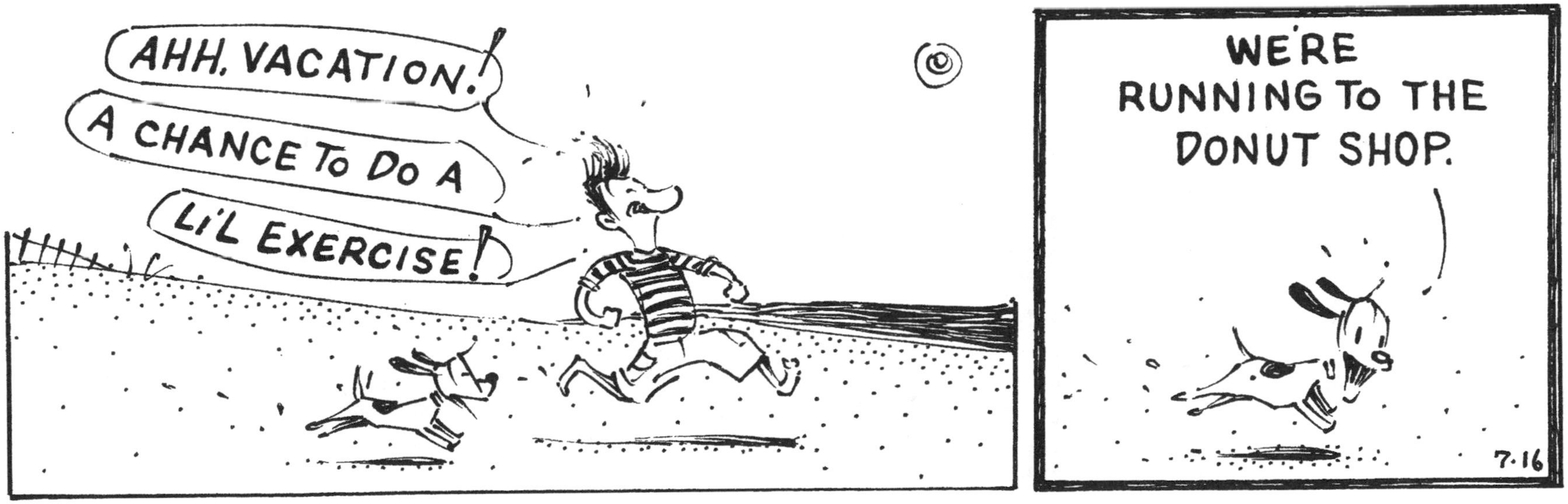
AHH, VACATION!
A CHANCE TO DO A
LI'L EXERCISE!
WE'RE RUNNING TO THE DONUT SHOP.
7.16

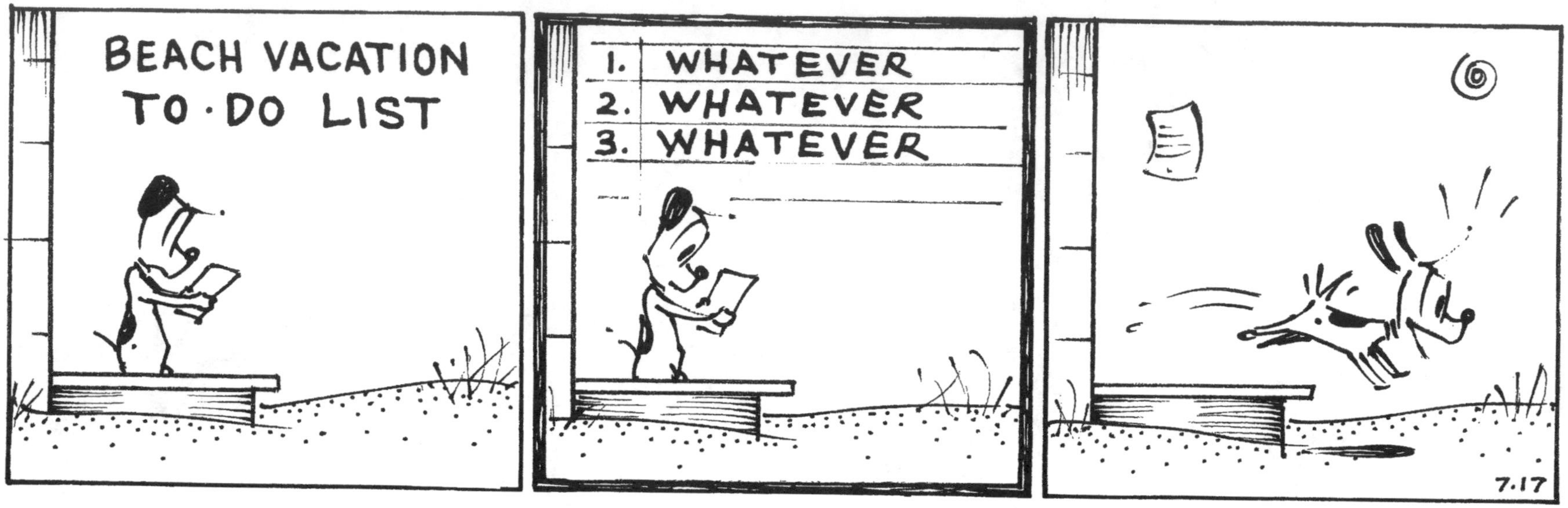
BEACH VACATION TO·DO LIST
1. WHATEVER
2. WHATEVER
3. WHATEVER
7·17

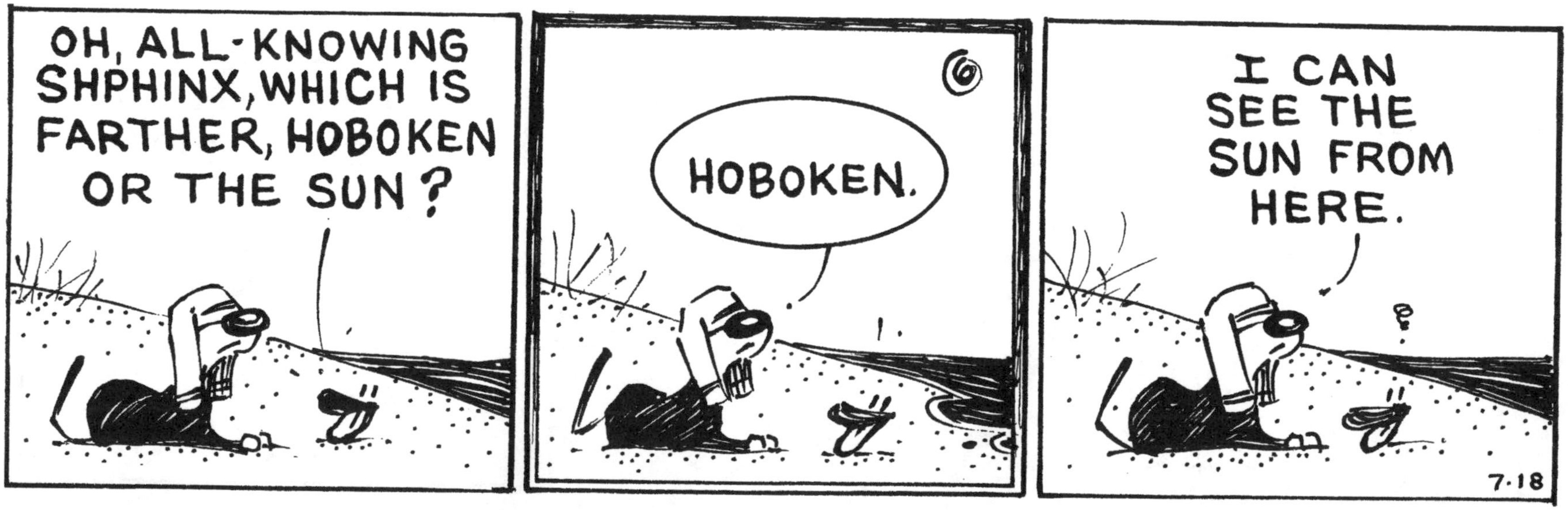
OH, ALL-KNOWING SHPHINX, WHICH IS FARTHER, HOBOKEN OR THE SUN?
HOBOKEN.
I CAN SEE THE SUN FROM HERE.
7·18

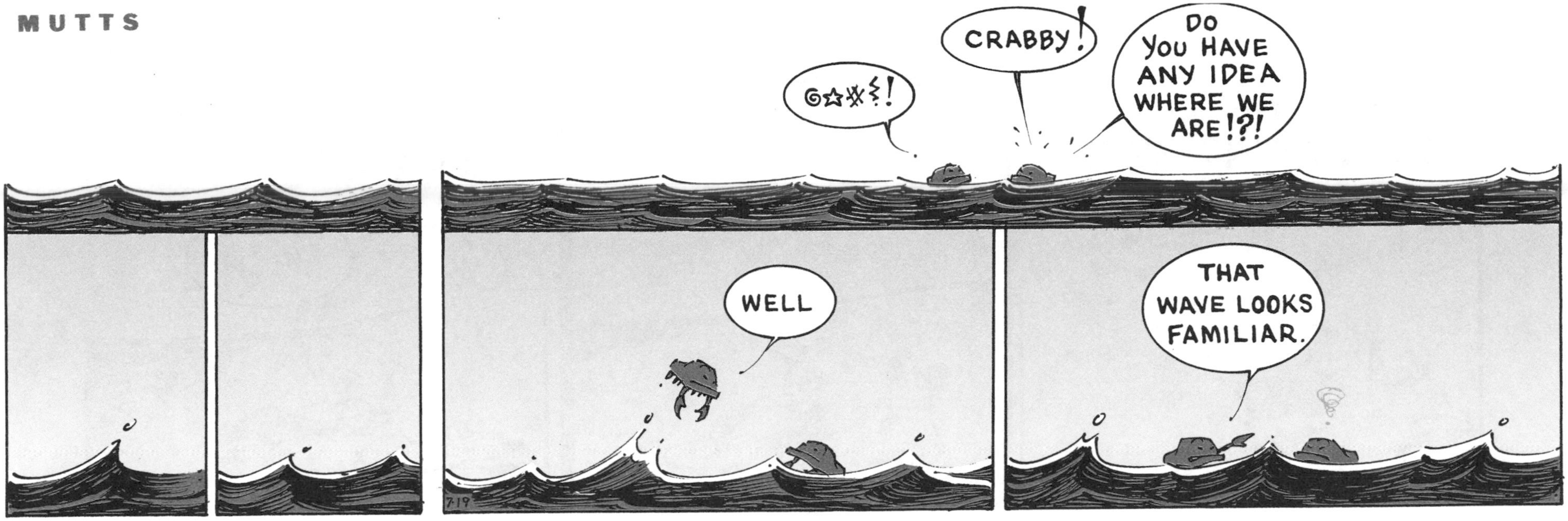
WELL
CRABBY!
DO YOU HAVE ANY IDEA WHERE WE ARE!?!
THAT WAVE LOOKS FAMILIAR.
7-19

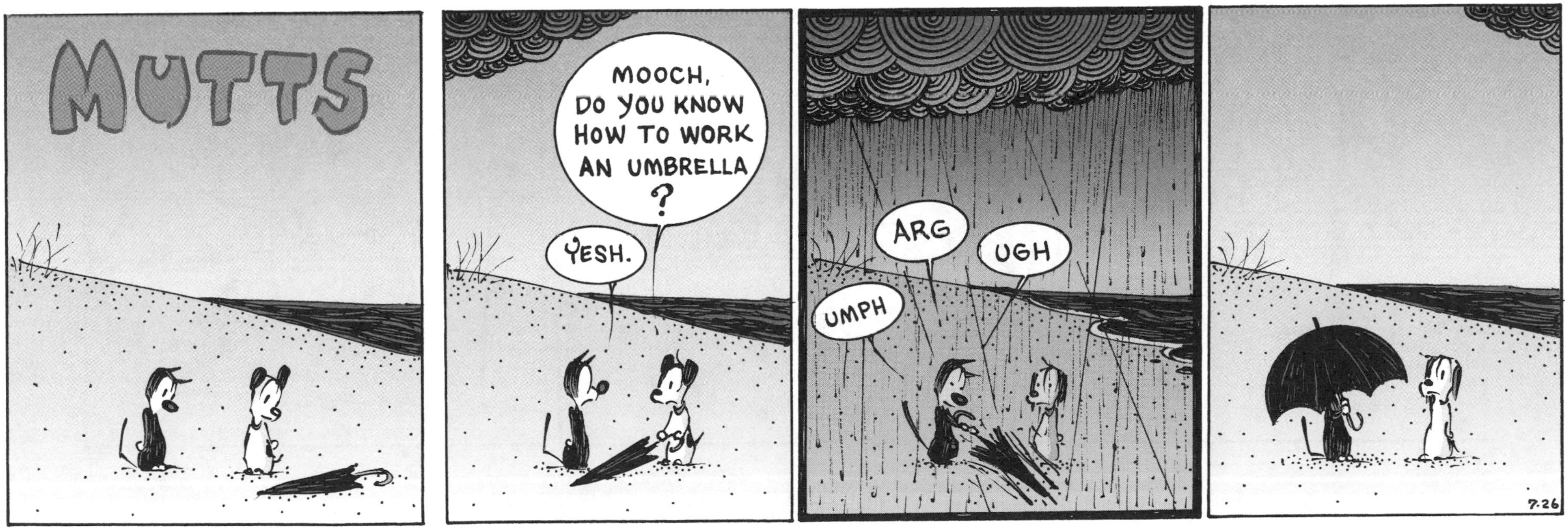
MUTTS
MOOCH, DO YOU KNOW HOW TO WORK AN UMBRELLA?
YESH.
ARG
UGH
UMPH
7-26

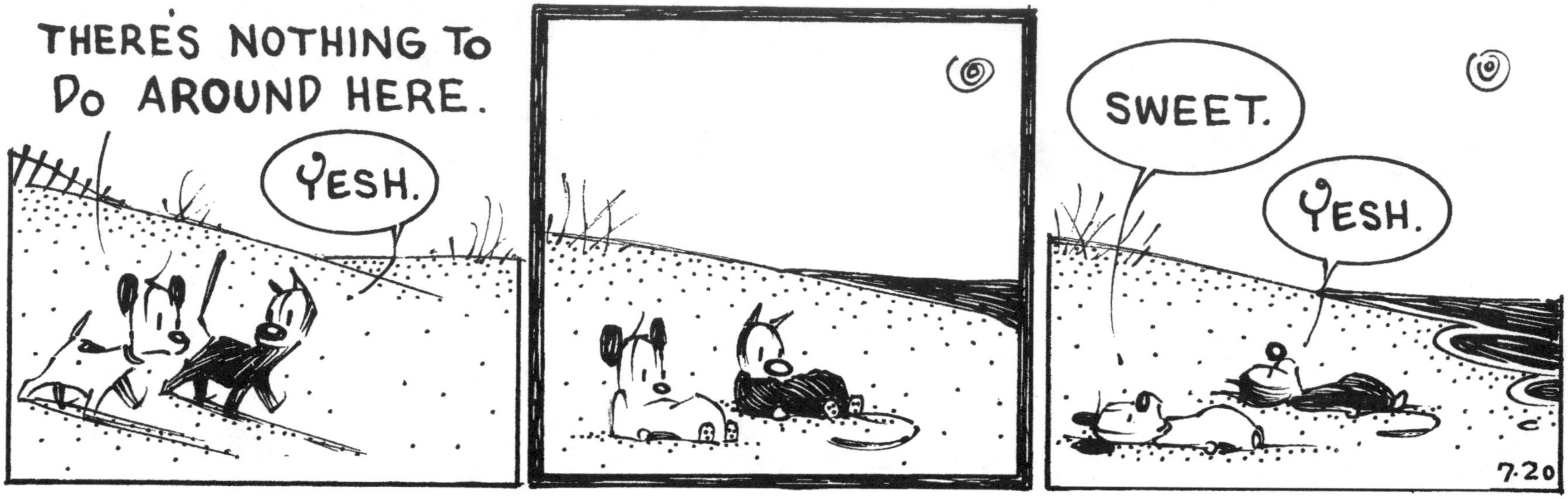
THERE'S NOTHING TO DO AROUND HERE.
YESH.
SWEET.
YESH.
7·20

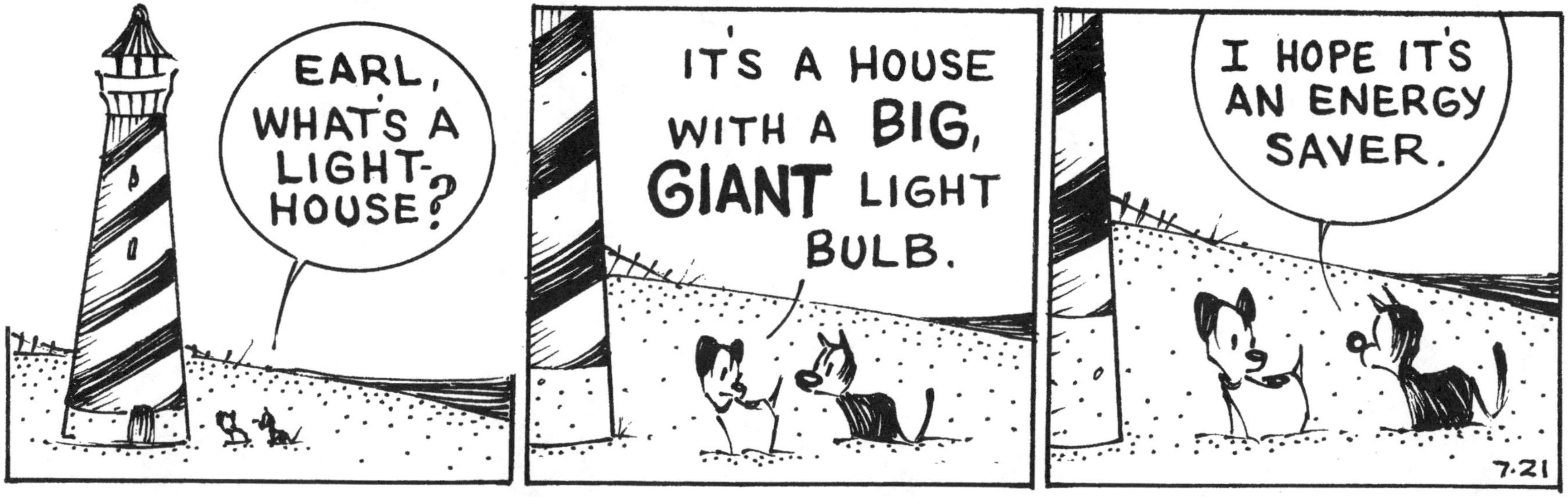
EARL, WHAT'S A LIGHT-HOUSE?
IT'S A HOUSE WITH A BIG, GIANT LIGHT BULB.
I HOPE IT'S AN ENERGY SAVER.
7·21

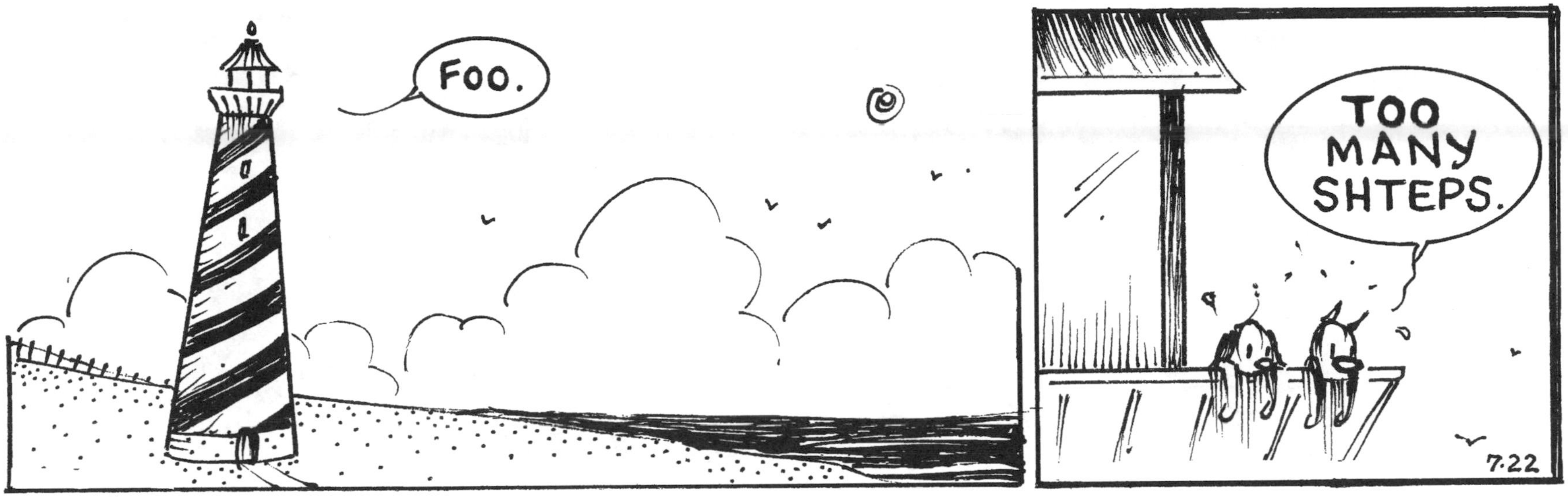
FOO.
TOO MANY SHTEPS.
7.22

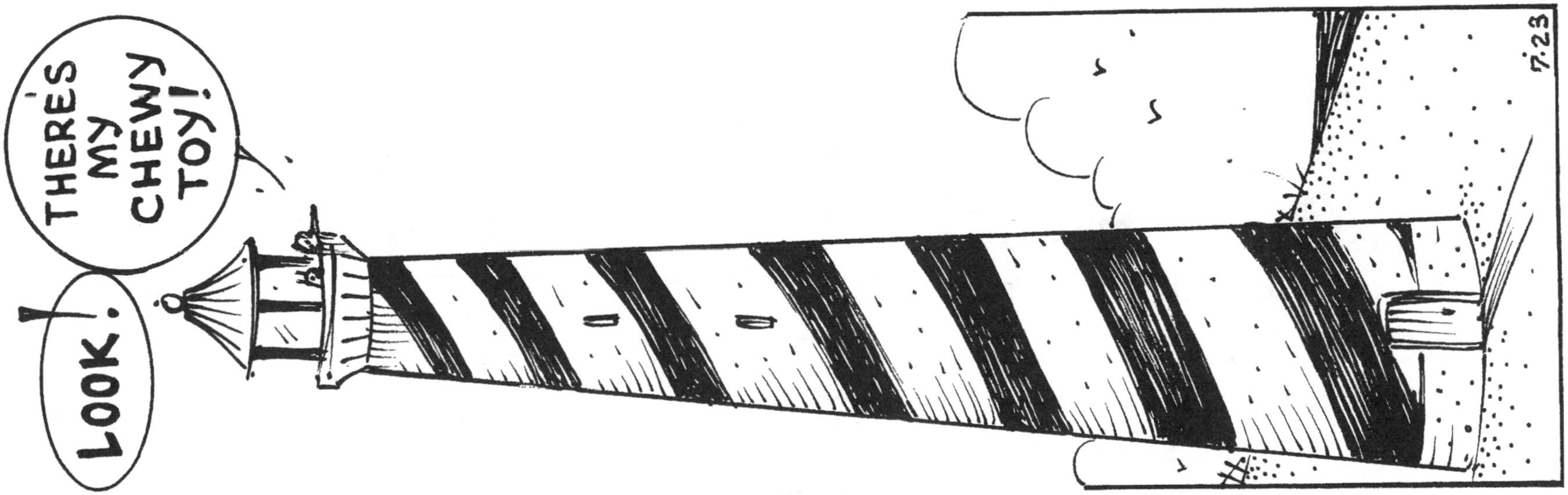
LOOK!
THERE'S MY CHEWY TOY!
7.23

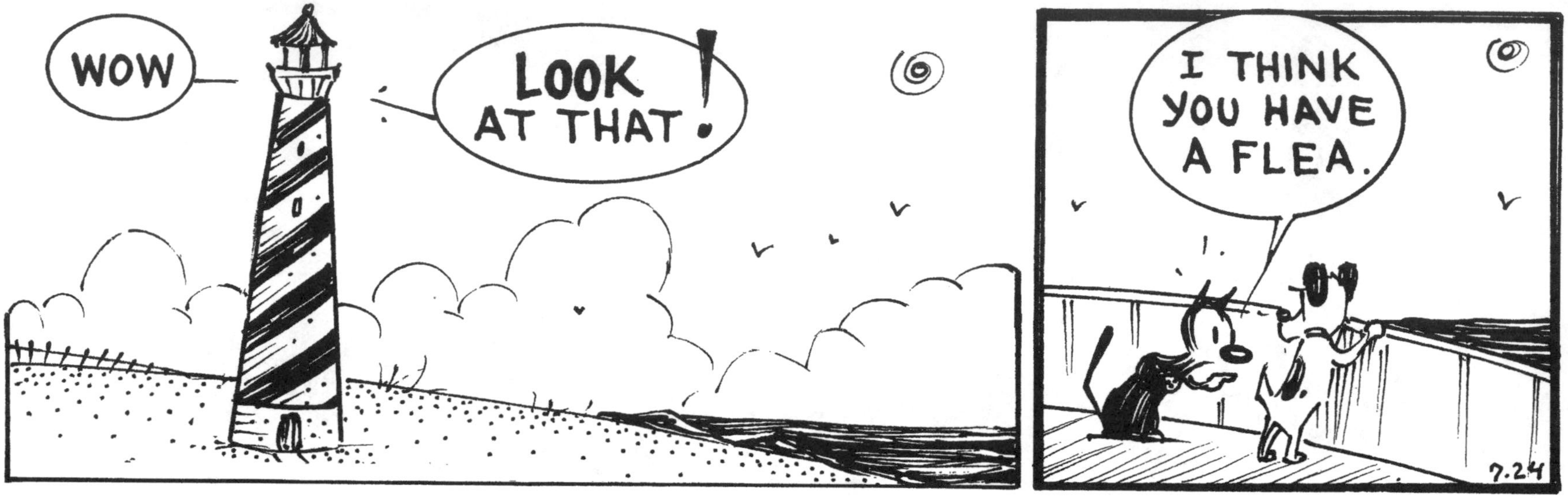
WOW
LOOK AT THAT!
I THINK YOU HAVE A FLEA.
7.24

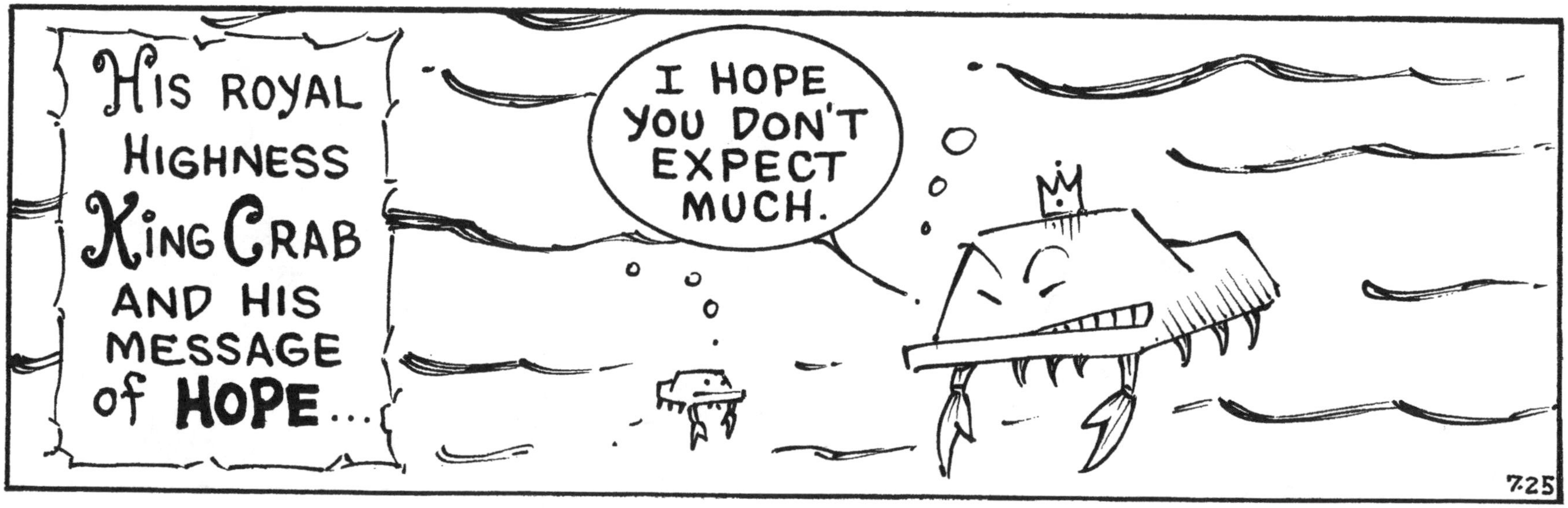
HIS ROYAL HIGHNESS KING CRAB AND HIS MESSAGE of HOPE...
I HOPE YOU DON'T EXPECT MUCH.
7.25

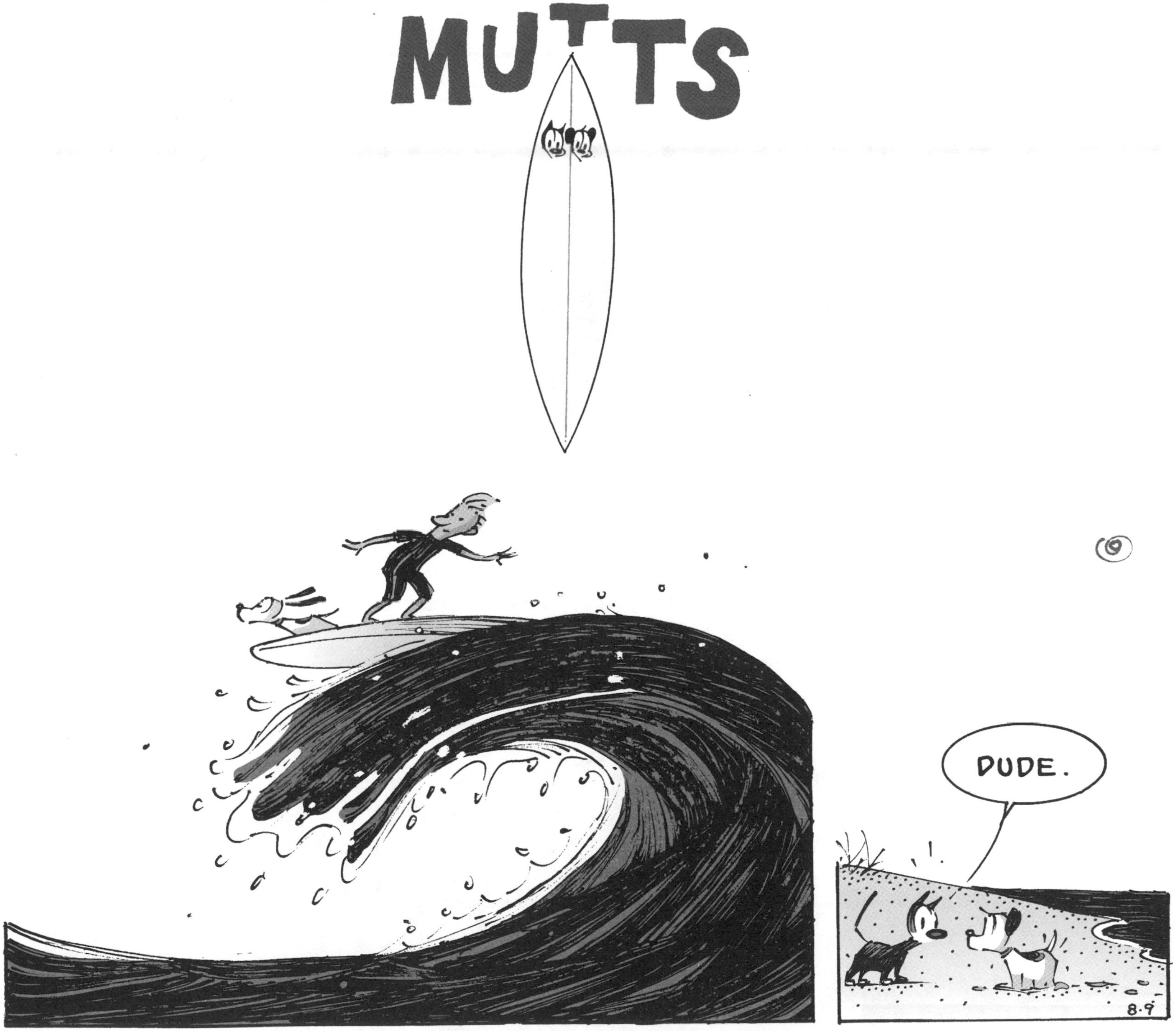
MUTTS
DUDE.
8·9

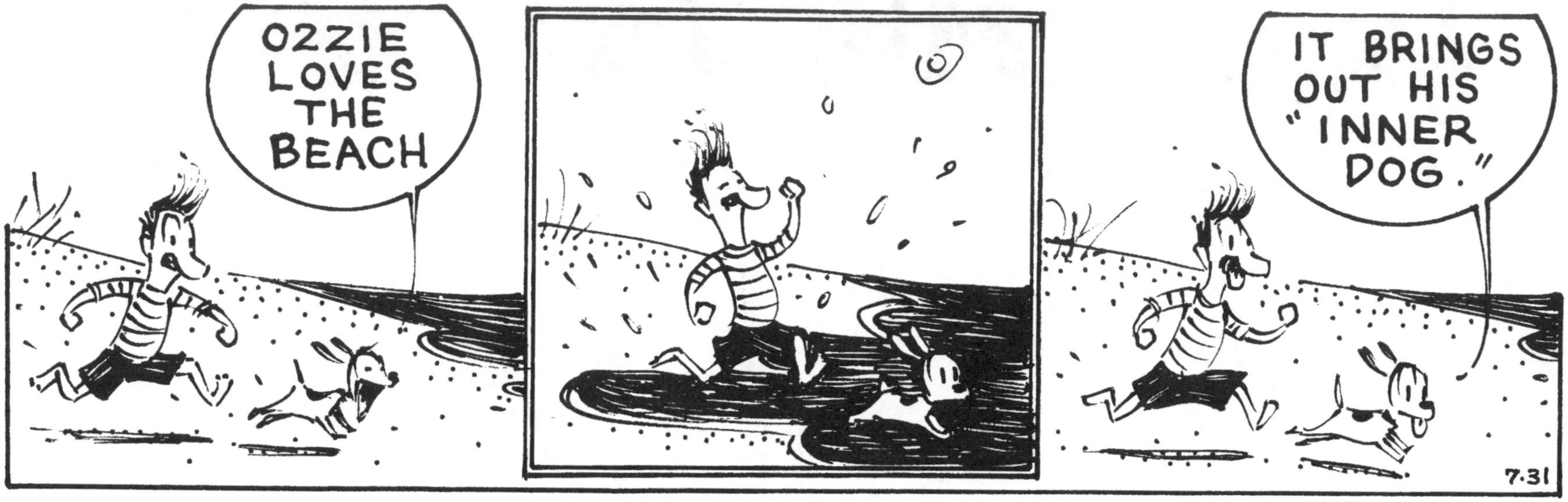
OZZIE LOVES THE BEACH
IT BRINGS OUT HIS "INNER DOG."
7·31

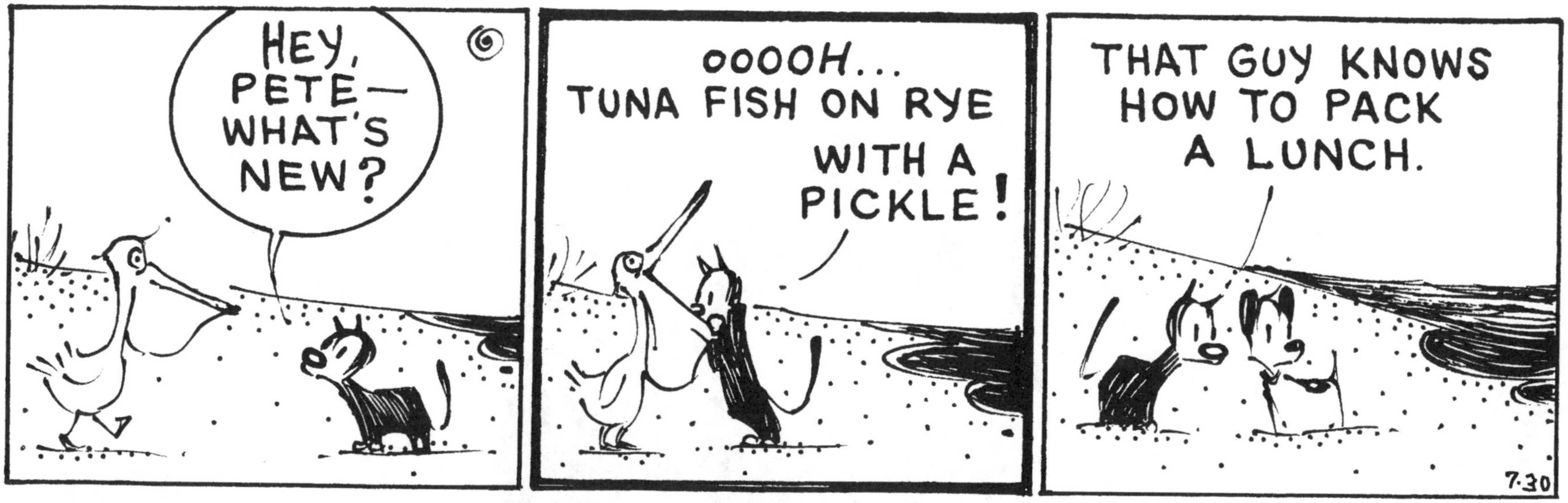
HEY, PETE—WHAT'S NEW?
OOOOH... TUNA FISH ON RYE
WITH A PICKLE!
THAT GUY KNOWS HOW TO PACK A LUNCH.
7·30

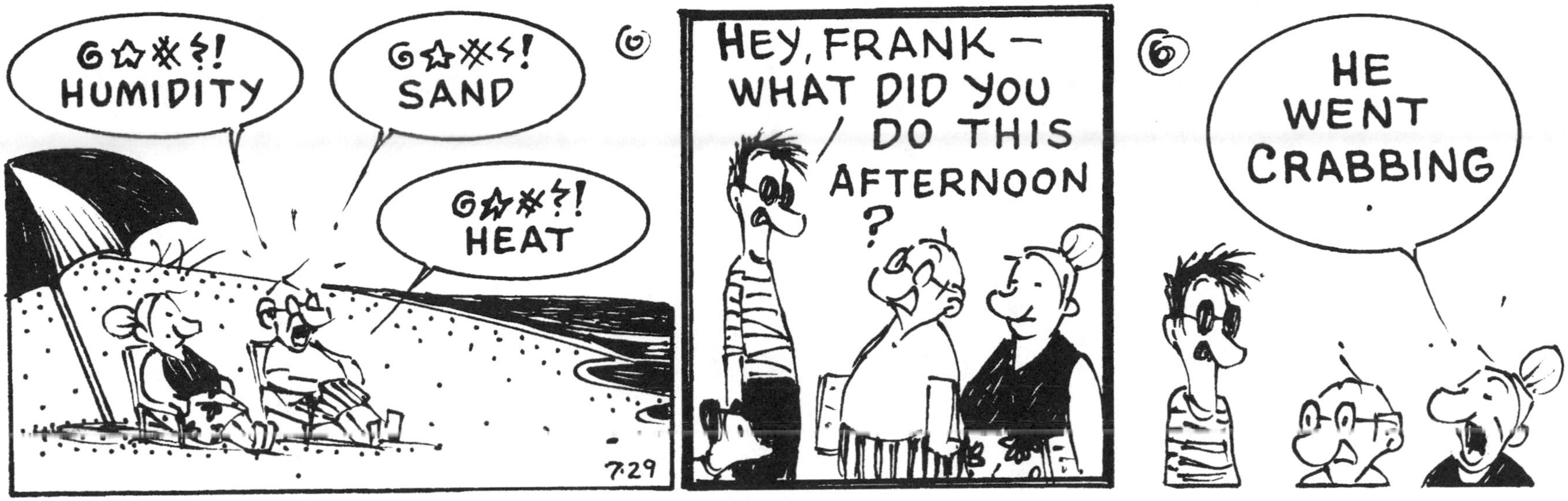
G☆※?! HUMIDITY
G☆※?! SAND
G☆※?! HEAT
7·29
HEY, FRANK — WHAT DID YOU DO THIS AFTERNOON
?
HE WENT CRABBING

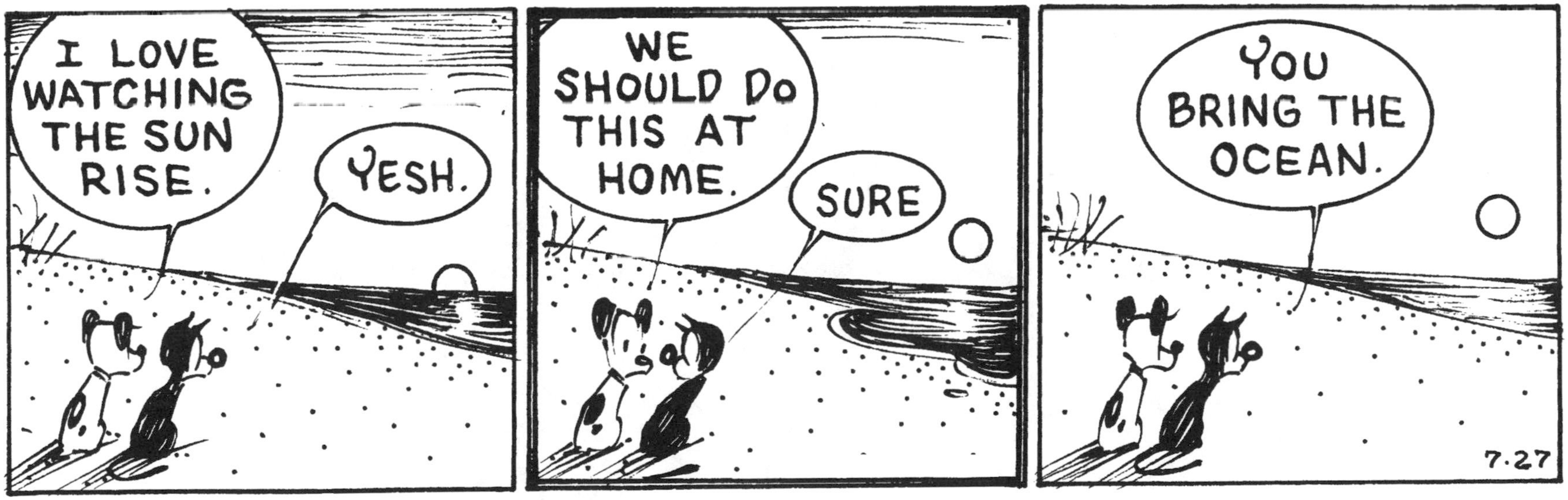
I LOVE WATCHING THE SUN RISE.
YESH.
WE SHOULD DO THIS AT HOME.
SURE
YOU BRING THE OCEAN.
7·27

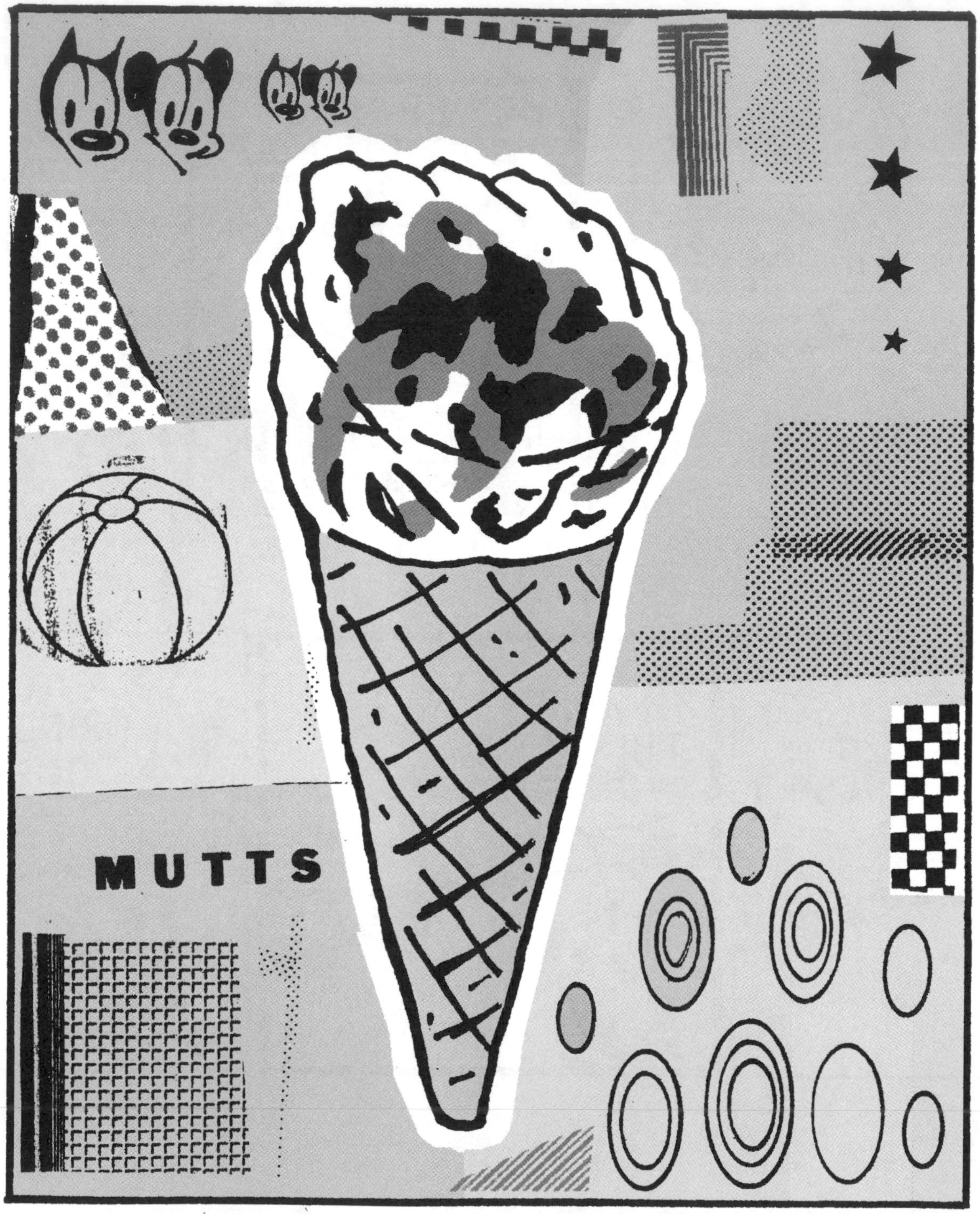
MUTTS

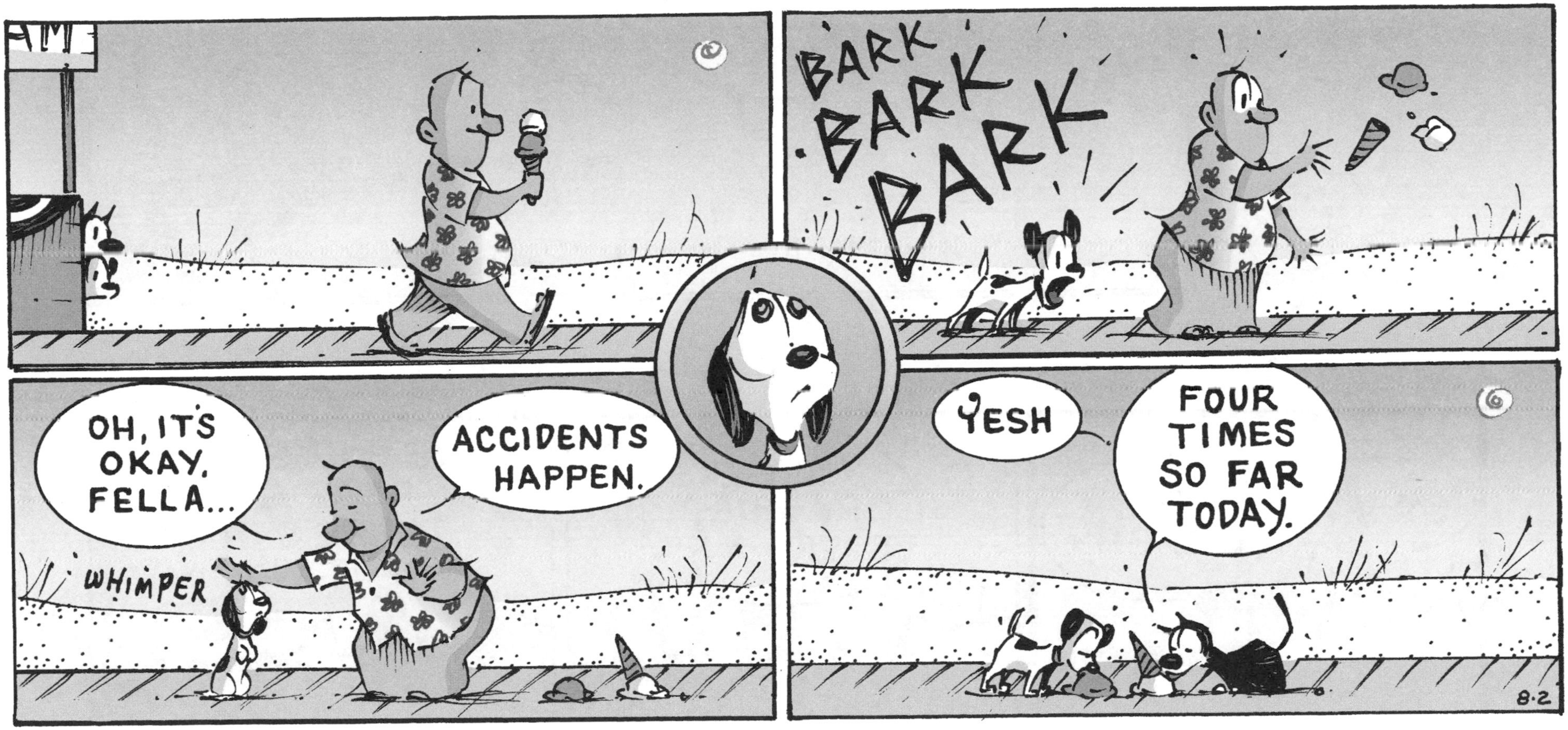
AM
BARK
BARK
BARK
OH, IT'S OKAY, FELLA...
ACCIDENTS HAPPEN.
WHIMPER
YESH
FOUR TIMES SO FAR TODAY.
8·2

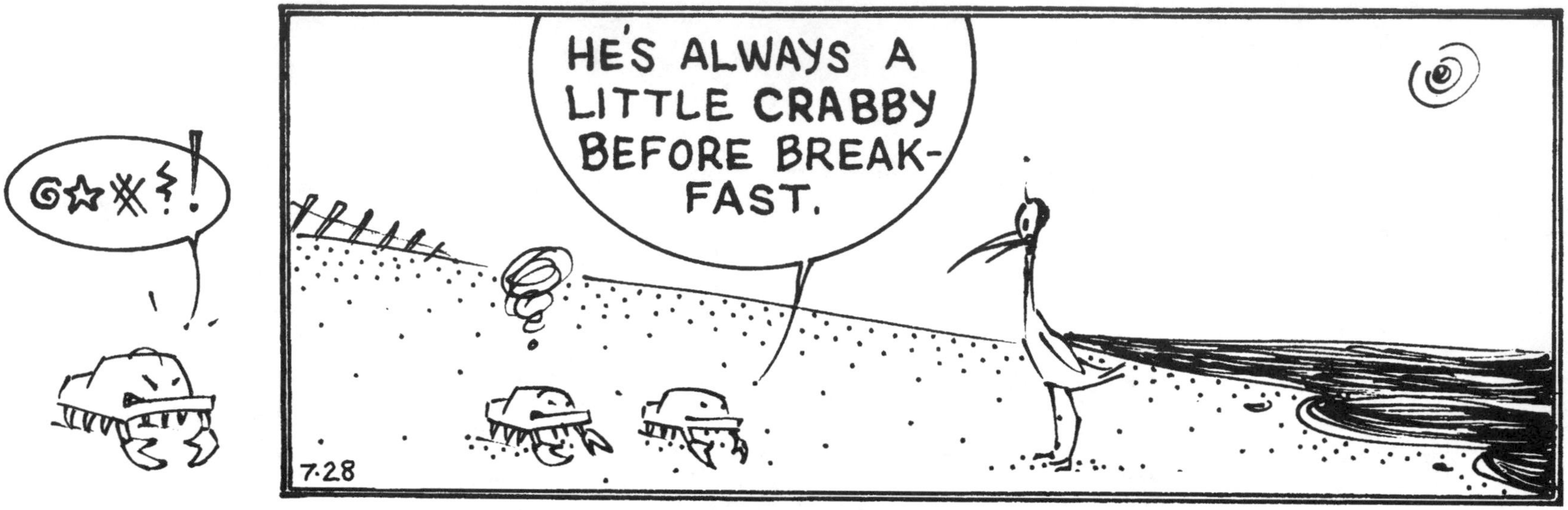
HE'S ALWAYS A LITTLE CRABBY BEFORE BREAK-FAST.
7·28

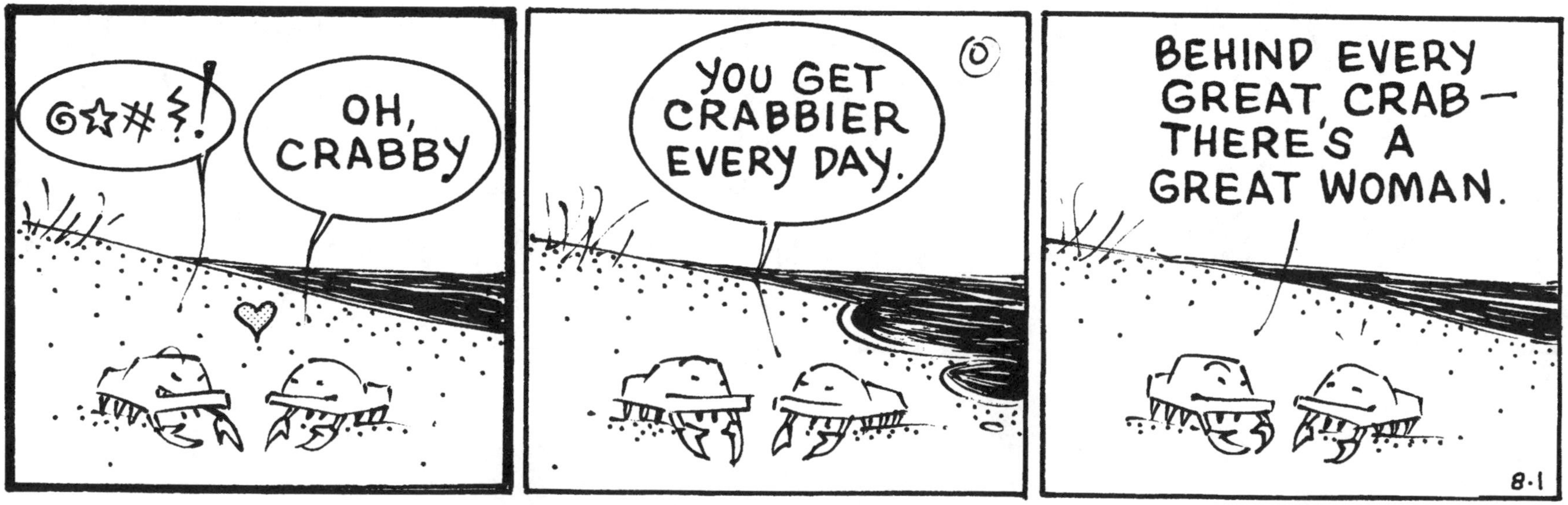
OH, CRABBY
YOU GET CRABBIER EVERY DAY.
BEHIND EVERY GREAT CRAB— THERE'S A GREAT WOMAN.
8·1

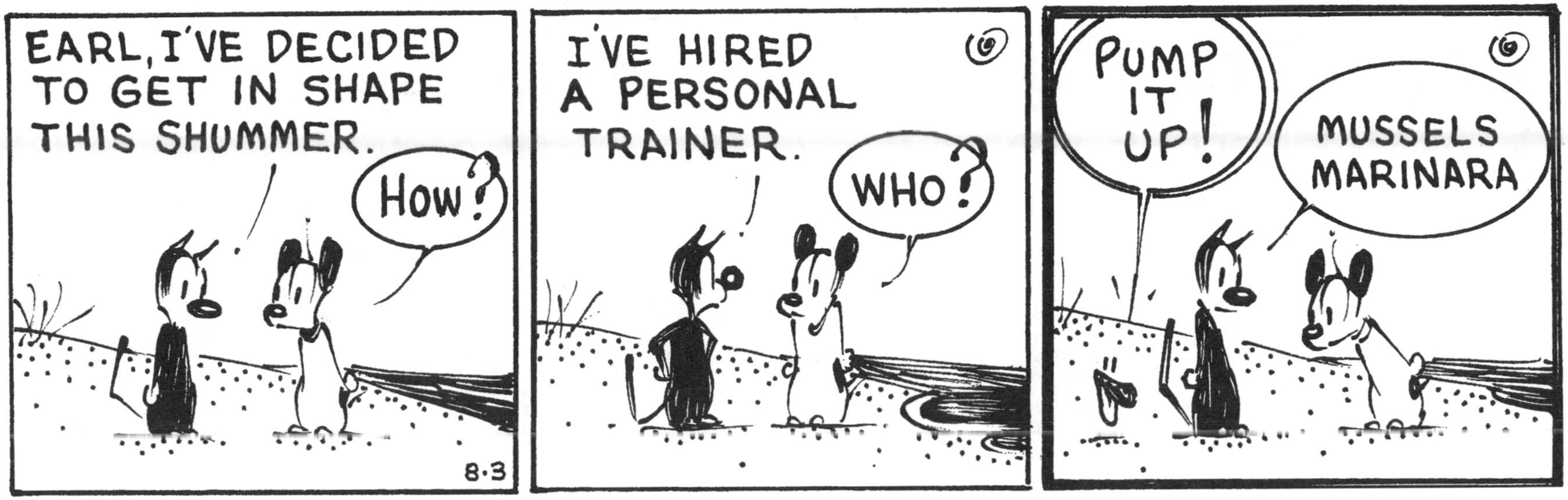
EARL, I'VE DECIDED TO GET IN SHAPE THIS SHUMMER.
HOW?
8·3
I'VE HIRED A PERSONAL TRAINER.
WHO?
PUMP IT UP!
MUSSELS MARINARA

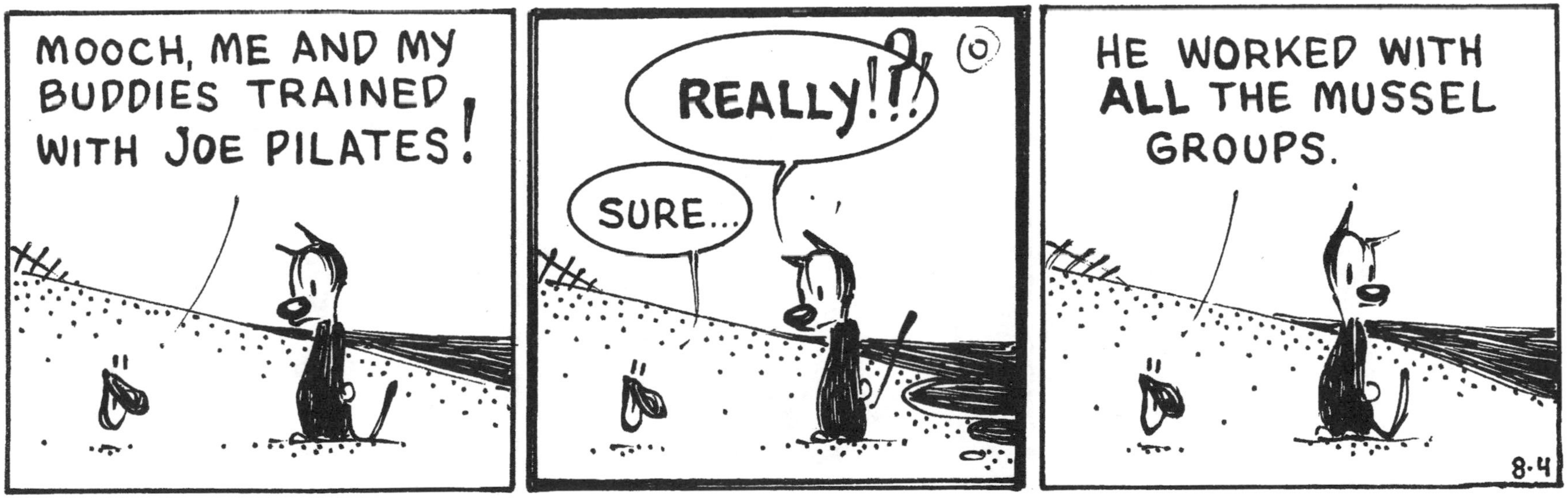
MOOCH, ME AND MY BUDDIES TRAINED WITH JOE PILATES!
REALLY!?!
SURE...
HE WORKED WITH ALL THE MUSSEL GROUPS.
8·4

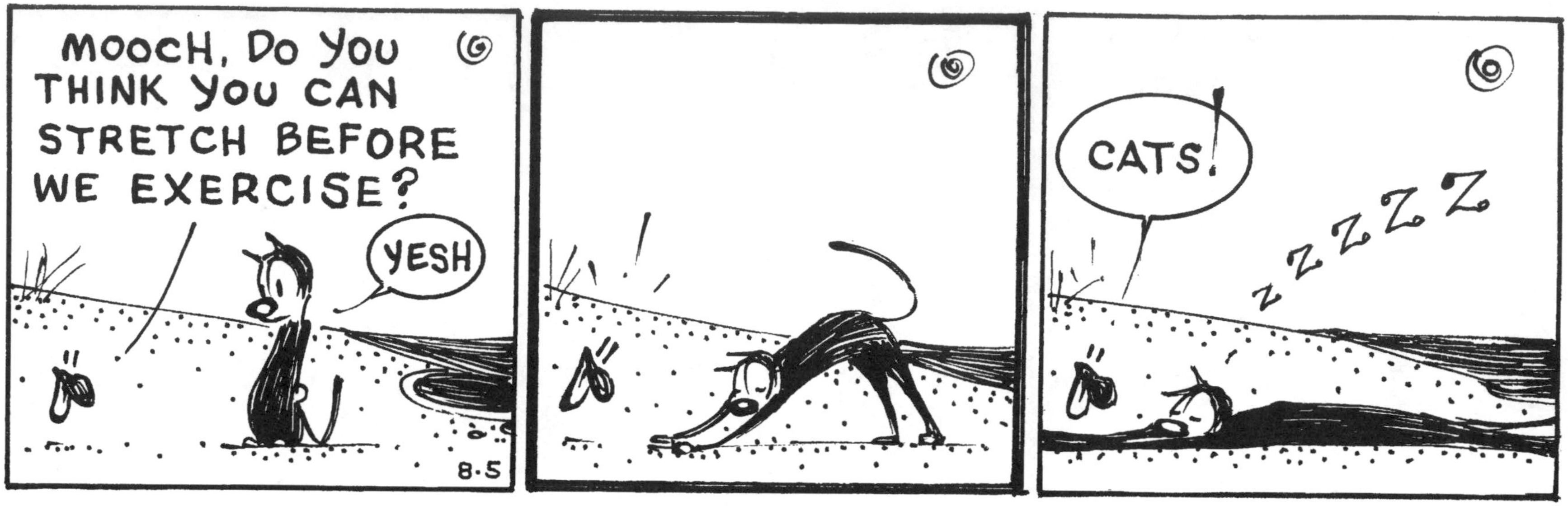
MOOCH, DO YOU THINK YOU CAN STRETCH BEFORE WE EXERCISE?
YESH
CATS!
ZZZZZZ
8·5

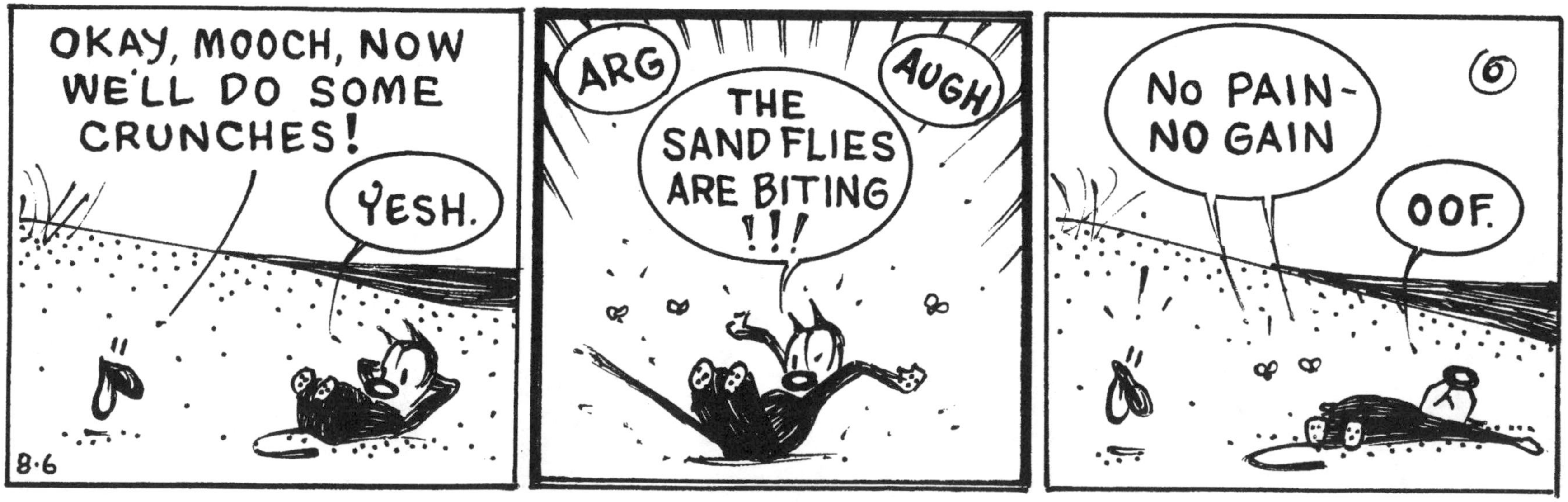
OKAY, MOOCH, NOW WE'LL DO SOME CRUNCHES!
YESH.
8·6
ARG
AUGH
THE SAND FLIES ARE BITING !!!
NO PAIN-NO GAIN
OOF.

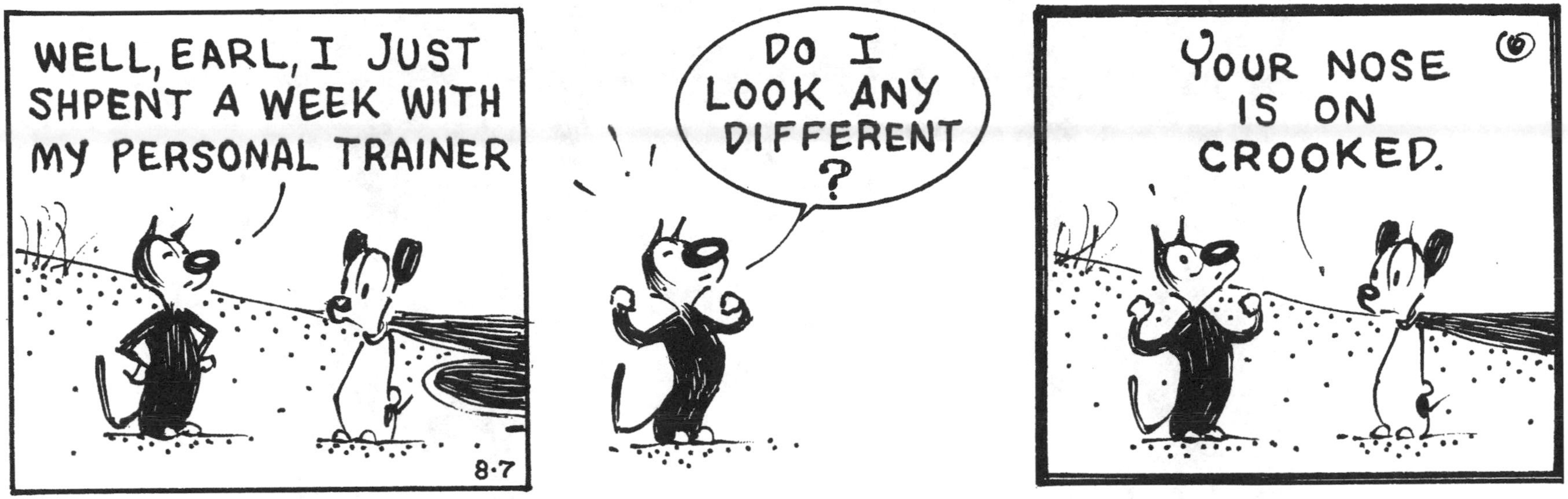
WELL, EARL, I JUST SHPENT A WEEK WITH MY PERSONAL TRAINER
8·7
DO I LOOK ANY DIFFERENT ?
YOUR NOSE IS ON CROOKED.

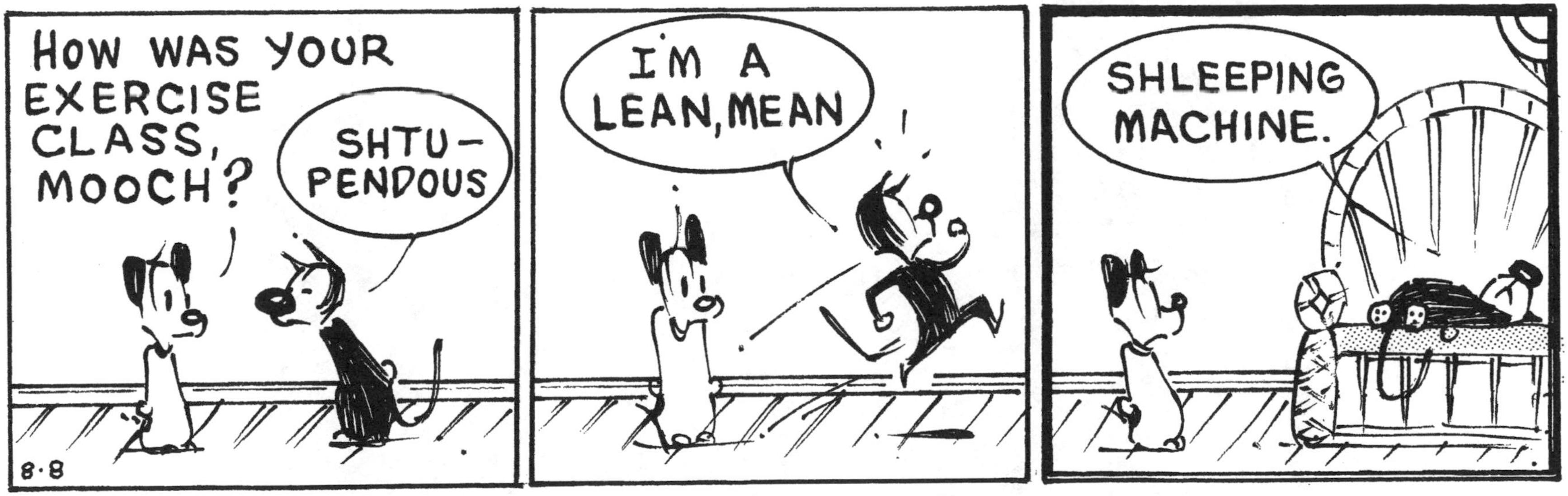
HOW WAS YOUR EXERCISE CLASS, MOOCH?
SHTU-PENDOUS
8·8
I'M A LEAN, MEAN
SHLEEPING MACHINE.

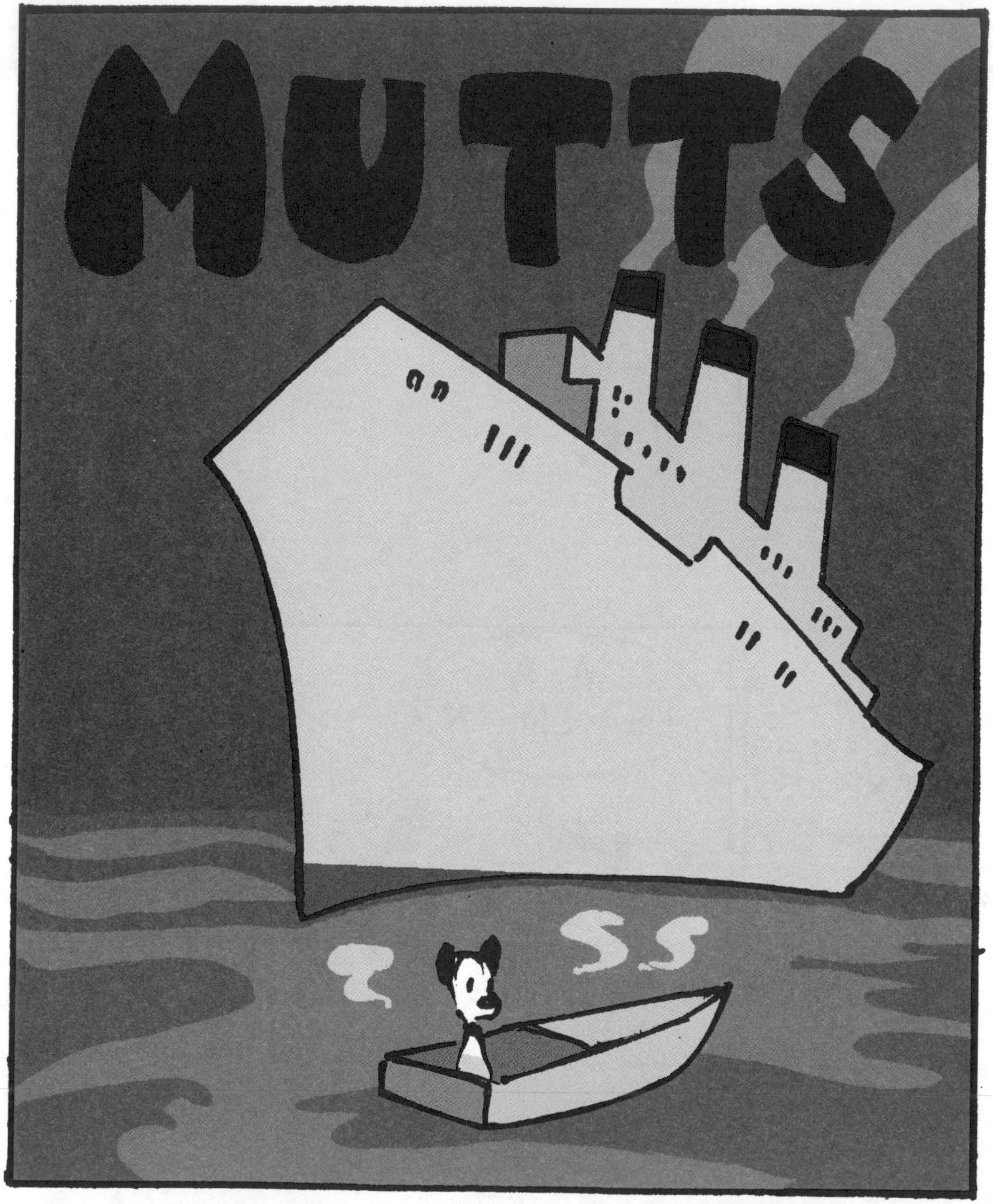
MUTTS

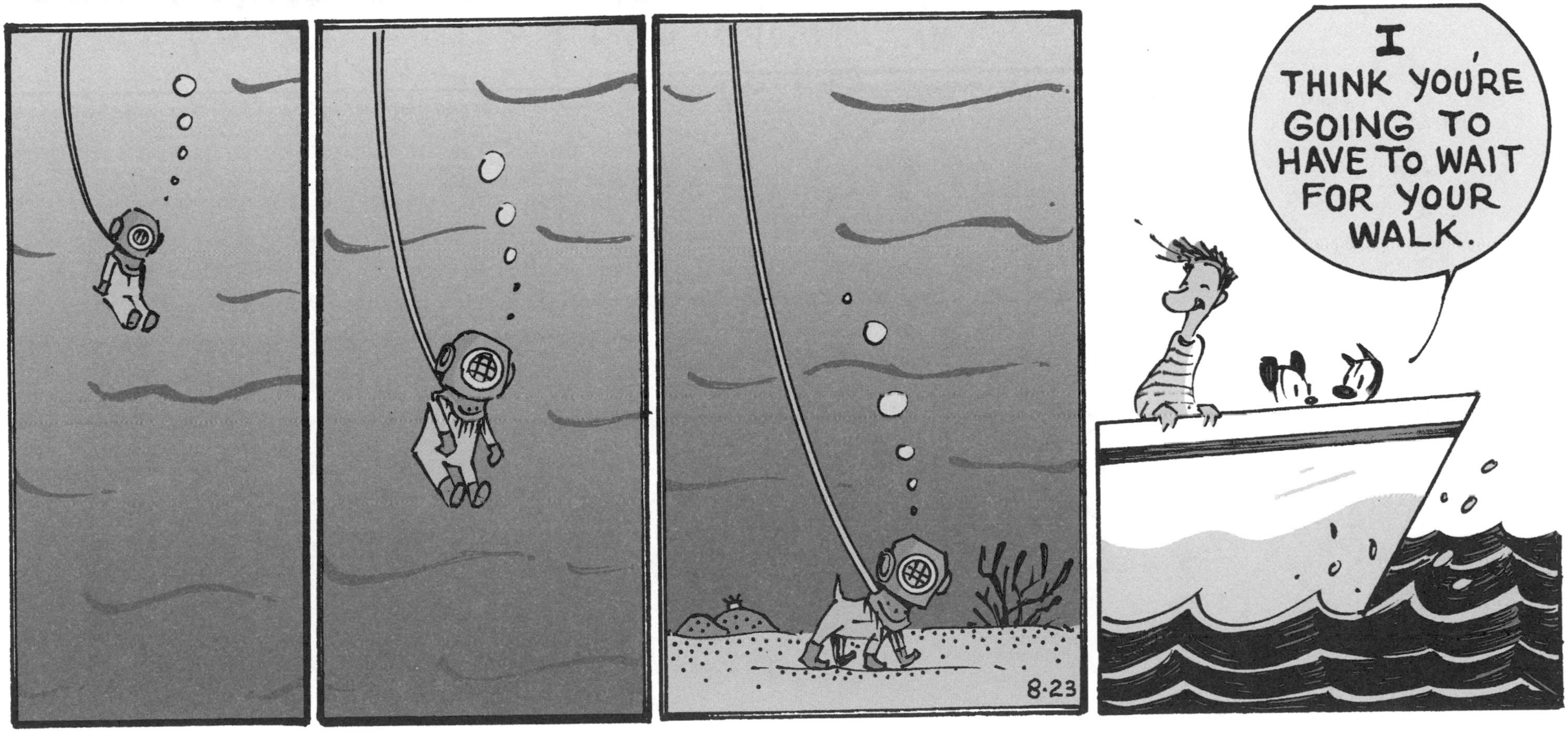
8·23
I THINK YOU'RE GOING TO HAVE TO WAIT FOR YOUR WALK.

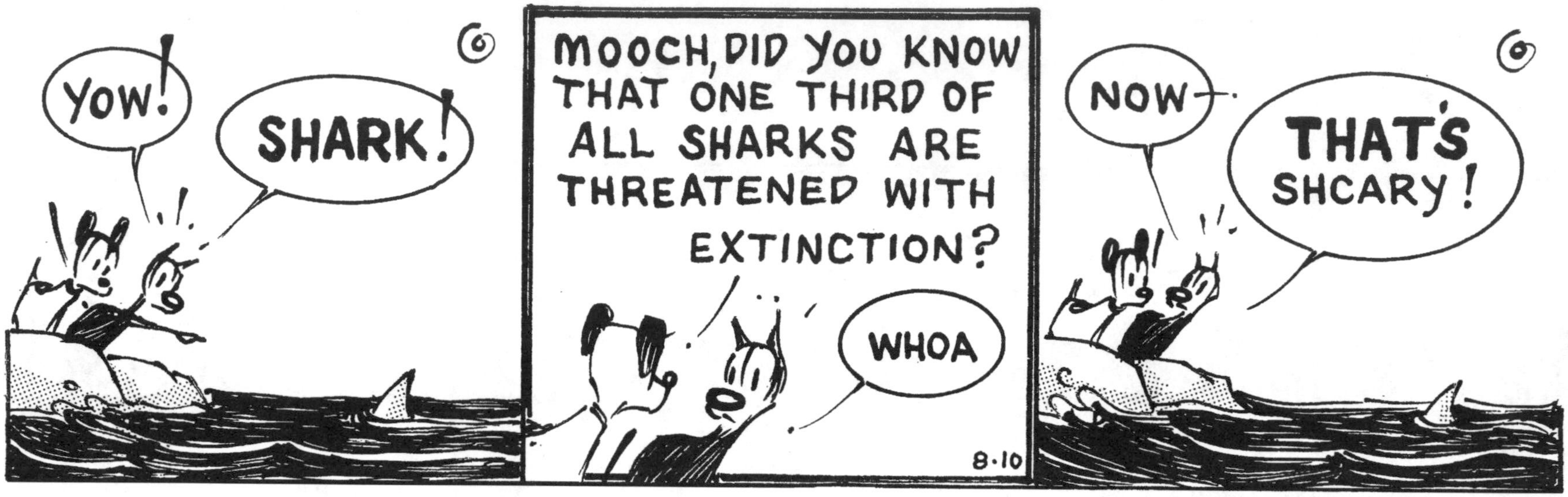
YOW!
SHARK!
MOOCH, DID YOU KNOW THAT ONE THIRD OF ALL SHARKS ARE THREATENED WITH EXTINCTION?
WHOA
8·10
NOW-
THAT'S SHCARY!

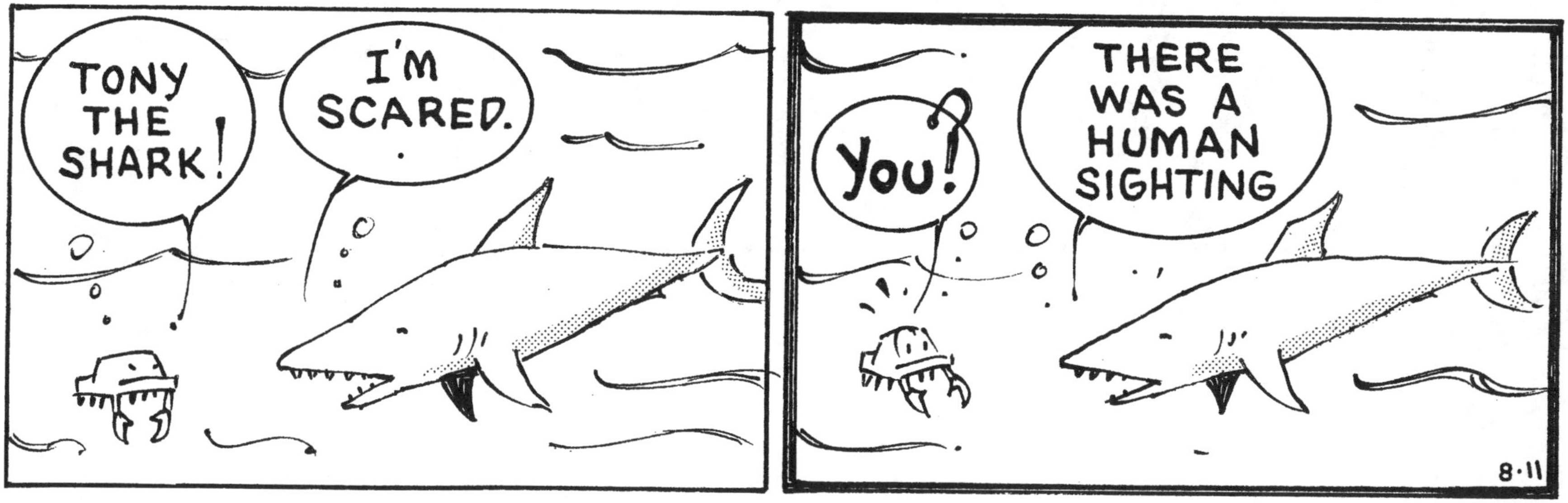
TONY THE SHARK!
I'M SCARED.
YOU!
THERE WAS A HUMAN SIGHTING
8·11

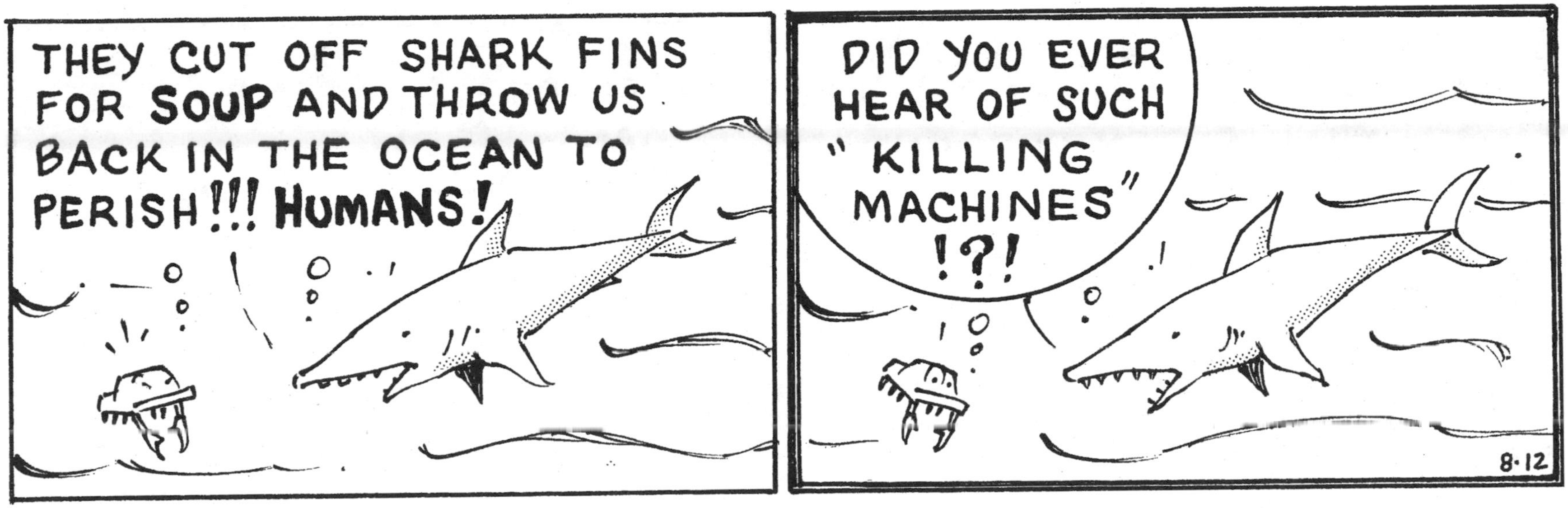
THEY CUT OFF SHARK FINS FOR SOUP AND THROW US BACK IN THE OCEAN TO PERISH!!! HUMANS!
DID YOU EVER HEAR OF SUCH "KILLING MACHINES" !?!
8·12

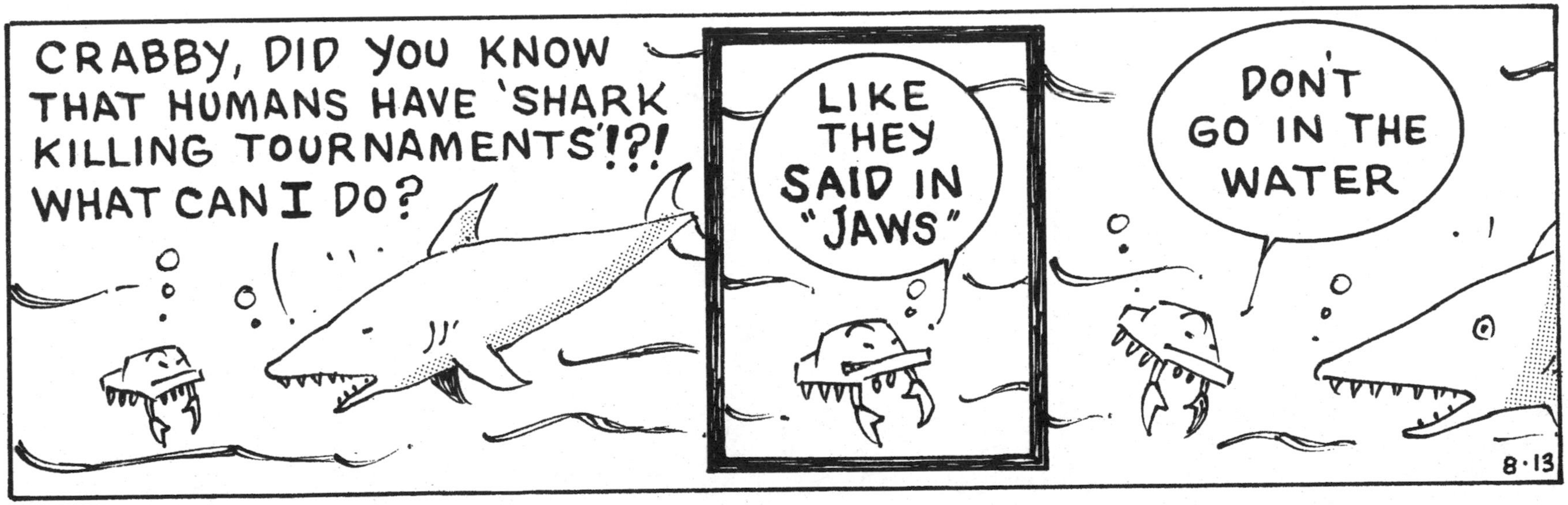
CRABBY, DID YOU KNOW THAT HUMANS HAVE 'SHARK KILLING TOURNAMENTS'!?! WHAT CAN I DO?
LIKE THEY SAID IN "JAWS"
DON'T GO IN THE WATER
8·13

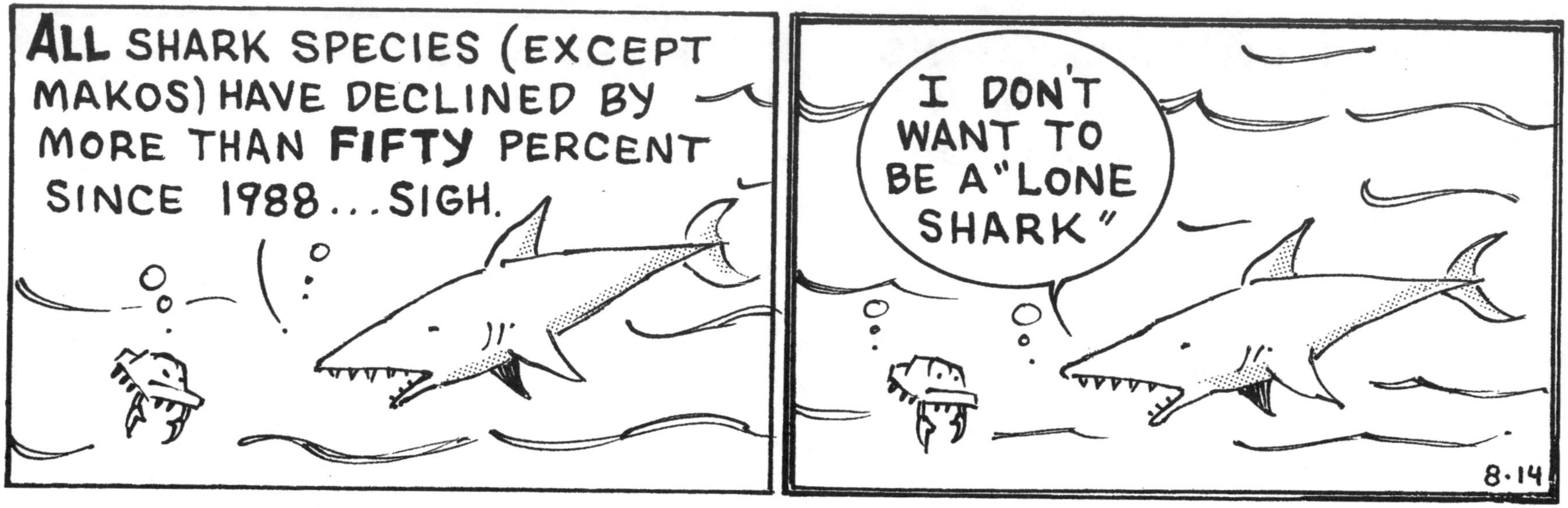
ALL SHARK SPECIES (EXCEPT MAKOS) HAVE DECLINED BY MORE THAN FIFTY PERCENT SINCE 1988... SIGH.
I DON'T WANT TO BE A "LONE SHARK"
8·14

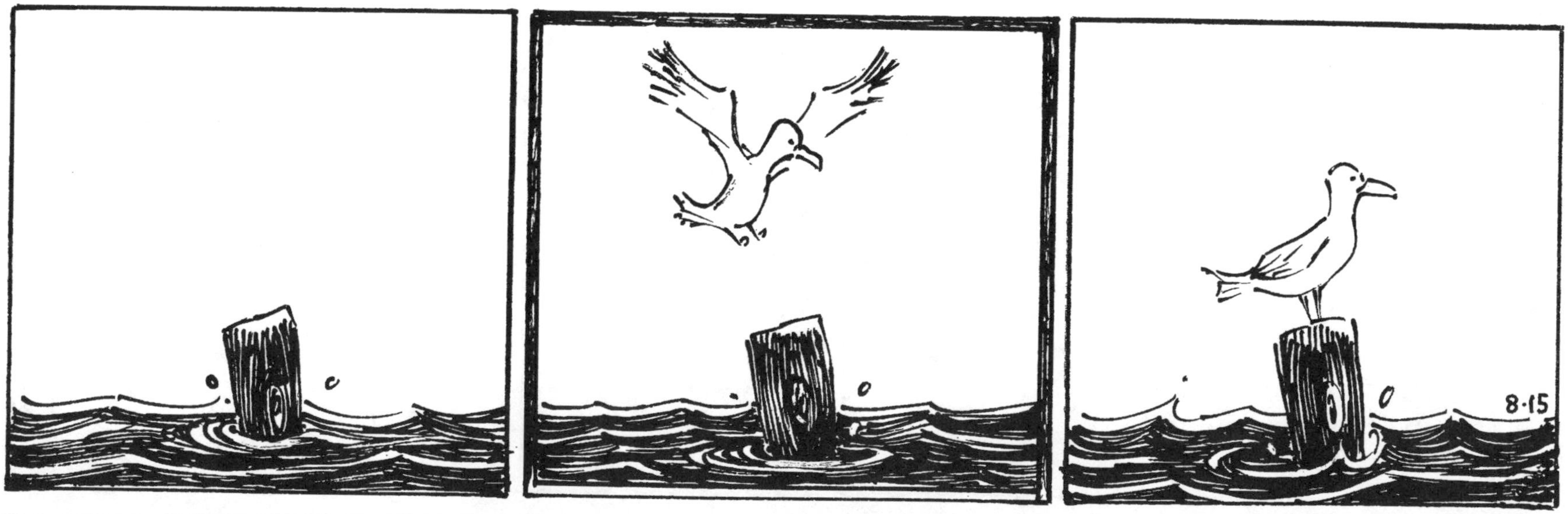
8·15

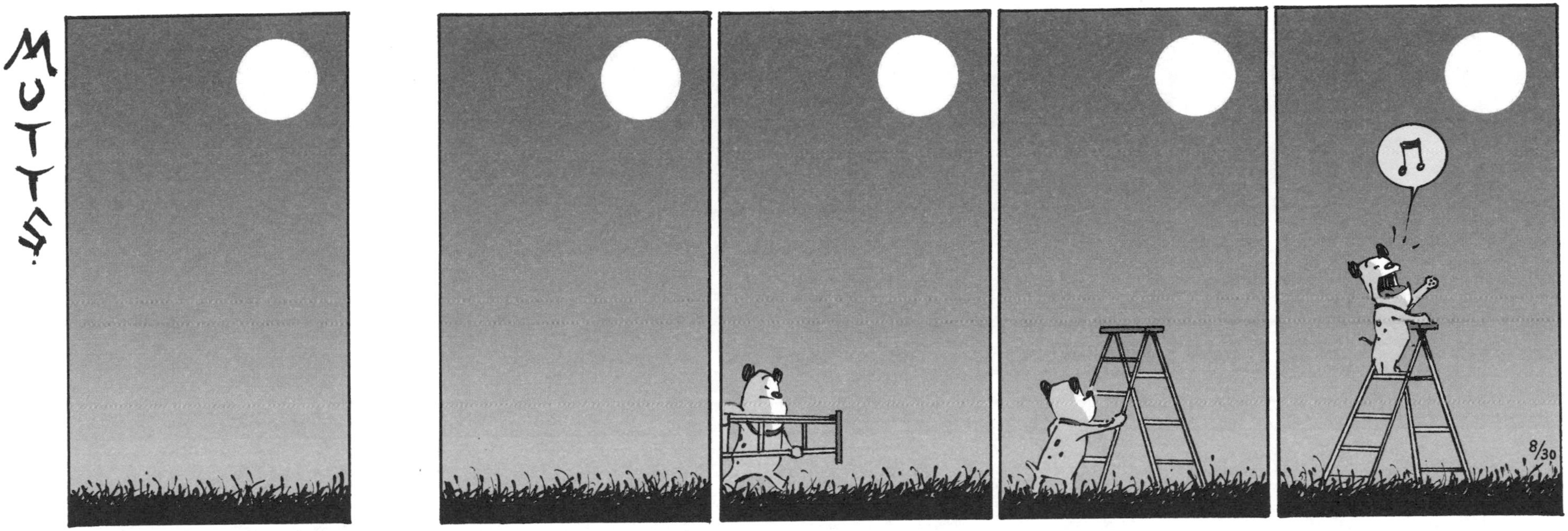
MUTTS
8/30

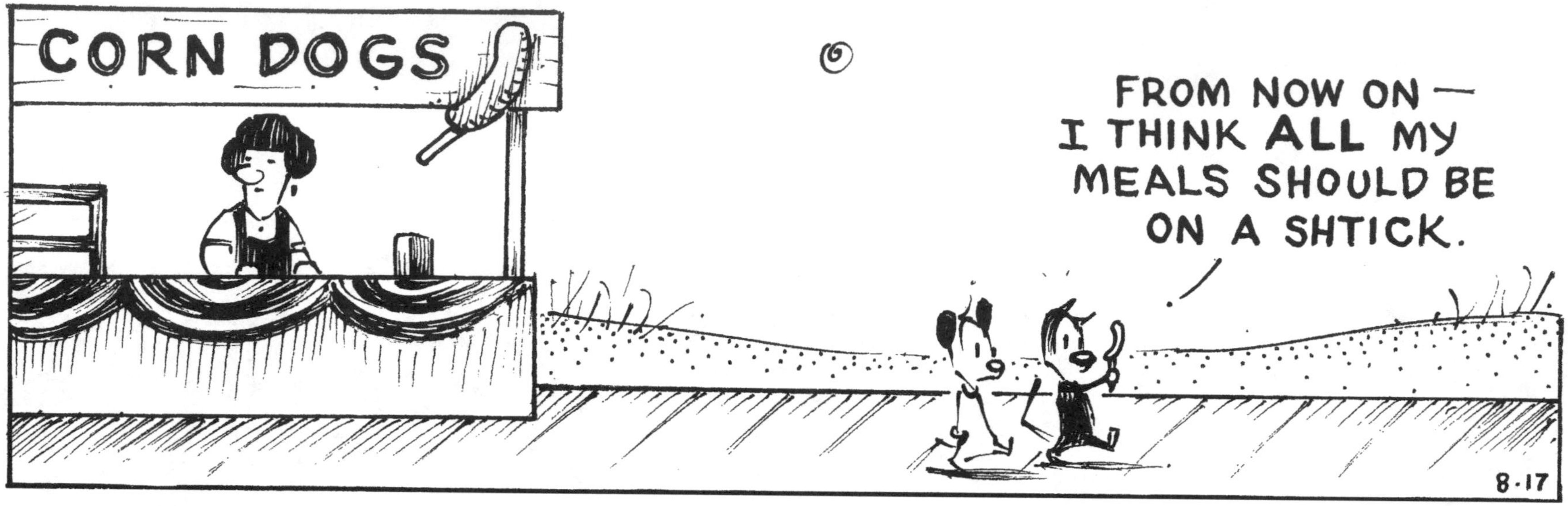
CORN DOGS
FROM NOW ON — I THINK ALL MY MEALS SHOULD BE ON A SHTICK.
8·17

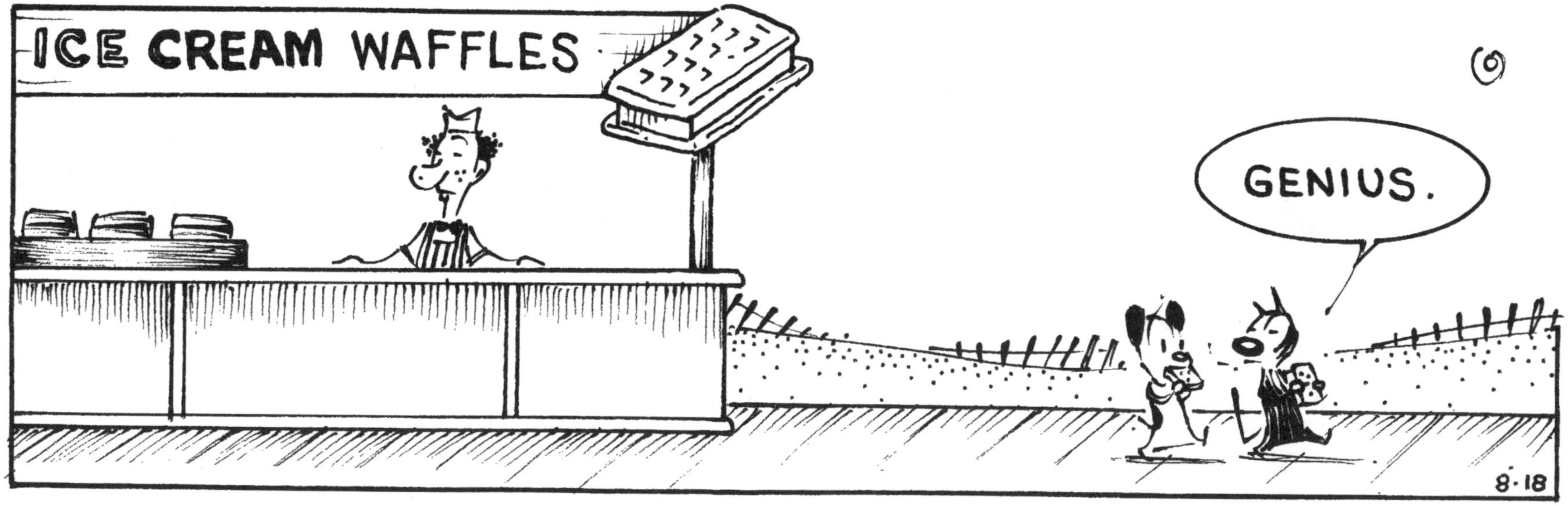
ICE CREAM WAFFLES
GENIUS.
8·18

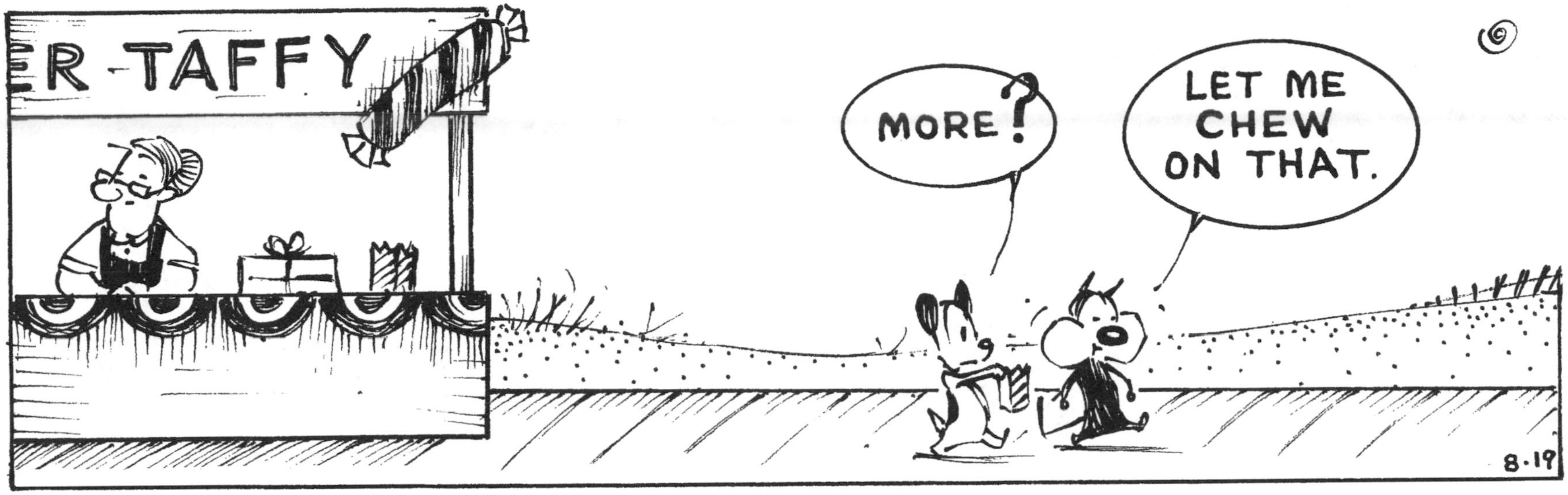
ER TAFFY
MORE?
LET ME CHEW ON THAT.
8·19

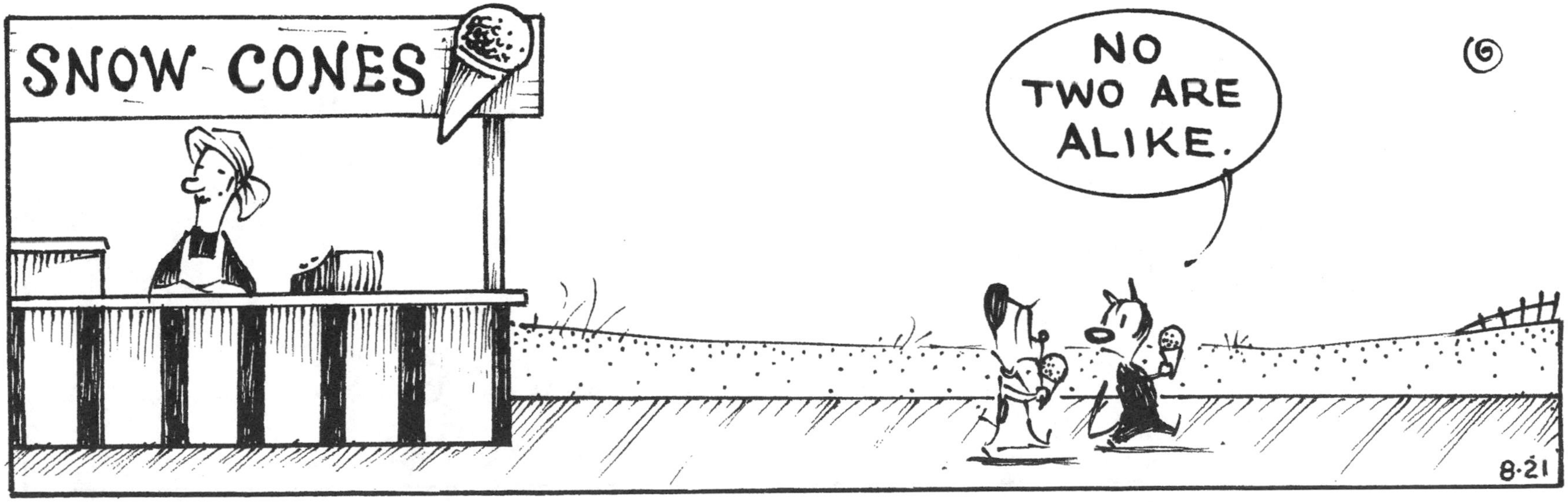
SNOW CONES
NO TWO ARE ALIKE.
8·21

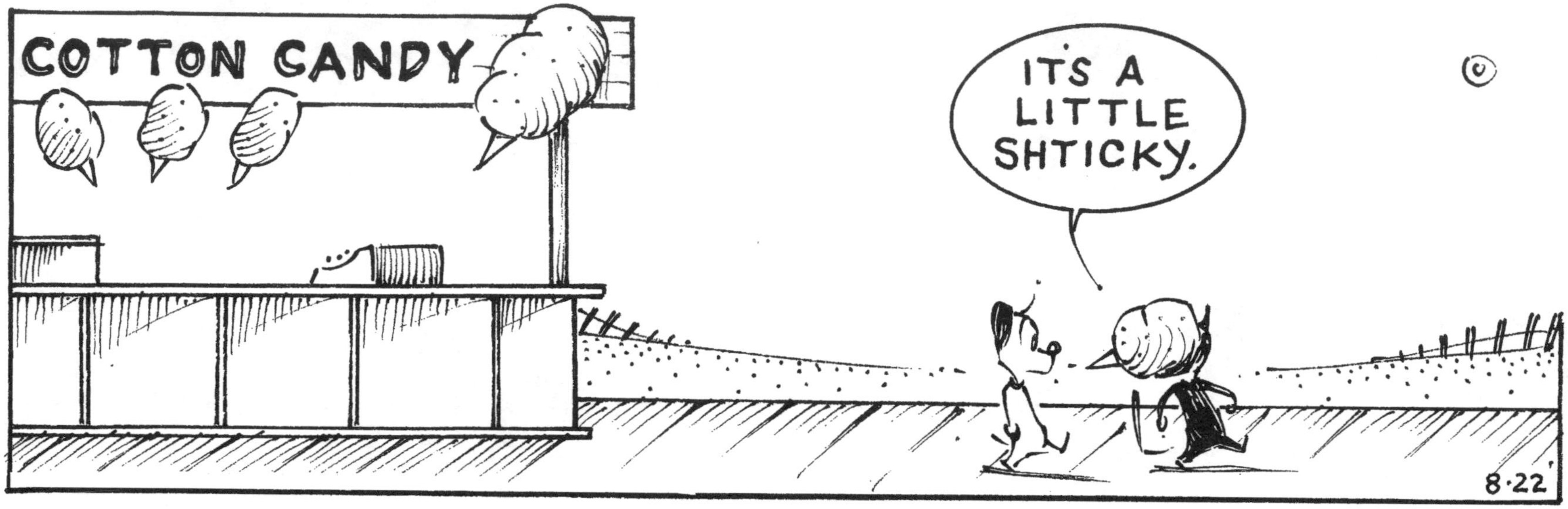
COTTON CANDY
ITS A LITTLE SHTICKY.
©
8·22

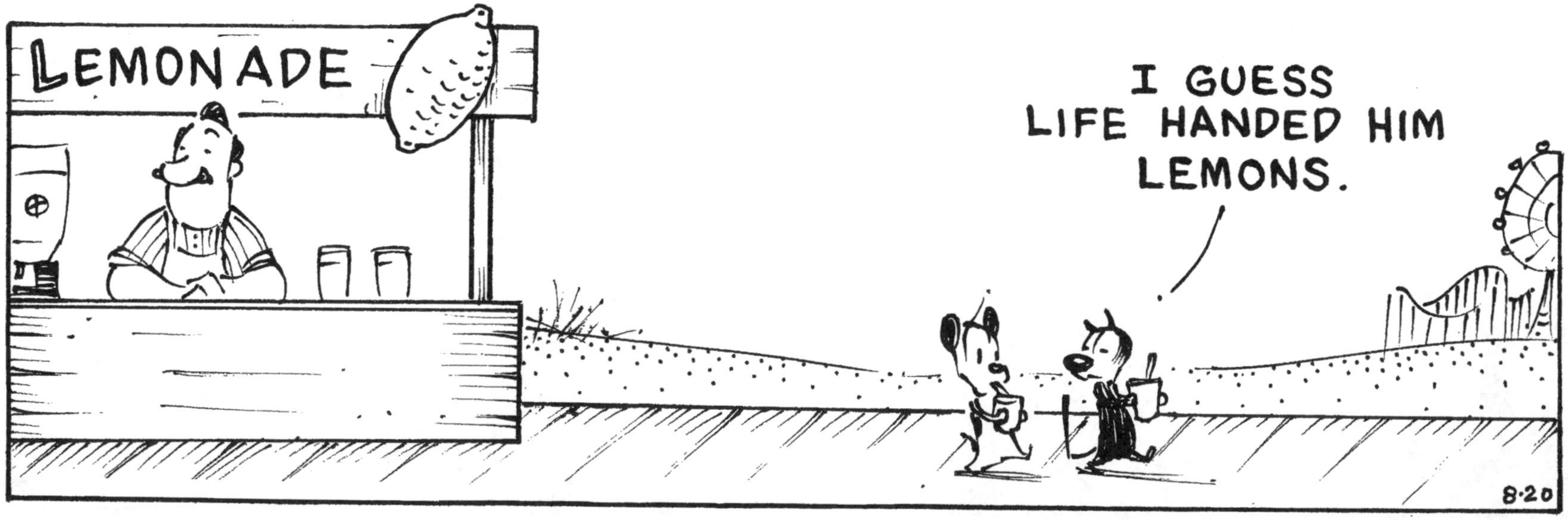
LEMONADE
I GUESS LIFE HANDED HIM LEMONS.
8·20

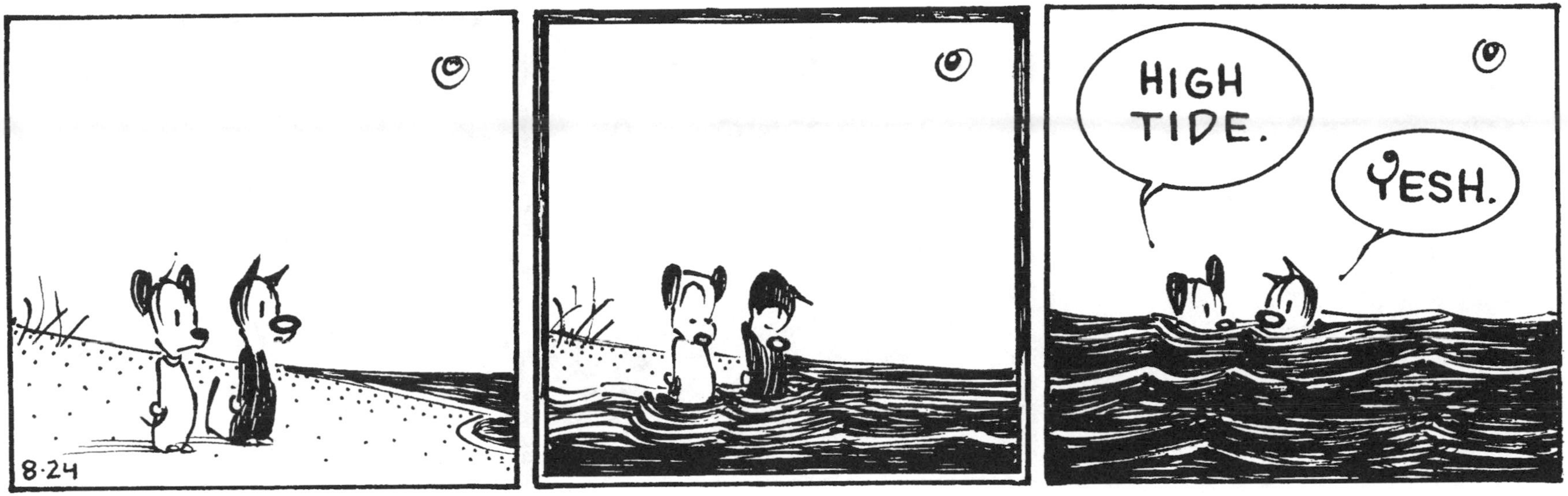
8·24
HIGH TIDE.
YESH.

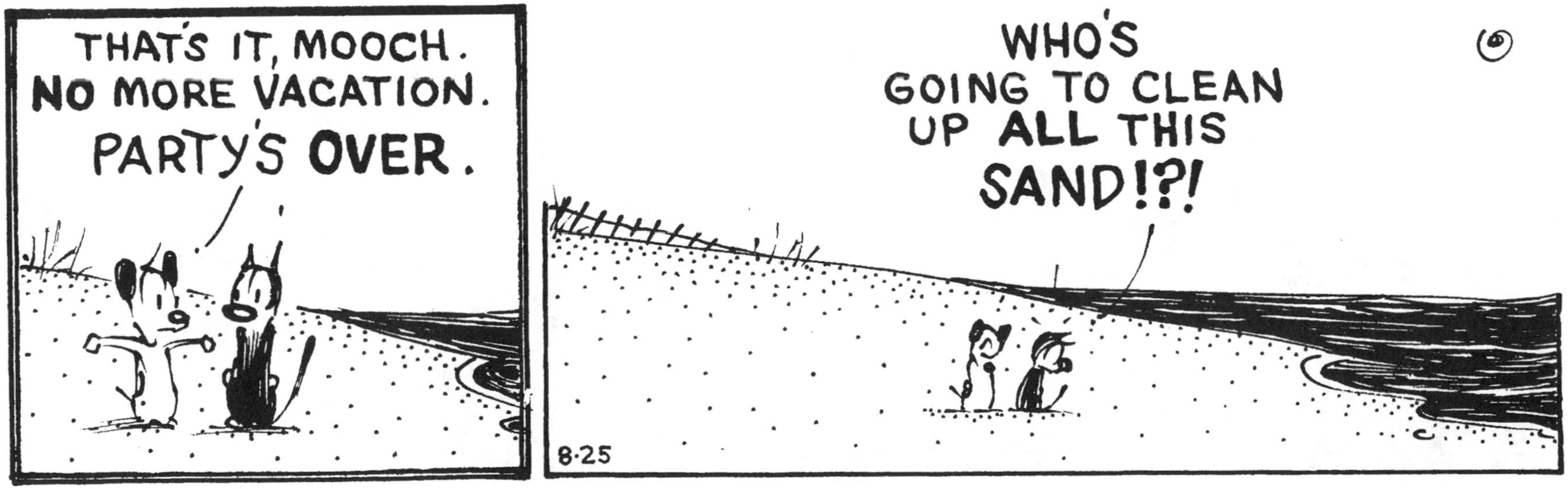
THAT'S IT, MOOCH. NO MORE VACATION. PARTY'S OVER.
8·25
WHO'S GOING TO CLEAN UP ALL THIS SAND!?!

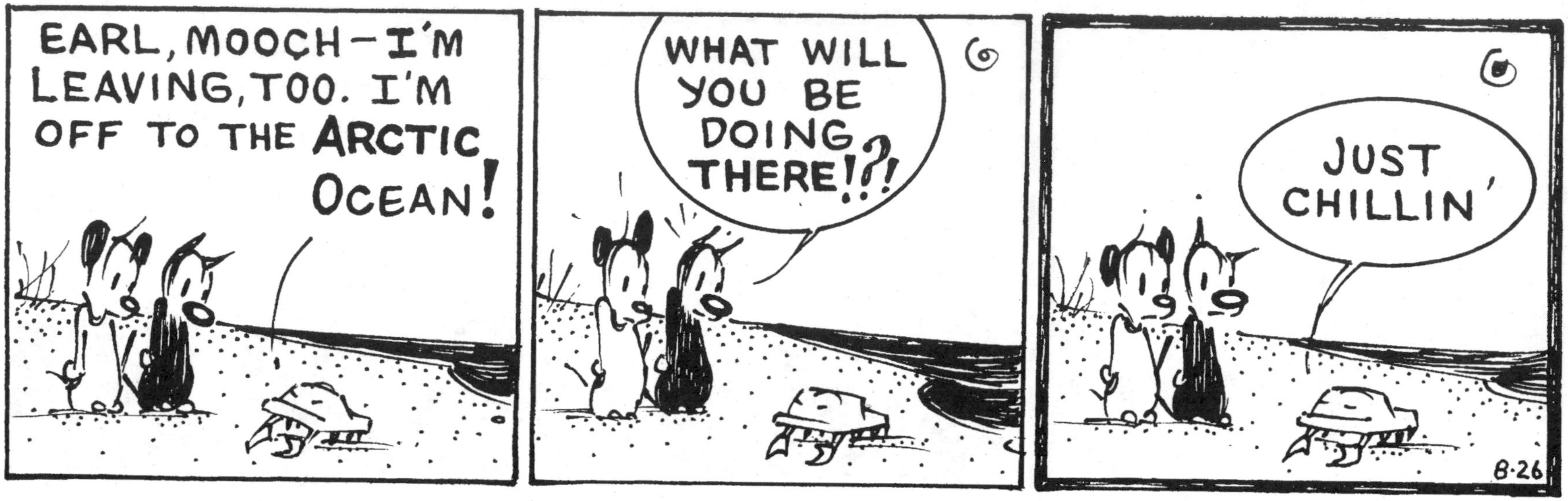
EARL, MOOCH – I'M LEAVING, TOO. I'M OFF TO THE ARCTIC OCEAN!
WHAT WILL YOU BE DOING THERE!?!
JUST CHILLIN'
8·26

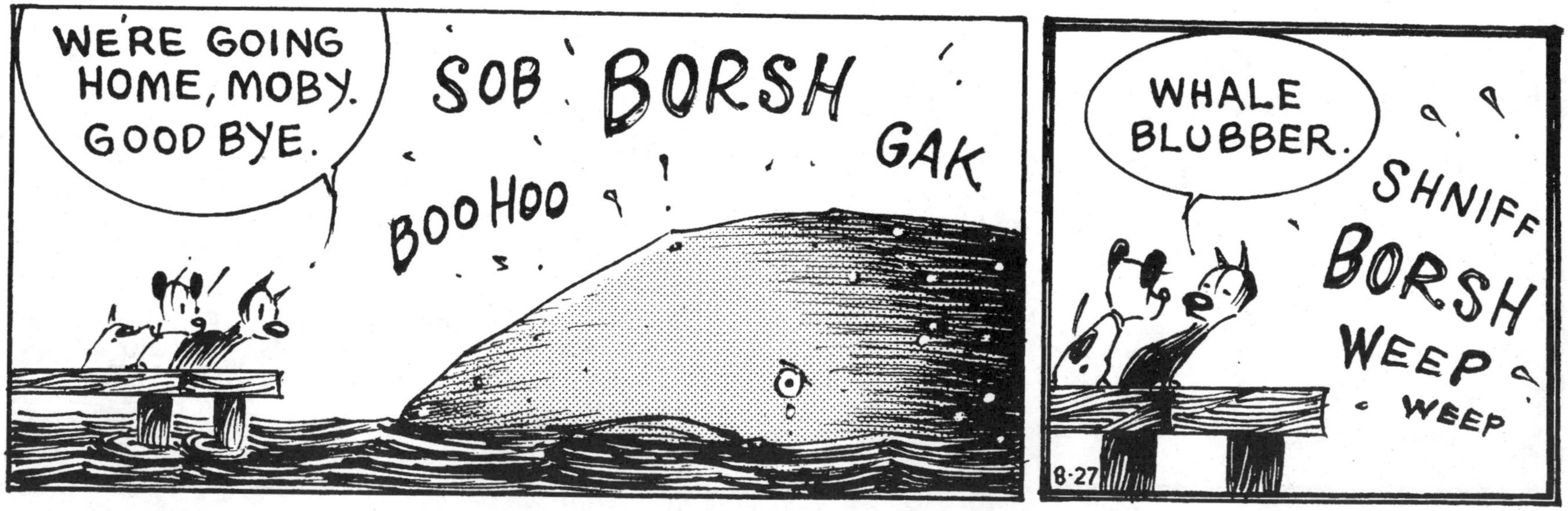
WE'RE GOING HOME, MOBY. GOODBYE.
SOB
BORSH
GAK
BOOHOO
WHALE BLUBBER.
SHNIFF
BORSH
WEEP
WEEP
8·27

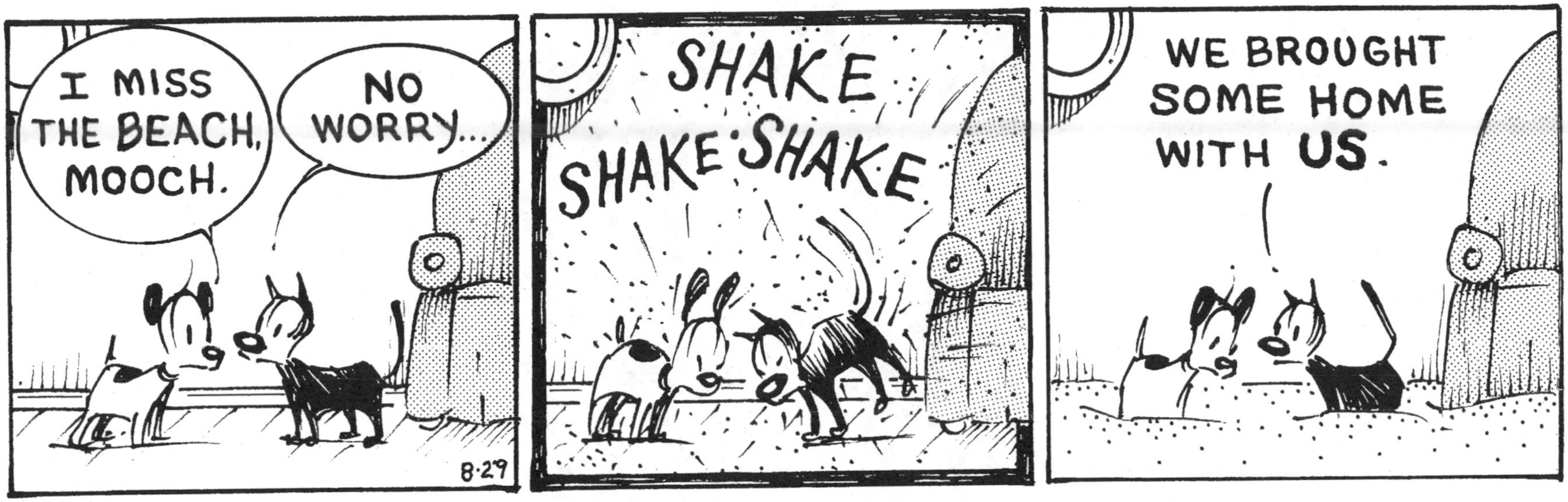
I MISS THE BEACH, MOOCH.
NO WORRY...
8·29
SHAKE SHAKE·SHAKE·SHAKE
WE BROUGHT SOME HOME WITH US.

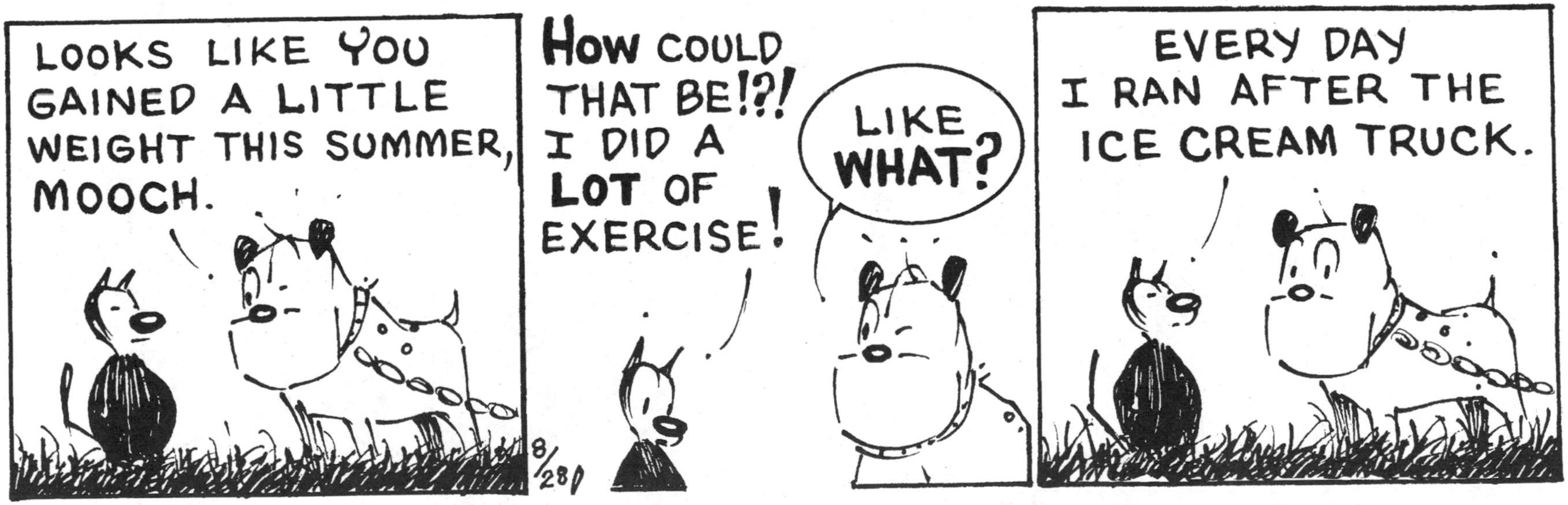
LOOKS LIKE YOU GAINED A LITTLE WEIGHT THIS SUMMER, MOOCH.
8/28
HOW COULD THAT BE!?! I DID A LOT OF EXERCISE!
LIKE WHAT?
EVERY DAY I RAN AFTER THE ICE CREAM TRUCK.

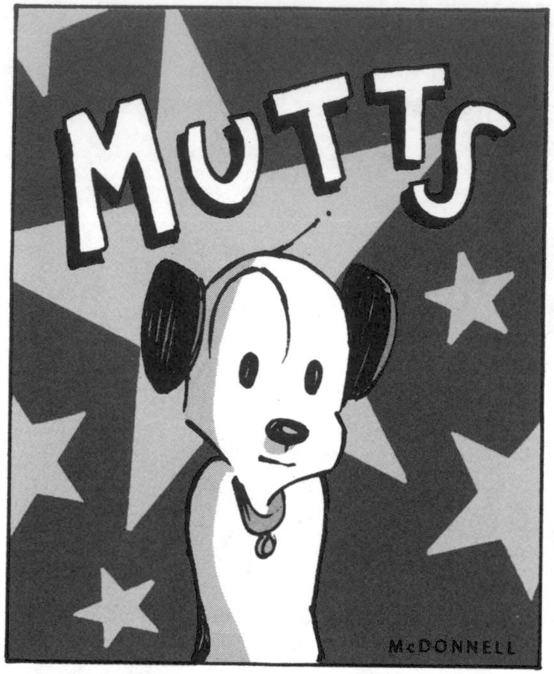
MUTTS
McDONNELL

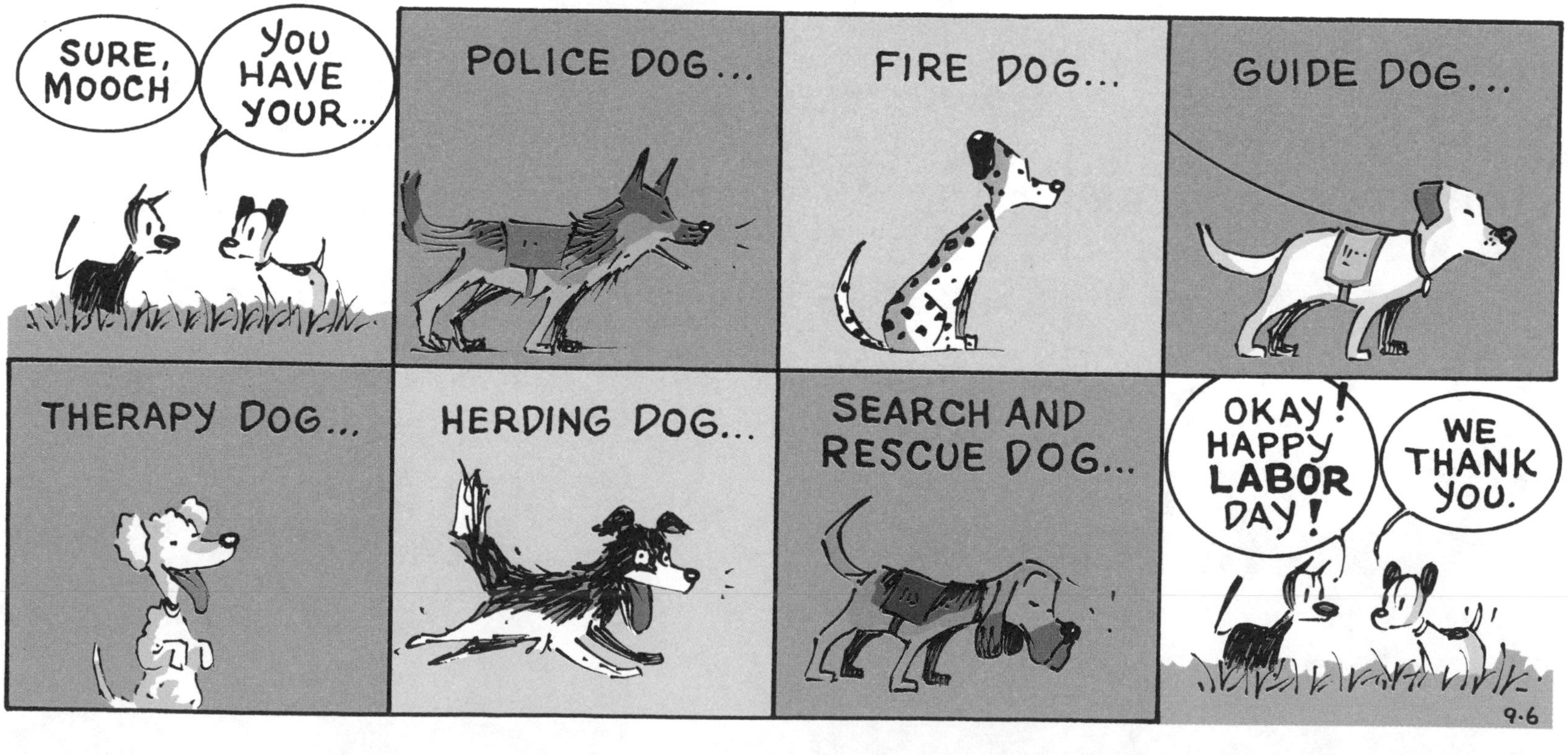
SURE, MOOCH
YOU HAVE YOUR...
POLICE DOG...
FIRE DOG...
GUIDE DOG...
THERAPY DOG...
HERDING DOG...
SEARCH AND RESCUE DOG...
OKAY! HAPPY LABOR DAY!
WE THANK YOU.
9·6

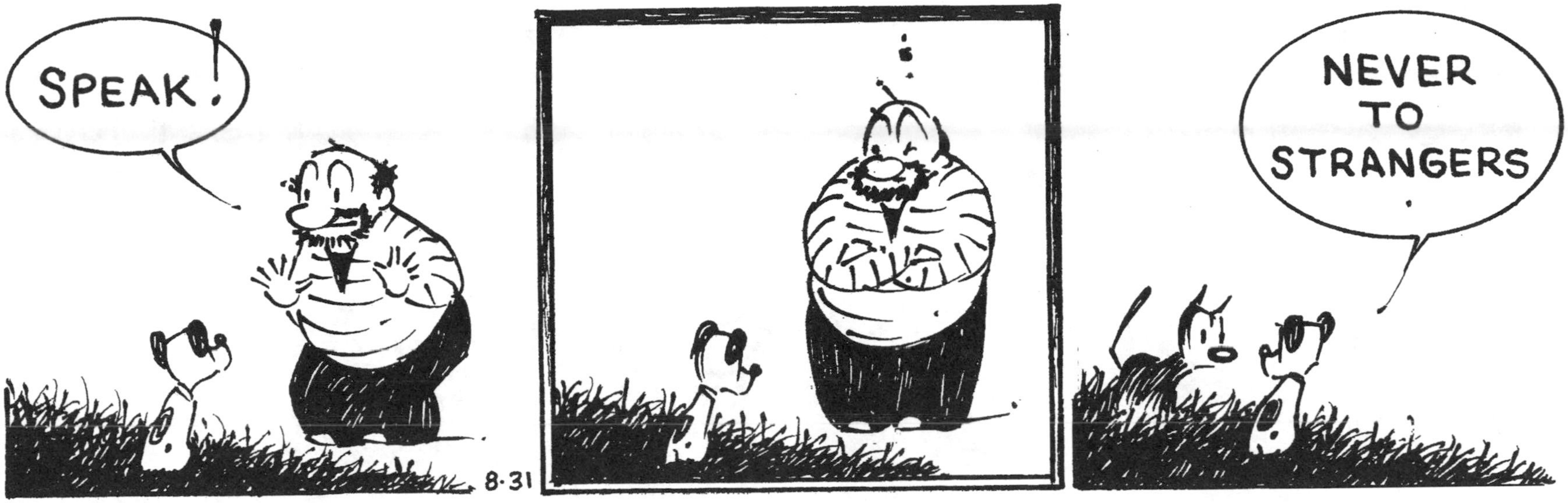
SPEAK!
8·31
NEVER TO STRANGERS.

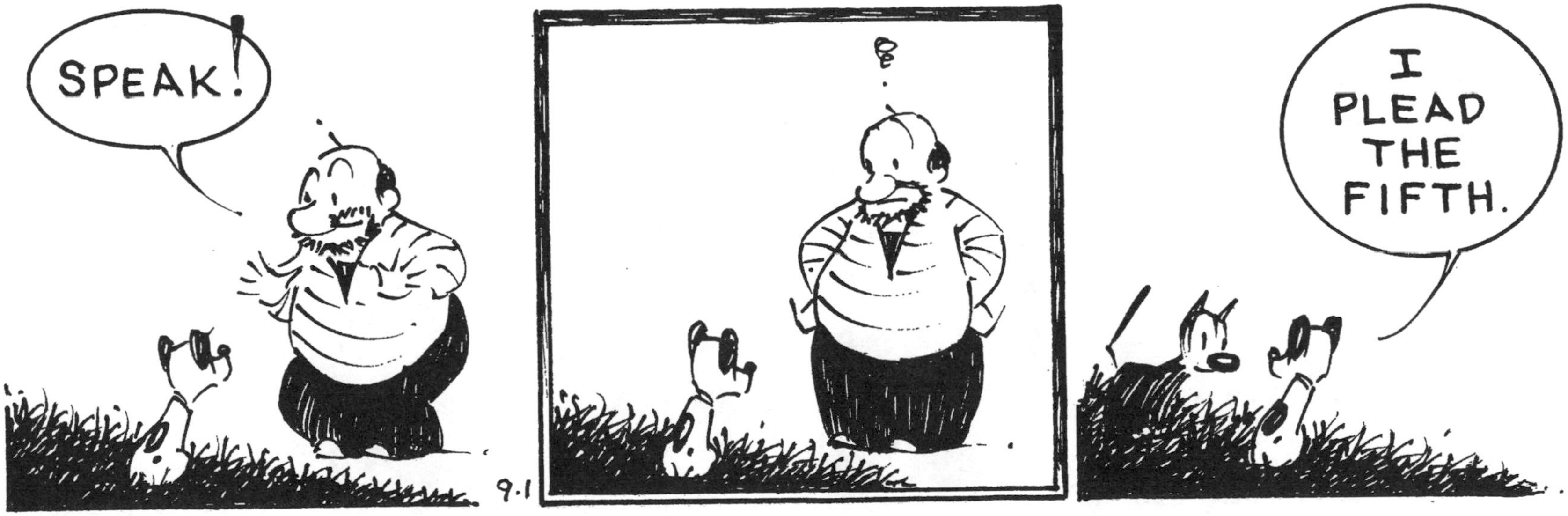
SPEAK!
9·1
I PLEAD THE FIFTH.

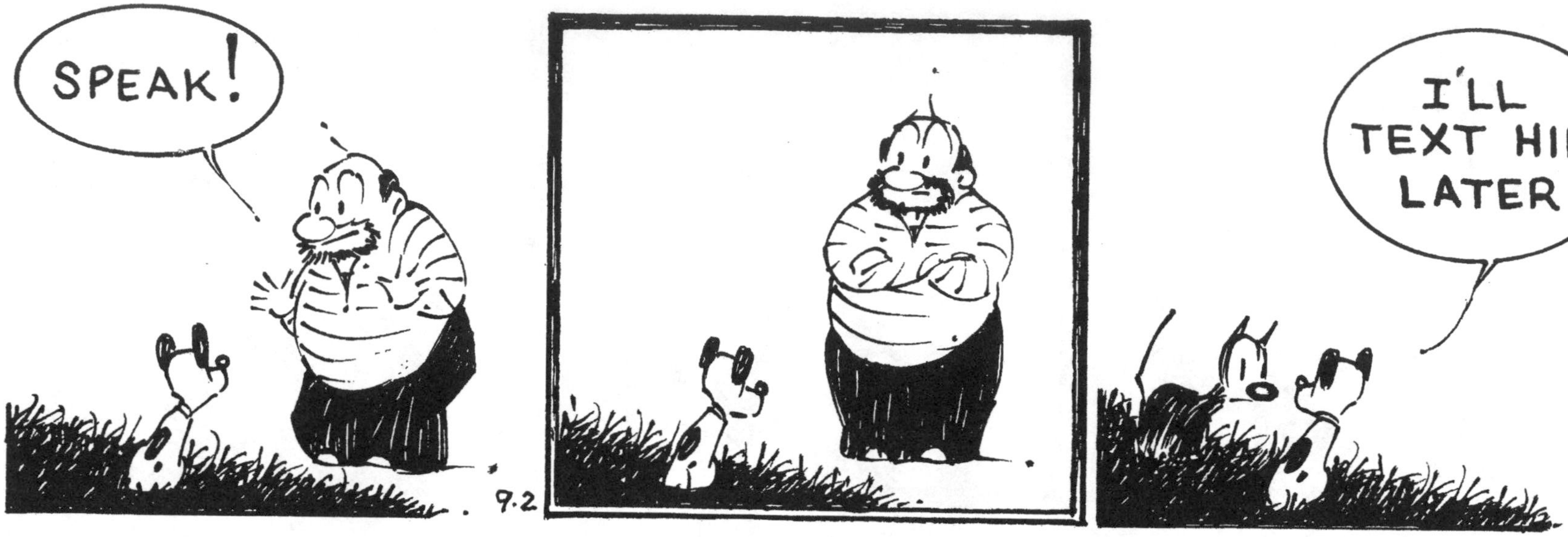
SPEAK!
9.2
I'LL TEXT HIM LATER.

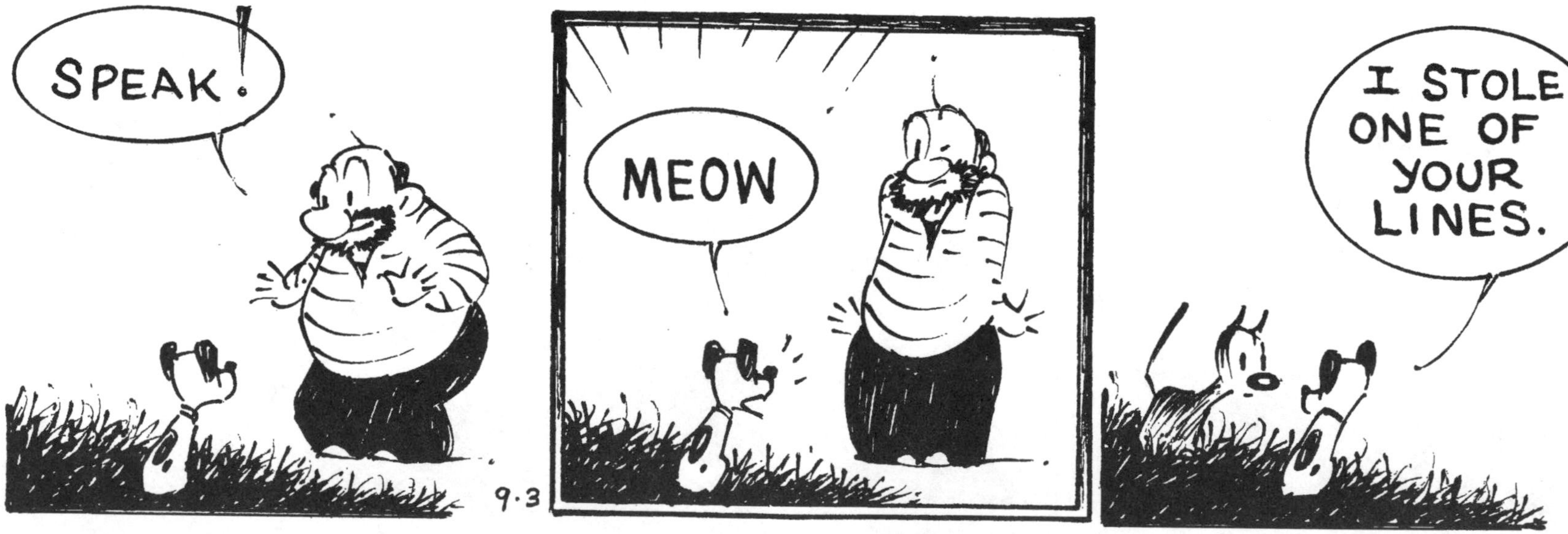
SPEAK!
9.3
MEOW
I STOLE ONE OF YOUR LINES.

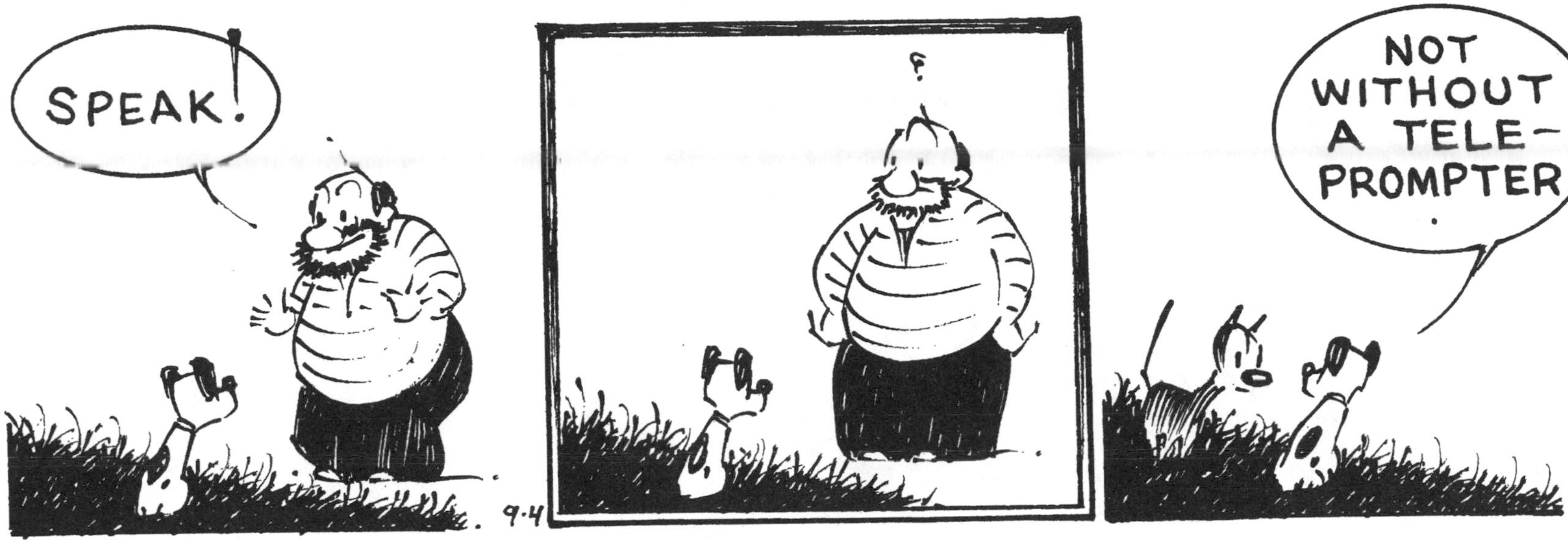
SPEAK!
9·4
NOT WITHOUT A TELE-PROMPTER.

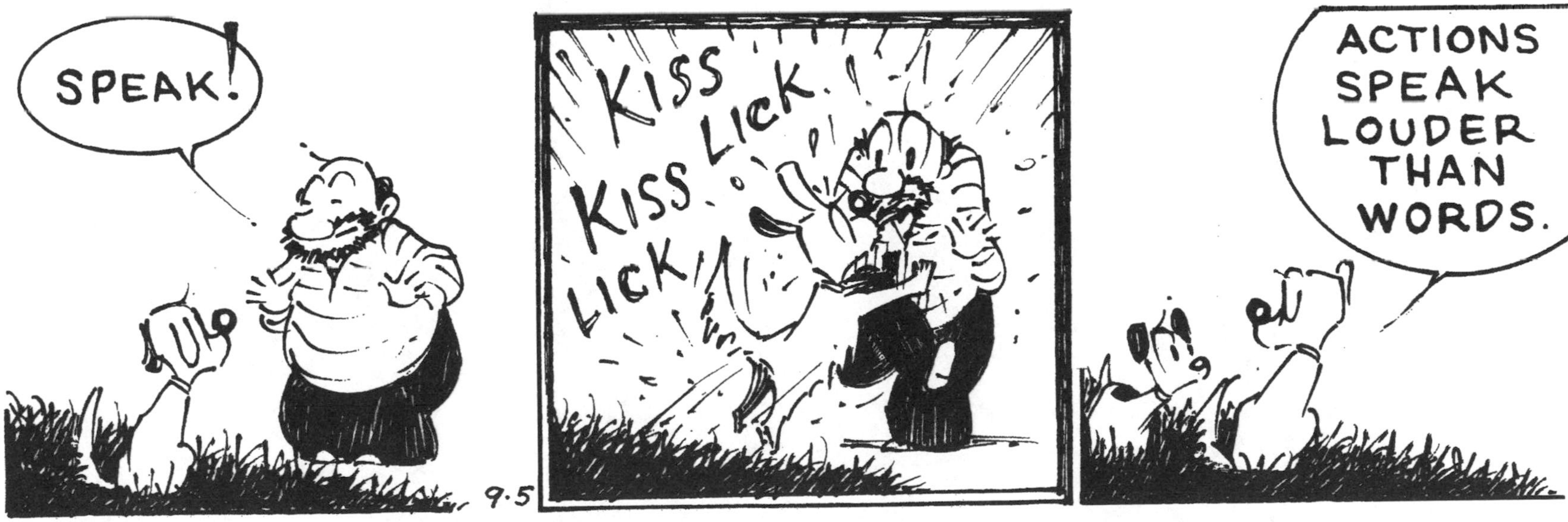
SPEAK!
9·5
KISS KISS LICK LICK
ACTIONS SPEAK LOUDER THAN WORDS.

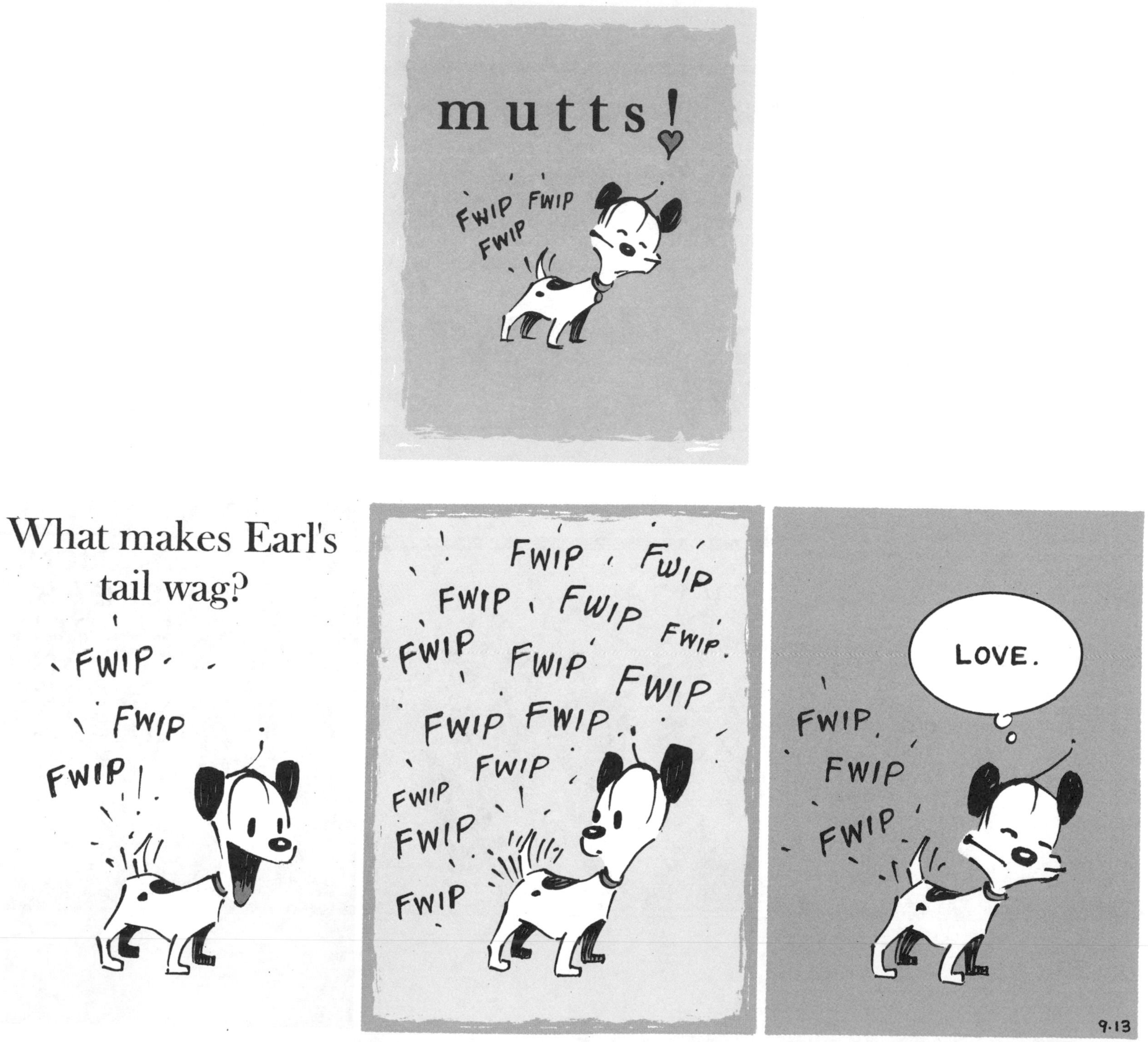
mutts!
FWIP FWIP FWIP
What makes Earl's tail wag?
FWIP FWIP FWIP
FWIP FWIP FWIP FWIP FWIP FWIP FWIP FWIP FWIP FWIP FWIP FWIP FWIP FWIP FWIP FWIP
LOVE.
FWIP FWIP FWIP
9.13

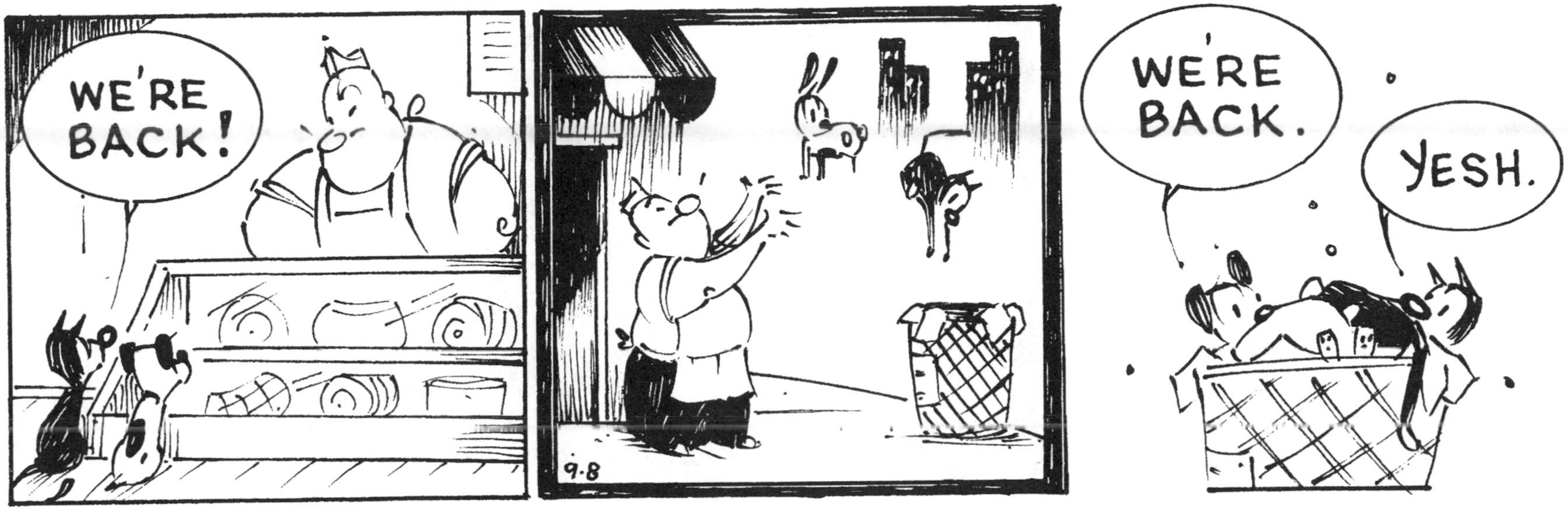
WE'RE BACK!
9.8
WE'RE BACK.
YESH.

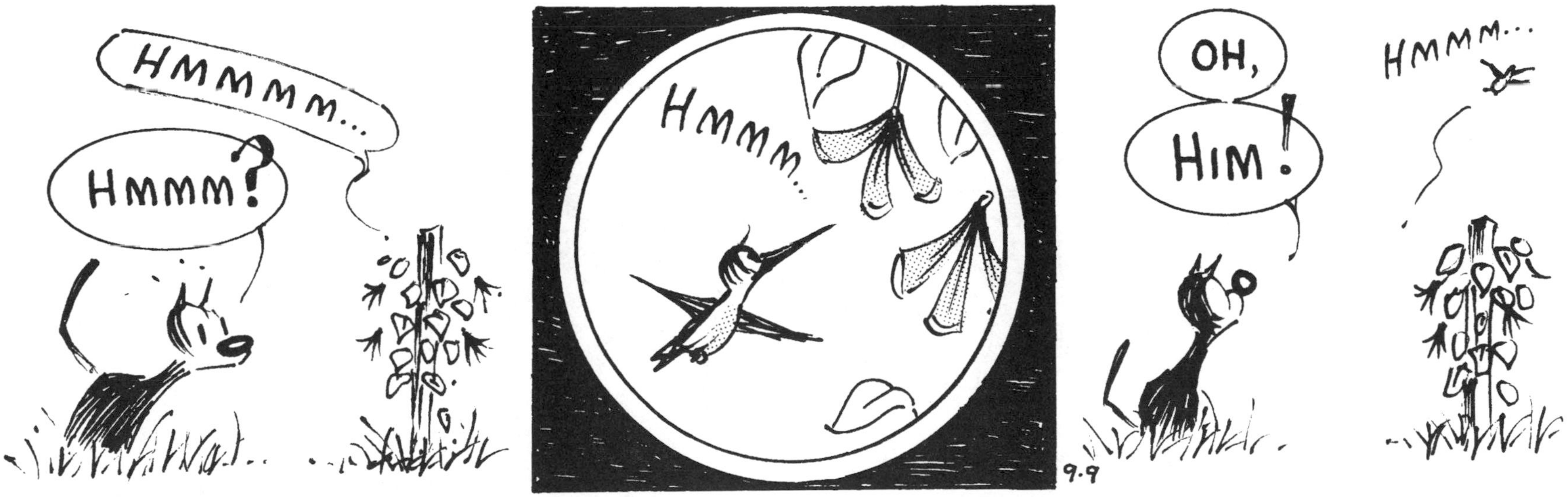
HMMMMM...
HMMM?
HMMM...
9.9
OH,
HIM!
HMMM...

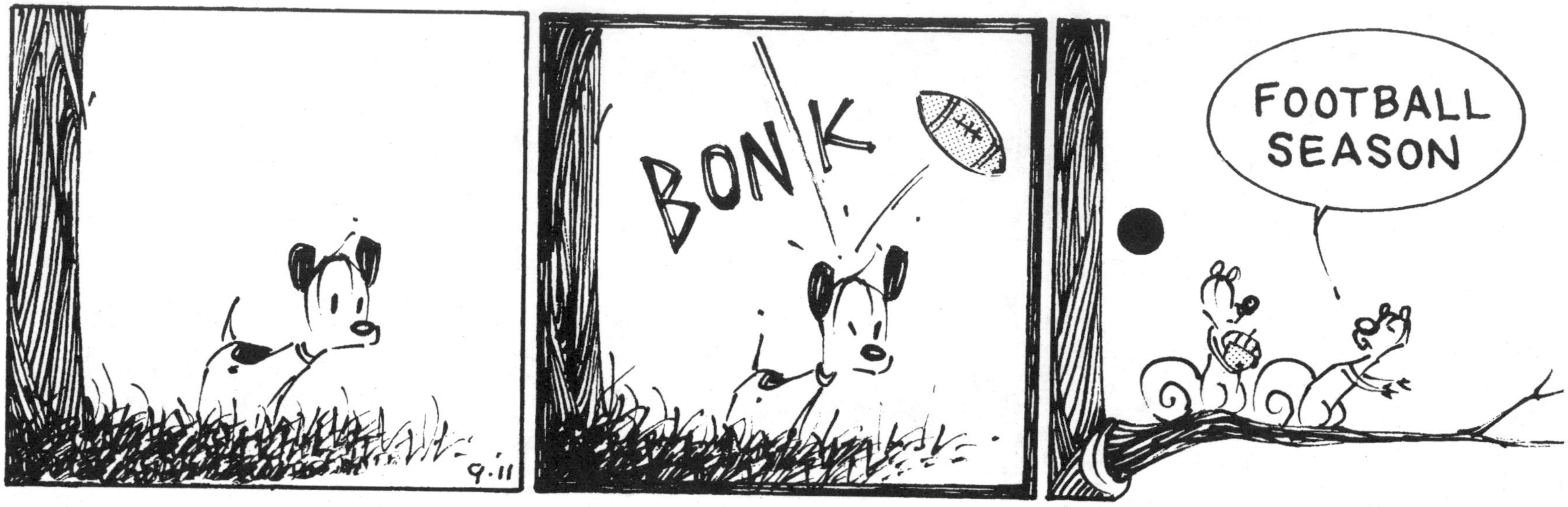
9.11
BONK
FOOTBALL SEASON

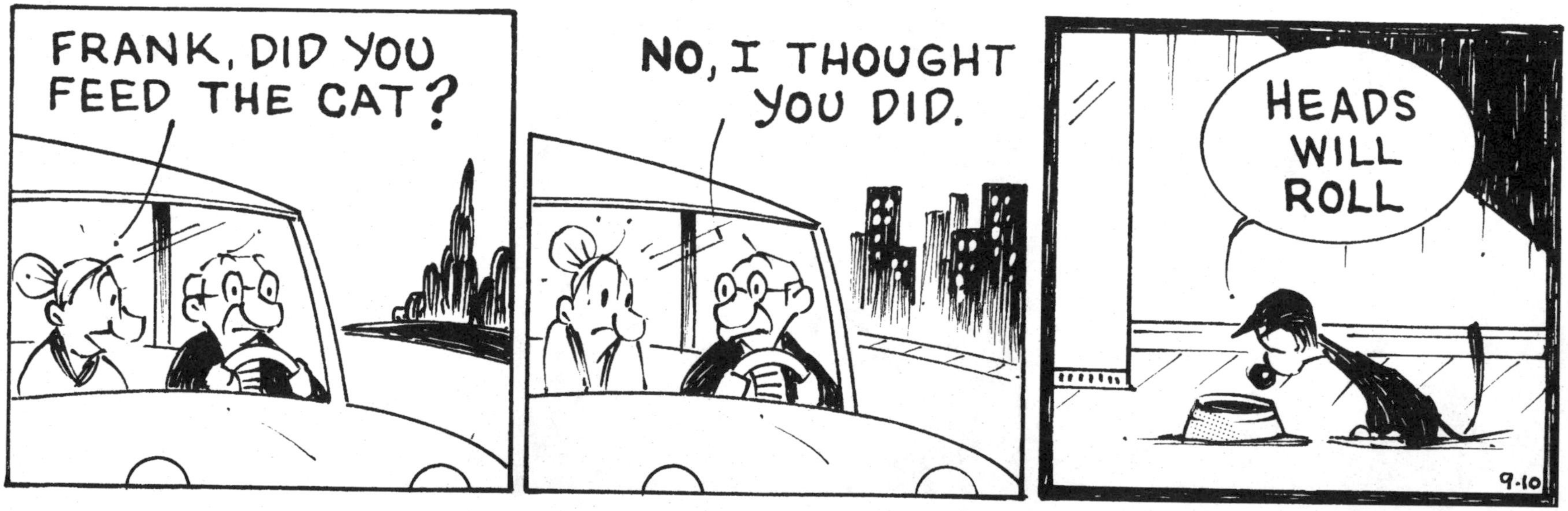
FRANK, DID YOU FEED THE CAT?
NO, I THOUGHT YOU DID.
HEADS WILL ROLL
9.10

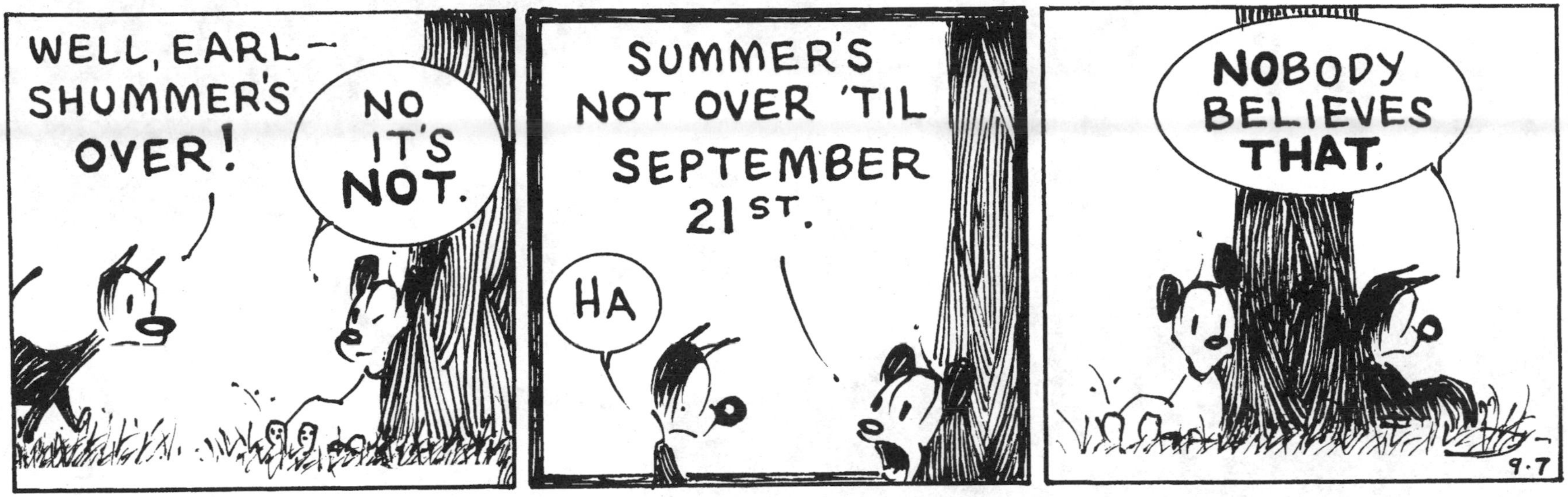
WELL, EARL- SHUMMER'S OVER!
NO IT'S NOT.
SUMMER'S NOT OVER 'TIL SEPTEMBER 21ST.
HA
NOBODY BELIEVES THAT.
9·7

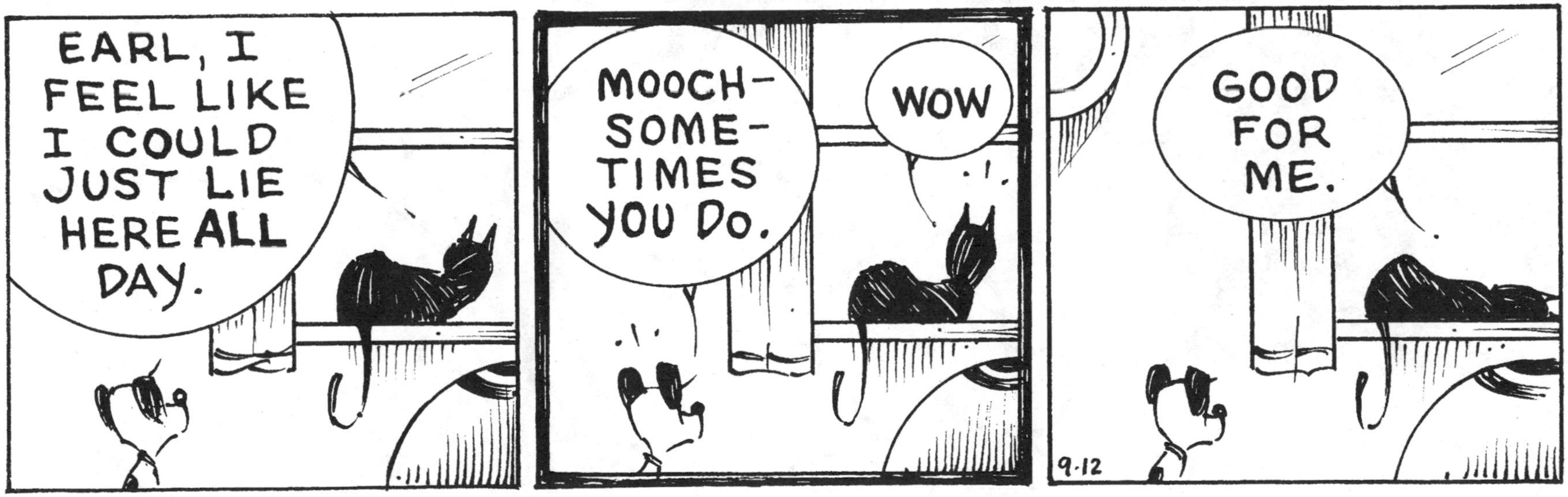
EARL, I FEEL LIKE I COULD JUST LIE HERE ALL DAY.
MOOCH- SOME- TIMES YOU DO.
WOW
GOOD FOR ME.
9·12

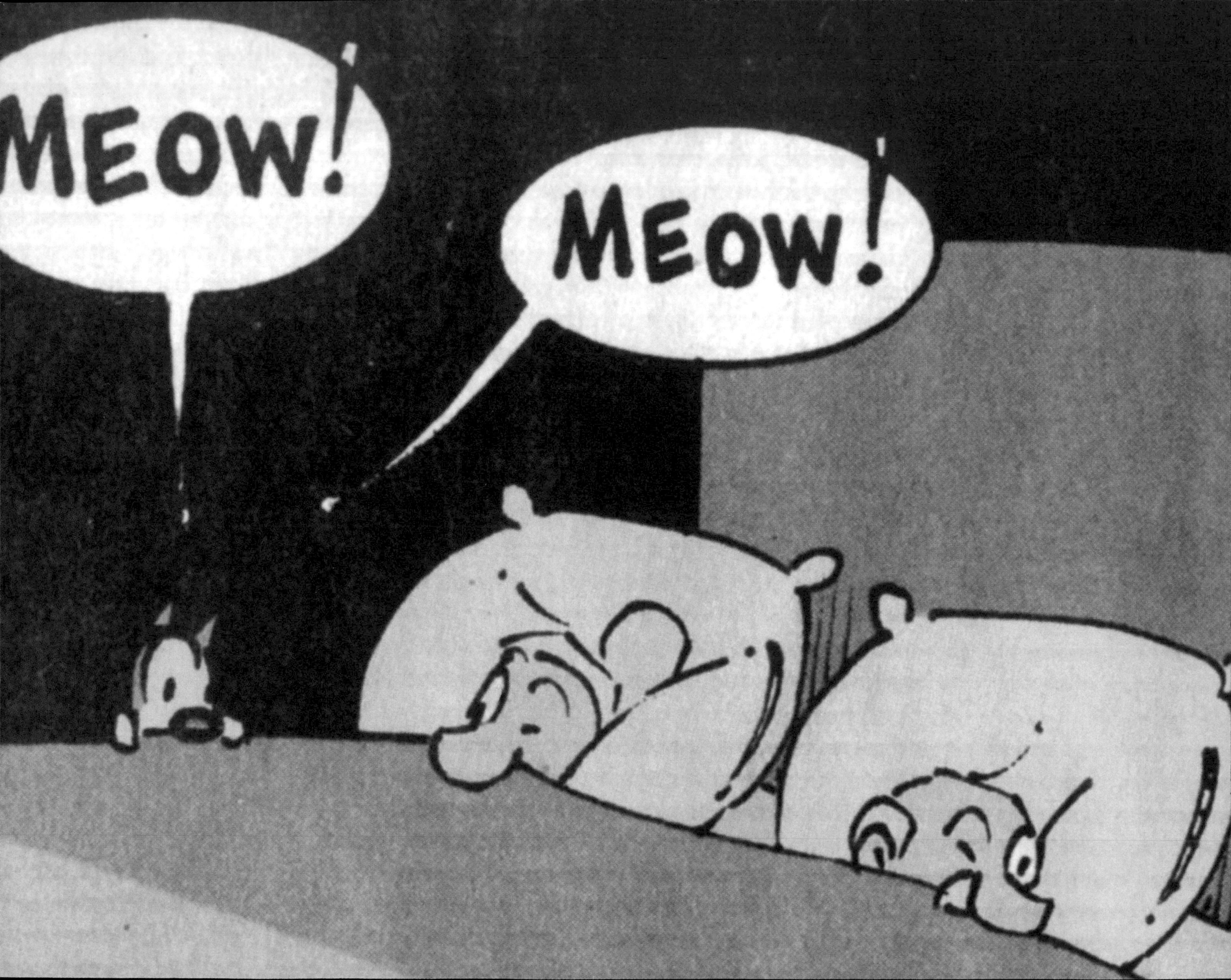
MEOW!
MEOW!

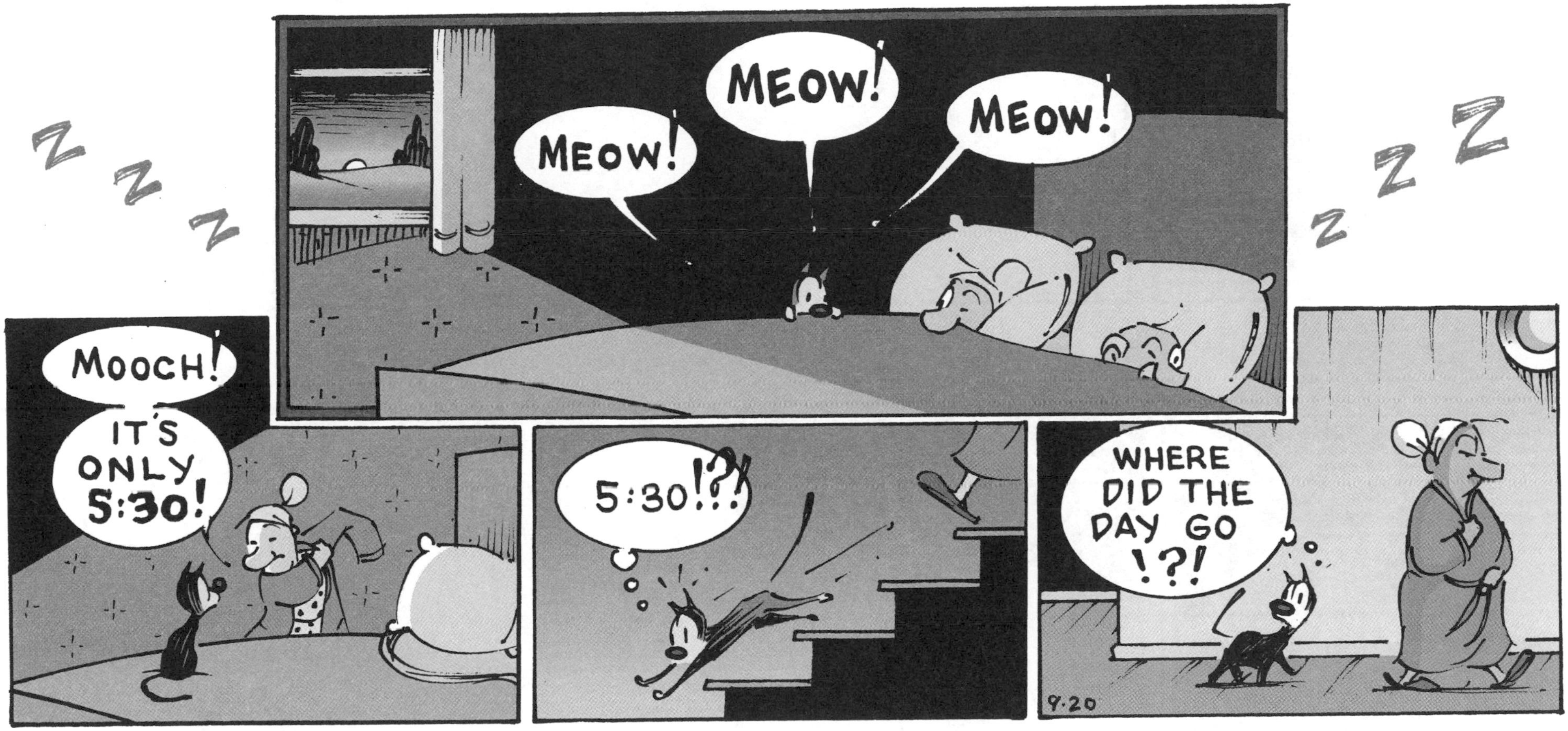

Z Z Z
MEOW!
MEOW!
MEOW!
Z Z Z Z
MOOCH!
IT'S ONLY 5:30!
5:30!?!
WHERE DID THE DAY GO !?!
9·20

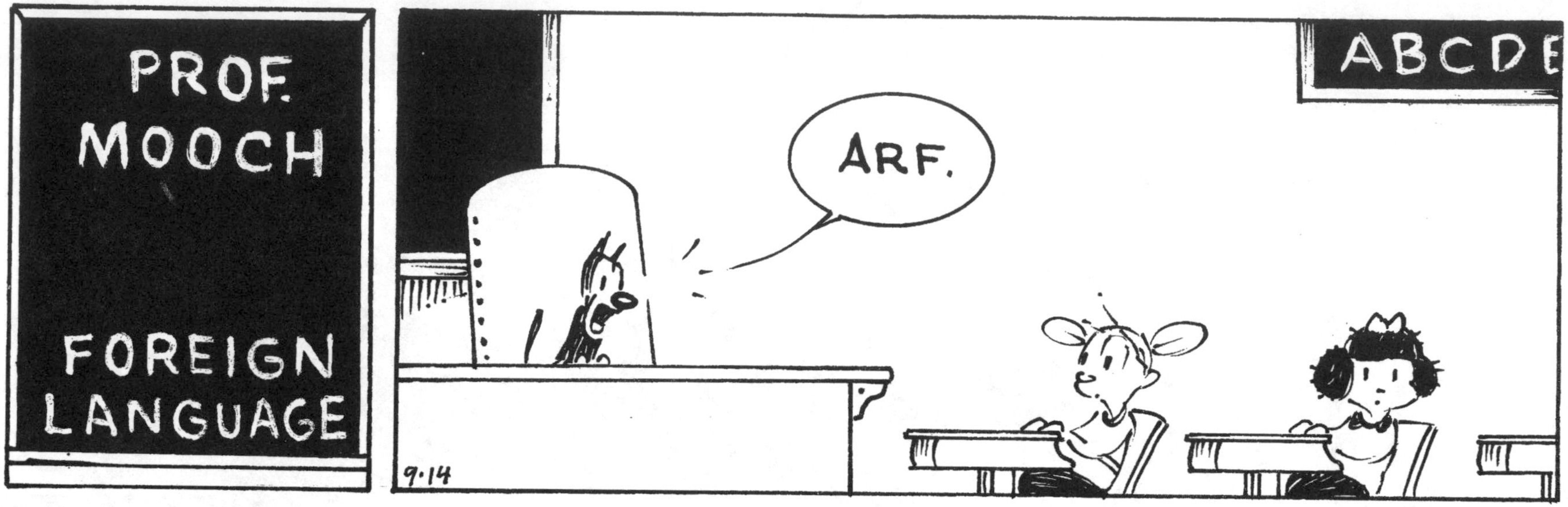
PROF. MOOCH
FOREIGN LANGUAGE
ABCDE
ARF.
9·14

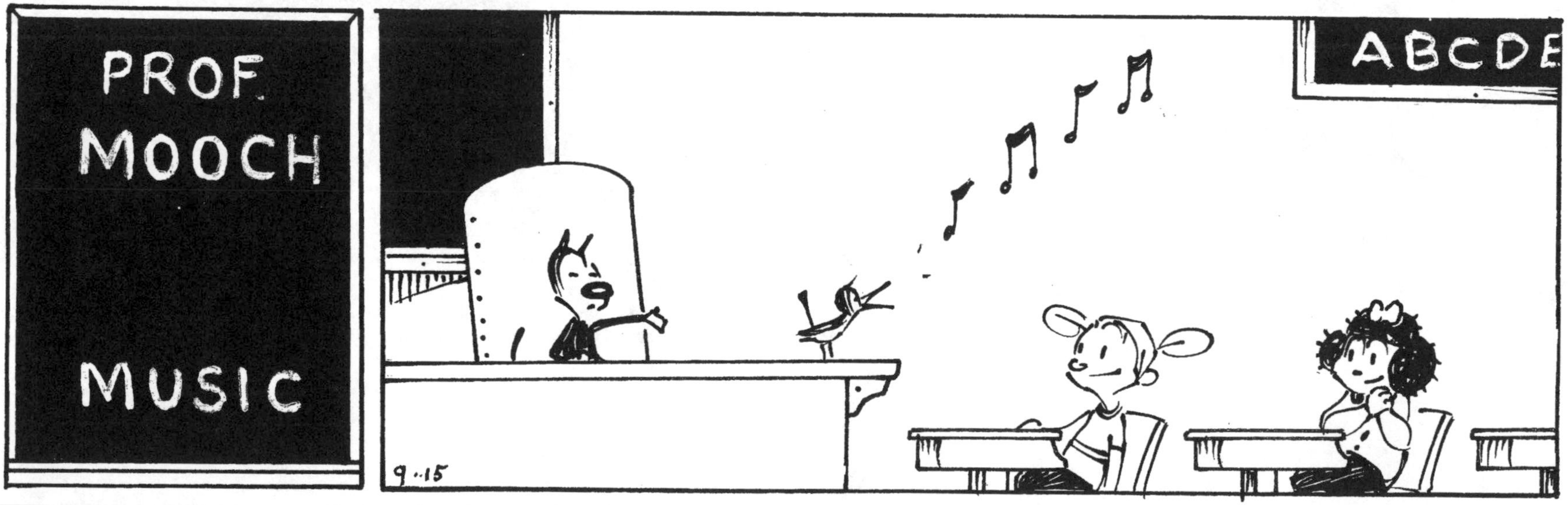
PROF. MOOCH
MUSIC
ABCDE
9·15

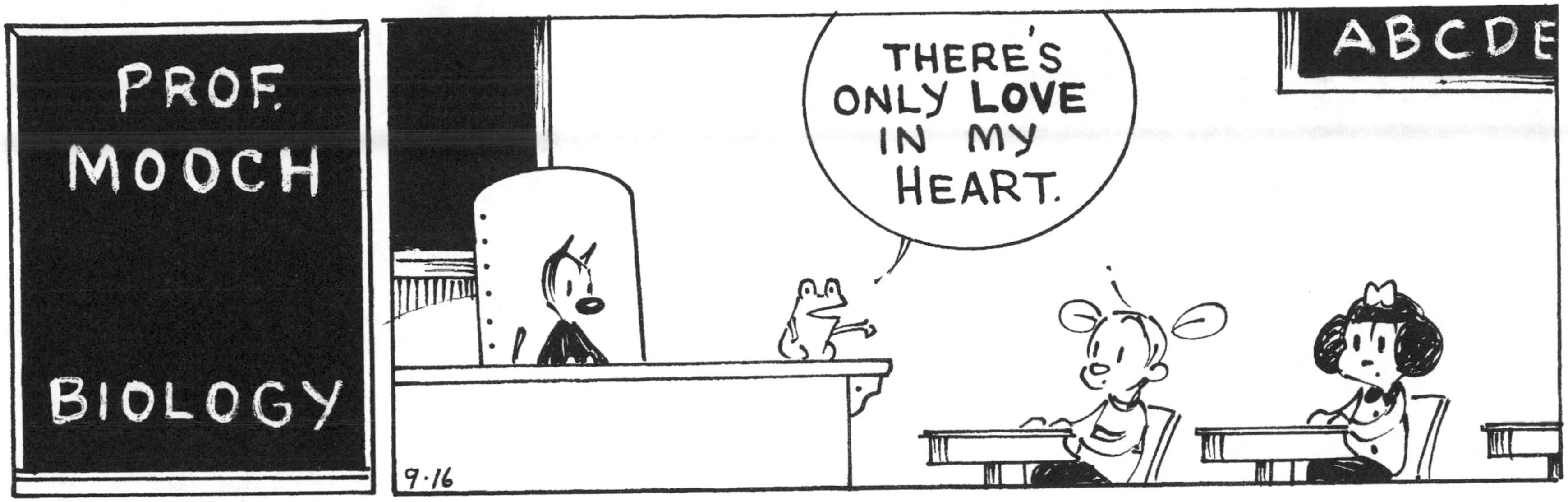
PROF. MOOCH
BIOLOGY
ABCDE
THERE'S ONLY LOVE IN MY HEART.
9·16

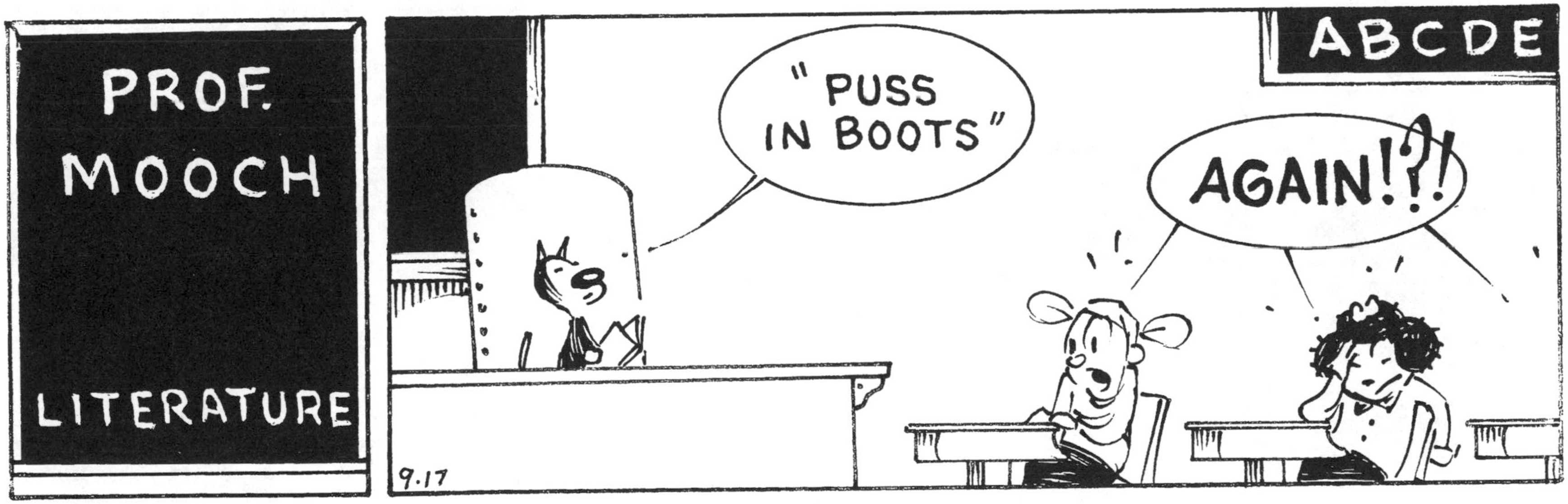
PROF. MOOCH
LITERATURE
ABCDE
"PUSS IN BOOTS"
AGAIN!?!
9·17

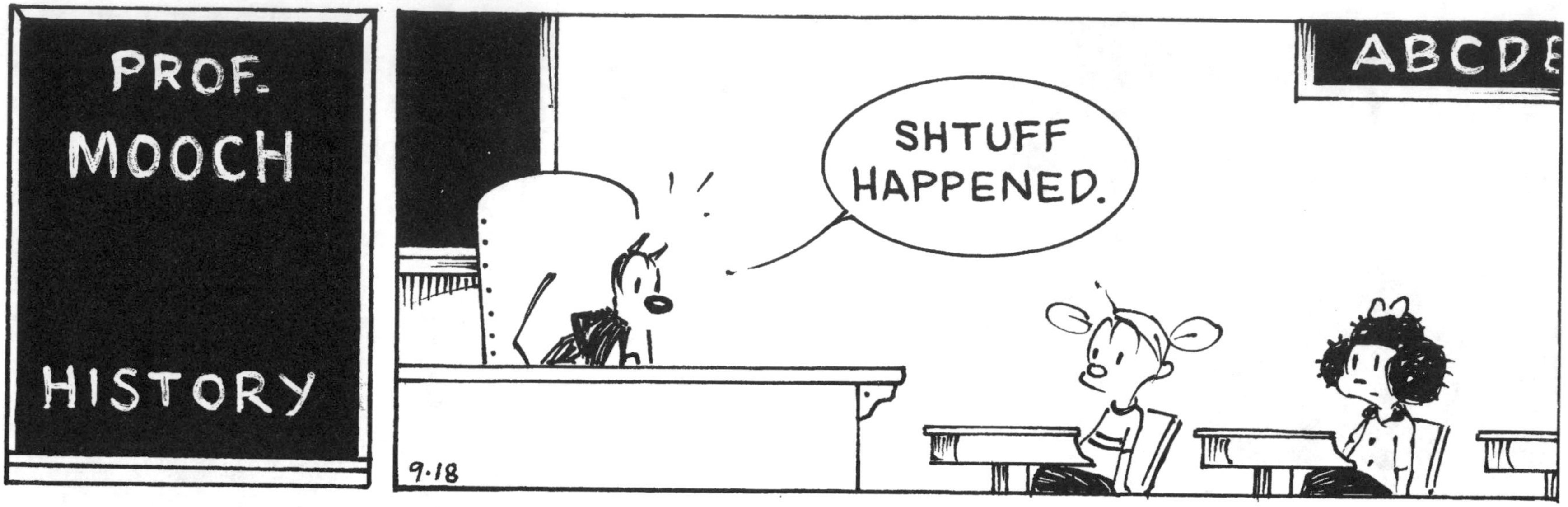
PROF. MOOCH
HISTORY
ABCDE
SHTUFF HAPPENED.
9.18

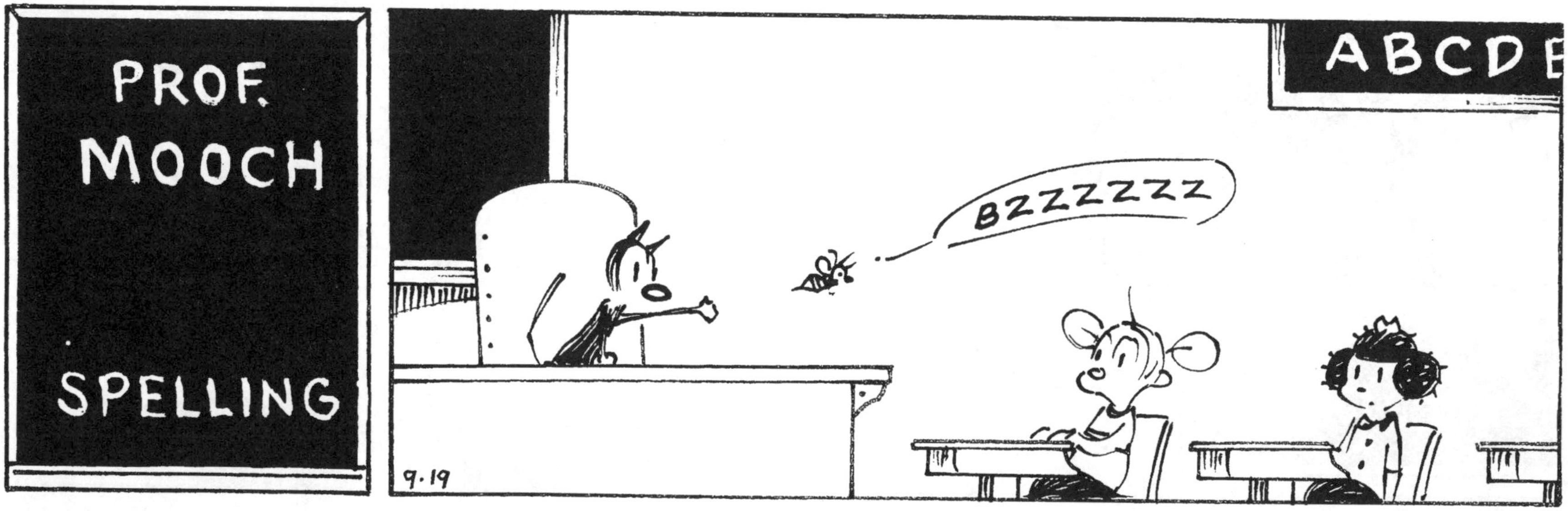
PROF. MOOCH
SPELLING
ABCDE
BZZZZZZ
9.19

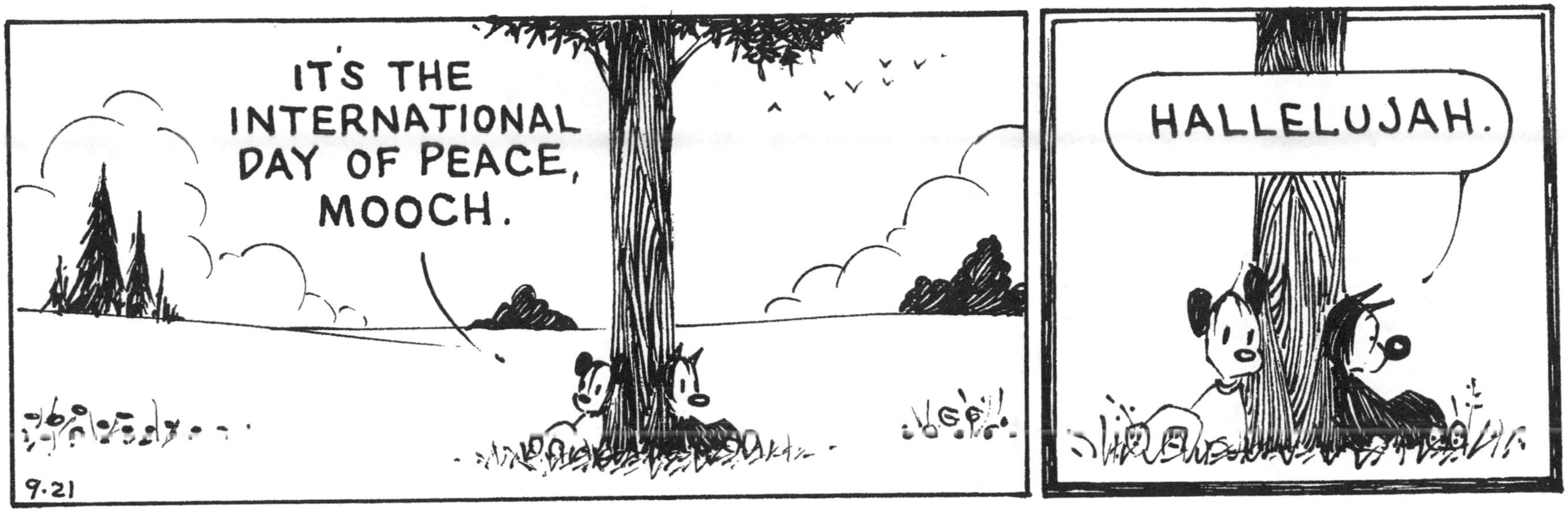
IT'S THE INTERNATIONAL DAY OF PEACE, MOOCH.
9·21
HALLELUJAH.

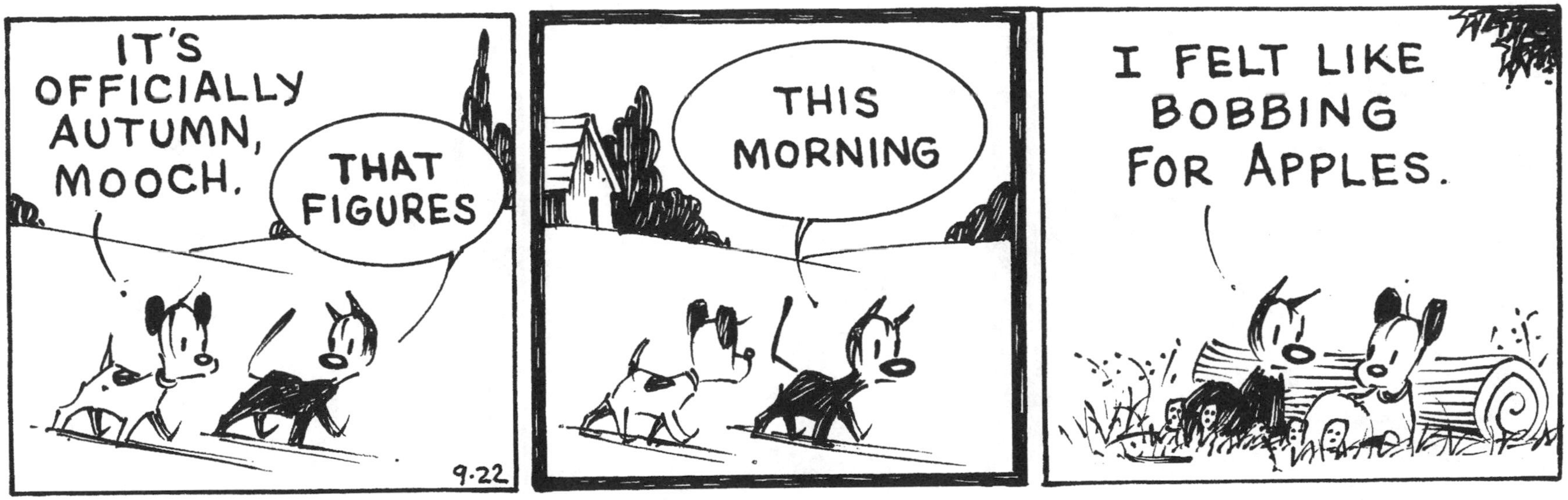
IT'S OFFICIALLY AUTUMN, MOOCH.
THAT FIGURES
9·22
THIS MORNING
I FELT LIKE BOBBING FOR APPLES.

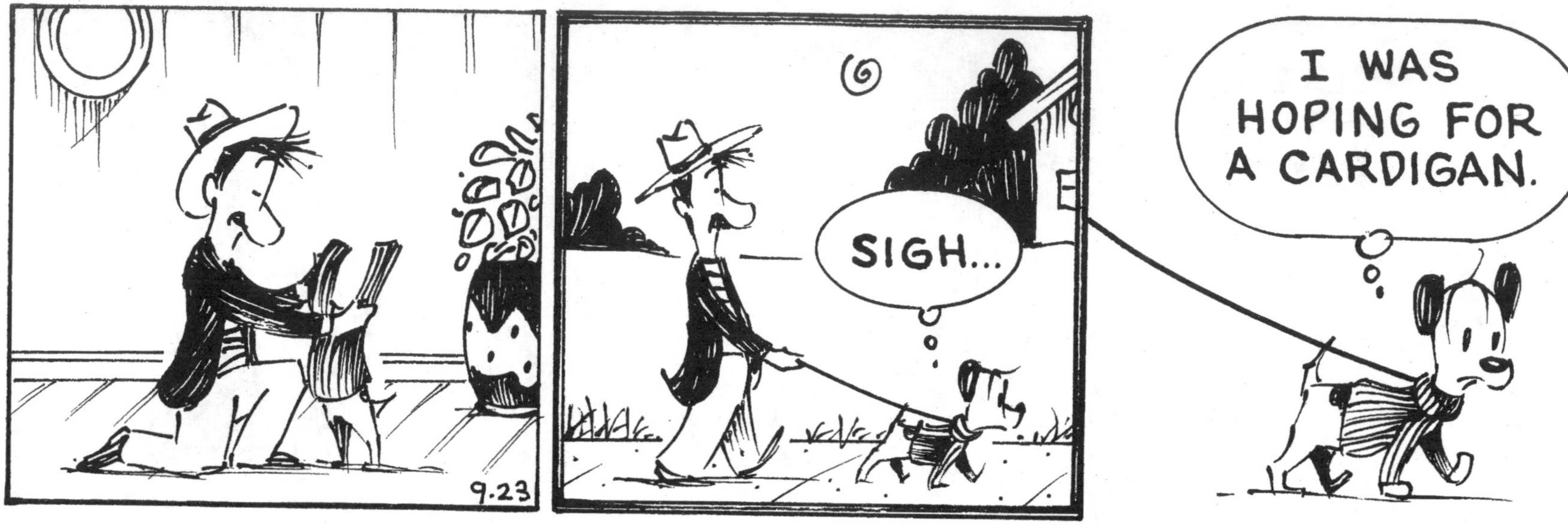
9.23
SIGH...
I WAS HOPING FOR A CARDIGAN.

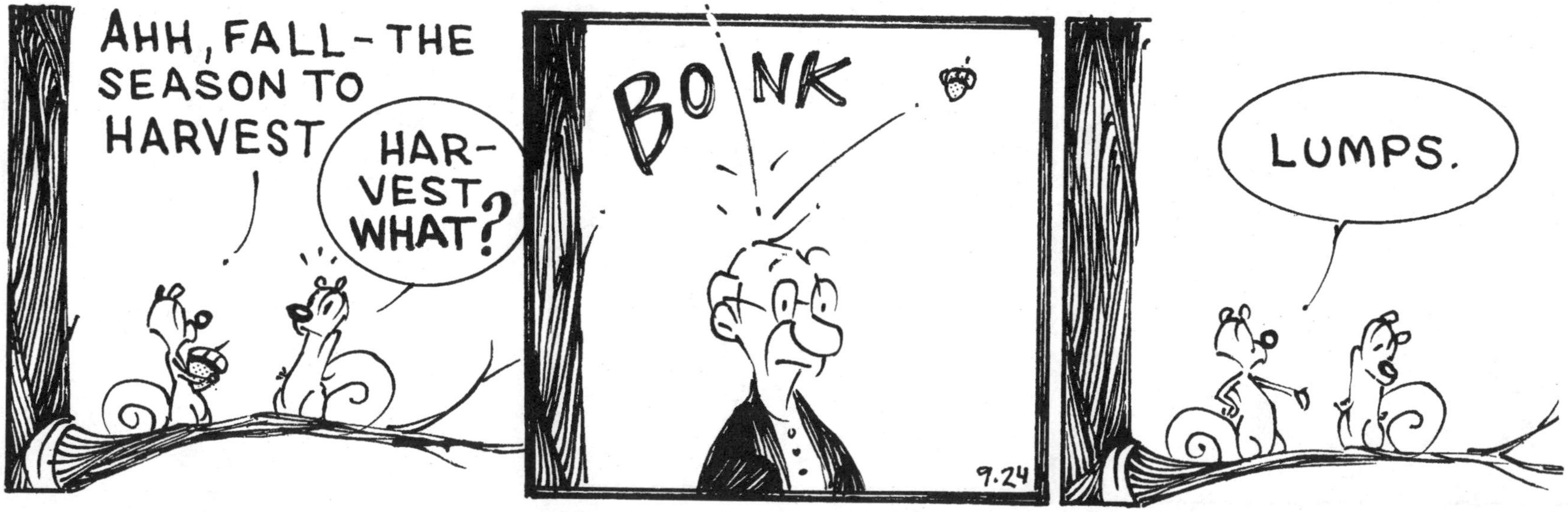
AHH, FALL - THE SEASON TO HARVEST
HAR-VEST WHAT?
BONK
9.24
LUMPS.

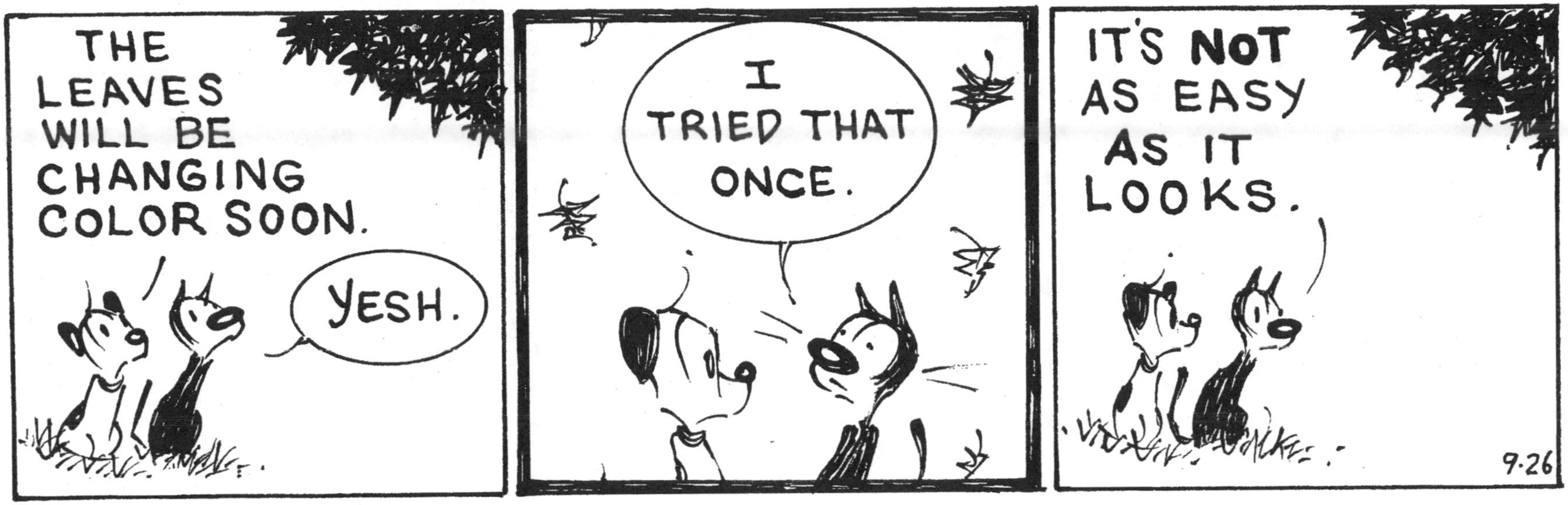
THE LEAVES WILL BE CHANGING COLOR SOON.
YESH.
I TRIED THAT ONCE.
IT'S **NOT** AS EASY AS IT LOOKS.
9·26

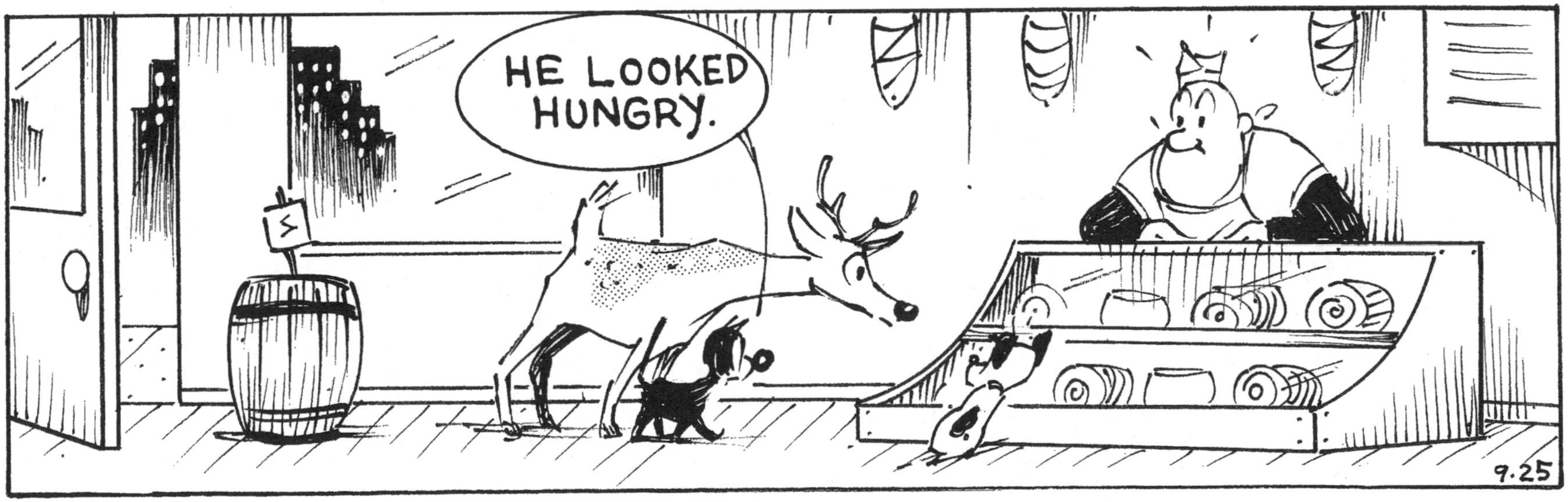
HE LOOKED HUNGRY.
9·25

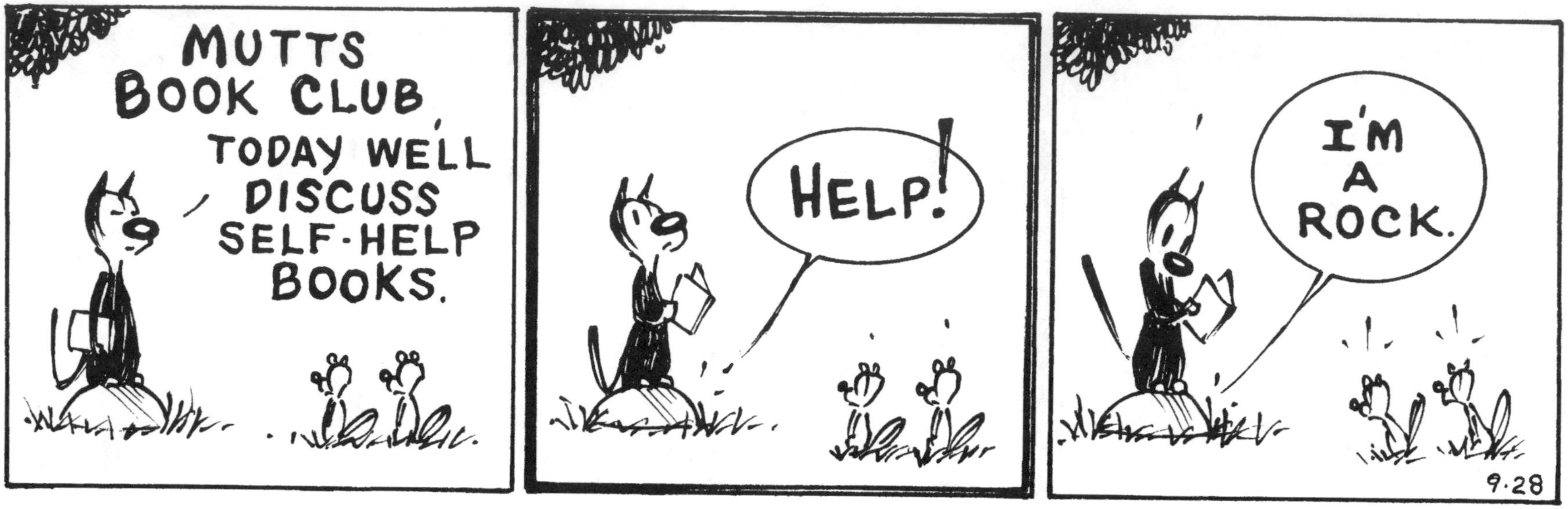
MUTTS BOOK CLUB,
TODAY WE'LL DISCUSS SELF-HELP BOOKS.
HELP!
I'M A ROCK.
9.28

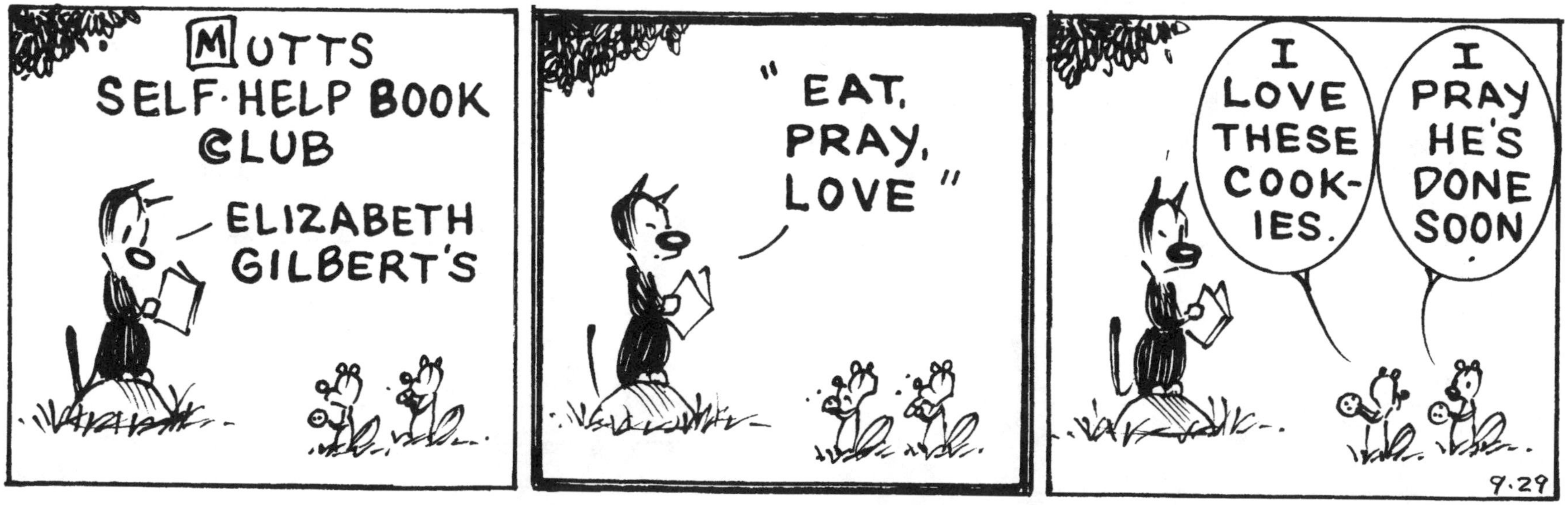
MUTTS SELF-HELP BOOK CLUB
ELIZABETH GILBERT'S
"EAT, PRAY, LOVE"
I LOVE THESE COOK-IES.
I PRAY HE'S DONE SOON.
9.29

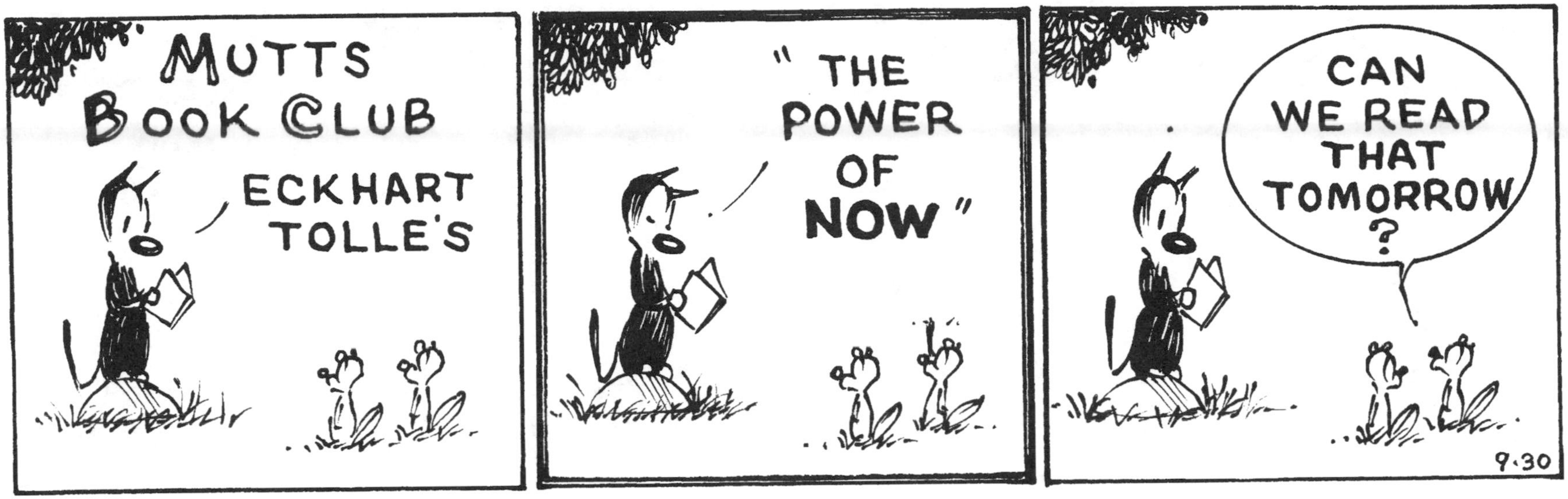
MUTTS BOOK CLUB
ECKHART TOLLE'S
"THE POWER OF NOW"
CAN WE READ THAT TOMORROW ?
9·30

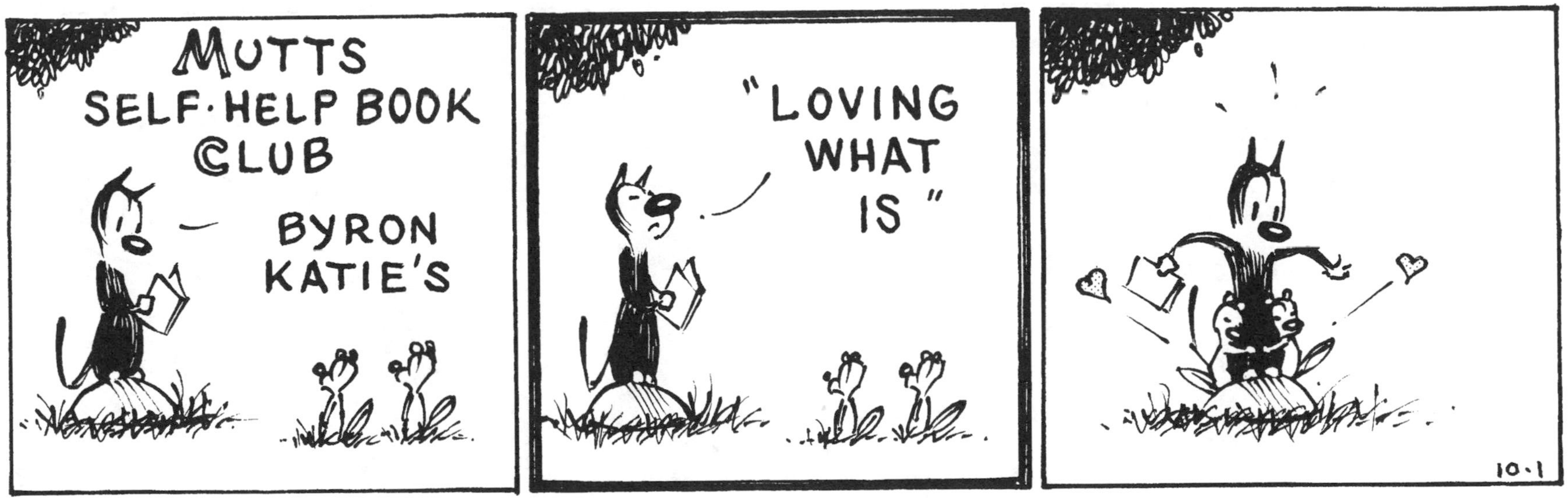
MUTTS SELF·HELP BOOK CLUB
BYRON KATIE'S
"LOVING WHAT IS"
10·1

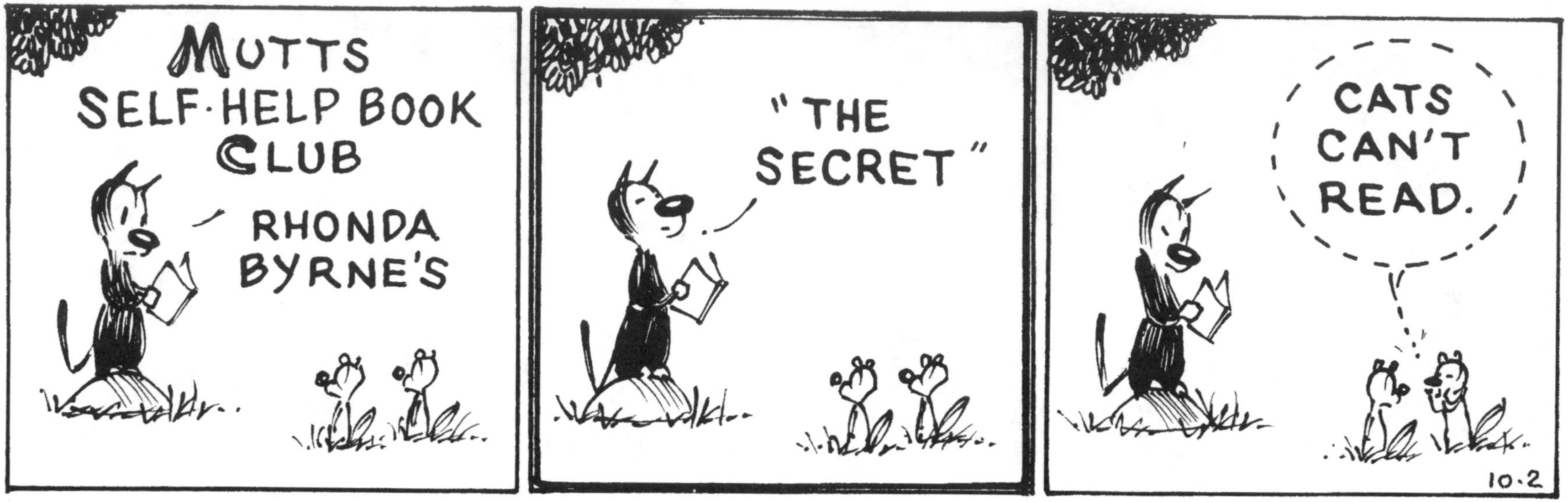
MUTTS SELF-HELP BOOK CLUB
RHONDA BYRNE'S
"THE SECRET"
CATS CAN'T READ.
10·2

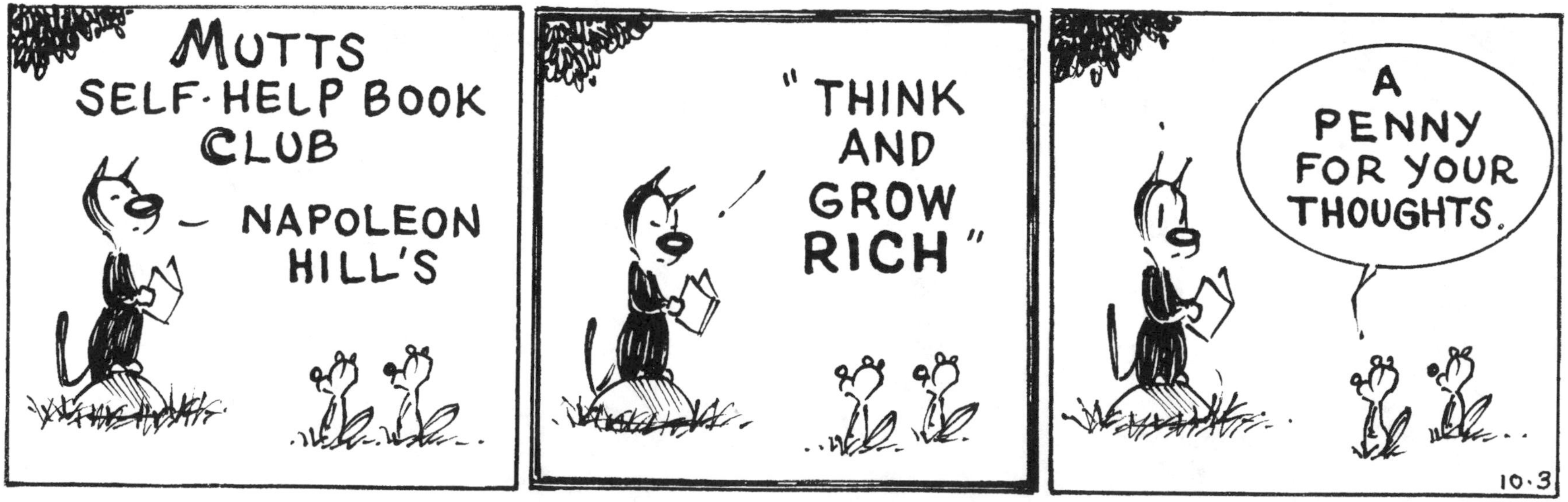
MUTTS SELF-HELP BOOK CLUB
NAPOLEON HILL'S
"THINK AND GROW RICH"
A PENNY FOR YOUR THOUGHTS.
10·3

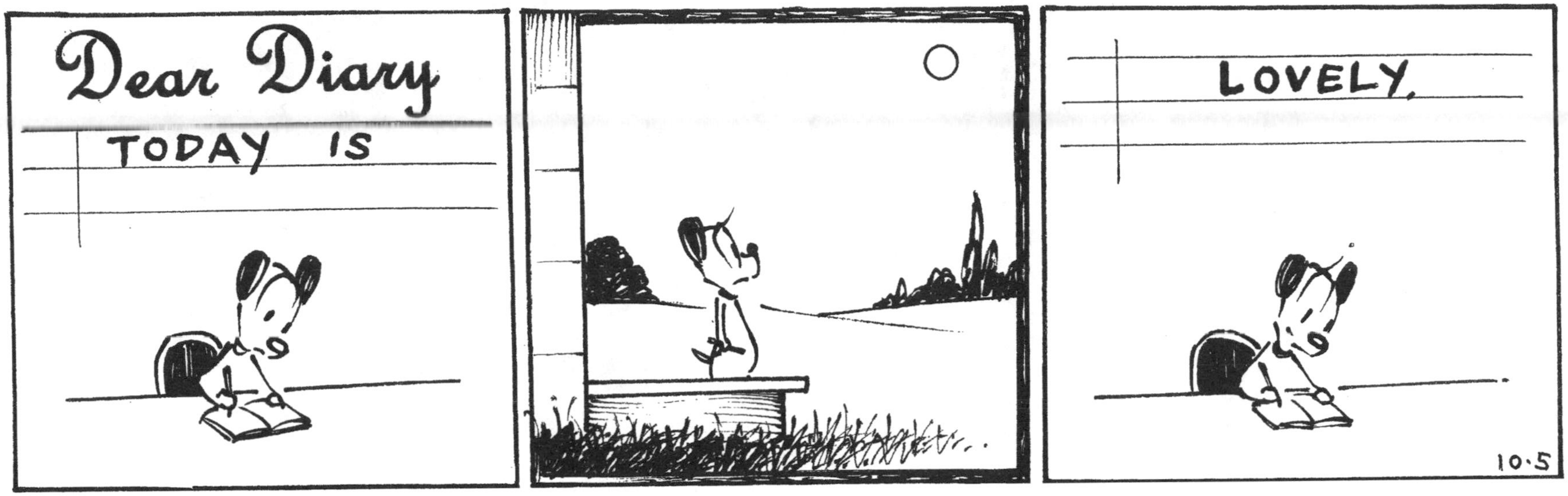
Dear Diary
TODAY IS
LOVELY.
10·5

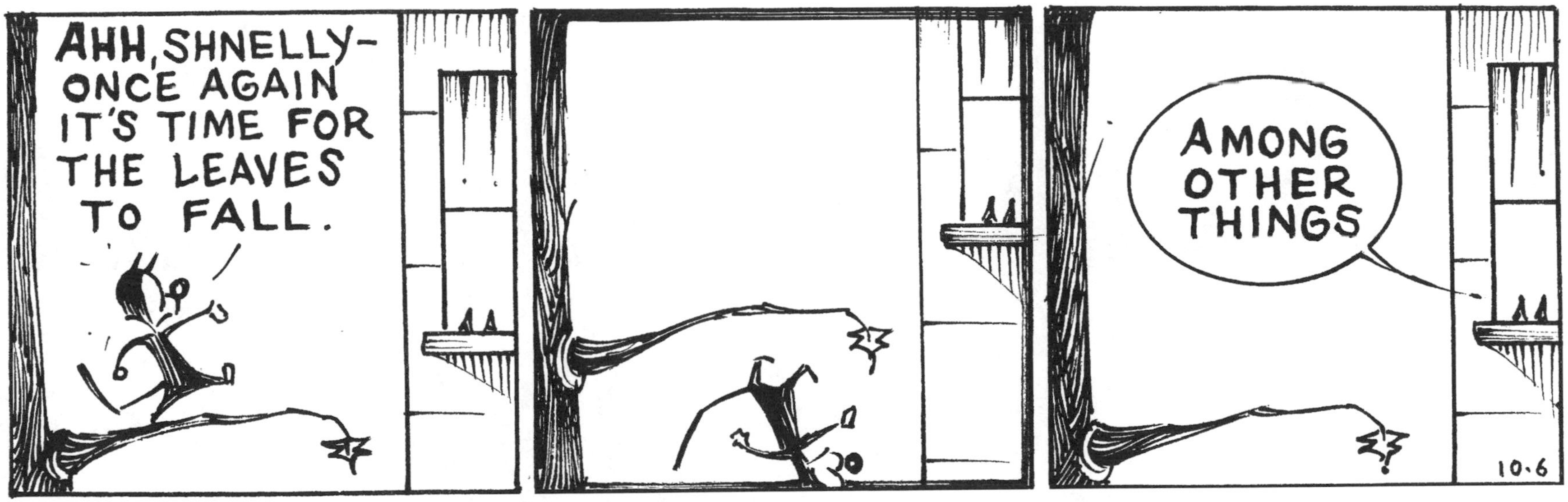
AHH, SHNELLY-
ONCE AGAIN
IT'S TIME FOR
THE LEAVES
TO FALL.
AMONG
OTHER
THINGS
10·6

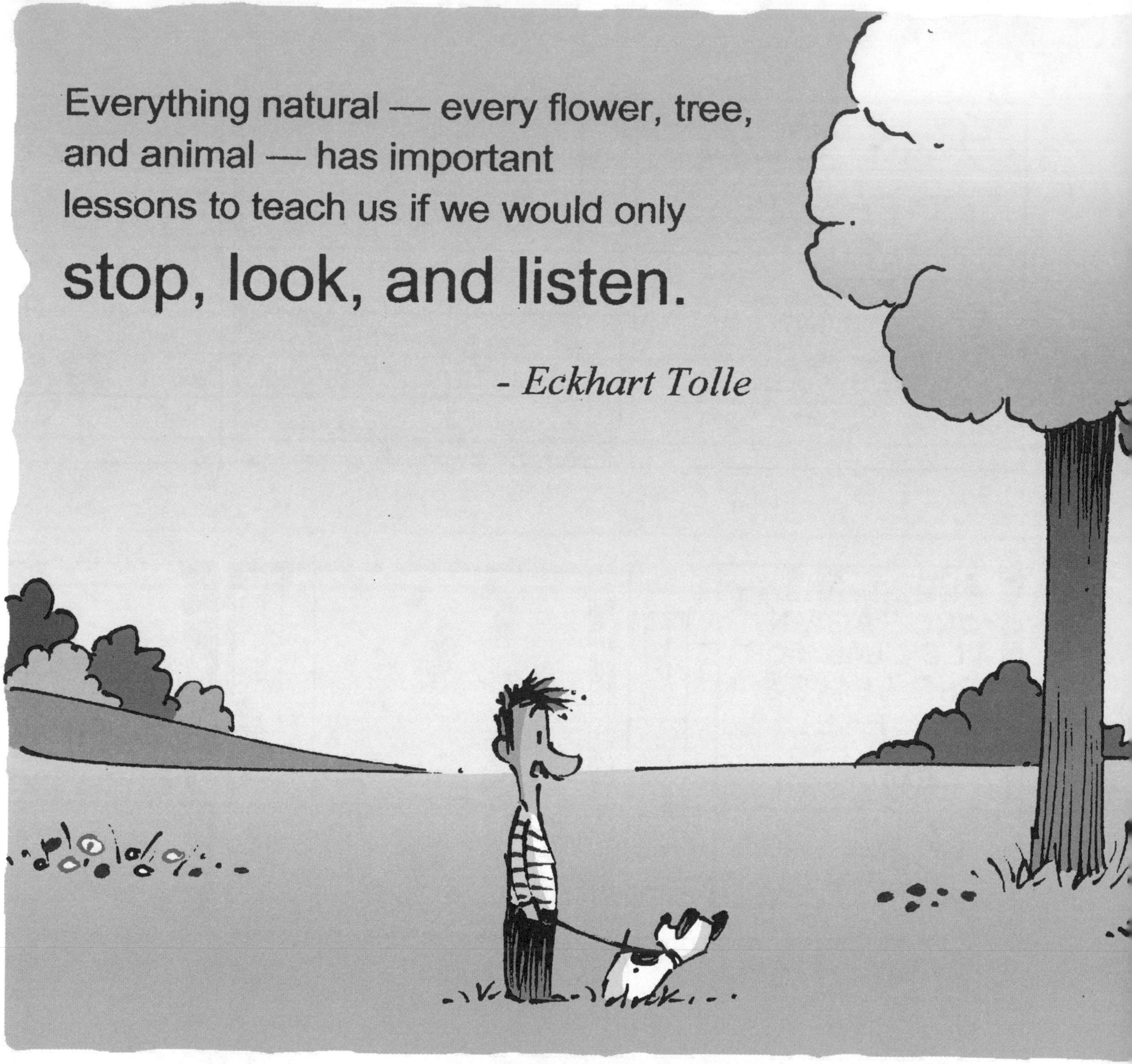
Everything natural — every flower, tree, and animal — has important lessons to teach us if we would only
stop, look, and listen.
- Eckhart Tolle

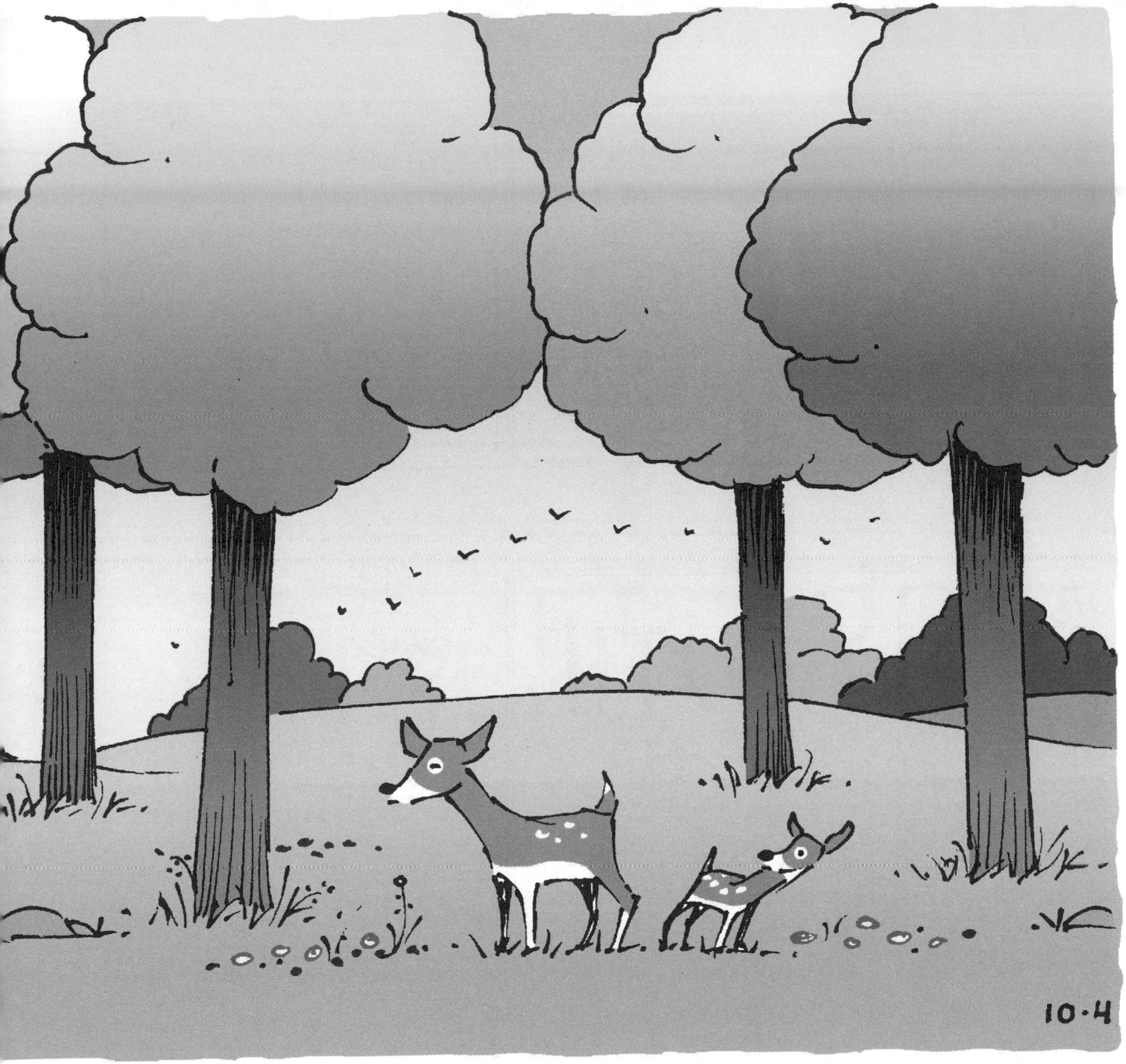
10-4

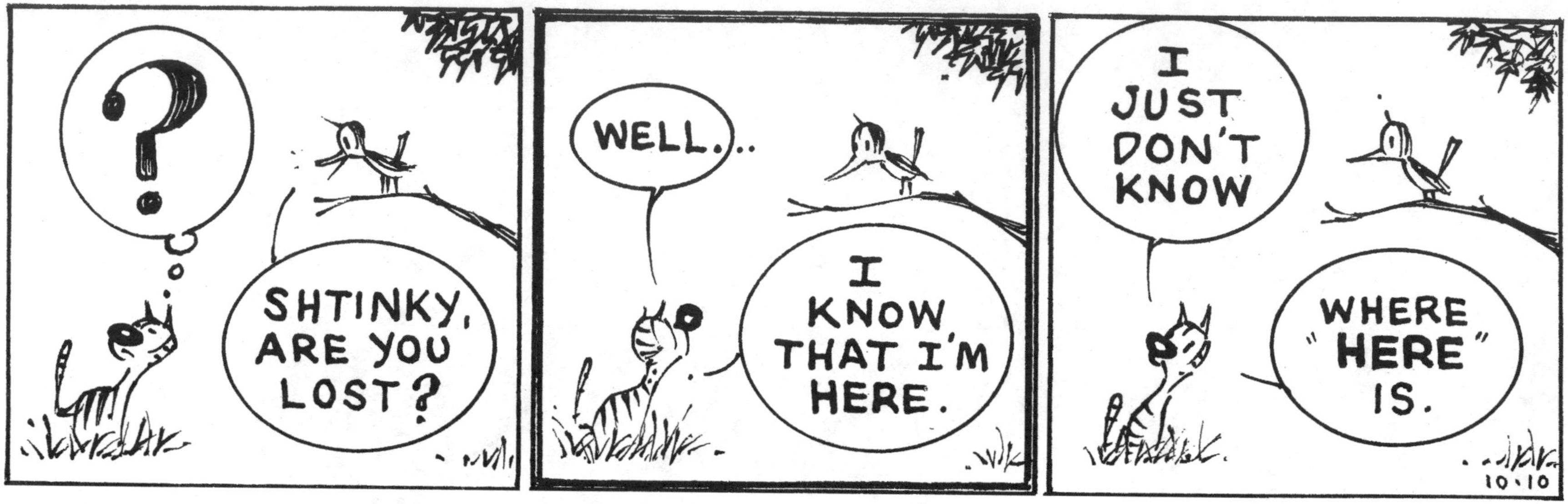
?
SHTINKY, ARE YOU LOST?
WELL...
I KNOW THAT I'M HERE.
I JUST DON'T KNOW
WHERE "HERE" IS.
10·10

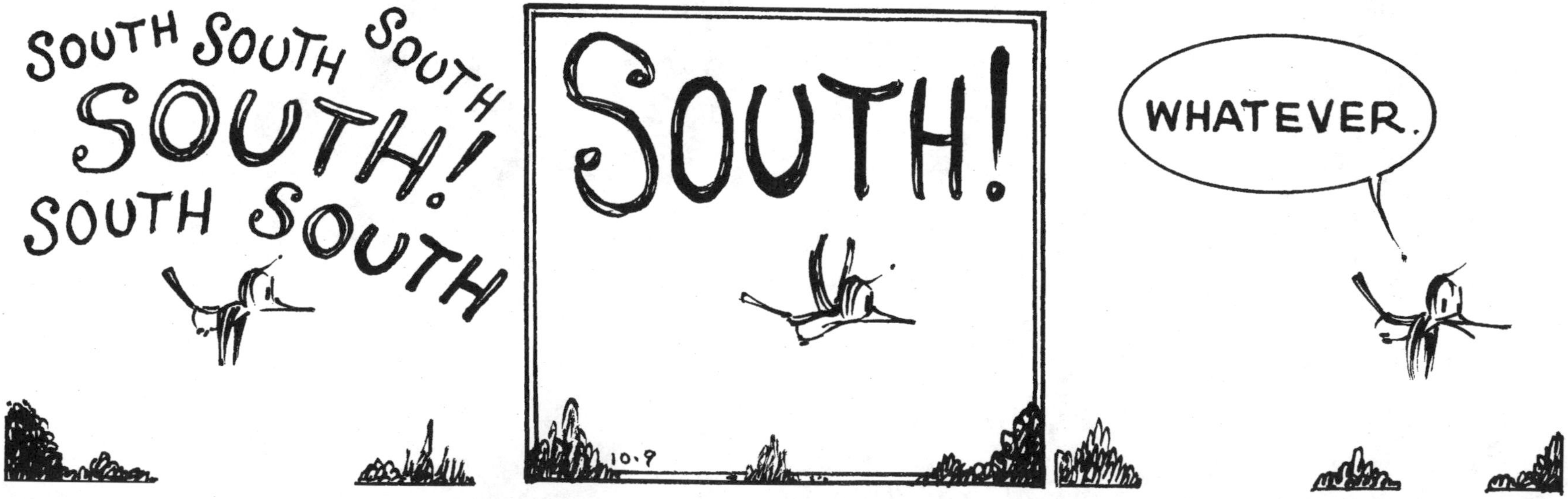
SOUTH SOUTH SOUTH SOUTH! SOUTH SOUTH
SOUTH!
10·9
WHATEVER.

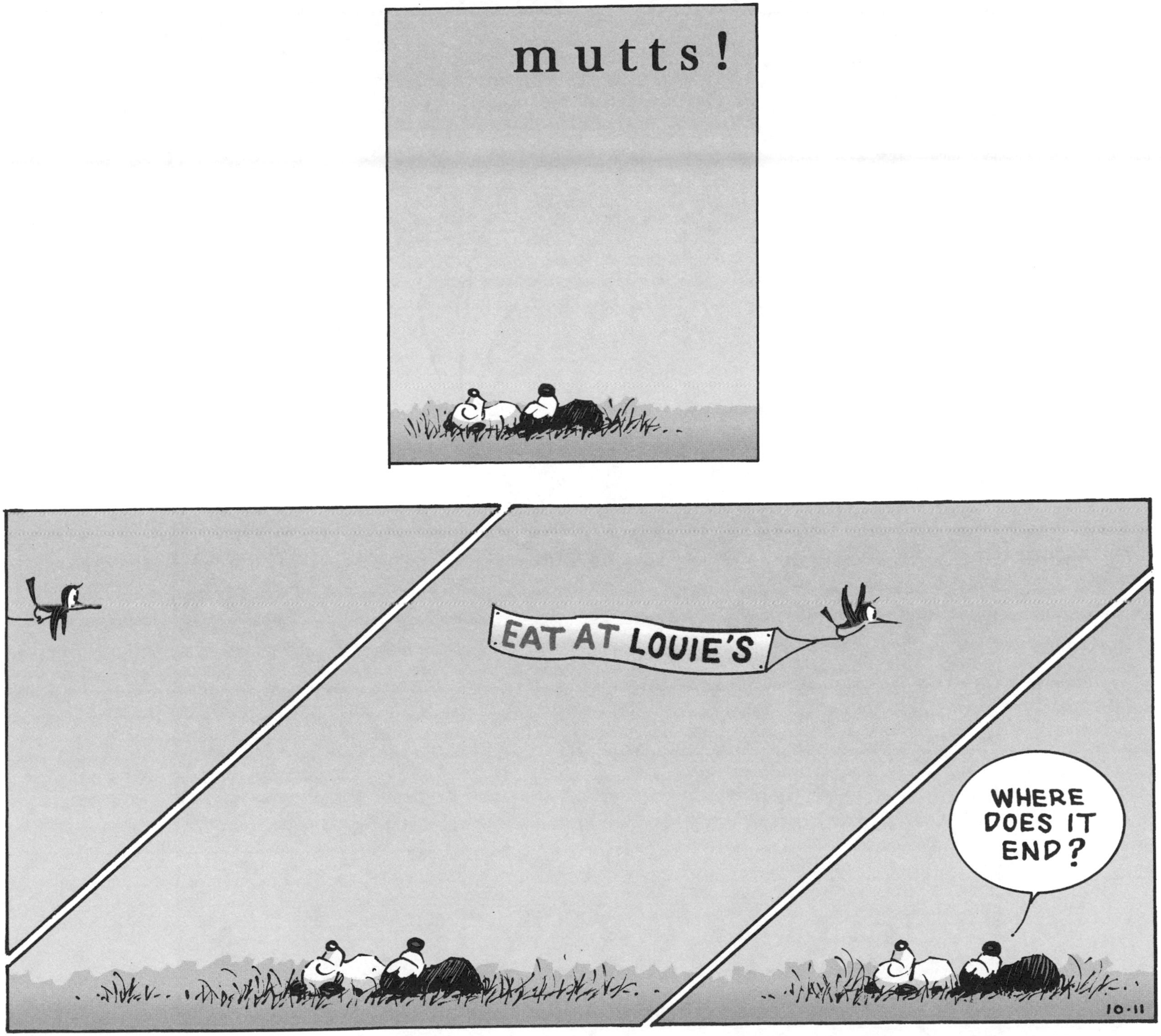
mutts!
EAT AT LOUIE'S
WHERE DOES IT END?
10-11

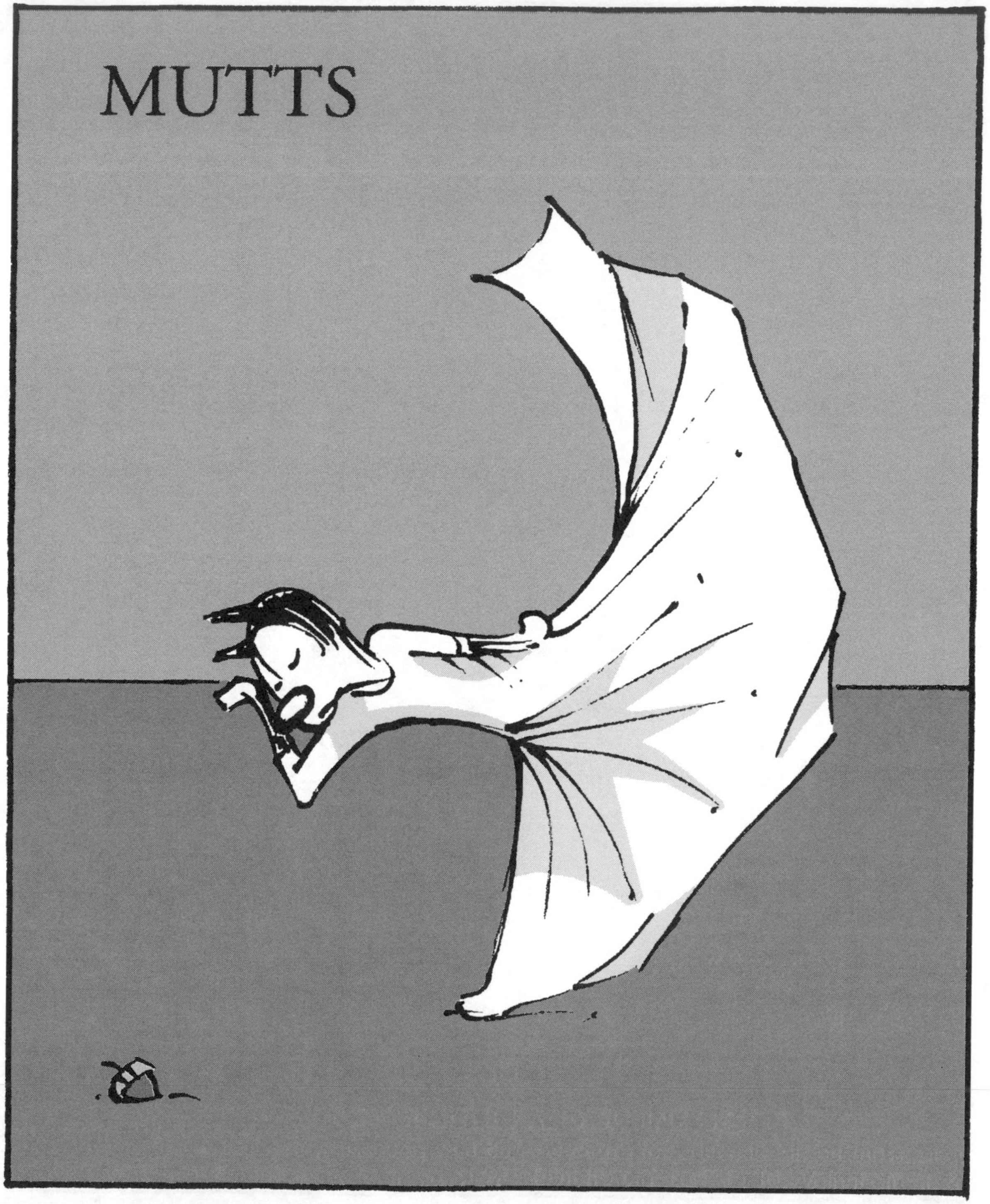
MUTTS

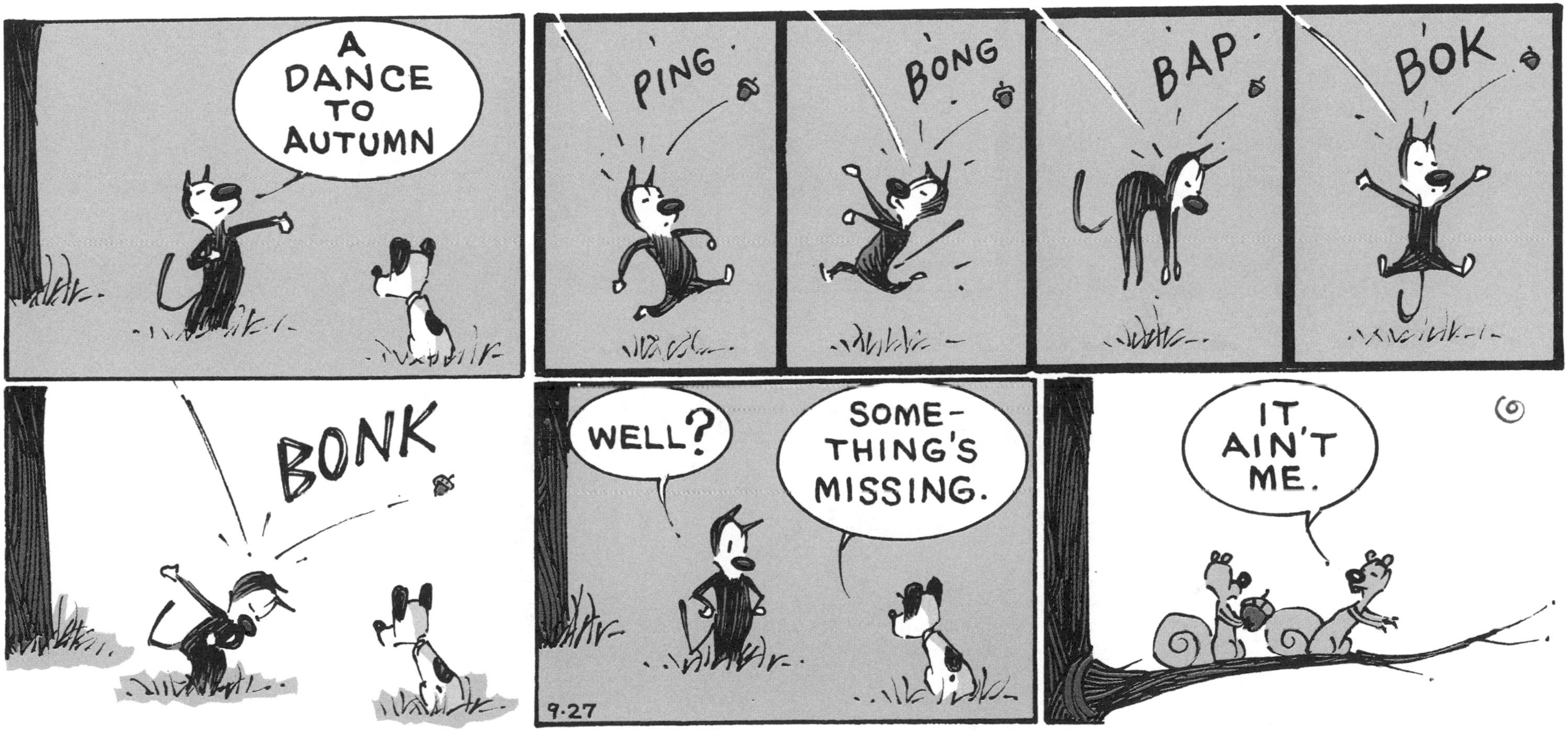
A DANCE TO AUTUMN
PING
BONG
BAP
BOK
BONK
WELL?
SOME-THING'S MISSING.
9·27
IT AIN'T ME.

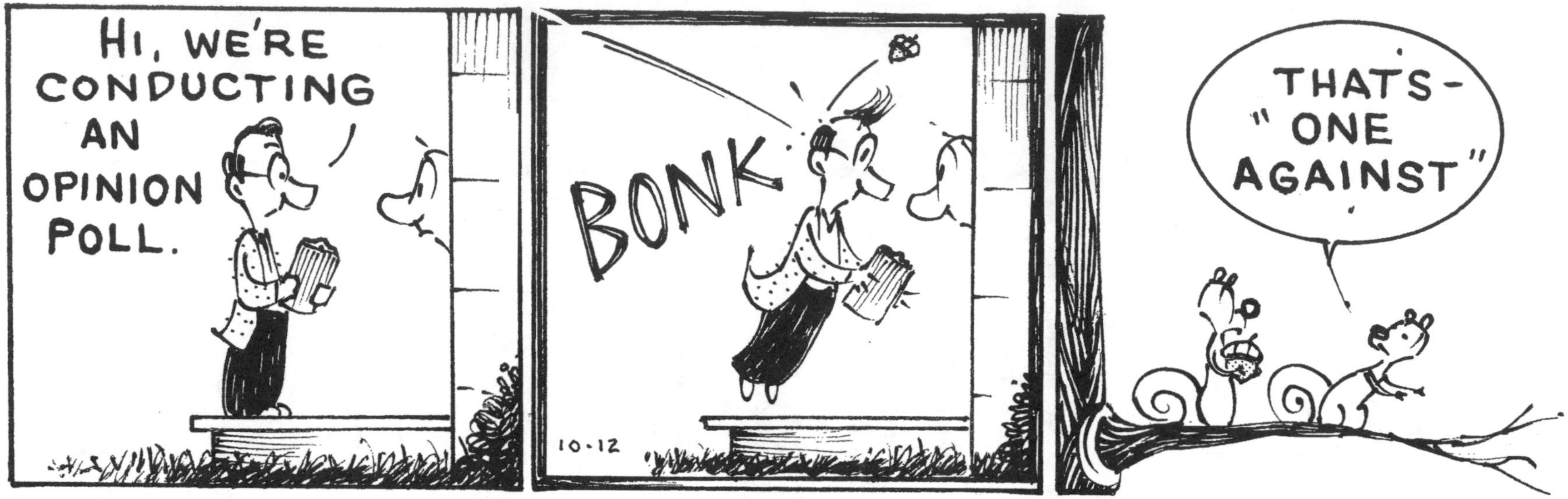
HI, WE'RE CONDUCTING AN OPINION POLL.
BONK
10-12
THAT'S "ONE AGAINST"

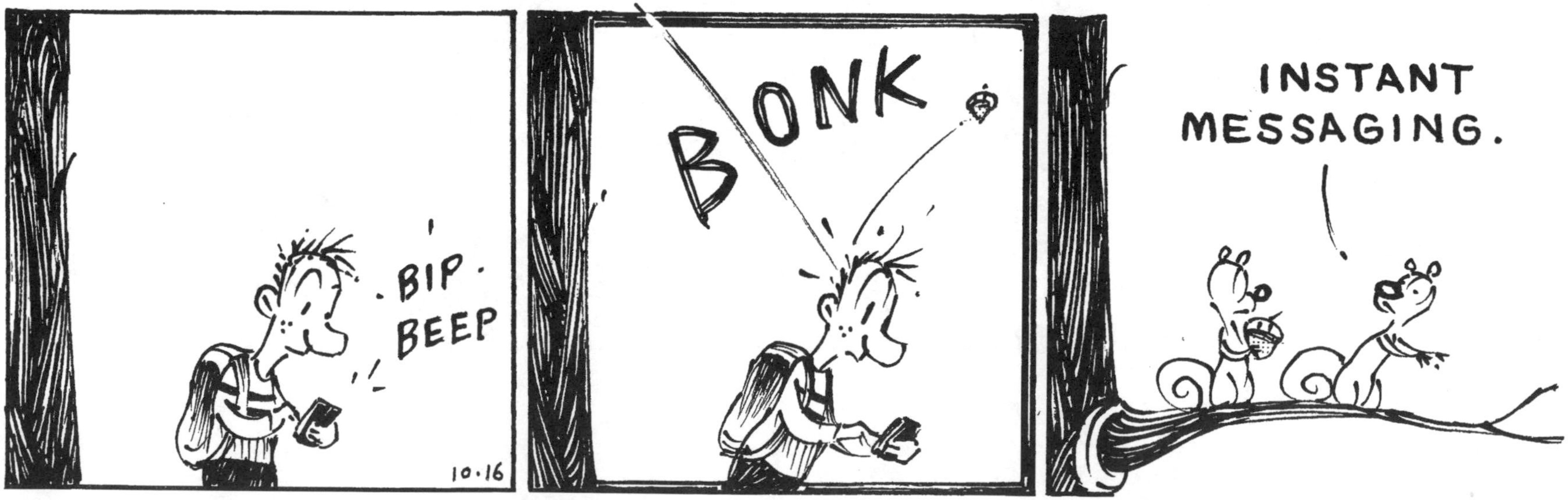
BIP BEEP
10-16
BONK
INSTANT MESSAGING.

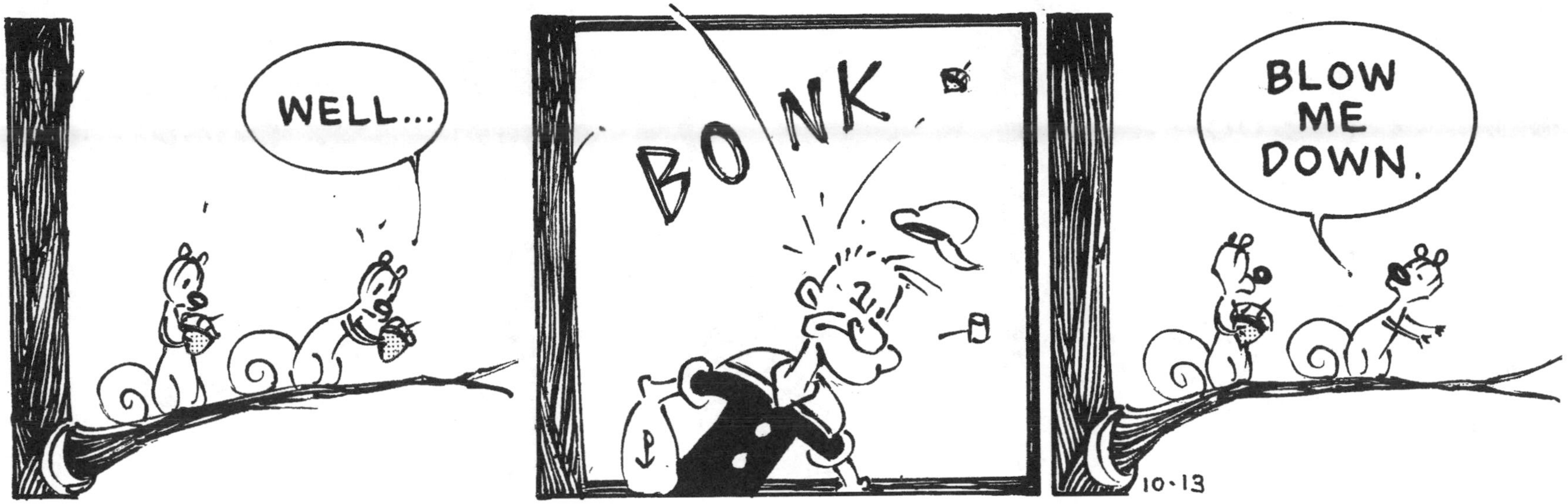
WELL...
BONK
BLOW ME DOWN.
10-13

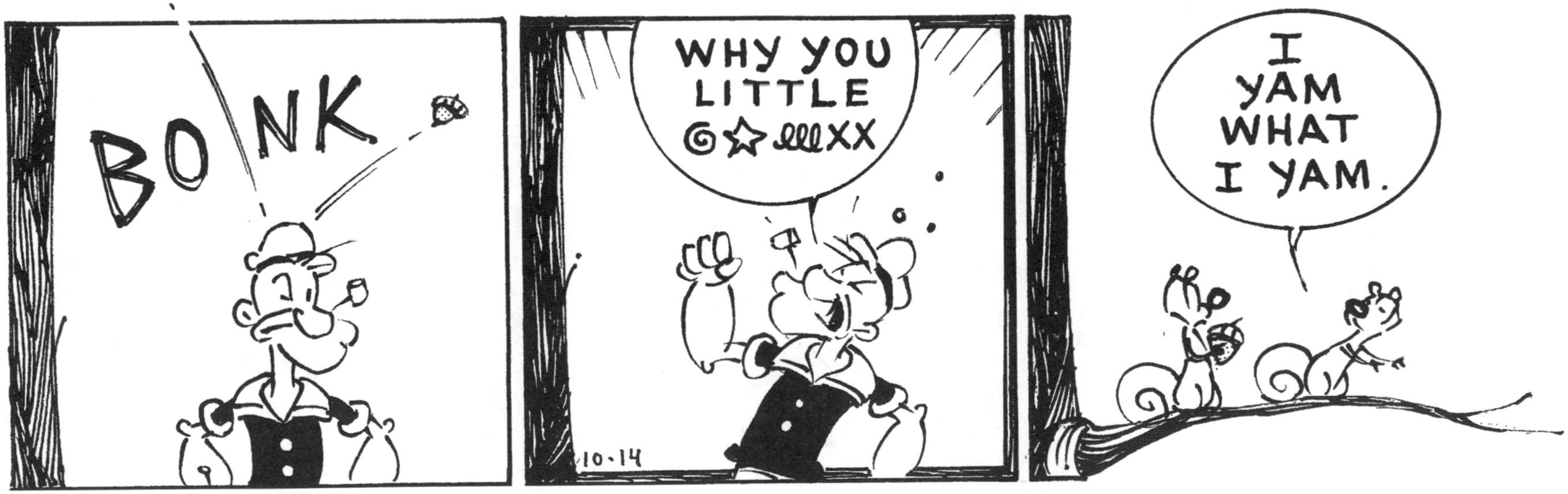
BONK
WHY YOU LITTLE
10-14
I YAM WHAT I YAM.

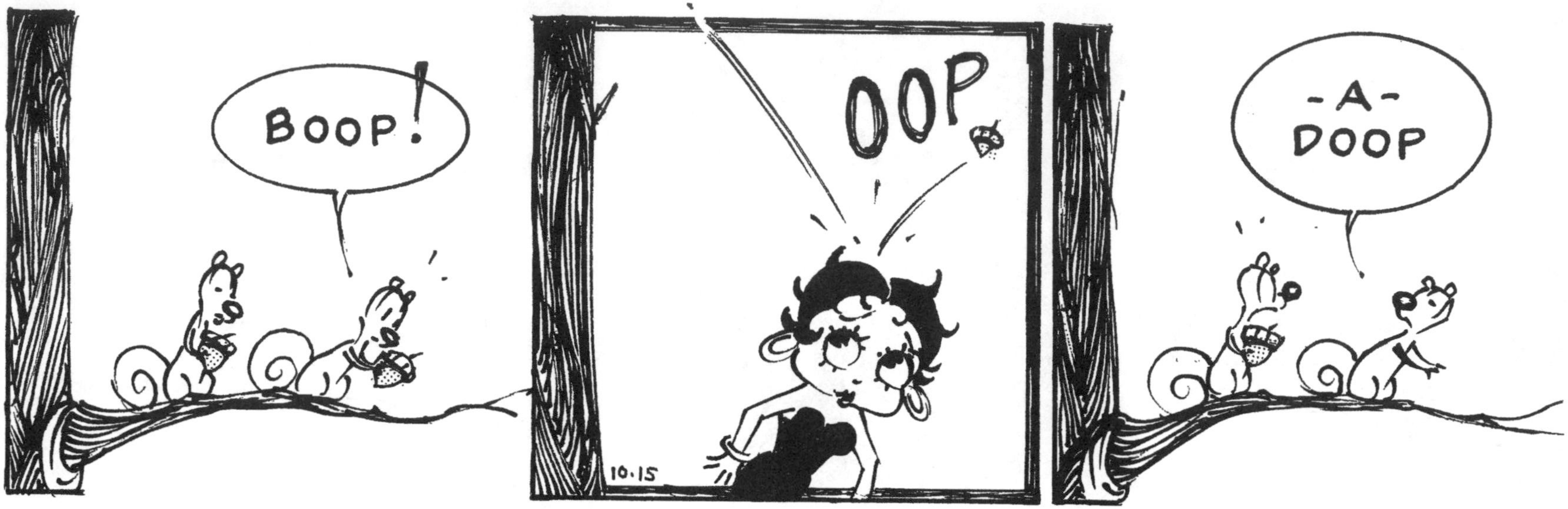
BOOP!
OOP
-A-
DOOP
10.15

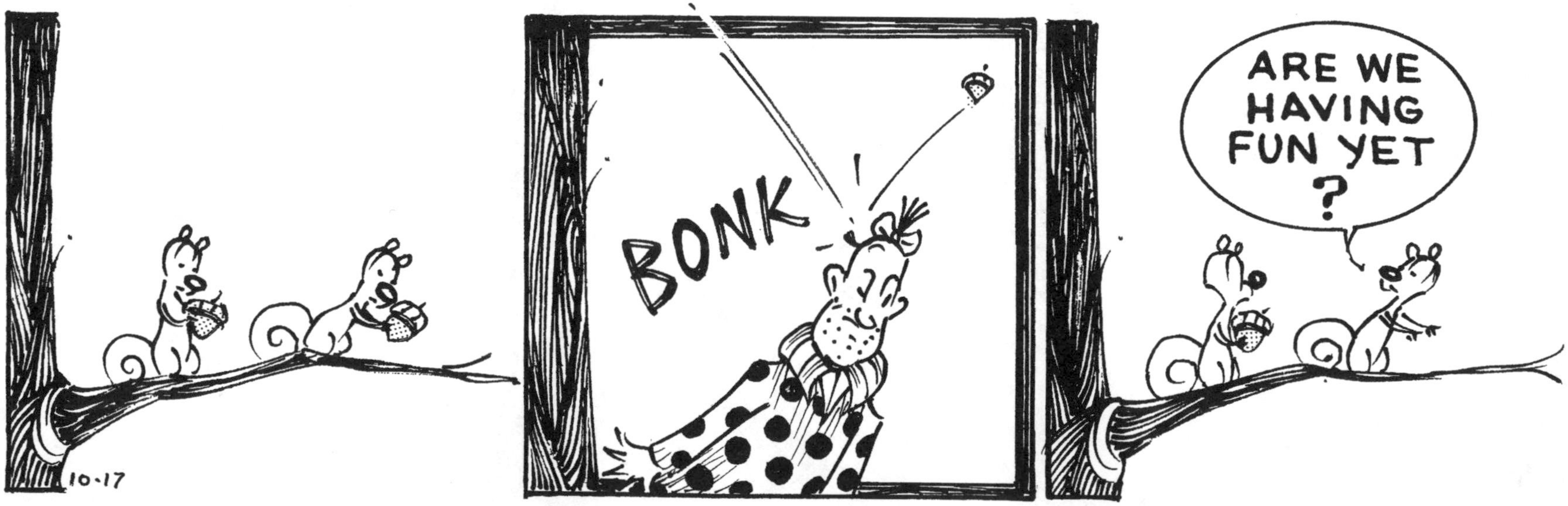
10-17
BONK
ARE WE
HAVING
FUN YET
?

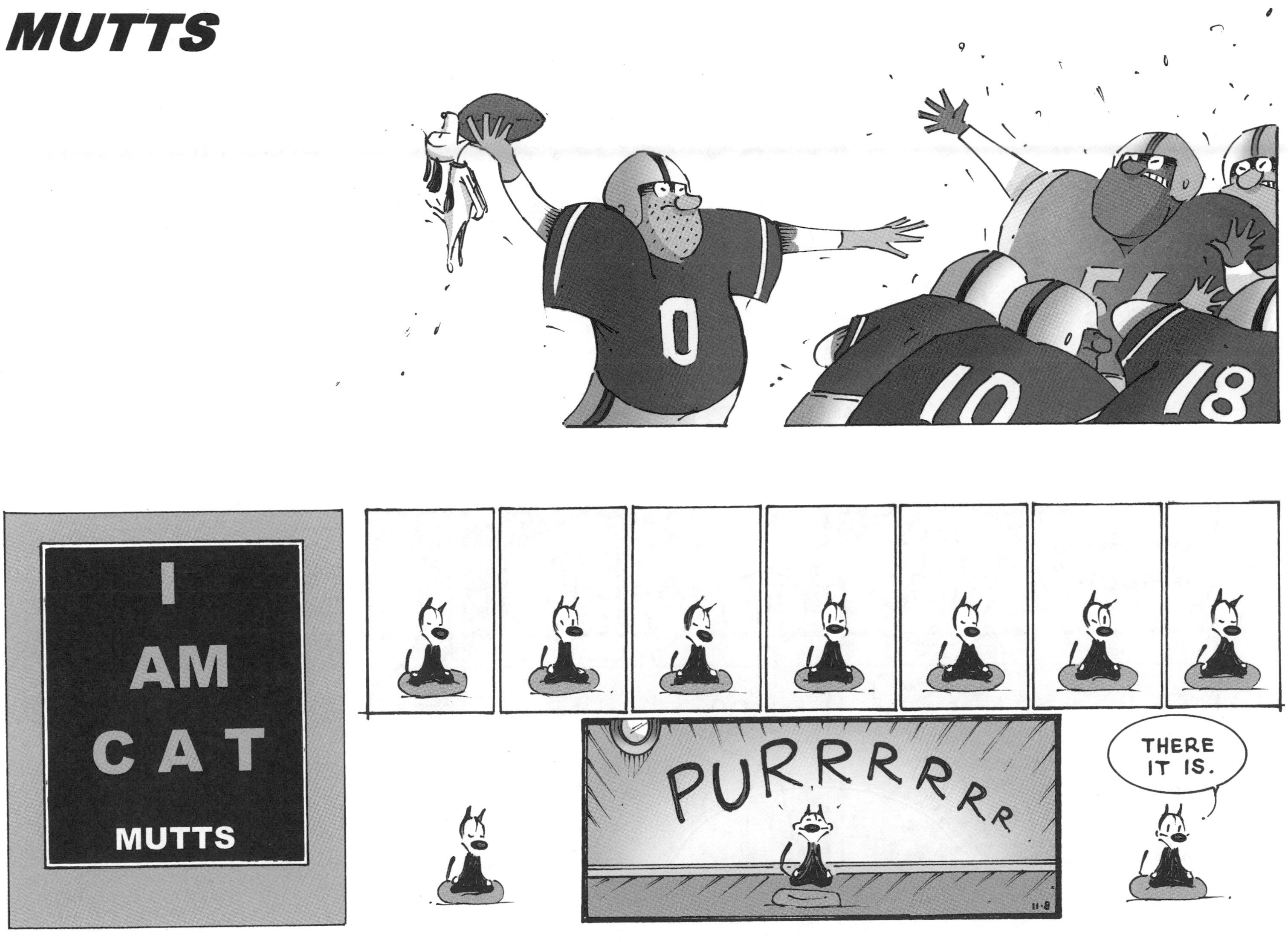
MUTTS
0
10
18
I
AM
CAT
MUTTS
PURRRRRRR
THERE IT IS.

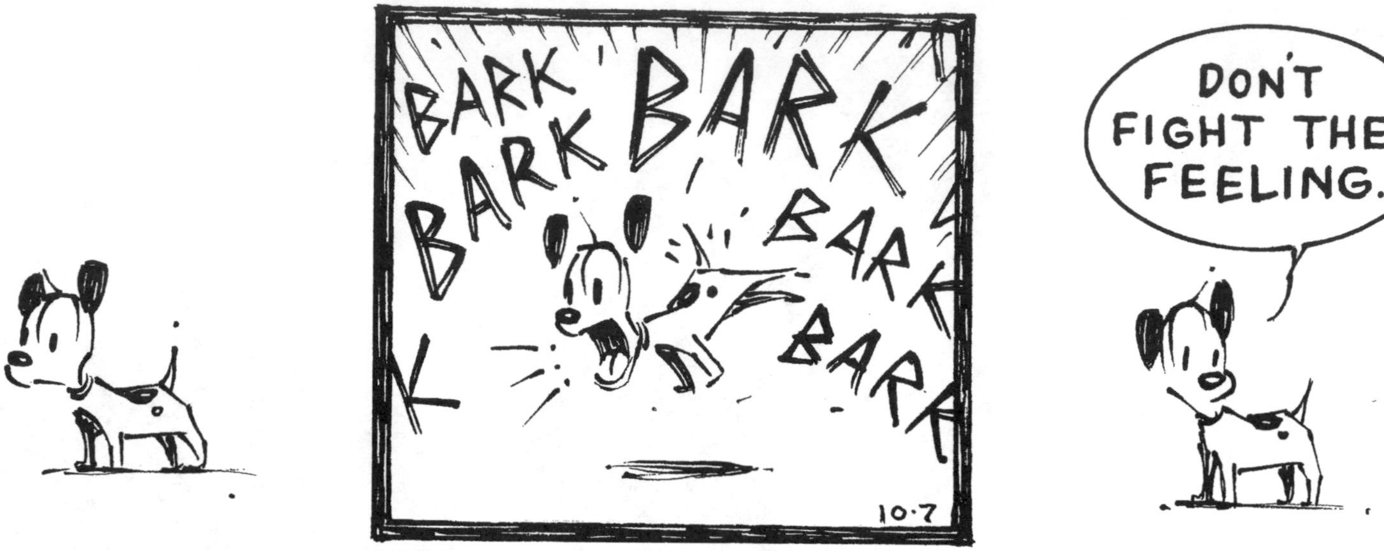
BARK
BARK
BARK
BARK
BARK
10·7
DON'T FIGHT THE FEELING.

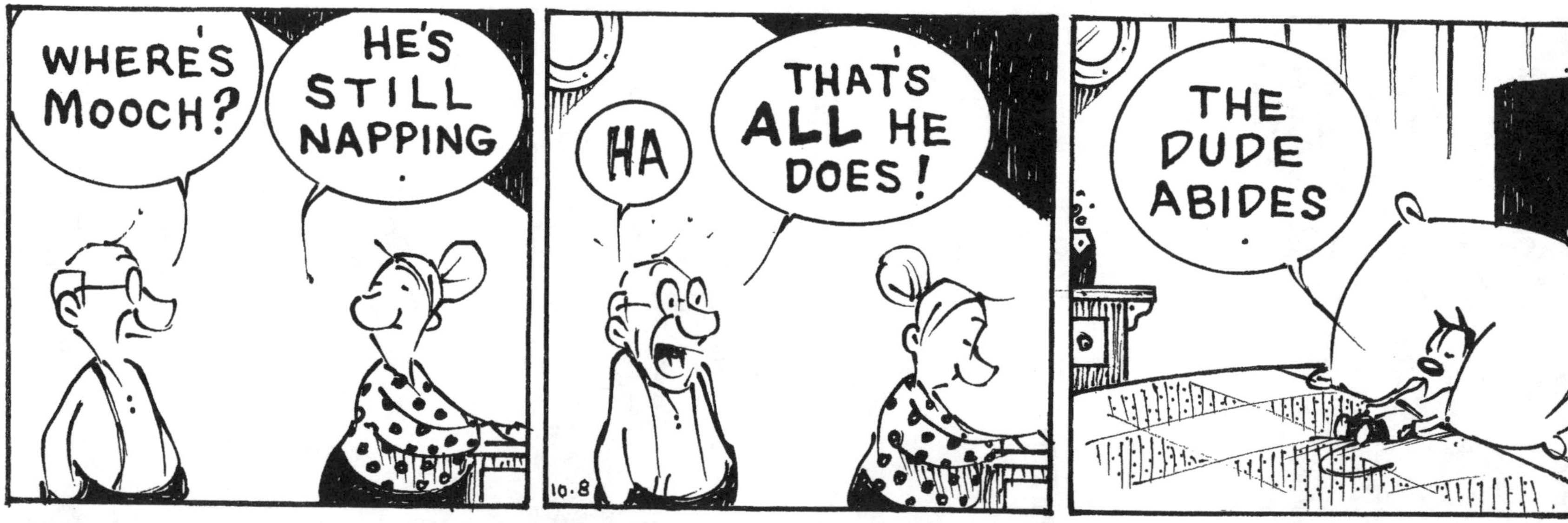
WHERE'S MOOCH?
HE'S STILL NAPPING.
HA
THAT'S **ALL** HE DOES!
10·8
THE DUDE ABIDES.

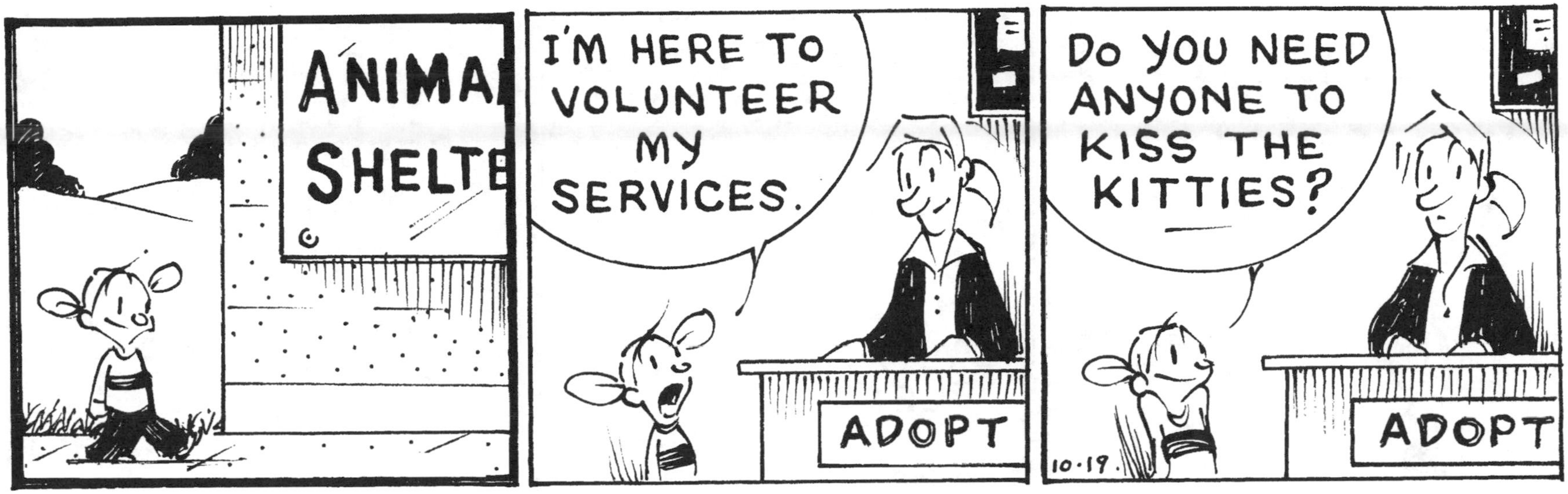
ANIMAL SHELTE
I'M HERE TO VOLUNTEER MY SERVICES.
ADOPT
DO YOU NEED ANYONE TO KISS THE KITTIES?
ADOPT
10·19

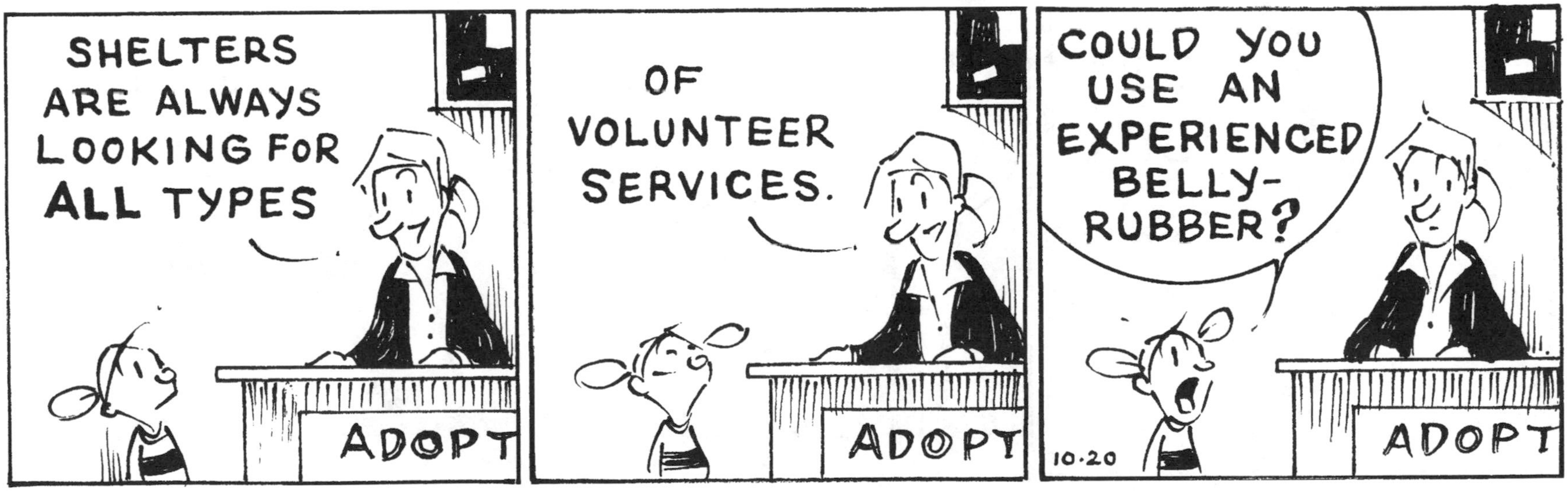
SHELTERS ARE ALWAYS LOOKING FOR ALL TYPES
ADOPT
OF VOLUNTEER SERVICES.
ADOPT
COULD YOU USE AN EXPERIENCED BELLY-RUBBER?
ADOPT
10·20

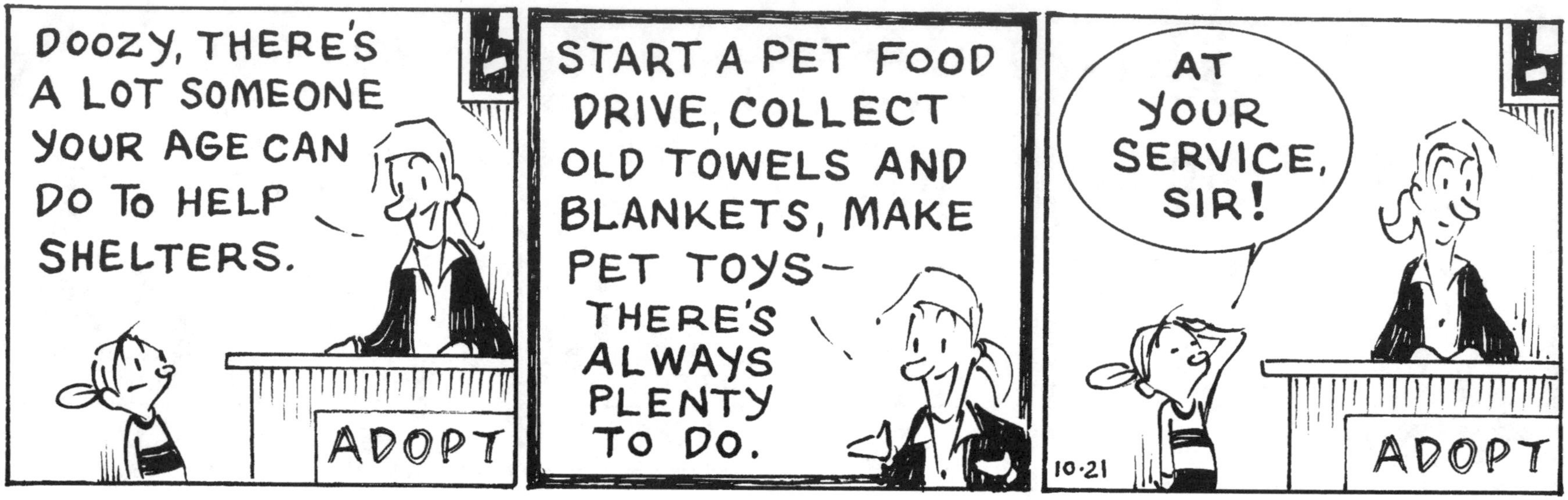
DOOZY, THERE'S A LOT SOMEONE YOUR AGE CAN DO TO HELP SHELTERS.
ADOPT
START A PET FOOD DRIVE, COLLECT OLD TOWELS AND BLANKETS, MAKE PET TOYS—
THERE'S ALWAYS PLENTY TO DO.
AT YOUR SERVICE, SIR!
ADOPT
10·21

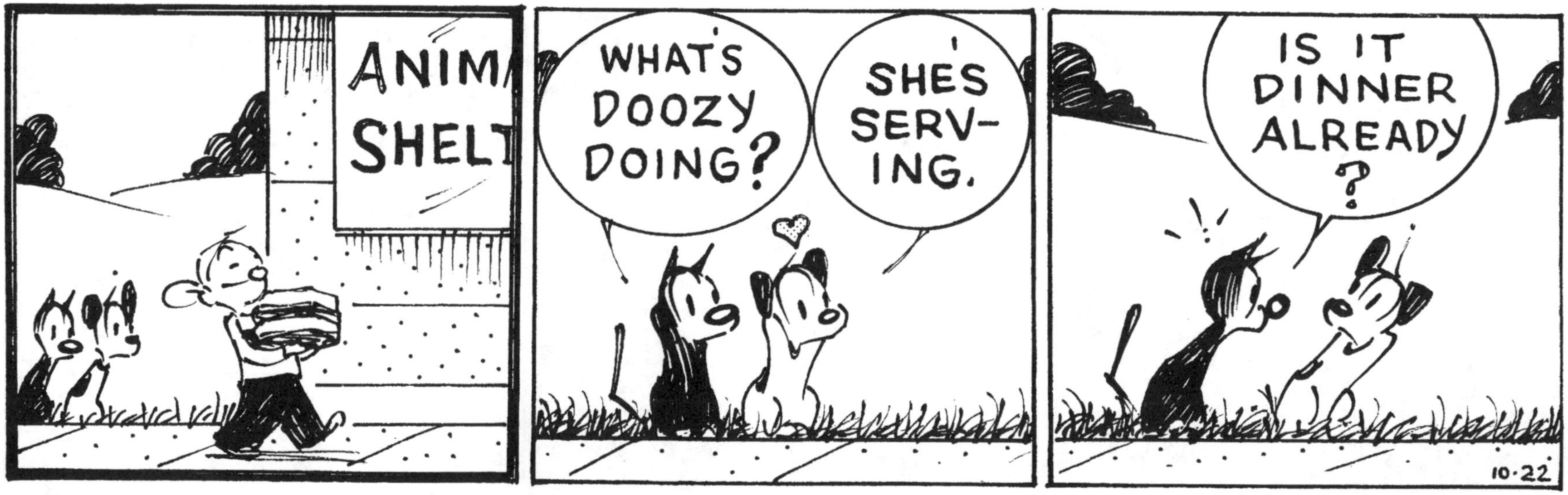
ANIM
SHELT
WHAT'S DOOZY DOING?
SHE'S SERV-ING.
IS IT DINNER ALREADY?
10·22

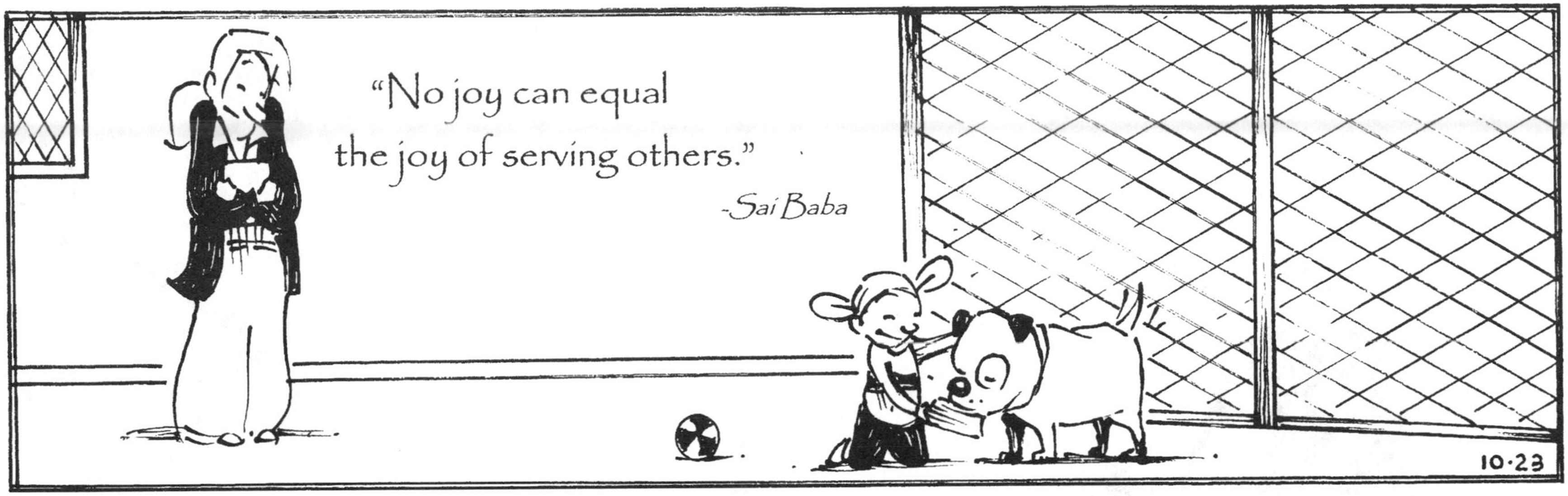
"No joy can equal the joy of serving others."
-Sai Baba
10·23

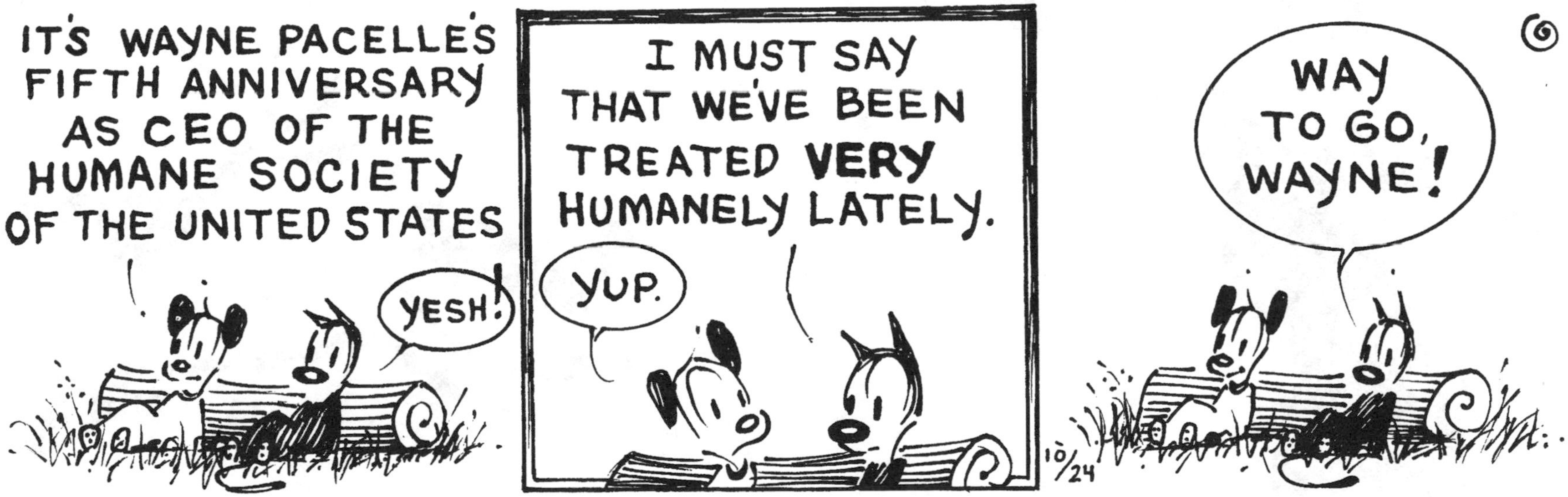
IT'S WAYNE PACELLE'S FIFTH ANNIVERSARY AS CEO OF THE HUMANE SOCIETY OF THE UNITED STATES
YESH!
I MUST SAY THAT WE'VE BEEN TREATED **VERY** HUMANELY LATELY.
YUP.
WAY TO GO, WAYNE!
10/24

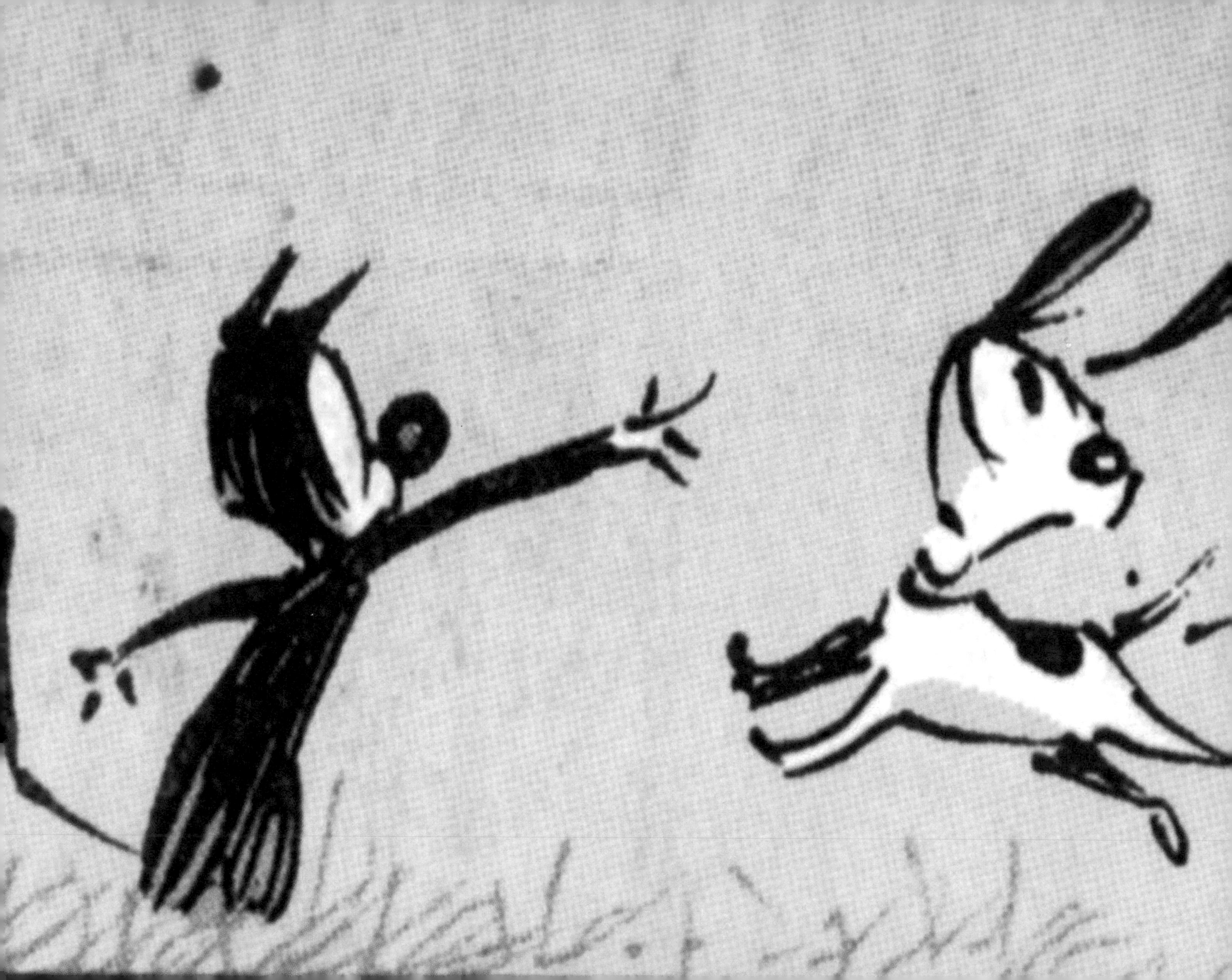

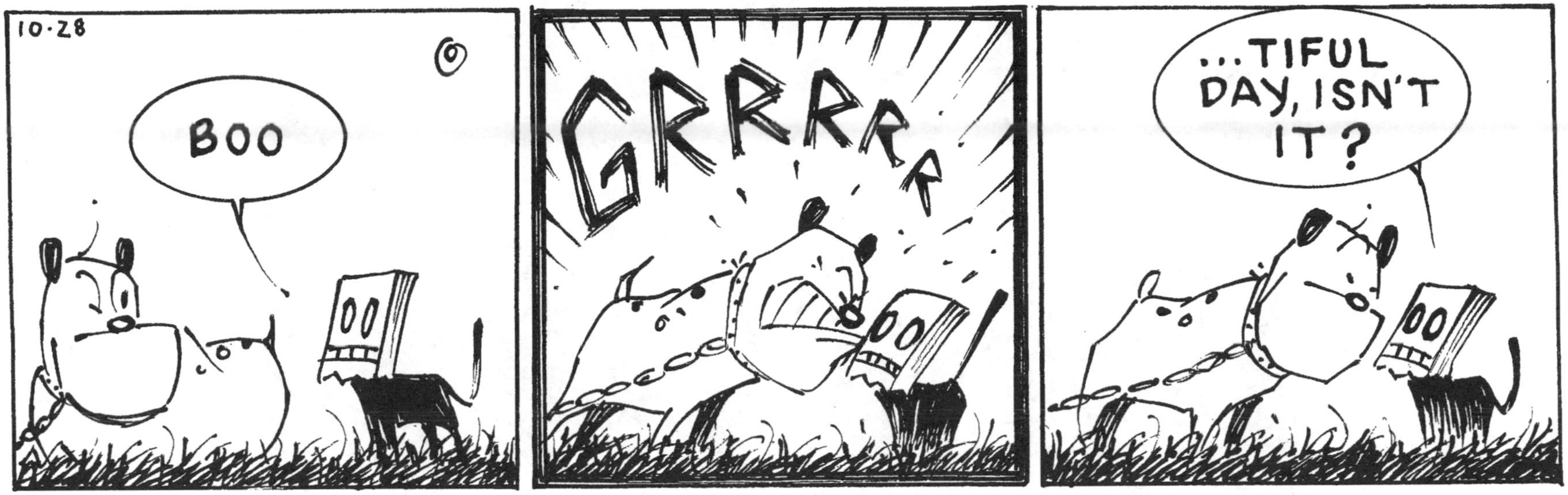
10·28
BOO
GRRRRR
...TIFUL DAY, ISN'T IT?

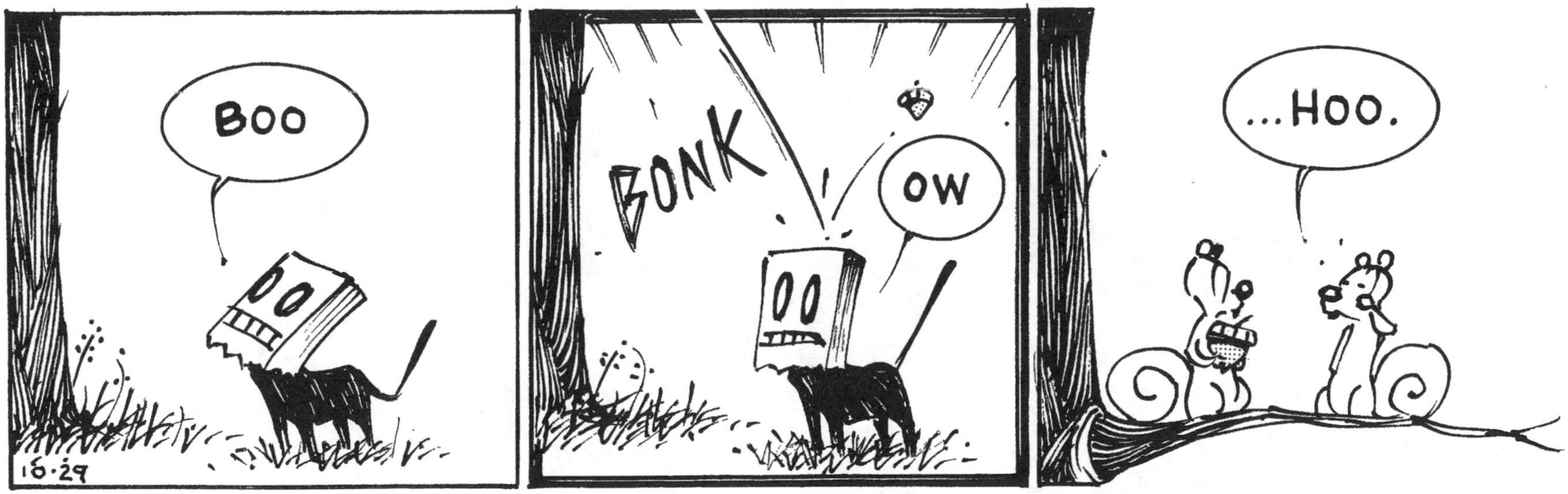
BOO
10·29
BONK
OW
...HOO.

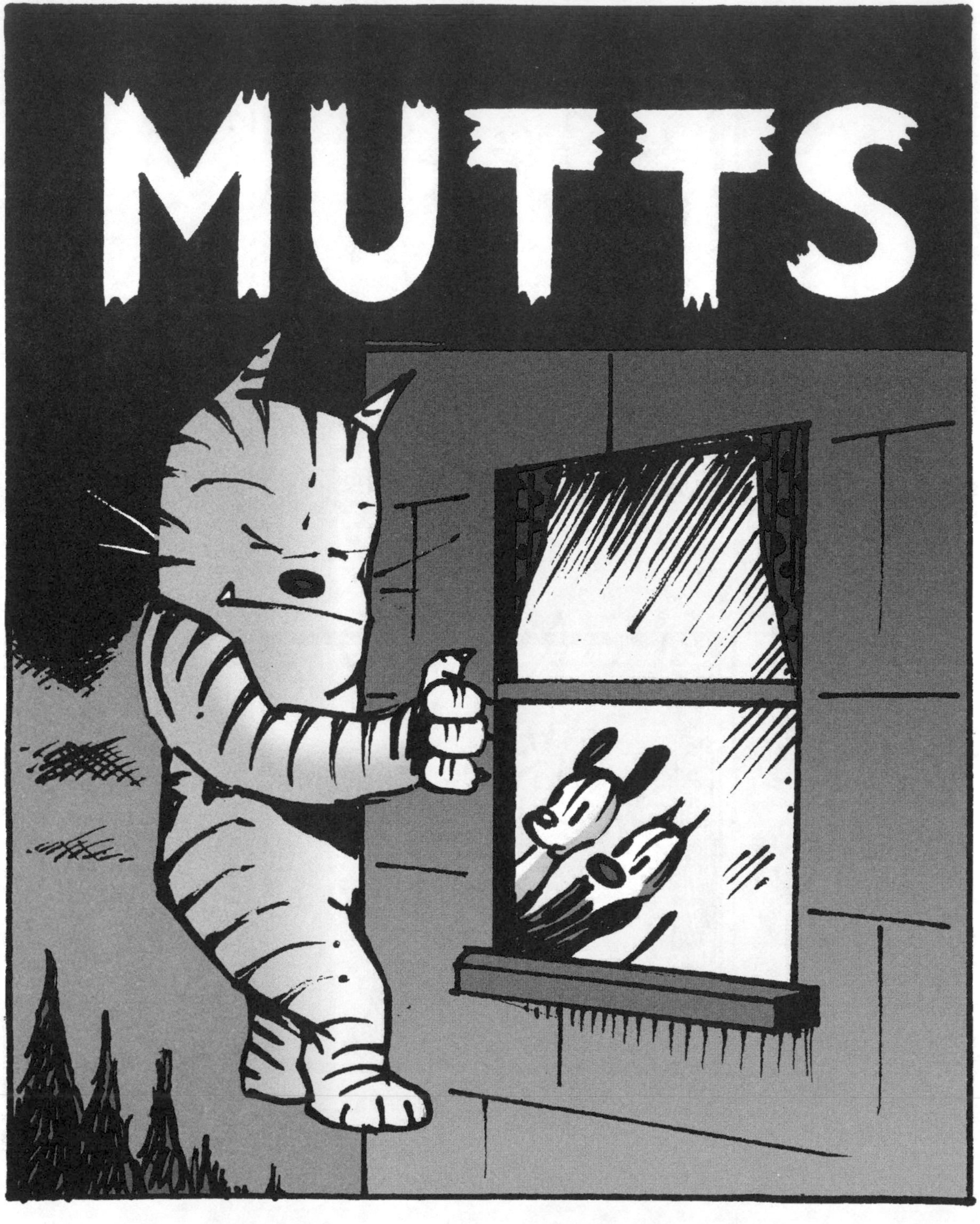
MUTTS

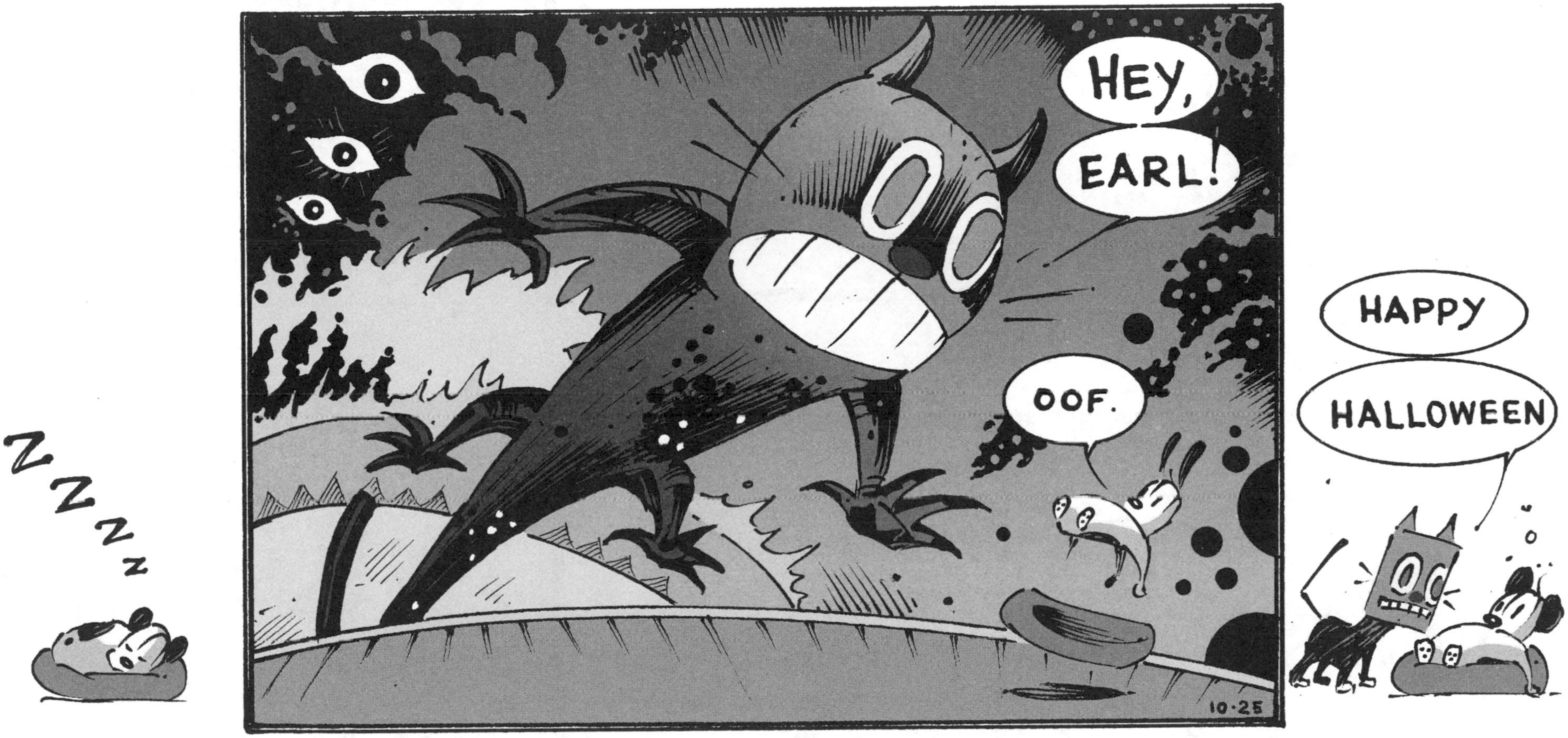
Z Z Z Z Z
HEY, EARL!
OOF.
10-25
HAPPY
HALLOWEEN

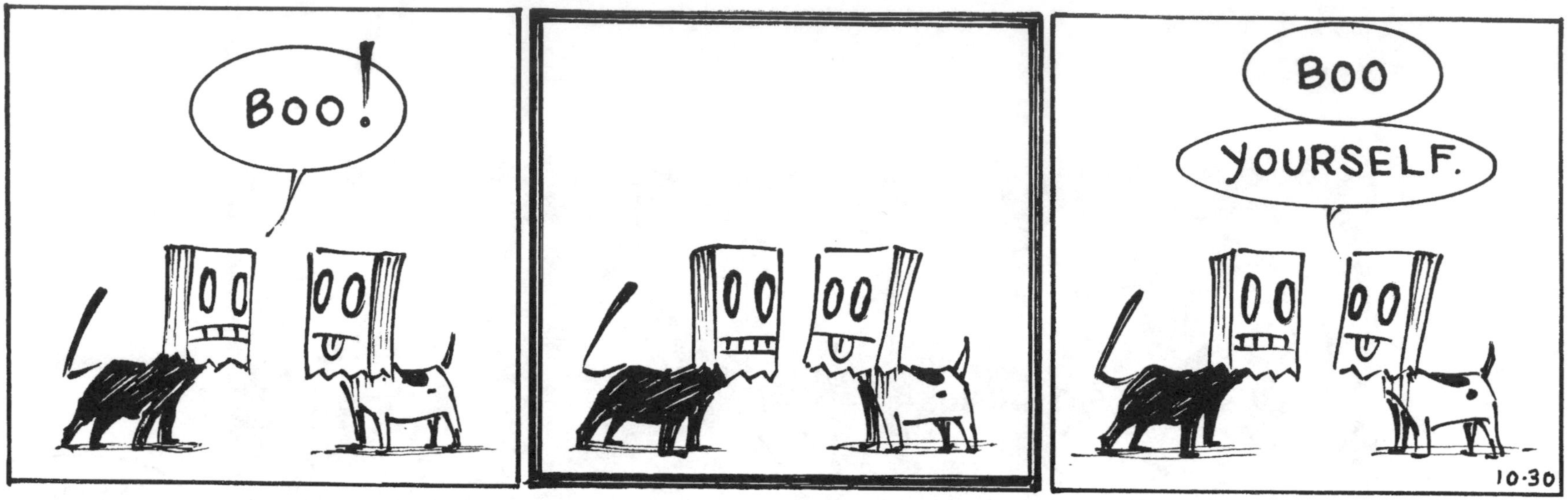
BOO!
BOO
YOURSELF.
10·30

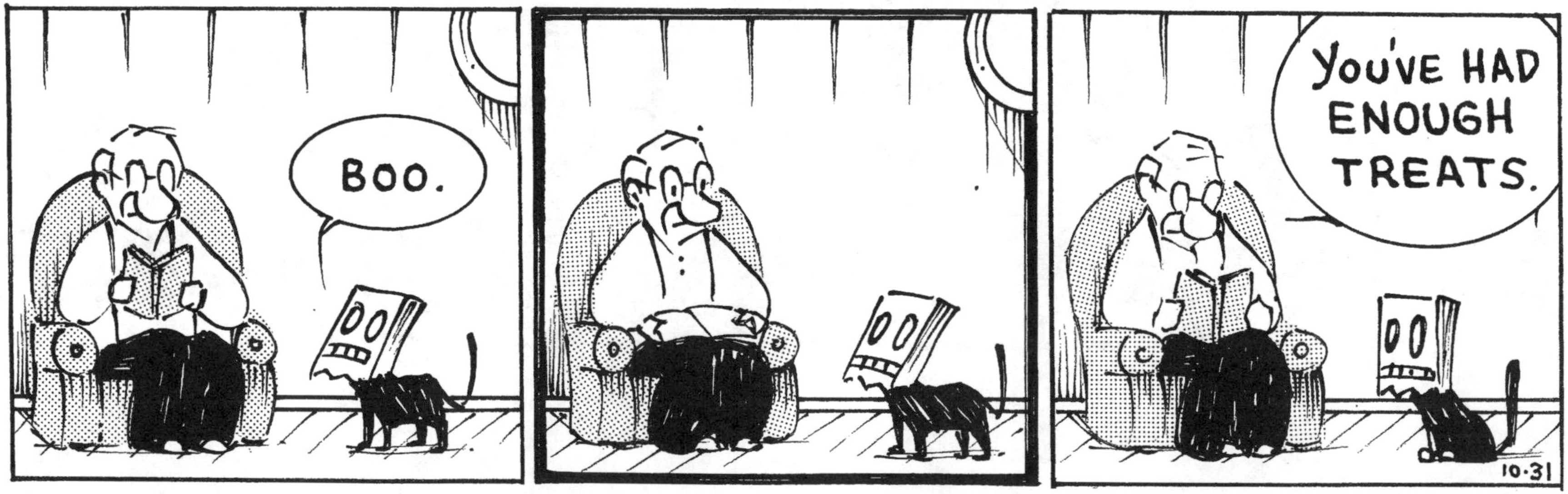
BOO.
YOU'VE HAD
ENOUGH
TREATS.
10·31

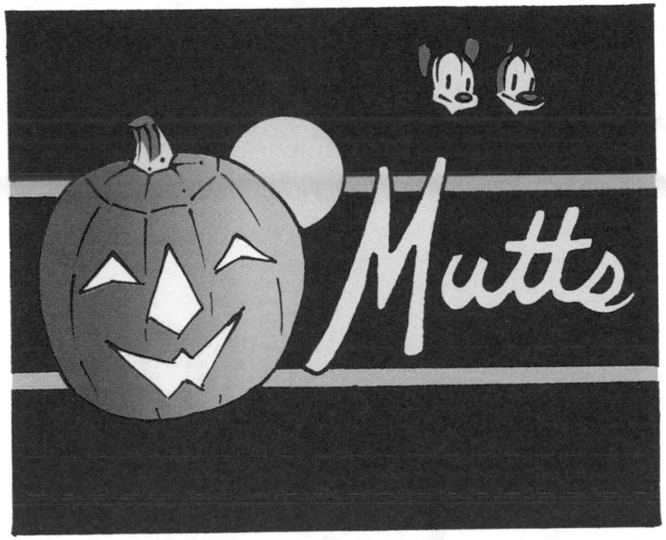
Mutts

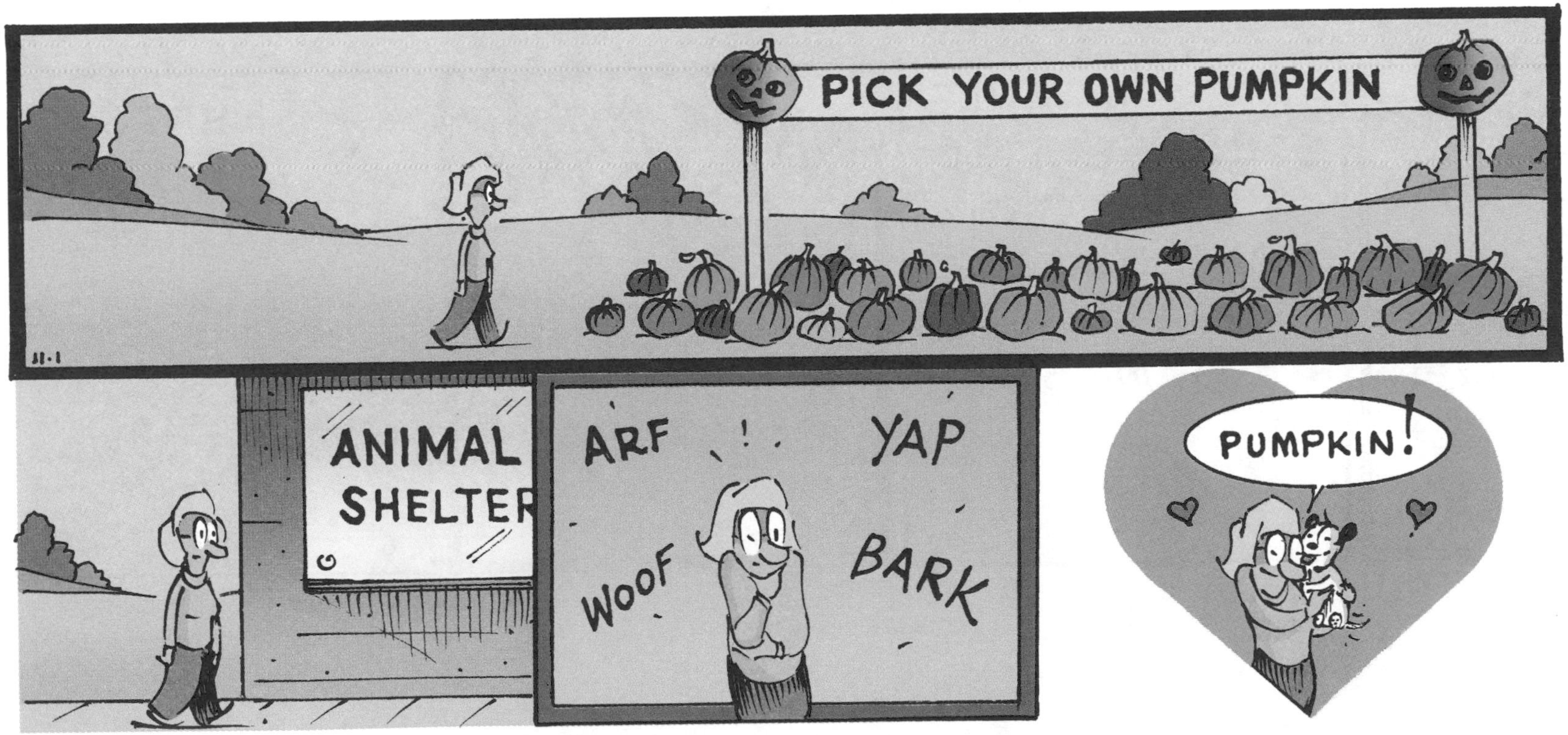
PICK YOUR OWN PUMPKIN
ANIMAL SHELTER
ARF
!
YAP
WOOF
BARK
PUMPKIN!

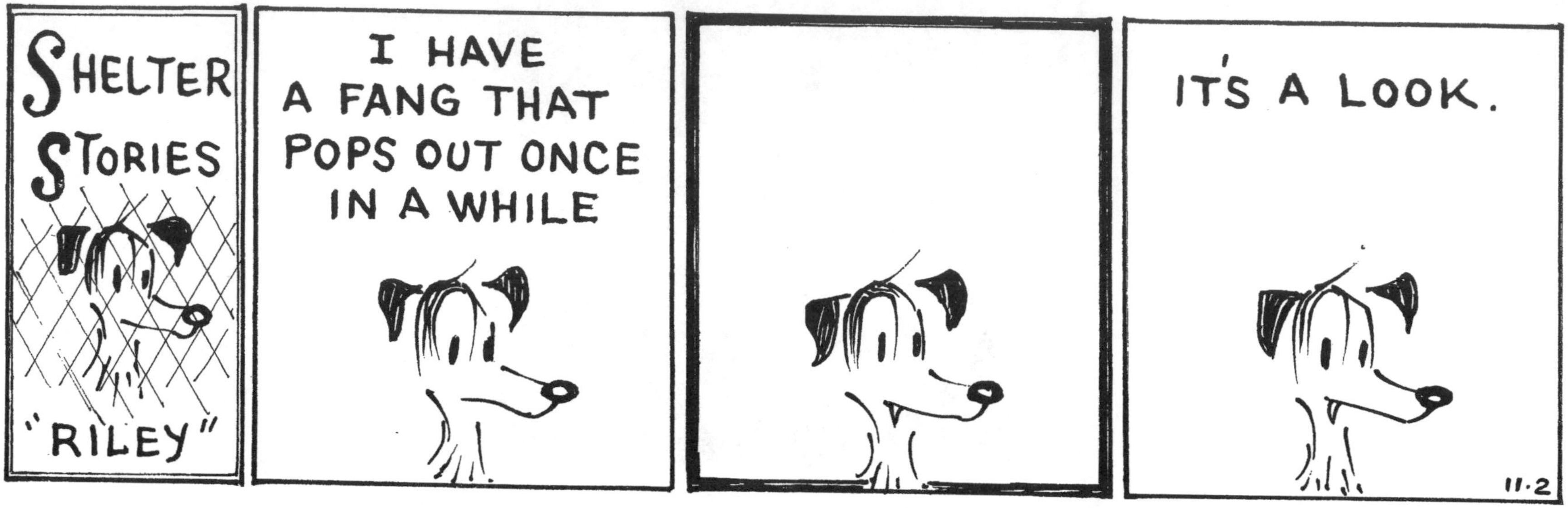
SHELTER STORIES
"RILEY"
I HAVE A FANG THAT POPS OUT ONCE IN A WHILE
IT'S A LOOK.
11·2

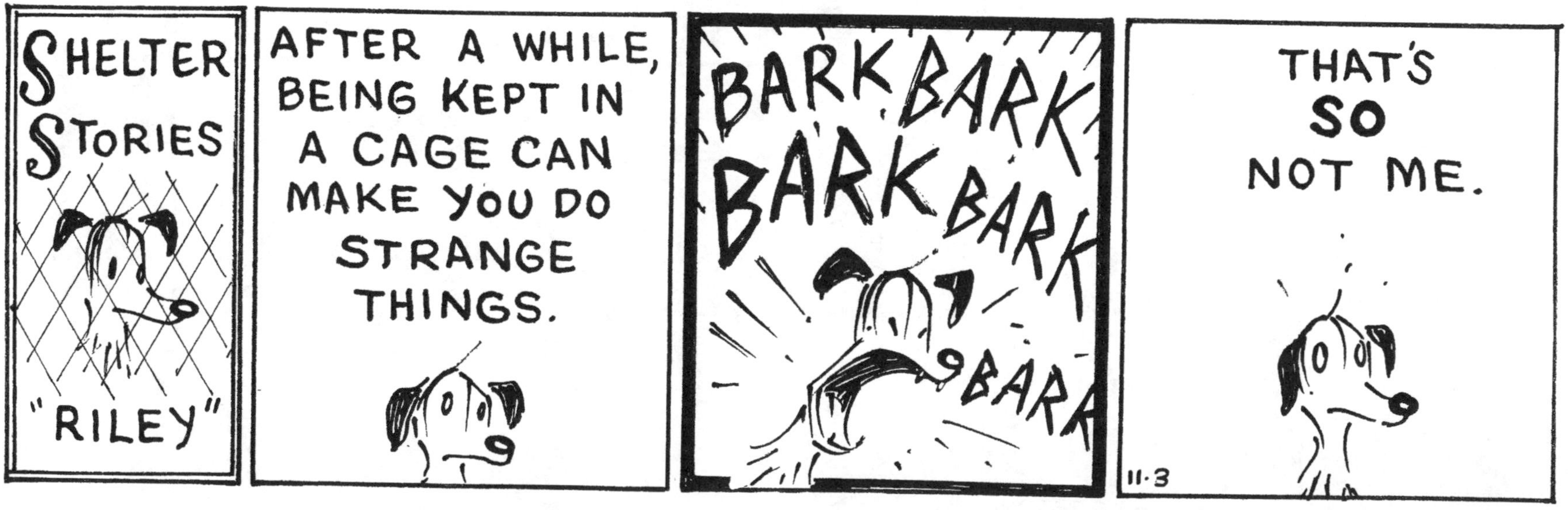
SHELTER STORIES
"RILEY"
AFTER A WHILE, BEING KEPT IN A CAGE CAN MAKE YOU DO STRANGE THINGS.
BARK BARK
BARK BARK
BARK
THAT'S **SO** NOT ME.
11·3

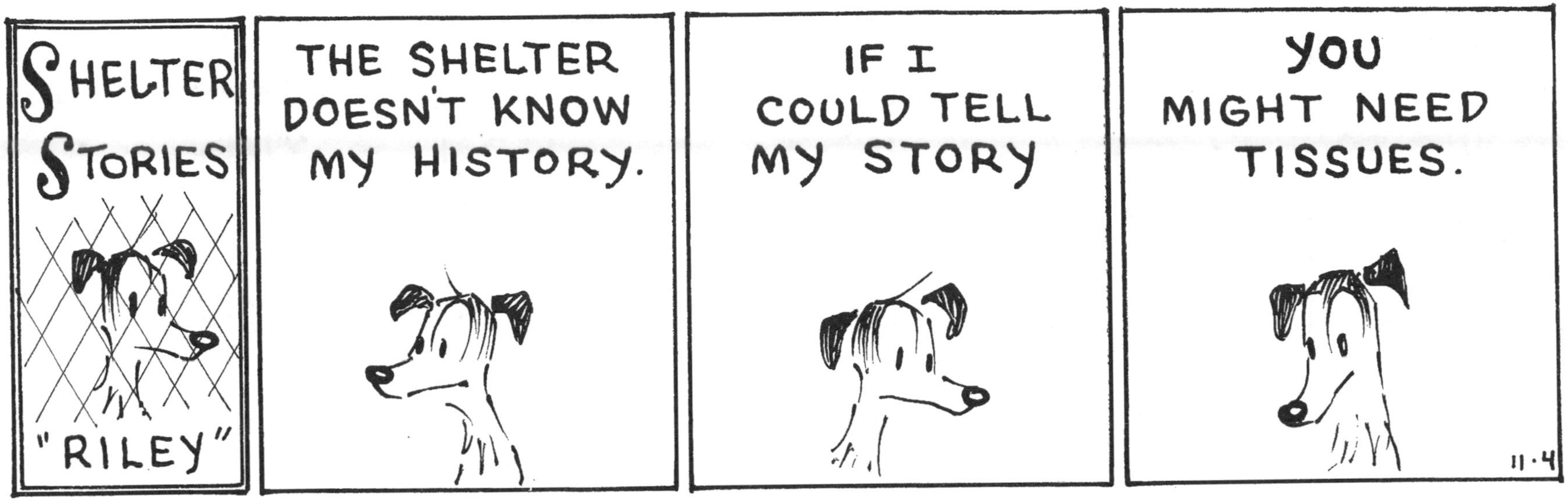
SHELTER STORIES
"RILEY"
THE SHELTER DOESN'T KNOW MY HISTORY.
IF I COULD TELL MY STORY
YOU MIGHT NEED TISSUES.
11·4

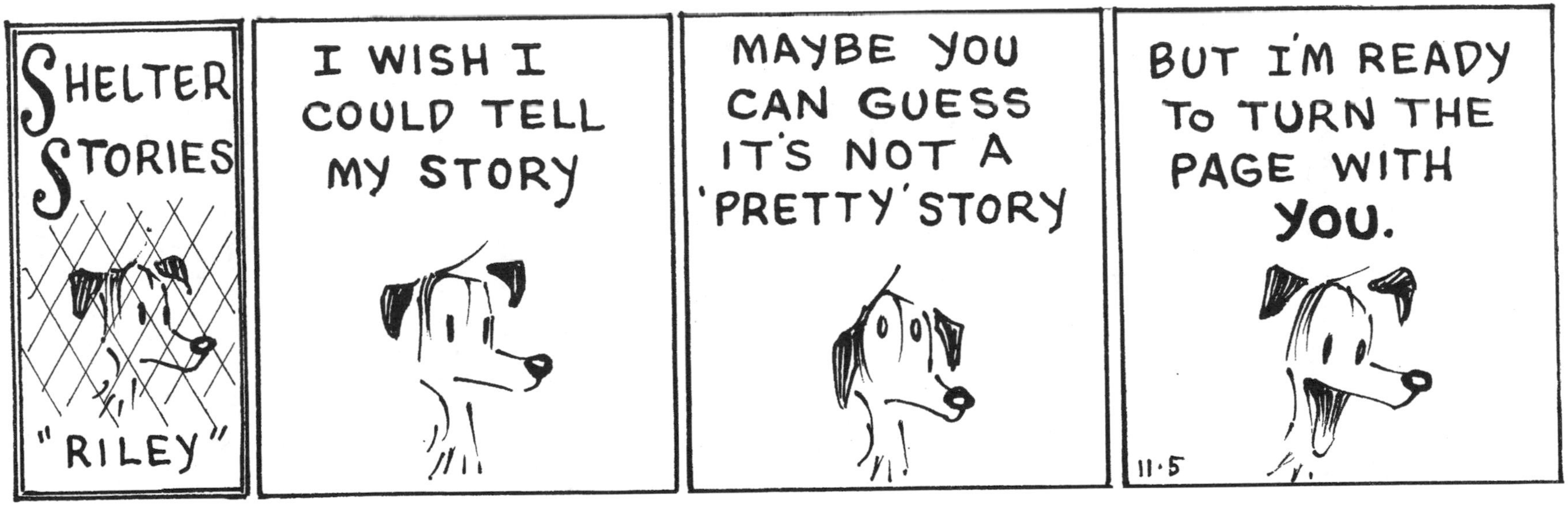
SHELTER STORIES
"RILEY"
I WISH I COULD TELL MY STORY
MAYBE YOU CAN GUESS IT'S NOT A 'PRETTY' STORY
BUT I'M READY TO TURN THE PAGE WITH YOU.
11·5

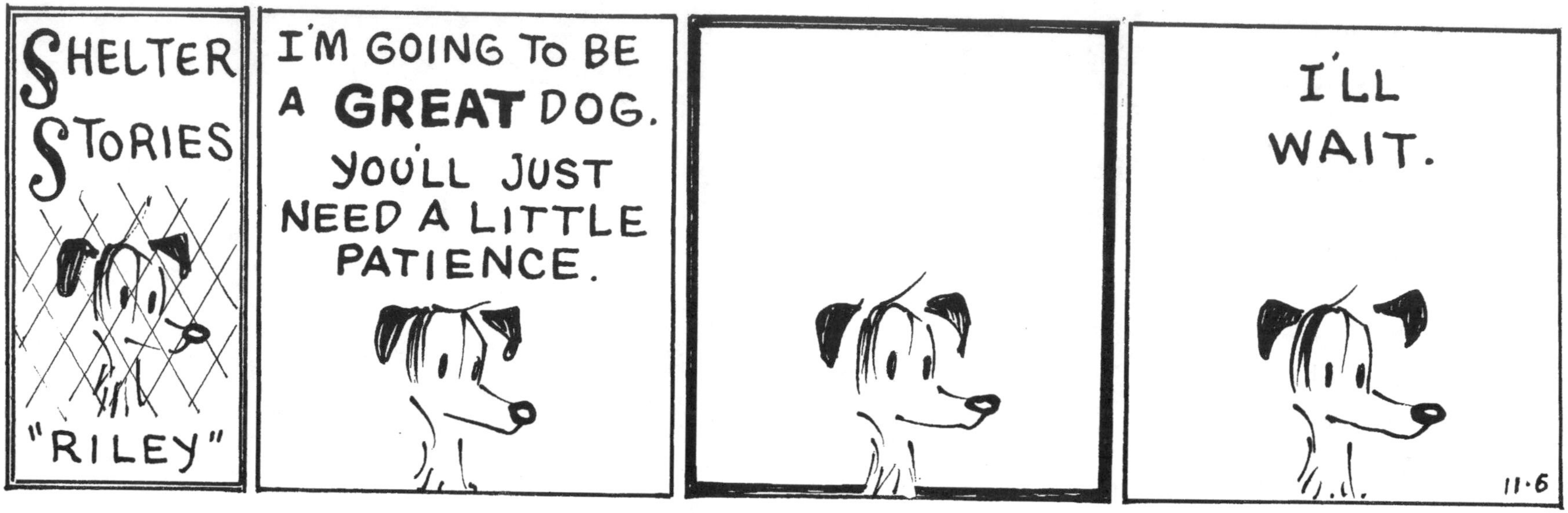
SHELTER STORIES
"RILEY"
I'M GOING TO BE A GREAT DOG.
YOU'LL JUST NEED A LITTLE PATIENCE.
I'LL WAIT.
11·6

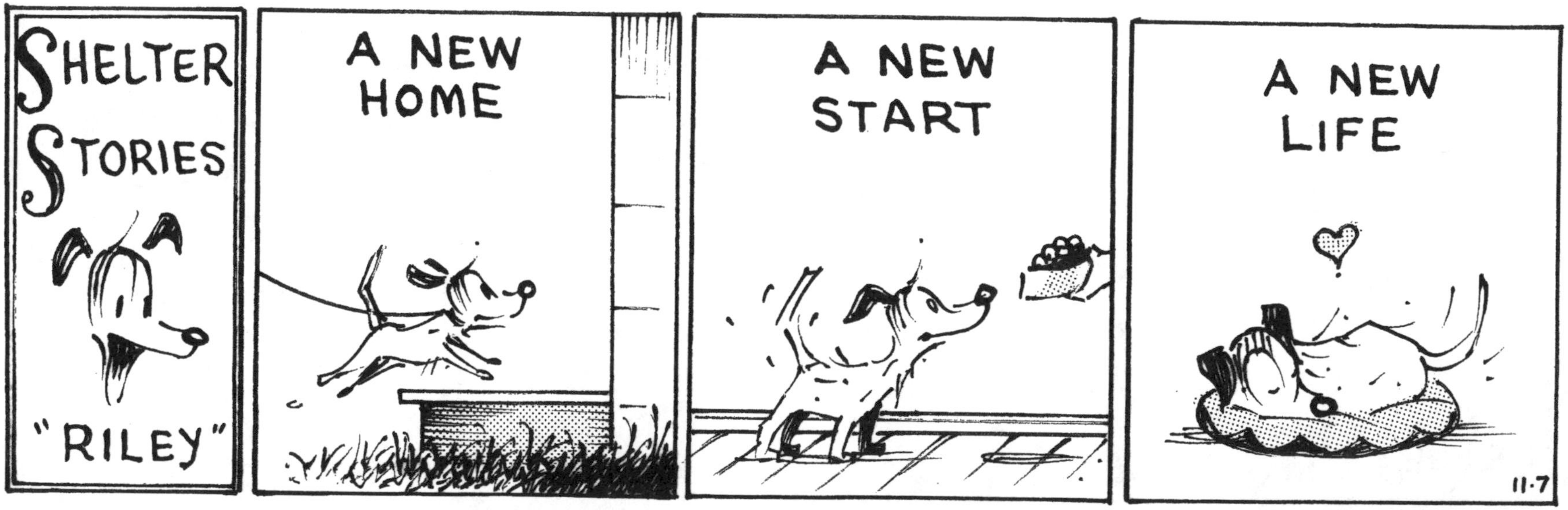
SHELTER STORIES
"RILEY"
A NEW HOME
A NEW START
A NEW LIFE
11·7

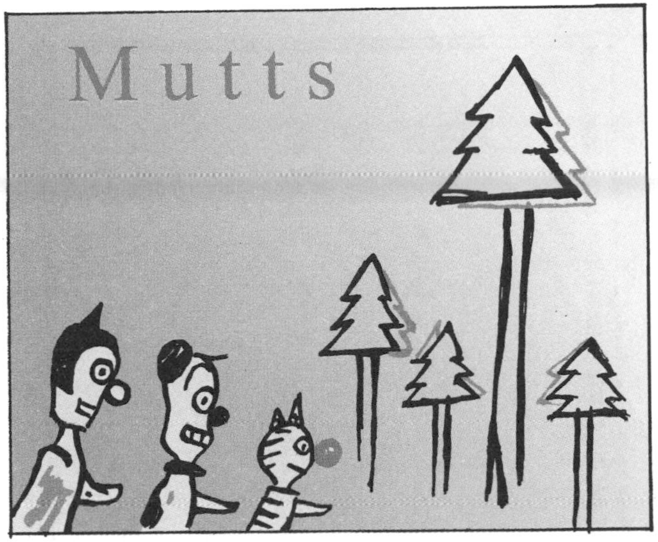
Mutts

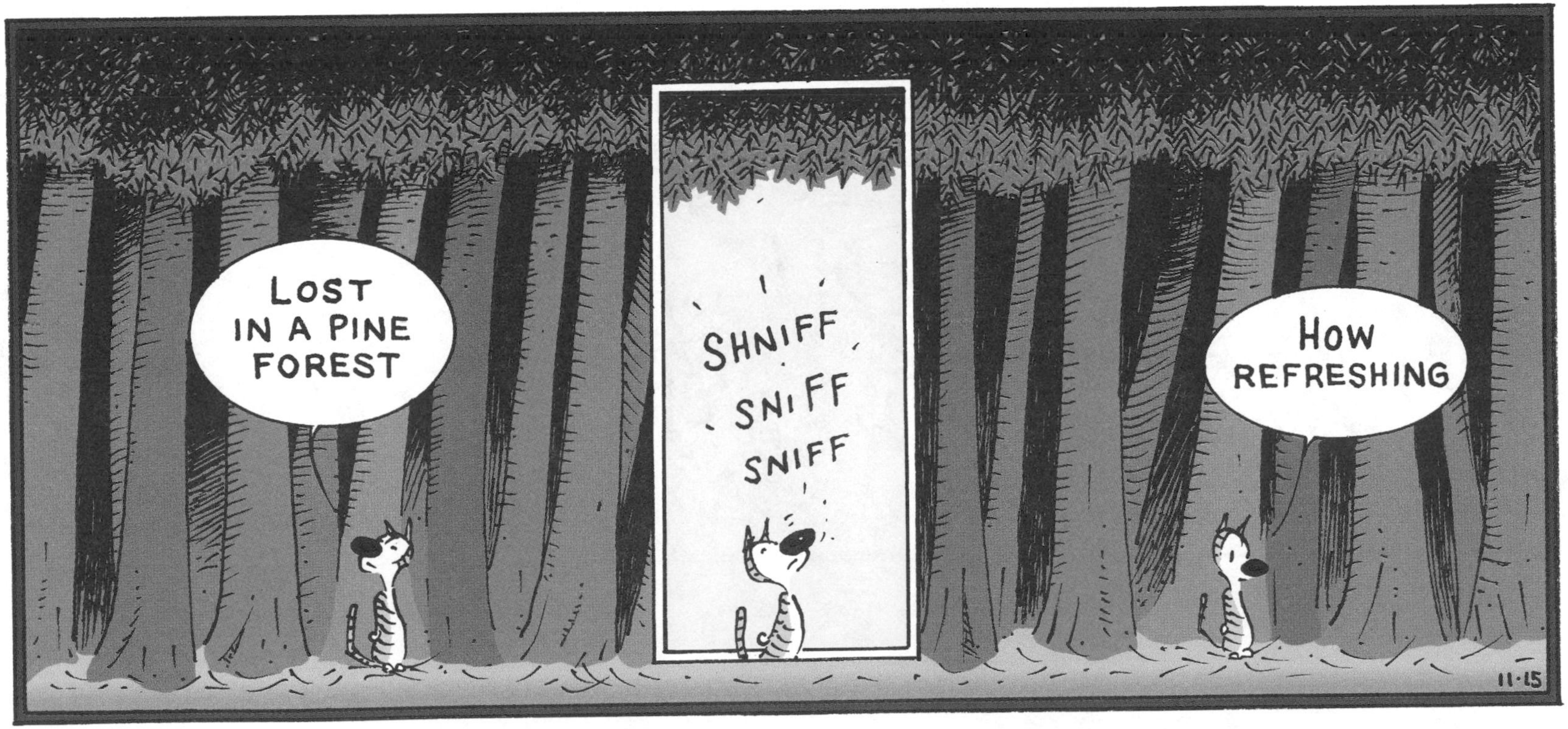
LOST IN A PINE FOREST
SHNIFF SNIFF SNIFF
HOW REFRESHING
11-15

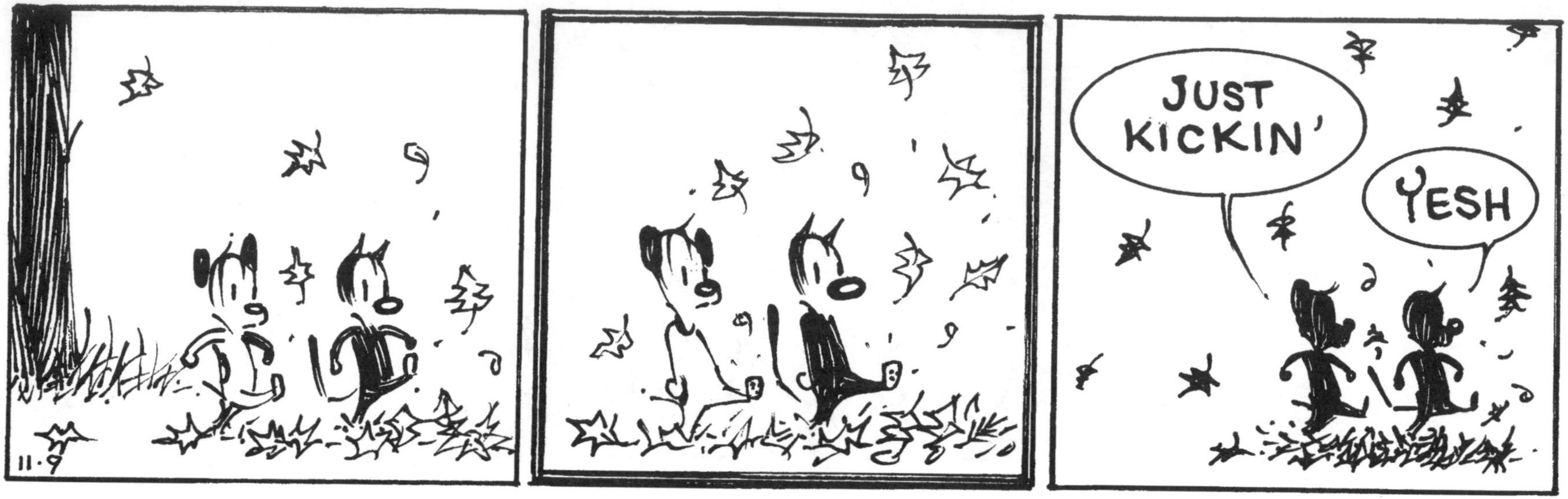
11·9
JUST KICKIN'
YESH

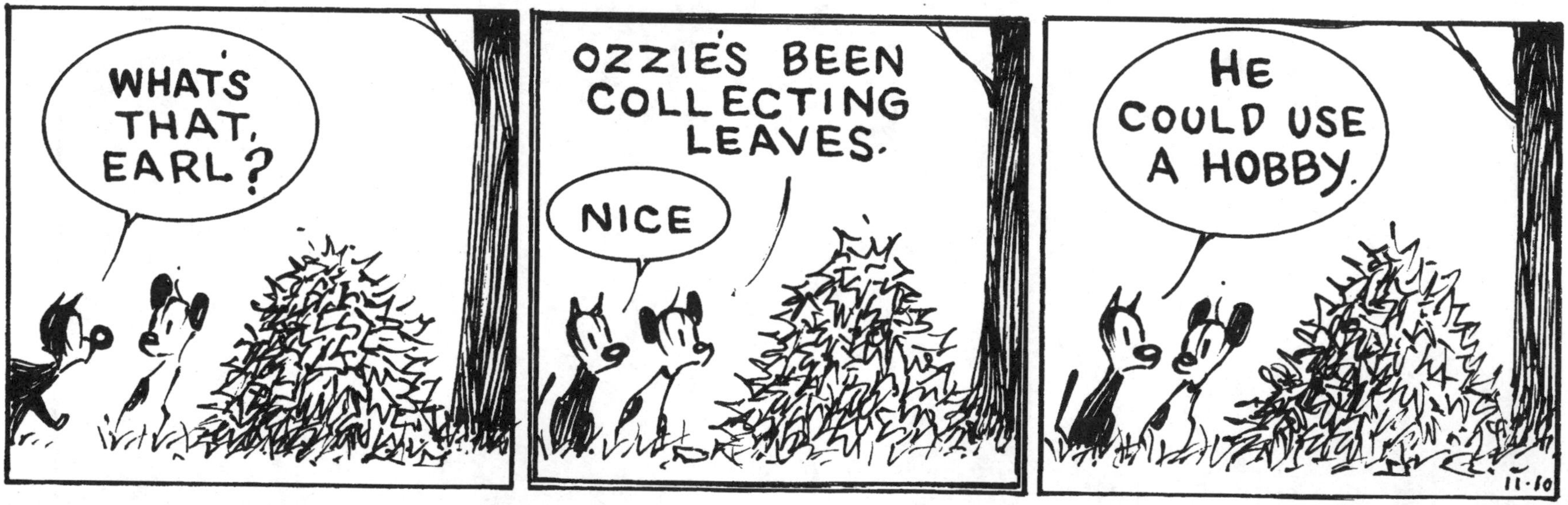
WHAT'S THAT, EARL?
OZZIE'S BEEN COLLECTING LEAVES.
NICE
HE COULD USE A HOBBY.
11·10

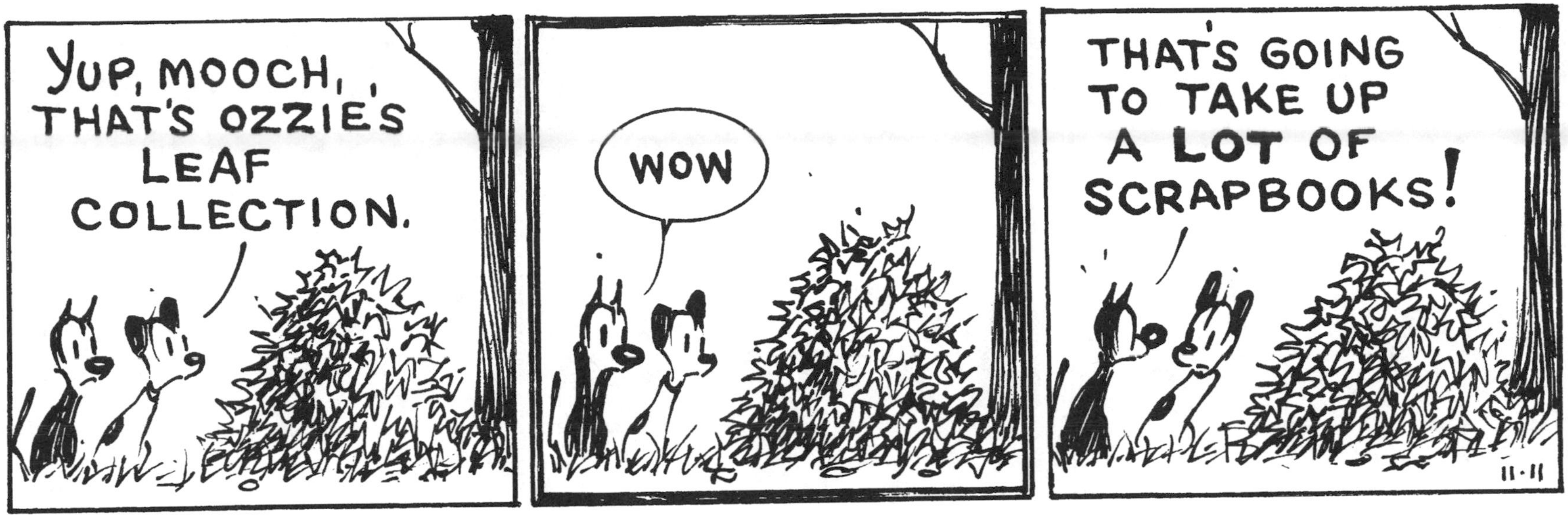
YUP, MOOCH, THAT'S OZZIE'S LEAF COLLECTION.
WOW
THAT'S GOING TO TAKE UP A LOT OF SCRAPBOOKS!
11-11

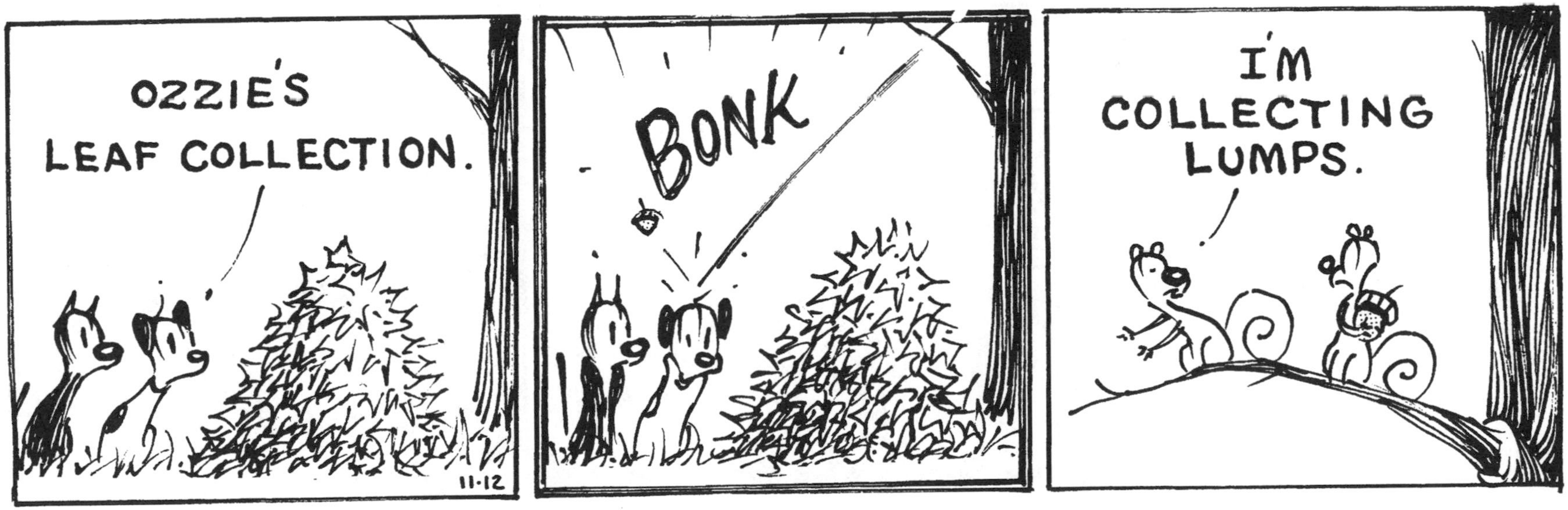
OZZIE'S LEAF COLLECTION.
11-12
BONK
I'M COLLECTING LUMPS.

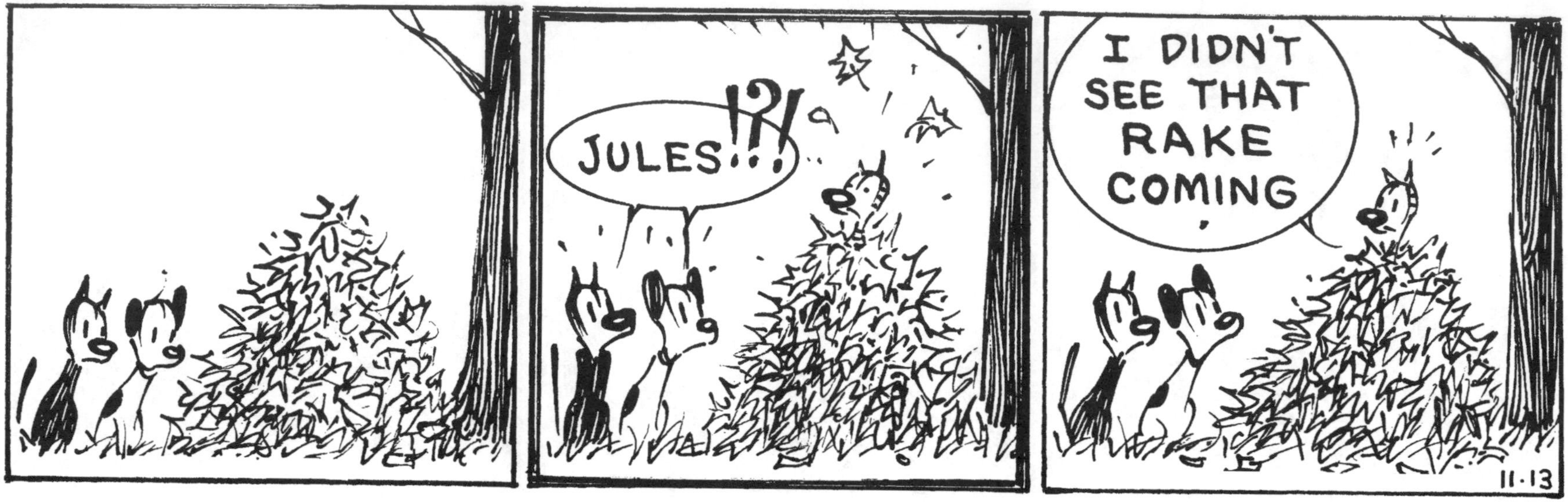
JULES!?!
I DIDN'T SEE THAT RAKE COMING
11-13

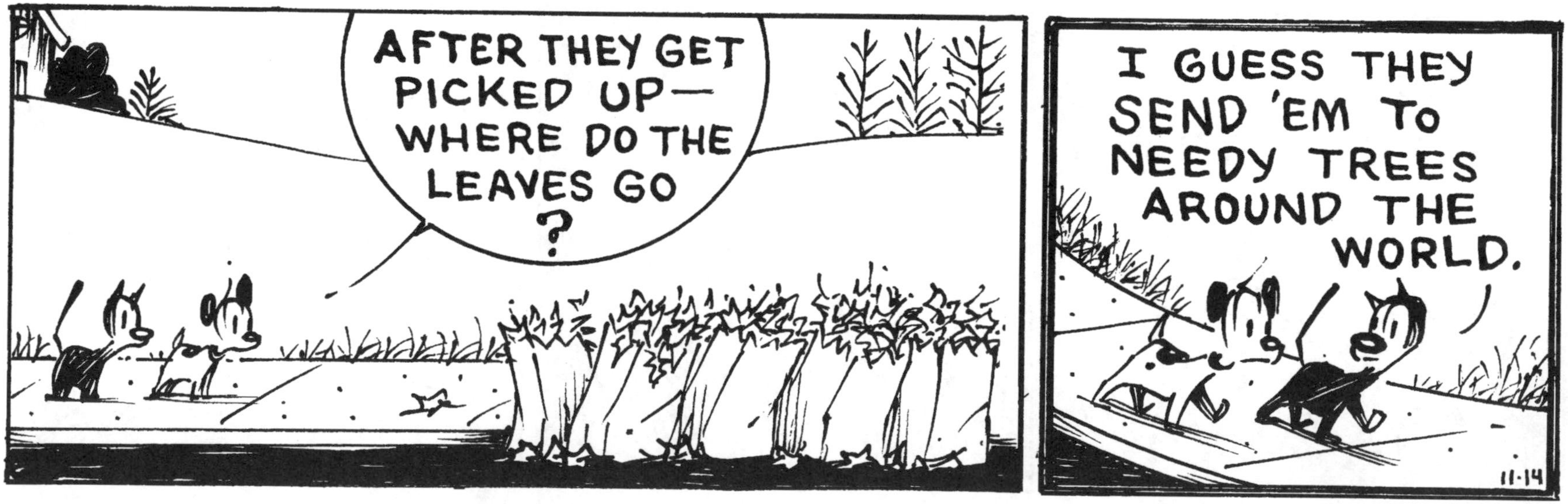
AFTER THEY GET PICKED UP— WHERE DO THE LEAVES GO ?
I GUESS THEY SEND 'EM TO NEEDY TREES AROUND THE WORLD.
11-14

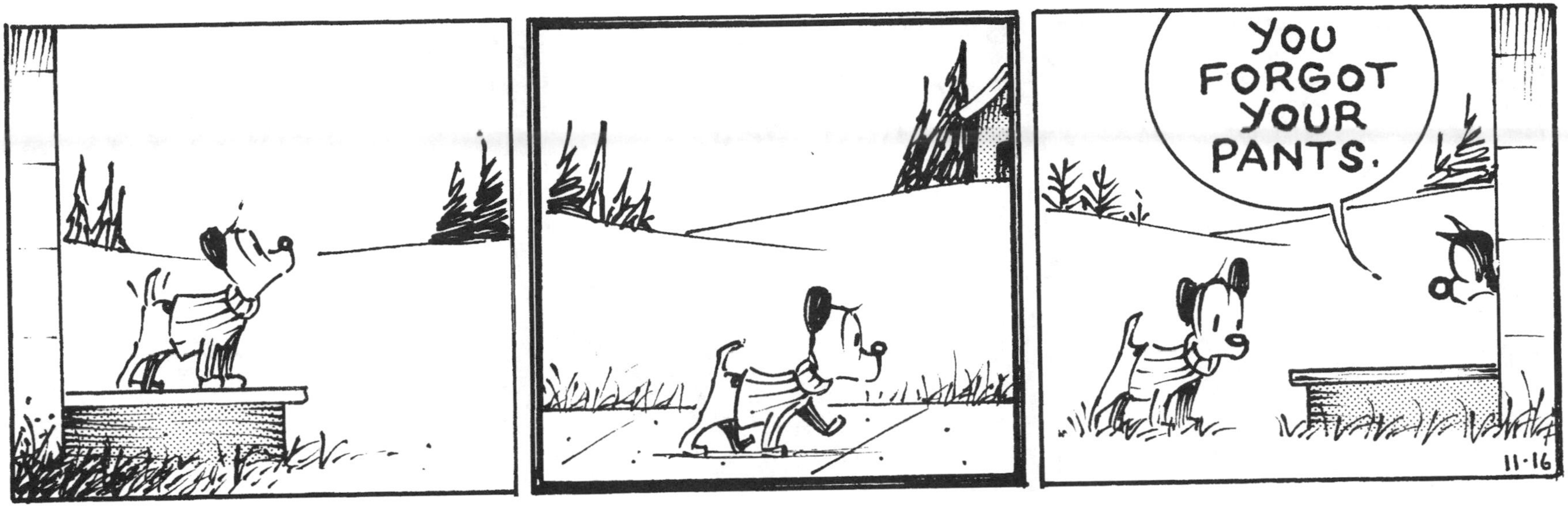
YOU FORGOT YOUR PANTS.
11-16

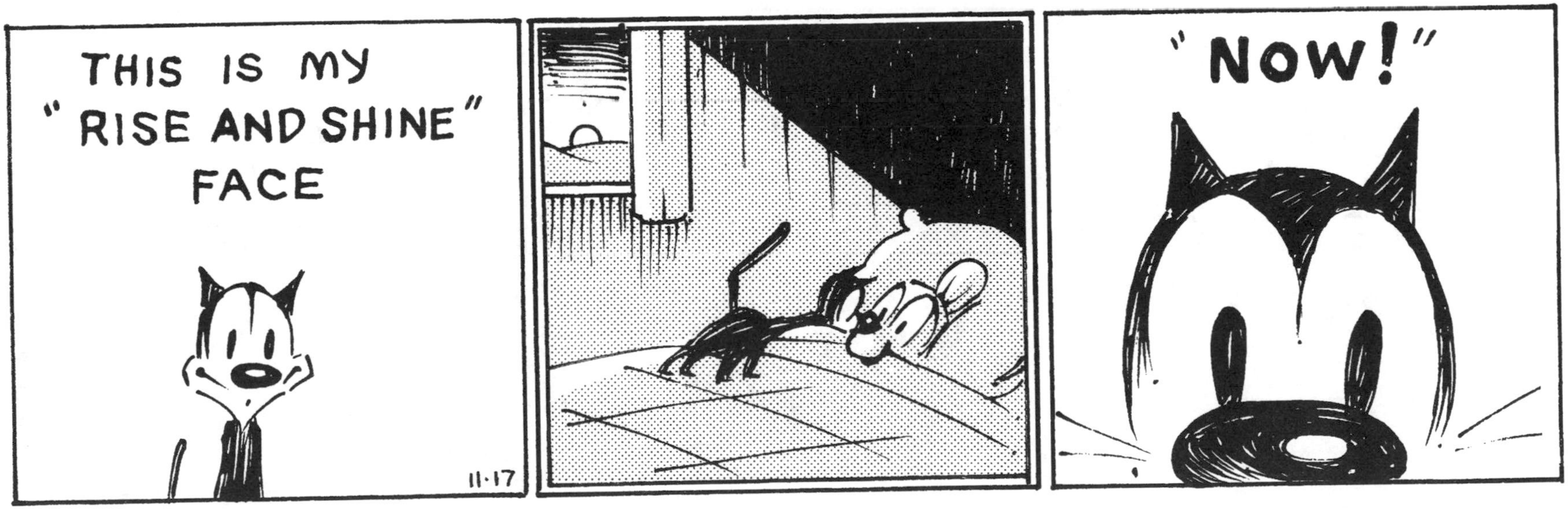
THIS IS MY "RISE AND SHINE" FACE
11-17
"NOW!"

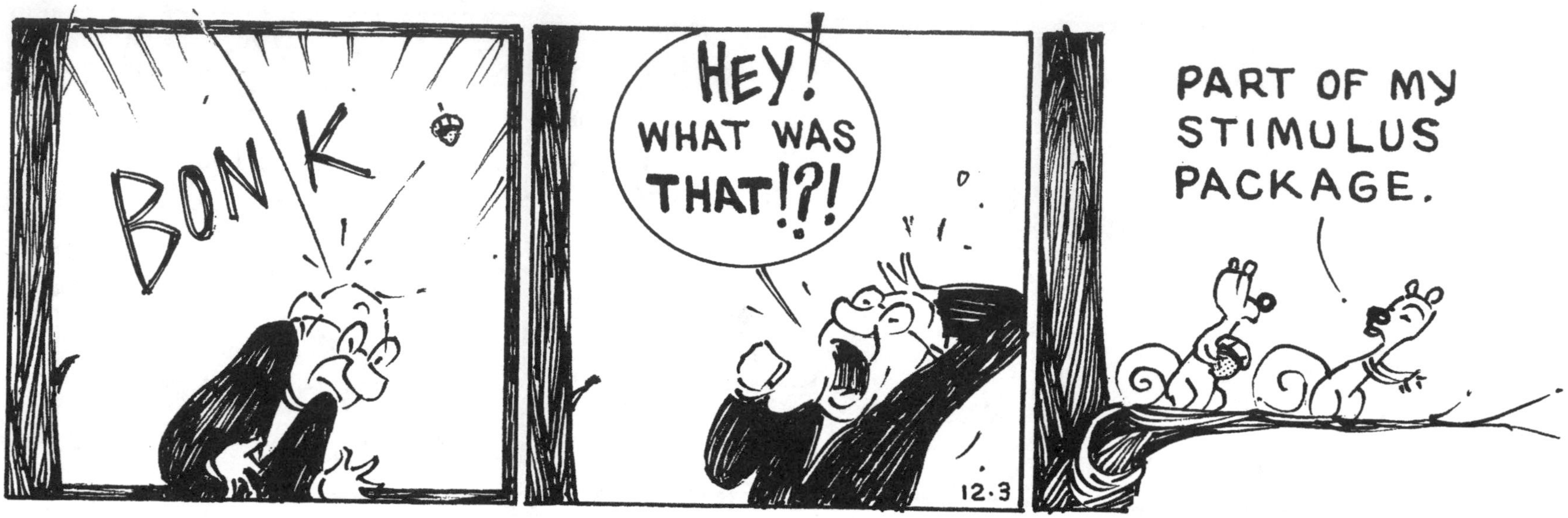
BONK
HEY! WHAT WAS THAT!?!
12·3
PART OF MY STIMULUS PACKAGE.

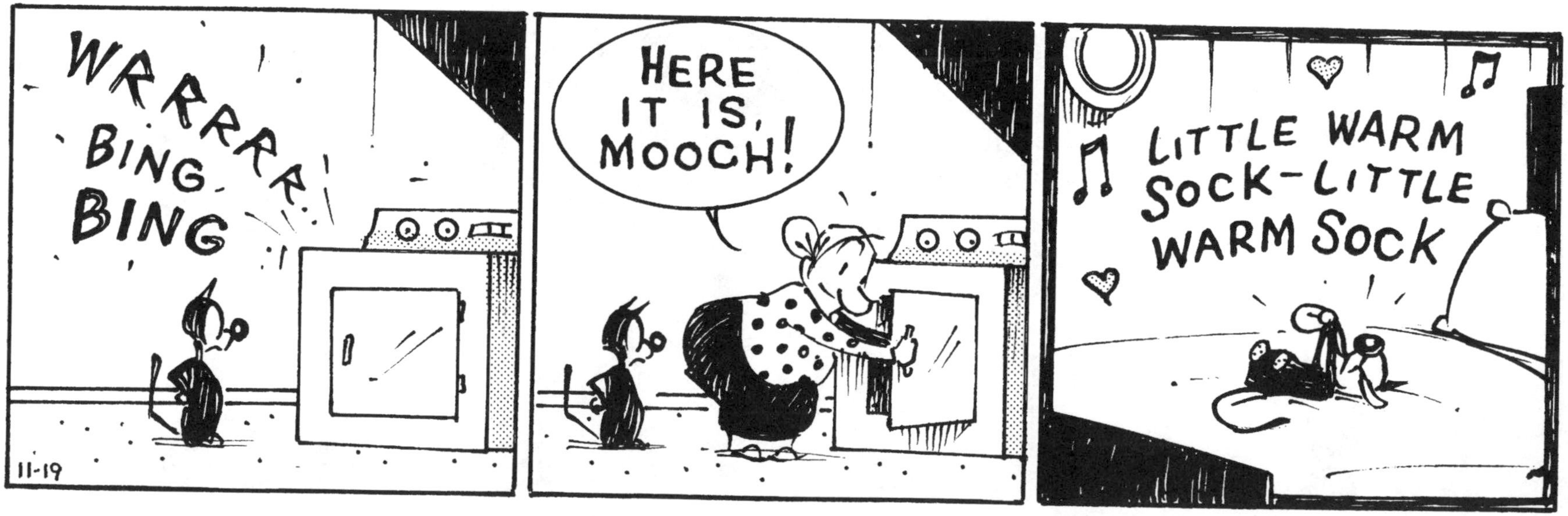
WRRRRRR BING BING
11-19
HERE IT IS, MOOCH!
LITTLE WARM SOCK-LITTLE WARM SOCK

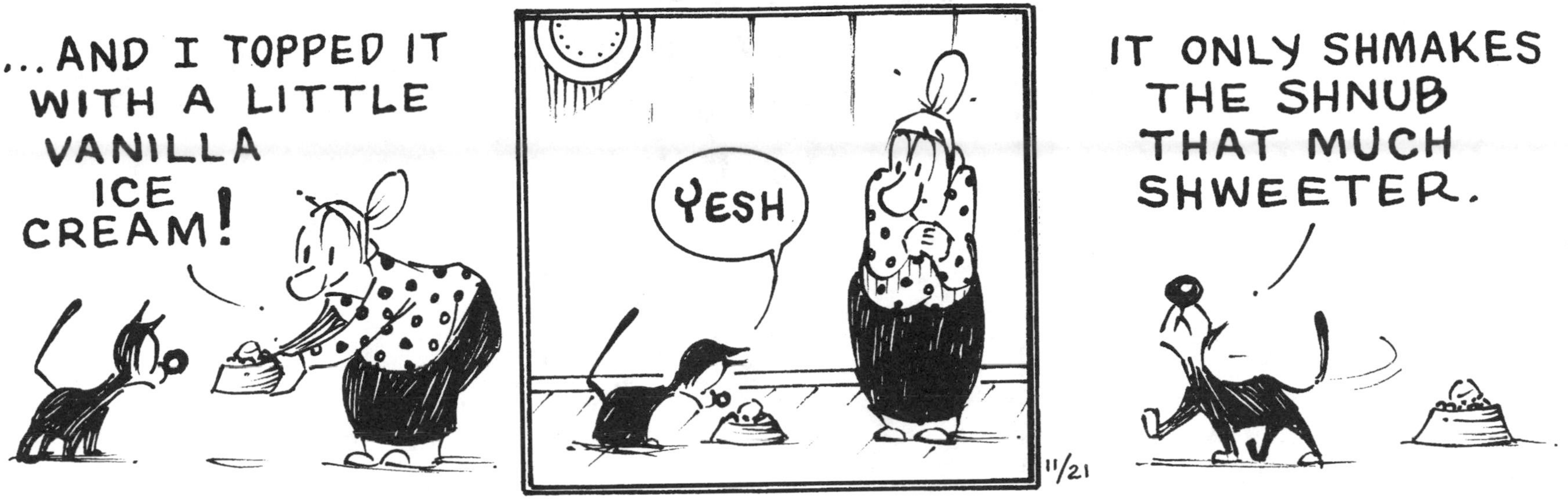
...AND I TOPPED IT WITH A LITTLE VANILLA ICE CREAM!
YESH
IT ONLY SHMAKES THE SHNUB THAT MUCH SHWEETER.
11/21

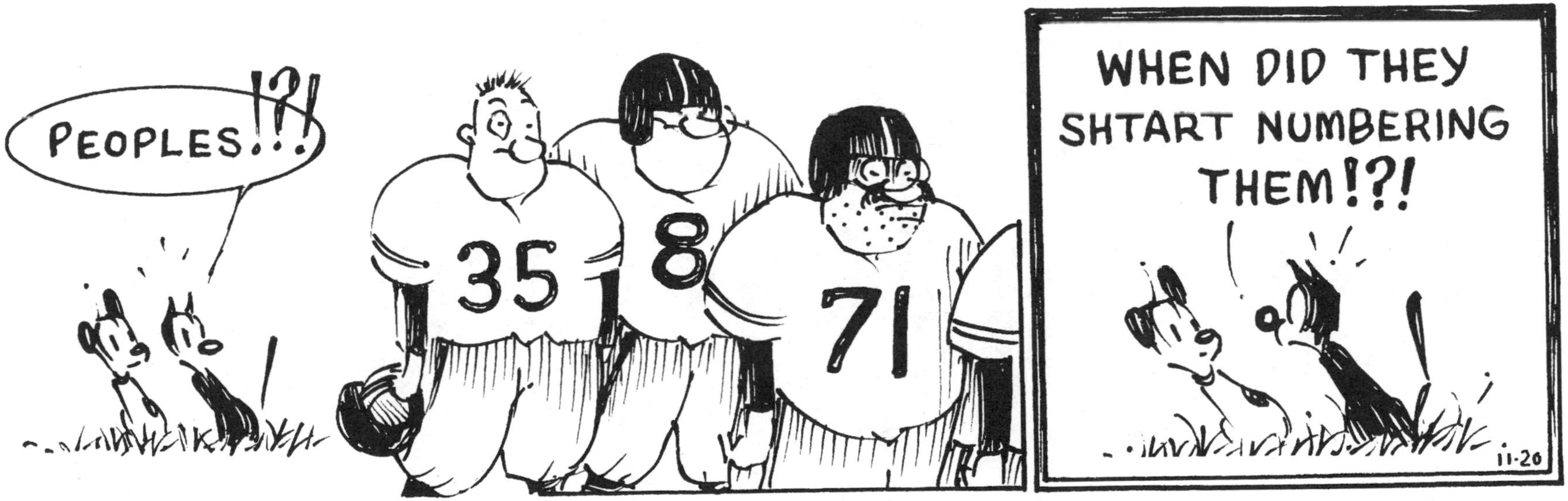
PEOPLES!?!
35
8
71
WHEN DID THEY SHTART NUMBERING THEM!?!
11·20

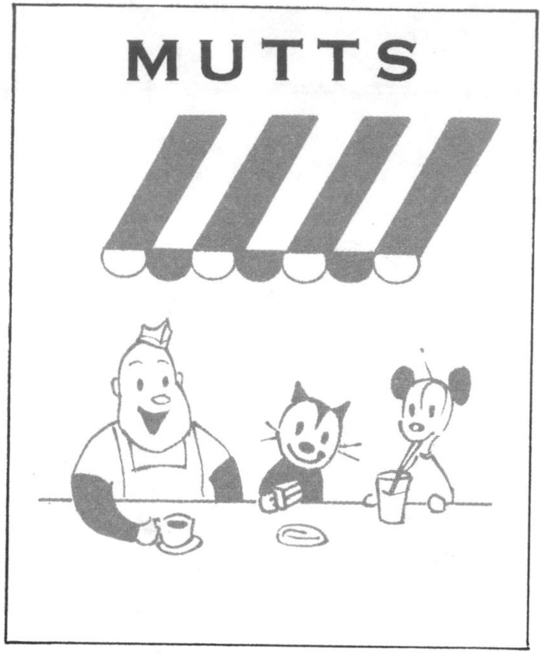
MUTTS

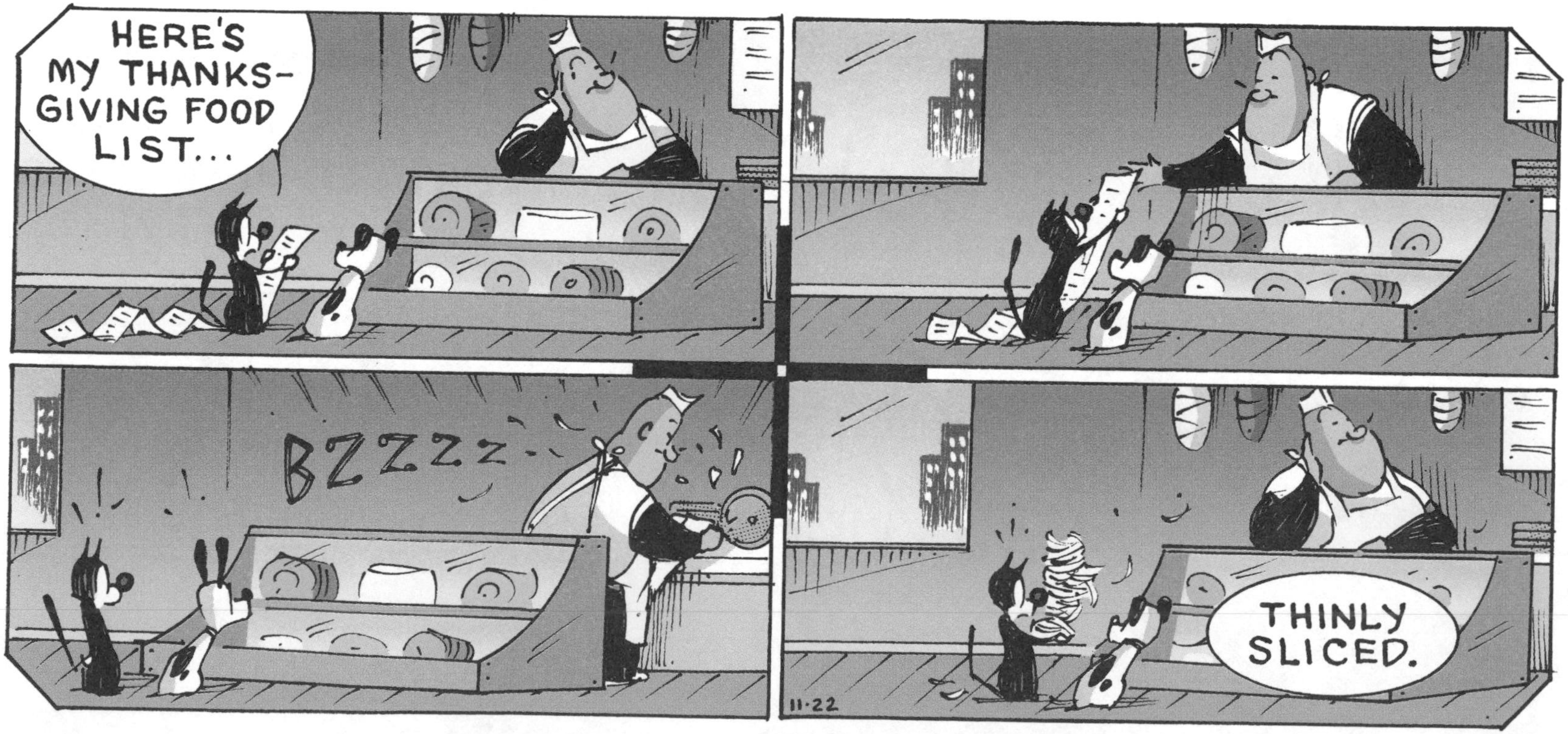
HERE'S MY THANKS-GIVING FOOD LIST...
BZZZZ
THINLY SLICED.
11·22

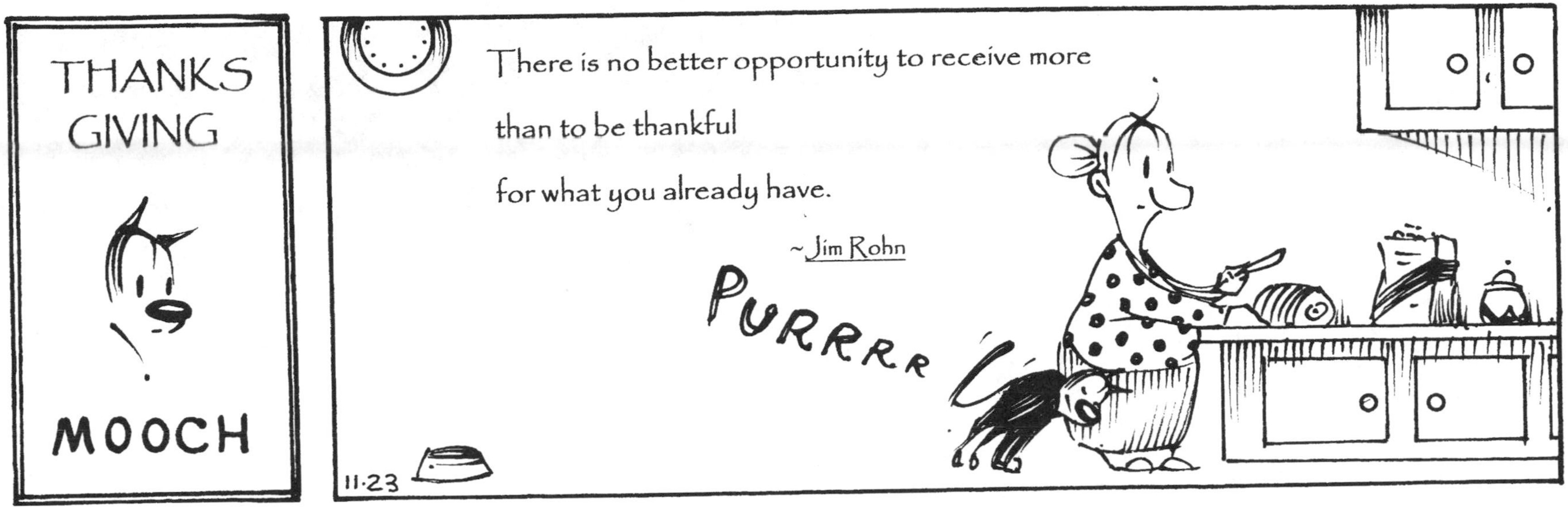
THANKS GIVING
MOOCH
There is no better opportunity to receive more than to be thankful for what you already have.
~Jim Rohn
PURRRRR
11·23

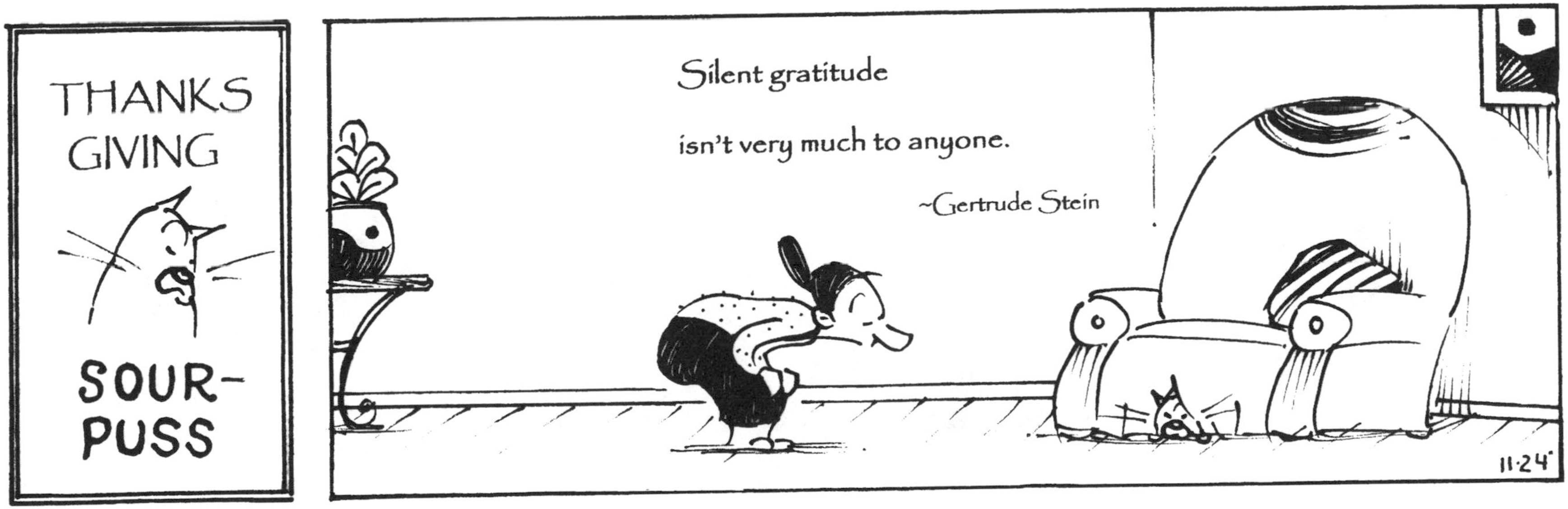
THANKS GIVING
SOUR-PUSS
Silent gratitude isn't very much to anyone.
~Gertrude Stein
11·24

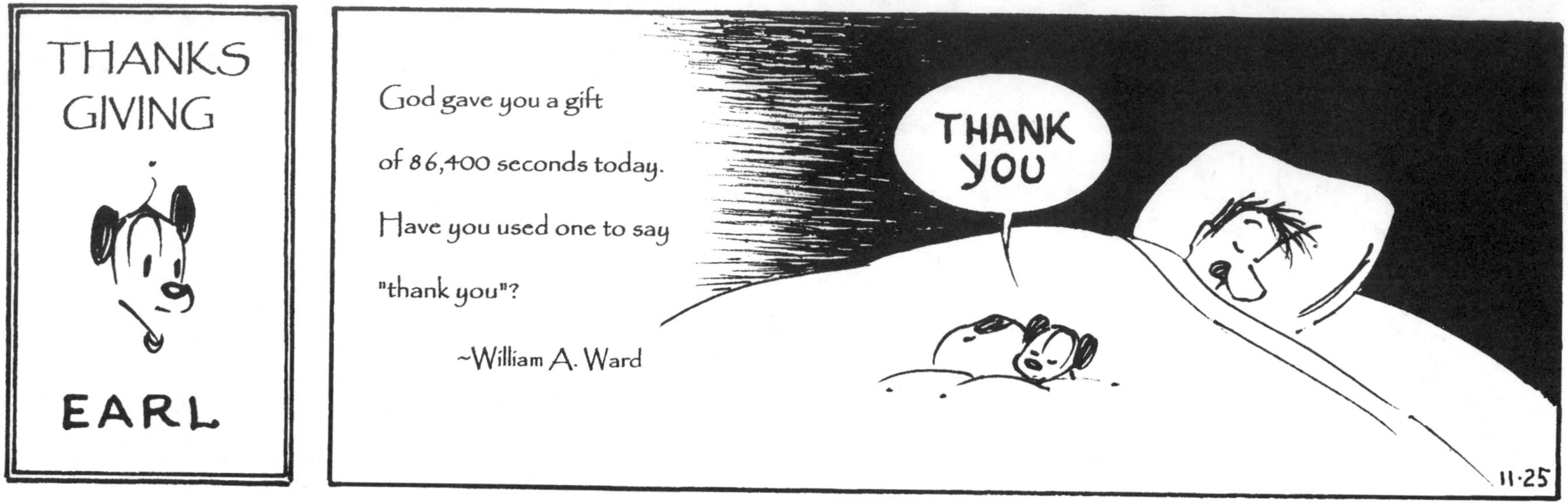
THANKS GIVING
EARL
God gave you a gift
of 86,400 seconds today.
Have you used one to say
"thank you"?
~William A. Ward
THANK YOU
11·25

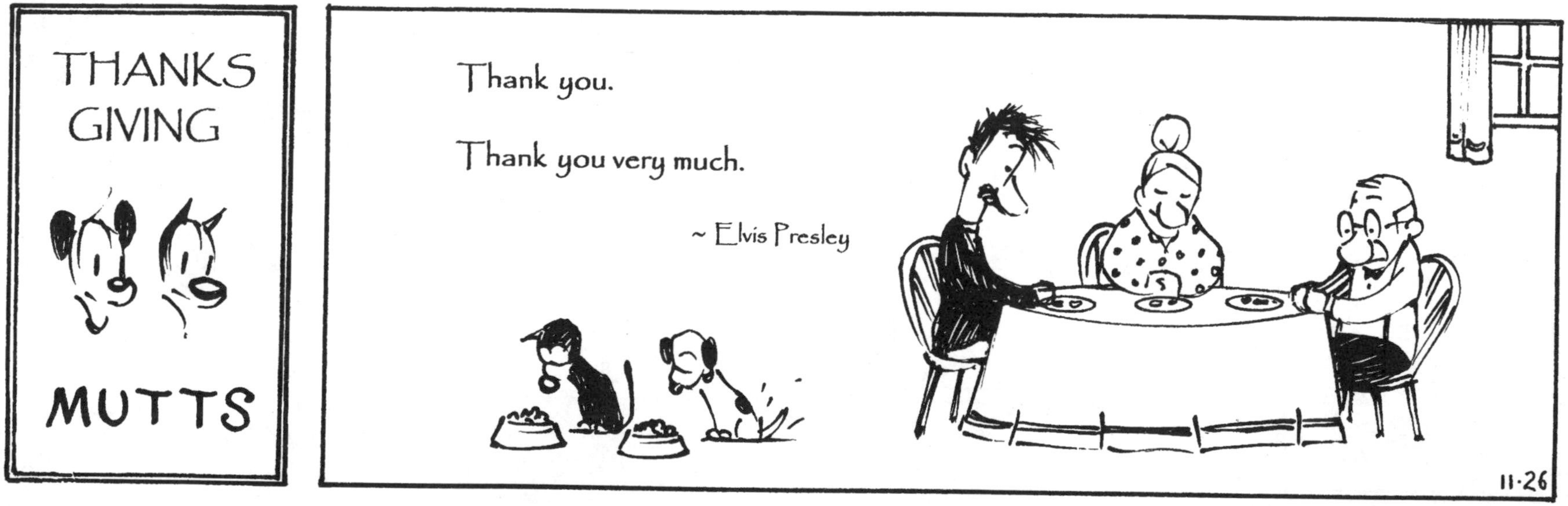
THANKS GIVING
MUTTS
Thank you.
Thank you very much.
~ Elvis Presley
11·26

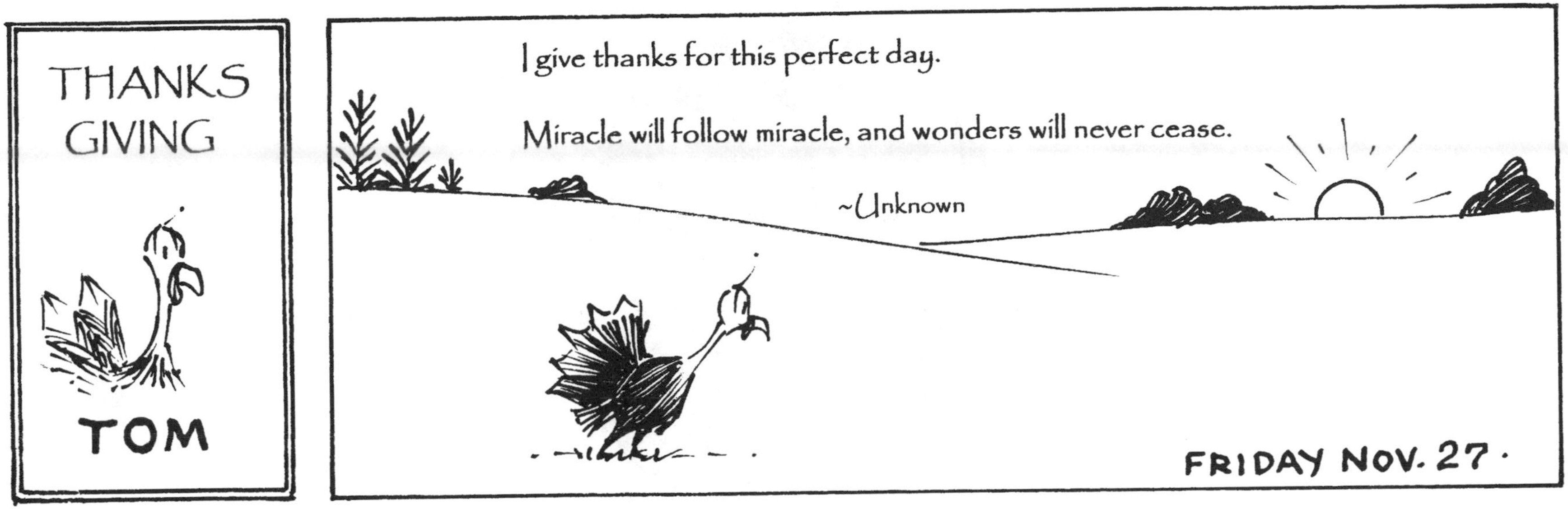
THANKS GIVING
TOM
I give thanks for this perfect day.
Miracle will follow miracle, and wonders will never cease.
~Unknown
FRIDAY NOV. 27.

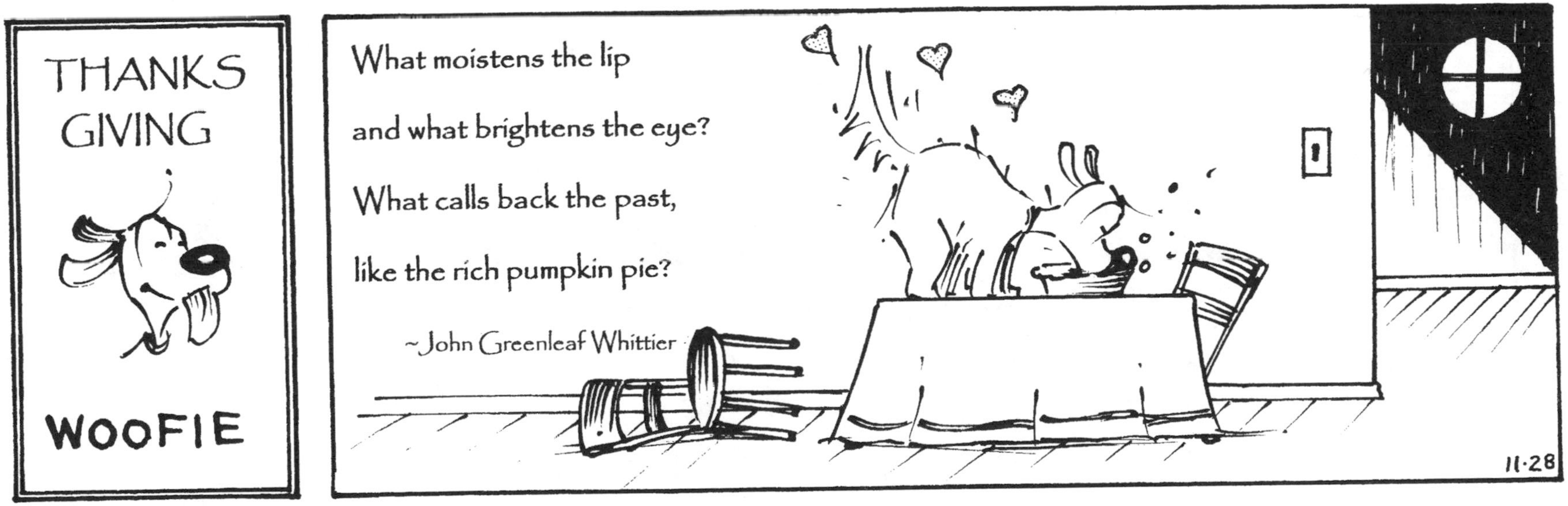
THANKS GIVING
WOOFIE
What moistens the lip
and what brightens the eye?
What calls back the past,
like the rich pumpkin pie?
~John Greenleaf Whittier
11·28

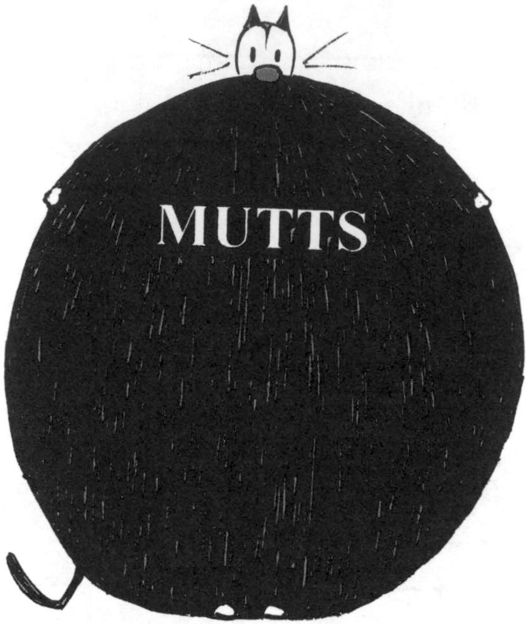
MUTTS

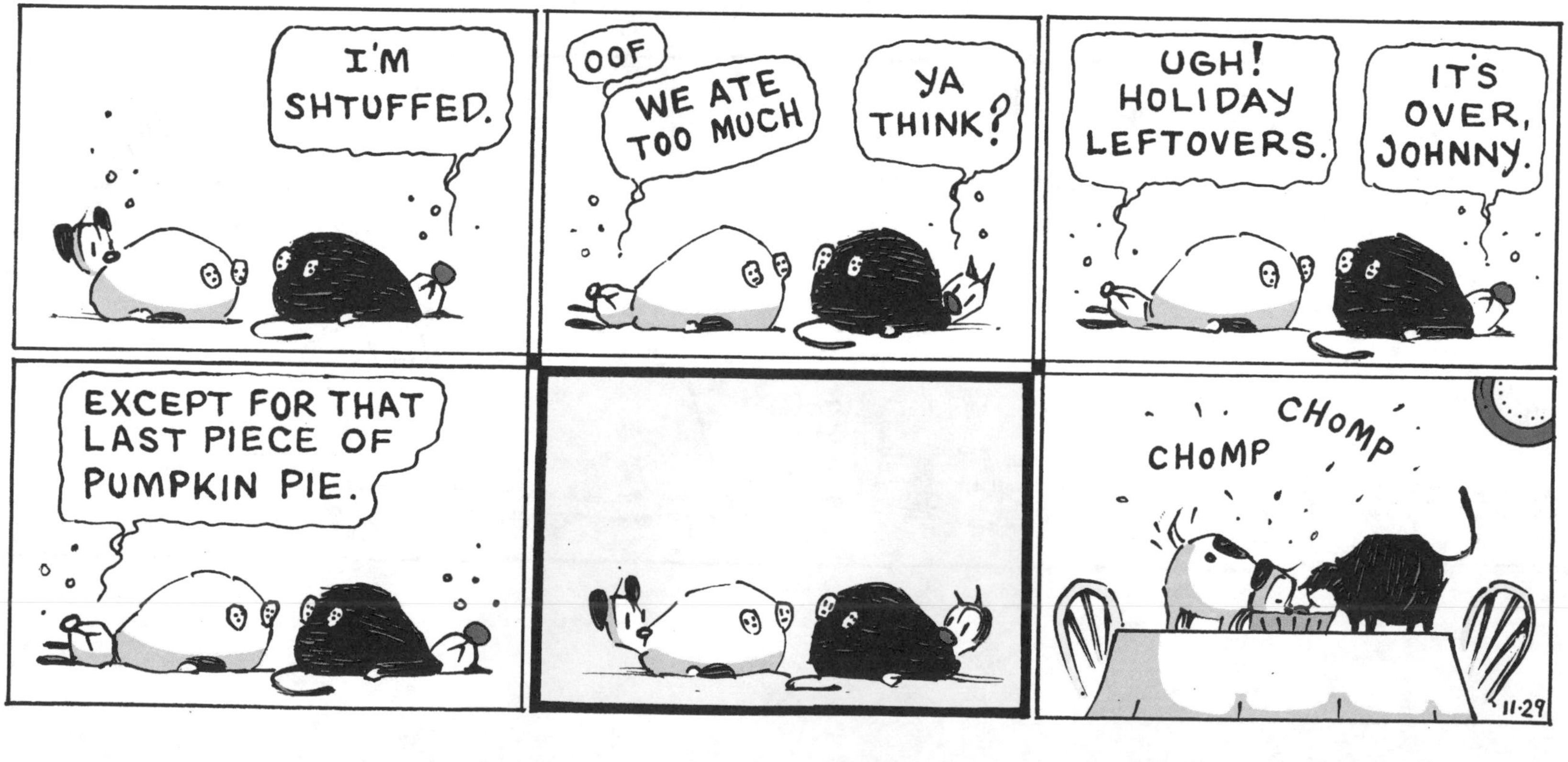
I'M SHTUFFED.
OOF
WE ATE TOO MUCH
YA THINK?
UGH! HOLIDAY LEFTOVERS.
IT'S OVER, JOHNNY.
EXCEPT FOR THAT LAST PIECE OF PUMPKIN PIE.
CHOMP
CHOMP
11·29

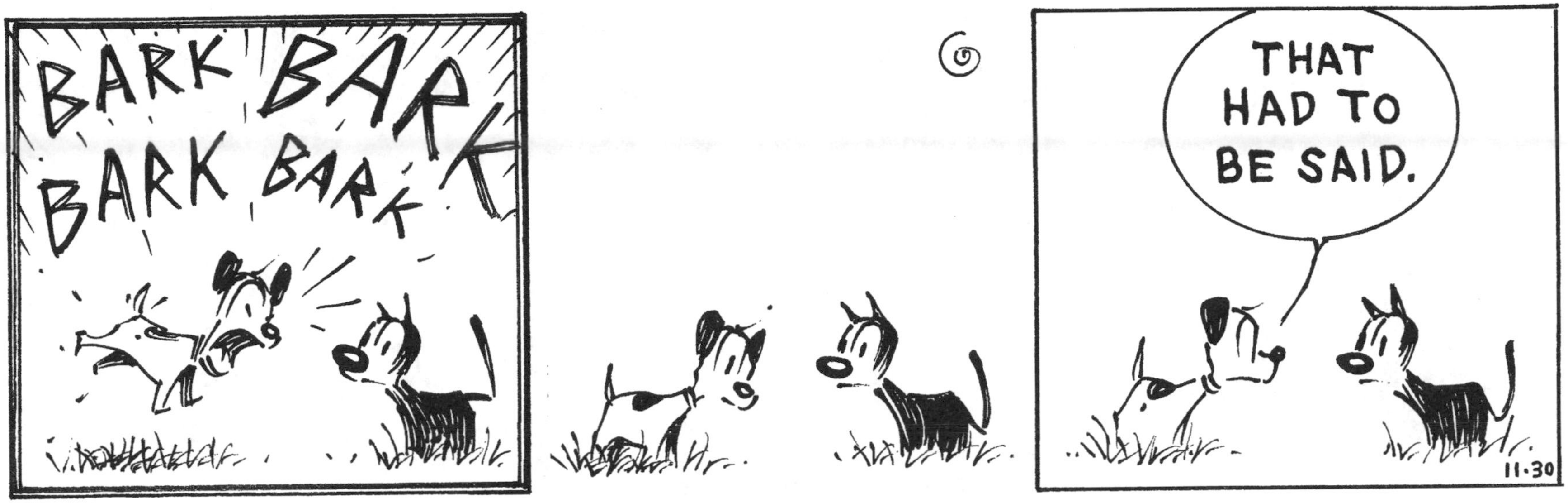
BARK BARK
BARK BARK
THAT HAD TO BE SAID.
11·30

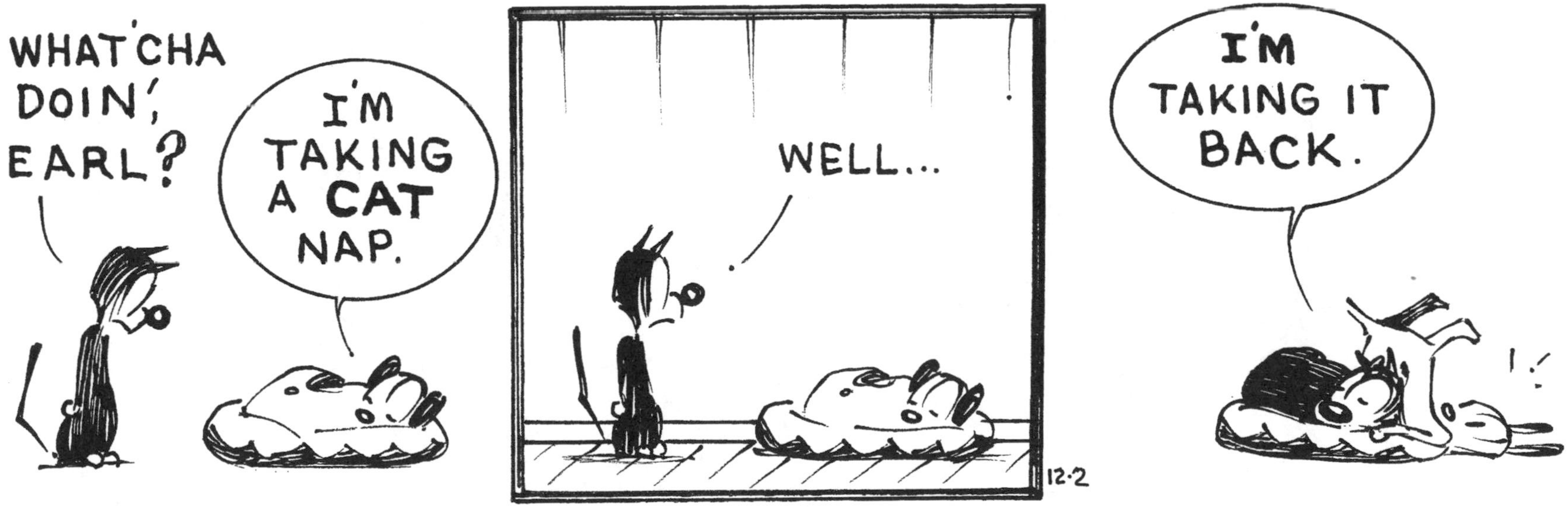
WHAT'CHA DOIN', EARL?
I'M TAKING A CAT NAP.
WELL...
I'M TAKING IT BACK.
12·2

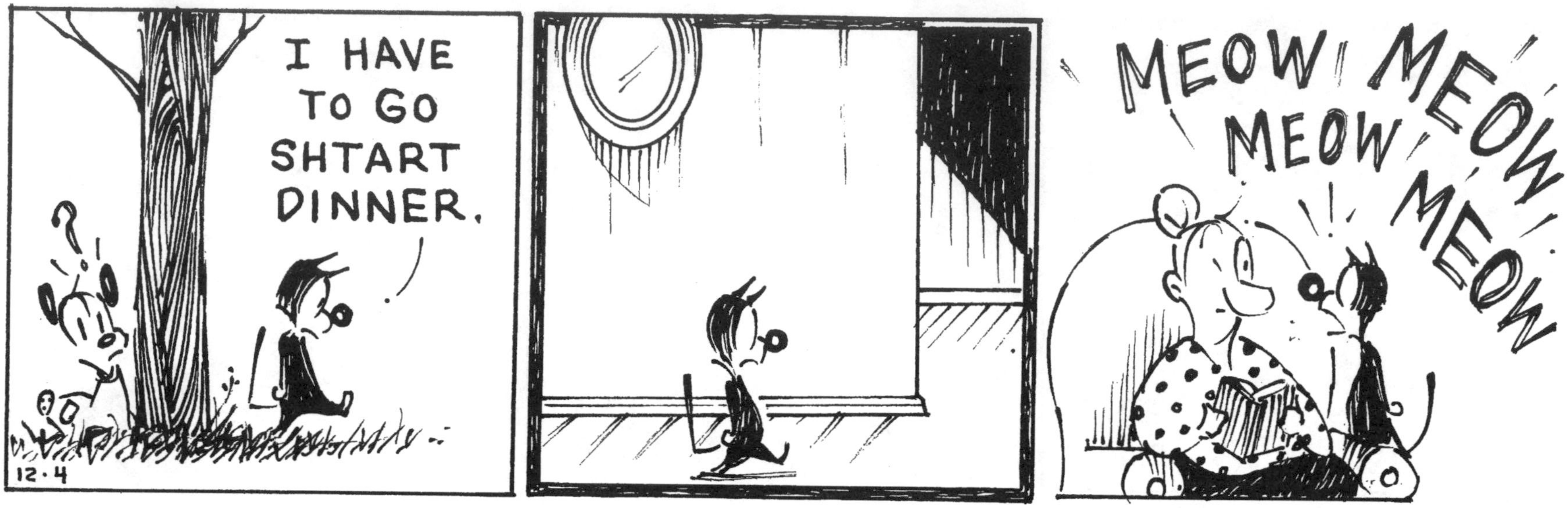
I HAVE TO GO SHTART DINNER.
12·4
MEOW MEOW MEOW MEOW MEOW

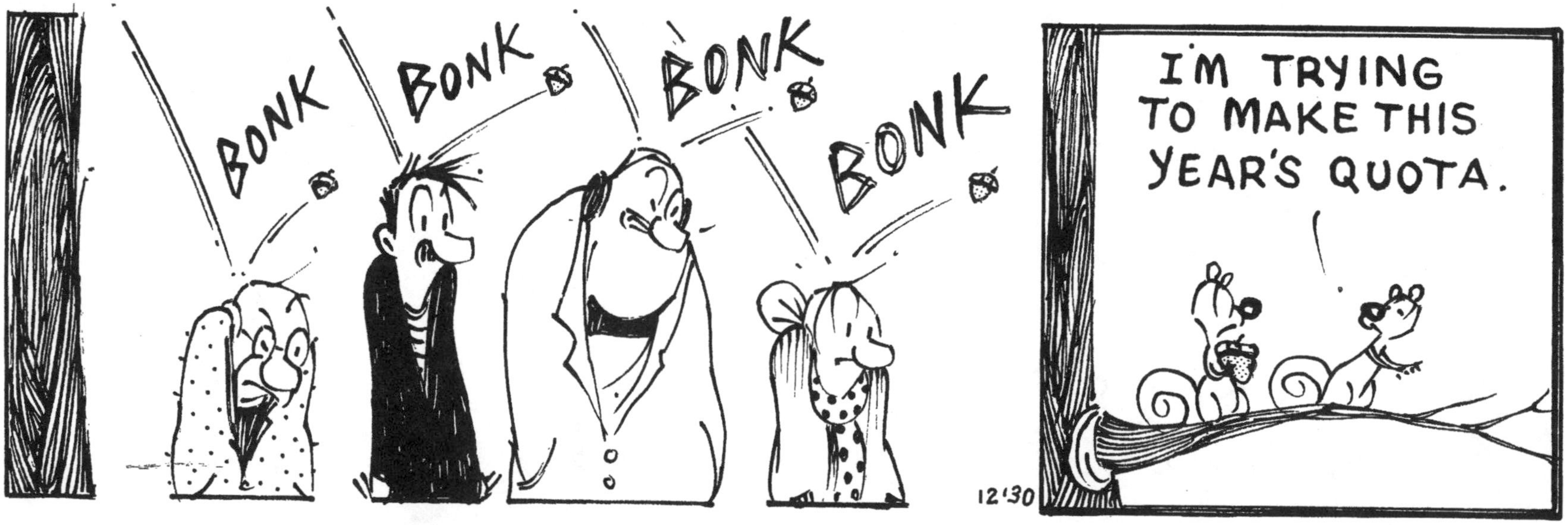
BONK
BONK
BONK
BONK
12·30
I'M TRYING TO MAKE THIS YEAR'S QUOTA.

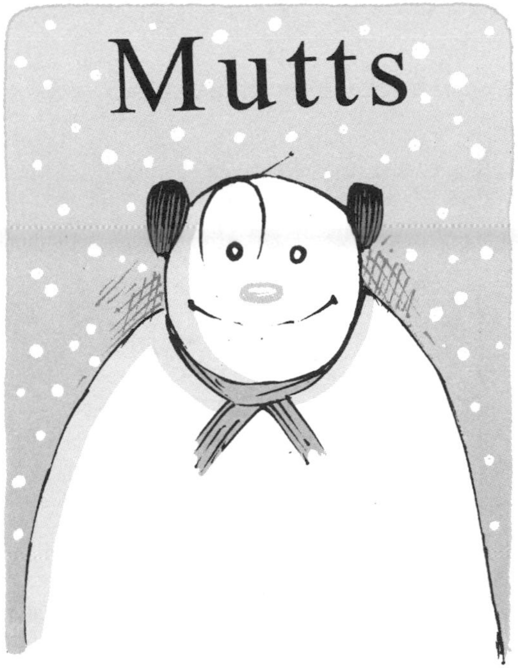
Mutts

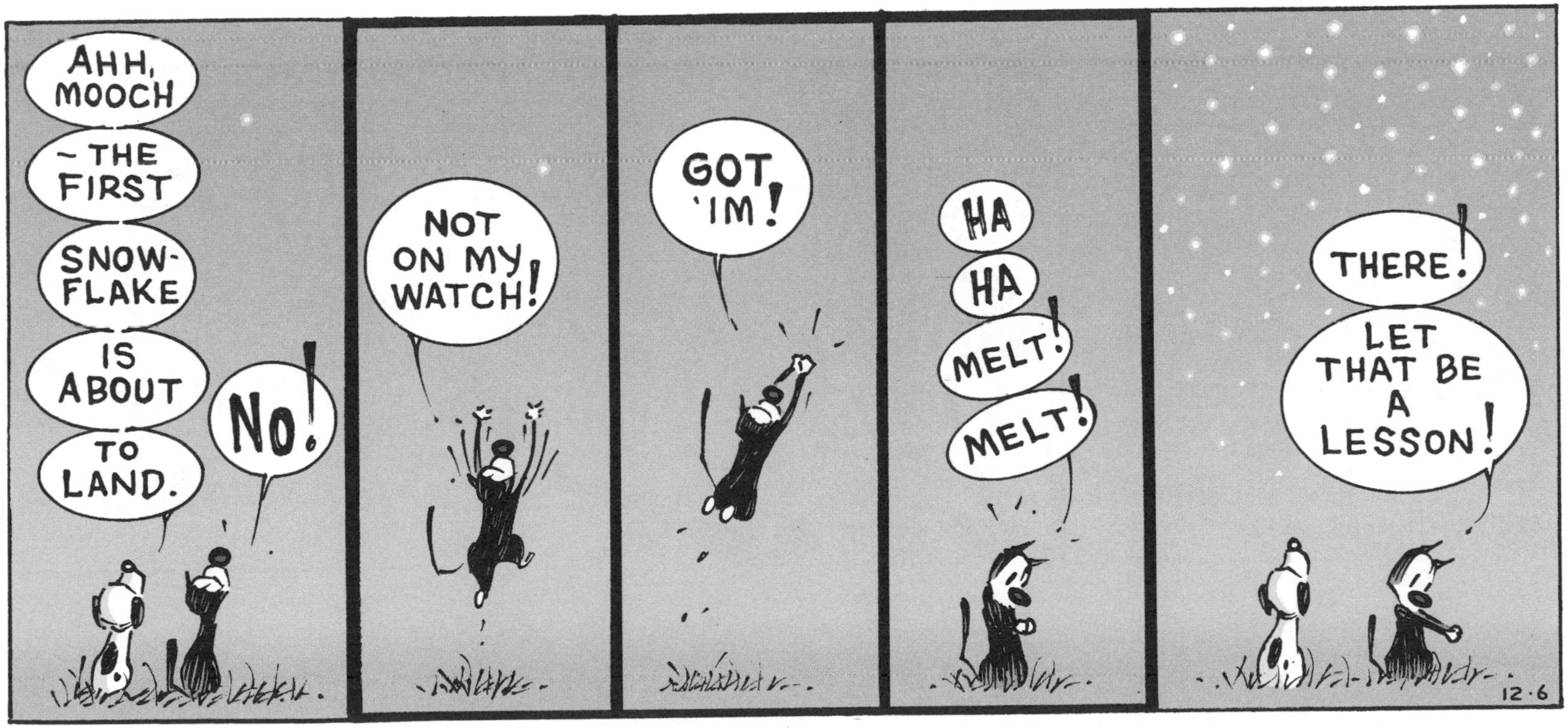
AHH, MOOCH
- THE FIRST
SNOW-FLAKE
IS ABOUT
TO LAND.
No!
NOT ON MY WATCH!
GOT 'IM!
HA
HA
MELT!
MELT!
THERE!
LET THAT BE A LESSON!
12·6

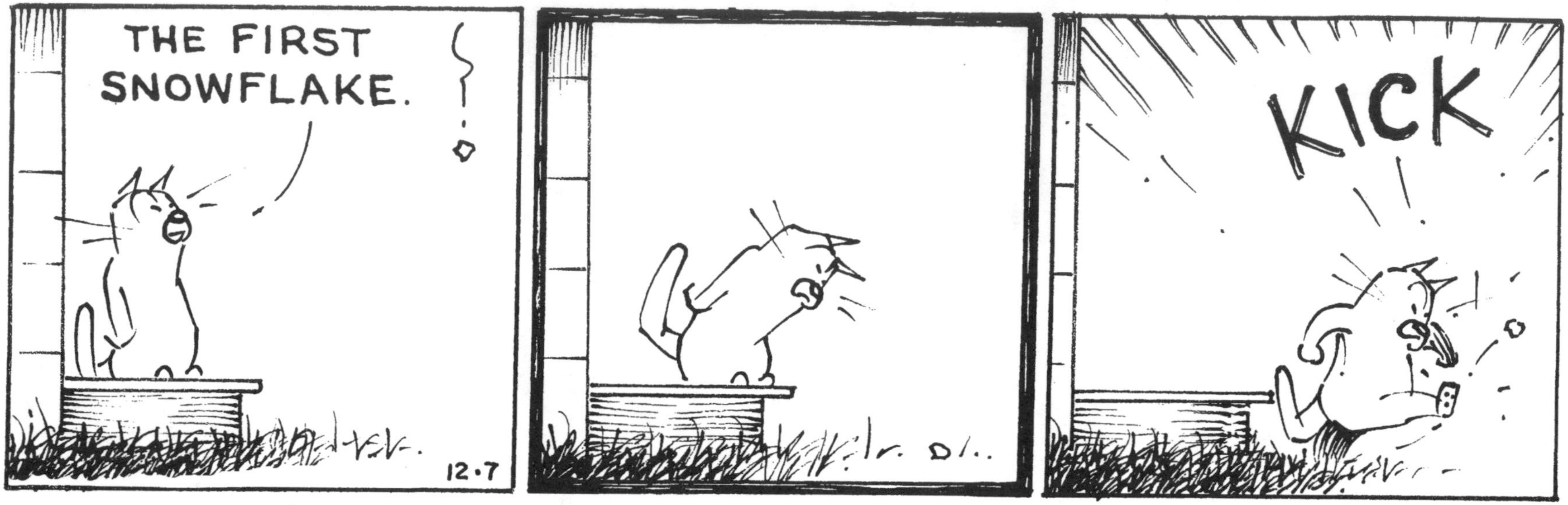
THE FIRST SNOWFLAKE.
KICK
12·7

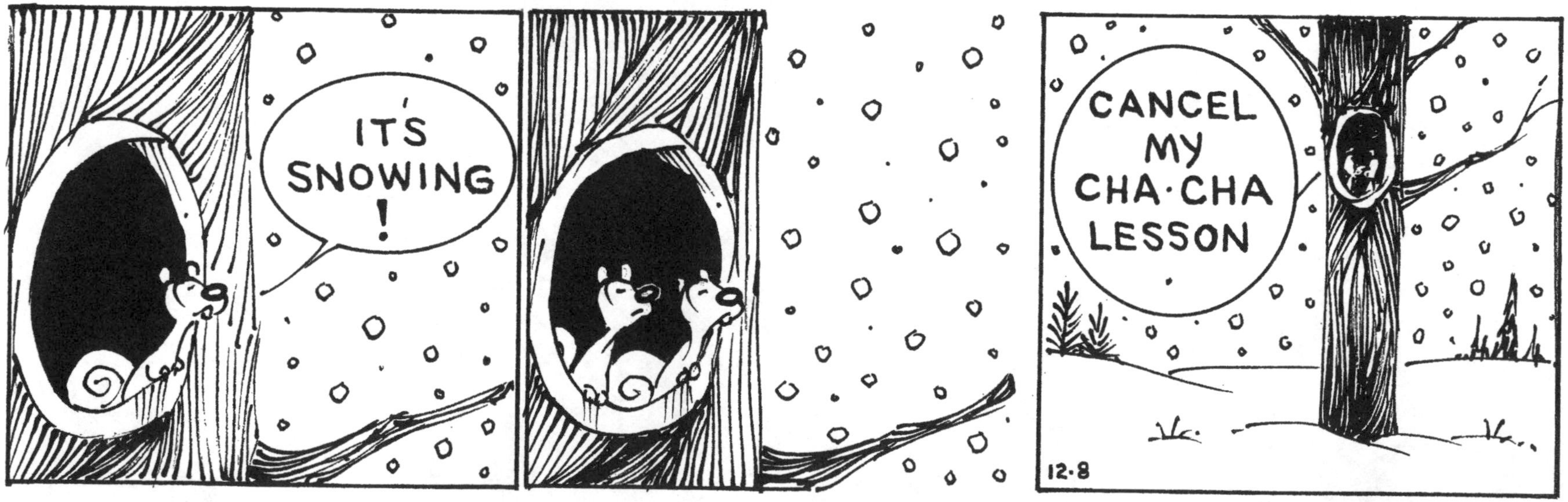
IT'S SNOWING!
CANCEL MY CHA·CHA LESSON
12·8

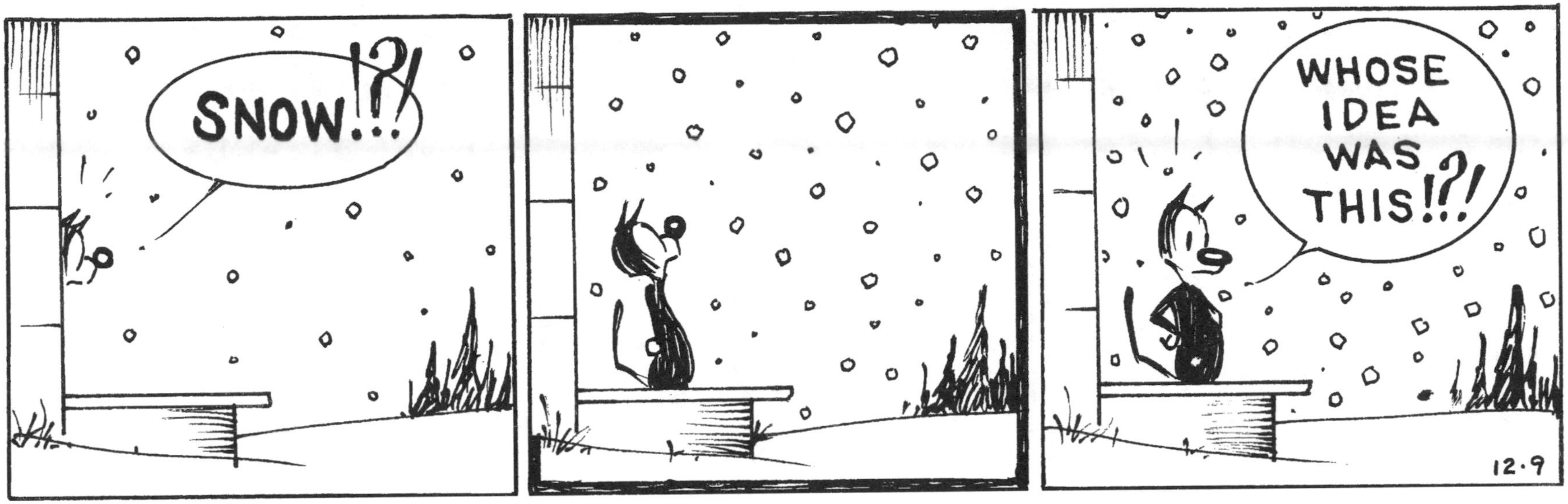
SNOW!?!
WHOSE IDEA WAS THIS!?!
12·9

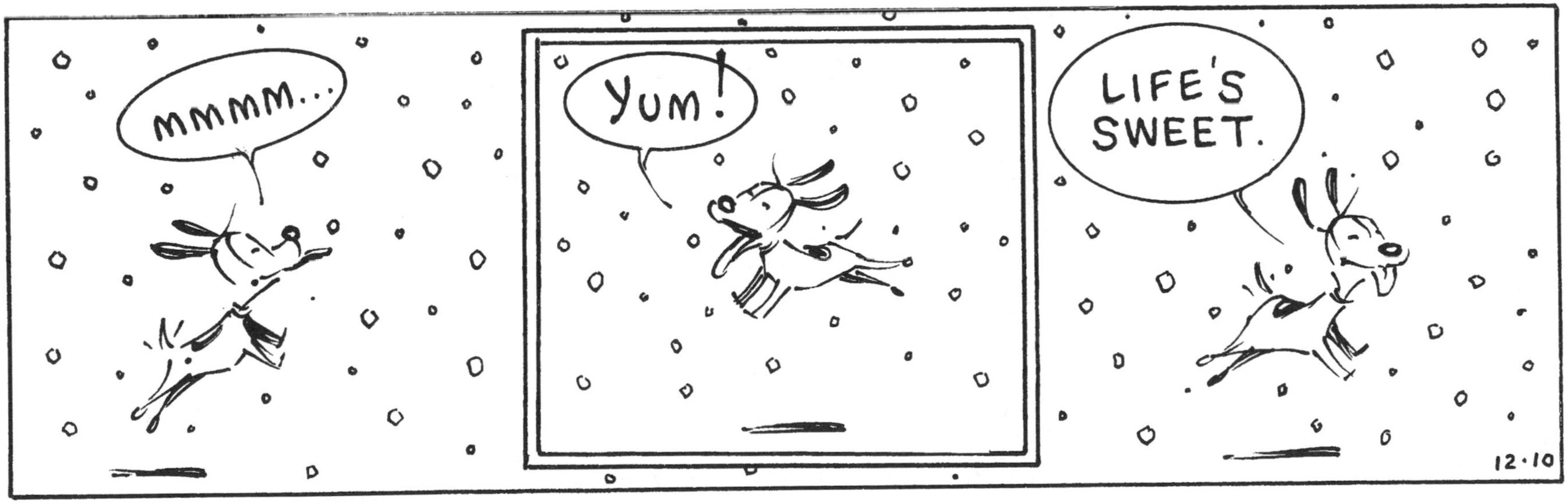
MMMM...
YUM!
LIFE'S SWEET.
12·10

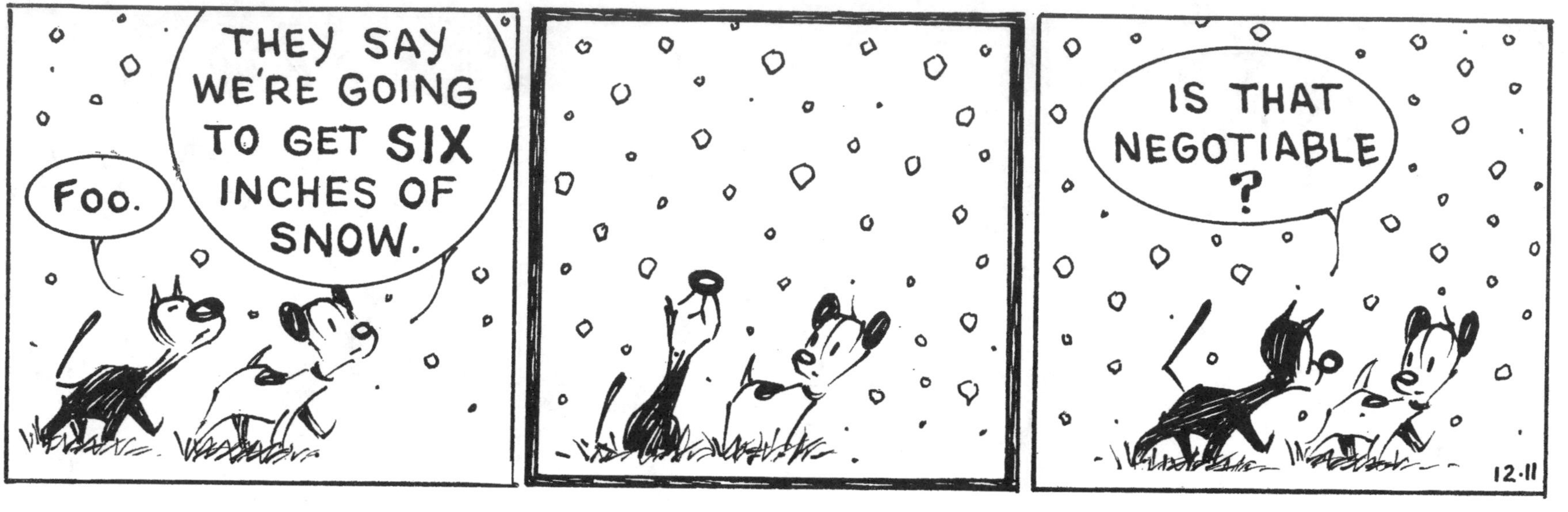
THEY SAY WE'RE GOING TO GET SIX INCHES OF SNOW.
Foo.
IS THAT NEGOTIABLE ?
12·11

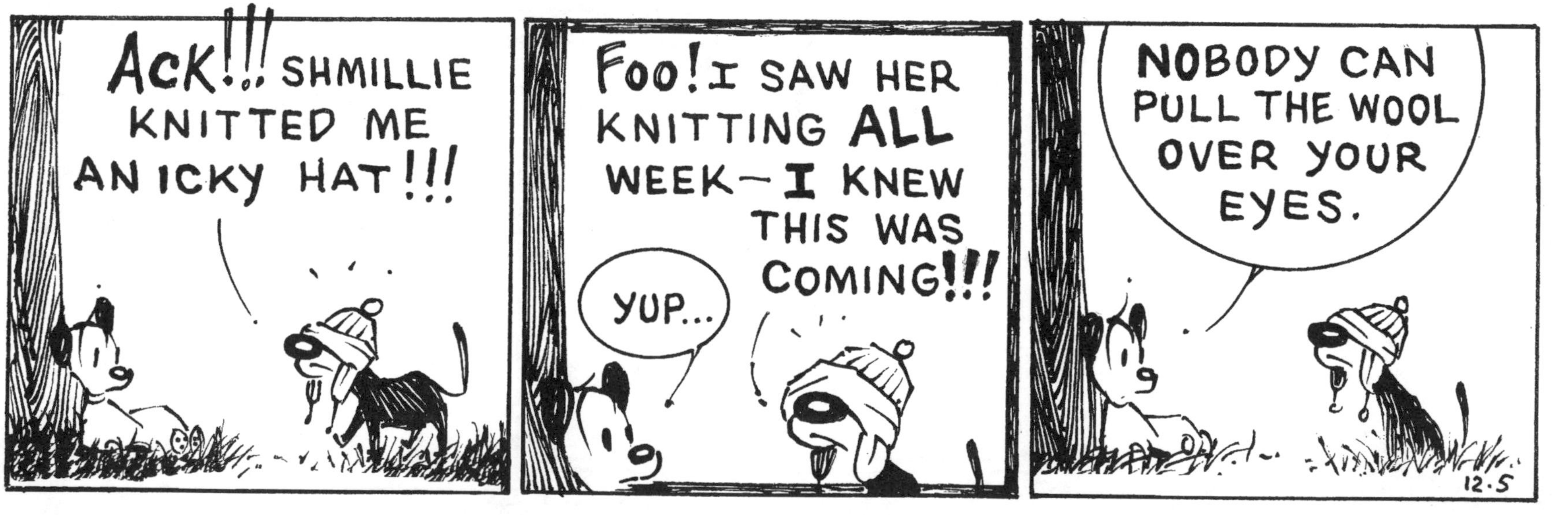
ACK!!! SHMILLIE KNITTED ME AN ICKY HAT!!!
Foo! I SAW HER KNITTING ALL WEEK—I KNEW THIS WAS COMING!!!
YUP...
NOBODY CAN PULL THE WOOL OVER YOUR EYES.
12·5

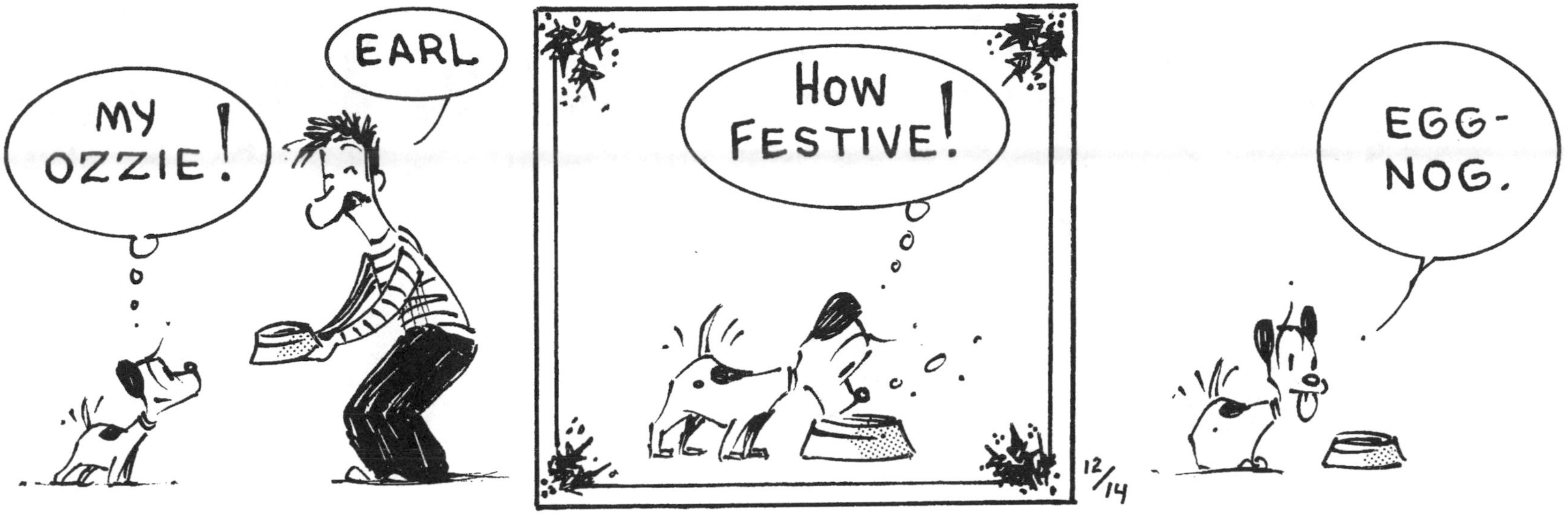
EARL
MY OZZIE!
HOW FESTIVE!
EGG-NOG.
12/14

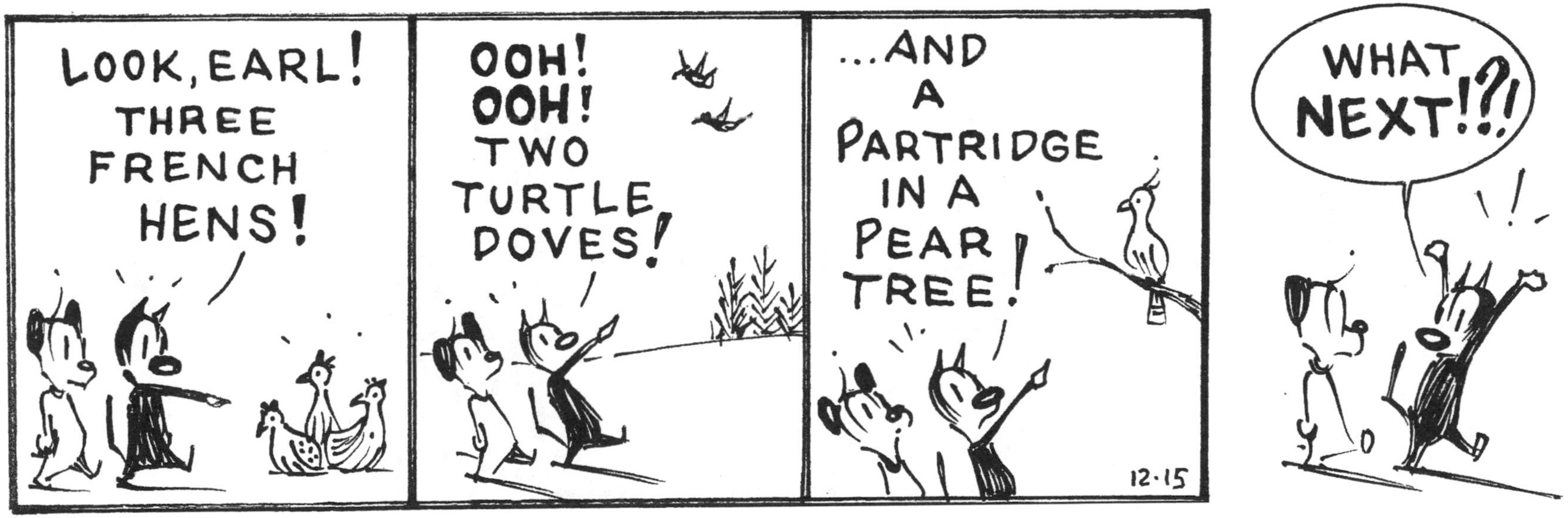
LOOK, EARL! THREE FRENCH HENS!
OOH! OOH! TWO TURTLE DOVES!
...AND A PARTRIDGE IN A PEAR TREE!
12-15
WHAT NEXT!?!

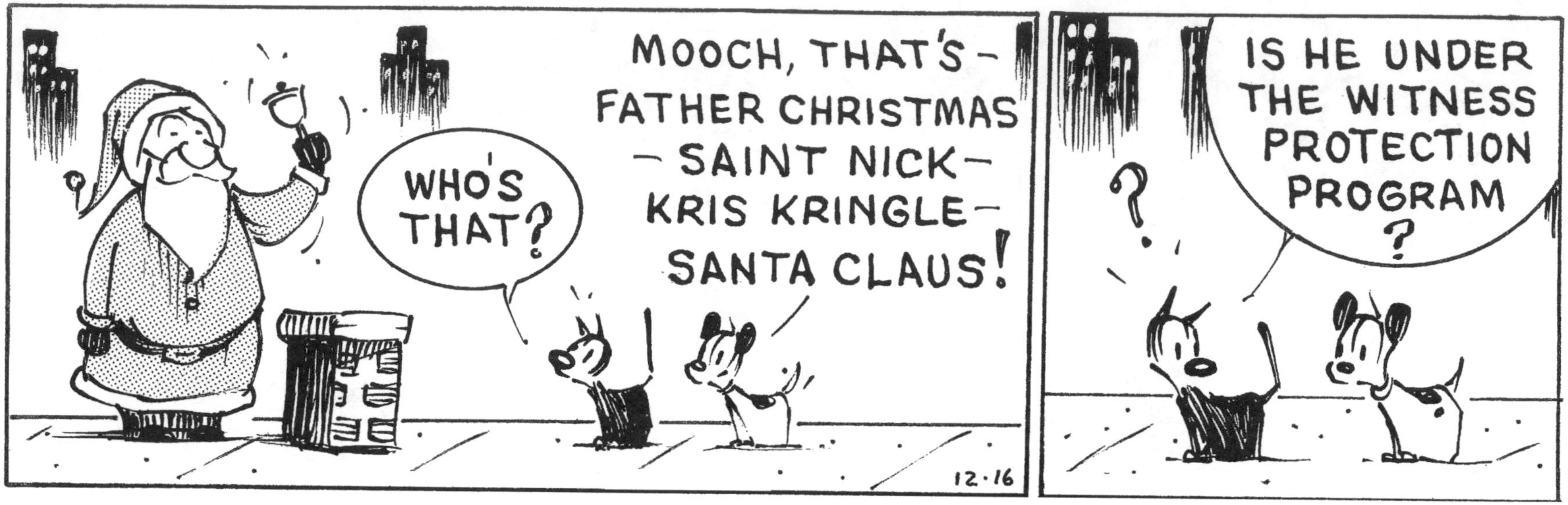
WHO'S THAT?
MOOCH, THAT'S — FATHER CHRISTMAS — SAINT NICK — KRIS KRINGLE — SANTA CLAUS!
IS HE UNDER THE WITNESS PROTECTION PROGRAM?
12·16

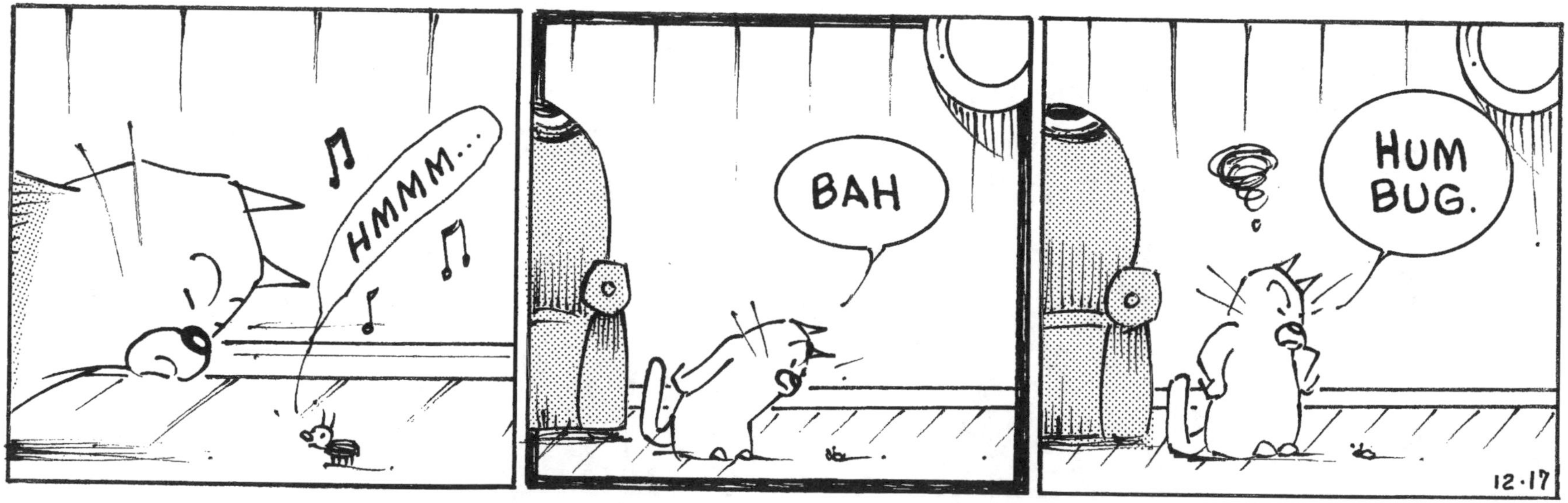
HMMM...
BAH
HUM BUG.
12·17

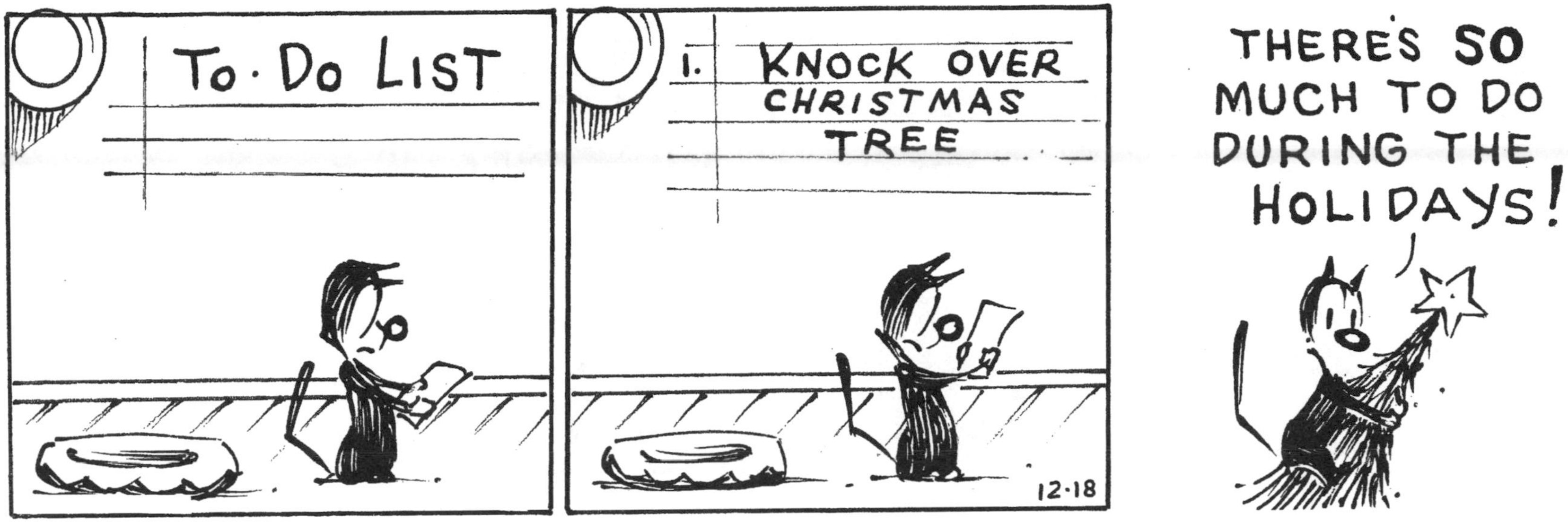
TO·DO LIST
1. KNOCK OVER CHRISTMAS TREE
12·18
THERE'S SO MUCH TO DO DURING THE HOLIDAYS!

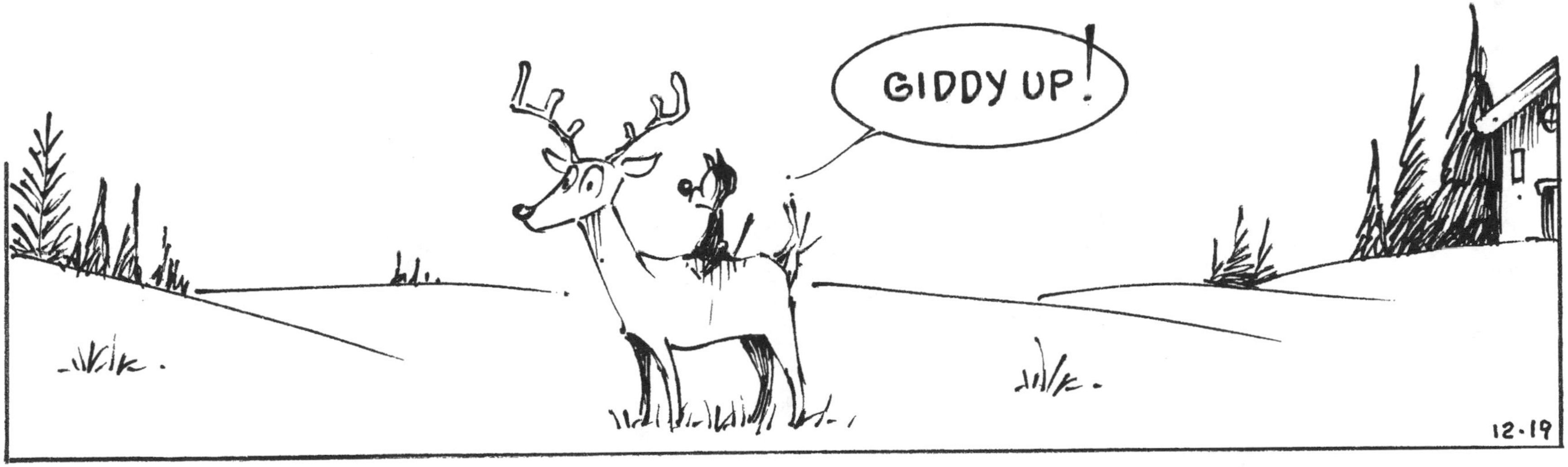
GIDDY UP!
12·19

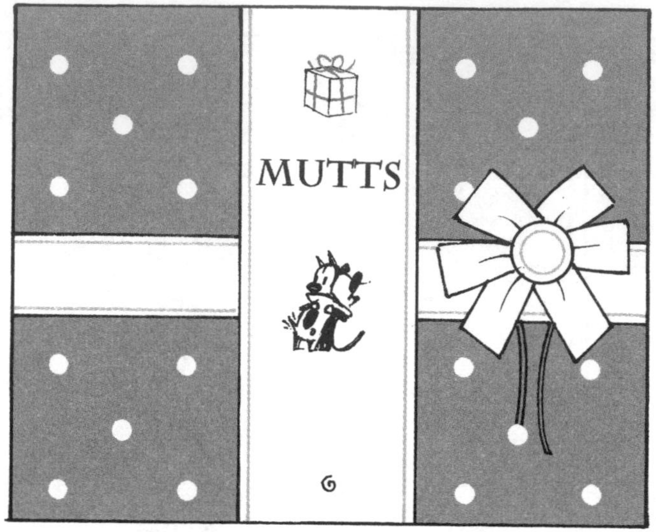
MUTTS

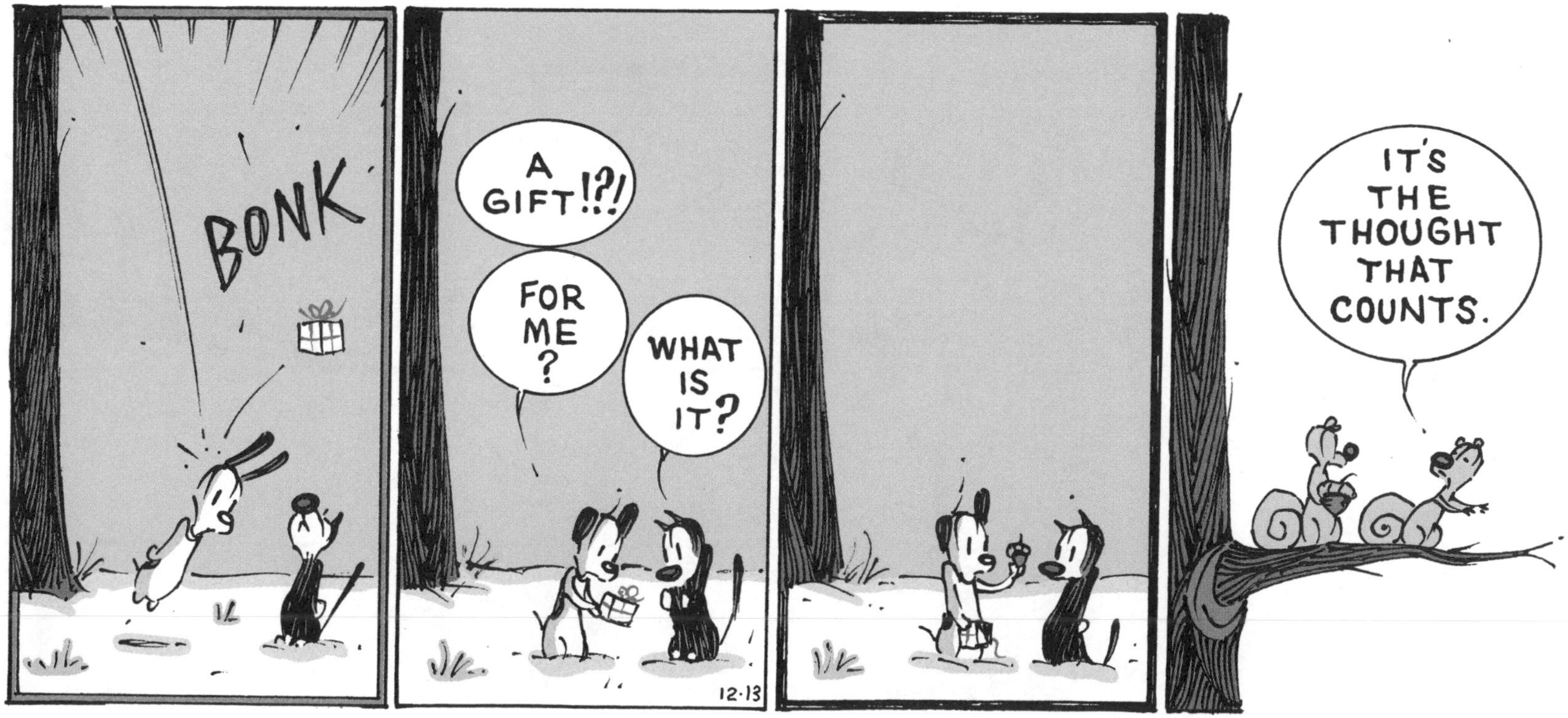
BONK
A GIFT!?!
FOR ME?
WHAT IS IT?
12·13
IT'S THE THOUGHT THAT COUNTS.

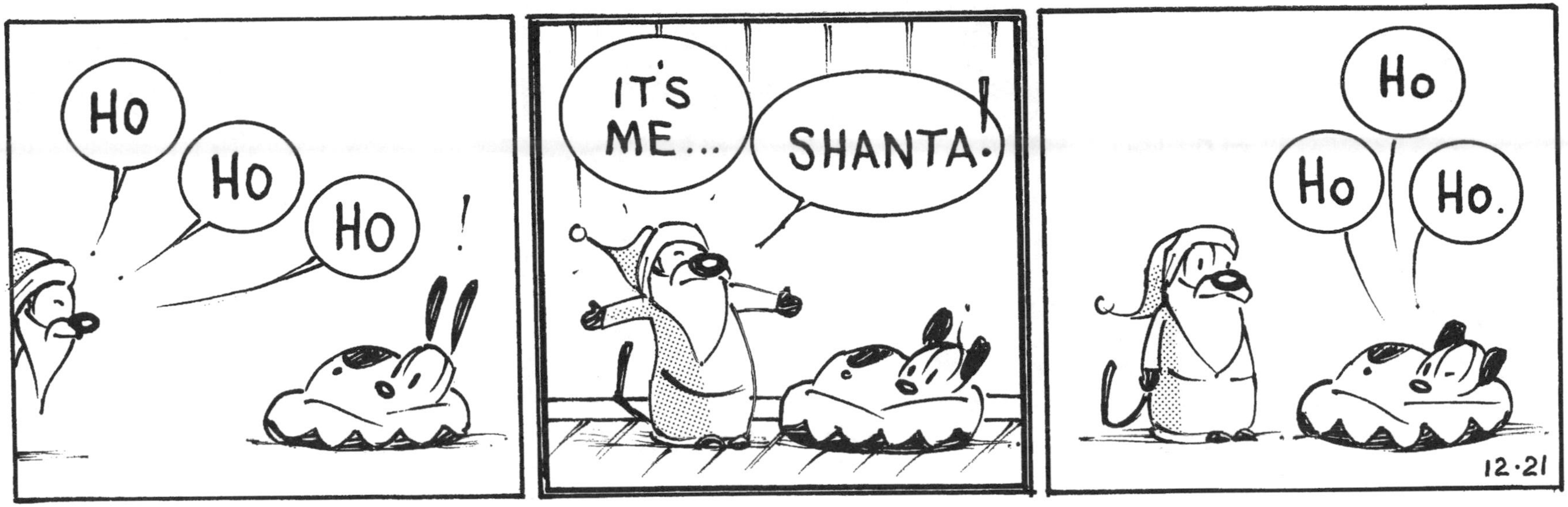
HO
HO
HO
!
IT'S ME...
SHANTA!
Ho
Ho
Ho.
12·21

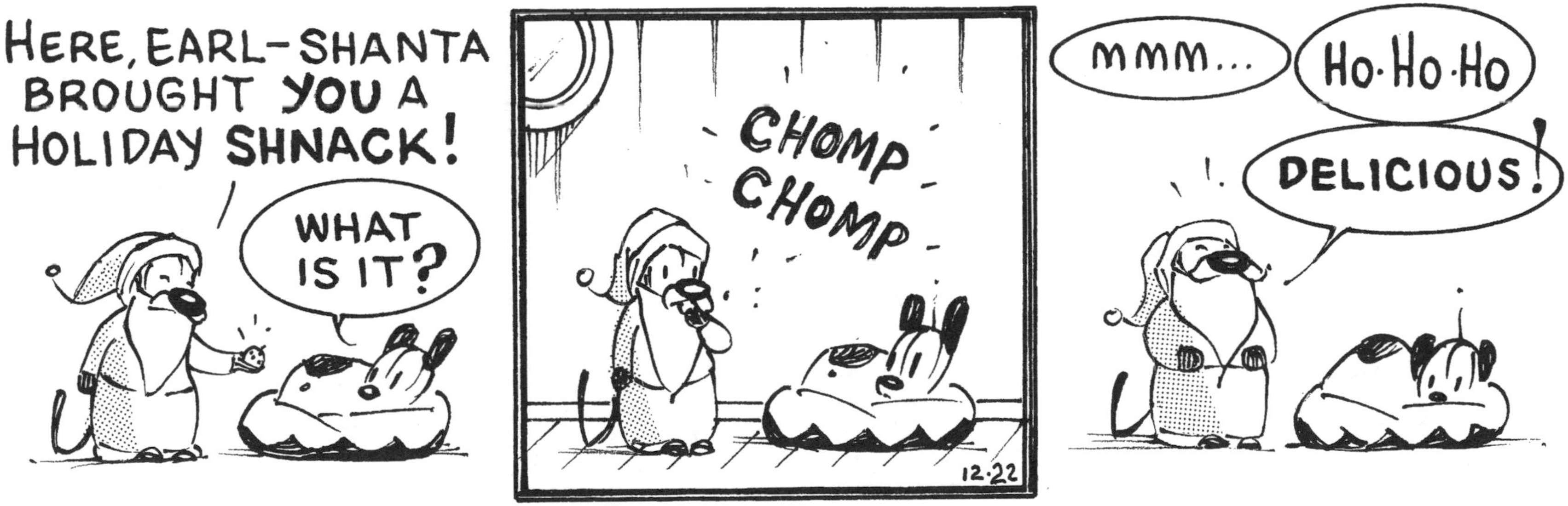
HERE, EARL–SHANTA BROUGHT YOU A HOLIDAY SHNACK!
WHAT IS IT?
CHOMP
CHOMP
12·22
MMM...
Ho·Ho·Ho
DELICIOUS!

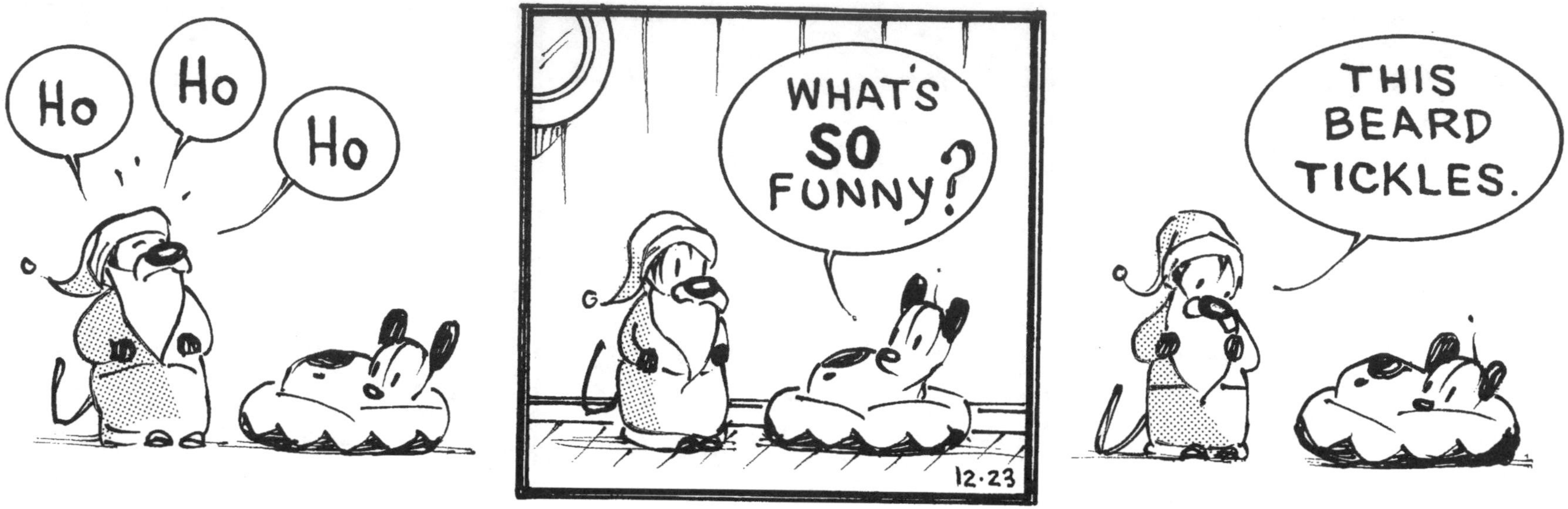
Ho
Ho
Ho
WHAT'S SO FUNNY?
THIS BEARD TICKLES.
12·23

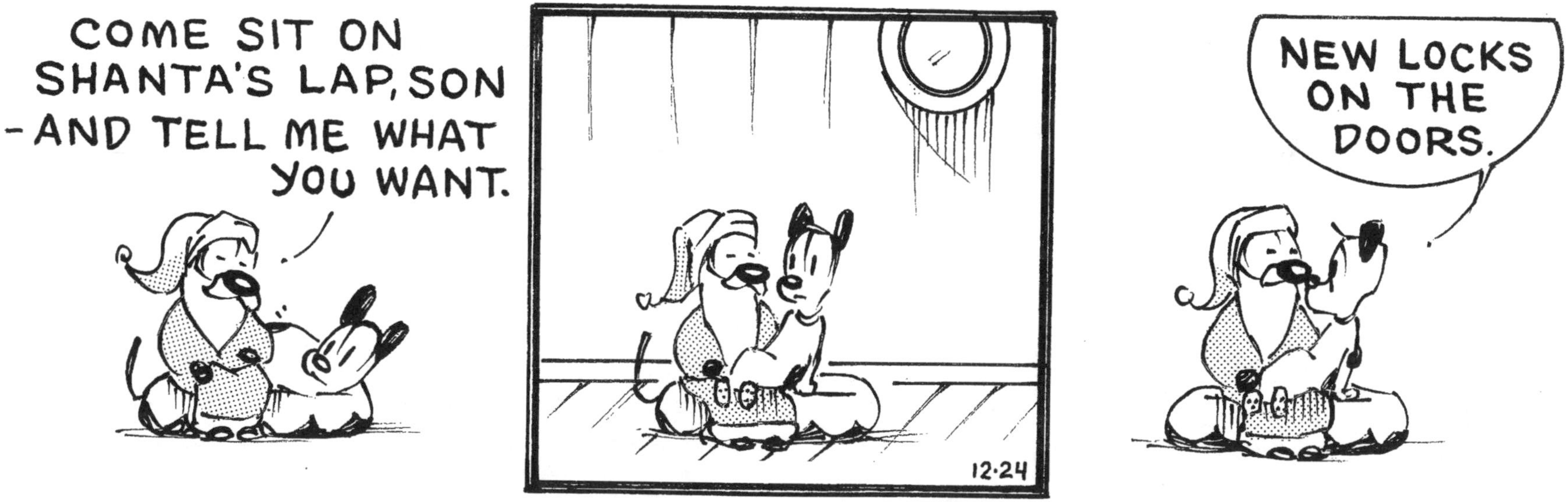
COME SIT ON SHANTA'S LAP, SON - AND TELL ME WHAT YOU WANT.
NEW LOCKS ON THE DOORS.
12·24

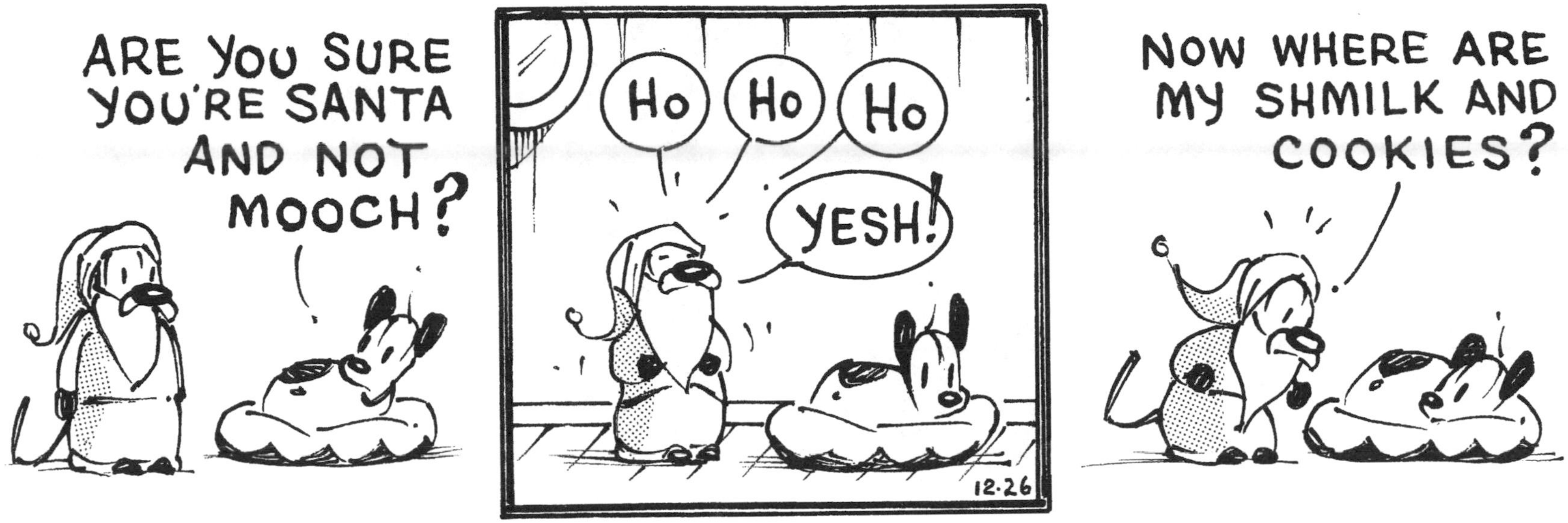
ARE YOU SURE YOU'RE SANTA AND NOT MOOCH?
Ho
Ho
Ho
YESH!
NOW WHERE ARE MY SHMILK AND COOKIES?
12·26

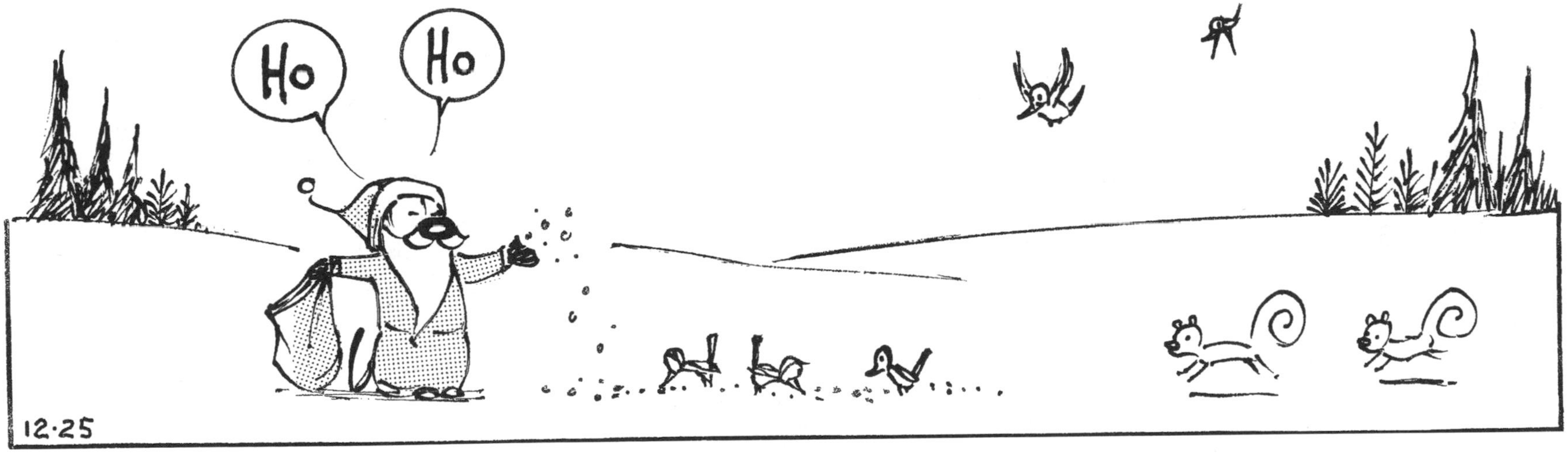
Ho
Ho
12·25

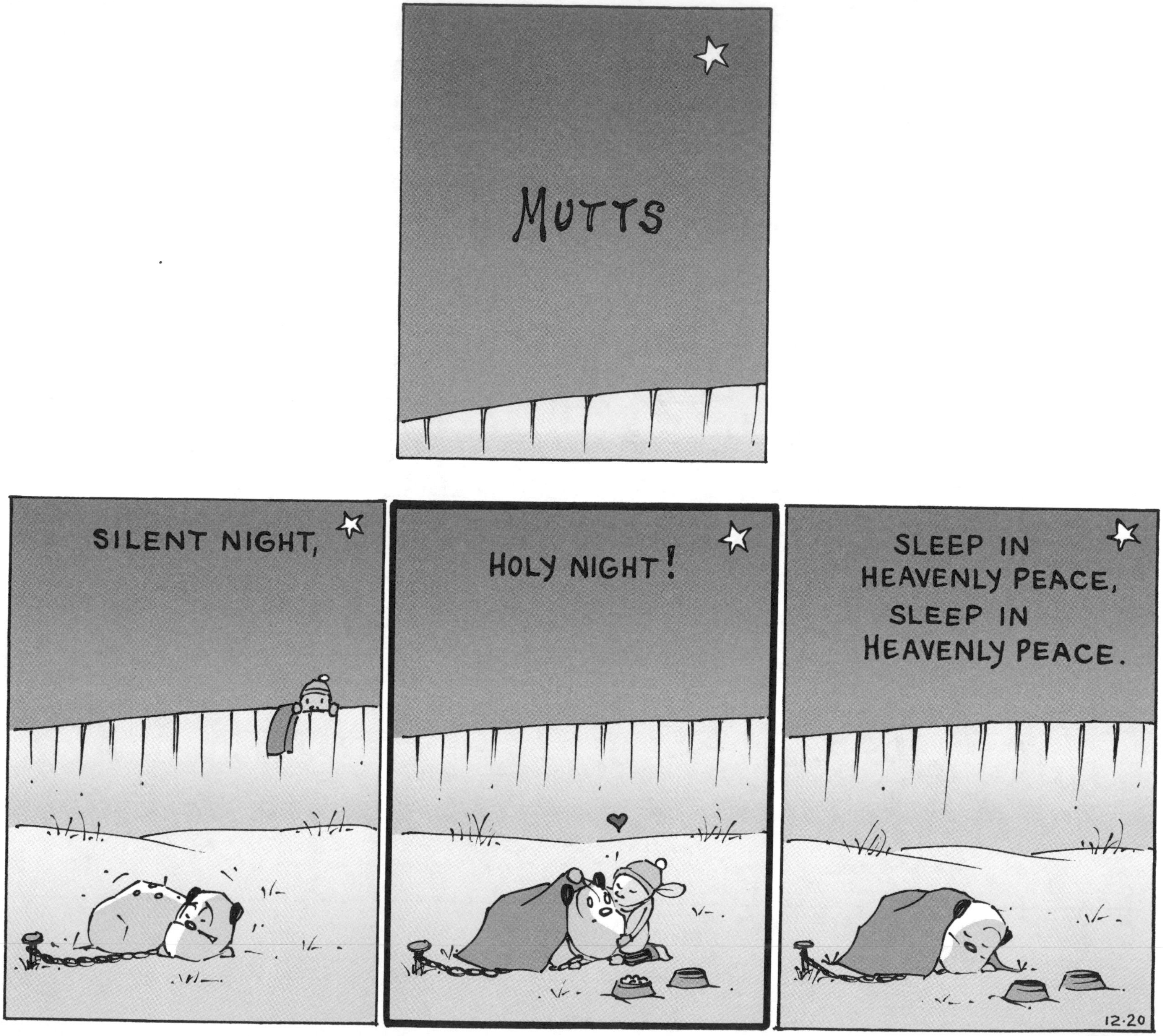
MUTTS
SILENT NIGHT,
HOLY NIGHT!
SLEEP IN HEAVENLY PEACE, SLEEP IN HEAVENLY PEACE.
12·20

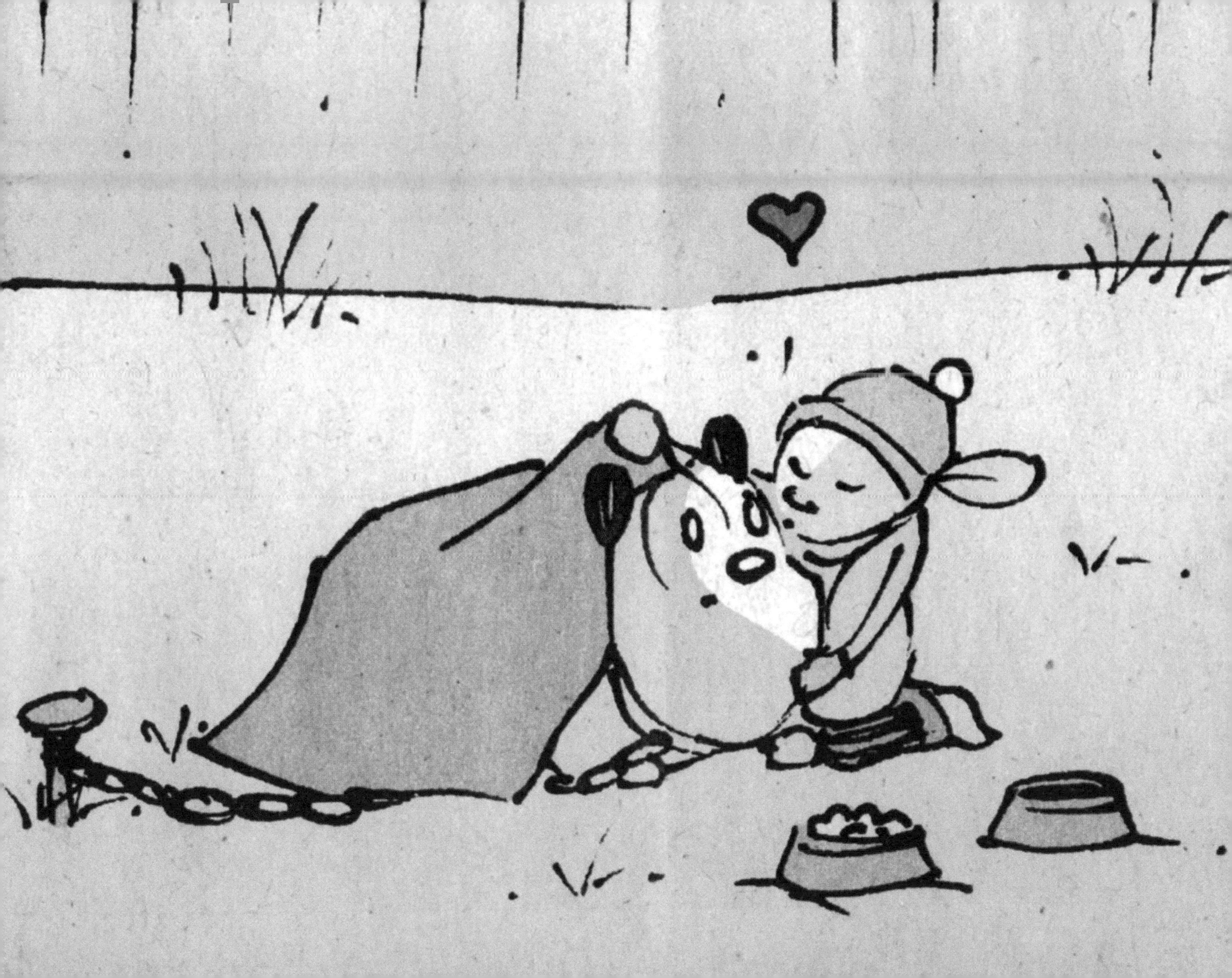

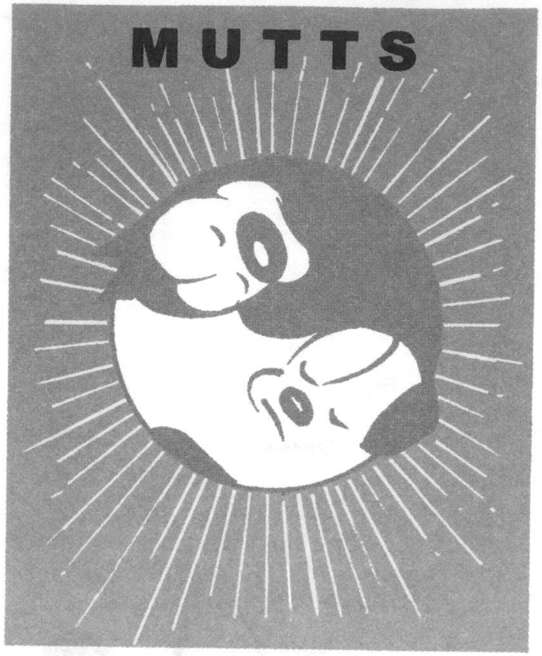
MUTTS

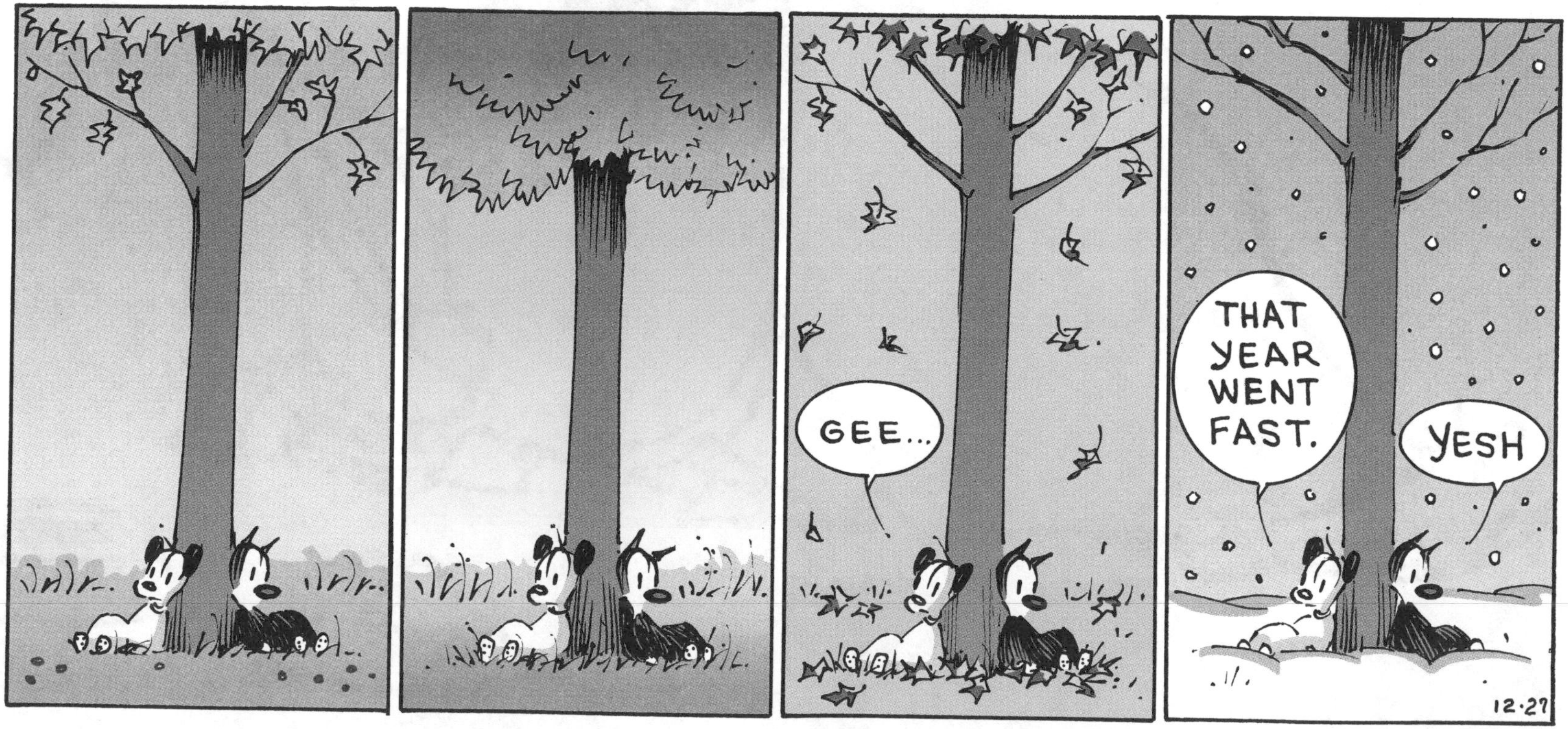
GEE...
THAT YEAR WENT FAST.
YESH
12·27